CW00369607

# 部首索引

# 目　錄

# 出版說明

這本《袖珍漢英詞典》是參攷了多種英語和漢語小詞典編輯而成的。目的使研習英語的讀者獲得適切的英語詞彙。同時，對讀者研習漢語的含義，也有所幫助。

本書共收基本單字四千多個；詞彙二萬四千多條。每一單字皆附有若干詞句，包括日常用語、專有名詞和成語等等。

本書按漢字部首排列，同時編有筆劃檢字表及漢語拼音檢字表，便於讀者查閱。

本書單字用漢語拼音注音，一字有兩音或以上的，均分別註明。單字譯成英文字義時，依照單字的詞性詳細解釋。一字可數用的（如普通的、轉音的、轉換詞意的等等），亦分別予以說明。

本書取材範圍，包括各種詞書、科學著作，以及報紙雜誌等，包括政治、經濟、文化、軍事等各方面。對一般教師、中學生及自學英語者，基本適用。

限於我們的編輯水平，如有不當之處，望讀者們指正。

中華書局編輯部

一九七七年十一月

# 一 部

一 (n.)- Unit. Union.
yī (adj.)- One; a; an. First. Same; identical. All.
(v.)- Unite into; unify.

一片 A piece; a slice; a bit.
一代 An age; one generation.
一切 All; wholly.
一半 One half.
一生 A lifetime; one's whole life.
一次 Once.
一再 One by one; each separately. Once and again.
一同 Together with; altogether.
一行 A party, a company.
一束 A bundle.
一刻 A quarter of an hour; a short time.
一周 A round; a circumnavigation.
一定 Certainly; surely.
一則 In the first place; first; an item.
一些 A little; some.
一班 A class; a squad.
一致 Unitedly; with one accord; unanimously.
一般 Generally (of a class of persons, etc.)
一紮 A bundle.
一部 A part; a copy; a volume.
一概 Summarily.
一對 A pair; a couple.
一種 A kind of; a sort of.
一齊 All together; simultaneously.
一層 A clause. A layer. A storey.
一樣 Alike; similarly; in the same manner; of the same sort.
一月份 January.
一會兒 Soon.
一卷(部)書 A volume of book.
一疋布 A piece of cloth.
一首詩 An ode; a poem. An interview.
一席話 A single remark.
一塊錢 One dollar.
一齣戲 A play.
一覽表 A table; a list.
一片胡言 Broad nonsense.
一丘之貉 Birds of a feather; foxes of the same dye.
一成不變 Invariable; immutable; fixed and unchangeable.
一目瞭然 Clear at a glance; self-evident.
一利一弊；一利一害 There is no fire without some smoke.
一見鍾情 Fall in love with one at first sight.
一言不發 Without a word.
一言難盡 It is a long story.
一事無成 Not a thing completed.
一知半解 Superficial knowledge; smattering.
一表人材 A man of great talents.
一致行動 Unanimous action.
一氣呵成 At one effort; in a breath.
一無所有 Without a single thing.
一絲不掛 Stark naked; utterly naked.
一盤散沙 A plate of loose sand; utterly lacking cohesion.
一網打盡 Make a wholesale arrest; round up.
一氧化碳(化) Carbon monoxide.
一氧化物(化) Monoxide.
一篇文章 An essay.
一舉一動 Every movement.
一舉兩得 Killing two birds with one stone.
一舉成名 Spring to fame.

一觸即發 A touch-and-go affair; a delicate situation.
一次方程式(代) Equation of the first degree; simple equation.
一言以蔽之 In a word; in short.
一年級學生 A first-year student; a freshman.
一面倒勝利(選舉) A landslide victory.

丁 (n.)- An adult. A servant. An individual.
dīng 丁口 People; population.
丁香(植) Cloves.
丁字尺 T square.
丁字形 T-shaped.
丁字街 A cross street.
丁字管 T pipe.
丁香花(植) Eilac. Mace; honey stalk.
丁字鐵條(工) T iron.

七 (adj.)- Seven.
七十 Seventy.
qī 七夕 The 7th night of the 7th month; Festival of the Weaver.
七月 July.
七色(光) Spectrum.
七折 Thirty per cent discount.
七倍 Sevenfold.
七角形(幾) Heptagon; septangle.
七弦琴 Lyre.
七面體(幾) Heptahedron.
七顛八倒 Topsy-turvy.

丈 (n.)- Ten Chinese feet. An elder; a senior.
zhàng 丈人 Father-in-law. An elder.
丈夫 A husband. A man of spirit; a hero.
丈母 Mother-in-law.

三 (adj.)- Three.
三十 Thirty.
sān 三月 March.
三次 Thrice; three times.
三更 Midnight; the dead of night.
三倍 Treble; triple; threefold.
三等 The third class.
三合土 Concrete.
三岔路 Junction of three roads.
三角形 Triangle.
三角洲 A delta.
三重奏 Terzetto; trio.
三等車 A third-class (railway) carriage.
三等客 A third-class passenger.
三等艙 Steerage.
三週年 The third anniversary.
三稜鏡 A prism.
三輪車 Tricycle; a tricar.
三K黨 The Ku Klux Klan.
三文治 Sandwiches.
三分之一 One third.
三心二意 Hesitant; undecided.
三角函數 Trigonometrical function.
三級跳遠 Hop, step and jump; triple jump.
三部合奏 A trio.
三氧化氮(化) Nitrogen tri-oxide.
三氧化硫(化) Sulphur trioxide.
三氧化錋(化) Molybdenum trioxide.
三百年紀念 The three hundredth anniversary; a tercentenary.

上 (n.)- Superiors. Top; summit.
(adj.)- Upper; high. Superior; excellent. Previous; last.
shàng (v.)- Go up; ascend; mount. Esteem; exalt.
(adv.)- Up; upward; above. Before.
(prep.)- On; upon; above.
上下 Up and down; above and below; rise and fall.
上午 Forenoon; A.M.
上古 Antiquity; ancient time.
上司 Superior; superior officers.
上旬 The first decade of a month.
上肢(解) Upper extremities (limbs).

上卷 Volume I; the first volume.
上帝 God; the Lord; Heaven.
上述 The above-stated; above mentioned.
上樓 To go upstairs
上校(陸) Colonel. (海) Captain.
上浣 The first decade of a month.
上海(地) Shanghai.
上尉(陸) Captain. (海) Lieutenant commander.
上船 Take (catch) a ship; embark.
上訴(法) Appeal.
上游 The upper course of a river.
上策 A good plan.
上等 First class; of the best quality.
上進 Make progress; get on.
上當 Cheated; imposed upon; taken in.
上演 Play on the stage; presentation; on show.
上算 It pays; profitable.
上學 Enter school; go to school.
上半夜 Before midnight.
上古史 Ancient history.
上議院 The Upper House; the House of Peers; the Senate.
上岸准單(商) Landing order; landing permit.
上岸碼頭 A landing pier.

下 xià (v.)- Go down. Descend. Fall (rain). Lay (eggs). Issue, as orders. Promulgate.
(adv. or prep.)- Below; beneath; under.

下人 Servants.
下午 Afternoon; P.M.
下水 Launch, as a ship.
下令 Give orders.
下旬 ; 下浣 The last decade of a month.
下降 Descend; come down.
下班 Go off duty; retire from duty.
下馬 Dismount.
下梯 Go down stairs.
下船 Leave (get off) a ship; land; disembark.
下野 Government office.
下等 Inferior; low; mean; vulgar.
下賤 Mean; base; vile.
下錨 Drop or cast anchor.
下屬 Subordinates.
下水禮 The launch; the launching ceremony.
下半旗 Flag to be half-masted.
下貨單(商) Shipping order.
下議院 House of Commons; Houses of Representatives.
下等客艙(商) Steerage.

不 bù (adj.)- Not; no; never; nay.
不久 Pretty soon; before long.
不日 Ere long; in a few days.
不安 Uneasy; uncomposed.

不但 Not only but.
不利 Disadvantage; improfitable.
不幸 Unlucky; unfortunate.
不忠 Disloyalty; infidelity.
不便 Inconvenience.
不祥 Ominous; ill-omened.
不料 Out of expectation; unexpected.
不能 Incompetence; impossibility.
不敢 I do not presume; I dare not.
不然 Not so. Or else.
不慎 Heedless; careless.
不該 Ought not; it is not proper.
不過 But.
不對 Not right.
不敵 No match for; not equal to.
不論 No matter.
不及格 Incapable; disqualified.
不可能 Impossibility.
不正當 Unlawfulness; impropriety.
不合格 Fail; disqualification.
不合理 Unreasonable.
不如意 Not favourable to one's wishes.
不高興 Displeased.
不知道 I don't know.

不要緊 It doesn't matter; never mind.
不倒翁 A tumbler.
不凍港 An ice-free port.
不耐煩 Impatient.
不能言 Inexpressible; beyond expression.
不健康 Unhealthiness; ill health.
不動產 Immovable property; real property.
不景氣 Depression; dullness.
不道德 Immoral; wicked; vicious.
不滿意 Not satisfied.
不衞生 Insanitation.
不銹鋼 Stainless steel.
不可思議 Mystery; incomprehensibility.
不合法的 Unlawful.
不好意思 Ashamed to; embarassed; reluctant to.
不但如此 Not only this way.
不肖之徒 Worthless characters.
不良導體(電) A poor conductor.
不法之徒 Outlaw.
不宣而戰 Undeclared war.
不祥之兆 A bad omen.
不動之款(商) Idle money.
不許動手 Hands off.
不許停車 No parking.
不許擅入 No admittance.
不速之客 An uninvited guest.
不勞而獲 Get without any labor.
不發光體 Non-luminous body.
不管部長 A minister without portfolio.
不擇手段 By fair means or foul; by any means.
不導熱體(物) Non-conductor.
不可戰勝的 Invincible.
不平等條約 An unequal treaty.
不列顛聯邦(地) British Commonwealth.
不兌現支票 Dishonoured cheque.
不定期航線 Irregular line; Irregular occasional route.
不侵犯條約 A treaty of non-aggression.
不信任投票 The vote of non-confidence.
不記名支票 Cheque to bearer.
不規則動詞 An irregular verb.
不設防城市 An open city.
不入虎穴焉得虎子 Nothing venture, nothing gain.

**丐** gài
(n.)- A beggar; a mendicant; a suppliant.
(v.)- Beg; request; ask for alms.
丐頭 The chief of beggars.

**丑** chǒu
(n.)- A clown; a jester; a buffoon; a comedian.
丑角 A merry-andrew; a merry-man; a clown; a comedian.

**且** qiě
(adv.)- More than that; in addition. On the point of; about. For the present; for the time being. Still yet; temporarily.
(conj.)- Moreover; besides; furthermore; but; still. Yet; also.
且說 By the way.

**世** shì
(n.)- The world. An age; a generation.
世世 From generation to generation; forever.
世代 Generations; ages.
世故 Worldly affairs; ordinary events.
世界 The world.
世紀 A century.
世間 In the world.
世界語 Esperanto.
世界觀 World view.
世界大勢 World situation.
世界大戰 World War.
世界末日 Doomsday; last day.

世界和平 Universal peace; world peace.
世界紀錄 World record.
世界恐慌 World crisis.
世界經濟 World economy.

**丘** qiū (n.)- A mound; a high place.
丘陵 A mound; a hill.

**丙** bǐng (n.)- The third of the Ten Stems (天干).

**丞** chéng (n.)- An assistant; a deputy.
丞相 A prime minister.

**丟** diū (v.)- Cast away; throw; leave to lose.
丟下 Lay it down; leave behind.
丟去 Throw off.
丟臉 Lose face.

**並** bǐng (adj.)- And; and also; as well as.
(adv.)- Together; side by side; at the same time; mean-while.
(conj.)- And; and also.
並不；並非 Not at all; in no sense.
並列 Coordinate.
並坐 Sit together.
並肩 Shoulder to shoulder; side by side.
並聯 Connection in parallel.
並行線(幾) Parallel lines.

# 丨 部

**丫** yā (n.)- A fork. A crotch.
丫頭；丫鬟 A young slave girl; maid-servant.

**中** zhōng (n.)- The middle; the center; the heart; core (in fruit).
(prep.)- In the middle of; within; in; between; among.
中士(陸) Sergeant.
中午 Noon; midday.
中心 The center; the heart.
中文 Chinese.
中立 Neutral.
中年 Middle age; mid-life.
中指 The middle finger.
中波 Medium wave.
中東(地) Middle East.
中秋 The mid-autumn festival.
中計 Fall into a snare; fall a prey to another's stratagem; be entrapped.
中風(醫) Apoplexy. Be seized with apoplexy.
中校(陸) Lieutenant colonel. (海) Junior captain.
中將(陸) Lieutenant general. (海) Vice admiral.
中尉(陸) Lieutenant. (海) Sub-lieutenant.
中等 Middle class.
中暑 A sunstroke.
中間 Midium; intermediate.
中飯 Tiffin; lunch; noon meal.
中意 Like; suit; please one's fancy.
中途 Halfway; midway.
中彈 Hit by the bullet.
中歐(地) Central Europe.
中醫 Chinese doctors.
中世紀 Middle ages.
中立國 Neutral country.
中耳炎 Otitis media.
中音部 Alto.
中學校 Middle school; secondary

school.
中央政府 Central Government.
中外貿易 Chinese-foreign trade.
中立地帶 A neutral zone.
中立態度 A neutral attitude.
中國代表 China's delegate.
中國銀行 The Bank of China.
中國製造 Manufactured (made) in China; Chinese made; Chinese production.
中亞細亞 Central Asia.
中途退學 Leave school in mid-course.
中等教育 Secondary education.
中篇小說 Novelette.
中亞美利加(地) Central America.
中國紅十字會 The Red Cross Society of China.
中華人民共和國 The People's Republic of China.

丰 (adj.)- Graceful; fine; good looking.
fēng 丰姿 Beauty; grace; handsome looking.

串 (n.)- A string.
(v.)- String together; connect; league together.
chuàn 串計；串謀 Plot or conspire together; collusion.
串通 Connivance.
串聯(物) Connection in series.
串門兒 To visit one neighbour after another.

# 丶 部

丸 (n.)- A pill; a small ball; a bullet; a pellet.
wán 丸藥 Pills; tablets.

丹 (n.)- A carnation or cinnabar colour. A pill.
dān 丹色 Light red.
丹青 A painting.
丹麥(地) Denmark.

主 (n.)- A ruler; a lord; a host; a master; an owner; the chief; the head; God; Almighty.
zhǔ (v.)- rule; manage.
主人 A master; an owner; a host.
主力 Main force; stamina.
主婦 A mistress. Housewife.
主旨 Essential point; object.
主犯 Principal offence; principal offender.
主客 Host and guest.
主持 An abbot. In charge of an affair.
主要 Importance; essence; important; essential; chief; leading; major.
主音 A keynote.
主任 Director; supervisor; principal.
主席 A chairman; a toastmaster. President.
主動 Promote; take the initiative.
主婚 An affiancer.
主張 Advocacy; maintain; hold; contend; insist; bear in mind.
主教 A bishop.
主筆 An editor.
主義 Principle; theory; doctrine.
主調 The key-note; the fundamental note.
主謀 The contriver of a plot.
主顧 Customers; a patron; a client.
主權 Sovereignty.

主觀 Subjective.
主力艦 Capital ship.
主席團 Presidium.
主題歌 A theme song.
主任委員 A committee chairman.
主治效能 The chief virtues.
主治醫生 A physician in charge.
主要目的 Supreme end.

## 丿 部

乃 nǎi (adj.)- That; those. Your. (conj.)- But; however. And; also. Moreover.
乃若 As to.
乃爾 Just that way; thus.

久 jiǔ (adj.)- Long; lasting.
久已 Long since; for a long time.
久別 Long separated.

之 zhī (pron.)- He; she; it. This. That. (prep.)- Of; for.
之外 Besides; in addition.
之字路 A zigzag course.

乍 zhà (adv.)- Unexpectedly; suddenly; abruptly. At first; for the first time.
乍雨 Rain suddenly.
乍晴 Clean up all in a sudden.

乏 fá (adj.)- Defective; empty. Poor. Lacking. (prep.)- Without; in want of.
乏味 Monotony; insipid.
乏術 At the end of one's wit.

乒 pīng
乒乓 Ping-pong; table-tennis.

乖 guāi (adj.)- Cunning; artful; crafty; wily. Odd; perverse; obstinate; quaint. Strange.
乖巧 Clever; tricky; ingenious; artful.
乖僻 Odd; cranky; base hearted; arrant; perverse; queer.
乖孩子 A good child.

乘 chéng (v.)- Ride; mount. Seize a chance or an opportunity.
乘車 Take a ride in carriage; ride in a car.
乘法 Multiplication.
乘馬 Ride a horse; take a ride.
乘涼 Enjoy the cool air; take an airing.
乘機 Avail oneself of an opportunity; improve an opportunity.
乘其不備 Catch one unprepared.

## 乙 部

乙 yǐ (n.)- The second of the Ten Stems. (adj.)- One. Second.
乙等 Class II; grade B; second class.

九 jiǔ (adj.)- Nine. Ninth.
九十 Ninety.
九月 September.
九泉 Hell; Hades.

九十歲人 A nonagenarian.
九死一生 A narrow escape; a hair breadth escape.

乞 (v.)- Ask alms. Beg; pray humbly; entreat.
qǐ 乞丐 A beggar.
乞求 Beg; entreat.
乞恕 Beg pardon.

也 (conj.)- And; also; besides; still.
也可 It may be done.
yě 也許 Perhaps; probably.

乳 (n.)- Milk. Breasts; the nipple; a teat; pap.
rǔ 乳水 Whey.
乳牛 Milk cow.
乳汁 Milk.
乳母 A wet nurse.
乳白 Milk white.
乳房(解) Mamma. The breast; milk.
乳齒 Milk teeth.
乳罩 Brassiere.

乾 (adj.)- Dry. Exhausted. Clean. Dried.
gān 乾旱 Drought.
乾兒 An adopted son.
乾枯 Dried up; withered.
乾燥 Parched.
乾洗(乾燥洗濯法) Dry cleaning.
乾娘 An adopted mother.
乾草 Hay.
乾淨 Clean. Entirely. Neat.
乾裂 Split from dryness.
乾爺 An adopted father.
乾糧 Dry provisions.
乾電池 Dry battery or cell.
乾燥劑 Drier.
乾燥木材 Air wood.
乾燥無味 Dry and insipid; cut and dry; flat; platitudinous.

亂 (adj.)- Confused; perplexed; agitated; disarranged; ravelled.
luàn (v.)- Put out of order; throw into disorder; confuse; disturb.
(adv.)- Out of order; out of sorts; in a mess.
亂世 A stirring period; a chaotic period.
亂言 Babble; talk wild.
亂倫 Incest.
亂殺 Slaughter.
亂衝 Rush.
亂七八糟 In disorder; untidy.
亂說一頓 Idle chatter.

# 亅 部

了 (adj.)- Finished; concluded. Intelligent.
liǎo (v.)- Understand. Complete; finish.
了然 Clearly; plainly.
了結 Have completed; be through with; have done with.
了解 Come to an understanding; see the point of; apprehend.
了不得 Marvellous; wonderful.

予 (pron.)- I; me.
yǔ (v.)- Give; confer; grant; bestow.

**事** shì (n.)- A thing; a matter; an affair. Business. A work; a service. Duties; functions. A subject. An occupation; a case.
事後 Afterward.
事件；事故 Matter; business; circumstances; occurrence.
事務 Affairs; matters.
事業 Occupation; career.
事態 Course of thing; current of event.
事實 A matter of fact; the facts.
事機 Schemes. Opportunity.
事務所 Office.
事務員 Clerk.
事實上 In fact.
事半功倍 With half the effort to achieve double result; an effective means.

# 二 部

**二** èr (adj.)- Two; both; the second; twice.
二十 Twenty; a score.
二手 Second-handed.
二月 February.
二次 Two times; twice. The second time.
二者 Both.
二倍 Two times; double; two-fold; duplicate.
二週；二星期 A fortnight.
二等 Second class.
二樓 Second storey; first floor.
二重奏 A duet.
二頭肌 Biceps.
二十世紀 The twentieth century.
二次大戰 The Second World War.
二氧化氮(化) Nitrogen dioxide.
二氧化硫(化) Sulphur dioxide.
二次方程式 A quadratic equation.
二百年紀念 Bicentenary.
二星期一次 Biweekly; fortnightly.
二等邊三角形 Isosceles triangle.

**于** yú (v.)- Go; proceed.
(prep.)- In; at; to; through.
于是 Thereupon; accordingly; consequently.

**云** yún (v.)- Say; speak; talk.
云云 And so on; and so forth; etc; so and so.

**互** hù (pron.)- Each other; one another.
(adj.)- Mutual; reciprocal.
互助 Mutual help.
互愛 To love each other.
互換 Exchange.
互選 Mutual election.
互相通知 To keep each other informed.
互相影響 Interaction.
互不侵犯條約 Treaty of non-aggression.

**五** wǔ (adj.)- Five.
五十 Fifty.
五月 May; the Fifth Month.
五味 Five tastes: acrid, sour, salt, sweet, and bitter.
五官 The five senses.
五金 Metals.
五星 The five planets: Venus (金星), Jupiter (木星), Mercury (水星), Mars (火星), Saturn (土星).
五大洋 The five oceans.

五大洲 The five continents.
五弦琴 A pentachord.
五線譜 Music paper.
五年計劃 Five years plan.
五項運動 The pentathlon.
五氧化氮(化) Nitrogen pentoxide.
五氧化二磷(化) Phosphorus pentoxide.
五十年紀念會 A golden jubilee.

井 jǐng (n.)- A well; a deep pit; a shaft.
井底蛙 A frog at the bottom of a well; a man of very limited experience; a person of narrow view; one ignorant of the world.
井井有條 Orderly; well-regulated; well-arranged; neat.

亙 héng (adj.)- Universal.
亙古 From ancient time.

些 xiē (adj.)- A little; some; a few.
(adv.)- Slightly; a small degree; not much.
些少 Any; a bit of.

亞 yā (adj.)- Second; next to. Junior. Inferior.
亞軍 To come in second; a first runner-up.
亞細亞(地) Asia.
亞硝酸(化) Nitrous acid.
亞硫酸(化) Sulphurous acid.
亞氯酸(化) Chlorous acid.
亞熱帶 The subtropical zone.
亞馬孫河(地) Amazon River.
亞硝酸鈉(化) Sodium nitrite.
亞硝酸鉀(化) Potassium nitrite.
亞硫酸鈉(化) Sodium sulphite.
亞硫酸銅(化) Copper sulphite.
亞非國家 Afro-Asian countries; African and Asian countries.
亞洲運動會 The Asian Games.

# 亠 部

亡 wáng (adj.)- Lost; dead; ruined; destroyed; gone; extinct.
(v.)- Lose. Die; perish. Escape; run away. Cease; decay; decease.
亡國 Subjugated state.
亡國奴 Persons subject to foreign rule.
亡命之徒 A ruffian; a desperado; a fugitive.

交 jiāo (adj.)- Contiguous. Crossed.
(v.)- Join. Deliver up; hand over to.
交叉 Intersection.
交友 Make friends.
交代 To hand over things to one's successor; give over charge; explain.
交尾 Coition.
交易 Exchange commodities; business dealings.
交界 The boundary; the frontier. Adjoining; bordering upon.
交情 Friendship; mutual affection; relationship.
交涉 Negotiate with.
交通 Communication.
交際 Intercourse; social functions.
交鋒 Engage in battle; cross swords.
交易所 Bourse; change; exchange.

交流電(物) Alternating current.
交貨港 Port of delivery.
交通部 Ministry of Communications.
交際花 A belle; a prominent society woman.
交戰國 Belligerent countries.
交響樂 Symphony; symphonic music.
交付日期 Day of delivery.
交貨付欵(商) Cash on delivery.
交貨證書 Delivery note.
交感神經(解) Sympathetic nerve.
交響樂隊 A symphony orchestra.

亦 (adv.)- Also; too; and.
yì

亨 (adj.)- Successful; prosperous; fortunate.
hēng 亨通 Prosperous; successful.

享 (n.)- Relish; pleasure.
(v.)- Enjoy; receive; sacrifice.
xiǎng 享受 To enjoy.

享有 To prosses.
享壽 Aged; at the age of; having lived.
享樂主義 Dilettantism.

京 (n.)- A capital.
(adj.)- Great; exalted; excellent.
jīng 京式 Peking fashions.
京城 The capital; the capital city of a nation.
京腔 A Peking accent.
京都 The capital or metropolis.
京戲 Peking opera.

亭 (n.)- An arbor; a pavilion; a portico.
tíng 亭台 Pavilions and galleries.
亭長 A constable of a village.
亭亭 Standing majestically, said of a tree or a woman.

亮 (adj.)- Bright; brilliant; clear; shining; splendid; sparkling; radiant; resplendent; vivid.
liàng

# 人部

人 (n.)- A man; a person; a human being; mankind.
rén 人人 All men; mankind.
人口 Population. Members of a family.
人才 Men of talents.
人心 Public sentiment; public opinion.
人民 People; the masses.
人性 Human nature.
人品 Character; disposition; behaviour.
人格 Personality.
人參(植) Ginseng.
人情 Human feelings; human sympathies; human nature. Favour; kindness.
人猿 Ape; anthropoid.
人種 Human races; races; races of mankind.
人類 Mankind; human beings.
人權(法) Human right.
人質 A hostage; a pawn.
人力車 A ricksha; a Jinrikisha.
人民幣 Jenminpiao; JMP; Y.
人行道 Sidewalk; foot path.
人造的 Artificial.
人造絲 Artificial silk; rayon.

人頭稅；人口稅 A poll-tax; a capitation tax.
人口統計 Population statistics.
人口調查 Population census.
人工呼吸 Artificial respiration.
人云亦云 Say as other people do.
人文地理 Political geography.
人民公社 People's commune.
人名辭典 A biographical dictionary.
人事行政 Personnel administration.
人事管理 Personnel administration.
人面獸心 A brute in man's shape.
人造牛油 Margarine; artificial butter.
人造汽油 Synthetic gasoline.
人造肥料 An artificial fertilizer.
人造(地球)衞星 Man-made (earth) satellite; artificial moon.
人造纖維 Synthetic textile; staple fibre.
人道主義 Humanitarianism.
人壽保險 Life insurance.
人民解放軍 People's Liberation Army.
人民大會堂 The Great Hall of the people.
人民民主國家 People's Democratic States.
人民民主專政 People's democratic dictatorship.

什 shí (n.)- A file of ten soldiers. Sundries. A tithe. A number of ten together.
(adj.)- Sundry; miscellaneous.
什物 Things; sundries.
什貨 Sundries.
什麼 What?
什錦小菜 Condiments.

仁 rén (adj.)- Human; kind; merciful. Charitable; benevolent; tender.
仁心 A kind heart.
仁兄 My good Sir!
仁義 Benevolence and justice.
仁至義盡 Magnanimous.

仄 zè (n.)- An oblique tone; consonant; inclined.
(adj.)- Inclined; slant.
仄字 A word in oblique tone.
仄聲 An oblique tone. Deflected, as opposed to even tones.

仆 pū (v.)- Fall to the ground.
仆倒 Fall down. Prostrate.

仇 chóu (n.)- An enemy; an opponent; a rival; an antagonist; a foe. Hatred; enmity; hostility.
仇恨 Hatred; enmity; hostility; spite.
仇敵 An enemy.

今 jīn (adj.)- Present; recent; modern.
(adv.)- Now; at present; nowadays; presently.
今日 To-day; this day.
今世 This world; this age; this generation.
今年 This year; the current year.
今夜 To-night.
今昔 Modern and ancient; present and past.
今後 Here-after; henceforth; from now on.
今早 This morning.

介 jiè (n.)- Scales; armour; mail. An attendant; an assistant.
(v.)- Lie between; border on. Assist. Introduce; recommend.
介詞(文) Preposition.
介紹 Introduce; recommend.
介意 Care; pay heed to; take to heart.
介紹書 A letter of introduction or recommendation.

仍 (adv.)- As; according. As before. However. Still. Again. Just so; thus.
réng
仍然 Still; the same as before.
仍舊 As of old; as usual; as formerly. Usual; customary.

仕 (n.)- An officer.
(v.)- Fill an office; serve the government.
shì

他 (pron.)- He; she; it.
(adj.)- Another; other.
tā
他人 Others; another person.
他日 Another day.
他的 His; hers; its.
他們 They; them.
他處 Elsewhere.
他項 Other items.
他自己 Himself; herself.

仗 (n.)- Arms; weapons of war. Battle.
zhàng (v.)- Rely on; depend on; look up to.
仗恃 Rely upon.
仗勢 Trust to power in influence.
仗義 For righteousness' sake.

付 (v.)- Pay; give to; send; deliver over to another; transfer; entrust to the care of; hand over.
fù
付印；付梓 Be sent to press; be published.
付郵 To deliver by mail.
付託 Commission; confide; charge one with; trust.
付訖 Paid; settled.
付清 Pay in full; clear off an account.
付還 Payback ; repay.
付款單 Bill payable.
付出…代價 To pay a price ; at the cost of.

仙 (n.)- An immortal; a fairy; a genius.
xiān
仙人 A genius; an immortal; fairy.
仙女 A fairy; an elf; angel.
仙景 A fairy scene; faerie.
仙人掌(植) The cactus.

仞 (n.)- A measure of eight feet.
(v.)- Measure. Fill.
rèn

代 (n.)- A generation. A dynasty. A reign. Subrogation.
dài
(v.)- Substitute; supersede; take the place of; replace; change ; alter.
(prep. )- In place of; instead of; on behalf of; as a substitute for.
代步 Substitute for walking—as horse, vehicle, etc.
代表 A representative; a delegate. Represent.
代勞 Do something for another; lend a hand.
代替 Substitute for; instead of.
代價 Price; expense.
代辦；代理公使 Charge d'affaires.
代名詞(文) Pronoun.
代表團 Delegation.
代理人 An agent; an attorney.
代理商 A commission agent.
代數學 Algebra.
代謝作用(生) Metabolism.

令 (n.)- A law; a rule; an order.
(v.)- Command; order. Cause; make; occasion.
lìng
令尊 Your father.
令郎 Your son.
令愛 Your daughter.
令人興奮的 Exciting.
令人震驚的 Shocking; frightening.

**以** (v.)- Use. Do. Consider; regard as.
yǐ (prep.)- By; with; by means of; in order to; so as to; because of; on account of; for. to the (conj.)- Because; that; effect that.

以上 Above.
以下 Below.
以內 Inside; within.
以外 Besides; beyond.
以此 Thus; in order to.
以免 Avoid. Lest.
以便 For the convenience of.
以前 Before; previous; formerly.
以致 So that; in order that.
以後 Afterwards; later; after; hence.
以故 Therefore.

**仰** (v.)- Look up. Expect. Regard with respect; admire. Rely upon. Let.
yǎng 仰光(地) Rangoon.

仰角 Angle of elevation.
仰望 Long for; expect.
仰慕 Regard with veneration; esteem; respect; admire.
仰臥 To lie on one's back.

**仲** (n.)- The second; middle man. The middle one.
zhòng 仲秋 The eighth month; mid-autumn.

仲夏 Mid-summer.
仲秋節 The Mid-Autumn Festival.

**件** (n.)- An article; an item; a subject. An affair; a case.
jiàn 件件 Everything.

**任** (n.)- An office. Responsibility; duty. Trust; confidence. A burden.
rèn (v.)- Bear; sustain. Undertake. Appoint; employ.

任用 Employ; engage.
任何 What? whatever?
任命 Appointment; designation.
任性 Follow one's own inclination; have one's own way.
任務 Role; duty; responsibility.
任期 Term of office.
任意 As he pleases.
任何人 Anyone.
任命狀 Certificate of appointment.
任何事物 Anything.
任勞任怨 Bear responsibility and blame.

**份** (n.)- A part; a portion; a share.
fèn

**仿** (adj.)- Similar; resembling.
fǎng (v.)- Imitate; copy.
仿佛 Similar; resembling.
仿造 Imitate.

**企** (v.)- Work; hope; expect; long for; stand and look for.
qǐ 企望 Look up to; hope; be on tip toe.

企業 Enterprise.
企圖 Intention; endeavour; seek; propose; contemplate.
企鵝 Penguin.
企業家 Enterpriser; industrialist; business man.

**伉** (v.)- Compose; match; oppose.
kàng 伉儷 A married couple.

**伊** (pron.)- He; she; it; that; one.
yī 伊朗(地) Iran.
伊拉克(地) Iraq.

伊索寓言 Aesop's Fables.
伊斯蘭教；回教 Mohammedanism.

伍 (n.)- A file of soldiers; a squad. A company.
wǔ 伍長 Corporal.

伏 (v.)- Lie or fall prostrate. Humble; subject; suppress. Hide.
fú 伏兵 Soldiers in ambush; an ambush. Lay a force in ambush.
伏卵 Hatch.
伏倒 Lay down on the ground.
伏特 Volt.
伏牛花(植) Barberry.

伐 (v.)- Attack; invade. Beat; strike. Cut down. Brag; boast; make a show of. Punish.
fá 伐木 Fell trees. Lumbering.
伐鼓 Beat a drum.

休 (v.)- Rest; take rest. Cease for a while; pause; stop. Spare; retire.
xiū 休手 Leave off work.
休息 To rest.
休假 Leisure. Have a holiday.
休養 Recreate; refresh.
休止符(樂) Rest.
休息室 Refreshment room or refreshment booth. A resting-room (place).
休假日 Holiday.
休息時間 Rest time; a recess.
休假半日 Half holiday.
休戚相關 Share joys and sorrows together.
休業時間 Recess time.

伙 (n.)- A comrade; a companion.
huǒ 伙伴 A comrade; a companion.
伙食 Food; provision; supplies.

伯 (n.)- An uncle. The eldest of brothers. A husband's elder brother.
bǎi 〔bó〕 伯父 A paternal elder uncle.
伯母 An elder aunt.
伯爵 A count; an earl.
伯爵夫人 A countess.

估 (v.)- Estimate; set a price on. Guess; think; consider; appraise; compare.
gū 估計；估量 Suppose; conjecture; reckon; estimate.
估價 Estimate the value of; quote a price on.
估定價目 Estimated price.
估價發單 A pro forma invoice.
估價過低 Undervaluation.

你 (pron.)- You.
nǐ 你我 You and I.
你的 Your; yours.
你們 You (plural).
你自己 Yourself.

伴 (n.)- A comrade; a partner; a companion; an associate; a chum; a mate.
bàn (v.)- Follow; attend on; accompany. Associate.
伴娘 A bridesmaid.
伴郎 A bestman.
伴侶 A partner; a companion.

伶 (n.)- An actor; a musician; a droll; a mummer; a player.
líng (adj.)- Clever; skilful.
伶仃 Lonely; isolated; desolate.
伶俐 Clever; acute; ingenious.

伸 (v.)- Stretch; extend; straighten out; dilate.
shēn 伸手 Stretch out the hand.

伸直 Straighten.
伸長 Lengthen.
伸張 Enlarge; widen; extend; spread.
伸訴 Make a statement; complain.
伸縮 Expand and contract; dilate and shrink.

**伺** (v.)- Wait upon; serve. Spy; watch; detect.
cī 伺候 Wait upon; serve.
伺探 Spy; pry into; detect.

**似** (adj.)- Like; similar; resembling; seeming.
shì (v.)- Seem; resemble.
(conj.)- As; as if.
似此 Like this; thus.
似乎 Look like; seeming; appearing.
似或 Probably.
似是而非 Apparently; seemingly. Paradoxical.

**佃** (v.)- Hunt. Plow; till the ground. Lease.
diàn 佃農 A husbandman.

**但** (adv.)- Only; merely; simply.
(conj.)- But; still; yet; however;
dàn nevertheless.
但是 But; but the fact is that.
但若 But if.
但願如此 I simply wish it so.

**佈** (v.)- Extend; spread; diffuse.
佈告 Declare; announce. Notice;
bù announcement; declaration.
佈景 Scene.
佈置 Make orderly; arrange; bring into order; set.

**位** (n.)- A seat; a place; a position; a situation; a post. A throne.
wèi 位居 A position. An abode.
位置 Position; situation.

**低** (adj.)- Low; down. Base; vulgar.
dī (v.)- Incline; lower; droop; stoop.
低地 Low land.
低垂 Hang down.
低音 Base.
低能 Mental deficiency; imbecility.
低速 Low speed.
低微 Low; lowly; low and mean.
低價 Cheap; low in price.
低潮 Low tide; ebb-tide.
低頭 Bow the head.
低音部 Base.
低氣壓 Low pressure; atmospheric depression.
低價貨 Low priced goods.
低級趣味 A bad (vulgar)taste.

**住** (v.)- Halt; stop; cease. Detain. Live in; dwell.
zhù 住口 Stop talking; cease to speak.
住宅 House; residence; dwelling place.
住址 Address.
住手 Stop.
住宅區 Residential district; residential quarter.
住址不定 Of no fixed address.
住址不明 One's address is unknown.
住址姓名 One's name and address.

**佐** (n.)- An assistant; helper; deputy.
zuǒ (v.)- Assist; help; aid.
佐證 Corroborative evidence.
佐理 An assistant.

**佑** (v.)- Aid; assist; help; to bless.
yòu

佔 (v.)- Occupy; take possession of.
zhàn 佔有 Occupy; possess; hold.
佔領 Seize.
佔據 Occupy by force; take possession of.
佔便宜 Take advantage of.
佔領區 Occupied area.
佔優勢 Get the better hand of.

何 (pron.)- Who? which? what?
(adv.)- How? why?
hé 何人 Who? what man?
何不 Why not?
何以 Wherefore? why?
何必 Why must it be? What necessity?
何事 What is the matter?
何物 What? Which?
何故 Why? For what reason?
何者 Which?
何時 When? At what time?
何處 Where? In what place?

余 (pron.)- I; me; myself.
yú

佚 (n.)- Ease; rest; repose; retirement.
yì (adj.)- Idle; leisurely.
(v.)- Omit; neglect.
佚名 Anonymous.

佛 (n.)- Buddha.
佛國(地) India.
fú 佛教 Buddhism.
佛塔 A pagoda.
佛廟 Temple.
佛教徒 Buddhist.

作 (n.)- Operation; work; workmanship.
zuò (v.)- Make; do; act. Become. Write; compose.
作文 Composition. Write an essay.
作用 Function; operation.
作伴 Keep company.
作品 A piece of work; writing.
作家 Author; writer.
作爲 Acts; doings.
作亂 Rebel; rise up in revolt.
作嘔 Turn the stomach.
作廢 Terminate; cancel; nullify; invalidate.
作弊 Cheat.
作戰 Fight; war.
作證 Give evidence; testify.
作曲家 Composer.
作威作福 To domineer.
作戰基地 A base of operations.

佝 佝僂病 Rachitis.
gōu

佩 (n.)- A pendant; things worn on the girdle.
pèi (v.)- Wear; gird on; carry.
佩服 Respect.
佩帶 Wear at the girdle.
佩勳章 Wear a medal.

佯 (v.)- Pretend; make believe; feign; simulate; counterfeit;
yáng affect; profess; dissemble.
佯笑 Pretend to laugh.

佳 (adj.)- Beautiful; pretty; fine; splendid; excellent; exquisite;
jiā nice; good; superior; handsome; fair.
佳人 A beauty; a pretty woman; a belle.
佳作 A fine work; a masterpiece.
佳音 Good news.
佳期 A happy occasion; an auspicious time.

佳景 Beautiful view; fine scenery.
佳節 A festival.
佳運 Lucky; fortunate.
佳麗 Handsome; beautiful.

佻 (adj.)- Slender; weak.
tiāo 佻達 Frivolous; impertinent; volatile; flighty.

使 (n.)- A messenger; an envoy.
shǐ (v.)- Send; commission. Employ; use; expend. Order; command. Cause; effect; occasion.
(conj.)- If; supposing.
使用 Make use of; spend; expend. Employ; use.
使節 An envoy; an ambassador.
使館 A legation; an embassy.

來 (v.)- Come; reach; effect; bring about.
lái 來月 Next month.
來去；來往 Going and coming.
來因；來源 Origin; source; cause.
來年；來歲 The coming year; next year.
來客；來賓 A guest; a visitor; a caller.
來訪 Visit; call.
來電 Telegram from.
來歷 Antecedents. Basis; foundation. Record of a person; curriculum vitae.
來臨 Presence; attendance.
來因河(地) The Rhine.
來回票 Return ticket.
來賓室 A reception-room.
來賓席 The guests seats; the seats for invited guests.
來往帳目 A current account.

侈 (adj.)- Extravagant; luxurious; wasteful; profuse; prodigal.
chǐ 侈言；侈談 Wild talk; exaggeration.

例 (n.)- Rules; regulations; bylaws. Custom; usage.
lì 例如 For instance; for example. Give an example.
例外 An exception.
例題 An example.

侍 (v.)- Wait on; serve; attend. Follow; accompany.
shì 侍者 An attendant; a boy; a waiter.
侍從 An attendant; a servant.

侏 (v.)- A pigmy; a dwarf.
zhū 侏儒 A pigmy; a dwarf; a Tom Thumb; a manikin; a midget.

供 (v.)- Supply; provide with; offer to; present to. Contribute.
gōng 供招；供認 Confess one's own crime.
供給 Supply (furnish) something; supply (furnish, serve, provide) one with.
供詞 Depositions; a statement.
供職 To hold an appointment.
供給不足 Short supply.
供給過多 Over supply; overstock.

依 (v.)- Trust to. Conform to; accede to; comply with. Rest
yī against; depend on.
(prep.)- According to; in accordance with; in conformity to; in agreement with.
依照 According to.
依次 In order; in succession.
依附 Adhere to; agree with.
依然 Still; as before; as it was; as ever; as it used to be.
依賴 Depend on; rely upon.

依舊 As before; as usual.
依賴心 Dependence; reliance.
依依不捨 Unwilling to part with.

侮 wǔ (n.)- Neglect. Contempt; disrespect.
(v.)- Insult. Despise. Ridicule.
侮弄 Make game or sport of; mock at; humbug.
侮辱 Insult; put to shame; disgrace.
侮蔑 Despise; hold one in contempt; scorn.

侯 hóu (n.)- A marquis. A marquess.
侯爵夫人 A marchioness.

侵 qīn (v.)- Invade; make an incursion into.
侵入 Invasion; a raid; intrusion.
侵犯 Invade; offend; aggress.
侵佔 Occupy.
侵略 Aggression; invasion; an inroad.
侵蝕 Erode. Erosion.
侵略政策 An aggressive policy.
侵略戰爭 Aggressive war.

侶 lǚ (n.)- A companion; a mate; a comrade.

便 biàn (adj.)- Convenient; handy; expedient; advantageous. Ready at. Ordinary; common.
(adv.)- Then. So; thus. Readily; forthwith.
便衣 Ordinary dress; plain clothes.
便利 Convenience; facilities; handiness.
便宜 Suitable; convenience; cheap; reasonable.
便所 A latrine; a water-closet (W.C.); a toilet; a lavatory.
便條 A note.
便帽 A cap.
便宜處分 Disposed of at one's discretion.
便衣警察 A policeman in plain clothes; a bull.

係 xì (n.)- Concern; consequences.
(v.)- Be. Bend. Belong to; attach to; connect with.
係數 Coefficient.
係屬 Connected with; belong to.

促 cù (adj.)- Urgent; hurried. Near; close.
促迫 Urge; press; hurry on.
促進 Promote; accelerate; spur; stimulate; hasten.
促膝談心 Cross knees and talk over matters —as friends.

俄 é (adv.)- All of a sudden; abruptly. Instantly; presently.
俄文 Russian; the Russian language.
俄國；俄羅斯(地) Russia.

俊 jùn (adj.)- Superior; eminent; remarkable; distinguished; Refined; handsome.
俊俏 Graceful; elegant.

俏 qiào (adj.)- Handsome; beautiful; pretty; excellent.
俏皮 Attractive; pretty; smart.
俏麗 Beautiful; pretty.

俐 lì (adj.)- Clever; intelligent; smart; sharp.

俑 yǒng (n.)- A wooden figure; a puppet.

**俗** sú (adj.)- Inelegant; unrefined; uneducated. Common; vulgar.
俗名 A common name.
俗氣 Vulgar taste; vulgarity; worldliness.
俗話 The vulgar dialect; a colloquial expression.
俗傳 Vulgar tradition.
俗稱 A popular name.
俗語 Colloquial language.
俗不可耐 Nauseating.

**俘** fú (n.)- A prisoner of war; a captive.
(v.)- Capture alive; take prisoner; make a prisoner of; captivate.
俘虜 Captives; prisoners of war.

**俚** lǐ (adj.)- Unpolished; vulgar; low-bred; rustic; rude; rough.
俚俗 Vulgar; rustic; rude; rough.
俚謠 A ballad; a folk-song.

**保** bǎo (n.)- A guardian; a protector. A guarantee; a bail. A servant; a waiter.
(v.)- Depend; protect; guard. Be surety for; guarantee; warrant. Secure; keep safe; insure. Feed; nourish.
保母；保姆 A nurse; a governess.
保存 Preserve; keep.
保守 Keep; maintain.
保持 Maintain; keep up; hold.
保留 Reserve; shelve.
保管 In charge; take custody of.
保障 A defense; a barrier.
保養 Nourish; take care of one's health.
保險 Insurance. Assurance.
保證 Guarantee; certify; secure; give security for.
保鏢 Escort; convoy.
保釋 Bail on security; stand bail.
保護 Protect; guard; defend.
保守黨 Conservative party; the conservatives.
保險單 An insurance policy.
保險費 Premium.
保險箱 A safe; a strong box.
保險絲 Fuse.
保險杠(槓)(緩衝器) The bumper.
保證金 A deposit as security; caution money.
保護色(動) Protective colour.
保護國 A protectorate.
保加利亞(地) Bulgaria.
保守主義 Conservatism.
保險公司 An insurance company.
保險金額 Insurance amount.

**俠** xiá (adj.)- Generous; noble-minded; public-spirited.
俠客 A chivalrous person; a gallant. One who champions a just casue.
俠義 Heroic; chivalrous; gallant.

**信** xìn (n.)- Faith; sincerity; truthfulness. Confidence; trust. A letter; a note. A seal; a stamp. Tidings; news. A security; a pledge.
(v.)- Trust; believe; have faith in; put trust in; give credit to; confide. Accord; follow.
(adj.)- Sincere; faithful; true.
信心 Piety; worship; devotion.
信片 A post card.
信用 Credit; confidence.
信任 Trust; confident of; confidence.
信仰 Faith; belief; conviction; worship.
信局 A post office.
信念 Belief; faith.
信封 An envelope.
信徒 Believers; followers; disciples.

信息 News; information.
信號 Signals.
信箋 Letter paper; note paper.
信箱 A post box
信賴 Trust; put trust in; place confidence in; rely on.
信口開河 Talk at random.
信守諾言 To keep one's promise.
信用滙票 A bill of credit.
信任投票 A vote of confidence.
信仰自由 Freedom of faith (belief).
信心百倍地 With unbounded confidence.

修 xiū (adj.)- Long; regular; neat; tidy. (v.)- Reconstruct; repair; mend; rebuild.
修正 Amend; revise; modify; correct.
修剪 Shear.
修理 Repair; regulate; prune.
修飾 Dress elaborately; adorn; decorate.
修業 Study; make a study of; pursue the course of.
修葺 Rebuild; repair.
修養 Moral culture; cultivation.
修築 Repair; restore; renew.
修飾語 A modifier.
修道院 A monastery; a cloister.
修辭學 Rhetoric.
修業文憑 A certificate of attendance.
修正主義 Revisionism.

俯 fǔ (n.)- Stoop; condescend; bow.
俯角 Angle of depression.
俯瞰 Overlook; look out upon; command a view of.
俯衝轟炸機 Dive bomber.

俱 jū (adj.)- All; whole. Both. (adv.)- Altogether; wholly.
俱備 Complete.
俱樂部 A club; a club-house.

俳 pái (n.)- Dissipation; theatrical show.
俳小 Irresolute; undetermined.
俳諧 Humorous speech.
俳優 Actors.

俸 fèng (n.)- Salary; remuneration; allowance; compensation.
俸金 Salary; stipend.
俸金及津貼 Salaries and allowances.

俾 bǐ (v.)- Cause; let; enable. Allow; follow; accord.
俾得 So that; so as to enable.

併 bǐng (adj.)- Equal; even. (v.)- Unite; combine.
併合 Annex; amalgamate; absorb.
併呑 Annex; swallow up; conquer.
併發 Occur at the same time.

倆 liǎng (n.)- Two.

倉 cāng (n.)- A granary; a barn; a storehouse; a bin.
倉庫 A warehouse.
倉卒間 In a hurry.

個 gě (gè) (n.)- A piece.
個人 An individual.
個別 One by one; separately; individually.
個性 Individuality.
個人主義 Individualism.
個人經濟 Individual economy.

倌 guān (n.)- A groom. Assistant in a wine-shop.

倍 (n.)- Time, as 三倍 three times (fold); as 十倍 ten-fold.
bèi (adj.)- Double; twofold; twice.
倍大 Double size.
倍增 Double; increase by 100 per cent.
倍數 A multiple.

們 (n.)- A word added to HE, SHE, YOU, I, or IT to express
men its plural number, as we or us.

倒 (v.)- Fall; Lie down; prostrate; Pour.
dào (adv.)- Then. Indeed. On the
〔dǎo〕 contrary.
(conj.)- But; still.
倒下 Fall down.
倒退 Recede; beat-a-retreat; withdraw.
倒閉 Become bankrupt.
倒進 Pour in.
倒運；倒霉 Bad luck; unlucky.
倒斃 Fall down dead; fall dead.
倒懸 Hang upside-down.

倔 (adj.)- Obstinate; stubborn; perverse. Hard to please.
jué 倔强 Crabbed; stubborn.

倖 (adj.)- Fortunate; lucky.
(adv.)- By a good chance.
xìng 倖免 Escape by mere luck; narrow escape.
倖運 Luck; fortune.

倘 (conj.)- If; supposing that; in the event of.
tǎng 倘有 In case of; in the event of.
倘若 If it be so; in that case.

候 (n.)- Season; time.
(v.)- Wait for; await; expect.
hòu Inquire after; visit.
候命 To await orders.
候車室 Waiting room, as of a railway station.
候補者；候選人 A candidate.

倚 (v.)- Rely on; depend upon. Lean against.
yǐ 倚勢 Rely on authority.
倚靠 Lean back; rely on.

借 (v.)- Lend to; borrow from.
(conj.)- If; supposing.
jiè 借約；借單；借據(商) A promissory note; an I. O.U.
借款；借債 Make loans.
(向……)借錢 Borrow money from.
借出款 Loan.

倡 (n.)- A leader; a guide.
(v.)- Introduce; promote; lead.
chàng Start; take the initiative.
倡導 Advocate; propagate; espouse.
倡議 Make a motion.

倣 (v.)- Imitate; model; take after; copy. Resemble.
fǎng (adj.)- Like; resembling.
倣造 Make according to pattern.

值 (n.)- Price; cost.
值日 On duty for the day.
zhí 值得 Worthwhile.
值錢 Worth; costly; valuable.
值夜班 On night duty.

倦 (adj.)- Tired; fatigued; worn out; exhausted.
juàn 倦怠 Tired; fatigued; weary; remiss.

倫 (n.)- natural relationship.
(adj.)- Constant; regular; ordin-
lún ary.

倫理 Moral principles.
倫敦(地) London.
倫巴舞 Rumba dance.

倮 luǒ (adj.)- Naked.

假 jiǎ (n.)- Holidays.
(adj.)- False; unreal; not genuine; hypocritical.
(conj.)- If; in case of.
假充 Pretend to be.
假名 A pseudonym. Assumed name.
假定；假設 Hypothesis. Supposition. Supposing that. Assume; persume. Postulate.
假冒 Sham; counterfeit.
假造 Counterfeit; invent a story; forge.
假期 Vacation; holiday.
假意 Falsely. Pretending.
假裝 Pretend to be; feign; disguise.
假話 Lies; falsehood.
假髮 A wig; a periwig.
假釋 Conditional release.
假面具 A mask.
假牙 Artificial teeth.
假仁假義 Pretended kindness and goodness.
假公濟私 Jobbery. Jobbing for selfish ends; seek one's own profit in public affairs.

偉 wěi (adj.)- Admirable; distinguished. Great; gigantic; magnificent. Powerful; strong; mighty.
偉人 A great man; a distinguished person.
偉大 Great; noble.

偎 wēi (v.)- Hug; cuddle together.
偎傍 Cuddle closely together.

偏 piān (adj.)- Partial; prejudiced. Inclined to one side; bent on (used in a bad sense). Selfish; leaning; onesided.
偏心 Prejudice; partiality.
偏私 Selfish; partial.
偏見 A partial view.
偏僻 Secluded.
偏差 Deviation. Declination.

偕 xié (v.)- Accompany; go along with; associate with.
(adj.)- Jointly; together.
偕同 With; together.
偕行 Walk together.

做 zuò (v.)- Do; act; perform. Work.
做作 Stiff; unnatural, as of a style of writing.
做官 Be an official; be in office.
做生意 Engage in trade.

停 tíng (v.)- Stop; cease; discontinue; halt; pause; hold up; stand still. Rest. Delay.
停工 Rest from work; suspend work; knock off.
停止 To stop; cease.
停刊 Cease to publish; suspension of publication; discontinuation of publication.
停留 Stay.
停業 Close down.
停學 Suspension from school; rustication.
停戰 Truce; cease fire.
停車場 A parking-place; a taxi-stand.
停戰條約 An agreement of truce (armistice); an armistice agreement.

健 jiàn (adj.)- Strong; vigorous; robust; hearty; stout.
(v.)- Strengthen; invigorate.

健全 Perfect; sound and safe.
健忘 Forgetful; bad memory.
健壯 Strong; vigorous; in good health.
健美 Bonny.
健康 Health.
健全的 Wholesome.
健身房 Gymnasium.
健身操 Sitting exercise.
健康證明書 Health certificate.

側 (n.)- The side.
(adj.)- Lateral. Inclining. Mean; low.
cè
(v.)- Incline; turn toward; lean.
側臥 Sleep on one side.
側門 A side door.
側視 Side look.

偵 (v.)- Spy; detect; explore; scout; discover; inspect.
zhēn
偵探 A spy; a detective. Detect; make secret inquiry.
偵察 Inspect; investigate. Searching for the enemy; searching operations.
偵查器 Detector.
偵察機 Reconnaissance plane.
偵探小說 Detective stories.

偶 (n.)-An image; an idol; a puppet; a statue. A pair; a couple.
ǒu
(v.)- Marry. Accord with; harmonize. Fit.
(adv.)- Occasionally; expectedly.
偶人；偶像 A wooden figure; a puppet; an idol; a statue; an effigy.
偶然 Accidentally; by chance.
偶數 An even number.
偶戲 A puppet show; marionette.

偸 (v.)- Steal; obtain unfairly; pilfer; take without right.
tōu
偸運 To smuggle.
偸看 Peep at; steal a glance, cast a sheep's eye.
偸盜 Steal and rob.
偸懶 Idle; shirk work.
偸聽 Overhear; eavesdrop.

傀 (n.)- A puppet; an idol.
傀儡 Puppets; doll.
kuĭ
傀儡政府 A puppet government.

傅 (v.)- Help; superintend. Assist; guide; support.
fù
傅顏色 Paint; colour.

傍 (n.)- The side.
(prep.)- Near.
bàng
傍晚 Dusk; sunset; evening. At nightfall.
傍徨 Wander about. Irresolute; undecided.
傍觀者 Third person; onlooker; bystander.
傍系親族 Collateral relatives.

傑 (n.)- A hero.
(adj.)- Heroic; famous.
jié
傑出 Eminent.
傑作 A masterpiece.

傘 (n.)- An umbrella; a parasol.
傘兵 Paratroops; a parachutist.
sǎn

備 (v.)- Prepare; make ready; provide; equip; supply.
bèi
(adj.)- Ready; prepared. Complete; entire; all; whole.
備用 For use.
備戰 Prepare for war.
備忘錄 Memorandum.

傢 (n.)- Furniture; utensils.
傢伙 Guy; fellow.
jiā
傢俬 House hold furniture.

催 (v.)- Urge; press; hasten. Importune.
cuī 催促；催迫 Urge; press; impel; expedite. Quicken; put on; hasten.
催眠 To hypnotise.
催化劑 Catalyst.
催眠曲 A cradle (nursery) song; a lullaby.
催眠劑 Opiate.
催淚彈 A tear-shell (-bomb); a lachrymatory gas shell.

傭 (v.)- Hire; engage. Serve.
yōng 傭人 Workmen; hiredmen; a servant.
傭工 Hired labourers.
傭兵 Mercenary.

傲 (n.)- Pride. Rudeness.
ào (adj.)- Proud; haughty. Scornful; insolent; arrogant.
傲視 Proud look.
傲慢 Scorn; arrogant; haughty; insolence.

傳 (n.)- A record; a biography.
chuán (v.)- Transmit; pass; transfer; carry forward. Interpret; explain. Spread. Send for. Tell; narrate.
傳下 Hand down; bequeath.
傳令 Issue orders; give out orders.
傳說 A legend; to allege.
傳統 Tradition.
傳奇 A story book; a romance; a saga.
傳染 Infect; contaminate. Infections.
傳記 Biography; memoir; life.
傳授 Instruct.
傳單 Circulars; handbills.
傳播 Propagation.
傳遞 Pass from one to another; transmit.
傳聞 It is said; it is stated; it is reported; as the story goes. Hearsay; rumour.
傳染病 A contagious or infectious disease.
傳家寶 An heirloom.
傳教士 A preacher; a missionary.
傳染病院 Epidemic hospital.

傴 (adj.)- Hump backed; hunchbacked.
yǔ 傴僂 Hump backed; crooked back; hunchbacked; stooping.

債 (n.)- A debt; an obligation.
zhài 債戶；債務人 A debtor.
債主；債權人 A creditor.
債券 Debenture.

傷 (n.)- Wound; injury; harm. Bruise; hurt.
shāng (adj.)- Sad at heart; mortified.
(v.)- Injure; hurt; wound; harm. Grieve; distress; mourn.
傷口 The mouth of a wound; a gash; a stab; lips of a wound.
傷亡 Casualties.
傷心 Great sorrow; a broken heart; grieved at heart; distressed in mind; break the heart.
傷兵 Wounded soldier.
傷風(醫) Catarrh. Catch cold.
傷痛 Mourn.
傷害 Hurt.
傷痕；傷疤 Scars.
傷損 Damage.
傷寒症(醫) Typhus or typhoid fever.
傷感情 Tread on one's corn; hurt the feelings of.

傾 (v.)- Turn over. Lean towards.
qīng 傾吐 Pour out; make a clean breast of; give vent to one's

thought.
傾向 Inclination; tendencey; disposition. Incline; trend; bend; dip.
傾斜 Obliquity; declivity.
傾銷 Dumping.
傾聽 Incline the ear; listen attentively; hear out; give an ear to.
傾斜角(物) Angle of inclination.
傾盆大雨 Pouring rain; to rain cats and dogs.
傾家蕩產 Disperse one's fortune.

僂 lóu (adj.)- Hunchbacked; bent-backed. Stooping; curved; bending.
僂佝 Deformed; short and ugly.

僅 jǐn (adj.)- Mere.
(adv.)- Only; merely; scarcely; simply; barely; just.
僅係 It is merely.
僅僅 Barely.

像 xiàng (n.)- A figure; a likeness; a portrait; a photo. An idol; an image; a statue.
(adj.)- Like; similar; resembling.
(v.)- Resemble; look like.
像片 Photograph.
像似 Resemble; look like; resembling; similar to.
像貌 Figure; form; countenance; looking.

僑 qiáo (v.)- Lodge; settle; emigrate; sojourn; dwell; reside.
僑民 Emigrants.
僑居；僑寓 Make a brief sojourn in.

僕 pū (n.)- A servant; a menial; a footman.
僕人 A servant.

僚 liáo (n.)- A companion; a colleague. An associate. A class.

僞 wěi (adj.)- False; unreal. Hypocritical; simulated; pretended. Counterfeit.
僞裝 Comouflaged; to pretend.
僞鈔 Fake banknote.
僞幣 False coin.
僞證 Perjury.
僞君子 A hypocrite.
僞政權 A bogus government; puppet government.

僥 jiǎo (adj.)- Lucky; fortunate.
僥倖 Lucky; fortunate; by chance.

僧 sēng (n.)- A Buddhist priest; a monk; a friar.
僧俗 The clergy and laity.
僧侶 Monk.
僧教(宗) Buddhism.

僭 jiàn (v.)- Assume; arrogate to oneself; usurp. Overpass one's duty. Seize without right.

僮 tōng (n.)- A slave boy; a boy servant.
僮僕 A young slave; a page; a foot boy; an errand boy; a bond servant.

僱 gù (v.)- Hire; engage; employ.
僱主 An employer.
僱用 Engage; charter.
僱員 Employee.

僵 jiāng (adj.)- Stiffened; rigid.
僵屍 A corpse; an indecomposed corpse.
僵局 Deadlock.

**價** (n.)- Price; value; cost; worth.
jià　價值；價錢 Price; value; charge; worth; cost.
價格 A standard of value.
價廉；價賤 Cheap. Low price.
價目表 Price list; price current.
價格上漲 The price is advancing.
價廉物美 Low prices and fine quality; fine wares at low prices.

**僻** (adj.)- Private; secluded.
pì　僻巷 A side lane; a private alley.
僻處 Live in seclusion; retire.
僻靜之地 A lonely place; an out-of-the-way place; a remote place; a secluded spot.

**儀** (n.)- Ceremony; rite. A rule; a principle. A present. Form.
yí　儀型 A good example or pattern; paragon.
儀容 Deportment; fashion; outward appearance.
儀態 Bearing; appearance.
儀器 Instrument; apparatus.
儀式 Ceremony.
儀仗隊 Guard of honour.

**儂** (pro.)- I; me. Thou; you.
nóng

**億** (adj.)- A hundred millions.
yì　億萬 Innumerable; numberless; many.

**儈** (n.)- A broker; an agent.
kuài

**儉** (adj.)- Moderate; economical.
jiǎn　儉約 Economy; thrift; frugality.
儉樸 Thrifty; frugal.

**儌** (adj.)- Lucky; fortunate.
jiǎo　儌倖 Lucky; fortunate.

**儍** (adj.)- Foolish; stupid; thoughtless; brainless. Dull; silly.
shǎ　儍子 A simpleton; a fool; a dunce; a foolish fellow.
儍話 Nonsense.

**儐** (v.)- Arrange; put properly. Entertain.
bìn　儐相 Bridegroom's best man or bride's maid of honour.

**儘** (n.)- The utmost; the extreme.
jǐn　儘力 Do the best; with all the strength.
儘夠 Quite enough.

**償** (n.)- An indemnity. Reward.
(v.)- Return; requite. Revenge; retaliate.
cháng　償金 Indemnity.
償還 Repay; compensate; make good.
償心願 Fulfill one's wishes.

**優** (adj.)- Abundant; excessive. Excellent; superior.
yōu　優先 Preference; priority.
優良 Best; superior.
優秀 Superior; superfine; excellent.
優待 The preferential treatment. Give special privileges to.
優美 Excellent; elegance.
優勝 Superiority; predominance.
優雅 Grace; elegance.
優勢 Superior power; superiority; preponderance.
優點 A point of superiority; features.
優待券 Complimentary ticket.
優勝組 A winning (victorious) team.
優等生 An honour-student; a classman.

優良作風 Excellent (fine) working style.
優良傳統 Excellent (fine) tradition.
優秀領袖 Brilliant leader.
優良道德品質 Fine moral character.

儲 (v.)- Store; to save.
chǔ 儲君 The heir king; the crown prince.
儲貨 Stored; warehoused.
儲蓄 Save money; accumulate.
儲蓄金；儲蓄存款 Savings deposit.
儲藏庫 A store house; a warehouse.
儲蓄銀行 Savings bank.

儷 (n.)- A pair; a couple.
lì

# 儿 部

允 (v.)- Consent; assent; promise; accept; permit; allow; grant;
yǔn agree.
允許；允准 Permit; allow; grant; approve; authorize.
允諾 Assent; promise; answer affirmatively.

元 (n.)- Beginning. Dollar (a unit of money in China).
yuán (adj.)- Original; primary. First. Eldest. Principal.
元月 January; the first month.
元旦 New year's day.
元帥 Commander-in-chief; field marshal; generalissimo.
元首 The head of state.
元素 Element.
元寶 Large ingots of silver.
元老院 The House of Elder Statesmen.
元素週期律 Periodic law of element.

兄 (n.)- An elder brother. A senior.
兄弟 Brothers. I; myself.
xiōng 兄妹 Brother and sister.
兄長 An elder brother; a senior.
兄弟黨 Fraternal Parties.
兄弟之邦 Fraternal states.

充 (v.)- Fill. Satisfy. Carry out.
充分 Enough; sufficient.
chōng 充足 Ample; enough; well supplied.
充飢 Satisfy one's hunger.
充當 Act for another; allot for.
充電 Charge with electricity.
充滿 Be full of; be filled with; be crowded with.
充實 Fullness; completeness.

兆 (n.)- A million. An omen.
兆象 An omen; augury; sign.
zhào

兇 (adj.)- Cruel; unmerciful; violent; savage; fierce.
xiōng 兇手 A murderer; a cutthroat.
兇猛 Fierce; ferocious; furious.
兇暴 Violence; ferocity.
兇器 A murderous weapon; deadly weapon.

先 (adj.)- First. Previous; former; past. Late; deceased.
xiān (adv.)- Before; formerly; past. Early; soon. Ahead.
先夫 My late husband.

先生 Teacher; master; tutor. Sir; Mr.
先考；先父 My deceased father.
先見 Foresight; anticipation.
先例 A precedent; a previous instance.
先烈 Meritorious predecessors.
先輩 A senior; an elder; older graduates from one's Alma Mater.
先鋒 A forerunner. Vanguard; advance guard.
先導 Guidance; leadership.
先驅 A forerunner; a pioneer; a harbinger.
先天的 Inherent, congenital.
先鋒隊 The van; the leading troop.
先决條件 A prerequisite.
先决問題 The first consideration.
先見之明 Have foresight; have a long head; be far-sighted.

光 guāng (n.)- Light; luster; brilliancy; brightness. Glory; honour; splendor.
(adj.)- Bright; brilliant; light; gleaming; radiant; illustrious. Bare; naked.
(v.)- Illumine; light; reflect.
光年(天) A light year.
光明；光亮 Bright; light; clear; lucid; luculent.
光波(光) Light wave.
光彩 Brilliancy; luster; glitter.
光陰 Time.
光景 State of affairs; circumstances; condition; an aspect.
光源(光) Source of light.
光滑 Smooth; polished.
光棍 A miscreant; a rogue; a scoundrel; a villain; a rascal.
光榮 Glory; honour. Make illustrious.
光線 Ray of light.
光輝 Brilliancy; splendour; glory; brightness.
光學 Optics; light; photology.
光頭 Bald; bareheaded.
光臨 The coming of a guest. Be so kind as to come.
光譜 Spectrum.
光榮榜 Board of honour.
光天化日 In broad daylight.
光合作用 Photosynthesis.
光明正大 Straight forward; frank; with open and unprejudiced mind; fair and square.
光明前途 Bright future.
光芒萬丈 To be forever glorious.
光陰如箭 Time flies like an arrow.

克 kè (n.)- Gram.
(adj.)- Adequate; able.
(v.)- Subdue; overcome; conquer; repress. Control.
克制 Control; restrain.
克服 Overpower; overcome; overmaster, conquer; prevail over; restore (country).
克什米爾(地) Kashmir.
克服困難 Overcome the difficulty.
克勤克儉 To save and be economic.
克里米半島(地) Crimea Peninsular.

兌 duì (v.)- Barter; exchange; give an equivalent.
兌交；兌給 Weigh out; pay to.
兌稅 Pay duty.
兌換 Change money; exchange.
兌換表 Exchange table.

免 miǎn (v.)- Get off; avoid; free from. Dismiss.
免役 Exemption from conscription.
免疫 Immunity.
免除 Exemption; remission.
免稅 Duty free; remission of taxes.
免費 Free of charge.
免職 Dismiss from office; discharge.

免不了；必定 Cannot be avoided; invariably.
免稅品 Free goods.
免稅單 Certificate of exemption.

兒 (n.)- A boy; a lad; a child; an infant; a son.
ér 兒女 Children; boys and girls.
兒子 Sons.
兒孫 Children and grandchildren; posterity.
兒童 Children; a boy.
兒時 Childhood.
兒戲 Boy's play. Trifling.
兒童心理 Child psychology.
兒童文學 Juvenile literature.

兔 (n.)- A hare; a rabbit.
tù 兔脫 Run away; get off; escape.

兜 (v.)- Wrap up; obtain.
兜風 To go joy-riding.
dōu 兜圈子 To take a round.

兢 (adj.)- Cautious; anxious; attentive.
jīng 兢兢 Fearful; terrified; wary.

# 入 部

入 (v.)- Enter; go into; come in; penetrate. Become a member
rù of. Receive.
入口 Importantion; import. Enter the harbour. Entrance; way in.
入伍；入隊 Join the army; fall into the ranks.
入考；入場 Take the public examination.
入座 Take a seat.
入息 Income; earning.
入院 Be removed to a hospital; go to hospital; admitted to hospital.
入場 Enter; admittance.
入會 Become member of a society (club).
入境 Enter a country.
入獄 Be sent to prison (jail, gaol).
入閣 Be appointed a cabinet member.
入學 Enter a school; matriculate.
入選 Be accepted for; be selected.
入殮 Be put in the coffin.
入籍 Be naturalized.
入口貨 Import.
入場券 An entrance ticket; a ticket of admission.
入會費 The entrance fee.
入學新生 A new student; an entering student; a freshman.

內 (adj.)- Inner; inside; internal; interior. Inclusive.
nèi (prep.)- Within; in. Among; in the midst of; inside of.
內心 One's inmost heart; real intention. (幾) Center of an inscribed circle.
內外 Home and abroad; native and foreign. In and out; within and without; inside and outside. Inclusive and exclusive.
內因 Internal cause.
內行 Skilful; expert in; versed in.
內助 Better half; wife.
內服 Internal use.
內政 Home administration; internal

affairs.
內科 Medicine, as opposed to surgery.
內容 Contents.
內海 Inland sea.
內部 The inside; the interior.
內傷(醫) An internal injury.
內港 Inland waters.
內幕 Private circumstances; inside facts.
內閣 The cabinet; a ministry.
內臟 The internal organs.
內分泌 Internal secretion.
內出血 Internal bleeding.
內服藥 Internal medicine.
內燃機 Internal combustion engine.
內科醫生 A medical man; a physician.
內容充實 Richness in contents; substantiality.
內容貧乏 Poor in substance; meagre in contents.
內閣改組 Reshuffle of a cabinet.
內閣會議 A cabinet council; a ministerial conference.
內閣總理 The Prime Minister; the Premier.
內憂外患 Troubles from within and without; troubles at home and abroad.

全 (adj.)- Whole; complete; entire; perfect; total.
quán (adv.)- Totally; wholly; fully; entirely; altogether.
全力 All one's strength (power, energy).
全才 Universal abilities. Versatile; all-round.
全文 The full text.
全局 The general situation.
全夜 Throughout the night.
全面 The whole surface.
全音(樂) A whole note.
全套 Full suit; full set.
全盛 The height (zenith) of prosperity.
全勝 A complete victory.
全景 The whole view; a panorama.
全集 One's complete (collected) works; a complete collection.
全程 All along.
全體 In a body; unanimously.
全世界 The whole world; the world at large.
全身像 A full-length portrait (figure).
全力以赴 All out.
全民投票 Universal suffrage.
全身不遂 Total paralysis; become completely paralysed.
全身武裝 Be armed to the teeth.
全權大使 An ambassador plenipotentiary.
全權公使 Minister plenipotentiary.
全權代表 A plenipotentiary.
全體一致 Unanimously; with one consent; without a dissenting vote (voice).
全體大會 A mass meeting.

兩 (n.)- A pair; a couple. A tael. An ounce.
liǎng (adj.)- Two; both; double.
(adv.)- Twice; again.
兩方 Both sides; the two parties.
兩次 Two times; twice; again.
兩院 The two Houses of Parliament.
兩月刊 Bimonthly.
兩相情願 Both parties are willing.

# 八　部

**八** (adj.)- Eight.
bā
八月 August; the 8th month.
八折 Twenty per cent discount.
八卦 The eight diagrams.

八倍 Octuple; eight times.
八哥(動) The raven.
八角形(幾) Octagonal.
八開本 Octavo.
八大行星 The eight major planets.
八分之一 An eighth part; one-eighth.
八分音符 A quaver.
八面玲瓏 Crystalline. Amiable; affable.
八小時勞動 Eight-hour labour.
八小時三班制 The 8-hour 3-shift system.

**公** (n.)- A duke; a lord. The male of animals. Gentleman. Sir; You. Husband. Father-in-law.
gōng
(adj.)- Public; common; general; open.

公分 Centimeter; gram.
公升 Liter.
公文 Documents; public papers.
公斤 Kilogram.
公主 A princess.
公司 A company; a corporation.
公出 Absence on duty; go out on public affairs.
公正 Impartial; just; upright.
公民 Citizen.
公式 A formula; a form.
公有 In common.
公佈 Make known to the public; promulgate.
公告 Public notification.
公里 Kilometer.
公尺 Meter.
公事 Official duties.
公使 A minister.
公約 Convention.
公寓 Apartment house. Boarding house.
公海 High seas; open seas.
公報 The official gazette; public report, or news. Communique; bulletin.
公款 Public funds.
公衆 Community; common people.
公證 Testimony.
公費 Public expenditure.
公路 Public roads; highway.
公開 Open to the public.
公債 Public debt.
公園 Park; garden.
公僕 A public servant.
公認 Public approval; general compact.
公請 A joint invitation.
公論 Public opinion.
公憤 Public indignation.
公選 Public election.
公爵 A duke.
公正人 Referee; umpire.
公安局 Bureau of Public Safety.
公使館 A legation.
公務員 A public officer; a civil servant.
公德心 Public spirit; the sense of public duty.
公積金 Reserve fund.
公平價目 Fair price.
公民大會 Mass meeting.
公民投票 Plebiscite.
公用事業 A public utility; communal affairs.
公立小學 Public elementary school.
公立學校 Public school.
公立醫院 Public hospital.
公共汽車 Omnibus; bus.
公共衛生 Public health; public sanitation; public hygiene.
公平合理 Fairly and reasonably.
公衆電話 A public telephone; a call box; a telephone booth.
公開展覽 Public exhibition.
公開秘密 Open secret.
公爵夫人 Duchess.
公立圖書館 The public library.
公共建築物 The public building.

六 (adj.)- Six.
liù 六十 Sixty.
六月 June; the 6th month.
六折 Forty per cent discount.
六倍 Six times.
六角形(幾) Hexagon.
六絃琴 Guitar.

兮 (interj.)- An interjection of admiration, doubt, or inquiry used in poetry.
xī

共 (v.)- Share; participate.
(adv.)- All; altogether; in all; collectively; wholly; totally.
gòng 共用 Common use.
共同 Mutual; in common.
共事 Work together; be associated with.
共計 The sum total; in all. Reckoning the whole.
共振(物) Resonance.
共處 Co-existence.
共鳴 Resonance; sympathy; feel sympathize with; respond to; be of the same mind with.
共和國 A republic.
共和黨 Republican party.
共產黨 Communist party.
共同市場 Common market.
共同行動 United action.
共同利益 Common interest.
共同目標 A common purpose; common cause.

兵 (n.)- Soldiers; a force; an army. Arms; weapons; Fighter; man in the ranks.
bīng (adj.)- Military; warlike.
兵丁；兵士；兵卒 Soldiers; marines; militia; enlisted men.
兵力 Military strength (force).
兵役 Military service.
兵亂；兵變 Troops in mutiny.
兵營 A military camp.
兵艦 Men-of-war; a battleship.
兵工廠 An arsenal; an Armoury.
兵役年齡 Military age.
兵隊檢閱 Review troops.

其 (pron.)- He; she; it; they. His; her; its; their.
qí (adj.)- This; that; the.
其中 Among them; in the midst of; there in.
其次 The next. Moreover.
其後 Afterwards; hereafter; eversince.
其實 Really; truly; in truth; in fact; in reality.
其餘 The rest; the remainder. Over and above.

具 (n.)- Tools; instrument.
(adj.)- Prepared; ready. All; every; throughly; throughout.
jù (v.)- Prepare; furnish; arrange; draw up; do.
具有 Have; possess.
具領 Receive.
具體 Concrete; definite.
具體辦法 A definite plan.

典 (n.)- Law; rule; ordinances. A story; legend; literary quotations. Ceremony; rite.
diǎn (v.)- Mortgage; pledge. Take oversight of. Manage; lease; contract; pawn.
典型 A prototype; an example; a pattern; a type.
典故 Literary quotations; allusions.
典當 A pawnshop Pawn; pledge.
典禮 Ceremony; rite; celebration.

兼 (adj.)- Both. Additional.
(adv.)- Together. Equally.
jiān (conj.)- Moreover; and; also.

兼用 Double use.
兼併 Absorb; annex.
兼理；兼攝 Manage several duties; concurrently.
兼顧 To give attention to both . . . and.
兼愛主義 Altruism.

# 冂 部

**冉** (adj.)- Tender; weak.
(adv.)- Gradually.
rǎn 冉冉 Gradually; imperceptibly.

**册** (n.)- A register; a record. A book; a volume. A copy; a pamphlet. An inventory; a list.
cè
册子 Records.

**再** (adv.)- Again; twice; second time. Also; further.
zài 再三 Time after time; again and again; repeatedly.
再生(生) Regeneration.
再版 Reprint; second edition.
再思 Think again.
再者 Moreover; again; furthermore.
再試 Try again; make another attempt.
再會 Good-bye.
再審 Retrial; re-examination. Rehearing; try a case over again.
再教育 Re-education; re-orientation; retraining.

**冒** (v.)- Rush; venture; risk; dare. Disguise; pretend.
mào 冒失 Rash; rude.
冒犯 Offend; affront.
冒充 Pretend to be.
冒雨 In spite of the rain.
冒昧 Take the liberty; rude.
冒牌 Imitate a trade- mark.
冒險 Brave danger; run the risk; run into danger.
冒失鬼 A blunderer; a rash fellow.
冒險者 An adventurer.
冒險主義 Adventurism.

**冑** (n.)- A helmet.
zhòu

**冕** (n.)- A crown; a coronet; a hat.
miǎn

# 冖 部

**冠** (n.)- A cap; a hat; a crown. The crest or comb of a bird; a derby.
guān (v.)- Cap. Excel; surpass.
冠巾 A headdress.
冠軍 Champion.
冠詞(文) Article.
冠戴 Dress; put on the hat.
冠冕堂皇 Have a bold and noble bearing.

冤 (n.)- Oppression; ill-usage; wrong; injustice; grievance.
yuān (v.)- Injure; wrong; oppress.
冤仇 Enmity; hatred.
冤枉；冤屈 An injustice; wrong; grievance. Implicate falsely.
冤家 An enemy; an opponent; a foe.
冤家聚頭 Enemies meet face to face.

冥 (n.)- The under world; Hades. (adj.)-Dark; dim; obscure; dusk;
míng gloomy; doleful.
冥海 The deep sea.
冥想 Contemplation; deep in thought.
冥頑 Stupid; unreformable; obstinacy; doltish.
冥王星 Pluto.

## 冫部

冬 (n.)- Winter. The cold season. (adj.)- Wintry.
dōng 冬季 Winter.
冬瓜(植) White gourd.
冬至；冬節 The winter solstice or festival.
冬青(植) Holly; Ilex pedunculosa; evergreen.
冬眠；冬蟄 Hibernation; winter sleep.
冬作物 Winter crops.
冬蟲夏草(植) Cordyceps roberti.

冰 (n.)- Ice.
(adj.)- Icy; cold; freezing.
bīng 冰山 An iceberg; a floating mass (mountain) of ice.
冰川 A glacier.
冰凍 Frozen.
冰島(地) Iceland.
冰袋 An ice-bag or ice-poultice.
冰棒 Frozen sucker.
冰塊 A lump (cake, block) of ice.
冰雹 Hailstones.
冰箱 A refrigerator; an ice-box.
冰戲 Skating.
冰糖 Sugar candy; crystal sugar.
冰點 Freezing point.
冰霜 Frost; ice.
冰淇淋 Ice cream.
冰河時代 The Glacial epoch; the ice age.

冶 (v.)- Fuse; melt.
冶匠 A founder; a smelter.
yě 冶坊 A foundry.
冶鐵 Forge; cast.
冶金術 Metallurgy.
冶金爐 Blast furnace.

冷 (adj.)- Cold; icy. Quiet; lonesome; solitary.
lěng (v.)- Cool; chill.
冷汗 A cold sweat.
冷門 Dark horse.
冷笑 A sardonic grin; a sneer.
冷淡 Cool; indifferent; unconcerned.
冷眼 A cold look; indifference.
冷落 Lonely; solitary. (商) Depression.
冷酷 Cruelty; cold-heartedness.
冷瘡 Chilblain.
冷戰 A cold war.
冷盤 Cold dishes.
冷藏 Cold storage.
冷水浴 Cold bath.
冷凝器 Condenser.
冷氣機 An air-conditioner.
冷藏庫 An ice-safe-chamber; an ice-pit.

冷血動物 Cold blooded animals.
冷氣設備 Air-conditioning; a cooling-apparatus.
冷淡態度 A lukewarm attitude.
冷眼旁觀 Look askance at.

冽 (n.)- Cold air; chill.
(adj.)- Very cold; chilly.
liè 冽風 A cold wind.

准 (v.)- Permit; grant; allow; consent; approve; authorize; promise.
zhǔn 准假 Leave of absence.
准將 A brigadier-general.
准尉 A sub-officer; a non-commissioned sublieutenant.
准許 Sanction; grant; approve of.
准予免稅 Grant exemption from duty.

凋 (adj.)- Fading; falling; withered; declined.
diāo (v.)- Become withered; fade; fall (leaves).
凋落；凋謝 Fallen; faded; withered.
凋零 Declined fallen.

凍 (adj.)- Cold; icy; freezing; frozen.
dōng (v.)- Cool; freeze.
凍死 Frozen to death; die of cold.
凍結 Freeze; coagulate.
凍僵 Benumbed with cold.
凍瘡 Chilblains.
凍結解除 Unfreeze.

凜 (adj.)- Cold. Bleak; desolate. Trembling.
lǐn 凜冽 Piercing cold; intense cold.
凜然 Stern; severe.

凝 (v.)- Freeze; coagulate; consolidate.
níng 凝固 Hardened; consolidated; congealed; coagulated. Solidification.
凝思 Meditate; be lost in thought.
凝視 Gaze at; stare fixedly.
凝結 Freeze; congeal; clot; consolidate; fix. (物) Coagulation; congelation.
凝固點(物) Solidifying point.
凝聚器；凝縮器 Condenser.

# 几 部

几 (n.)- A small table; a side table; a tea stand.
jī

凡 (adj.)- All. Every. Common; usual. Mortal; human.
fán (adv.)- Generally.
凡才 Common ability.
凡事 Every thing; all affairs.
凡例 General rules.
凡間 The world. In human life. Secular.
凡庸 Ordinary; mediocre.
凡士林 Vaseline.
凡陀林 A mandolin.

凭 (v.)- Lean. Trust to; rely on.
píng

凰 (n.)- The female phoenix.
huáng

**凱** (n.)- A victory. The triumphant return of an army.
kǎi 凱旋 Return in triumph.
凱歌 Victory song.
凱風 The south wind.
凱旋門 Triumphant arch.

**凳** (n.)- A bench; a stool.
dèng 凳子 A seat without a back.

# 凵 部

**凶** (adj.)- Unlucky. Unhappy; sad; evil. Cruel; fierce.
xīong 凶手；凶徒；凶身 A murderer; a cutthroat; an assassinator; an assassin.
凶日 Black day.
凶兆 Evil-boding; bad omen.
凶宅 A haunted house.
凶器 The deadly weapon.

**凸** (adj.)- Convex; projecting.
凸牙 Projecting teeth.
tū 凸出 Project; swell up; protrude.
凸字 Characters cut in relief; a raised type.
凸起 Convexity.
凸眼 Prominent eyes.
凸鏡 Convex mirror.
凸透鏡(物) Convex lens.
凸板印刷 Relief printing.

**凹** (n.)- An indentation; a hollow; a depression or cavity.
āo (adj.)- Concave; hollow.
凹下 Arched vault; recess.
凹凸 Concave and convex; unevenness.
凹地 A hollow.
凹坑 A pit.
凹眼 Deep eyes.
凹面鏡(物) Concave mirror.
凹透鏡(物) Concave lens.

**出** (v.)- Go out. Appear. Produce; spring from. Pay.
chū (adv.)- Out; abroad; forward.
出入 In and out. Income and expenditure.
出力 Make an effort; take the trouble.
出口 Export. Exit; way out; outlet.
出世 Be born; enter the world.
出名 Become famous. Celebrated; well-known; noted.
出汗 Perspire; sweat.
出血 Bleed.
出身 Qualification.
出版 Publish. Publication.
出芽 Bud; sprout; put forth a shoot; shoot; germinate.
出門 Travel.
出品 Manufactures; products; exhibits.
出洋 Go abroad.
出席 Attendance; presence.
出庭 Appear in court.
出租 Let; for rent.
出動 Dispatch; set out.
出產 Natural products.
出現 Appear; make an appearance.
出發 Set out; start; make a start; leave; depart.
出嫁；出閣 Marry a husband.
出路 An outlet; an outgate.
出演 Come on the stage; perform; appear before the footlights.
出獄 Released from prison; be set free.

出賣 For sale.
出醜 Incur disgrace; bring shame to oneself.
出殯 A funeral.
出版物 A publication.
出版界 The publishing world.
出口稅 Export duty.
出版業 Publishing business.
出口商 Exporter.
出納員 A cashier.
出世紙 Birth certificate.
出版自由 Liberty of the press.
出席人數 Number of attendances.
出租汽車 Hired car.

**函** hán (n.)- A letter. An envelope. A case.
(v.)- Contain. Write.
函件 A letter.
函洞(鐵道) Tunnel.
函授 Teach by correspondence.
函數(算) Function.
函覆 In reply.
函授學校 A correspondence school.

# 刀 部

**刀** dāo (n.)- A knife; a sword. An ancient coin.
刀口 The edge of a knife; blade.
刀片 Razor blade.
刀尖 The point of a knife.
刀豆(植) French beans.
刀柄 The knife handle.
刀背 The knife back.
刀鋒 The point of a knife or sword.
刀鞘 A sheath; a scabbard.

**刁** diāo (adj.)- Wicked; artful; cunning; crafty; knavish.
刁野；刁蠻 Barbarous; savage; unruly.
刁難 Obstructive.

**分** fēn (n.)- Duty; function. Cent; a minute.
(v.)- Divide; separate; distribute; part. Share. Distinguish.
分力(物) The resolution of forces.
分子 A share; an individual. (物) Molecule. (算) Numerator.
分工 Divison of labour.
分手 Depart; take leave; say good-bye.
分付 Pay by installments.
分母 (算) Denominator.
分米 Decimeter.
分佈 Distribution; spread.
分別 Classify; distinguish; parting.
分局 A branch bureau.
分店 A branch shop.
分析 Analysis; assay.
分歧 Diverge; branch off; ramify.
分派 Apportion duties; appoint; dispatch.
分界；分限 The boundary; the frontier; demarcation; delimitation. Extent.
分娩 Give birth to a child; delivery; childbirth.
分校 A branch school.
分家；分產 Divide the property.
分班 By turns.
分租 Rent part of a house.
分配 Distribute; divide.
分散 Disperse; scatter.
分裂 Split; divided; break up. (生) Seg-

mentation.
分量 Measure; capacity; weight; quantity.
分發 Send to different places.
分詞(文) A participle.
分解(化) Decomposition. Resolution.
分課 A subdivision of a section.
分擔 Bear a part of; share in.
分類 Classify; assort.
分公司 Sub-office.
分光器；分光鏡 Spectroscope.
分列式 A march past; defile.
分角器；分度規 A protractor.
分界線 The boundary-line; the line of demarcation.
分解作用 Disintegration.
分清是非 To thrash out questions of right and wrong.
分期付款 Installment; hire purchase; pay by installment.
分工合作 Proper division of labour and cooperation.

切 qiē 〔qiè〕 (v.)- Cut; carve; mince; slice; chop.
切己 Self-concern. Of personal consequence.
切肉 Mince meat.
切忌 Prohibited; interdicted.
切迫 Urgent; impending; imminent.
切脈 Feel the pulse.
切碎 Cut to pieces.
切腹 Disembowelment; harakiri.
切實 Strongly; sincerely; heartily.
切線(幾) Tangent.
切點(幾) A point of contact.
切斷 Cut off.
切斷面 A section.

刊 kān (v.)- Cut; carve; engrave. Print; publish.
刊印 Print; publish.
刊物 A periodical; a magazine.

刎 wěn (v.)- Cut; kill oneself.
刎頸 Cut one's own throat.

刑 xíng (n.)- Punishment. A law.
刑具 Implements of punishments.
刑場 An execution-ground.
刑期 Term of penalty; prison term.
刑罰 Punishment; penalty.
刑事案 Criminal case.
刑事法庭 Criminal court.

划 huà 〔huá〕 (v.)- Pole; paddle; oar.
划船 Pole a boat. A small boat.
划艇 A rowboat; an openboat.

列 liè (n.)- A rank; a file; a series. A row; a line; a class.
(v.)- Distinguish. Put in order. Arrange.
列入 Be arranged; be included in; fall under.
列下；列後 As follows; in the following; enumerated below.
列位 Gentlemen; sirs. Ladies and gentlemen.
列車 Train.
列表 List.
列席 Sit; attend.
列隊 Dress ranks.
列傳 Biography.
列舉 Enumerate; enumeration.

初 chū (n.)- Commencement.
(adj.)- First; beginning; early; original.
(adv.)- Originally; at first; firstly.
初一 The first day of the month.
初生 The first born; the first growth.
初次 The first time.

初旬 The first decade of a month.
初版 First edition.
初級 Elementary; primary.
初期 Infancy.
初學 Begin study. Elementary instruction; primary education.
初學者 A beginner; an abecedarian; a novice.
初次登台 Debut.
初等教育 Elementary education.
初開天地 At the creation.
初級中學校 Junior middle school.
初等小學校 Primary school.
初等教科書 Primary school text books.
初級師範學校 Junior normal school.
初級實業學校 Junior technical school.

删 (v.)- Cancel; expunge; erase; reject; eliminate.
shān 删去；删削 Expunge; cancel; erase; eliminate.
删減 Abridge; cut short.

判 (n.)- Judgment; decision. A verdict.
pàn (v.)- Separate; divide into parts; halve. Judge; decide; give a sentence. Distinguish.
判決(法) Decision; sentence; determination; verdict. Judge; decree.
判官(法) A judge.
判罪 Conviction.
判斷 Give judgment; judge.

別 (n.)- Separation; departure.
(adj.)- Special. Different; unlike. Another; other.
bié
〔biè〕 (v.)- Separate; divide; part. Distinguish. Differ. Leave; depart.
別人 Another man.
別名 Another name; an alias; pseudonym.
別後 After our parting.
別致 Rare; unusual; special.
別針 Pin.
別處 Another place. Elsewhere.
別墅；別業 A villa; a country seat; a summer house.
別扭 Stubborn.
別離 Leave; separate; part; depart.
別動 Don't move.

刨 (n.)- A plane.
(v.)- Plane; level; make smooth.
páo 刨子 Carpenter's plane.
〔bào〕 刨花 Shavings; wood chips.

利 (n.)- Gains; profit; advantage. Interest.
lì (adj.)- Sharp; acute; advantageous; beneficial; useful. Happy; fortunate.
利己 Benefit oneself. Selfish.
利用 Utilize; avail; use; take advantage of.
利害 Severe; serious.
利息；利率 Profit; interest.
利益；利潤 Gain; profit; interest.
利器 Cutlery; arms; edge-tool.
利物浦(地) Liverpool.
利斯本(地) Lisbon.
利比亞(地) Libia; Libya.
利己主義(哲) Egoism.
利比里亞(地) Liberia.
利害關係人 Person interested.

刮 (v.)- Pare; scrape off; plane off; rub; brush away; raze.
guā 刮刀 A scraping knife.
刮平 Raze; level down.
刮鬍 Shave the beard.
刮鬍刀 A razor.

到 (v.)- Reach; arrive; make way to; get at; attend to; come
dào to.

(prep.)- To; at; from; till; until.
到了 Be arrived.
到今 Until now; up to the present.
到手 Come to hand; in hand. Receive.
到任 Take the post.
到底 After all; at last; finally; in the end.
到處 Everywhere; in every place; in all directions; far and wide; on every side; all about; all round.
到期 In due time.
到達 Reach; arrive; come at.

**剁** duò
(v.)- Chop; cut into fine pieces; mince.
剁成肉漿 Make into fine mince-meat.

**制** zhì
(n.)- Rule; law. System.
(v.)- Regulate; control; govern. Make; invent. Prevent; press; hinder.
制止 Withhold; suppress; inhibit.
制作 Create; make; do.
制定 Enactment; set down.
制服 Uniform.
制度 Rules; regulations; system; policy.
制法 Laws; rules; orders.

**刷** shuà 〔shuā〕
(n.)- A brush; a scraper.
(v.)- Scrub; rub; wipe off; brush.
刷牙 Brush the teeth.
刷印 Print.
刷衣 Brush the cloth.
刷子 A brush.
刷鞋 Brush shoes.

**券** quàn
(n.)- A bond; a certificate; a contract. A ticket. A deed.
券契 A bond or deed.
券據 A certificate; a coupon.

**刹** shā 〔shà〕
(n.)- An abbey; a monastery.
刹那 A very short moment.

**刺** cì
(v.)- Stab; pierce; thrust; cut into.
刺入 Pierce.
刺刀 Bayonet; dagger.
刺客 An assassin; a stabber.
刺傷 Wound by stabbing.
刺蝟(動) A hedgehog.
刺激 Stimulus; provoke; excite.
刺諷 Mock; satirize.
刺繡 Embroidery.
刺激品 A stimulant; a stimulus; an incentive.

**刻** kè
(n.)- A quarter of an hour.
(v.)- Carve; engrave; cut. Devote oneself to.
(adj.)- Illtreat; maltreat.
刻刀 A carving knife.
刻下 At present; now.
刻字 Engrave characters.
刻板 Cut blocks.
刻苦 Painstaking. Suffer hardship.
刻畫 Carved; cut; laboured.
刻薄 Treat harshly; illtreat.

**剃** tì
(v.)- Shave.
剃刀 A razor.
剃頭 Haircutting.
剃鬚 Shave the beard; shave the whisker.
剃頭匠 A barber.
剃頭店 A barber's shop; hair-dressing saloon.

**則** zé
(n.)- A rule; a law. A system. A standard.
(v.)- Pattern.
(adv.)-Consequently. After that.

In that case.
(conj.)- Then; and so; therefore.
則例 By-law.
則傚 Imitate; model.

削 (v.)- Cut; shave; scrape off. Sharpen; pare off.
xiāo 削皮 Peel the skin.
〔xuē〕 削尖 Sharpen.
削除 Deduct; take away.
削薄 Scrape thin.
削筆刀 A pen knife.

前 (adj.)- Front; former; previous.
(v.)- Advance; progress; go
qián forward; go ahead.
(adv.)- Before; ago; formerly; previously; ahead.
(prep.)- Before; in front of.
前人 A predecessor; an antecessor.
前方 The front.
前日 The day before yesterday.
前月 The previous month; ultimo; months ago.
前任 The former incumbent; predecessor.
前次 A previous occasion; last time.
前年 The year before last.
前言 Foreword; preamble.
前足；前脚 Forelegs; forefoot.
前門 A front door.
前後 Before and after; first and last; forward and backward.
前者 Formerly; previously; the former.
前述 Above mentioned.
前面 In the front; before; anterior.
前哨 Advanced post; outpost.
前景 The foreground.
前途 The future.
前程 Future; future career.
前進 March; proceed; advance; progress; go ahead; set forward.
前線 The front line.
前鋒 The advance guard.
前輩 Seniors; elders; forerunners.
前臂(解) Forearm.
前奏曲 An overture; a prelude.
前置詞(文) Preposition.
前途有望 Promising; of great promise; hopeful.
前程萬里 Bright future.

剔 (v.)- Scrape off. Pick out.
剔出 Get rid of; reject.
tī 剔清 Pick clean.

剖 (v.)- Explain; argue. Cut up. Halve; split. Judge.
pōu 剖析 Solve.
剖屍；剖解 Cut up a dead body; dissect; anatomize.
剖開 Rip open; cut open.

剛 (n.)- Strength. Intrepidity.
(adj.)- Solid; hard; stiff; firm.
gāng Steady; strong; unyielding.
(adv.)- Just now; recently; only a moment ago; just.
剛果(地) Congo.
剛直 Straight; upright; inflexible.
剛柔 Hard and soft.
剛强 Wilful; obstinate.
剛毅 Resolute; unyielding.
剛才 Just now.

剜 (v.)- Cut out; scoop out.
剜肉補瘡 A makeshift to tide
wān over a present difficulty.

剝 (v.)- Split; tear; peel off; strip. Pull off; rind. Extort; fleece;
bō demand by force.
〔bāo〕 剝皮 Peel. Extort; fleece. Skin.
剝削 Oppress; squeeze; extort.
剝奪 Strip; deprive.
剝落 Dilapidated.

剩 (n.)- An overplus; a residue; a remainder.
shèng (v.)- Remain; be left.
剩下 Remain over; left over.
剩出 Put aside.
剩錢；剩銀 Money remaining. Balance.
剩餘價值 Surplus value. Residual value.
剩飯殘羹 Remains of food.
剩餘利潤 Surplus profit.

剪 (n.)- Shears; scissors; clippers.
jiǎn (v.)- Cut; clip; shear; cut off; smooth; extirpate.
剪刀 Shears; scissors; clippers.
剪貼 Clipping.
剪短 Clip; curtail.
剪碎 Cut into pieces.
剪斷 Cut asunder.
剪髮 Haircutting.
剪草 Mow grass.
剪影 Silhouette.

剮 (v.)- Cut the body into pieces; hack.
guǎ

副 (n.)- An assistant; an associate. A set or suit of things.
fù (adj.)- Vice; second.
(v.)- Assist; second; aid.
副手 An assistant.
副本 A duplicate copy.
副官 Aide-de-camp; adjutant.
副業 Subsidiary business; a side job.
副主席 A vice-chairman.
副作用 Secondary reaction; harmful byeffects.
副食品 A subsidiary (supplementary) food; a side-dish.
副產物 By-product.
副經理 Sub-manager; assistant manager.
副領事 Vice consul.
副總統 Vice president.

割 (v.)-Cut. Divide. Take off; cede.
gē
割禾 Reap grain; cut rice.
割草 Cut grass; mow.
割開 Rip open; cut asunder.
割傷 Cut; wound.
割除(手足) To amputate.

創 (v.)- Begin; commence; start. Establish; found. Create; invent.
chuàng Wound; cut; gash.
創立；創設 Found; establish; set up.
創刊 The first publication.
創作 Invent; originate; create.
創始 Begin; start; initiate; take the first step; make a beginning.
創造 Create.
創傷 A wound; a cut; the part hurt; scar.
創業 Start a business; open a firm.
創辦 Institute.
創辦人 The founder; promoter.
創新紀錄 Make (establish) a new record.

剷 (v.)- Spade; hoe.
chǎn
剷子 A spade; a hoe.
剷平 Raze.
剷除 Obliterate.
剷土機 Scraper.

剿 (v.)- Attack; destroy; put down.
jiǎo
剿匪 Put down bandits.
剿捕 Arrest; catch; suppress.

劃 (v.)- Carve; engrave; cut. Mark. Divide.
huà 〔huá〕
劃分 Divide; distinguish between.
劃去 Cross off.
劃界 Draw a line or demarcation.
劃破 Scratch.
劃一 Uniform.

劃定價目 Cost mark.
劃線支票(商) Crossed cheque.

**劇** jù (n.)- A play; an act; a drama.
(adj.)- Annoying; distressing; severe.
(adv.)- Extremely; very; seriously.
劇本 A play; a scenario; a dramatic composition.
劇烈 Strong; pungent; drastic.
劇場 A theater; a playhouse; the stage.
劇痛 Torture; pang.
劇中人 Characters in a play; the cast.

**劈** pY 〔pĭ〕 (n.)- A wedge.
(v.)- Cut; split.
劈柴 Split wood.
劈開 Split open; cleave. (鑛) Cleavage.
劈碎 Split into pieces.

**劊** guì (v.)- Cut off; amputate; execute.
劊子手 An executioner: one who is ordered to kill a criminal.

**劍** jiàn (n.)- A sword; a rapier; a dagger.
劍客；劍俠 A knight; a fencer.
劍術 The art of fencing; swordsmanship.
劍魚(動) A swordfish.
劍鋒 The point of a sword; sword blade.
劍鞘 A scabbard.
劍擊 Fencing.

**劑** jì (n.)- Dose; prescription.

# 力 部

**力** lì (n.)- Strength; power; energy; spirit; might; vigour. Force.
力士 A man of great muscular strength.
力求 Request earnestly.
力壯 Robust; vigorous; strong and healthy.
力量 Physical strength; force; power.
力强 Strong.
力學(物) Dynamics. Study with diligence.
力點(物) Point of application of force.
力量對比 Balance of force.
力戒驕傲 To guard against arrogance.
力爭上游 To aim high.
力求進步 Struggle for improvement; spare no pains in making improvements.
力所不及 Not within one's power.

**功** gōng (n.)- Merit; a good service. Honour; reward. Virtue; effect; achievement; accomplishment.
(adj.)- Meritorious; worthy; virtuous.
功夫 Work; service; kungfu.
功用 Use; effect. Function.
功效 Merit; effect; efficiency.
功勞 Merit; meritorious services.
功課 Task; work; service; lesson.
功勳 Achievement.

功績 Distinguished services; a meritorious deed.
功課表 Time table.
功利主義 Utilitarianism.

加 jiā (n.)- Addition. Enlargement; increase.
(adj.)- Extra; additional.
(v.)- Add; increase. Advance; promote.
加工 Extra work.
加稅 To levy an extra tax; a higher tax rate.
加油 Come on!
加法(算) Addition.
加侖(量) Gallon.
加倍 Twice; double; twofold; two times.
加冕 Coronation.
加深 Deepen.
加速 Hasten; quicken.
加減 Increase and decrease; addition and subtraction.
加薪 Feed with fuel. Increase salary.
加厘粉 Curry-powder.
加拿大(地) Canada.
加速度(物) Acceleration.
加爾各答(地) Calcutta.
加利福尼亞(地) California.

劣 liè (adj.)- Feeble; weak. Bad; inferior; poor; humble. Depraved; mean.
劣紳 Deprived gentry.
劣貨 Low-grade goods; an inferior article.
劣等 Inferior grade; of poor quality.
劣等生 A backward pupil.

助 zhù (v.)- Help; aid; assist; render assistance; co-operate.
助手 An assistant; a helper.
助教 Assistant teacher.
助捐 Contribute; subscribe.
助理人 Staff.
助產士 A midwife.
助動詞(文) Auxiliary verb.
助一臂之力 Lend a helping hand.

努 nǔ (v.)- Exert; strive; endeavour.
努力 Exertion; great efforts; endeavours. Make an effort; try hard; strive.

劫 jié (v.)- Rob; snatch; plunder.
劫去 Snatched away.
劫案 A case of robbery.
劫掠；劫奪 Harry; rob; plunder; loot; pillage.
劫匪 Robbers; plunderers; highwaymen; bandits.
劫機 To hijack a plane.
劫機者 A hijacker.
劫掠一空 Make a clean sweep.

効 xiào (n.)- Result; effect.
効力 Render service. Effect.
効用 Function.
効勞 Serve in return for some favour received; offer one's service.

勁 jìn 〔jìng〕 (adj.)- Strong; powerful. Hard.
勁力 Great strength.
勁敵 Powerful enemy.

勃 bó (adj.)- Confused; flourishing; prosperous.
(adv.)- Suddenly; hastily; unexpectedly; abruptly.
勃然 Suddenly; abruptly.

勇 yǒng (n.)- Bravery; courage; daring.
(adj.)- Adventurous; daring; heroic; brave; courageous; val-

iant; fearless.
勇士 A brave man; a man of courage.
勇氣 Courage; valour; vigour; stout heart; brave spirit.
勇猛 Fearless; fierce; desperate.
勇敢 Courageous; daring; bravely. Be courageous.
勇往直前 March boldly forward; aggressive.
勇於作戰 Fight bravely.

勉 miǎn (v.)- Force; compel; urge. Stimulate; encourage. Persuade.
勉强 Forced; compelled; constrained; urged; pressed.
勉勵 Encourage; stimulate. Energize; excite; give energy.

勒 lè (n.)- A bridle; the reins. (v.)- Bridle; rein in. Force. Bind; curb; cease.
勒令 Force compliance; insist on.
勒死 Strangle.
勒索 Extort; squeeze; screw out; blackmail.
勒馬 Check a horse; clap spurs to a horse; bridle a horse.

動 dǒng (n.)-Motion. Movement. Action. (adj.)- Movable. Restless. (v.)- Move; affect; induce; influence. Stir; shake.
動人 Charming.
動力 Motive power; dynamic force.
動工 Begin work; commence a work.
動手 Begin; start; strike the first.
動作 Action; operation; movement.
動向 A trend; movement.
動身 Set out; start.
動物 Animals.
動怒 Excite one's anger; enrage; become angry.
動脈(醫) Artery.
動員 Mobilize.
動詞(文) A verb.
動搖 Be in commotion; shake; tremble.
動機 Motive; cause.
動蕩 Vibrate; shake.
動靜 Moving and resting; state; condition.
動聽 Eloquent; convincing. Please to the ears.
動物界 Animal kingdom.
動物園 Zoological garden; zoo; menagerie.
動物學 Zoology.
動畫片 Cartoons.
動脈硬化症 Arteriosclerosis; sclerosis of the arteries.

勘 kān (v.)- Survey; locate; examine by comparison; collate.
勘探 Detect.
勘究 Investigate thoroughly.
勘誤 Correct errors.
勘驗 Investigate; examine.
勘誤表 Corrigenda; errata.

務 wù (n.)- Business; work; affairs; concerns; function. (v.)- Attend to; devote oneself to.
務必 Must. Have to; necessary.
務農 Devote oneself to agriculture.

勝 shēng (v.)- Conquer; have the victory; win.
勝仗 Victory.
勝任 Equal to the task; adequate to the post; competent.
勝利 Victory; triumph.
勝負；勝敗 Victory and defeat.
勝迹 Famous places of ruins.
勝過 Excel; surpass; out strip; transcend; run before.
勝利軍 A victorious army.

勝負不分 A draw game; a draw; a dead heat.

勞 (n.)- Merit; worthy actions; services; pains; toil; diligence.
láo (adj.)- Careworn; burdened; fatigued.
(v.)- Labour; to work.
勞力 Labour.
勞役 Hard labour. Laborious task; drudgery; toil.
勞神 Weary oneself. Trouble another; bother.
勞苦 Toilsome; laborious; hardship.
勞動 Labour; toil; drudgery.
勞碌 Toil. Busy.
勞駕 Excuse me for putting you to the trouble of coming.
勞工局 Labour office.
勞動黨 Labour Party.
勞動力 Labour power.
勞動者 A worker; a labourer.
勞動節 May Day.
勞工保險 Workmen's insurance.
勞工神聖 The diginity of labour.
勞工部長 The Minister of Labour; the Secretary of Labour.
勞動改造 Reform through labour.
勞動階級 Labour class. Proletariat.

募 (v.)- Invite to do. Raise. Beg; call upon.
mù 募捐 Ask for subscriptions; raise contributions.
募款 Raise fund.

勢 (n.)- Power; influence; authority; strength; force. States;
shì condition; circumstances.
勢力 Strength; influence; force; power.
勢利 Snobbish.
勢力均衡 Balance of power.
勢力爭奪 A struggle for power.
勢如破竹 Their strength is like splitting bamboo—once it starts it is sure to go on.

勤 (n.)- Diligence.
(adj.)- Diligent; attentive.
qín (v.)- Work hard.
(adv.)- Diligently; steadily; laboriously.
勤勉 Industrious; hardworking; diligent.
勤勞 Hardworking; toilsome; industrious; laborious.
勤儉 Diligent and frugal; thrift.
勤學 Study hard; learn diligently; learn by heart; studious; assiduous.
勤懇 Very diligent; painstaking. In good earnest.

勦 (v.)- Suppress; crush; put down by force; destroy. Plagiarize.
jiǎo 勦匪 Destroy rebels or robbers.

勳 (n.)- Loyal merit.
勳位 Order.
xūn 勳章 Decoration; medal; order of merit.
勳業 Distinguished services; merit.

勵 (v.)- Stimulate; encourage; urge.
lì

勸 (v.)- Advise; exhort. Persuade; induce. Encourage; stimulate.
quàn 勸告 Recommend; advice.
勸阻 Dissuade.
勸解 Exhort to peace; compromise.
勸慰 Soothe; console.
勸導 Exhort and teach; induce.
勸勉 Encourage by advice; persuade; exhort.
勸人爲善 Incite people to do good.

# 勹 部

勺 (n.)- A spoon; a ladle. A small quantity; a little bit; a spoonful — of a pint (升).
sháo
勺子 A spoon; a ladle.

匀 (adj.)- Equal; even; average; alike; same.
yún (v.)- Divide equally.
(adv.)- Equally; in equal parts; evenly.
匀正 Uniform.

勾 (n.)- A hook.
(v.)- Cancel; annul. Hook on with; connect. Entice; draw.
gōu
〔gòu〕 勾引 Entice; seduce; inveigle.
勾消 Cancel.
勾除 Cancel; reject; repeal; make void.
勾結 Connive; in league with. Join in a plot; secretly connected.
勾當 Business; affairs. Manage affairs.

勿 (adv.)- Not; never; no.
wù 勿用 Not necessary; not to use.
勿動 Don't touch; don't move.
勿灰心 Do not be downcast.
勿隨地吐痰 No spitting.

包 (n.)- A wrapper. A parcel; a bundle; a bale; a package.
bāo (v.)- Wrap; pack; envelope. Contain; hold; embrace; include.
包件 A parcel; a package.
包含 Include; comprise; contain.
包庇 Screen; harbour; protect.
包括 Include; involve; embrace; cover.
包紮 Bundle.
包圍 Surround; invest.
包廂 Boxes or stalls in a theatre.
包裝 Pack; wrap up.
包辦 Undertake. Contract.

匆 (adj.)- Hurried; hasty.
匆匆 In hurry.
cōng 匆忙 Hasty. In haste.

匈 (n.)- Name of a tribe which was under the suzerainty of the Han dynasty.
xiōng
匈牙利(地) Hungary.

匍 (v.)- Crawl; creep. Lie prostrate; scramble.
pú 匍匐；匍行 Crawl; creep.

# 匕 部

匕 (n.)- A ladle; a spoon. A knife; a short sword.
bǐ 匕首 A dagger; a stiletto.

化 (n.)- Change; alteration; transformation.
huà (v.)- Change; alter; transform;
〔huā〕 transmute; convert. Reform;

influence. Dissolve; melt.
化石 Fossil.
化合(化) Chemical combination.
化妝 Toilet. Dressing.
化費 Expenditure.
化學 Chemistry.
化膿 Suppurate; maturate; fester.
化驗 Test. Chemical examination.
化合力 Chemical affinity.
化合物 Compounds.
化妝品 Toilet supplies; cosmetics.
化妝室 Dressing room; make-up room; parlour.
化妝檯 A dressing table.
化學式 Chemical formula.
化學家 Chemist.
化學工業 Chemical industry.
化學反應 Chemical reaction.
化學平衡 Chemical equilibrium.
化學性質 Chemical property.
化學物品 Chemicals.
化學肥料 Chemical fertilizer.
化學現象 Chemical phenomena.
化學變化 Chemical change.
化學方程式 Chemical equation.

北 běi (n.)- The north.
(adj.)- Northern.
北方 The northern regions.
北京(地) Peking.
北風 North wind.
北海(地) The North Sea.
北部 The northern part; the north.
北極 The north pole.
北歐(地) Northern Europe.
北半球 The Northern Hemisphere.
北冰洋 The Arctic Ocean.
北美洲(地) North America.
北海道(地) Hokkaido, Japan.
北寒帶 North frigid zone.
北極光 Aurora borealis.
北極星(天) The Polar Star.
北極圈 Arctic circle.
北極熊(動) Polar bear.
北溫帶 North temperate zone.
北回歸線 Tropic of Cancer.

匙 shi 〔chí〕 (n.)- A spoon. A key.
匙子；匙羹 A spoon.

# 匚 部

匝 zā (n.)- A circuit. Revolution.
(adj.)- Rounding.
匝月 A whole month.

匠 jiàng (n.)- A worker; a maker; a mechanic; an artificer.
匠人 A workman; an artificer; a mechanic.

匡 kuāng (adj.)- Regular; correct; square; right.
匡正 Correct; rectify; right.
匡救 Deliver; rescue.

匣 xiá (n.)- A box; a chest; a trunk; a case; a coffer.

匪 fěi (n.)- Highwayman; robber; rebels; bandits.
匪首 The head of bandits.
匪徒 Bandits; rebels; insurgents.
匪巢 A rebel stronghold.
匪幫 A gang.

**匯** (n.)- A bank draft; a check; remittance; exchange.
huì (v.)- Remit. Draw on.
匯付 Pay to.
匯合 Concourse.
匯兌 Exchange; remit money by bank drafts.
匯單；匯票 An order of money; a bill of exchange; a bank draft; a letter of credit.
匯款 Drafts; remittances.
匯費 Remittance charge.

# 匸 部

**匹** (n.)- A numerative for houses. A piece of cloth.
pǐ (v.)- Match; pair; compare; fit; together.

**匿** (v.)- Hide; conceal; keep away from sight. Abscond; secret.
nì 匿名 Anonymous.
匿名信 An anonymous letter.

**區** (n.)- A locality; a quarter; district; zone; a boundary.
qū (v.)- Classify; sort; separate; discriminate.
區別 Discriminate; distinguish; differ.
區長 Head police of the district.
區處 A place to dwell in. Distinguish and decide.
區域 A region; a location; a district.

# 十 部

**十** (adj.)- Ten. Tenth. Complete.
十分 Perfect. Quite; very; full;
shí not less than.
十月 October; the tenth month.
十年 A decade; decennary.
十足 Complete. Pure.
十倍 Decuple; tenfold; ten times.
十萬 A hundred thousand.
十億 A billion; a milliard.
十一月 November; the eleventh month.
十二月 December; the twelfth month.
十字架 A cross.
十字軍 The Crusades.
十字路 Crossroads; crossways.
十點鐘 Ten o'clock; ten hours.
十二指腸 The duodenum; the duodena.
十分之一 One-tenth.
十字架像 A crucifix.
十全十美 Perfect.
十項運動 Decathlon.
十滴藥水 Chlorodyne.
十六分音符 A semiquaver.
十四行詩體 Sonnet.

**千** (adj.)- Thousand; ten hundred.
千古 Ancient times. Forever;
qiān eternity.
千金 Daughter.
千萬 A large indefinite number. By all means.
千里眼 Clairvoyance.
千里鏡 A telescope.

千千萬萬 Hundreds and thousands; thousands and thousands.
千山萬水 Land and sea.
千方百計 All sorts of schemes; by one means or another.
千辛萬苦 Suffer many (innumerable) hardships; have no end of trouble.
千鈞一髮 Hang by a thread.
千載一時；千載一遇 A golden opportunity; a rare chance.
千篇一律 Monotonous.
千變萬化 Innumerable (incalculable, kaleidoscopic) changes; wonderful variety.

升 shēng (n.)- A pint.
(v.)- Advance; rise; promote.
升降 Ascend and descend; rise and fall.
升級 Promote; rise in rank; be advanced.
升高 Lift; heighten; advance.
升旗 Hoist a flag. Flag-raising.
升學 Promoted to a higher school.
升降機 An elevator; a lift.
升旗禮 Flag-raising ceremony.

午 wǔ (n.)- Noon; twelve o'clock in daytime.
午日 Dragon boat festival.
午夜 Midnight.
午前 Forenoon; A. M.
午後 Afternoon; P. M.
午飯 Lunch; a luncheon.
午睡 A noontide (midday) nap; siesta.

卉 huì (n.)- Plants; herbs.
卉木 Plants and trees.
卉草 Flowering plants.

半 bàn (n.)- Half.
(v.)- Divide.
(adj.)- Half.
半百 Half of a hundred; fifty.
半夜 Midnight.
半音 Semitone; half-note.
半島 A peninsula.
半徑(幾) Radius.
半球 Hemisphere.
半票 Half-ticket.
半圓 Semicircle.
半路 Halfway.
半旗 Flag at half-mast.
半數 Half the total number.
半價 Half price.
半月刊 Half-monthly.
半身像 Bust.
半導體 Semi-conductor.
半透明 Semi-transparent; translucent.
半學年 Semester.
半斤八両 Six of one and half a dozen of the other.
半生半熟 Half-raw and half cooked.
半身不遂 Hemiplegia; hemiplegy.
半信半疑 Half in doubt; doubtfully.
半途而廢 Stop halfway.
半殖民地 Semi-colony.
半封建社會 Semi-feudal society.

卑 bēi (adj.)- Low; base; vulgar; humble.
(adv.)- Below; beneath; under; humbly; vulgarly.
卑劣 Inferiority.
卑汚 Base; filthy; mean.
卑陋 Low; mean; base; worthless.
卑鄙 Mean; low; vulgar; base; submissive.
卑賤 Mean; ungentlemanlike; vulgar; vile; mean.
卑劣感 Inferiority complex.

卒 zú (n.)- A servant. A follower; a footman.
(v.)- Conclude. Die.
(adv.)- Hurriedly; hastily. Sud-

denly; unexpectedly. Finally; at last.
卒伍 Troops.
卒急 In haste; in a great hurry.
卒然 All at once; suddenly; abruptly; unexpectedly.
卒業文憑 A diploma.

卓 (adj.)- High; lofty; tall. Distinguished. Prominent. Upright.
zhuō 卓見 Clear-sightedness; foresight.
卓絕 Super-eminent.
卓越 Distinguished; excellence; greatness.

協 (n.)- Agreement; concord. Mutual help.
xié (v.)- Agree; harmonize with; bring into harmony. Aid; help; assist; cooperate; unite; combine; agree with.
(adj.)- Harmonious; jointed.
協力 United effort; cooperate.
協助 Help; aid; assist; side with.
協定 Concert. Cooperation.
協約 Alliance; convention.
協商 Negotiate with; treat with.
協會 Association.
協調 Harmonization; conciliation.
協議 Mutual consent.
協約國 Allies; Entente Powers.

南 (n.)- South.
(adj.)- South; southern.
nán 南方 The South.
南瓜(植) Pumpkin.
南京(地) Nanking.
南非(地) South Africa.
南洋(地) The South Seas.
南美(地) South (Latin) America.
南風 South wind.
南海(地) The South China Sea.
南極 The south pole.
南半球 Southern Hemisphere.
南極洲 Antarctic regions.
南極圈 Antarctic circle.
南溫帶 South temperate zone.
南回歸線 Tropic of Capricorn.
南洋羣島(地) South Sea Islands.
南斯拉夫(地) Jugoslavia.

博 (adj.)- Extensive. Universal; general. Learned; intelligent;
bó well educated. Spacious; wide; extended.
(v.)- Gamble; play for money.
博士 A doctor degree. A learned scholar.
博學 Extensively read; well read.
博識 Wide knowledge.
博物院 A museum.
博覽會 An exhibition; an exposition; a fair.
博士論文 A thesis for a doctorate.

# 卜 部

卜 (n.)- Divination; sortilege.
(v.)- Divine; foretell; guess;
pǔ bode.
〔pū〕 卜卦 Divine by the eight diagrams.

占 (v.)- Divine; foretell. Take possession of; occupy.
zhān 占卜 Divine; cast lots; soothsaying.
占有 Take possession of.

占卦 Divine by diagrams.
占領 Occupation. Taking possession of; seizure.
占據 Occupy; seize.

**卡** (n.)- A guardhouse; a station. A customs' barrier; a pass.
kǎ 卡片 Visiting cards.
卡紙 Cardboard.
卡通；漫畫 Cartoon.
卡片索引 Card index.
卡式錄音帶 Cassette (tape).
卡式錄音機 Cassette (tape) recorder.
卡式錄音座 Cassette deck.

**卦** (n.)- Divination. Diagrams.
guà 卦命 Divine.

# 卩 部

**印** (n.)- A seal; a stamp. A mark; an impression. Printing.
yìn (v.)- Print; impress. Seal; stamp.
印尼；印度尼西亞(地) Indonesia.
印刷 Printing.
印板 Block type.
印度(地) India.
印象 Impression.
印鑑 Signature. Seal.
印尼人 An Indonesian.
印花稅 Revenue tax; stamp duty.
印刷人 Printer.
印刷所 Printing office; printing department; printery.
印刷品 Printed matters.
印刷紙 Printing paper.
印刷機 A printing-machine; a printing-press.
印度人 Hindu; Indian.
印度洋(地) The Indian Ocean.
印圖紙；複寫紙 Tracing paper.
印度支那(地) Indo-China.
印象主義 Impressionism.

**危** (n.)- Peril; danger; hazard.
wēi (adj.)- Dangerous; unsteady; risky.
危迫 Dangerous and pressing.
危害 Injure; do an injury to.
危途 A dangerous road.
危機 Crisis; crititcal point.
危險 Dangerous.
危難 In peril; in danger.
危在旦夕 Death is expected at any moment. In imminent danger.
危地馬拉(地) Guatemala.
危險地帶 A danger zone.
危險區域 Dangerous zone.

**卵** (n.)- An egg. Testicles of animals. Oospore.
luǎn 卵子 Testicles. An egg; an ovum.
卵形 Oval; egg-shaped.
卵巢(解) Ovary.
卵黃(動) The yolk; the yellow of an egg.
卵生動物 The ovipara; an oviparous animal.

**卷** (n.)- A book; a volume. A roll.
(adj.)- Curved; curled; rolled.
juàn (v.)- Roll up.
卷尺 Measuring tape.
卷毛 Curly hair.

卷舌 Keep silent.
卷首 An introduction; the commencement of a book.

卸 (v.)- Get rid of; put off; unload; discharge. Deliver over to; hand
xiè over charge; resign; give up.
卸肩；卸責 Give up the control of an affair. Hand over charge of. Rest the shoulder; lay down responsibility. Put the blame on others.
卸脫 Keep off.
卸貨 Break bulk; unload; discharge. Deliver goods.
卸貨日(商) Lay days.
卸貨港 Port of discharge.

即 (v.)- Approach; reach.
(adv.)-Now; immediately; pres-
jī ently; at once.
(conj.)- Even; though.
即午 Near noon. This noon.
即日 To-day; this day; the same day.
即付(商) At sight.
即使 Even if.
即刻 Immediately; at once; outright; as soon as.
即速 Quickly; speedily; be quick.
即付裝運(商) Prompt shipment.
即時運費(商) Immediate shipment.

卿 (n.)- A high official; a minister. Lord; peer. You.
qīng 卿士 The minister of state.

# 厂 部

厄 (n.)- Difficulty; distress; affliction.
è (adj.)- Cramped; distressed; afflicted.
厄運 In miserable condition.
厄瓜多爾(地) Ecuador.

厘 (n.)- The thousandth of a Chinese foot or a tael.
lí

厚 (adj.)- Thick; compact; dense. Faithful; sincere; honest. Rich.
hòu 厚板 A thick plank.
厚待 Treat well; good treatment; kind treatment.
厚恩 Great favour.
厚紙 Thick paper.
厚情；厚意 Sincere feelings; good will.
厚惠 High favours.
厚禮 Handsome present.
厚顏 Thick-skinned; barefaced; brazen faced; shameless; impudent.
厚顏無恥 Shamelessness; brazen; impudence.

原 (n.)- A plain; a field. An origin; a source; a beginning.
yuán (adj.)- Natural; original. Proper; primary.
(v.)- Forgive; remit; excuse; pardon.
(adv.)- Primarily; originally.
原子(化) Atom.
原文 The text; the original.
原本 Origin; source. First copy.
原由 Reasons; causes; circumstances.
原因；原故 Cause; reason; origin.
原告(法) Plaintiff; accuser.
原來 As a matter of fact; in fact;

originally.
原則 Principle; law.
原料 Raw materials.
原素 Element.
原理 Original principles; theory.
原野 Moorland; wild; plains.
原意 Original intention; motive.
原價 The prime cost; original value.
原稿 Original manuscript or draft.
原諒 Excuse; forgive; pardon.
原籍 One's own native place.
原子序 Atomic number.
原子核 Atomic nucleus.
原子能 Atomic energy.
原子量 Atomic weight.
原子彈 Atomic bomb.
原子價 Atomic value.
原始人 The primitive man.
原著者 The author.
原稿紙 Copy-paper.
原子武器 An atomic weapon.
原子時代 Atomic age.
原原本本 From first to last. From the very beginning; entirely.
原價計算 Costing.
原子物理學 Atomic physics.

**厠** cè (n.)- A privy; a water-closet; a toilet; lavatory.
(v.)- Put in a row; insert.
厠所；厠坑 A privy; water-closet; toilet room; a latrine.

**厦** xià (n.)- A great house; a mansion; an edifice.
厦門(地) Amoy.

**厭** yàn (v.)- Dislike; hate; sicken at; get tired of; be tired of.
(adj.)- Disagreeable; disgustful; hateful.
厭世 Pessimistic; weariness of life.
厭倦 Fatigued; weary; outdone.
厭惡 Hate; loathe; be disgusted at; distaste.
厭煩 Hate to be troubled; troublesome; wearisome; vexations.

**厲** lì (adj.)- Severe; harsh; stern; cruel. Oppressive.
厲害 Severe.
厲聲 Speak sternly; harsh tone.

# ㄙ 部

**去** qù (v.)- Go; leave; quit; depart from. Remove; cancel. Dismiss.
(adj.)- Apart; off; away.
去世 Dead; passed away; deceased.
去年 Last year.
去垢 Cleanse.
去罷 Be off; begone.
去職 Give up one's post; resign.
去邪歸正 Repent; leave the evil and follow the good.

**參** cān [shēn] (v.)- Take part in; participate. Advise; consult with.
參加 Participate.
參考 Refer to; compare. Reference.
參軍 To join the military force.
參照 Refer to.
參與 Take part in; participate; share; join in.
參戰 Participation in war. Enter (join) a war.

參謀 Staff officers.
參觀 Visit; take a view of; pay a visit to.
參見；參謁 Have an interview with.
參考書 Reference books.
參謀長 Chief of staff.
參議員 Senator.
參議院 Senate.

# 又 部

又 yòu (adv.)- More; again; further; also; too.
(conj.)- And. But while.
又來 To come again.
又及 Postscript (P.S.).

叉 chā 〔chá〕〔chǎ〕 (n.)- A crotch; a fork.
(adj.)- Diverging; branching.
(v.)- Cross the arms. Fork.
叉子 A fork.
叉手 Interlace the hands.
叉腰 Put the arms akimbo.
叉路 A fork in a road; crossing.
叉燒肉 Carbonado; roast pork.

及 jí (v.)- Reach; attain; extend; connect; toward.
(prep.)- To; until; till. With. Concerning; regarding.
(conj.)- And; as well as; also.
及早 While it is early.
及時 Seasonable. In time.
及格 Up to standard; capable; qualified.

友 yǒu (n.)- A friend; a companion; an associate; a comrade.
(adj.)- Friendly; fraternal; kind; cordial.
友人 Friend; acquaintance.
友邦 A friendly country; neighbouring states.
友善 Kindly; familiar.
友愛 Fraternal; friendly; amity.
友誼 Friendship.
友好協定 A friendship pact.
友好團結 Friendship and unity.
友好訪問 Friendly visit.
友好關係 Friendly relations.
友誼比賽 A friendly game or contest.

反 fǎn (adj.)- Contrary; opposite.
(v.)- Return. Turn. Send back. Rebel; revolt.
(adv.)- Against.
反口 Retract; deny one's words; disown.
反之 On the contrary; on the other hand.
反攻 Counter attack.
反抗 Defy; oppose; resist; set against.
反省 Introspection; reflection; perception with consciousness of self. Collect one's thought.
反叛 Revolt; rebel.
反映 Reflection; reflect. Foreshow.
反胃 Turn the stomach.
反面 The opposite side; the other side. Turn the cold shoulder.
反射 Reflection. Reflect.
反動 Reaction.
反常 Out of order. Unusual.
反感 Reflex influence; ill feeling; antipathy.
反對 Oppose; object to; protest against.
反語 Irony.
反駁 Retort; refute.

反擊 A counter-attack; a counter-charge.
反應(化) Reaction.
反覆 Repeatedly; over and over; again and again; reiterate.
反比例(算) Inverse proportion.
反射作用 Reflex action.
反貿易風 Anti-trade wind.
反殖民主義 Anti-colonialism.
反貪汚浪費 Against corruption and waste.

叔 shū (n.)- An uncle.
叔父 An uncle.
叔母 An aunt.

取 qǔ (v.)- Take; get. Receive. Choose; select. Lay hold on.
取出 Take out; draw out.
取回 Get back.
取消 Annul; nullify; cancel; take back.
取勝 Win; come over; get a victory.
取暖 Warm; bask.
取樂 Persue pleasure; to enjoy; to make fun.
取鬧 Cause a row.
取決 Decide; rely on.
取暖設備 Heating installation; heating system.

受 shòu (v.)- Receive; accept. Bear; endure; suffer.
受享 Enjoy.
受命 Be content with one's lot; be ordered.
受屈 Be wronged.
受苦 Suffer hardships.
受害 Suffer injury; be injured.
受益 Be benefited; be the better for.
受累 Be involved in.
受寒 Suffer from cold.
受聘 Receive wedding present; be engaged.
受賄 Receive bribes. Take bribes.
受精 Be fertilized (fecundated, impregnated).
受熱 Get fever.
受罰 Be punished; pay the forfeit.
受賞 Receive a reward.
受禮 Receive a salutation or gift.
受寵 Find acceptance.
受騙 Be deceived or taken in.
受委曲 Suffer injury.
受益者 Person enriched. Beneficiary.
受託人 Trustee.
受託者 Mandatory.
受難日 Good Friday.
受權書 A power of attorney.
受讓人 Assignee.

敘 xù (n.)- Preface; introduction. Interview; meeting.
(v.)- State; narrate; describe.
敘事 Notes of explanation; statement.
敘述 Narrate; quote from; describe.
敘談 Chat; talk; converse with; gossip; discuss.
敘利亞(地) Syria.

叛 pàn (v.)- Rebel; revolt.
叛背 Conspire against.
叛謀 Plot a rebellion.
叛徒 A rebel; renegade.
叛亂 Rebellion.
叛變 Mutiny.

叟 sǒu (n.)- An elder; a senior; an old man; an aged person.

叢 cóng (n.)- A bushy place; a copse.
(adj.)- Crowded. Thick; dense.
叢生 Growing together; luxuriant; overgrow.
叢書 A collection of books; series.

# 口 部

**口** kǒu (n.)- The mouth; an entrance; an opening; a hole. A gorge; a pass. A port.
口才 Eloquence.
口令 A vocal signal; a password; a watchword.
口吃 Falter; stammer; stutter.
口技 Mimicry; ventriloquism.
口角 Quarrel; dispute.
口供 Testimony; statement.
口味 Taste.
口岸 A port; a harbour.
口沫 Spittle; saliva; spit; mouth spray.
口信 A verbal message.
口紅 Rouge; a lip-stick.
口述 Dictate.
口音 Accent; enunciation.
口徑 Caliber.
口渴 Thirsty.
口袋 A sack; a bag.
口試 Oral examination.
口號 A slogan.
口腔(解) Mouth cavity.
口脣(解) Lips.
口糧 Food; rations. Victuals.
口琴 Harmonica; a mouth organ.
口頭語 Commonplace sayings; conventional expressions.
口是心非 Double-faced. Hypocrisy.
口蜜腹劍 A honeyed mouth but with a sword in the belly.

**古** gǔ (n.)- Antiquity; ancient times.
(adj.)- Ancient; old; antiquarian.
古人 The ancients; the men of old.
古巴(地) Cuba.
古文 Ancient literature; classics.
古代 Antiquity; old ages.
古色 An aged look; an antique appearance.
古典 Classics.
古怪 Curious; strange; peculiar; odd; quaint.
古玩；古董 Curios; antiques; articles of virtue.
古板 Old-fashioned; conservative.
古城 Ancient city.
古畫 An old painting or picture.
古象(動) The mammoth.
古都 An ancient city; a former capital.
古塔 An ancient pagoda.
古語；古諺 Old sayings; an adage.
古蹟 Remains of antiquity; relics; historic ruins; ruins.
古玩店；古董店 An antiquarian shop; art curio store or curio shop.
古色古香 Wear the rust of antiquity.
古往今來 In (through) all ages; in all history.
古典主義 Classicism.

**句** jù (n.)- A sentence; a clause; a phrase.
句子 A sentence.
句法 Syntax; sentence construction; phraseology.
句讀 Punctuation.

**另** lìng (adj.)- Another; separate; distinct; extra.
(adv.)- More.
(conj.)- And.

另一 Another one.
另日 Another day.
另外 Still; again; in addition to; besides; further.

叨 (v.)- Desire; crave; long for. Enjoy; receive; feel grateful.
dāo
〔tāo〕

叩 (v.)- Ask; inquire; pray for. Knock. Kotow; bow; implore.
kòu
叩見 Visit a superior.
叩門 Knock at the door.
叩謝 Offer hearty thanks; thank sincerely.

只 (adv.)- Merely; only; simply.
(conj.)- But; however; yet.
zhī
〔zhǐ〕
只怕 Probably. The only thing to fear is.... .
只是 But; however; nevertheless.
只要 If only.
只須 It is only necessary to . . . ; have only to ... .
只此一次 Only this time and no more.

叫 (n.)- The cries or voices of animals.
jiào
(v.)- Shout; exclaim; cry out. Send for. Name. Sing, as an insect.
叫門 Knock at a door.
叫喚 Call; order.
叫喊 Shout; cry aloud.
叫化子 A beggar.
叫救命 Cry for help.

召 (v.)- Call; summon; cite.
召見 Summon to audience; grant an audience.
zhào
召租 For rent; to let.
召喚 Summon; call; send for.
召集 Call a meeting; convene. Assemble; convoke.
召請 Invite.
召租房屋 House to let.

叮 (v.)- Reiterate; give charge to; order. Sting, as a mosquito.
dīng
叮囑 Reiterate; repeat an order; enjoin on.

可 (v.)- Be able; can; may. Permit; tolerate.
kě
可口 Palatable; pleasing to the taste; delicious.
可以 Possibe. May.
可可 Cocoa.
可見 Visible; evident; apparent.
可怕 Terrible; dreadful; horrible; awful.
可恥 Shameful.
可笑 Laughable; ridiculous.
可能 Possible.
可惱 Irritating.
可惡 Detestable; disgustful; abominable.
可愛 Lovely; pleasant; sweet.
可敬 Worthy of respect; respectable.
可厭 Distasteful; hateful; disgustful; disagree able; loathsome; fulsome.
可疑 Suspicious; doubtful.
可憐；可憫 Pitiable; pitiful.
可靠 Reliable; trustworthy.
可能性 Possibility.
可溶性(理) Solubility.
可燃性(理) Inflammability.
可蘭經 Koran.

台 (n.)- Terrace. Your honour.
台灣 Taiwan.
tāi
台函 Your note; your favour.

叱 (v.)- Hoot at; scold.
叱責 Blame; censure.
chì

史 (n.)- A history; chronicles; annals; story.
shǐ 史家 An historian.
史記 A history.
史學 Historiology.

右 (n.)- The right.
(adj.)- High; noble; honourable.
yòu Right hand.
右手 The right hand; the sword arm.
右岸 The right bank of the river.
右傾 Pro-right; right deviation.
右翼 The right wing.
右邊 Right side.
右傾機會主義 Right opportunism.

叶 (v.)- Harmonize; rime.
叶韻 Rhyme; put into rhyme.
yè

司 (n.)- A commissioner; a superintendent; an officer. A court
sī or office; a bureau.
(v.)- Control; manage.
司令 A commander.
司法 Administration of justice; the judicature.
司長 The head of a bureau.
司庫 A treasurer.
司儀 Marshal.
司機 A driver; a chaffeur.
司鐸 Catholic priest.
司令部 The headquarters.
司閽人 A door-keeper.
司法部長 The minister of justice.
司法機關 Judicial organ; judiciary.
司法警察 Judicial police.

吃 (v.)- Stutter; stammer. Eat.
吃力 Feel tired.
chī 吃飯 Take dinner.
吃虧 Bear an injury; suffer a loss; incur loss.
吃驚 Frightened; startled.

各 (adj.)- Each; every. Separate; various.
gè 各人 Each person; each one; every one.
各方 Every side.
各地 Various districts; in every place.
各式 All kinds; various sorts.
各樣；各種 Various or different kinds; every sort; every form.
各方面 Every directions; all directions.
各就位 On your marks!
各等價目 Class prices.

合 (adj.)- Agreeable; accordant; suitable; harmonious.
hé (v.)- Close; fold up. Join; unite. Match; pair. Collect; meet; convene.
(prep.)- In accordance with.
合一 Unite; concur; bring together.
合同 An agreement; a contract.
合成 Composition. Resultant.
合併 Annex; embody; bring together. Amalgamation; union.
合作 Co-operate.
合適 Suitable; proper.
合法 Lawful; legal; right.
合股 Co-partnership. Join in a stock in trade.
合金 An alloy.
合計 Sum up; add up; total up.
合格 Up to the standard; qualified; competent.
合唱 Chorus.
合理 Reasonable; rational.
合意 Agreement; agreeable.
合謀 Plot together; conspire.
合作社 Co-operative society; co-op.
合衆國際社 United Press International (UPI).

吉 (adj.)- Fortunate; lucky; auspicious.
jí 吉日 A lucky day; red-letter day.

吉凶 The bright and the black side of things; good and evil.

吉祥 Fortunate; auspicious; great fortune.

吉期 An auspicious occasion; a lucky day. A wedding day.

吉他琴 Guitar.

吉普車 A jeep car.

吉隆坡(地) Kuala Lumpur.

同 (adj.)- Same; equal; similar; identical.
tóng (v.)- Unite. Harmonize. Share in. Assemble; combine.
(adv.)- Alike; altogether; in common.
(prep.)- With; in company with.
(conj.)- And; as well as; with.

同一 Identical; the same.

同上 Ditto.

同化 Amalgamate; incorporate; assimilate.

同日 The same day.

同伴 A companion.

同年；同庚 Of the same year; in the same year.

同位；同格(文) Apposition.

同志 Comrade; fraternity.

同事；同僚 Fellow officials; colleagues.

同姓 Of the same surname.

同居 Fellow-lodger; co-habitant. Live with; lie with; cohabit.

同胞 Brothers; fellow countrymen.

同時 Meanwhile; simultaneously; at the same time; the same breath.

同級 Same rank; same class.

同情 Like feeling; sympathy.

同意 Agree; assent; accord; accept.

同鄉 Fellow countrymen; natives.

同輩 Compeer.

同樣 Of the same kind; alike; similar; equal.

同學 A schoolmate; a classmate; fellow students.

同甘苦 Share in one's joy and sorrow.

同門會；同學會 Alumni association.

同音字 Homophone.

同高線；等高線 Contour-line.

同溫層 Stratosphere.

同鄉會 Association of fellow provincials.

同盟軍 The Allied Forces.

同盟國 Allies; allied powers.

同義字 Synonym.

同化作用(生) The process of assimilation.

同胞兄弟 Brothers of the same mother; own brother; full brother.

同流合汚 Go with the stream.

同病相憐 Fellow sufferers pity each other.

名 (n.)- A name; an appellation; a title. Fame; honour; reputation. Merit; credit.
míng (adj.)- Famous; well-known.
(v.)- Name; designate.

名人 Famous or eminent men; great man; people of distinction.

名片；名刺 A visiting card.

名册 A list of names; a muster roll.

名字 The name or style by which a shop, a person, or a thing is known.

名言 A wise saying; a witty remark.

名將 A famous general; a great commander.

名產 A noted product; a staple.

名單 A list.

名勝 Famous places of scenery.

名詞(文) A noun. A term.

名貴 Valuable.

名媛 A lady.
名著 A fine work; a masterpiece.
名義 The name. Under the name of; in the capacity of; nominal.
名稱 Name; term; style.
名聲 Fame; reputation.
名譽 An honour, or mark of distinction; credit.
名勝古蹟 Noted places and historic sites.
名滿天下 Name is wide-spread.
名譽會長 An honorary president.
名譽學位 An honorary degree.

后 (n.)- A queen; an empress. A ruler; a sovereign.
hòu

吏 (n.)- An officer. Government official.
lì
吏治 Administrative rules.
吏員 Official attendants.

吐 (v.)- Spit; vomit. Disclose.
tǔ
(tù)
吐出 Cast forth.
吐沫 Spit.
吐痰 Spit phlegm.
吐瀉 Vomit and purge.
吐露 Utter; express.
吐露秘密 Disclose secret.

吋 (n.)- An English inch.
cùn

向 (n.)- Direction; course.
xiàng
(v.)- Used to be. Face; point to.
(adj.)- Facing; opposite to; former; preceding.
(prep.)- Toward; to.
向上 Upward. Advance; improve; progress.
向日 Formerly; previously. Facing the sun.
向北 Northward.
向外 Outward.
向西 Facing or toward the west; westward.
向來 Hitherto; heretofore.
向東 Toward the east; eastward.
向南 Southward; facing the south.
向前 Forth; outward; forward.
向後 Backward.
向心力 Centripetal force.
向日葵 The sunflower.
向右轉 Right turn.
向左轉 Left turn.
向前進 Go straight ahead; go on ahead.
向後轉 Left wheel.
向右看齊 Eyes right.
向左看齊 Eyes left.
向左邊行 Keep to the left.

君 (n.)- A ruler. Gentleman; sir; Mr.; you.
jūn
(adj.)- Honourable.
君子 A perfect gentleman.
君主 King or queen; a ruler.
君國 One's sovereign and country.
君主國 A monarchy.
君主立憲 Constitutional monarchy.
君主政體 Monarchy; monarchical government.
君主專制 Absolute monarchy.

吝 (adj.)- Stingy; closefisted; close; parsimonious; miserly.
lìn
(v.)- Grudge; spare.
吝惜 Stingy. Give reluctantly.
吝嗇者 A miser; a niggard; a Jew.

吞 (v.)- Swallow; devour; gulp.
tūn
吞丸 Bolt down (swallow) a pill.
吞下；吞食 Gulp; swallow.

吞併 Engross all; seize the whole.
吞沒公款 Embezzlement. Embezzle public funds.

**吟** yín (n.)- Hum; intone; recite. Sigh; moan.
吟詩 Hum verses; recite poems.

**吠** fèi (n.)- The bark of a dog.
(v.)- Bark; yelp; howl; cry.
吠聲 The noise of barking.

**否** fǒu (adj.)- Negative. Bad; wicked.
(v.)- Deny; refuse; decline.
(adv.)- No; not. Else; otherwise; never; neither.
否定 Deny; reply in the negative.
否決 Veto; vote down; reject; decide against.
否則 Otherwise; else; or.
否認 Deny; disallow; renounce; disown.
否決權 A veto; the right of veto.
否定語 A negative.

**吩** fēn (v.)- Order; command; bid.
吩咐 A command. Command.

**含** hán (v.)- Hold; contain; embrace. Bear. Hold in the mouth.
含有 Have; contain; hold; include.
含恨 Cherish resentment; harbour a grudge.
含笑 Smile; chuckle.
含混；含糊 Careless; indistinct; muttering; not clear; confused.
含羞 Feel bashful or bear ashamed.
含悲 Feel sorry.
含意 Implication; meaning; shade.
含蓄 Connotation. Imply; implicit; implication.
含羞草(植) Sensitive plant.

**吮** shǔn (v.)- Lick; suck.
吮味 Test the flavour; taste.

**呈** chéng (n.)- A petition.
(v.)- Present; offer. Show; discover. State to a superior; hand in a petition.
呈上 Present to; hand in.
呈交 Tender; deliver to; present.
呈送；呈遞 Send; transmit; send up.
呈現；呈露 Manifested; disclosed.
呈報 Submit a report.
呈請 Request; apply.
呈繳 Proffer.
呈獻 Offer.

**吳** wú (n.)- The State of Wu, one of the Three Kingdoms (229-280 A.D.). The province of Kiangsu. The surname of Chinese.

**吵** chāo [chǎo] (v.)- Quarrel; dispute; make a noise.
吵鬧 Make a disturbance or quarrel.

**吶** nà (adj.)- Slow of speech.
(v.)- Stammer; speak cautiously.
吶喊 The din of battle; shout.

**吸** xī (v.)- Inhale; make an inspiration. Imbibe; suck in; absorb. Attract; draw.
吸引 Draw; attract.
吸收 Absorption; suction.
吸烟 Smoke.
吸氣 Inspire; inhale; draw in the breath.
吸盤 A sucker.
吸龍(物) Siphon.
吸血鬼 A vampire; a blood-sucker.
吸烟室 Smoking room.

吸墨紙 Blotting paper.
吸濕物；吸濕藥 Absorbent.

**吹** chuī (n.)- A puff; a blast; a gust.
(v.)- Blow; puff; blast.
吹牛 Brag; boast.
吹求；吹毛求疵 Find fault with; pick fault; nag.
吹起 Blow up.
吹笛 Play the flute.
吹號 Give a signal, as by blowing a horn.
吹滅 Extinguish; blow out.
吹管 A blowpipe.
吹噓 Praise; puff; recommend.
吹嘯 Whistle.
吹喇叭 Blow the trumpet.
吹奏樂隊 A brass band.
吹奏樂器 A wind-instrument.

**吻** wěn (n.)- The lips.
(v.)- Kiss.
吻合 Agreeing; coinciding.

**吼** hǒu (n.)- An angry tone. The roar of animals.
(v.)- Roar; howl.
吼叫 Roar; howl.

**吾** wú (pron.)- I; me; my.
吾子 My son.
吾兄 You; sir. My elder brother.

**告** gào (v.)- Announce; proclaim; inform; tell.
告示 An official proclamation.
告別；告辭 Take leave; bid farewell to; say good-bye to.
告知 Notify; inform; tell.
告急 Report the danger.
告病 Ask for sick leave.
告假 Ask for leave of absence.
告密 Give confidential information.
告訴 Complain; accuse.
告誡 Warn; enjoin on.
告示板 A bulletin board; a notice board.
告別會 A farewell party; a parting ceremony.

**呂** lǚ (n.)- A kind of sword. A tube. A musical note.
呂宋(地) Luzon.
呂宋烟 Manila cigars.

**呆** dāi (n.)- A fool; a dunce.
(adj.)- Silly; simple; idiotic; foolish.
呆人 A dunce; a fool; a ninny; a noddy; a stupid fellow.
呆笨 Brainless; without understanding; foolish.
呆話 Nonsense.
呆滯 Clumsy.

**呢** ní (n.)- A low sound; a murmur. Woolen cloth.
呢絨 Woolen cloth; woolen goods.
呢絨線 Woolen yarn.

**周** zhōu (n.)- Circumference; a circuit.
(adj.)- Enough. Close; secret. Thoughtful.
(v.)- Supply. Assist. Extend everywhere. Make a circuit. Surround.
(adv.)- Entirely; completely. Everywhere. The end.
周折 Deviation. Roundabout; circuitous. Difficult.
周知 Well-known; widely-known.
周密 Secret; hidden; close together.
周刊；周報 Weekly.
周圍 All round; surrounding; circuit.
周末晚會 Week end party.

周年紀念 Anniversary.
周密、廣泛的調查 Minute investigation.

**咒** zhòu (n.)- An incantation; an imprecation. A charm to hurt or protect any person; a spell.
(v.)- Curse. Swear an oath.
咒詛；咒罵 Curse; imprecate.

**呱** gū (n.)- The cry of an infant.
(v.)- Cry.
呱呱墮地 Be born; come into the world; see the light.

**味** wèi (n.)- Taste; flavour; savour; relish. Smell; scent. Interest.
(v.)- Relish; take pleasure.
味美 Gustable; delicious; nice.
味道 Flavour; taste.
味淡 A slight taste; a raw flavour.
味濃 A rich taste; a ripe flavour.
味覺 Sense of taste.
味覺器官 Organ of taste.

**呵** hē (v.)- Expel the breath.
呵欠 Yawn.
呵責 Blame; scold.
呵呵大笑 Laugh heartily.

**呻** shēn (v.)- Groan; moan; lament.
呻吟 Groan; moan.

**呼** hū (v.)- Breathe out; expire the breath; exhale. Call. Address. Shout; cry out loudly.
呼吸 Breathe; inhale and exhale.
呼救 Cry for help.
呼喊 Call aloud; shout out; bawl.
呼嘯 Roar.
呼應 In response to; in concert (unison) with.
呼吸作用(生) Respiration.
呼吸系統 Respiratory system.

**命** mìng (n.)- A decree; an order. The span of life.
(v.)- Order; command; charge.
命令 A command; orders.
命名 Give a name; christen.
命案 A case of murder.
命根 One's own life; inmost self.
命運 A horoscope; destiny.

**咀** jǔ (v.)- Chew.
咀嚼 Chewing.

**咄** duō (v.)- Hoot; scold.
(interj.)- An exclamation of surprise or of joking. Tut!
咄咄怪事 How strange!

**咆** páo (v.)- Roar. Bluster.
咆哮 A roar.

**和** hé (n.)- Harmony; union; agreement. Peace.
(adj.)- Mild; peaceful. Harmonious; amiable.
(v.)- Be on friendly terms; be at peace. Fit. Unite; harmonize. Mix; compound.
(prep.)- With.
(conj.)- And.
和平 Peace.
和好 Reconcile; agree; be on good terms.
和尚 A Buddhist priest; a monk; a friar.
和暖 Warm.
和氣 Agreeable. Friendly feeling; gentle.
和睦 Reconciliation.

和諧 Harmonious. Connubial harmony.
和平會議 Peace conference.
和平解決 A peace settlement.

**咏** yǒng
(v.)- Sing; intone.
咏詩 Hum verses.

**咐** fu
(v.)- Order; instruct; bid.

**咖** kā
咖啡 Coffee.
咖侖 Gallon–a measure used for liquids.
咖啡壺 A coffee pot.
咖啡館 Cafe; coffee-house.

**咨** zī
(v.)- Consult about. Inquire and find.
咨文 An official dispatch between equals.
咨行 Notify; inform.
咨送 Send to.
咨問；咨詢 Write to inquire; put questions to.

**咫** chǐ
(n.)- A measure of length used during the Chou dynasty; eight inches.
咫尺之間 Very close; within a foot of.

**咬** yǎo
(n.)- Bite; gnaw; chew; masticate.
咬傷 Be wounded by biting.
咬斷 Bite into two.
咬嚼 Chew; masticate.
咬牙切齒 Gnash the teeth in anger.

**咯** kǎ
(v.)- Cough; spit out; emit from the mouth.
咯血 Spit out blood.

**咳** ké
(v.)- Cough.
咳吐 Cough and spit.
咳嗽 Cough.
咳嗽藥 A cough medicine.

**咸** xián
(adj.)- All; whole; together.
(adv.)- Altogether.

**咽** yān
(v.)- Swallow; gulp.
咽喉 The gullet; the throat; a narrow pass.

**哀** āi
(n.)- Sorrow; grief; pity; commiseration; lament.
(adj.)- Sad; distressing; sorrowful.
(v.)- Grieve for; sympathize.
哀求；哀請 Appeal to one's feelings; implore.
哀悼 Condolence; mourning; the deepest regret (sympathy).
哀愁 Sorrow; sadness.

**品** pǐn
(n.)- A class; a kind; a sort. An article.
品行 Actions; conduct; behaviour.
品性 Temper; disposition; nature.
品詞(文) Parts of speech.
品評 Criticize.
品種 A variety; a kind; a sort; a grade.
品貌 Conduct and appearance.
品質 Quality.
品性修養 Development of character; character-building.
品端學優 Morally upright and highly educated.

**哄** hǒng (hōng)
(n.)- The hum of a crowd.
(v.)- Cheat; trick; deceive; tempt.
哄笑 Roar with laughter; burst

out laughing.
哄鬧 Make an uproar; clamourous; noisy.
哄騙 Cheat.

**哇** wā
(v.)- Spit out; vomit.
哇哇 A child's voice.

**哈** hā
(v.)- Laugh.
哈巴狗 Pekingese dog.
哈爾濱(地) Harbin.

**哎** āi
哎喲 Oh! Good gracious! Dear me!

**員** yuán
(n.)- An officer; a member.
員司 Staff.

**哥** gē
(n.)- An elder brother.
哥哥 An elder brother.
哥嫂 Brother and sister-in-law.
哥本哈根(地) Copenhagen.
哥爾夫球 Golf.

**哨** shào
(n.)- An outpost; a guard station. A whistle.
(v.)- Whistle. Patrol; act the scout.
哨子 A whistle.
哨兵 A sentinel; a sentry; a picket.

**哩** lǐ
(n.)- A mile, English unit of length.

**哭** kū
(v.)- Cry; wail; scream and groan; weep.
哭泣 Cry; weep.
哭喊 Cry out in pain.
哭喪臉 A melancholy face.

**哮** xiāo
(v.)- Howl; bellow; roar. Cough.
哮喘病 Asthma.

**哲** zhé
(n.)- A sage; a wise man.
(adj.)- Wise; sagacious; perspicacious.
哲學 Metaphysics; philosophy.
哲學家 Philosopher.

**哺** bǔ
(v.)- Suckle a child.
哺育 Bring up.
哺乳動物 A mammal.

**哽** gěng
(n.)- Choking from grief.
(v.)- Choke.
哽咽 A lump in the throat.

**唁** yàn
(v.)- Moan or grieve.
唁弔 Mourn other's death; lament for; condole with.
唁電 A telegram (telegraphic message) of condolence.

**唆** suō
(v.)- Incite; stir up.
唆使 Instigate to evil; incite.

**唉** āi
(interj.)- Ah ! Alas !

**唐** táng
(adj.)- Rude. Hasty. Wild; boastful.
唐人 A Chinese.
唐朝 The T'ang Dynasty (618-905. A.D.).
唐詩 Poems of T'ang Dynasty.
唐人街 The China Town.

**售** shòu
(v.)- Sell; dispose of; trade; bargain.
售主 The purchaser.

售出 Sell out.
售價 The selling price.
售罄 Sell off.
售票房 Booking office; ticket office.
售票員 Booking clerk; conductor.
售貨員 Salesman.
售貨學 Salesmanship.
售出通知書 Sale note.
售貨總清賬 Account sales ledger.

**唯** wéi (n.)- An answer.
(adv.)- Only.
唯一 The only; unique.
唯心派 Idealists.
唯心論 Spiritualism; idealism.
唯物派 Materialists.
唯物論 Materialism.
唯物史觀 Historical materialism.
唯一代理人(商) Sole agent.

**唱** chàng (v.)- Sing. Lead; go before. Give or pass the word.
唱片 A record; a disc.
唱咏 Sing; chant.
唱歌 Singing; join the singing.
唱詩班 A choir; a glee club.

**唾** tuò (n.)- Saliva; spittle.
(v.)- Spit; salivate; eject.
唾出 Spit out.
唾沫 Saliva; spit.

**啄** zhuó (v.)- Peck at; pick up.
啄木鳥 A wood-pecker.

**商** shāng (n.)- A merchant; a dealer; a tradesman. Trade; commerce.
(v.)- Trade; carry on commerce.
商人 Merchants.
商店 A shop; a store; a firm.
商品 Goods; wares; articles of merchandise; commodity.
商家 A shop; a mercantile house.
商界 Commercial world; business circle.
商科 Commercial course.
商訂 Decide; arrange.
商埠；商港 Commercial ports.
商船 A trading vessel; a merchant ship.
商會 A chamber of commerce.
商業 Commerce; trade; business.
商量；商議 Consultation; consult; confer.
商標 A trade-mark; a brand.
商業區 The business section of a city.
商業文件 Business document.
商業信件 Commercial correspondence; business letter.
商業英文 Business ( commercial ) English.
商業註册 Commercial registration.
商業道德 Commercial morality; business ethics.
商業管理 Business management ( administration ).
商業學校 School of commerce.
商業簿記 Commercial bookkeeping.
商品出口處 Commercial outlet.
商品陳列窗 Show window.
商業中心區 Down town; trade center.

**問** wèn (v.)- Ask; question; inquire.
問候 Inquire about a person's health; pay a visit to; greet; regard; remember.
問路 To ask the way.
問答 Dialogue; conversation; questions and answers.
問詞 A question; an interrogation.
問號 Question mark.
問題 A problem; a question; enquiry.
問事處 Information office; inquiry office.
問明白 Ask distinctly.
問題的關鍵 Key to the question.

**啓** qǐ (v.)- Open. Explain. Tell; announce; notify. Begin. Develop; instruct.
啓行 Start; set out.
啓事 A notice.
啓封 Break a seal. Open a letter.
啓發 Develop; enlighten; educate.
啓信機 Mail opener.
啓蒙運動 An enlightenment movement.

**啕** táo (v.)-Wail; weep.

**啖** dàn (v.)- Bite; eat; taste; swallow.

**啞** yǎ (adj.)- Dumb.
啞子 Dumb-man; mute.
啞鈴 Dumb-bell.
啞鈴操 Dumb-bell drill.

**啤** pí
啤酒 Beer.

**啡** fēi
咖啡 Coffee.

**啃** kěn (v.)- Bite; gnaw; munch.

**啼** tí (v.)- Howl; cry; crow; scream; bewail.
啼哭 Weep and wail.

**喀** kā (v.)- Vomit; spit out.
喀什米爾 (地) Kashmir.

**善** shàn (n.)- Goodness; virtue; excellence; splendidness.
(adj.)- Good; virtuous. Clever; expert; skilful; handy. Fine; excellent.
(v.)- Praise; admire.
善於 Skilled in.
善良 Kind; good; gentle; virtuous.
善事；善舉 Benevolent actions; charitable work.
善意 Bona fide; in good faith; friendliness; good will; good faith.
善有善報 Good act will be well rewarded.
善始善終 A good beginning and a good end.
善與人交 Be good in making friendly intercourse.

**喇** lǎ (n.)- Jabbering noise; sound of a trumpet.
喇叭 A horn or trumpet; a bugle.
喇嘛 Lama.
喇叭花 (植) The morning glory.
喇嘛教 Lamaism.
喇嘛僧 A Lama priest.

**喉** hóu (n.)- Throat; the gullet.
(adj.)- Guttural.
喉音 A guttural sound.
喉風；咽炎 Pharyngitis.
喉症；白喉 Diphtheria.
喉痛 Throat-ache.
喉管；枝氣管 Bronchia.
喉嚨 The gullet; the throat; the windpipe.

**喊** hǎn (n.)- A call; a cry.
(v.)- Cry; call; shout.
喊苦 Wail.
喊救 Cry for help; call on to rescue.

喊痛 Cry out from pain.
喊賣 Cry goods for sell, as hawkers.
喊救之聲 Alarm of danger of life.

**喋** dié (v.)- Chatter; babble; prattle.
喋喋不休 To chatter ceaselessly; gabble.

**喔** wū (n.)- The crowing or cackling of fowls.
喔喔 The crowing of a cock.

**喘** chuǎn (n.)- Breath.
(v.)- Pant.
喘息 Pant; wheeze.
喘氣 Gasp.

**喚** huàn (v.)- Call; hail. Invite; order; summon; bid. Name; designate.
喚醒 Awaken.

**喜** xǐ (n.)- Joy; delight; gladness; pleasure; happiness.
(adj.)- Glad; cheerful; happy; joyous; delightful; elated.
(v.)- Be pleased with; like; be fond of; rejoice; take delight in.
喜事 A wedding; an occasion of joy.
喜訊 Happy tidings; good news; good message.
喜悅 Joy; gladness; pleasure.
喜酒；喜筵 A wedding feast.
喜愛 Be fond of.
喜劇 A comedy.
喜鵲(動) The magpie.
喜色滿面 Beam with joy; be all smiles with joy.
喜馬拉亞山(地) Himalayas.

**喝** hē 〔hè〕 (v.)- Call out aloud; shout. Sip; drink.
喝水 Drink water.
喝令 Set on. Shout an order.
喝采 Cry up; cheer; salute; clap the hands in applause; give cheers.
喝醉 Get drunk; become tipsy; intoxicated.
喝倒采 Make cat-calls; boo.

**喧** xuān (n.)- Clamour; noise; uproar; brawl.
(adj.)- Noisy; boisterous.
喧嘩 Brawling; noisy talk; clamour.
喧嚷 Noisy.

**喻** yù (v.)- Instruct; explain. Illustrate.
喻言 Metaphor; fable; allegory.
喻譬 Illustrate with example.

**喪** sāng 〔sàng〕 (n.)- A funeral. A mourning; a grief.
(adj.)- Bereaved. Forgotten. Mourning.
(v.)- Mourn; lament. Lose; miss. Die.
喪心 Insane.
喪失 Loss; fail; miss.
喪命 Die.
喪服 Mourning clothes (dress).
喪禮 Funeral rites; obsequies.
喪鐘 Death bell.
喪家狗 A homeless dog—an outcast.
喪心病狂 Have cracked brains; as mad as a March hare.
喪失自由 Loss of liberty.

**喫** chī Same as 吃.
(v.)- Swallow; eat. Drink. Suffer; bear.
喫苦 Suffer hardships.
喫酒 Drink wine.
喫飯 Eat; take a meal.
喫煙 Smoke.
喫虧 Suffer loss.
喫齋 Fast.

喫驚 Frightened; be taken aback; be surprised.

喬 (adj.)- High; stately; lofty. Pretended; concealed; disguised.
qiáo 喬木 Stately trees.
喬裝 Disguise. Under the guise of.
喬遷 Remove. Removal.

單 (n.)- A check; a bill. A receipt. A recipe. Writing paper.
dān (adj.)- Alone; single; isolated. Odd; singular.
(adv.)- Only; but; nothing but; merely.
單子 A list; a bill.
單位 Unit.
單軌 Monorail.
單槓 A simple lever; horizontal bar.
單價 Simple price; unit price.
單數 An odd number. Singular.
單線 A single line (track).
單調 Monotony; dullness; monotone.
單據 A receipt; documentary proof.
單獨 Alone; single; solitary.
單薄 Thin; poor; weak.
單行本 A separate (special) volume.
單身漢 A bachelor; a single man.
單思病 Lovesickness.
單人床 A single bed.
單程票 A single ticket; a one-way ticket.
單軌鐵路 The centripetal railway; the mono-railway.

啣 (v.)- Hold in the mouth.
xián

嗅 (v.)- Smell; scent; nose.
嗅覺 Sense of smell; olfactory.
xiù 嗅覺器官(生) The organ of smell; olfactory organ.

嗆 (v.)- Cough.
qiāng

嗎 (n.)- An interrogative sign; what (?).
ma (v.)- Reproach.
〔má〕 嗎啡 Morphia; morphine.
〔mǎ〕

嗓 (n.)- The throat; the larynx.
嗓子 The throat; the voice.
sǎng 嗓子啞 Hoarse.

嗚 (interj.)- Welladay! Ah! Alas! Eh!
wū 嗚呼 Alas! Alack!
嗚咽 A sob; whimpering.
嗚嗚 Sound of a horn or a whistle.

嗜 (v.)- Relish; take delight in; have an appetite for; be fond of; indulge in; like.
shì 嗜好 Fond of; addicted to.
嗜酒 Addicted to drinking.
嗜賭 Fond of gambling.
嗜音樂 Fond of music.

嗟 (v.)- Sigh; grieve.
嗟嘆 Sigh; deplore.
jiē

嗡 (n.)- The hum of insects.
wēng

嗣 (n.)- Heirs; posterity; descendants; child; offspring.
sì (adj.)- Following.
嗣後 Hereafter; henceforth.
嗣業 Inherit a property.

**嗤** chī
(v.)- Laugh at.
嗤笑 Laugh at.

**嗽** sòu
(n.)- A cough.
(v.)- Clear the throat. Cough.

**嘅** kǎi
(v.)- Sigh; regret; grieve at.
嘅嘆 Sigh.

**嘆** tàn
(v.)- Sigh; regret; mourn. Praise; applaud.
嘆息 Regret.
嘆氣 Heave a sigh.

**嘉** jiā
(adj.)- Good; excellent; fine; admirable.
(v.)- Admire; approve; commend; praise.
嘉偶 A happy couple.
嘉許 Commend; appreciate; approve.
嘉獎 Praise and reward.
嘉賓 Respected guests; guests of honour.
嘉餚 Excellent food; fine dishes; delicacy.

**嘔** ǒu
(n.)- A child's prattle.
(v.)- Vomit; spit out; disgorge.
嘔吐 Vomit; throw up; puke.
嘔血 Spit blood; bleed at the lungs.
嘔氣 Vent one's anger or spleen.

**嘖** zé
(v.)- Cry and bawl; make an uproar. Quarrel; dispute; wrangle. Praise.

**嘗** cháng
(v.)- Taste. Test. Try; attempt.
(adv.)- Already; formerly; ever; once.
嘗味 Taste.
嘗試 Try; attempt; make trial of; endeavour.

**嘘** xū
(v.)- Breathe; puff; breathe softly. Speak well of; speak in favour of; praise; recommend.
嘘氣 Blow with the breath. Belch. Expire; exhale.

**嘮** láo
(v.)- Chatter.
嘮叨 Chattering; loquacious.

**嘯** xiào
(n.)- A whistling, hissing sound.
(v.)- Whistle. Roar. Hiss.
嘯吟 Sing in chorus.

**嘲** cháo
(v.)- Ridicule; laugh and joke with; mock at; jest at.
嘲弄 Put joke upon one; make fun of; make fool of.
嘲笑 Jeer at; mock at; laugh; jest; ridicule.
嘲罵 Abuse; rail at; scold.

**嘴** zuǐ
(n.)- A bill; a peak; a mouth.
嘴唇 The lips.
嘴饞 Gluttonous.

**嘶** sī
(n.)- The neighing of a horse. A crashing noise.
(v.)- Neigh.
嘶喊 Cry out. Uproaring noise.

**嘹** liáo
嘹喨 Loud and clear—of sounds.

**嘻** xī
(v.)- Laugh with the short catches of the breath.
嘻笑 Laugh; giggle.

噤 (v.)- Shut the mouth; unable to speak.
jìn 噤口 Seal the lip; hold one's tongue.

器 (n.)- A vessel; a tool; an implement. An article; a utensil. Ability; capacity.
qì 器皿 Plates; dishes; crockery.
器材 Materials; stuffs.
器具；器械 Furniture; utensils; tools; implements.
器官 Organ.
器重 Have a high opinion of.
器械 Arms; weapon; apparatus; instrument.
器容量 Capacity.
器械體操 Heavy gymnastics.

噩 (n.)- Surprisal.
(v.)- Surprise.
è 噩耗 Startling (unlucky) news, as of a death.
噩夢 A dreadful dream.

噪 (n.)- The hum of voices.
(v.)- Chirp.
zào 噪音 A noise; a din.

噴 (v.)- Spurt; blow out; puff; snort.
pēn 噴出 Spout; spurt; jet; gush out.
噴泉 A geyser; a fountain.
噴香 Sweet-scented; fragrant.
噴嚏 Sneeze.
噴水池 A fountain.
噴射器 A sprayer.
噴射機 A jet plane.

噸 (n.)- Ton, English unit of weight.
dūn 噸量 Ton of weight.

嚇 (v.)- Threaten; scare; alarm; frighten; terrify.
xià 嚇死 Frightened to death.
嚇唬 Intimidate.

嚏 (v.)- Sneeze.
tì

嚮 (v.)- Incline to; follow. Guide; approach.
xiàng (prep.)- Toward; near.
嚮往 Long for; desire; think of.

嚴 (adj.)- Severe; stern; relentless; rigid; strict; solemn. Close.
yán (adv.)- Extremely; very.
嚴防 Take care sternly; closely guard.
嚴重 Severe; strict; stern; rigorous.
嚴格 Strict; stern; rigorous.
嚴寒 Extremely cold; intense cold.
嚴密 Close; secret; precise.
嚴肅 Solemn; grave; austere.
嚴厲 Strict; stern; stringent.
嚴酷 Severe; tyrannical; oppressive.
嚴肅之貌 A solemn face; a long face.

嚷 (v.)- Make a clamour; cry out; shout.
rāng 嚷鬧 Quarrel.

嚼 (v.)- Chew; ruminate; bite, masticate.
jiáo 嚼口 Wooden tongue for horse.

囂 (n.)- Hubbub; clamour.
xiāo

囈 (v.)- Mutter or talk in one's sleep.
yì 囈語 Silly talk; talk in delirium.

**囉** luó (adj.)- Annoying; talkative.
囉唆 Vexatious; annoying; talkactive; prattle.

**囊** nóng (n.)- A bag, a sack; a purse; a case.
(v.)- Put in a bag.
囊括 Wrap up; envelop.
囊中 In one's purse.

**囑** zhǔ (v.)- Bid; order; ask another to do; enjoin upon.
囑咐 Instruct; bid; charge one to do.
囑託 Give in charge; commission; request.

# 囗 部

**囚** qiú (n.)- Imprisonment; confinement. A prisoner; a criminal. A prison; a jail.
(v.)- Imprison; put in prison; put in jail.
囚犯 A felon; a convict; a prisoner; a jailbird.
囚禁 Shut up in prison.
囚籠 A cage to carry prisoners.

**四** sì (adj.)- Four; fourth.
四十 Forty.
四川（地）Szechwan.
四方 In every direction; in all directions; everywhere; on all sides; all over. The four quarters.
四月 April.
四角 Four-cornered; square.
四肢 The limbs; the legs and arms.
四季；四時 The four seasons.
四面 The four sides. On all sides.
四倍 Four times; fourfold; quadruple.
四海 The whole world.
四重奏 A quartet.
四邊形 A quadrilateral.
四聲道 4-channel.
四分之一 One-fourth; a quarter.
四分五裂 Go to pieces; be torn up; be disrupted.
四通八達 Accessible from all directions.
四面八方 On all sides; in all directions.

**回** huí (n.)- A time; a turn. A chapter in a novel.
(v.)- Return; turn back; go back; revert to. Alter.
回去 Return; go back.
回來 Return; come back.
回音；回答 A reply; an answer.
回家 Return home; go home.
回航；回駛 Sail back.
回教；伊斯蘭教 Mohammedanism.
回報 Reply.
回單；回執 A receipt.
回復 Recovery; restoration; reestablishment.
回想 Recall; reflect; consider.
回國 Return to one's native country.
回避 Avoid; evade; shun. Avoid visitors.
回聲 An echo; reverberation of sound.
回覆 Return. Reply; answer.
回顧 Look back; retrospect.
回憶錄 Memoirs; recollections; reminiscences.
回教徒 Moslem.
回教寺院 A mosque.
回頭是岸 Repentance is salvation.

**因** yīn (n.)- Cause; reason. Foundation, base.
(prep.)- For; owing to; because of; for the sake of; in order to; for the purpose of.
(conj.)- Because; for; as. So; therefore.

因子；因數(算) Factor.
因此 On this account; for this purpose.
因為 Because.
因緣 Origin; fate.

**囤** dùn (n.)- A grain bin.
囤積 Hoard.

**囫** hú (n.)- Round; entire; the whole.
囫圇吞棗 Swallowed a date whole—do a thing without thought.

**困** kùn (adj.)- Confined. Needy; poor.
(v.)- Confine.
困苦 Poverty-stricken; in deep poverty; in distress.

困倦 Fatigued; tired; weary.
困惱 Vexation.
困惑 Puzzled.
困窮 Poverty; destitution.
困難 Perplexity; difficulty; distress.

**固** gù (adj.)- Strong; firm; sturdy. Strengthened.
(v.)- Make firm.
(adv.)- Firmly; assuredly.

固定 Settle; be fixed.
固執 Hold fast; stick to; insist upon. Pig-headed.
固然 Surely; certainly; unquestionably; of course.
固體 A solid.
固有名詞 A proper noun.
固定收入 A regular (fixed) income.
固定資產 Fixed assets.

**圃** pǔ (n.)- A vegetable garden; an orchard.

**圇** lún 囫圇 Complete; whole.

**圈** quān (n.)- A circle; a sphere; a scope. A ring.
(v.)- Punctuate. Encircle; surround.

圈子 A circle; a range.
圈套 A snare; a plot; a trap.
圈點 Circles and dots; punctuation marks.

**國** guó (n.)- A state; a country; a kingdom; an empire; a nation.
國土 The territory; the domain; the realm.

國內 Internal; domestic.
國王 The king; the sovereign.
國史 Records of the country; national history.
國外 Outside the country; abroad; overseas.
國民 People; citizens.
國交 Diplomatic relations.
國防 National defence.
國事 National affairs.
國花 The national flower.
國家 A state; a country; a nation.
國庫 The national treasury; the treasury of the state.
國產 Home products.
國貨 Native products; home-made goods.
國都 The capital; the metropolis.
國會 National assembly; a parliament; a diet.

國葬 State burial (funeral).
國賊 A traitor; a rebel.
國際 International.
國境 The frontier; the border.
國旗 The national flag.
國歌 National anthem; national song.
國粹 The spirit of a nation.
國語 Mandarin; national language; one's mother tongue.
國慶 The national celebration.
國營 State operation; nationalization.
國籍 Nationality; citizenship.
國務院 State Council.
國務卿 The Secretary of State (美).
國際法 International law.
國際歌 Internationale.
國慶日 National holiday.
國民經濟 National economy.
國立學校 Government school.
國家主權 Right of sovereignty.
國家機關 Organ of the state.
國家銀行 National bank.
國務總理 Premier.
國會議員 A member of Parliament (M. P.).
國際主義 Internationalism.
國際列車 An international train.
國際貨幣 International money.
國際貿易 International trade.
國際郵政 International post.
國慶紀念 National anniversary celebration.
國際通信社 The International News Service (INS).

**圍** (n.)- An inclosure. Circumference.
wéi (v.)- Surround; besiege; circumscribe; inclose.

圍巾 A muffler; a scarf or a wrap.
圍困 Surrounded; hemmed in; besieged; shut in.
圍攻 Lay siege to; beleaguer.
圍棋 A kind of Chinese chess.
圍裙 Petticoat. Apron.
圍牆 A surrounding wall.
圍繞 Environ; surround; encircle; hem in.
圍桌而坐 Sit around a table; ring round (about) a table.

**園** (n.)- An inclosure; a yard; a garden; a park; an orchard.
yuán A theater. A tea house.
園丁 A gardener.

園亭 An alcove; a garden bower.
園藝 Horticulture; gardening.
園遊會 A garden-party.
園藝植物 A garden-plant.

**圓** (n.)- A circle. A dollar; a Yuan.
(adj.)- Round; circular.
yuán (v.)- Make round; cut off corners.

圓球 A sphere.
圓規 Compasses.
圓心 Centre of a circle.
圓月 Full moon.
圓形 Round; circular.
圓周 Circumference.
圓桌 The round table.
圓柱 A column.
圓圈 A circle; a ring.
圓筒 Cylinder.
圓滑 Smoothness; accommodating.
圓滿 Perfection; harmony.
圓舞；華爾姿舞 A round (circle) dance; a waltz.
圓周角 An inscribed angle.
圓周率 The ratio of the circumference of a circle to its diameter.
圓桌會議 A round-table conference.
圓滿解決 A peaceful (an amicable) settlement; a satisfactory close.
圓滿家庭 A harmonious household; a happy home; a happy family.

**圖** tú (n.)- A figure; plan; drawing; diagram or chart; an illustration; a picture.
(v.)- Plan; scheme.

圖形 The sketch; an illustration; the contour.
圖表 Diagram.
圖案 A design; a sketch.
圖書 Library; a collection of books.
圖章 A seal.
圖畫 Maps and pictures; pictures.
圖解 An illustration; an explanatory diagram.
圖像 A portrait; a picture.
圖樣 An illustration.
圖謀 Plan; plot.
圖書館 A library.
圖書目錄 A catalogue of books.
圖書館長 The chief librarian.
圖書管理員 A librarian.
圖書閱覽室 A reading-room.

**團** tuán (n.)- A globular mass; a sphere. A lump. A body. A guard.
(adj.)- United. Round; globular.
(v.)- Collect; group.

團長 Chief of a regiment; colonel. The head of a party.
團員 A member of a party (an association).
團結 Unite closely; band together.
團聚 Unite.
團體 Unity; union; a body of ; a party; an organization.
團體操 Mass drills.
團體生活 Group life.
團體旅行 Travel in a party.
團體會議 A mass meeting.
團體精神 Team spirit.

**圜** huán (n.)- A circle. A ball. Heavenly bodies; a star.

# 土 部

**土** tǔ (n.)- Earth; ground; soil; land. A region; a place. Territory; possessions.
(adj.)- Native; local; typical; crude.

土人；土著 The aborigines; the people of the land; natives.
土地 Land; territory; country.
土星(天) Saturn.
土音 Local accent; brogue; dialect.
土匪 Bandits.
土產 Native products.
土話 Local dialect; patois.
土棍；土豪 Local rowdies.
土壤 Soil.
土耳其(地) Turkey.
土地國有 Land nationalization.
土崩瓦解 A collapse; break-down; utter disorder.
土豪劣紳 Local rascals and oppressive gentry.
土木工程師 A civil engineer.

**在** zài (v.)- In or at. Remain. Alive; exist; be present.
(prep.)- In; on; at; within.
在世 Alive.

在上 Above; up.
在下 Below.
在內 Within; inside.
在外 Without; outside.
在前 Before; ahead.

在後 Behind; after.
在家 At home; indoors.
在船 On board.
在場 Present; on the spot.
在職 Be in office.
在學校 At school.
在夢中 In a dream.

**地** dì (n.)- The earth; ground; place; land; field; space; territory; locality; spot.
地心 The center of the earth.
地方 A place; the locality; the region; some-where.
地主 A landholder; a landlord.
地瓜(植) Sweet potatoes.
地穴 A hole.
地名 The name of a place; a place-name.
地位 Place; situation; position; rank.
地址 Address.
地形 Configuration; geographical position; natural features.
地角 A cape.
地板 A floor.
地表；地面 The surface of the earth.
地域 A tract of land; an area; a region.
地基 A foundation.
地殼 The earth's crust.
地理 Geography.
地球 The globe; the earth.
地產 Estate.
地稅 Land tax; revenue derived from the ground.
地窖 Basement; cellar.
地勢 The nature of a country; physical features; topography.
地道 Subterranean passages; a subway; a tunnel.
地雷 Mines.
地圖 A map; an atlas.
地獄 Hell; Hades.
地蓆 Matting.
地租 Rent; land tax.
地鐵(鑛) Terrestrial iron.
地盤 The foundation; the ground; the base.
地震 An earthquake.
地氈 A carpet; a rug.
地點 Location.
地中海(地) The Mediterranean Sea.
地方稅 Local tax.
地平線 Horizon.
地球儀 A globe.
地理學 Geography.
地質學 Geology.
地下鐵道 Underground railways; a subway.
地心吸力 Gravitation.
地方政府 Local Government.
地方警察 Local police.
地文地理 Physical geography.
地理掛圖 A wall-map.
地理學家 Geographer.
地產公司 A realty company.
地質學家 Geologist.
地球的公轉 Revolution.
地球的自轉 Rotation.

**址** zhǐ (n.)- A foundation. Address.

**坂** bǎn (n.)- A hillside; a slope; a cliff. A bank.

**坊** fāng (n.)- A lane; an alley; a street. A store; a workshop. A monument.
坊里 A street. A neighborhood. Hamlets.

**坍** tān (v.)- Fall into ruins; collapse; tumble down.
坍台 Lose one's face.

**坎** kǎn
(n.)- A pit.
坎穴 A hole; a pit.

**坐** zuò
(v.)- Sit; be seated. Be situated; be located.
坐位 A seat; one's position.
坐船 Travel by boat.
坐落 Situation. Situated; located.
坐監；坐牢 Be in prison.
坐褥 A cushion.

**坑** kēng
(n.)- A trench; a pit; an excavation; a hollow; a quarry.
坑谷 A valley.

**均** jūn
(adj.)- All; equal, fair.
均勻 Uniformity; even.
均勢 Balance of power.
均等 Equality.
均分 To share equally.

**坡** pō
(n.)- A slope; a hill-side.
坡度 Grade.

**坦** tǎn
(adj.)- Level; plain; smooth.
坦平 Level; smooth.
坦白；坦率 Frankness; open-heartedness; straightforward.
坦克車 A tank; an armoured motor-car.

**坩** gān
(n.)- A pot.
坩堝 A crucible; a melting-pot.

**坼** chè
(v.)- Burst; open; tear; chap; rend asunder.
坼裂 Crack; split.

**垂** chuí
(adj.)- Suspended; hanging.
(v.)- Suspend; hang down; drop. Condescend; bend down; bow.
垂下 Drop; hang down; dangle.
垂危 In great danger; imminent; critical.
垂死 At death's door.
垂直 Perpendicular.
垂直線 A perpendicular; a vertical line.
垂涎三尺 Eagerly covet; gloat on.
垂頭喪氣 Downcast; dejected.

**垃** lā
垃圾 Rubbish.
垃圾箱 A dust-bin.

**坪** píng
(n.)- A level ground.

**型** xíng
(n.)- A mould of earth for castings. A statue; a law.

**垢** gòu
(n.)- Dirt; filth. Immorality. A stain.
(adj.)- Dirty; filthy. Disgraceful.
垢穢 Dirt; filth.

**埃** āi
(n.)- Dust; dirt.
埃及（地） Egypt.
埃塵 Dirt; dust.
埃及人 An Egyptian.

**埋** mái
(v.)- Bury; inter. Cover; conceal. Store up; lay up.
埋伏 Lay an ambush.
埋沒 Hide; conceal.
埋怨 Murmur; complain.
埋葬 Bury; inter.
埋藏 Lay up; store up.
埋設地雷 Lay mines.

**城** chéng
(n.)- A city; a town.
城門 A castle-gate; a city gate.
城堡 Bastion; castle.

城牆 The city-walls; the rampart.
城市生活 City life.

**埔** pǔ (n.)- A plain; an arena. A port; a mart.

**域** yù (n.)- A frontier; a boundary. A region; lands.

**埠** bù (n.)- A port; a trading place; a city.
埠頭 A wharf; a port ; a trading place; a jetty.
埠際賽 Interport match.

**執** zhí (v.)- Hold; grasp. Seize; apprehend; arrest. Attend to; manage. Maintain; retain; keep.
執友 An intimate friend; a comrade; a chum.
執行 Execute; carry out.
執政 Manage the government. Statesmen; premier.
執筆 Write.
執照 A certificate; a pass; a licence; a passport.
執政黨 The party in power; ruling party.
執照費 Licence fee.
執行委員會 The executive committee.

**培** péi (v.)- Cultivate; nurse. Strengthen.
培植 Cultivate; grow; raise. Support; assist.
培養 Nourish; invigorate the body; cultivate.

**基** jī (n.)- The foundation; a base; a basis. A beginning.
(adj.)- Fundamental; principal.
(v.)- Commence. Found.
基本 A foundation; a basis; a base.
基地 A base.
基金 An endowment; a fund; a foundation.
基準 A standard; a basis.
基層 Base; basement.
基礎 Foundation; basis; beginning; starting point.
基本上 Fundamentally.
基督教 Christianity.
基本工業 Basic industries.
基本原理 Fundamentals; a basic principle.
基本英語 Basic English.
基督教徒 Christians.
基督教青年會 The Young Men's Christian Association ( Y.M.C.A.).
基督教女青年會 The Young Women's Christian Association (Y.W.C.A.).

**堂** táng (n.)- A hall. A court; a public establishment.
堂皇 Magnificent.
堂兄弟 Cousins of the same surname.
堂姊妹 Female cousins of the same surname.
堂堂正正 Fair and square; with dignity and impartiality.

**堅** jiān (adj.)- Strong; hard. Determined; resolute.
堅決 A strong determination; a fixed purpose.
堅定 Fixed; decided.
堅固 Immovable; hard; firm; strong.
堅信 Convince.
堅持 Manifest persistent obstinacy; hold on; insist on.
堅實 Hard and solid.
堅忍不拔 Indomitable; indefatigable; persevering.

堅持到底 Hold on to the very end.
堅强不屈 Unyielding and firm resistance.

堆 (n.)- A heap; a mass; a pile. A mound. A crowd.
duī 堆土 Bank up with earth.
堆積 Accumulate; store up; pile up.

堊 (v.)- Whitewash; plaster.
è

堡 (n.)- A station for defense; a castle.
bǎo 堡壘 A fort; a fortification.

堤 (n.)- A dike; an embankment; a dam.
dī 堤岸 A bank; a dike.

堪 (adj.)- Able; adequate to.
堪用 Useful; fit for use.
kān

堰 (n.)- An embankment; a levee, a dike.
yǎn 堰壩 An embankment.

報 (n.)- A reward. A report. A newspaper.
bào (v.)- Recompense; revenge. State; report.
報仇 Revenge oneself on an enemy.
報名 Register.
報考 Register for examination.
報告 Inform; make a report.
報到 Report one's arrival.
報恩 Requite favours; repay one's kindness.
報紙 Newspaper.
報復 Retaliate; revenge.
報單 A notice. An application to pass goods through the customs.
報答 Recompense; repay.
報喜 Report good news.
報酬 A pay; a reward; a fee.
報館 A newspaper office.
報警 Sound an alarm; report to the police.
報名處 Office of registry.
報告人 Informer.
報告書 A report; returns; a journal.
報紙夾 A newspaper-holder.
報館主筆 Editor of a newspaper.
報館記者 A correspondent. A journalist; a reporter; a newsman.

場 (n.)- An open space; a field; a yard. An arena.
chǎng 場面 A stage. Social standing. The scene.
場地 A courtyard; a lawn.

堵 (n.)- A low wall.
(v.)- Obstruct; stop. Close. Guard.
dǔ 堵口 Stuff the mouth.
堵塞 Block up.

塊 (n.)- A piece; a fragment; a part; a lump.
kuài 塊狀 Lumpy; massive.
塊根 Tuberous root.
塊莖 Tuber.

塑 (v.)- Model in clay.
塑像 An earthen (a clay) figure.
sù 塑膠 Plastic.

塔 (n.)- A tower; a pagoda. A pyramid.
tǎ 塔斯通訊社 Telegraphonye Agentstvo Sovyetskovo Soyuza (Tass).

塗 (v.)- Daub; smear. Blot out; cancel; scratch out; wipe off.
tú 塗改 Blot out; alter.
塗抹 Rub out.
塗面 Paint the face.
塗飾 Plaster in colour.
塗脂抹粉 Rouge and powder.
塗搽藥水 An embrocation; a liniment; a lotion.
塗搽藥膏 An ointment.

塘 (n.)- A pool; a pond. A bank.
táng 塘沽(地) Tangku.

塞 (n.)- A pass. A frontier. A stopper.
sāi (v.)- Stop up; close. Hinder.
塞口 Stop a hole.
塞子 A cork; a stopper.
塞住 Close; shut (choke, stop, block) up.
塞滿 Fill; stuff full.

塡 (v.)- Fill up; complete; supply enough.
tián 塡平 Fill up.
塡充 To fill in the blank spaces.
塡滿 Become full; fill up.
塡補 Make good; supply enough.
塡海 Reclaim land from the sea.
塡寫 Fill in—as particulars.
塡履歷 Note in the register of the age, residence, etc. Write a curriculum vitae.

塢 (n.)- A ship-yard.
wù

塵 (n.)- Dust; dirt. Rubbish; garbage.
chén 塵污 Soiled with dust; defiled with dust.
塵埃 Dust.

塹 (n.)- Moat around a city.
qiàn

塾 (n.)- A domestic or village school; a family school.
shú

境 (n.)- A limit; a boundary. State; circumstances; condition.
jìng 境內 In the locality; within the boundary.
境地 Territory.
境界 Boundary; limit; frontier.
境遇 Circumstances; condition.
境況 Situation.
境界線 The boundary line.

墅 (n.)- A cottage; a country-seat; a villa; a summer house.
shù

墊 (n.)- A cushion.
diàn (v.)- Place on. Advance money. Fill up.
墊子 A cushion.
墊平 Fill up and make even.
墊款 Advance in cash. Money advanced.

墓 (n.)- A burial place; a tomb; a grave.
mù 墓地 Church-yard; cemetery.
墓碑 A gravestone; a tombstone; a stone monument.
墓誌 An epitaph; the inscription at a grave.

墜 (v.)- Fall down; tumble down; sink; crumble; collapse.
zhuì 墜下 Fall down.

墜胎 A premature birth; a miscarriage.
墜馬 To fall off a horse.
墜入陷阱 Fall into a trap.

**增** zēng (v.)- Increase; augment; add to.
增入 Add to.
增大 Enlarge.
增加 Add; increase; raise.
增光 Do honour.
增多 Multiplication.
增兵 Reinforce; send more troops.
增刪 Make corrections.
增刊 Supplement.
增租 Raise the rent.
增高 Make higher; bring up.
增產 Increased production (output).
增盛 Increasing prosperity.
增設 An increase of institutions.
增減 Increase and decrease; add and reduce (deduct); rise and fall; vary; fluctuate.
增訂 Improve on or upon; make amendments to.
增强 Strengthen; fortify.
增補 Add on; supplement.
增進 Grow; advance; improve.
增加工資 Increased wages.

**墟** xū (n.)- A mound; a waste. A market.
墟場 An open arena where fairs are held.

**墨** mò (n.)- Ink.
(adj.)- Dark; black.
墨水；墨汁 Ink; writing fluid.
墨油 Printing ink.
墨魚(動) The cuttle-fish.
墨硯 An inkstone.
墨綠 Dark green.
墨西哥(地) Mexico.

**墩** dūn (n.)- A mound; a heap.
墩台；墩堡 A beacon mound.

**墮** duò (v.)- Sink; let fall. Destroy.
墮後 Fall behind.
墮胎 Abort; cause abortion. Miscarry.
墮馬 Fall off a horse.
墮落 Sink; fall into decay; lose reputation.

**墳** fén (n.)- A grave. A mound.
墳山；墳墓 A grave.
墳場 A cemetery; a graveyard.

**墾** kěn (v.)- Develop new land; plow; cultivate; exploit.
墾地 Plow.
墾荒 Develop barren lands.

**壁** bì (n.)- A wall. A defence; a fortress. A precipice; a cliff.
壁櫥 A built-in cabinet.
壁虎(動) House lizard; gecko.
壁紙 Printed hangings; wall paper.
壁報 A wall newspaper.
壁畫 Fresco; wall painting.
壁燈 A wall lamp.
壁爐 A fireplace; a grate.

**壅** yōng (v.)- Block up with earth; close up. Hinder.
壅塞 Obstruct; block up; impediment.

**壇** tán (n.)- An open altar. An arena; a stage; a pulpit.
壇場 An altar in the open air.

**壑** hè (n.)- A valley. A pit. A pond; a pool.
壑谷 A valley.

**壓** (v.)- Press; oppress; keep down; suppress.
yā 壓力(物) Pressure. (工) Compression; stress.
壓死 Crush to death.
壓抑 Take a peg lower or to take down.
壓制 Tread on the neck; control.
壓服 Bring under; beat down; overpower.
壓迫 Oppress; coerce.
壓倒 Upset; throw down; overturn.
壓榨 Squeeze, compress; press.
壓碎 Crush; squash.
壓縮 Compress; constrict.
壓破 Break by crushing.
壓水機 Hydraulic press.
壓氣機(機) Air compressor.
壓榨機 A press; a compressor.
壓倒的多數 An overwhelming majority.
壓倒的勝利 A sweeping victory.

**壕** (n.)- A moat around a city wall; a ditch; a trench.
háo 壕溝 A ditch; a trench.

**壘** (n.)- A rampart; a fort; a fortress.
lěi 壘球 Baseball.

**壞** (adj.)- Dilapidated; broken down. Useless.
huài (v.)- Ruin; injure; destroy.
壞名 Notorious; bad reputation.
壞處 Bad points; defect.
壞意 Bad thoughts; malice.
壞血病 Scorbutus.
壞運氣 Bad luck.
壞脾氣 Bad temper.

**壟** (n.)- A small hill.
(v.)- Monopolize.
lǒng 壟斷 Monopolize.

**壤** (n.)- Soil. A territory. Earth.
壤質沙土 Loamy sand soil.
rǎng

**壩** (n.)- An embankment; a dike; a breakwater; a dam.
bà 壩頭 A mart; a port.

# 士 部

**士** (n.)- An officer. A soldier. A gentleman. A scholar.
shì 士兵；士卒 Soldiers.
士氣 Morale.
士女 Man and woman; gentlemen and ladies.

**壯** (adj.)- Strong; robust; healthy; hardy.
zhuàng 壯丁 An adult.
壯大 Strong; lusty.
壯士 A strong person; a brave soldier.
壯年 Manhood; youth; in the prime of life.
壯志 Resolute; strong-minded; firm.
壯健 Healthy. In strong health; in fine spirits or health.
壯麗 Splendid; glamour; grand; great and glorious.
壯觀 A magnificent view.

**壳** (n.)- Husk; covering; crust; shell.
ké

**壹** yī
(adj.)- Uniform; alike. One.

**壺** hú
(n.)- A pot; a cup.
壺蓋 The lid of a pot.

**壻** xù
Same as 婿.
(n.)- A son-in-law.

**壽** shòu
(n.)- Age. Longevity.
壽衣 A burial dress; a shroud.
壽辰；壽誕 A birthday.
壽命 Age.
壽酒 A birthday feast.
壽終 Die a natural death.
壽險 Life insurance.
壽禮 Birthday presents.
壽數 The span of life.
壽木；壽器 A coffin.
壽險單 Life insurance policy.

# 夂 部

**夏** xià
(n.)- Summer.
夏季 Summer.
夏至 The summer solstice.
夏令營 Summer camp.
夏作物 Summer crops.
夏威夷(地) Hawaii.
夏枯草(植) A labiate plant which dries up in the summer, used in medicine.
夏威夷人 A Hawaiian.

# 夕 部

**夕** xī
(n.)- Evening; twilight. Sun-set.
夕陽；夕照 The setting sun.

**外** wài
(adj.)- Out; outside.
(prep.)- Without; beyond; outside.
外人 An outsider. A foreigner.
外公；外祖 A mother's father; a maternal grand-father.
外皮(生) The skin.
外交 Diplomacy; foreign intercourse.
外行 Unexperienced. A raw hand; layman; new hand.
外衣；外套 An outer coat; an overcoat.
外形 Feature; outlook; appearance.
外洋 Overseas; abroad.
外科 Surgery.
外界 External; the outside world.
外面 Surface; outside; exterior.
外國 A foreign country.
外埠 An outport.
外號 A nickname.
外援 Foreign aid.
外滙 Foreign exchange.
外甥 A nephew; sister's son.
外貌 Countenance; appearance.
外賓 A foreign guest.
外觀 Aspect.

外文系 Department of foreign languages.
外交官 Diplomatic officers.
外交界 Diplomatic circles.
外交家 Diplomats.
外交部 The Ministry of Foreign Affairs.
外祖母 Maternal grandmother.
外甥女 A niece; sister's daughter.
外敷藥 Fomentations.
外交政策 A foreign policy.
外交部長 The Minister of Foreign Affairs.
外交機關 Diplomatic organ.
外國使節 A foreign envoy.
外科醫生 Surgeon.
外國語學校 School of foreign languages.

多 (n.)- Plenty; a great number.
(adj.)- Many; numerous; plentiful; much.
duō
(adv.)- Often; mostly.

多士 Toast.
多少 How many? A certain quantity.
多半 The greater part; in a greater degree.
多次 Many times.
多年 For many years.
多見；多聞 Experienced; well informed.
多病 Sickly; of delicate health; weak and tired.
多能 Capable; talented; versatile.
多情 Passionate; affectionate.
多智 Wise; sagacious.
多量 A great (large) quantity; a vast volume.
多種 Many kinds; a large variety.
多數 A large number; a majority; a plurality.
多謝 Many thanks. Thank you very much.
多難 Full of trouble (difficulties).
多讀 Read much (widely, extensively).
多方面 Many directions (quarters).
多見識 Of wide information. Well informed.
多數黨 A majority party.
多才多藝 Many-sided; versatile.
多產作家 A prolific writer (author).
多管閒事 Be a meddlesome busybody.
多多益善 The more the better.

夜 (n.)- Night; darkness.
夜市 Night market.
yè
夜半 Late in the night; midnight.

夜色 The shades of night.
夜車 A night train.
夜夜 Nightly; night after night; every night.
夜盲 Day-sight; night blindness.
夜班 Night shift.
夜景 A night-view; a night-scene.
夜飯 Supper; the evening meal.
夜學 Study at night. An evening school.
夜靜 The stillness of night; the dead of night.
夜鶯 The nightingale. A street-walker.
夜光蟲 A noctiluca.
夜總會 Night clubs.
夜行軍 Night march.
夜光表 A watch with a luminous dial.
夜來香（植） The tuberose.
夜盲症 Nyctalopia.
夜禮服 An evening dress.
夜以繼日 Night and day.

夢 (n.)- A dream.
(v.)- Dream; see visions.
mèng
夢幻 A dream; fantasy.
夢見 See in a dream.

夢想 Dream of.
夢醒 Awaken from a dream.
夢魘 Nightmare.
夢遊病 Sleep-walking; somnambulism.

**夥** (n.)- A band; a party. A partner; a companion.
huǒ (adj.)- Numerous; many.

夥伴 A partner in business.
夥計 A shop assistant. A clerk. An employee.

# 大 部

**大** (adj.)- Great; big; huge.
dà (adv.)- Highly; extremely; greatly.
大小 Great and small. Size.

大夫(醫生) A physician.
大方 Generous. On a large scale.
大王(石油大王等) Magnate; baron.
大半 For the most part; largely; mostly.
大衣 A cloak; an overcoat.
大臣 A high official; a minister of state; a chancellor.
大作 A great work; a masterpiece.
大局 The general situation; political condition.
大志 High aims; elevated mind.
大旱 A severe (long) drought.
大豆 Soya bean.
大阪(地) Osaka.
大事 An important affair.
大使 An ambassador; an envoy.
大雨 A heavy (pouring) rain; a downpour.
大便 Faeces; excrement; dung.
大怒 Great anger; in a great rage.
大洋 The ocean.
大風 A strong wind; a gale.
大家 We all; all of us.
大宴 A grand banquet.
大氣 The atmosphere; the air.
大海 An ocean; the high seas.
大浪 Surge; billows.
大班 Manager.
大病 A serious illness.
大笑 Laugh heartily.
大國 A powerful nation; a great power.
大約 About.
大將 A general (陸); an admiral (海).
大尉 A captain (陸); a lieutenant (海).
大赦 A general pardon; amnesty.
大略；大概 General outline; general sketch. For the most part.
大連(地) Dairen.
大陸 A continent.
大麥 Barley.
大蔴 Hemp.
大厦 A big house; a mansion; an edifice; magnificent buildings.
大衆 The whole party. The masses.
大街 The main street.
大意 General idea. Careless.
大會 A great meeting; a mass meeting.
大煙 Opium.
大腦 The cerebrum.
大舅 A wife's elder brother.
大道 The highway; the highroad.
大腿 The thigh.
大蒜(植) Garlic.
大寫 The large type of writing; capital letter.
大學 A university.
大橋 Major bridges.
大聲 In a loud voice; at the top of one's voice.
大膽 Very courageous; bold; daring; fearless.
大體 In general; on the whole; almost.
大廳 The main hall; the auditorium.
大人物 VIP (very important person).

大力士 A man of great strength; a Hercules.
大主教 An archbishop.
大本營 Army base; headquarters.
大多數 Great majority; the great number.
大西洋(地) The Atlantic Ocean.
大使館 An embassy.
大前提 A major premise.
大洋洲(地) Oceania.
大宴會 A banquet.
大理石 Marble.
大部分 The greater part; the best part.
大規模 On a large (grand) scale.
大減價 Cheap sale; great sale.
大猩猩(動) Troglodytes gorilla.
大學生 A university student; a collegian.
大總統 President.
大不列顛(地) Great Britain.
大公無私 Just and equal.
大材小用 Use a talented man in an inferior capacity.
大事年表 A chronology.
大街小巷 Streets and lanes.
大量輸出 Export in large quantities.
大量生產 Mass production; production on a large scale.
大學校長 A university (college) president.
大學教授 A university (college) professor.
大西洋公約 The Atlantic Pact.
大學畢業生 Graduate.
大學一年級生 Freshman.
大學二年級生 Sophomore.
大學三年級生 Junior.
大學四年級生 Senior.

天 tiān (n.)- The sky. Nature. A day. (adj.)- Celestial; natural.
天下 The world. The empire.
天才 Genius; a natural talent.
天主 The Creator; the lord of Heaven.
天平 A pair of scales; a balance.
天旱 Drought; dry weather.
天災 Calamity; catastrophe.
天使 An angel.
天性 Instinct; natural dispositon.
天河(天) The Milky Way.
天空 The heavens; the sky; the air; space.
天花(醫) Smallpox.
天亮 Daylight; dawn; daybreak.
天津(地) Tientsin.
天時 Seasons; the weather.
天氣 Weather; climate.
天眞 Innocence; naive.
天堂 Land of the leal; Heaven; Paradise.
天涯 The horizon.
天陰 A dull day; a cloudy day.
天資 Natural quality.
天線 Antenna; aerial line.
天險 A natural barrier (stronghold).
天文臺 An astronomical observatory.
天文學 Astronomy.
天王星(天) Uranus.
天主堂 A cathedral; a church.
天主教 The Roman Catholic Church.
天花板 The ceiling.
天然美 Natural beauty; the beauties of nature.
天演論 The theory of evolution.
天鵝絨 Velvet.
天下聞名 World-famous.
天文學者 An astronomer.
天主教王 Pope.
天主教徒 A Roman Catholic.
天方夜譚 The Arabian Nights' Entertainment.
天氣預報 Weather forecast; a weather report.
天然資源 Natural resources.
天淵之別 Be as far apart as heaven and earth.

天文望遠鏡 An astronomical telescope.

太 (adv.)- Very; too; extremely.
tài 太大 Too big.
太子 The Heir; apparent; the Crown Prince.

太太 Madam; her ladyship.
太平 Great peace.
太后 The emperor's mother; the empress dqwager.
太多 Too much; too many.
太空 The sky; space.
太陽 The sun.
太監 A eunuch.
太平門 Safety-exit in theatres, etc.
太平梯 Safety ladder.
太平洋 The Pacific Ocean.
太陽穴(解) The temple.
太空人 Spaceman; astronaut.
太空船 Space-ship.
太陽系 The solar system.
太陽神 The sungod; Helios (希臘神話); Phoebus (羅馬神話). Apollo.
太晤士河(地) River Thames.
太陽黑點 A sun-spot; a macula.

夫 (n.)- A husband. A labourer. A man.
fū 夫人 Mrs., Madame; a married woman.

夫婦 Husband and wife; a couple.

夭 (n.)- An early death.
yāo (adj.)- Young; fresh-looking; tender.
(v.)- Die young.

夭死；夭折 Die young. An early death.

央 (n.)- The middle or center. The half of.
yāng (v.)- Entreat; request; beg. Finish.

央求 Entreat; solicit; beg; request.

失 (v.)- Lose; miss; omit.
shī 失火 Catch fire; fire breaks out.
失主 The loser—of property.
失色 Lose colour (countenance); turn pale.

失言 Make a slip of the tongue; speak wrongly.
失足 Slip; lose one's footing.
失事 Get into trouble; meet with an accident.
失明 Lose one's eyesight. Blind.
失信 A breach of promise or faith. Break faith.
失約 A breach of contract. Break one's promise.
失神 Absent-minded.
失效 Losing effect; invalidation.
失眠 Lose one's sleep; have a restless night.
失措 Lose presence of mind; flustered.
失敗 Fall to the ground; fail of success. Failure.
失望 Lose hope; be disappointed. Hopeless.
失業 Drop from an employ. Out of job. Unemployment.
失策；失算 An error; a mistake; commit a blunder.
失踪 Disappear, run away; abscond.
失機 Lose the chance; lose one's opportunity.
失禮 Be rude to. Disrespectful.
失戀 Love-lorn; disappointment in love.
失面子 Lose one's face.
失眠症 Insomnia.
失業者 Unemployed workers; the workless; the unemployed.
失踪者 A disappearing person.

夾 (adj.)- Lined, doubled.
jiá (v.)- Press; squeeze. Hold with pincers.
夾子 Clamp forceps; pincers.

夾衣 A lined coat; a doubled garment.
夾攻 Attack from both sides.
夾雜 Mixed; ill-assorted.
夾髮針 Hairpin.

奄 (v.)- Stop; cover. Remain; tarry.
yǎn 奄奄一息 Gasping for breath.

奇 (adj.)- Rare; strange; wonderful; curious; uncommon. Unusual.
qí 奇人 A strange person.
奇事 A miracle; a strange affair.
奇怪 Strange; odd; queer; curious.
奇特 Peculiar.
奇異 Unusual; remarkable.
奇聞 Strange news.
奇數 An odd number.
奇談 Strange talk.
奇蹟 Wonders; miracle.
奇觀 Spectacle.
奇巧 Curious; clever; ingenious.
奇奇怪怪 Most strange; extremely odd.

奈 (conj.)- But. How.
nài 奈何 What remedy is there? What shall be done?

奉 (v.)- Receive. Offer. Deliver; send. Serve. Obey.
fèng 奉公 Serve; in the service of.
奉行 Carry out orders.
奉命 Receive a command or order.
奉承 Flatter; pay court to. Look after.
奉送 Offer; present.
奉陪 To bear another company.
奉獻 Dedication; presentation.

奎 奎甯(藥) Quinine.
kuí

奏 (v.)- Play music; function.
zòu 奏效 Have a beneficial result; be successful; take effect.
奏樂 Play music; strike the band.
奏凱 Sing the song of triumph.

契 (n.)- A bond; an agreement; a deed; a certificate; a contract.
qì (adj.)- Adopted.
契約 A written contract; a bond.
契據 Title deed.

奔 (v.)- Run away; flee; hurry off.
bēn 奔走 Hurry off. Move actively in.
奔波 Wearied in travelling; bustle.
奔流 A rushing stream; rapids.
奔逐 Drive out.
奔馳 Hurry off; hasten; travel quickly.
奔騰 Furious. Jump.

套 (n.)- A case; an envelope. A set. A suit of clothes.
tào (v.)- Encase; envelop. Imitate.
套褲 Overalls; leggings.
套鞋 Overshoes.
套房 Suite.

奠 (v.)- Make a libation. Determine; settle. Put down.
diàn 奠定 Quiet. Settled.

奢 (adj.)- Extravagant; profuse; luxurious.
shē 奢侈 Extravagant; lavish; profuse.
奢望 Entravagant hopes.
奢侈品 Luxuries.

奧 (adj.)- Deep. Difficult to understand. Marvelous.
ào 奧妙 A mystery. Mysterious.
奧秘 Subtle; hidden.
奧地利(地) Austria.

奪 (v.)- Seize. Grasp; capture; catch.
duó 奪目 Attractive to the eyes.
奪回 Get back by force; recover; recapture.
奪取 Capture; seize; take.
奪權 Disqualify; deprive of power or right. Foul.

獎 (n.)- A prize; a reward.
(v.)- Encourage. Commend; praise.
jiǎng
獎券 Lottery.
獎金 Bounties. A prize; a reward.
獎品 A reward; a prize.
獎章 A medal.
獎賞 Commend and reward.
獎勵 Stimulate to exertion.
獎學金 Scholarship.

奮 (adj.)- Zealous; violent; spirited. Vigorous. Courageous; daring.
fèn (v.)- Rouse; excite; stir up. Cheer; awaken.
奮力;奮勉 Ardent effort. Exert strength. Energetic.
奮勇 Take heart. Ardent courage.
奮發 Burst forth; arouse.
奮激 Excite; stir up.
奮鬥 Fight desperately; struggle.

# 女 部

女 (n.)- A girl; a maid. A woman.
女士 A lady; mistress. Miss.
nǚ 女友 A lady friend.
女王 A queen.
女主 A mistress; a hostess.
女生 A school girl.
女兒 A daughter.
女性 Femininity; womanhood.
女孩;女童 A girl; a lass.
女神 A goddess.
女郎 A young lady.
女將 A female warrior; an Amazon.
女婿 A son-in-law.
女傭 A maidservant.
女權 Woman suffrage; rights for women.
女外套 Mantle.
女司機 Female operative or machinist.
女作家 A female writer; an authoress.
女店員 A shop-girl; a saleswoman.
女英雄 A heroine.
女校長 A school mistress; a woman president.
女記者 A lady writer (reporter).
女教員 A lady (woman, female) teacher; an instructress; a schoolmistress.
女學校 Girl schools.
女儐相 Bridesmaid.
女子師範學校 Girls' normal school.

奴 (n.)- A slave; a servant; a menial.
nú 奴才 A bondman; a slave.
奴役 Slavery.
奴婢 Male and female slaves.
奴隸 A slave; a bondsman.
奴隸制度 Slavery.

奴隸解放 Emancipation of slaves.
奴隸販子 A slaver.

**奶** nǎi (n.)- Milk. Term of respect for woman.
(v.)- Suckle.
奶奶 A grandmother. A woman.
奶油 Butter; cream.

**奸** jiān (adj.)- Wicked; treacherous; deceitful; false.
(v.)- Violate.
奸人 An artful villain.
奸計 A crafty device; a wicked plot.
奸商 A dishonest merchant; a profiteer.
奸細 A spy; a traitor.
奸惡 Vicious; wicked; villainous.
奸淫 Treacherous and lecherous.
奸猾 Deceptive; double-handed.
奸賊 A traitor.

**好** hǎo (adj.)- Good; well; nice; fine; excellent. Dear; friendly; kind.
(v.)- Love; fond of; wish for; take delight in; incline.
(adv.)- Well; extremely.
好人 A good man; a nice fellow.
好久 A very long time.
好天 A fine day; sunny weather.
好友 Good friend.
好心 A kind intention; a good heart. Kindhearted.
好手 An adept; a skillful workman; an expert.
好多 A great many; very many.
好看 Good-looking; nice-looking; handsome.
好食 Good to eat; edible.
好酒 Bibacious; fond of liquor; given to wine.
好笑 Laughable; ridiculous; funny.
好勝 Ambitious of excelling; competitory.
好評 Favourable comment (criticism).
好意 Good will; kindness.
好感 Good feelings; a favourable impression.
好話 A complimentary remark; kind words.
好運 Good luck; good fortune.
好漢 A brave fellow; a hero.
好學 Studious; fond of study.
好聽 Pleasing to the ear.
好奇心 Curiosity.
好消息 Good news.
好望角(地) The Cape of Good Hope.
好脾氣 A good temper.
好結果 A good result; a success.
好機會 Good chance; rare opportunity.
好好先生 A good-natured (simple-minded, soft-hearted) person.
好酒之徒 A winebibber; tippler; drinker.
好善不倦 Not to be weary in the pursuit of virtue.

**如** rú (adj.)- Like; similar. Alike.
(prep.)- According to.
(conj.)- If. As if; as though; as; suppose.
如一 Much alike; same.
如下 As follows.
如今 Now; nowadays; at present; at this time.
如有 If there be; should it happen that.
如此 So; thus; such; like this.
如何 How! Why? What has become of.
如果 If; suppose; provided that.
如常 As usual; as customary.
如期 At time; on time; in due time; punctually.
如意 As you wish.
如此云云 They say so and so.
如何是好 What is the best thing to do?
如膠如漆 Very deep love.

**妊** (adj.)- Pregnant.
(v.)- Conceive; become pregnant.
rèn
妊娠 Pregnancy; conception.
妊婦 A pregnant woman; an expectant mother.

**妒** Same as 妬.
(adj.)- Jealous; envious.
dù (v.)- Be jealous of; be envious of.
妒忌 Envy; jealousy. Grudge.

**妓** (n.)- A whore; a prostitute; a courtesan; a hackney.
jì
妓女 Prostitutes; whores.
妓院；妓館 A brothel; a bawdy-house.

**妖** (n.)- A phantom; a spirit; an elf; a fairy.
yāo (adj.)- Strange; magical; supernatural. Heretical.
妖冶；妖嬈 Fascinating; bewitching.
妖怪；妖精 An apparition; a bugbear; a goblin.
妖魔 A devil; a demon; a monster.
妖魔鬼怪 Evil spirits of all kinds.

**妙** (adj.)- Excellent; admirable; spiritual; wonderful.
miào
妙手 An expert; a skilled artist or physician.
妙年 The prime of life. Young; youthful.
妙法；妙計 An admirable plan; a capital scheme.
妙齡女子 A young blooming girl.

**妝** (v.)- Adorn oneself; beautify.
妝扮 Costume. Decorate; dress.
zhuāng
妝飾 Adorn; make one's toilet. Ornaments.
妝飾品 Ornaments.

**妥** (adj.)- Firm. Ready; prepared. Satisfactory.
tuǒ
妥協 Make a compromise; meet one halfway; settle by mutual concession.
妥善 Satisfactory; properly arranged for; well-managed.
妥當 Propriety; appropriateness.

**妨** (v.)- Hinder; obstruct. Injure. Interfere with. Deter.
fāng
妨害 Interfere with; disturb.
妨礙 Hinder; obstruct.
妨害睡眠 Disturb one's sleep.
妨害衞生 Offence against public health.

**妹** (n.)- A younger sister.
mèi
妹夫 A younger sister's husband; a younger brother-in-law.

**妻** (n.)- A wife.
qī
妻子 A wife; wife and children.
妻母 A mother-in-law.
妻弟 A wife's brother; a brother-in-law.
妻族；妻黨 Wife's family.
妻親 Relatives on the wife's side.

**妾** (n.)- A concubine; a secondary wife.
qiè

**姊** (n.)- An elder sister. A miss.
jiě
姊夫 An elder brother-in-law—elder sister's husband.
姊妹 Sisters.

**始** (n.)- The beginning; commencement.
shǐ (v.)- Start; begin.

始末；始終 From beginning to end; during the whole time; throughout. Beginning and end.
始祖 Founder; first ancestor.
始基 The origin; the foundation.
始創 Invented; first made. Originate.
始業式 Inauguration; the opening ceremony.
始創人 Originator; the first person in doing something.

姍 shān (adj.)- Good; beautiful.
姍姍 A slow gait; walk slowly.

姑 gū (n.)- A paternal aunt.
姑丈 Father's sister's husband; uncle.
姑且 For the time being; in the meantime.
姑母 Paternal aunt – a father's sister.
姑娘 A young lady; a girl; a lass.
姑嫂 Sisters-in-law.

姓 xìng (n.)- A surname; a family name.
姓氏 The surname.
姓名 A full name; a name.
姓名錄 A name-list; a register of names.

委 wěi (v.)- Put in charge of. Appoint; depute. Give up; abandon.
(adv.)- Really; indeed.
委任 Appoint; delegate or appoint to an office.
委屈 Treat with injustice.
委員 A deputy; a special commissioner.
委託 Give in charge; entrust; deliver to another's care and exercise.
委婉 Circuitous; circumlocutory.
委靡 Dispirited. Lethargy.
委員長 Chairman of a committee.
委員會 A committee meeting.
委內瑞拉（地） Venezuela.

姚 yáo (adj.)- Handsome.
姚冶 Fascinating; bewitching; charming.

姣 jiāo (adj.)- Handsome; pretty; lascivious.
姣美 Beautiful; fascinating; captivating.
姣態 Attractive; coquettish.

姥 lǎo (n.)- A matron; a tutoress. An old woman.

姦 jiān Same as 奸.
(n.)- Fornication.
(v.)- Debauch; ravish; violate.
姦淫 Adultery; liaison; illicit sexual intercourse.
姦婦 An adulteress.

姨 yí (n.)- A wife's sister. Maternal aunts.
姨父 An uncle (husband of mother's sister).
姨母 An aunt (mother's sister).

姪 zhí (n.)- A nephew – a brother's child.
姪女 A niece.
姪婿 A niece's husband.

姸 yán (adj.)- Beautiful; handsome; elegant; pretty.
姸美 Excellent; pretty; beautiful.

姻 yīn (n.)- Relationship by marriage.
姻緣 Marriage affinity.
姻親 A wife's relatives.
姻族關係 Relationship by affin-

ity.

姿 zī
(n.)- Manner; carriage.
姿勢 A posture; a pose.
姿態 Carriage; manner; style; pose.
姿容秀麗 Graceful; elegant.

威 wēi
(n.)- Majesty; intimidating power.
(adj.)- Stately; majestic; grave.
(v.)- Threaten; awe.
威力 Might; power; authority.
威武 Martial-looking.
威信 Prestige; dignity; authority.
威風 An imposing air; dignified manners; majesty and pomp.
威脅 Coerce; intimidate.
威望 High reputation; influence and popularity.
威逼 Tyrannical; despotic. Intimidate.
威震 Strike terror into; awe.
威嚴 Dignified; majestic; august; commanding.
威尼斯(地) Venice.
威爾斯(地) Wales.
威士忌酒 Whiskey.
威風凜凜 Awe-inspiring; dignified manners.

娃 wá
(n.)- A baby. A beautiful woman.

娉 pīng
(adj.)- Graceful.
娉婷 Elegant and graceful.

娘 niáng
(n.)- A girl; a miss; a young lady. A mother.
娘子 A young lady. A wife.
娘家 My wife's family.
娘子軍 A Joan of Arc; a female soldier.

娛 yú
(n.)- Joy; delight; amusement.
(v.)- Amuse; rejoice; give pleasure; delight.
娛樂 Pleasure; amusement.
娛樂場所 An amusement park.
娛樂雜誌 Magazine for amusements.

娟 juān
(adj.)- Beautiful; graceful.

娠 shēn
(adj.)- Pregnant; conceived.
娠婦 A pregnant woman.

娣 dì
(n.)- A younger sister. A bridesmaid.
娣婦 A younger brother's wife.

娥 é
(n.)- Angel; a goddess.

娩 miǎn
(v.)- Deliver a child; bear a child.

娶 qǔ
(n.)- Marriage.
(v.)- Marry; take a wife.
娶妻；娶親 Marry a wife.

姘 pīn
(n.)- Illicit intercourse.
姘夫 A paramour.
姘頭 A lover; a paramour.

娼 chāng
(n.)- A whore; a prostitute; a strumpet.
娼妓；娼婦 A whore; a prostitute.

婀 ē
婀娜 Elegant; graceful.

**婆** (n.)- An old woman; a dame. Mother-in-law.
pó 婆娑 Dance.
婆婆 Grandmother. A husband's mother.
婆媳 Mother-in-law and daughter-in-law.
婆羅洲(地) Borneo.
婆羅門 A Brahman.
婆羅門教 Brahmanism.
婆羅門教徒 A Brahmanist.

**婉** (adj.)- Beautiful; graceful.
wǎn 婉言 Entreaties. Speaking in a pleading way.
婉轉 Speak in a roundabout way; euphemistically.

**婊** 婊子 A prostitute.
biǎo

**婚** (n.)- Marriage; wedding.
(v.)- Marry a wife.
hūn 婚姻 Marriage; wedding; matrimony.
婚期 A wedding date.
婚筵 Wedding-feast.
婚禮 A wedding (marriage) ceremony.

**婢** (n.)- A slave girl; a maidservant.
bǐ 婢女 A maid; a slave girl.

**婦** (n.)- A wife. A married woman.
(adj.)- Female.
fù 婦人 A woman; the fair sex.
婦女 Women; ladies.
婦科 Gynaecology.
婦人病 Women's diseases.
婦女會 A women's society.
婦女便所 Ladies' lavatory.
婦女解放 Emancipation of women.
婦女運動 The woman's (feminist) movement.
婦科醫生 A gynaecologist.

**婷** (adj.)- Graceful and ladylike.
tíng

**媒** (n.)- A go-between; match-maker.
méi 媒人 A go-between; a match-maker.
媒介 Mediate; go-between.
媒介物 A medium; an agent; a carrier.

**媚** (adj.)- Attracting; charming; fascinating.
mèi 媚人 Fawn upon one; make advances to a person.
媚眼 Bewitching eyes.

**媳** (n.)- A daughter-in-law.
xí 媳婦 A daughter-in-law; a son's wife.

**媽** (n.)- A mother. An old woman; an old woman servant.
mā 媽媽 A mother; mamma.

**媾** (n.)- A second marriage.
(v.)- Wed. Make peace.
gòu 媾和 Conclude peace; make peace with.

**嫁** (v.)- Marry a husband. Impute to.
jià 嫁人;嫁夫 Marry a husband.
嫁女 Marry off a daughter.
嫁妝 A marriage portion.
嫁接法(農) Grafting buddage.
嫁禍於人 Shift evil on another maliciously; impute a fault to a person.

**嫂** sǎo (n.)- An elder brother's wife; a sister-in-law.

**嫉** jí (v.)- Dislike; hate.
嫉妬 Jealous; envious.
嫉忌 Dislike; hate.
嫉妬心 Jealousy.

**嫌** xián (n.)- Dislike. Dissatisfaction.
(v.)- Dislike; have an aversion to.
嫌小 Object to a thing as being too little.
嫌少 Consider an amount too small.
嫌惡 Hatred; dislike; loathing; disgust.
嫌棄 Reject; despise.
嫌疑 Suspicion; distrust.
嫌疑犯 A suspect. A suspected offender.

**嫖** piáo (n.)- Whoring.
(v.)- Whore; frequent a brothel; see a whore.
嫖妓 Visit prostitutes.
嫖客 A whoremaster; a whoremonger; a brotheler.
嫖賭 Prostitution and gambling.

**嫡** dí (n.)- The consort of a man; a proper wife.
嫡親 Blood relatives.
嫡堂兄弟 First cousins.

**嫣** yān (adj.)- Winning; attractive; charming.
嫣紅 Crimson.
嫣然一笑 The smile of a beauty.

**嫦** cháng 嫦娥 Name of a fairy who stole the elixir of immortality and fled with it to the moon.

**嫩** nèn (adj.)- Tender; weak; delicate; young; slender.
嫩皮 A soft skin.
嫩肉 Tender meat.
嫩芽 Tender shoots; young shoots; a scion.
嫩葉 A young leaf; a cotyledon.
嫩色 A light colour.

**嫺** xián (adj.)- Elegant; accomplished; refined.
嫺熟 Skilled in.

**嬉** xī (n.)- Pleasure; amusement; sport.
(v.)- Amuse.
嬉玩 Play; sport.
嬉笑 Make fun.
嬉戲 Fun; pleasure.
嬉皮笑臉 Grinning.

**嬋** chán (adj.)- Graceful; pretty.
嬋娟 Graceful; beautiful; pretty.

**嬌** jiāo (adj.)- Beautiful; lovely. Dear. Delicate.
嬌生；嬌養 Bring up delicately; nurse tenderly.
嬌兒 A pet; a spoiled child.
嬌妻 My dear wife; my dear.
嬌羞 Bashful; shy; modest; blushing.
嬌嫩 Delicate.
嬌艷 Pretty; fresh and beautiful.
嬌生慣養 Spoilt.

**嬰** yīng (n.)- An infant; a baby.
嬰兒；嬰孩 A baby; a newborn child.

**嬸** shěn (n.)- A father's younger brother's wife; an aunt.
嬸娘 An aunt.

# 子 部

子 (n.)- A son. A boy. A person.
(v.)- Treat as a son.
zˇ 子女 Children; sons and daughters.
子夜 Midnight.
子音 A consonant.
子孫 Sons and grandsons; offspring; descendants.
子時 11 P.M. to 1 A.M.
子彈 Bullets; shot.
子爵 A viscount.
子午線 Meridian.
子宮出血 Metrorrhagia.

孑 (n.)- A halberd.
(adj.)- Only; single. Solitary.
jié Alone.
孑孓(動)The larvae of mosquitoes.
孑然一身 Lonely.

孔 (n.)-A hole; an opening; a cave.
孔雀(動) The peacock.
kǒng 孔雀屏 A peacock - feather screen.

孕 (adj.)- Conceived; pregnant.
(v.)- Be pregnant.
yùn 孕育 Be with young; give birth to.
孕婦 A pregnant woman; an expectant mother.
孕期 Gestation.

字 (n.)- A written character; a writing; a word. A name.
zì 字句 Words and phrases; expressions; wording.
字本；字帖 A copy book.
字母 Syllabics; an alphabet.
字典 A dictionary.
字首 Prefix.
字條 A note or memorandum.
字原；部首 Radicals.
字彙 Vocabulary; glossary.
字跡 Handwriting.
字義 The meaning of a word.
字幕 A title; a subtitle.
字據 A written proof; a receipt; documents.
字體 Shape of words; the form of a character. A type; print.
字紙簍 Waste-paper basket.
字母拼音 Phonetic spelling.

存 (adj.)- Alive; extant.
(v.)- Remain; exist. Keep; deposit.
cún 存下 Put away; keep; place in deposit.
存亡 Alive or dead. Saved or lost.
存在 Being in existence; survive.
存放 Deposit.
存查；存案 Keep on record; keep for reference.
存根 The counterfoil of a check, etc.
存貨 Goods kept in stock; stock.
存備；存藏 Keep in store.
存款 A balance in hand; deposit.
存摺 A bank pass book; a deposit book.
存款人 Depositor.
存款單 Deposit slip.
存款簿 Pass book; deposit slip book.

**孝** (n.)- Filial piety.
(adj.)- Filial; obedient.
xiào 孝服 Mourning clothes.
孝順 Obedient.
孝敬 Filial and respectful.

**季** (n.)- The youngest of brothers. A season.
jì 季刊 A quarterly publication; quarterly.
季票 Season ticket.
季節 A season.
季候風 Monsoon.

**孤** (n.)- An orphan.
(adj.)- Fatherless. Alone; single.
gū Lonesome.
孤女 An orphan girl; fatherless girl.
孤兒 An orphan.
孤立 Unassisted; single handed. Alone. Isolated.
孤軍 A doomed battalion; an isolated force.
孤島 A solitary island.
孤寂 Lonely; lonesome.
孤單；孤獨；孤寒；孤零 Solitary; single; alone.
孤癖 Eccentric; peculiar.
孤孀 A lonesome widow.
孤兒院 An orphanage; an orphan asylum.
孤苦伶仃 Poor and destitute.

**孩** (n.)- A child; a baby.
孩氣 Childishness.
hái 孩童；孩兒 Children.

**孫** (n.)- A grandson; a grandchild. Descendants.
sūn 孫女 A granddaughter.
孫子 A grandson.
孫文；孫逸仙（中山） Dr. Sun Yat-sen.

**孰** (pron.)- Who? whom? which? what?
shú 孰言 Who says?
孰能 Who is able?
孰輕孰重 Which is more important?

**學** (n.)- Learning; study; science. Doctrines. A school.
xué (v.)- Learn; study; practise.
學力 Knowledge.
學士 Bachelor degree (B.A., etc.). A scholar.
學友 Schoolfellows; schoolmates.
學生 A student; a pupil; a schoolboy.
學年 Academic year.
學位 Academic degree.
學制 Educational system.
學派 School; sect.
學科 Courses of studies; subjects; curriculum.
學者 A scholar; a man of learning.
學徒 An apprentice.
學習 Learning and practising (exercising); study.
學級 Class; grade.
學院 Institute; college.
學校 A school; a college; an institution.
學期 A semester; a term; a session.
學費 School fees (expenses); tuition.
學問 Knowledge; learning.
學監 A proctor; a school superintendent.
學說 Doctrine; theory.
學壞 Become corrupted.
學齡 School-age.
學生服 A school uniform.
學士學位 The Bachelor degree (B.A., etc.).
學年考試 An annual examination.
學位文憑 A diploma.
學校生活 School life.
學校教育 School education.
學校董事 Directors of a school board.

學以致用 To learn in order to practise.
學校管理 School management.
學期試驗 A terminal examination.
學齡兒童 Children of school age; schoolable children.
學生聯合會 Students' union.
學校結業禮 Commencement day; speech day.
學校創立紀念日 Anniversary of the founding of a school.

孺 rú (n.)- A child; a suckling; a baby.

孿 luán (v.)- Bear twins.
孿生子 Bear twins.
孿生兄弟 Twin brothers.

## 部

它 tā Same as 牠.
(n.)- It.

宅 zhái (n.)- A house; a residence; a dwelling. A site; a locality.
(v.)- Fix upon. Reside; dwell.
宅地 Building land; a house-lot.
宅院 A courtyard.

宇 yǔ (n.)- House. The canopy of heaven; universe.
(adj.)- Wide; vast; extensive.
(v.)- Cover; spread over; brood over; shelter.
宇宙 The universe; the cosmos.
宇宙學 Cosmology.
宇宙引力(物) Universal gravitation.
宇宙火箭 Cosmic rocket.
宇宙飛船 Space ship.

守 shǒu (n.)- A charge; a post. A prefect. A guard.
(v.)- Keep; maintain. Protect; defend. Watch over; attend to; guard; supervise; wait for.
守夜 Keep watch at night. Night watch.
守信 Remain faithful.
守城 Guard a city.
守約 True to one's word. Keep one's word.
守望 Keep watch; look out.
守寡 Remain a widow; chastity.
守衛 Keep guard.
守中立 Observe neutrality.
守秘密 Keep secret; refrain from telling others.
守財奴 A miser; a Jew; a niggard.
守望台 Watch-tower.
守門員 Goal keeper.
守口如瓶 Keep the mouth closed like a bottle.

安 ān (adj.)- Peaceful. Comfortable; safe; quiet; silent.
安心 Put the mind at rest; feel easy; have no anxiety about; make oneself quiet.
安全 Safe; free from danger; safety; security.
安危 Safety; welfare; fate.
安好 Well; in peace; in good health.
安步 Walk slowly.
安身 Stay in; settle down.
安定 At rest; tranquilly.
安居 Settle down.

安抵 Arrive in safety.
安放 Put in a safe place; lay; put.
安家 Support the family.
安息 Rest peacefully. Take a rest; repose.
安排 Set in order; arrange; adjustment; arrangement; compose; set.
安設 Establish.
安插 Find a place for one; get a position for one.
安逸 Indolent. Take things easily.
安置 Place. Appoint to.
安葬 Bury.
安寧 Peace; tranquillity.
安睡 Placid sleep; sound sleep.
安慰 Comfort; soothe; afford consolation; set at ease.
安樂 Joy; comfort; ease.
安靜 Repose; peaceful; quiet.
安徽(地) Anhwei.
安全感 A sense of security.
安眠藥 A sleeping-draught (-potion, drug); a soporific.
安樂椅 An easy-chair; an arm-chair.
安分守己 Keep one's duty and self-restraint.
安全地區 Zone of safety.
安全第一 Safety first.
安居樂業 Live in prosperity and contentment.
安全理事會 Security Council.

宋 (n.)- Name of a dynasty.
sǒng 宋朝；趙宋 The Sung dynasty (960–1280 A.D.).

完 (adj.)- Done; completed; finished. Used up; all gone. Perfect.
wán (v.)- Finish; complete.
(adv.)- Finally; wholly; entirely; altogether; absolutely.
完了 Done up; finished.
完工 Finish a job or work.
完全 Complete; perfect; whole.
完成 Completion; perfection. Bring the matter to an end.
完美 Perfect.
完婚 Marry.
完畢 Concluded; settled. Come to an end. Finished; done.
完備 Well-prepared; all ready.
完結 Conclude; be completed (finished, concluded); be brought to a conclusion.
完滿 End; culminate; satisfaction.
完全失敗 Complete failure.
完全發達 Well developed.
完全獨立國 An independent state; a sovereign state.

宏 (adj.)- Vast; wide; spacious. Great. Large.
hǒng 宏壯 Magnificent; splendid.
宏亮 Sonorous.
宏業 An extensive business.
宏圖 Ambitious plans.
宏麗 Magnificent; grand; fine; spacious; rich.
宏偉 Elegant.
宏才碩學 Profound learning and great abilities.

宗 (n.)- An ancestor; a family. A matter.
zōng 宗旨 The leading idea; purpose; principle.
宗派 The branches of a family; a sect; a denomination.
宗教 A religion; a faith.
宗族；宗親 Kindred.
宗主權 Suzerainty.
宗教界 The religious world.

官 (n.)- An officer. The government; the authorities; official.
guān (adj.)- Governmental; official;

public.
官方 Of the government; the authorities.
官司 A lawsuit; litigation.
官吏；官員 Officers.
官費 Government expense.
官僚 Fellow officials. Officialdom.
官銜 Brevet; an official title.
官價 Official fixed price.
官廳 Government office. Administrative organs.
官費生 Government supported student.
官立學校 Government school.
官費留學生 A student sent abroad by the government.

宙 zhòu (n.)- All ages; a universe. ( see 宇).

定 dìng (adj.)- Fixed; firm; secure; steady.
(v.)- Fix; determine; arrange. Order; settle; decide.
定向 Direction.
定形 A fixed form; a regular shape.
定要 Insist on.
定律 The statute law; theory; canon; law.
定約 A contract or agreement. Make an agreement.
定座 Reserve seat; booking seat.
定案 Decide a case.
定理 Theorem; theory.
定貨 Order goods.
定單 A contract; an agreement; an order.
定期 At stated periods; at a fixed time.
定量 Quantitative. A fixed quantity.
定罪 Sentence; condemn; convict.
定義 Definition.
定價 Settle the price. A fixed price; set price; listed price.
定額 A fixed quantity or number.
定貨單 An order for goods.
定價表 A price list; a priced catalogue.
定時炸彈 Time bomb.
定期刊物 Periodical.
定期交貨 Delivery on term.
定期存款 A fixed deposit; a time deposit.
定期考試 A regular examination.
定期航空 Regular air service.
定期航線 Regular line.
定期滙票 Time draft.
定量配給 Ration.

宛 wǎn (adj.)- Courteous; obliging.
宛若；宛如 As if; very like.

宜 yí (n.)- Union; harmony; accord. Affair.
(adj.)- Fit; suitable; accordant; proper.

客 kè (n.)- A guest; a stranger. A customer.
客人 A guest; a visitor.
客串 Amateur player.
客車 Passenger car (train).
客店；客棧 A lodging house; a hotel.
客家 The Hakkas of South China.
客座 A private room for guest.
客氣 Polite; courteous; formal.
客廳 A reception room. A visitor's room.
客船 Passenger ship (vessel, boat).
客觀 Objectivity; an objective view.

宣 xuān (v.)- Proclaim; announce; make known; publish. Spread; expand.
宣布 Become public. Proclaim; declare; promulgate.

宣告 Declare. Sentence; judgment; pronounce sentence upon one; condemn to.
宣言 Manifesto; announcement; declaration.
宣揚 Publish; make known.
宣傳 Propaganda; propagation; publicity.
宣誓 An affidavit; take an oath; swear.
宣戰 Declare war.
宣讀 Read.
宣傳員 A publicity man; a propagandist.
宣傳部 The ministry of propaganda.
宣傳費 Advertising (publicity) expenses.
宣傳隊 Propaganda corps.
宣誓書 An affidavit; a written oath.
宣戰書 The declaration (proclamation) of war.
宣布獨立 Declaration of independence.
宣告破產 Declare bankruptcy.
宣告無效 Declare null and void.
宣告無罪 The verdict of not guilty; declare one not guilty.
宣誓就職 Swear in; induct into office by administrating an oath.

室 shì (n.)- A mansion. A chamber; a room. A home; a family. A wife.
室人 My wife.
室內 Interior of a room; indoor.
室外 Outdoor.
室內運動 Indoor exercise.
室內遊戲 An indoor game (amusement).
室外運動 Sport.

宦 huàn (n.)- An official; a dignitary. A eunuch.
宦海 The official world; official circles.
宦途 The government service.
宦學 Travel to study.

宮 gōng (n.)- The palace. An ancestral temple. A district college.
宮女；宮娥 Ladies of the palace; maids of honour.
宮殿 A palace.

宰 zǎi (v.)- Govern. Preside. Slaughter; kill.
宰相 A prime minister; a premier.
宰殺 Butcher; slaughter; kill.
宰割 Cut up—as meat.

害 hài (n.)- Evil; harm; danger; calamity.
(adj.)- Injurious; harmful.
(v.)- Injure; damage; harm. Suffer from.
害人 Do one harm.
害怕 Frightened; terrified. Fear; be afraid of.
害病 Suffer from sickness; be ill; be taken ill.
害羞 Shy; bashful.
害處 Injuries; evils; damages.
害蟲 A noxious (destructive) insect.
害自己 Injure oneself.

宴 yàn (n.)- A feast; a banquet.
(v.)- Entertain; feast.
宴客 To give a feast.
宴居 Live at leisure.
宴會 Give a party to; invite guests. A feast.
宴筵 A banquet; a dinner-party.
宴請佳賓 Entertain guests.

宵 xiāo (n.)- Night; evening.
宵夜 Night snack.
宵禁 A curfew.

家 (n.)- A household; a family; a home. A house; a dwelling.
jiā (adj.)- Domestic.
家人 The family; the inmates. A domestic.
家用 Family expenditure.
家私 Family property; furniture.
家事；家務 Household or domestic affairs.
家具 Furniture; household goods (utensils).
家課 Home work; assignment.
家長 The head of a family; a patriarch.
家信 A family letter; a home letter.
家政 The management of domestic affairs.
家庭 A family; home.
家畜 Domestic animals; live stock.
家族 The family.
家產 The family property; one's fortune.
家眷 Family; wife and children.
家鄉 One's native place.
家禽 Domestic fowls; poultry.
家業 Family estate or property.
家運 The fortune of a family; the family circumstances.
家具店 A furniture shop (store).
家庭工業 Domestic (home) industry.
家庭生活 One's home life.
家庭教育 Home education.
家庭教師 A private teacher; a tutor.
家常便飯 Ordinary plain food.
家喻戶曉 Everybody knows about it.

容 (n.)- Manner; conduct; appearance; the countenance.
róng (v.)- Contain. Endure; bear with. Admit. Forgive.
容忍 Endure; bear with; put up with.
容易 Easy; not difficult.
容納 Contain; have capacity.
容量 Capacity.
容貌 The personal appearance; external aspect; the countenance.
容器 A receptacle; a vessel.
容積 Volume; capacity.
容顏 Appearance; looks; demeanour.

宿 (n.)- Stars. A night. A halting place. A night's rest.
sù (adj.)- Kept overnight. Long-standing.
(v.)- Remain; lodge; sojourn. Keep.
宿舍 A lodging house; a dormitory.
宿夜 Stay over night.
宿費 The charge for lodging; lodging-charges; the charge of a hotel.
宿願 A long-cherished desire.
宿命論 Fatalism.

寂 (adj.)- Still; quiet; solitary. lonesome.
jì 寂寞；寂寥 Solitary; lonely; lonesome.
寂靜 Silent; quiet.

寃 (n.)- Wrong; grievance; oppression.
yuān (v.)- Ill-use. Wrong.
寃枉；寃屈 An injustice; grievance. Wrong; injure.
寃家 An enemy; an opponent.
寃孽 Vengeance; retribution.

寄 (v.)- Lodge at. Confide to. Send.
jì 寄生 Parasitism. Live upon.
寄來 Receive from.
寄放 Deposit.
寄信 Send a letter; mail or post a letter.
寄託 Commit in charge; entrust to.
寄宿 Lodge at; sojourn; board.

寄費 Postage.
寄望 Expect.
寄生蟲 Parasites.
寄件人 Name of sender.
寄宿生 A boarding student; a boarder.
寄宿舍 Boarding house; dormitory.
寄宿學校 A boarding school.

寅 yǐn (n.)- A fellow officer; a colleague.
寅月 The first month.
寅時 The early morning.

密 mì (adj.)- Thick; dense. Hidden; secret.
密友 An intimate friend; a bosom friend.
密切；密接 Close; intimate.
密佈 Closely spread over; covered completely.
密函 A secret letter or note.
密室 A secret apartment; a privy chamber; a private room.
密封 Seal closely (tightly).
密度 Density.
密探 A secret agent; a spy; an emissary.
密雲 Dense (heavy) clouds.
密會 Meet in secret; have a secret meeting.
密碼 Private code.
密談 A secret conversation (talk).
密謀 A plot; an intrigue.
密切關係 Be closely connected with; be on intimate relations with.
密碼電報 Code telegram.

寇 kòu (n.)- Bandits; highwaymen. An enemy.
寇盗 Robbers; bandits.

富 fù (n.)- Wealth.
(adj.)- Rich; wealthy.
(v.)- Enrich; become rich.
富有 Well off; rich in.
富翁 A man of means; a millionaire.
富强 Rich and powerful.
富裕 Wealth; opulence; prosperity.
富貴 Rich and noble; wealth and rank; prosperity.
富豪 A wealthy man; a millionaire.
富麗 Splendid; luxurious.
富士山（地） Fujiyama.
富貴花 The peony.

寐 mèi (v.)- Doze; sleep; slumber.

寒 hán (adj.)- Cold; chilly; Shivering. Poor; needy.
寒冷 Cold; coldness.
寒風 A cold wind.
寒家 A poor family.
寒流 Cold currents.
寒假 Winter vacation.
寒帶 The frigid (arctic) zone.
寒酸 The poverty-stricken circumstances of poor man.
寒熱 Fever.
寒暑表 Thermometer.

寓 yù (n.)- A residence; a home; a lodging.
寓言 Fables; metaphors.
寓所 A lodging; a dwelling.
寓言故事 A fable; an allegory.

寞 mò (adj.)- Still; silent.
(adv.)- Lonely.

察 chá (v.)- Examine; observe. Discover.
察究 Investigate.
察明 Examine into fully; ascertain clearly.

察核 Try; adjudicate.
察驗 Examine.

**寡** guǎ (n.)- A widow.
(adj.)- Few; single.
(adv.)- Rarely; seldom.
寡言 Habitually silent; taciturn.

寡婦 A widow.
寡聞 Have heard but little. Not well-informed; of poor information.
寡斷 Lack of judgment.

**寢** qǐn (n.)- Rest. A chamber.
(adj.)- Odd-looking; ugly.
(v.)- Sleep; rest. Stop.
寢具 Beddings.

寢室 A bedchamber; a bedroom; a dormitory.
寢息 Rest.
寢寐 Sleep.
寢食不安 No rest either in sleeping or eating.

**寥** liáo (adj.)- Empty; vacant. Scarce. Solitary.
寥寥 Very few.
寥闊 Wide; empty; vast.

**實** shí (n.)- Solidity. Fruit. Facts.
(adj.)- Real; actual. Solid. Honest; sincere. Fixed, as a price.
(v.)- Fill; cram; stuff.
(adv.)- Verily; in truth; in reality; truly; exactly.

實力 Energy; real strength; effective force.
實用 Practical use; utility.
實在 Really; truly; in truth; in fact; in reality.
實行 Put into operation; practise; execute; enforce.
實收 Actual receipts; real income.
實例 An actual example; an instance.
實況 The actual state; the real condition.
實物 The real thing; the actual object.
實施 Carry into effect; put into operation.
實效 Practical result; efficacy.
實習 Exercise; practise; training; drill.
實現 Realize; actualize; materialize.
實業 Industry.
實話 The truth.
實際 Reality; actuality.
實價 The fixed price; net price.
實彈 A real bullet; a loaded shell.
實數 The full number. (算) Concrete number.
實質 Substance; essence.
實踐 Practise; put into practice.
實據 Substantial proof.
實權 Real power.
實驗 Personal experience; experiment.
實用品 A useful article; necessaries; articles for practical use; notions.
實驗室 A laboratory.
實用主義 Pragmatism.
實用英語 Practical English.
實有其事 It truly is a fact.
實事求是 By verification of the facts to get the truth.
實際之人 A practical man; a man of action.

**寧** nǐng (adj.)- Peaceful; tranquil.
(v.)- Would rather.
寧靜 Quiet; peaceful; tranquillity.

寧死不屈 Rather die than surrender.

**審** shěn (v.)- Investigate. Discriminate. Try.
審判 Examine and decide cases; sentence.

審查 Examine; investigate; judge; review.

審美 Appreciation of the beautiful arts.
審問 Investigate; try. A judicial inquiry; a trial.
審慎 Careful.
審判者 An umpire; a judge; a referee.
審查官 An examiner; a judge.
審查手續 Trial procedure.
審美觀念 Aesthetic conception.

寫 xiě (v.)- Write; Draw.
寫生 Drawing. Paint on natural objects.
寫字 Write.
寫法 Rule of writing.
寫明 Write plainly; set forth clearly.
寫作 To write; to compose.
寫信 Write a letter.
寫意 A rough sketch; happy; comfortable carefree.
寫字紙 Writing paper.
寫字間 An office.
寫字檯 A writing desk.
寫實小說 A realistic novel.
寫實主義 Realism.

寬 kuān (adj.)- Spacious; broad. Gentle; lenient; forgiving; indulgent.
(v.)- Widen; enlarge. Relax. Forbear.
寬大 Generous; broad-minded.
寬容 Tolerance; indulgence; magnanimity.
寬恕 Clement; lenient; indulgent.
寬裕 In good financial standing; well-to-do.
寬餘 Abundant; overplus.
寬慰 Console; cheer; comfort.
寬闊 Wide; broad; extensive.
寬宏大量 Broad-minded and magnanimous.
寬軌鐵道 A broad (the standard) gauge railway.

寮 liáo (n.)- A small window. A small house.
寮國；老撾(地) Laos.

寶 bǎo (n.)- A coin. An imperial seal. A jewel. A gem.
(adj.)- Precious; valuable. Honourable; respectable; worthy.
寶石；寶玉 Precious stones; gems.
寶貝 Costly; precious. Jewels. My darling. A pet. Esteem; value; prize.
寶庫 Treasury; treasure house.
寶貴 Preciousness; costly.
寶塔 Pagoda.
寶劍 A valuable sword.
寶藍 Sapphire blue.
寶藏 Treasure.

寵 chǒng (n.)- Kindness; favour; love.
(v.)- Love; confer favours. Esteem; dote on; thinking highly of.
寵兒 A pet; a favourite child.
寵愛 Dote on; love; love ardently.

# 寸 部

寸 cùn (n.)- A Chinese inch. One tenth of a Chinese foot.
(adj.)- Little.
寸陰 Time.
寸步不離 Not to move a step from; not to let out of one's sight.

寸步難行 I can't go a step. It is difficult to move a step.

寺 (n.)- A chamber. A temple; a monastery.
si 寺院 Temples; fanes; mosques; monastery.

寺人 A eunuch.

封 (n.)- A domain; a boundary. An envelope.
fēng (v.)- Stamp; close; cover.
封入 Inclose; infold.

封面 Title-page; front cover.
封底 Back cover.
封船 Impress a boat.
封禁 Prohibit and seal up; blockade.
封爵 Knight.
封鎖 Blockade; block up.
封蠟 Sealing wax.
封建制度 Feudal system.
封建時代 Feudal age.

射 (v.)- Shoot; aim at.
shè 射中 Shoot and hit. Shoot at the mark.
射程 A range; a rifle-range.

射箭 Shoot arrows.
射擊 Firing; shooting.

將 (n.)- A leader; a general; a commander.
jiāng (v.)- Take. Shall; will; be ready to. Be going to; intend to.
(adv.)- Soon; then; in the immediate future; presently.

將來 In future; in the progress of time; in the course of time.
將到 About to come. Approach.
將近 Close to; nearly; hardly; almost.
將軍 A general; a military commander.
將功贖罪 Atone for a misdeed with meritorious services.

專 (adj.)- Single. Special; particular. Attentive; only.
zhuān (v.)- Assume; bend on; devote.
專心 With one mind; with the whole heart; whole heartedly.

專用 Private (exclusive) use.
專有 Sole ownership; exclusive possession.
專利 Monopoly.
專車 Special train; reserved car.
專制 Absolutism; an unlimited monarchy. Despotic.
專門 A specialist; an expert. A specialty; particular.
專科 A special course of study. A specialty, as in medicine.
專家 A specialist; an expert.
專利品 Patented articles.
專利權 Right of patent.
專門家 An expert.
專修科 A special course.
專心致志 A settled, inflexible will.
專制政體 Absolute monarchy; despotic government.
專門知識 Expert (technical) knowledge.
專有名詞 Proper noun.
專欄作家 A columnist.
專科醫生 A medical specialist.

尉 (n.)- A military official.
wèi 尉官 A company officer.

尊 (adj.)- High; eminent; noble; honourable; respectable.
zūn (v.)- Honour; dignify; adore; respect; esteem.

尊君；令尊 Your father.
尊姓 Your surname?
尊重；尊敬 Venerate and esteem. With great respect for; revere; adore; hold in esteem.

尊貴 Honourable; noble.
尊稱 A title of honour; an honourary appellation.
尊嚴 Dignity; solemnity; majesty.

尋 (v.)- Search for; seek; find; look for; investigate.
xún 尋人 Look for a man.
尋出 Find out; make out.
尋求 Look for; seek. In search of.
尋見 Search for.
尋物 Seek something.
尋思 Reflect; consider; meditate.
尋常 Usual; ordinary; common.
尋路 Find the way.
尋樂 Seek for amusement.
尋根究底 Make a thorough investigation; sift a matter to the bottom.

對 (n.)- Parallel. A pair; a couple. (adj.)- Consistent with; agreeing. Opposite. Correct; right.
duì (v.)- Front. Correspond to; suit; pair. Answer; respond; reply.
對手 A match for; an equal; a peer; a rival.
對比；對照 Contrast; comparison. Check; counter view.
對方 The other side; the opposite party.
對付 Deal with; match.
對半 Half-and-half.
對立；對峙 Confrontation; opposition. Stand face to face with; be opposed to.
對抗 Oppose; confront; stand against.
對岸 On the opposite bank of the river.
對門 The opposite door; over the way.
對待 Deal with.
對面 Opposite side; face to face.
對流(物) Convection.
對換 Exchange.
對象 Object.
對策 Counter measure.
對話 A dialogue.
對過 Opposite to; over the way; across the street.
對稱(幾) Symmetry. (文) The second person.
對數(數) Logarithm.
對質(法) Confront.
對證 Eyewitness in a lawsuit.
對不住；對不起 Excuse me; I am very sorry; I beg your pardon.
對角線 A diagonal line.
對頂角 Vertically opposite angles.
對數表 A logarithmic table; a table of logarithms.
對內政策 A domestic (home) policy.
對外政策 A foreign policy.
對外貿易 Foreign trade.
對外關係 Foreign (international) relations.

導 (v.)- Lead. Guide; direct. Exhort; persuade.
dǎo 導師 Tutor.
導演 Director.
導線 A leading wire.
導體(物) Conductor.
導火線 A fuse; a train of powder. An incentive.
導電體 Electric conductor.
導熱體 Heat conductor.
導向飛彈 Guided missile.

# 小 部

**小** (adj.)- Small; little; petty. Young.
xiǎo (v.)- Slight.
小人 A mean person. Common people.
小刀 A pocket (pen) knife.
小山 Hill.
小丑 A merry-man; a comedian; a mummer.
小牛 A calf.
小心 Be careful; take care; beware; look out; regardful; cautious.
小片 Scrap; small piece.
小包 A parcel.
小半 The lesser half; minority.
小名 Name given to a young child.
小曲；小調 A little ballad.
小舟 A small boat.
小池 Pool.
小米(農) Millet.
小羊 Lamb.
小村 Hamlet.
小事 A slight affair; a trifling matter; an incident.
小姐 Miss; a young lady; an unmarried woman.
小姑 Husband's sister.
小店 Stall.
小兒 A baby; a child.
小河 Creek; rivulet; brook.
小狗 A puppy.
小雨 A drizzle; a slight (light) rain.
小便 Make water; pass urine; urinate. Urine; water.
小型 Small pattern.
小巷 A small lane.
小室 Cabinet.
小指 The little finger.
小風 Breeze.
小食 Snack.
小時 Hour.
小屋 A hut; a shed; a log-cabin.
小島 A small island; an islet.
小馬 Colt.
小鬼 A devilkin.
小產 Premature birth; abortion; miscarriage.
小組 Squad.
小販 A petty tradesman; a peddler; a hawker.
小偷 A thief.
小麥 Wheat.
小量 Small quantity.
小費；小帳 Tips. Petty expenses.
小溪 Brooklet; creek.
小照 A miniature protrait; a photograph.
小腦 Cerebellum.
小腹 The belly.
小腸 Small intestines.
小路 Foot path; lane.
小睡 Nap.
小腿 Calf of the leg.
小說 Stories; novels; fictions.
小數(算) Decimal.
小器 A narrow minded man.
小學 Elementary (primary) schools.
小貓 A kitten; a kitty.
小錢 Cash; small coin.
小膽 Cowardly; timid; frightened at little things.
小點 Dot.
小聲 A low voice; a whisper.
小册子 A trait; a booklet; a bulletin; a pamphlet.
小行李 Luggage; baggage.
小汽船 Launch.
小兒科(醫) Pediatrics; a children's doctor.
小前提 Minor premise.
小品文 A short piece; a sketch; an essay.
小炸彈 A grenade.
小食堂 Grill.
小規模 A small scale.
小隊長 A section leader (commander).

小腸氣（醫） Rupture; hernia.
小說家 A novelist; a story-writer.
小數點（算） Decimal point.
小學生 School-children; a schoolboy; a schoolgirl.
小學校 Elementary or primary school.
小包郵件 A postal parcel.
小康之家 A well-to-do family.
小寫字體 Small letter.
小學教育 Primary education.
小學教員 An elementary school teacher; a schoolmaster（男）; a schoolmistress（女）.
小兒痲痺症 Infantile paralysis.
小資產階級 Petty-bourgeois.

少 shǎo 〔shào〕 (adj.)- Little; few; rare; scarce. Lack. Young.
(v.)- Disparage; detract.
(adv.)- In a little while. Seldom.
少女 A little (young) girl.
少年 Young. A youth.
少有 Rare; seldom; scarce.
少壯 Young; youthful.
少校 A major（陸）; a lieutenant-commander（海）.
少婦 A young lady.
少將 Major-general（陸）; rear-admiral（海）.
少尉 A sub-lieutenant (陸); a second sub-lieutenant（海）.
少許 A little.
少量 A small quantity.
少數 A minority; a small number.
少年時代 Boyhood.
少見多怪 Things seldom seen are strange.
少數民族 Minority.

尖 jiān (n.)- Tip; point.
(adj.)- Pointed. Sharp; poignant.
尖刀 A sharp-pointed knife.
尖利 Sharp; poignant.
尖頂 Peak; spire; apex.
尖塔 A pinnacle; a spire.
尖端 The extreme point; the extremity.
尖銳 Sharp; pointed; acute.
尖銳化 Become acute (intense).

尙 shàng (adj.)- Noble; high.
(v.)- Honour; respect; reckon; hightly; esteem.
(adv.)- However; nevertheless; yet; still.
(conj.)- Still; yet; but.
尙且 Still; however.
尙可 Barely possible.
尙有 There are still some.
尙未妥當 Not yet satisfactorily settled.

# 尢 部

尤 yóu (adv.)- More; very; furthermore.
尤其 Particularly.
尤佳 Better still.

就 jiù (v.)- Go to; follow. Approach. Complete; finish.
(adv.)- Then; just now. Immediately; forthwith. Thereupon; presently.
(conj.)- If; provided; then; even if.
就任 Take up a post; come into office.
就地 On the spot; off-hand.
就此 Just then; then.
就位 Take seat. Inaugurate.

就近 Near by. Take a short cut.
就是 That is; namely.
就義 Die for a righteous cause.
就寢 Go to bed; sleep.
就緒 Be in good order.
就醫 See a doctor.
就職 Take up one's office; inauguration.
就職宣誓 Swear in.
就職演説 Inauguration address.

# 尸 部

**尸** shī (n.)- A corpse.
(v.)- Superintend; arrange. Personate. Control; take charge of.
尸身；尸首 Corpse.

**尺** chě (n.)- A foot. A ruler.
尺寸 Feet and inches; dimensions; measurement; size.
尺度 Linear measure; gauge; scale.
尺牘 Letter writing.

**尼** ní (n.)- A nun.
尼姑 A Buddhist nun.
尼庵 A nunnery.
尼古丁 Nicotine.
尼泊爾(地) Nepal.
尼羅河(地) The Nile River.
尼加拉瓜(地) Nicaragua.

**尾** wěi (n.)- Tail. End.
(v.)- Follow.
尾巴 A tail.
尾末 The end; the bottom.
尾隨 Follow; dog one's steps.
尾隨而來 Come last. Follow.

**尿** niào (n.)- Urine.
(v.)- Urinate.
尿布 Diaper.
尿管；尿道 The urethra.
尿化驗；尿檢查 Uroscopy; examination of the urine.
尿道炎 Inflammation of the urethra; urethritis.

**局** jú (n.)- Situation. An office; a bureau. A department; depot.
(adj.)- Coiled; contracted; narrow; compressed; curly.
局長 Chief of a bureau; chief of an office. Commissioner.
局面 The state of affairs; the situation.
局部 A part; a section. Local; sectional.
局勢 The situation. The position of a game; condition.
局外人 An outsider; one not concerned with; bystanders.
局部麻醉 Local anaesthesia.

**屁** pì (n.)- A fart; wind from the bowels.
(v.)- Break wind.
屁股(解) The buttocks; the posteriors; rump.

**居** jū (v.)- Live; inhabit; lodge; stay.
居心 Intention.
居民 Inhabitants; residents; citizen.
居住 Live; dwell; reside.
居首 At the head of; lead.
居留 Stay.

居處 Dwelling.
居然 Contrary to expectation. After all; really.
居留地 Settlement.

屆 (n.)- Time; term; set time; termination.
jiè (v.)- Reach; arrive.
屆時；屆期 At the appointed time; in due time; when the time comes; in due course.

屈 (n.)- Grievance; wrong; injustice.
qū (v.)- Submit; subject. Crook.
屈曲 Crooked; bend by force.
屈服 Subdue; go under; keep under; surrender.
屈辱 Humiliation; disgrace.
屈從 Yield to; submit to.
屈膝 Bend the knee; truckle to another.
屈指一年 Reckoning with fingers one year has gone.

屋 (n.)- A house; a room; a building; a dwelling; a cabin.
wū 屋內 Within doors; indoors.
屋外 Out-of-door; outdoor.
屋主 Landlord.
屋契 The lease of a house.
屋租 House rent.
屋頂 Roof.
屋簷 Eaves.
屋宇招租 House to let.

屍 (n.)- A corpse; a carcass.
屍灰 Cinders; ashes.
shī 屍首；屍體 A corpse; a dead body.
屍骨 Bones of the dead.
屍體檢驗 Examine a corpse; make a post-mortem examination.
屍體解剖 Autopsy; necropsy; post-mortem dissection.

屎 (n.)-Filth; excrement.
屎坑 A privy; a latrine.
shǐ 屎桶 A close chair; a commode.

屑 (n.)- A fragment; a bit; rubbish; scraps.
xiè (v.)- Pound; break into pieces.
(adj.)- Light; trifling.
屑物 Waste.

展 (v.)- Open out; spread out. Look into.
zhǎn 展長 Prolong; lengthen.
展翅 Spread the wings—fly.
展望 A view; prospect. View; look upon.
展期 Postpone. Continuation; hold over.
展開 Open out; expand; outspread; unfold itself.
展舒 Spread out; expand.
展覽 Show; expose; exhibit.
展覽會 An exhibition; a show.

屏 (n.)- A screen. A defence; a protection; a shelter.
píng (v.)- Screen. Cover; shelter.
屏風 A screen.
屏息 Hold one's breath. Respectful.
屏除；屏絕 Get rid of.
屏除迷信 Remove superstitions.

屜 (n.)- A drawer. A tray.
tì

屠 (v.)- Butcher; slay; slaughter.
屠刀 A butcher's knife.
tú 屠夫；屠戶 A butcher.
屠殺 Slaughter; butcher.
屠場 A slaughter house; a butchery.

屢 (adv.)- Frequently; repeatedly; time after time; again and again. Always; often.
lǚ
屢次 Many times; repeatedly; frequently; often; once and again.
屢年 For many years.
屢戰 Frequent battles.

層 (n.)- A layer; a stratum. A bed; a course. A step. A storey.
céng
層次 Order. Degrees; gradations.
層樓 Storeys of a house.
層出不窮 Depth can't be exhausted.

履 (n.)- Shoes.
(v.)- Walk; tread. Fulfil; perform.
lǚ
履任 Enter on one's post.
履行 Carry out or perform—as an obligation. Give effect. Fulfill.
履歷 A curriculum vitae; a short account of one's previous experience.

屬 (n.)- A sort; a class. A grade.
(v.)- Join on; belong to.
shǔ
屬下 Subordinates. Under the jurisdiction of; inferiors.
屬地 Dependencies; colonial possessions colonies; dependent domain.
屬邦；屬國 Vassal (dependent) states; colonies.
屬性 An attribute.
屬於 Belong to; appertain to.

# 屮 部

屯 (n.)- A village.
(v.)- Collect together; assemble; store up; mass.
tún
屯紮；屯駐 Quarter; station at.
屯積 Amass; store up.
屯糧 Hoard up grain; store up grain.
屯積居奇 Store up goods and raise their price.

# 山 部

山 (n.)- Mountains; a range; a hill.
shān
山川 Mountains and rivers.
山水 Landscape. Mountain streams.
山穴；山洞 A cave.
山地 Hilly district; highlands.
山羊(動) A goat.
山西(地) Shansi.
山峽 Pass or gap in a mountain.
山谷 A valley; a ravine.
山兔(動) Hare.
山坡 A hillside; a slope.
山岳；山峯 Mountain peaks. Lofty mountain.
山林 A mountain grove; a woody hill. A forest.
山東(地) Shantung.
山脊 The ridge of a mountain.
山崩 A landslide; a landslip.

山脚；山麓 The foot or base of a mountain.
山頂 Summit; a mountain top; a peak.
山楂(植) The hill haw.
山腰 Half-way up a hill; hill-side.
山路；山道 A pass; a mountain path.
山歌 Folk-songs.
山寨 A hill fortress; a mountain stronghold.
山嶺 Range of hills; chain of mountain.
山海關(地) Shanhaikwan.
山水畫 Landscape painting.
山盟海誓 A solemn oath.
山窮水盡 Circumstances of extreme need.

**岔** chà
(n.)- The point where roads fork. Diverging path.
(v.)- Branch off.
岔道 A diverging path.

**岡** gāng
(n.)- The ridge of a hill. A mound; a peak; a summit; a hillock.

**岩** yán
Same as 巖.
(n.)- Rock.
(adj.)- Rocky.
岩石 Rocks.
岩漿(礦) Magma.

**岳** yuè
(n.)- A lofty mountain. A wife's parents.
岳丈；岳父 A wife's father; father-in-law.
岳母 A wife's mother; mother-in-law.

**岸** àn
(n.)- A shore; a beach; a bund; a bank.
岸上 On the bank; ashore.
岸然 In a lofty manner.
岸錨 Shore anchor.

**峙** shì
(v.)- Stand high; tower. Pile up.

**峭** qiào
(n.)- A steep hill.
(adj.)- Steep; strict. Straight; quick.
峭壁 A steep precipice or rock.

**峯** fēng
(n.)- The peak of a hill; a summit; a mount.
峯嶺 Mountain ranges.

**島** dǎo
(n.)- An island; an isle.
島國 An island country.
島嶼 Islands; islets.

**峻** jùn
(adj.)-High; steep; precipitous; lofty; severe; stern.
峻峭 Lofty and steep.
峻嶺 A lofty range.

**峽** xiá
(n.)- A gorge; a mountain pass; a valley; a strait.
峽口 A pass in mountains; a defile.

**崇** chóng
(adj.)- High; Lofty; dignified. Noble; honourable; eminent.
(v.)- Honour; worship; respect.
崇拜 Worship; adore; honour; glorify.
崇高 Lofty; sublime.
崇敬 Respect; look up to.
崇拜偶像 Idol-worship.

**崎** qí
(adj.)- Rugged; uneven; rough; irregular; craggy.
崎嶇 Rugged; uneven.

**崑** kūn
(n.)- A high mountain.
崑崙山(地) Kunlun Mountains.

崖 (n.)- A cliff. A bank; a precipice; a slope; a rock.
yá 崖角 The point of a cliff.
崖岸 A steep bank; dignified.

崗 (n.)- Ridge of a hill; a mound.
崗位 Beat of a policeman; a
gǎng post; a position.
崗亭 A police-box.
崗警 Police.

崛 (adj.)- Eminent; towering, as a peak.
jué 崛起 Become eminent.

崢 (adj.)- Elevated; dignified; conspicuous; prominent; stately.
zhēng 崢嶸 Elevated; dignified; eminent.

崩 (n.)- An emperor's death. The fall of a mountain; a land-
bēng slide.
(v.)- Collapse; fall in ruins.
崩口；缺脣 Harelip.
崩敗 Great defeat.
崩裂 Break open; fall in.
崩潰 Collapse; break-down.
崩壞 Rock and ruin.

崽 (n.)- A child. A servant; a waiter.
zǎi

嵌 (v.)- Inlay; set in; insert.
嵌工 Mosaic.
qiàn 嵌寶 Set or inlaid with jewels.
嵌鑲 Set, as a jewel. Inlay.

嵐 (n.)- Vapour; mist.
lán

嶄 (n.)- Eminence.
(adj.)- High; sublime; gigantic.
zhǎn 嶄然露頭角 Be preeminent above the rest; rise into eminence; cut a conspicuous figure.

嶇 (n.)- A difficult ascent up a hill (see 崎嶇).
qū (adj.)- Rugged; mountainous; hilly; steep; uneven; rocky.

嶸 (adj.)- Lofty; prominent.
róng

嶺 (n.)- A ridge; a mountain range. A pass in a mountain.
lǐng 嶺頭 The highest peak.

嶼 (n.)- An islet.
yǔ

巍 (adj.)- High; lofty; great.
巍然 Lofty; sublimely; con-
wēi spicuously.
巍巍 Lofty; towering; soaring.

巔 (n.)- The peak or apex of a mountain or hill; a summit;
diān a point.

巒 (n.)- Mountain peaks.
luán

巖 Same as 岩.
(n.)- A precipice; a cliff.
yán (adj.)- Lofty; steep; perilous; hazardous.
巖穴 A cave; a grotto.
巖石 Stone; rock.

# 巛 部

川 (n.)- A mountain stream; a river; a creek; a current.
chuān (v.)- Flow out; run through the ground.
川資 Travelling expenses; passage money; fare.
川綢 Szechuan silk; Szechuan crapes.
川澤 Marshes. A large volume of water.
川流不息 Uninterrupted flow; continually going on.

州 (n.)- A prefecture; a department; a state; a county.
zhōu 州官 A prefecture magistrate.
州長 A governor.
州城 A department city.
州縣 Department and district magistrate.

巡 (v.)- Go around for inspection; patrol; cruise.
xún 巡行 Parade.
巡更 Watch at night.
巡官；巡長 Police officers.
巡哨 Patrol; sentry-go.
巡迴 Circulation.
巡捕；巡警 Policeman; constable.
巡船 A revenue cruiser.
巡視 Go and look round.
巡邏 Patrol.
巡洋艦 A cruiser.
巡迴大使 Ambassador-at-large.

巢 (n.)- A nest. A haunt; a den; a lurking place.
cháo (v.)- Build a nest.
巢穴 A den; a lair.
巢居 Lodge; dwell; nestle.

# 工 部

工 (n.)- Work; a job. A workman; a labourer.
gōng (adj.)- Skilful in.
(v.)- Work; labour; service.
工人 Labourers; workmen.
工夫 Time; leisure. Labour.
工匠 A workman; an artificer; a mechanic; a handicraftsman.
工作 Job; work; task. Operate.
工兵 Engineers; engineering corps. A sapper.
工事(軍) Field work.
工具 A tool; an implement.
工程 Labour; workmanship; construction.
工費 Working expense; wages.
工會 Labour union.
工業 Manufacturing industry.
工藝 Technics.
工資；工錢 Wages; pay; the cost of labour.
工廠 A factory; a workhouse; a yard.
工頭 A foreman; an overseer.
工黨 Labour Party.

工務局 Bureau of public works.
工程師 An engineer.
工程學 Engineering.
工業化 Industrialization.
工業品 Industrial product; manufactured article.
工業國 An industrial nation.
工廠區 A factory district.
工人階級 The working class.
工作時間 Labour hour.
工作單位 Unit of work.
工科大學 College of engineering.
工商管理 Industrial and commercial management.
工業制度 Industrial system.
工業革命 Industrial revolution.
工業學校 Technical school.
工廠制度 Factory system.
工廠管理 Factory management.
工廠簿記 Factory book-keeping.
工學博士 A doctor of engineering (D. Eng.)
工業國有化 Nationalization of industry.
工廠監查員 Factory inspector.

左 zuǒ (n.)- The left-hand side.
(adj.)- Left.
左右 Near by; right and left.
左岸 The left bank of a river.
左派 The left wing (wingers). The left party.
左傾 Leftist-leaning; leftist-inclined. Left deviation; pro-left.
左翼 The left wing (flank).
左右爲難 In a dilemma.
左傾思想 Leftist thoughts.
左傾機會主義 Opportunism of left deviation.

巧 qiǎo (adj.)- Clever; skilful; ingenious. Cunning; artful. Dexterous; talented.
巧手；巧匠 A skilled workman. An adept.
巧妙 Ingenious; clever; skilful.
巧言 With honeyed words; persuasively; artful words.
巧妻 Clever wife.
巧計 An ingenious plan; a clever trick. A capital plan; artifice.

巨 jù (adj.)- Chief; mighty; large; gigantic; huge; big; vast; great; enormous.
巨人 A giant; a Titan.
巨大 Huge; gigantic; immense; colossal.
巨浪 Large or high waves; surge.
巨萬 Myriads; countless.
巨魁 A chief; a ring-leader.
巨禍 Great misfortunes or calamities.
巨額 A large amount.

巫 wū (n.)- An enchantress; an enchanter; a witch. A sorcerer; a conjurer; a magician.
巫咒 Spells.
巫婆 A witch; a sorceress.
巫術 Black art; witchcraft; sorcery.
巫醫 Wizards and quack doctors.

差 chāi (chà) (n.)- Order; service. An attendant; a messenger; a runner. Commission. Difference; wrong; mistake; blunder.
(adj.)- Unlike. Uneven; irregular; unequal.
(v.)- Send; commission. Err; mistake.
差別 Distinction; difference.
差役 Official servants; runners messengers.
差異 Various; different.
差等 Grades.
差號 Minus sign (−).

差誤 Make a mistake; commit an error; blunder.
差遣 Footman. Dispatch; send.
差額；差數 The balance; the difference.
差不多 Not much unlike; nearly the same; almost.
差別關稅 Differential duty.

# 己 部

**己** (n.)- Private; personal. Selfish.
(pron.)- I; myself; self.
jǐ 己力 One's own strength.
己身 My own self; one's own body.

**已** (adj.)- Done; finished; passed.
(v.)- Cease; come to an end. Stop.
yǐ (adv.)- Already.
已久 For a long time.
已而 That's all; it's all said.
已完 Already finished.
已故 Dead; deceased; late.
已經 Already.
已遲 It is too late.
已付支票 Paid up cheque.
已付運費 Carriage paid; freight paid.

**巴** (n.)- Name of an ancient state.
bā 巴西(地) Brazil.
巴結 Flatter; toady; curry favour.
巴掌 The open hand; the palm.
巴黎(地) Paris.
巴拿馬(地) Panama.
巴勒斯坦(地) Palestine.
巴基斯坦(地) Pakistan.
巴爾幹半島(地) Balkan Peninsula.
巴拿馬運河(地) The Panama Canal.

**巷** (n.)- A side street; a lane; an alley.
xiàng 巷口 Entrance to a lane.
巷戰 Urban warfare; street fighting.

# 巾 部

**巾** (n.)- A handkerchief; a neck-cloth; a towel.
jīn 巾帕 A handkerchief.
巾幗 Womankind.
巾幗英雄 A heroine; a brave woman.

**市** (n.)- A market; a square; a city; a town.
shì (v.)- Trade. Buy.
市上 On the market.
市內 The city proper.
市民 A citizen; the townsmen.
市立 Municipal establishment.
市況；市面 The state of trade; the commercial condition.
市長 A mayor.
市區 Downtown; a municipal district.
市郊 Suburb.

市政 Municipal administration.
市場 A market; a fair.
市價 The market price; the current price.
市政局 Municipal council.
市政廳 The City Administration Building; the city hall; the municipal office.
市議員 A member of municipal (city).
市價表 Quotation; sliding scale.
市外電話 A trunk call.
市立學校 Municipal schools.
市立醫院 City hospital.
市場商業 Trade in market.
市場價格 Market prices.
市場競爭 Competition of market.

布 bù (n.)- Cloth. Dungaree.
(v.)- Spread; scatter. Arrange; display. Publish; make known.
布匹 Piece-goods.
布衣 Cotton clothes. A common people.
布告 Announce; make known to the public. A decree; a proclamation.
布帛 Cotton and silk fabrics.
布袋 A sack.
布丁 Pudding.
布店 A draper's shop.
布商 A draper; a mercer.
布莊 A piece-goods store.
布置 Make preparation; arrange.
布魯塞爾(地) Brussels.
布達佩斯(地) Budapest.
布爾什維克主義 Bolshevikism or Bolshevism.

帆 fān (n.)- A sail. Canvas.
(v.)- Sail.
帆布 Sailcloth. Canvas.
帆船 Sailing vessels; a sail.
帆篷 Sail.
帆布鞋 Canvas shoes.

希 xī (adj.)- Few; scarce; rare. Unique.
(v.)- Hope; anticipate; expect.
(adv.)- Seldom; rarely.
希少 Few; unusual.
希奇 Curious; strange.
希望 Hope; expect.
希臘(地) Greece; Hellas.
希臘人 Greek; Hellenic; Grecian.
希臘文 Greek; the Greek language.
希有之物 Things rarely seen.
希伯來人；希伯來文 Hebrew.
希臘教會 The Greek Church.

帕 pà (n.)- A handkerchief. A veil.
帕米爾高原(地) The Pamir plateau.

帖 tiě 〔tiē〕 (n.)- A copybook. A placard; a card.
(adj.)- Settled; decided.
帖子 A card.
帖匣 A card-case.
帖套 A card envelope.

帘 lián (n.)- The flag-sign of a tavern. A cloth screen hung before a door or window.

帚 zhǒu (n.)- A besom; a broom.

帛 bó (n.)- Silk.

帝 dì (n.)- God. The emperor.
帝位 The throne.
帝制 Imperial government; monarchical rule.
帝國 An empire.
帝國主義 Imperialism.

帝國主義者 An imperialist.

**帥** (n.)- Leader; marshal; general; commander-in-chief.
shuài (v.)- Lead on; guide.
帥兵 Lead a troop.
帥旗 The flag of a commander-in-chief.

**師** (n.)- An army. A master; a teacher; an instructor.
shī (v.)- Imitate.
師母 The teacher's wife.
師表 A pattern; a leader.
師長 The commander of a division.
師傅 A teacher. A master; an expert.
師團 A division.
師範學校 A normal school.

**席** (n.)- A mat. A table; a banquet; a feast. A seat.
xí (v.)- Cover with mats. Spread out.
席次 The order of seats; precedence.
席捲天下 Rolled up the empire like a mat—conquered it.
席捲而逃 Absconded with everything.

**帳** (n.)- A curtain. A scroll. A tent. An account.
zhàng 帳子 Curtain; screen.
帳目 An account.
帳房 An accountant; a treasurer; bookkeeper's department.
帳單 Account note.
帳幕 A shelter-tent.
帳篷 Tents for soldiers; a mat shed.
帳櫃 A counter.
帳簿 Account book.

**帶** (n.)- A girdle; a belt; a bandage; a ribbon. A zone; a region.
dài (v.)- Take with one; bring; wear; carry. Lead.
帶子 A girdle; a belt; a ribbon.
帶出 Take out; carry out.
帶回 Bring back.
帶兵 Lead troops.
帶信 Carry letters.
帶魚 The hair-tail fish.
帶傷 Be wounded.
帶領 Lead; take in one's charge.
帶分數 A mixed number (fraction).
帶電體 A charged body; an electrified body.

**帷** (n.)- A curtain. A tent.
wéi 帷房 The bed chamber.

**常** (n.)- A rule; a principle. Constancy.
cháng (adj.)- Constant; frequent; common; usual; ordinary; general.
(adv.)- Always; constantly; frequently; usually.
常人 An ordinary person; a man of mediocrity.
常久 For a long time.
常例 Custom; common usage; an established practice.
常客 A regular customer (patron).
常軌 The regular (normal) course; the right way.
常規 A common custom; ordinary rules.
常備 Make preparations; standing.
常態 The normal (ordinary) state; normality; normalcy.
常數(算) A constant.
常談 Common talk.
常識 Common sense. General knowledge.
常用語 Current words; the vocabulary in daily use.
常備軍 A standing army.

常備藥 A household medicine.
常勝軍 An ever-victorious army.
常用對數(算) Brigg's or common logarithm.
常務委員 A standing member of an executive committee.
常務理事 A managing director.
常設國際法庭 Permanent International Court.

帽 (n.)- A hat; a bonnet; a cap.
mào 帽子 A hat; a cap.
帽店 A hatter's shop; a hat shop.
帽架 A hat-rack; a hat-tree.
帽沿 The brim of a hat.
帽商 A hatter; a milliner; a millinery.
帽舌 The visor.

幀 (n.)- A piece, as a piece of painting or a piece of calligraphy. A photograph.
zhèng

幅 (n.)- The width of cloth. A roll, as of paper. A hem.
fú 幅度 Range extent.
幅員遼闊 A wide area.

幕 (n.)- A tent; a screen. An act.
mù 幕下 Drop a curtain. The staff.
幕友 A private secretary to an official.
幕間 An interval.
幕拉開 Pull aside a curtain.
幕後主持人 Backroom boy.

幟 (n.)- A long narrow flag or pennon; a banner; a streamer.
zhì

幣 (n.)- Money; coins; currency.
bì 幣帛 Presents of silk; money and silk.
幣制統一 Unification of currency.

幫 (n.)- A group; a class; a party.
(v.)- Help; assist.
bāng 幫手 A supporter; a helper or helping hand.
幫兇 An accomplice.
幫助 Help; support; back up.
幫辦 A submanager. An assistant. A police inspector.

# 干 部

干 (n.)- A shield.
(v.)- Interfere; oppose.
gān 干涉 Interfere; have part in; have a finger in the pie. Concern; consequences.
干支 The system of the Stems and Branches.
干預 Interfere; meddle with.
干涉內政 Interfere in internal affairs.
干預政治 Mix in politics.

平 (n.)- Peace; tranquillity.
(adj.)- Even; level; smooth.
píng Peaceful. Just.
平凡 Common; ordinary.
平分 Bisection; equal division.
平方(算) A square.
平日 On ordinary days; usually.
平民 The common people.
平生 During the whole life.
平地 Flat ground; level land; a plain.

平安 Safe; peaceful. Prosperous.
平行 Parallel. Of equal rank.
平均 Average.
平定 Suppress; pacify; put down trouble.
平坦 Level; flat; even.
平易 Plainly; simply.
平治 A peaceful rule. Rule fairly.
平原 Plain; level land.
平面 Surface. A plane.
平時 Ordinary times.
平素 Daily; usual; habitual.
平常 Common; ordinary; usual.
平等 Equality.
平滑 Smooth.
平價 At par.
平靜 Calmness; peaceful; quiet.
平衡 Balance; equilibrium.
平穩 Peaceful; quiet; calm.
平分線 A bisecting line.
平方哩 Square mile.
平方根(算) A square root.
平行線 Parallel lines.
平均數 The mean number.
平面圖 A plane figure; a ground plan.
平滑肌 Smooth muscle.
平衡木 Balance beam.
平民教育 Mass education.
平安無事 In peace.
平均分數 The average mark.
平均年齡 The average age.
平均速度 Mean velocity.
平版印刷 Plain surface printing.
平面幾何 Plane geometry.
平等互惠 Reciprocity based on equality.
平等待遇 Equal treatment.
平等條約 Treaty of equality.
平行四邊形 A parallelogram.

年 (n.)- Year. Age.
(adj.)- Annual. Aged.
nián (adv.)- Yearly; annually.

年入 Annual income.
年內 Within the year; before the end of the year.
年少；年幼 Young; tender years.
年代 An age; an epoch; an era.
年年 Annually; yearly; year after year.
年利 An annual interest.
年尾；年底 At the end of the year; the year-end.
年表 A chronology; a chronological table.
年長 Seniority.
年紀；年齡 The years of one's age.
年級 Grade (小學); form (英); class.
年高；年邁 Advanced in age; aged; stricken in years.
年產 Annual output (product).
年號 The name of an era.
年輪(植) The annual ring.
年糕 New year dumpling of glutinous rice.
年鑑 A year-book.
年月日 The date.
年底獎金 The year-end bonus.

幷 (adj.)- Combined.
(v.)- Combine; unite.
bìng 幷合 United; combined.

幸 (n.)- Luck; good fortune.
(adj.)- Fortunate; lucky.
xìng (v.)- Hope for.
(adv.)- Fortunately; happily; luckily.

幸得 Happily succeeded in; fortunately got.
幸運 Good fortune; luck.
幸福 Happiness; felicity; welfare; well-being.
幸運兒 A lucky person; a fortune's favourite.
幸災樂禍 Take pleasure in the calamity of others.

幹 (n.)- The trunk of a tree.
(adj.)- Skilful; able.
gàn (v.)- Manage; transact; do.
幹部 Cadre.

幹線；幹路 A main line.
幹事員 Members of a committee; business officer. Manager; secretary.
幹事長 The chief manager.

# 幺 部

幻 (n.)- Deceit. Magic. Illusion.
huàn (adj.)- Deceptive; unreal. Changeable; imaginative.
幻想 Imagination; fancy; airy toys.
幻術 Magic arts; sleight-of-hand; black arts.
幻景 Fata Morgana; a mirage.
幻滅 Vanishment of an illusion; disillusion.
幻像 Virtual image; illusion.
幻影 A phantom; a vision; an illusion.
幻燈 A magic lantern.
幻想曲 A fantasia; a fantasy.
幻想家 A castle-builder; a dreamer.
幻燈畫 A lantern-slide.

幼 (n.)- Youth.
yòu (adj.)- Delicate; youthful.
幼女 A little girl.
幼子 A son; a little boy. The youngest son.
幼小 Infancy; childhood; juvenility.
幼年 Childhood.
幼兒 A baby; an infant; a child.
幼芽(植) Plumule; young sprout.
幼孩 Children.
幼細 Delicate; fine; pretty.
幼童 A boy; a kid; a lad.
幼稚 Infantile; childish; inexperienced.
幼稚園 Kindergarten.
幼年時代 In one's childhood (early days).

幽 (n.)- Deep recess. Hell.
yōu (adj.)- Gloomy; retired; mysterious; solitary; secret.
幽思 Contemplation; meditation.
幽雅 Retired and tasteful; graceful.
幽會 A stolen (secret) interview.
幽禁 In prison; in custody; in jail.
幽境 A secluded region; a nook.
幽靜 Retired and still; quiet; calm.
幽默 Humour.
幽靈 A ghost; a spirit; a spectre; a phantom.

幾 (n.)- The incipient tendencies to motion; the springs of action.
jī (jǐ) (adj.)- Subtle. A few; some; several. How much?
(v.)- Be near. Examine into.
(adv.)- Almost; about; somewhat; to a certain extent; rather; nearly.
幾及 Almost up to; nearly.
幾乎 Nearly; almost at the point of.
幾多 How many?
幾何 Little. How much? Geometry.
幾個 Some.
幾時 What time? when? For how long?
幾許 How much?
幾歲 How old?
幾何學 Geometry.
幾何公理 Axioms.
幾何學家 A geometrician.

# 广 部

庇 (n.)- Appentice; pentice; penthouse.
bǐ (v.)- Protect. Cover; shelter; shade; hide.
庇祐 Divine protection and assistance. Countenance; protection and support.
庇廕 Protect.
庇護 Protection; kindness; shelter. Hide; take by the hand.

序 (n.)- Order; precedence; series. A preface; a prologue. A school.
xù (v.)- Follow in order.
序文 A preface; an introduction.
序言 Preamble.
序次 Series; order; in due sequence.
序曲 An overture; a prelude.
序幕 The opening (first) scene (act); the curtain-raiser.
序論 An introduction; introductory remarks.
序數 An ordinal number.

底 (n.)-A rough draft. The bottom; base.
dǐ (adj.)- Low; menial.
(prep.)- Below; underneath; under.
底下 Under; below. Low; menial.
底子 A foundation; a shoe-sole.
底本；底稿 A draft; a first copy; manuscripts.
底座 Base; basement.
底細 In details. The gist of; the real story.
底價 Base price; bottom price.
底線 A base line.
底數(算) A base.

店 (n.)- A shop; a store. An inn; a tavern.
diàn 店主；店東 A storekeeper; a shopkeeper; the head of a firm.
店客 Guests; buyers; customers.
店面 The shop-front.
店家；店肆 Shops; firms.
店夥；店員 A shop assistant. A clerk.

庚 (n.)- Age; year. The seventh of the Ten Stems (天干). A
gēng path; a road.

府 (n.)- A prefecture; a department. A palace. A yamen.
fǔ (v.)- Store; collect.
府主 Master; host.
府尊 The prefect.
府上好否 Is your family well?

度 (n.)- A measure. A rule. A degree.
dù (v.)- Spend. Measure; estimate; guess; calculate. Pass; cross over.
度日 Spend or pass the day; make a living.
度測 Guess; estimate.
度量 Measure; capacity.
度數 The number of times; degress.
度量衡 Weights and measures.
度量寬宏 Broad-minded.

度量衡學 Metrology.

**座** (n.)- A seat; a cockpit; a stand; a bench.
zuò 座位 A seat; a chair; a cockpit (飛機)
座右銘 A constant guide; a motto.
座談會 A table-talk.

**庫** (n.)- A storehouse; a magazine. A granary; a depot; depository.
kù A treasury.
庫房 A treasury; a vault. Bursary.
庫倫；烏蘭巴托(地) Urga; Ulan Bator.
庫頁島(地) Sakhalin Island.

**庭** (n.)-A courtyard. A court of justice. A hall.
tíng (adj.)- Straight.
(v.)- Growth straight. Appear at court.
庭房 The principal hall.
庭院 Courtyard.

**庶** (n.)- The people; a multitude; the mass.
shù (adj.)- Various; all; numerous.
庶人 Ordinary people; commoners.
庶民 The people; the masses.
庶免 In order to avoid.
庶物 All things.
庶務員 Business manager.

**康** (n.)- Peace; happiness; joy.
(adj.)- Healthy; delightful;
kāng peaceful.
康泰；康寧 In good health; healthy.
康健；康强 Hale; healthy; vigorous.
康樂 Happiness; delight.
康復 Recover; recuperate.
康健證書 Certificate of health.
康莊大道 Avenue.

**庸** (n.)- Merit; service.
(adj.)- Meritorious. Ordinary;
yōng usual. Stupid; simple; common; foolish.
(v.)- Employ; use.
庸人 An insignificant person.
庸才 Ordinary talents; mediocre ability.
庸俗 Rude; vulgar.
庸醫 A quack doctor; a charlatan.
庸庸碌碌 With no achievement.
庸碌之相 Common-looking.

**廂** (n.)- A side room. A suburb.
廂房 A side room.
xiāng 廂座 A box seat.

**廉** (n.)- A corner; an angle; nook; side.
lián (adj.)- Honest; pure. Low-price.
廉恥 Modest; bashful.
廉售；廉賣 Sell cheap.
廉價 At a low price; cut price. Sale.
廉潔 Probity; integrity; uprightness.
廉價品 Low-priced goods; popular-priced goods.

**廊** (n.)- A veranda; a porch; a gallery; a corridor.
láng 廊房；廊廡 Corridors; passages; side room.

**廓** (adj.)- Wide; great; open; extensive; spacious; empty.
kuò (v.)- Enlarge; expand.
廓清 Swept away—as rebels.

**廕** (n.)- Shelter; shade; shadow; protection.
yìn 廕庇 Shelter.

廚 (n.)- A kitchen. A wardrobe; a case.
chú 廚師；廚子 A cook.
廚刀 Chopper.
廚具 Kitchen utensils.
廚房 A kitchen; a cook room.
廚櫃 A cupboard.
廚竈 A kitchen stove.

廝 (n.)- A menial; a servant; an attendant.
sī 廝吵 Quarrel.
廝殺 Fight desperately; slay.

廟 (n.)- Temples; shrine.
廟宇 Temples.
miào 廟祝 A temple curate or sexton.
廟堂 Shrine.

廠 (n.)- A factory; a plant; a workhouse; a manufactory.
chǎng 廠主 Manufacturer; owner of a factory.
廠所 A station. A plant.
廠家 Factories.
廠章；廠規 Factory regulations.

廢 (adj.)- Useless; wasteful; destroyed; discarded.
fèi (v.)- Throw away; abolish; disuse; depose; destroy; abandon; give up; cancel.
廢人 Cripples; disabled persons.
廢止 Abrogation; abolition. Make void or of no effect.
廢去 Thrown aside; abandoned.
廢物 Waste; refuse; useless things; rubbish.
廢氣 Exhaust steam.
廢紙 Waste paper.
廢除 Abrogate; annul; cancel; abolish; revoke; repeal; declare null and void.
廢票 Cancelled cheque; cancelled ticket.
廢棄 Abandon; thrown aside; discard; cast away.
廢話 Verbiage; nonsense.
廢寢 Lose one's sleep.
廢墟 Ruins; remains.
廢鐵 Scrap-iron.
廢氣管(工) Exhaust pipe.
廢紙簍 A waste-paper basket.
廢除舊俗 Abolish old customs.
廢寢忘餐 Forgetful of sleep and eating in doing something.
廢物利用 Utilization of waste products.

廣 (n.)- Breadth; width.
(adj.)- Wide; extensive; vast;
guǎng broad; spacious.
(v.)- Enlarge; make broad; extend; broaden; widen.
廣大；廣闊 Wide; vast; spacious; broad.
廣州(地) Canton. Kwangchow.
廣泛 Wide; extensive.
廣西(地) Kwangsi.
廣佈 Wide spread.
廣告 Advertisement; notice.
廣東(地) Kwangtung.
廣益 Great benefit.
廣遠 Far and wide.
廣播 Broadcast; speak over (through) the raido.
廣告版 A bill-board; a hoarding.
廣告部 Advertising department.
廣告費 Advertising expense. The advertisement charge.
廣告欄 Advertising column in papers.
廣播站 A radio-broadcasting station.
廣播員 An announcer.
廣播器 Microphone.
廣播電台 Broadcasting station.
廣播節目 A radio programme.

**廬** (n.)- A hut; a cottage.
lú 廬舍 A hut; a cottage; a hovel.
廬舍爲墟 Even cottages were ruined.
廬山眞面目 The real appearance of a person or thing.

**廳** (n.)-A hall; a parlour. A court.
tīng 廳堂 The main hall; the auditorium.

# 廴 部

**延** (adj.)- Slow; dilatory. Long; distant.
yán (v.)- Protract; delay; defer. Postpone. Invite. Extend; lengthen; continue in length.
延久 For a long time. Prolong.
延長 Prolong; protract; extend; spin out.
延期 Postpone; defer; put off; lie over.
延聘；延請 Engage; invite.
延遲 Slow; delay.
延擱 Neglect; detain; stay; lay aside.
延長線 An extension line.
延期貨 Demurrage.

**廷** (n.)- The court; the palace; the courtyard of a palace.
tíng 廷臣 Ministers; courtiers.

**建** (v.)- Establish. Found; construct; build; set up; organize; create.
jiàn 建立 Establish; build; erect.
建設 Construction; establishment.
建國 Found a state.
建築 Building; construction. Build; construct.
建議 Make a proposal for consideration.
建築物 A building; an edifice; a structure.
建築師 A builder; an architect.
建築學 Architecture.
建築工程 Construction works.
建築材料 Building materials.
建築條例 Building act.
建築工程師 Architect.
建築工程學 Architectural engineering.

# 廾 部

**弄** (v.)- Play or trifle with; perform. Handle; do.
lòng 弄死 Kill; put to death.
弄壞 Put out of order; spoil.
弄慣 Accustomed to some thing.
弄巧成拙 Get into trouble through clever means.
弄假成眞 Fulfil what was promised in joke.

**弊** (n.)- Abuses; corruption; defect; vices.
bì (adj.)- Distressed; corrupt; vicious.
弊病；弊端 Corruption; abuse; defects; viciousness.

# 弋 部

**式** (n.)- Form; formula; style; example. Law; system.
shì 式樣 An example; a pattern; a model.

**弑** (n.)- Murder a superior.
shì

# 弓 部

**弓** (n.)- A bow.
弓矢；弓箭 Bow and arrows; archery.
gōng 弓步 A measure of five feet.
弓形 Bow-shaped; arched; crescent.
弓弦 A bowstring; a chord.
弓箭手 Archers and bowmen.
弓弦樂器 A bowed instrument.

**弔** Same as 吊.
(v.)- Condole with; console; mourn; pity. Suspend; hang.
diào 弔井 A draw-well.
弔水 Draw water from a well.
弔死 Hang oneself.
弔孝；弔喪 Mourn for a dead.
弔牀 Hammock.
弔唁 Condole; lament with another.
弔起 Raise.
弔桶 Well-bucket.
弔慰 Sorrow; condolence; mourning.
弔電 A telegram (telegraphic message) of condolence.
弔橋 A drawbridge; a suspension bridge.
弔頸 Hang by the neck.
弔刑架 Scaffold; gallows.
弔鐘花(植) The bell flower; campanula.

**引** (n.)- A preface; an introduction. A fuse.
yǐn (v.)- Lead; conduct; guide. Introduce. Draw out.
引力(物) Attraction; gravitation.
引火 Light; set fire; strike a light.
引出 Elicit; lead out.
引用 Employ. Quote; refer to.
引例 Illustration; produce an instance.
引動 Stir up; instigate.
引港(航) Pilot.
引渡(法) Transfer; extradition.
引進 Introduce.
引路 Act as a guide; show the way; lead the way.
引號 Inverted commas; quotation marks.
引言 Introduction.
引誘 Entice; induce; seduce; tempt; lure; bring on.
引導 Lead; instruct; guide; conduct.
引擎 Engine.
引火器 Lighter.
引用語 Quotation.
引咎辭職 Take the responsibility upon

oneself and resign.
引狼入室 Bring a wolf into the house—bring disaster upon oneself.
引渡罪犯(法) Extradition of criminals.

弛 chǐ (adj.)- Lax; dissolute.
(v.)- Unstring bow; slacken; relax; loosen.
弛放 Unloose; let go.
弛緩 Lax; slack; loose.

弟 dì (n.)- A younger brother.
(v.)- Respect one's elder brother.
弟子 A pupil; a disciple.
弟兄 Brothers.
弟婦；弟媳 A sister-in-law—a younger brother's wife.

弦 xián (n.)- The string of a bow or fiddle.
弦月 A crescent moon; a moon in crescent, as 上，下弦月 a waxing or waning moon.
弦線 Chord.

弧 hú (n.)- A wooden bow; an arc.
(adj.)- Curved.
弧形 Bow-shaped.
弧線 An arch of a circle.
弧光燈 Arc lamp; arc-light.

弩 nǔ (n.)- A crossbow.
弩手 A crossbowman.
弩箭 A cross arrow.

弱 ruò (n.)- Weakness.
(adj.)- Weak; soft; young; delicate.
弱小 Small and weak.
弱者 The weak.
弱國 A weak state (nation).
弱點 A short-coming; a defect.
弱小民族 Small and weak nations.

張 zhāng (n.)- A leaf; a piece.
(v.)- Extend; open; expand. Set out. Boast.
張力 Tensile force; tension.
張大 Enlarge; make much of. Boast; arrogant.
張弓 Draw a bow.
張揚 Publish abroad; make widely known.
張開 Open; set out; display.
張家口(地) Kalgan.
張燈結綵 Decorate with lanterns and coloured hangings.

强 qiáng (adj.)- Strong; powerful; forcible.
(v.)- Compel. Strengthen.
强力 Strong; powerful; mighty.
强大 Great and powerful; influential; mighty.
强佔 Take by force; usurp.
强兵 A powerful army.
强忍 Be compelled to endure.
强求 Demand urgently.
强壯 Strong and healthy; vigourous; full of life or vigour.
强制 Constrain; compel; coerce.
强劫 Rob openly by force.
强弩 A stiff (strong) bow.
强姦 Violate; ravish; rape.
强度 Intensity.
强者 A strong man; a powerful man.
强迫 Coercion; compulsion.
强弱 Strong and weak.
强烈 Strong; severe; drastic.
强記 Try hard to remember. A retentive (tenacious) memory.
强健 Robust; sturdy; sound.
强盜 Robbers; highwaymen; bandits.
强盛 Powerful and flourishing, as a

nation.
强硬 Strong; firm; stubborn; uncompromising.
强奪 Extort; plunder; loot.
强敵 A formidable rival (foe, enemy).
强暴 Violent; overbearing.
强調 Stress; emphasis.
强辯 Sophisticate; quibble.
强心劑 A heart stimulant.
强迫教育 Compulsory education.
强硬手段 Rigorous measures.
强制管理 Compulsory administration.

彈 tán (n.)- A shot; a bullet.
(v.)- Shoot; snap; play an instrument.
彈力 Elasticity; flexibility.
彈丸 A shot; a ball; a bullet.
彈子 A pellet; a bullet; billiard balls; pools.
彈孔 A shot-hole; a bullet hole.
彈片 A shell splinter.
彈性 Elasticity.
彈奏 Play on; harp.
彈唱 Play and sing.
彈弦 Play the lute.
彈指 A very brief space of time.
彈壓 Suppress; put down; subdue by force.
彈簧 Springs.
彈子房 A billiard saloon; a pool room.
彈琵琶 Play the guitar.
彈鋼琴 To play on the piano.
彈簧鎖 Spring lock.
彈性限制 Elastic limit.
彈性綳帶 An elastic bandage.

彌 mí (adj.)- Distant; remote.
(v.)- Reach; spread. Close up.
彌月 The first month after confinement; one month after a baby's birth.
彌補 Make up; indemnify. Make good.
彌漫 Widespread.
彌撒 The mass.

彎 wān (adj.)- Curved; arched; bent.
(v.)- Draw a bow; bend.
彎曲 A curve; a bend; crookedness; curvature.
彎直 Straighten.
彎腰 Bend the body.

# 彐 部

彗 huì (n.)- A broom.
彗星 A comet.

彙 huì (n.)- A class. A collection.
(v.)- Group together; sort; collect.
彙報 Make a collective report.
彙集 Collect; gather.

# 彡 部

**形** (n.)- Form; figure. The body; appearance. Landscape.
xíng (v.)- Appear; show.
形式 A model; a form external appearance.
形成 Form; shape.
形狀 Manner; mode.
形容 Appearance. Modify; qualify; describe.
形勢 Outline; feature; configuration; the state of things.
形跡 Traces; signs; indications; marks.
形像 Shape; form; phase.
形體 The body; substance.
形態 Form; shape.
形容詞 An adjective.
形而上學 Metaphysics.
形式主義 Formalism.
形形色色 Many varieties.
形影不離 Hand and glove with one.

**彩** (n.)- A prize. Bright colours.
(adj.)- Brilliant; ornamental.
cǎi 彩色 Variegated; party-coloured.
彩排 A dress rehearsal.
彩票 Lottery ticket.
彩旗 Ornamented banners.
彩繡 Coloured embroidery.
彩色版 Printing in colours; colour-printing; a chromolithograph.
彩色電影 A colour-picture.

**彫** (adj.)- Fading; withered.
(v.)- Carve; engrave; cut.
dīao 彫刻 Carve; engrave; cut.
彫花 Carve figures.
彫琢 Cut and polish.
彫像 Carve an image. A statute.
彫刻刀 A carving-knife; a graver.
彫刻師 An engraver; a carver.
彫塑家 A sculptor.

**彭** (n.)- The sound of a drum.
彭亨 A swelling; expansion.
péng

**彬** (adj.)- Refined; gentle.
彬彬有禮 Very gentle and polite.
bīn

**影** (n.)- A shadow; an image. A picture.
yǐng (v.)- Copy; trace.
影子 A shadow; a silhouette.
影片 A cinema film.
影射 Copy another's mark.
影迷 A movie fan.
影戲 Moving pictures; movie; cinematograph.
影響 Influence; effect.
影戲院 A moving-picture theatre; a cinema.
影戲明星 Movie star.
影印副本 A photo-copy.

# 彳 部

**彷** (v.)- Be like; resemble.
彷彿 Somewhat like. Uncertain;
fǎng doubtful.
彷徨 Wander about; irresolute; don't know what to do.

**役** (n.)- A servant. A battle; engagement.
yì (v.)- Serve; employ.
役使 Employ.
役畜(農) Working animals.

**彼** (pron.)- He; she.
(adj.)- That.
bǐ 彼此 This and that. Now and then. You and I. Both parties.
彼處 There.
彼此相愛 Love one another.

**佛** (adj.)- Like; resembling. Indistinct. (see 彷).
fú

**往** (adj.)- Former; before; past.
(v.)- Go; leave; pass.
wǎng 往日 Formerly; days before.
往事 Past events; bygones.
往來 Intercourse; traffic.
往往 Often so; frequently; constantly.
往返；往復 Go and come back; to and fro; backward and forward.
往前 Go on; proceed.
往後 Hereafter; in the future.
往時 Old times; in old times; in the past.

**征** (v.)- Attack; invade. Go. Levy taxes; take duty.
zhēng 征兵 Raise troops.
征服 Subjugate; master; overcome; conquer.
征稅 Collect taxes.
征服者 A conqueror.

**待** (v.)- Wait; bide; expect. Treat.
待命 Be ordered to wait for
dài further orders.
待遇 Treatment; dealing; pay; salary.
待聘 Waiting for an engagement.
待車室 A waiting room.

**徇** Same as 殉.
(v.)- Comply with; accord with.
xùn Die for.
徇難 Sacrifice one's life to save country from troubles.

**很** (adv.)- Very; rather; quite.
很好 Very good.
hěn

**律** (n.)- Rule; discipline. Law; statute. Standard tubes, in music.
lǜ 律例 Law.
律師 A lawyer; an attorney; a barrister; a solicitor.
律師費 The lawyer's fee.

**後** (adj.)- Hind; posterior. Subsequent. Future. Late.
hòu (adv.)- Afterwards; at last; in future, backward.
後方 Rear; backward; in the back ground.
後日 Day after to-morrow.
後世；後代 Future generation; future days; posterity.
後半 The latter half (part).
後母 A step-mother.
後來 Afterwards; at last; finally.
後果 Consequence; effect.
後門 A rear-gate; a postern gate.
後盾 Backing; protection.
後者 The latter.
後悔 Repent; feel remorse; regret.
後退 Go back; recede; retreat.
後患 Disastrous aftermaths.
後備 The second reserve.
後嗣 Descendants; posterity. An heir.
後腦 The hindbrain.
後裔 Descendants; posterity; offsprings.
後衛 The rear-guard; the full back.
後輩 Juniors; inferiors.
後天的 Acquired.
後備兵 A second reservist.
後繼者 A successor; an heir.
後會有期 We shall meet again.

後備球員 Bench.

徐 (adj.)- Slow; steady.
(adv.)- Slowly; gently.
xú 徐州(地) Hsuchow.
徐步 Walk slowly; jog.

徐徐 Slowly; step by step; gradually.

徑 (n.)- A byway; a pass. Diameter.
(adj.)- Direct. Straight-forward.
jìng 徑到 Go direct to.
徑路 A path; a lane.

徑賽 Track athletics.

徒 (n.)- A follower; a pupil. A servant.
tú (v.)- Walk on foot.
徒手 With empty hands; unarmed.

徒刑 Penal servitude.
徒弟 A disciple; a pupil; an apprentice.
徒步 Going on foot; walking.
徒勞 Make a vain attempt; use vain efforts; labour in vain; come to nothing.
徒手操 Free-hand drill; free gymnastics.
徒步旅行 A walking (pedestrian) tour.
徒勞無益 Toil in vain; vain efforts.

得 (v.)-Get; gain; obtain; secure; acquire.
dé 得力 Be of service; capable.
得分 Marks; a point; a score.

得手 Have the upper hand of. Succeed.
得失 Success and failure; gain and loss.
得利 Reap profit; make money.
得病 Get sick.
得益 Gain; profit; benefit.
得悉 Become acquainted with; know; learn.
得救 Be saved; obtain salvation.
得票 The number of votes obtained; a polling score.
得勝 Win; get a victory.
得勢 In power.
得意 Exaltation; pride; self-complacency.
得罪 Offend; displease.
得策 A best policy; advisability.
得寵 Win favour; be in one's books.
得人心 Be popular.
得銷路 Find a market.
得寸進尺 Give him an inch and he'll take an ell.
得意洋洋 Triumphant; in triumph; with elation.

徘 (v.)- Walk about; wander.
徘徊 Walk to and fro. Irresolute; undecided.
pái

徙 (v.)- Move; remove; change.
徙任 Be moved to another post.
xǐ 徙居 Change one's house; move one's abode.

徙善 Change for the better; reform.

從 (adj.)- Inferior; subordinate.
(v.)- Follow; pursue; second.
cóng Agree with; obey. Manage.
(prep.)- By; from; through.
(conj.)- Since; whence.

從未 Never; at no time.
從事 Do business; engage in; pursue.
從來 Up to this time; so far; hitherto.
從俗 Conform to custom; swim with the tide.
從前 Hitherto; formerly; before.
從者 An attendant; a retinue; a follower.
從容 Be free; be at ease; with composure.
從新 Anew; begin afresh.
從嚴 Severely; strictly; with severity.
從屬 Be subordinate to; be attached to; depend on.

從今而後 Henceforth; from now on.
從古以來 Since the antiquity.
從早到晚 From early till late.
從來如此 As ever; as in the past.
從容不迫 An easy manner.
從頭至尾 From beginning to end.

**御** yù (adj.)- Imperial; royal.
(v.)- Drive a chariot. Manage.
御用 For imperial use.
御旨 An imperial decree.

**徧** biàn (adv.)- Everywhere; all round.
徧佈 Spread far and wide.
徧地 Everywhere.
徧身 The whole body.
徧世界 The whole world.

**復** fù (v.)- Return. Repeat. Answer. Restore.
(adv.)- A second time; again.
復仇 Take revenge; retaliate.
復原 Recover; become whole; return to health.
復生；復活 Revive; come to life again. Resurrection; revival.
復合 Reunite.
復命 Report the result of a mission.
復音 A reply; an answer.
復員 Demobilization; be demobilized; be discharged.
復業 Resumption of work.
復興 Revival. Recover prosperity.
復職 Be reinstalled in office; resume office.
復籍 Re-registration.
復活節 Easter.
復員令 Demobilization orders.

**循** xún (v.)- Follow; accord. Proceed in order. Go around.
循照 According to.
循環 Circulation; rotation.
循序漸進 Follow in proper sequence and make gradual progress.
循環系統(解) The circulatory system of blood.

**徭** yáo (n.)- Feudal labour of a serf; forced labour.
徭役 Force labour on government service.

**微** wēi (adj.)- Small; insignificant; tiny; slight. Mean.
微力 Small power; humble effort.
微小 Minute; little; petty.
微分(算) Differential calculus.
微光 Faint light; a slight glow; a glimmer.
微妙 Delicate; minute; exquisite.
微雨 A small rain; a drizzle; a slight shower.
微風 A slight breeze; a gentle wind.
微弱 Feeble; weak.
微笑 A smile.
微菌 Germs; bacteria.
微微 Slightly.
微熱 A slight fever.
微賤 Low; mean; inferior.
微積(算) Integral calculus.
微醺 Slightly flushed; mellow with drink.
微生物；微生蟲 A microbe; a micro-organism; bacterium.
微血管；毛細管 Capillary.
微積分 Differential and integral calculus.

**徵** zhēng (v.)- Summon; call. Seek. Collect; levy; raise.
徵召 Summon. An invitation to men of talents by government.
徵收 Collect; gather.
徵兵 Conscription. Enlist soldiers; re-

cruit.
徵求 Ask for.
徵信 Seek confidence.
徵稅 Levy a tax.
徵集 Call out; raise.
徵聘 Engage one in service by a present.
徵調 Transfer troops.
徵求意見 Seek the opinions of; ask for one's view.
徵求會員 Convass for members.

德 dé (n.)- Virtue; goodness; kindness; favour.
德文；德語 German.
德育 Moral education.
德政 Good (benevolent) administration.
德國；德意志(地) Germany.
德黑蘭(地) Teheran.

徹 chè (v.)- Penetrate; pervade; pass through.
徹夜 From sunset to dawn; all night long; all the night through.
徹底 Get at the root. Thoroughgoing; complete.
徹頭徹尾 From beginning to end; from head to foot.

徼 jiǎo (v.)- Demand; beg; seek for.
徼倖 Happily; luckily.

徽 huī (n.)- A flag. A symbol.
(adj.)- Excellent; beautiful; splendid.
徽章 Symbol; mark; badge; insignia.

# 心 部

心 xīn (n.)- Heart. Mind; sense. The centre.
心巧 Clever.
心血 Great endeavour.
心事 Cares; concerns.
心房(解) Atrium; heart chambers.
心思 Thoughts.
心情 One's feelings.
心悸 Throbbing; pulsation.
心理 Psychology. Mind. Idea.
心焦 Worried; vexed; agitated.
心痛 Grieved at heart; a sore feeling at the heart; mental sufferings. Cardialgia.
心慌 In a hurry (flurry).
心亂 Confused; perplexed.
心傷；心碎 Heartbroken.
心愛 Beloved; favourite.
心意 Ideas; aims.
心腹 A man (who is) to be trusted confidentially.
心腸 The heart; the feelings.
心境 A mental state; one's psychology.
心寬 Light-hearted.
心算 Mental calculation.
心酸 Sour-hearted.
心緒 The state of mind.
心願 Wish; desire; intention; hope.
心臟(解) Heart.
心靈 Intelligence; spirit; soul; inspiration.
心不死 Not to lose hope.
心理學 Psychology; mental philosophy.
心理戰 Psychological warfare.
心腹友 Bosom friends; close friends; intimate friends; good friends.

心臟病 Heart-trouble; heart-disease.
心不在焉 Absent-minded; inattentive.
心心相印 Our opinions exactly tally.
心甘情願 Heartily willings.
心理作用 Mental process.
心有餘而力不足 More than willing but lacking power.

必 (adj.)- Necessary; requisite.
(v.)- Be certain; be necessary; must; be sure.
bǐ
(adv.)- Certainly; surely.
必定；必然 Certainly; surely; by all means; necessarily; without fail; at all events.
必要；必須 Must. Absolutely; of necessity; essential.
必需 Require; need; put in requisition. Essential; necessary.
必修科 Required subjects; a compulsory course.
必然性 Inevitability.
必需品 Necessaries; necessities; requisities.
必要條件 An indispensable (necessary) condition.
必要機構 Necessary organ.

忌 (adj.)- Jealous; distasteful.
(v.)- Fear. Void; avoid. Hate. Dislike.
jì
忌食 Avoid eating.
忌憚 Afraid; apprehensive; dread; fear.
忌避 Shun; avoid.

忍 (adj.)- Harsh; hard-hearted; severe; hard; inflexible.
rěn (v.)- Endure; forbear; bear; allow.
(adv.)- Patiently.
忍心 Cruel; hard-hearted.
忍受 Endure hardship.
忍耐 Edure; bear; persevere.
忍笑 Repress laughter; keep one's countenance.
忍辱 Digest an insult; endure contempt.
忍淚 Refrain the tears.
忍痛 Bear pain.

志 (n.)- Will; resolution; aim; intention.
zhì 志向 Inclination; ambition; will; aim.
志願 Voluntary; willing; desire.
志願兵 A volunteer.
志願書 A written application.

忘 (adj.)- Absent-minded; forgetful.
wàng (v.)- Forget. Neglect; disregard.
忘本 Forget the origin. Forget one's parents or benefactors.
忘形 Forget oneself.
忘恩 Forget favours; ungrateful.
忘記 Forget; lose the memory of.
忘情 Forget affection.
忘我 Unselfish.
忘恩負義 Ungrateful; thankless.

忙 (n.)- Precipitation; haste; bustle.
(adj.)- Busy; hurried. Bustling;
máng occupied; stirring.
忙人 Busy man.
忙迫；忙碌 Be busy at work; urgently pressed.
忙亂 In hurry and confusion.
忙中有錯 Haste causes errors.

忠 (n.)- Loyalty.
(adj.)- Loyal; patriotic; sincere;
zhōng honest; devoted; faithful.
忠心 Faithfulness; loyalty.
忠臣 A loyal or faithful minister.
忠告 Advice; faithful admonition.
忠言 Kind advice; faithful saying.

忠良 Honest; virtuous.
忠信 Faithful.
忠厚 Honest; upright; faithful; trustworthy.
忠誠 Faithful and sincere.
忠言逆耳 Unpleasant advice is a good medicine.

快 (n.)- Cheerfulness. Rapidity; promptness.
kuài (adj.)- Glad; joyful; happy; cheerful. Quick; speedy; fast; rapid.
快車 Express train.
快門(攝影) Shutter.
快信 Express letter.
快活；快樂 Pleasure. Gay; cheerful; pleased; joyful; happy; glad.
快捷 Promptly; quickly; speedy.
快跑 Trot; gallop.
快感 Pleasant sensation; agreeable feeling.
快慢 Quick and slow. Speed; rate.
快暢 Refreshing; pleasant.
快鎗 Rifle.

忱 (n.)- Sincerity; honesty; heart.
chén (adj.)- Sincere; honest.

念 (n.)- Thought; reflection; consideration.
niàn (adj.)- Thoughtful. Twenty.
(v.)- Reflect on; remember; consider; think of. Read; recite.
念書 Learn books by heart; study; read books.
念頭 Thoughs; desires.
念想 Think about.
念經 Chant prayers; repeat the liturgies.
念熟 Learned by heart.
念念不忘 Bear in mind constantly.

忸 (adj.)- Blushing; ashamed. Used to; accustomed.
niǔ (v.)- Blush; feel ashamed.
忸怩 Be ashamed; shy.

忽 (n.)- The millionth part of a tael or ounce of silver.
hū (adj.)- Sudden. Careless; negligent.
(v.)- Disregard; neglect; slight.
(adv.)- Suddenly; unexpectedly.
忽略 Careless; forgetful. Disregard.
忽然；忽地 Suddenly; in a moment; on a blow; on a sudden; all of a sudden.
忽視 Neglect; disregard; make light of.
忽冷忽熱 Now hot, now cold; sudden changes of temperature.

忿 (n.)- Anger; rage; hatred; fury; wrath; indignation; resentment.
fèn (adj.)- Wrathful; angry.
忿恨 Deep malice; bitter hatred. Hate bitterly; hate.
忿怒 Angry; rage; wrath; indignation.

怎 (adv.)- How? Why? What?
zěn 怎生；怎麼 What? How is it? Why is it?
怎敢 How dare . . . ?
怎樣 How? in what way?

怒 (adj.)- Angry; wrathful; irritated.
nù (v.)- Be angry with; get into a passion.
怒色 An angry look; an angry face.
怒言 Angry words; high words.
怒氣 Anger; rage.
怒號 Scold; roar.
怒濤 Angry waves; raging billows.
怒髮衝冠 Hair standing on end; in a towering passion.

**怕** (v.)- Fear; dread; be afraid of.
pà 怕死 Afraid of death.
怕羞 Shy; bashful; blushing.

**怖** (adj.)- Afraid; frightened; alarmed.
bù (v.)- Frighten; threaten; terrify; scare.

**思** (n.)- Desire; thoughts; ideas; meaning.
sī (v.)- Think; consider; intend.
思考 Speculate; careful consideration.
思念 Remember; think of; anxiety.
思家 Think of one's home. Home sick.
思索 Muse; contemplate.
思欲 Wish to; intend to.
思想 Think about; reflect on; consider.
思慕 Longing; yearning.
思維 Thought; thinking; revolve; flect.
思慮 Serious thoughts of; serious thought.
思潮 The current (trend) of thoughts; current ideas.
思鄉病 Homesickness.
思想界 The thinking world; the world of thought.
思想家 Thinkers.
思想問題 The thought problem.

**怠** (adj.)- Heedless; careless; indolent; lazy.
dài 怠工 Sabotage.
怠惰 Idle; lazy; negligent.
怠慢 Rudely; carelessly; impolitely.
怠緩 Slow; sluggish; idle.
怠工運動 A go-slow strike; a "stay in" strike; sabotage; a sit down.

**怡** (adj.)- Pleased; joyful; pleasant; delighted; satisfied.
yí 怡悅 Take delight in; be pleased; rejoice; pleased at.
怡然自得 Happy and content.

**急** (adj.)- Hasty; impatient; pressing; anxious; uneasy. Fast; hurried; earnest; urgent; quick; rapid; swift.
jí (v.)- Hurry; hasten.
急切 Critical; urgent; pressing.
急用 Urgent need; pressing need.
急忙；急促 Hasty; hurried.
急步 Walk hastily.
急性 A hasty disposition; a quick temper; irritability.
急迫 Urgent; forced; impelled; urged; in a hurry.
急降 Quick dive. Drop suddenly (rapidly).
急流 A torrent; a rapid stream.
急症；急病 An acute disease; a virulent disease; a sudden illness.
急速 Fast; quick; swift; with celerity.
急喘 Gasping.
急電 Urgent telegrams.
急需 An urgent need; necessary.
急難 In straits. Difficulties; emergency.
急躁 Irritable; passionate.
急辯 Retort.
急行軍 A quick march.
急救法(醫) First-aid.
急性中毒 Acute intoxication.
急性肺炎 Acute pneumonia.
急性傳染病 Acute endemic disease.

**性** (n.)- Disposition; nature; property; temper; spirit; quality.
xìng Life. Sex.
性交 Sexual intercourse.
性能 Function.
性別 Sex.

性命 Life.
性急 Quick-tempered; hasty.
性柔 Tender nature.
性剛 Strong nature.
性格 Nature.
性病 Sexual disease; venereal disease.
性情 Temper; nature; dispositon; the passions; instinct.
性慾 Sexual appetite; sexual desires.
性暴 Violent nature; sanguine temperament.
性質 Quality; property; temperament; nature; character.
性教育 Sex education.
性關係 Sexual relations.

怨 (n.)- Ill will; resentment; hatred; spite.
yuàn (adj.)- Dissatisfied; repining; murmuring.
(v.)- Hate; repine; murmur against; blame; dislike; complain.
怨言 Spiteful words; grumbling complaints.
怨恨 Bear a grudge against; hate. Spite; hatred; ill-blood.
怨氣 Resentment. Spite; hatred.

怪 (n.)- A monster; a prodigy.
guài (adj.)- Strange; marvellous; miraculous; wonderful.
(v.)- Blame; find fault with. Wonder at.
(adv.)- Unusually; very.
怪人 A peculiar person.
怪事 A strange event; a miracle.
怪癖 Fantastical temper; strange and peevish.
怪異 Uncanny; supernatural; monstrous; whimsical.
怪責 Bring blame; reprimand.
怪談 Weird talk.
怪可憐 Pitiable indeed!

怯 (adj.)- Timid; cowardly; afraid; fearful; timorous.
qiè (v.)- Be afraid; lose heart.
怯畏 Timid; timorous.
怯懦 Show signs of fear; be a coward.

恆 (adj.)- Constant; permanent; regular.
héng (adv.)- Continually; perpetually; permanently.
恆久 For a long time; enduring.
恆心 Constancy; perseverance; steadiness of mind.
恆河(地) The Ganges.
恆星 Fixed stars.
恆等式(算) Identical equation.

恍 Same as 怳.
huǎng (adj.)- Wild. Absent-minded; confused; disturbed.
恍惚 Indistinct; dim; blurred; confused; at a loss.

恐 (n.)- Terror; fear; alarm; fright.
(adj.)- Apprehensive; fearful.
kǒng (v.)- Fear; threaten; apprehend; dread; be affraid of; terrify.
恐怕 Be afraid of; fear. Probably; perhaps.
恐怖 Horror; terror; consternation.
恐慌 Scare; horror; panic; crisis.
恐嚇 Threaten; scare.
恐懼 Fear; terror. Afraid; tremor; fright.
恐龍 Dinosaurs.
恐嚇信 A threatening letter.
恐怖時代 The Reign of Terror.

恕 (adj.)- Benevolent; merciful; sympathizing; considerate of.
shù (v.)- Excuse; pardon.
恕送 Excuse me not seeing you off.

恕罪 Forgive a fault; be indulgent to other's fault; beg pardon.
恕不另找 No change given.
恕不奉陪 Excuse me for leaving your company.

恢 huī (adj.)- Great; liberal.
(v.)- Enlarge. Recover; restore.
恢復 Recover; restore; make good.
恢復期 The period of convalescence; a convalescent stage.
恢復原狀 Restore to its former condition; revert to type.
恢復秩序 Restore order by effort.

恤 xù Same as 卹.
(n.)- Compassion; pity; sympathy.
(adj.)- Mournful; moved; compassionate.
(v.)- Give alms to. Pity; sympathize with.
恤老 Relieve the aged.
恤孤 Bring up the orphans.
恤款；恤金 Indemnity. Compensation.
恤孤院 Institute for destitute children.

恥 chǐ (n.)- Shame; disgrace.
(adj.)- Disgraced; shameful; ashamed.
(v.)- Feel shamed; blush. Insult; disgrace.
恥笑 Laugh at; ridicule.
恥辱 Shame; disgrace; dishonour.

恨 hèn (n.)- Hatred; dislike. Regret.
(adj.)- Sorry; vexed.
(v.)- Hate; dislike. Regret; resent; loathe.
恨毒 Malice.
恨怒 Animosity; resentment.
恨怨 Hate; abhor; dislike.
恨入骨髓 The deepest hatred.

恩 ēn (n.)- Favour; affection; benefit; grace; kindness.
(adj.)- Compassionate; gracious; kind.
(v.)- Oblige; show favour.
恩人；恩主 A benefactor; a patron.
恩仇 Love and hatred.
恩物 Kindergarten gifts; toys; playthings.
恩惠 Kindness; favour; grace; mercy.
恩情 Kindness; affection. Love.
恩惠 Mercy; benefection; favour.
恩愛 Affection; love.
恩賜 His (Her) Majesty's gift.
恩愛夫妻 An affectionate couple.

恫 dǒng (adj.)- Aching; moaning from pain. Sighing.
恫嚇 Threaten; scare; bully.

恬 tián (adj.)- Peaceful; quiet.
恬靜 Tranquil; quiet.
恬不知恥 Show no sign of shame; be impervious to shame.

恭 gōng (n.)- Reverence; respect.
(adj.)- Reverent; polite; courteous; respectful.
(v.)- Reverence; respect; esteem; honour.
恭候 Await respectfully; respectful compliment.
恭喜 Congratulate; wish one joy respectfully.
恭賀 Sincere or hearty congratulations.
恭敬 Respect. Polite; respectful.
恭維 Praise.
恭請 Invite.
恭賀年禧；恭賀新禧 I wish you a happy New Year. Happy New

Year.
恭賀聖誕 A merry Christmas to you. Merry Christmas.

息 (n,)- A full breath. Interest on money.
xī (v.)- Breathe. Sigh. Rest; suspend.
息怒 Appease anger; assuage wrath.
息票 A coupon.
息錢 Interest on money.

恰 (adj.)- Exact; just; in good time.
qià (adv.)- Just; fortunately; exactly; opportunely; seasonably.
恰巧 Fortunately; luckily; opportunely.
恰好 Just right.
恰遇 Meet with opportunity. In the nick of time.
恰當 Fitted; suitable.

恿 (n.)- Urge; incite.
yǒng

悄 (adj.)- Sad; sorrowful; disheartened. Silent; quiet; still.
qiāo 悄悄 Quietly.
悄然 In solitude; solitarily.
悄然而去 Go off quietly.

悅 (adj.)- Please; delighted; gratified.
yuè (v.)- Be pleased; please.
悅目 Pleasing to the eye; delightful to the eye.
悅耳 Pleasing to the ear.
悅樂 Enjoyment; pleasure.

悉 (adj.)- All; entire; total.
(v.)- Know; understand.
xī 悉心 With one's entire mind.

悍 (adj.)- Fierce; violent. Imperious. Brave.
hàn 悍然 Ruthlessly; unreasonably.
悍急 Hasty; violent; ardent.

悔 (n.)- Repentance; remorse; regret.
huǐ (adj.)- Penitent; repentant; contrite.
(v.)- Regret; reform; change.
悔心 Regret; remorse; contrition.
悔改 Repent; reform.
悔恨 Deep remorse. Regret bitterly.
悔悟 Awaken from sin and repent.
悔過 Repent of one's error.
悔過自新 Repent and make a new start; reform an evil habit; begin a new course of life.

悖 (adj.)- Perverse; unreasonable. Rebellious.
bèi (v.)- Rebel.
悖逆 Rebellious; refractory.
悖理 Unreasonable; contrary to principle.

悚 (adv.)- Frightened; terrified.
sǒng 悚然 Timorous; sudden fear.

悟 (v.)- Awake; become conscious of; notice.
wù 悟性 Intelligence; power of apprehension.
悟會 Understand; become aware of.
悟覺 Perceive; realize.

悠 (adj.)- Far; far reaching. Discontented.
yōu 悠然 Leisurely; calmly.
悠閒 Idly; indolently.
悠遠 Far-off; a long distance.
悠久 A long time.

**患** (n.)- Evil; affliction; misery. Grief.
huàn (adj.)- Sad; vexed; fearful.
(v.)- Suffer; grieve; sorrow for.

患者 A patient; a diseased person.
患病 Be ill; suffer from disease. Sickness; illness.
患害 Misfortune; calamity.
患處 The diseased (affected, sore) part.
患難 Misfortune; hardship.
患難朋友 A friend in need.
患得患失 A small-minded man.

**悲** (n.)- Grief; sympathy.
(adj.)- Tragic; sad; mournful.
bēi (v.)- Commiserate; grieve; sympathize.

悲壯 Touching; pathetic; tragic.
悲哀 Sorrow; sadness; grief.
悲痛 Grief and pain.
悲傷 Painted and wounded; take or lay to heart.
悲嘆 Grief; sorrow; lamentation.
悲慘 Extreme grief; deep sorrow.
悲歌 A sad tune; a sad piece of music.
悲劇 A tragedy; a tragic drama.
悲憤 Indignation; resentment.
悲聲 In a sad (tearful) voice.
悲觀 A pessimistic view.
悲喜劇 A tragi-comedy.
悲觀的 Pessimistic; gloomy.
悲觀者 Pessimist.
悲觀主義 Pessimism.

**悵** See 惆悵.
(adj.)- Despaired; disappointed;
chàng dissatisfied.
悵網 In low spirits; depressed; downcast.

**悶** (adj.)- Sad; grieved; unhappy.
(v.)- Be in agony; be much
mèn worried.

悶氣 Depressed; in low spirits; dull.
悶死 Die of vexation; die in agony.
悶斃 Suffocate; stifle; smother.
悶悶不樂 In distress; be much worried.

**悸** (adj.)- Uneasy; perturbed.
jì

**悼** (adj.)- Sorrowful; mournful.
(v.)- Lament; mourn; express
dào condolences.
悼嘆 Sigh mournfully.

**悽** (adj.)- Grieved; sorrowful; suffering.
qī 悽惶 Sad; sick at heart.
悽慘 Sorrowful; melancholy.

**情** (n.)- Passions; feelings; affection. Condition.
qíng 情人 A lover; a sweetheart; a fiance.

情形；情景 Aspects; circumstance; conditions.
情況 The state of affairs (things); a situation; circumstances.
情狀 Circumstances.
情面 Influence; favour; personal esteem.
情書 A love letter; a sugar report.
情婦 A mistress; a woman in love.
情深 Kind-heart; affectionate; tender.
情理 Reason; common sense; right.
情場 Realm of love.
情報 A report; information; intelligence.
情愛 Affection; love.
情意 Affection; kindness.
情歌 A love song; an amorous song.
情敵 A rival in love.
情節 Details of a case; circumstances.
情緒 Emotion; feeling.

情勢 The situation; the state.
情調 A mood; an atmosphere.
情誼 Friendship; kindness.
情趣 Mood; effect; sentiment.
情操 Abstract sentiments.
情願 Be willing. Voluntary.
情報局 An intelligence department; the information bureau.
情不自禁 Unable to restrain the emotions; no self-control.
情投意合 Come to a mutual understanding; understand each other; become intimate.
情節相同 A parallel case; details are similar.

**惆** chóu (adj.)- Annoyed; disappointed.
惆悵 Disappointed; sorry; dissatisfied.

**惑** huò (n.)- Suspicion; doubt; disorder.
(v.)- Doubt. Deceive lead into errors.
惑亂 Be confused; be bewildered.

**惕** tì (v.)- Stand in awe of; be alarmed.

**惘** wǎng (v.)- Lose one's self-possession.
惘然 Saddly; despairingly.

**惜** xī (adj.)- Sparing.
(v.)- Pity; feel for. Spare; save.
惜別 Sorrow of parting.
惜物 Careful of things; not wasteful.
惜錢 Save money.
惜光陰 Be spare of time; redeem the time.
惜老憐貧 Pity the aged and the poor.

**惟** wéi (v.)- Think over; plan.
(adv.)- Only; merely; simply.
(conj.)- But.
惟一 Only one; unique.
惟恐 Lest; fearing.
惟獨 Only; alone.
惟一代理人 Sole agent.

**惠** huì (n.)- Kindness; benefit; favour.
(adj.)- Benevolent; kind; liberal; complaisant.
(v.)- Give in charity; bestow. Be kind to.
惠函；惠音 Your favour; your esteemed letter.
惠愛 Benevolence; kindness.
惠賜 Bestow graciously.
惠臨 Honour with a visit; favour with your presence.
惠贈 Give; present. Gift.

**惡** è (n.)- Evil; wickedness.
(adj.)- Bad; wicked; unpleasant. Awkward.
(v.)- Hate; be averse to; slander.
惡人 A wicked or bad man.
惡化 Growing worse; aggravation; degeneration.
惡心 Evil intention; evil thoughts.
惡名 Ill fame; bad reputation.
惡劣 Very bad.
惡言 Abuse language; evil-speaking.
惡性 Malignant; malign; bad.
惡俗 Bad customs.
惡毒 Vicious; malicious; malignant.
惡相 Evil looks (physiognomy); countenance.
惡臭 An offensive odour; a nasty smell.
惡食 Bad or poor food.
惡徒；惡棍 Bad characters; undesirable characters.
惡疾 Noxious disease; malignant (virulent) disease.

惡耗 Bad news.
惡習 Bad habits; evil practices (manners); an evil habit (custom).
惡報 Ill recompense.
惡意 Ill will; bad intentions; malice.
惡運 Ill luck; unlucky; unfortunate.
惡夢 A nightmare.
惡魔 A devil. Satan. The old enemy.
惡作劇 Mischievous tricks or practices; a mad prank. Play pranks.
惡性循環 A vicious cycle (spiral).
惡戰苦鬥 A desperate fight; a hard battle.

惰 duò (n.)- Laziness; idleness.
(adj.)- Indolent; idle; careless; lazy.
惰性 Inertia.

惱 nǎo (n.)- Vexation; anger.
(adj.)- Indignant; annoyed.
惱恨 Hate and detest.
惱怒 Irritated.

想 xiǎng (n.)- An idea; a conception; a thought.
(v.)- Think; consider; hope; anticipate.
想念 Think of; think on.
想家 Think of home; homesick.
想起 Recollect; remember; recall.
想望 Hope; expect.
想像 Imagination; fancy.
想當然 Most probably; I think it is so.
想像力 Imaginative power; the power of imagination.
想入非非 Allow the fancy to run wild; give play to one's imagination.

惶 huáng (n.)- Fear; terror; apprehension.
(adj.)- Scared; terrified; frightened; timorous.
惶恐 Alarmed; frightened.
惶惶 Fearing; trembling.
惶惑 Doubtful; hesitating.

惹 rě (v.)- Provoke; rouse; excite; attract.
惹事 Make trouble.
惹起 Lead to; give rise to; cause.
惹禍 Incur mischief; induce calamities.
惹人注意 Cause others to take notice.
惹是生非 Make mischief.

惺 xīng (adj.)- Intelligent.
惺忪 Flickering; twinkling.

愁 chóu (n.)- Sorrow; sadness.
(adj.)- Mournful; sad; melancholy.
(v.)- Grieve; sorrow.
愁心 Sad heart.
愁眉 Contracted brows; anxious look.
愁容 A sad look; a mournful appearance; a sorrowful countenance.
愁悶 Sorrowing; chagrined; melancholy.
愁嘆 Grief; sorrow.

愈 yù (v.)- Surpass; be superior.
(adv.)- More; further. Healed.
愈加 Further; much more. Greatly increased. In addition to.
愈好 Recovered; quite well; better.
愈多愈好 The more... the better.
愈快愈好 The sooner... the better.
愈來愈多 More and more.

愉 yú (n.)- A cheerful countenance.
(adj.)- Contented; pleased; happy.
(v.)- Be pleased; be glad.
(adv.)- Joyfully; willingly.
愉快 Light of heart; delightful; joyful;

happy.
愉悅 Joyful; glad; happy; pleased.

意 (n.)- Thought; opinion; intention; idea; purpose. Meaning.
yì 意旨 View; mean; idea.
意向 Intention; inclination.
意志 Will; purpose.
意見 Idea; opinion; view; proposal.
意味 Meaning; signification; sense.
意思 Intention; intent; thought.
意料 Guess; conjecture; suppose.
意義 Meaning; import; purpose.
意圖 Intention; plan; aim at.
意態 Demeanour; bearing.
意識 Senses; consciousness.
意願 A wish; a desire.
意譯 A free translation.
意大利(地) Italy.
意外事 Accidents; unexpected events.
意志剛强 Iron will; resoluteness; purpose.
意見一致 Be of the same opinion; agree; see eye-to-eye with.
意味深長 Be full of meaning (significance).
意氣揚揚 In high spirits; elated; triumphantly.
意想不到 Unexpected; unthinkable.
意識形態 Ideology.
意大利字體(斜體字) Italics.
意志堅强者 A man of strong will; a man of iron.
意志薄弱者 A man of weak will.

愕 (v.)- Be startled; be astonished; be amazed.
è 愕然 In alarm; in surprise; in amazement.

愚 (n.)- Stupidity; folly; ignorance.
(adj.)- Silly; foolish; stupid.
yú (v.)- Deceive; make a fool of.
愚民 The ignorant people; the untaught people.
愚弄 Make sport of; make a fool of.
愚昧 Stupid; ignorance.
愚笨 Stupid; loutish; unskilled.
愚鈍 Silly; stupid; obtuse; dull.
愚蠢 Blunt-witted; beef-witted; block-like.

愛 (n.)- Love; affection.
(v.)- Love; take delight in;
ài be fond of; wish; desire; like.
愛人 One's love (女); one's lover (男); one's sweetheart.
愛女 One's beloved daughter.
愛用 Use regularly; patronize.
愛好 Be fond of; have a passion for.
愛妻 One's beloved (dearest) wife.
愛國 Patriotism; love one's country.
愛惜 Be sparing of; be economical of. Have mercy.
愛情 Love; a personal affection.
愛撫 Caress; fondle; cherish.
愛憎 Likes and dislikes; love and hatred.
愛慕 Take a real liking to; long for.
愛憐 Pity; compassion; fellow feeling.
愛護 Take care for; look after; protect with loving care.
愛讀 Love to read; read with pleasure (keen interest).
愛戀 In love; have a passion for.
愛面子 Keen on face-saving.
愛國心 Patriotism; patriotic feeling (spirit).
愛國者 An ardent patriot.
愛爾蘭(地) Ireland.
愛讀書 Be fond of reading books.
愛科學 To be interested in science.
愛沙尼亞(地) Estonia.
愛克司光 X-rays.
愛國運動 A patriotic movement.
愛國團體 A patriotic society (organiza-

tion).
愛惜光陰 Careful of time; redeeming the time.
愛國一家 Patriots belong to one family.
愛斯基摩人 An Eskimo; an Esquimau (多數-maux).
愛克斯光照片 An X-ray (Röntgen) photograph.
愛克司光療法 X-ray treatment; Röntgenotherapy.
愛好正義的人民 Just-minded people.

愜 qiè (adj.)- Satisfied; contented; gratify.
愜意 Satisfied and pleased.

感 gǎn (n.)- Feeling; sentiment.
(adj.)- Affected; moved. Grateful.
(v.)- Touch; move; feel; affect; excite.
感化 Influence; correct; reform.
感光 Sensitization; sensitivensss. Affected by light.
感冒 Cold; influenza.
感恩 Grateful; bound in gratitude.
感染 Infection. Be infected with; catch.
感動 Influence; stir the feelings; touch; rouse; excite.
感情 Feeling; emotion; passion.
感慨 Deep emotion.
感想 Thoughts; impressions.
感嘆 Sorry; mournful; feel melancholy.
感銘 A deep impression; a great sensation.
感激 Grateful; affected with gratitude.
感應 Induction. Sympathy.
感謝 Thanks; gratitude.
感覺 Sensation; sense; sensibility.
感觸 The sense of touch; feeling.
感化院 A reformatory; a house of correction.
感光紙 Sensitive (sensitized) paper.
感染性 Infectious; contagious.
感想錄 A record of impressions.
感嘆詞 An exclamation; an interjection.
感嘆號 The exclamation mark (point).
感應性 Irritability.
感應圈 Induction coil.
感謝語 Words of thanks.
感激涕零 So moved to gratitude that—words fail—and the tears fall.
感應作用 Induction; sympathy.
感應電流 Induced current.
感覺系統 Sensible system.
感覺神經 The sensory nerve.
感覺敏銳 Sensitive.
感覺器官 Sense organs; the sensorium.

愧 kuì (adj.)- Ashamed; bashful; mortified.
愧慚 Be ashamed; feel abashed.

愼 shèn (adj.)- Cautious; careful; prudent.
(v.)- Be careful; be prudent; be discreet.
愼言 Be careful of speaking.
愼重 Circumspect; careful.

慄 lì (adj.)- Afraid; terrified; fearful.

慈 cí (n.)- Maternal affection. Kindness; mercy.
(adj.)- Kind; tender-hearted; humane.
慈母 An affectionate mother; a tender (fond) mother.
慈姑(植) Caladium.
慈祥 Merciful; lenient.
慈善 Merciful; philanthropic.
慈悲 Mercy; benevolence; charity; compassion; pity.

慈愛 Affection; tenderness.
慈善家 A philanthropist; a charitable person.
慈善事業 Charitable work; charity and relief work.
慈善團體 A charitable corporation.
慈善醫院 A charity (social) hospital.

態 tài (n.)- Figure; gait; behaviour; manner; circumstances.
態度 Attitude; behaviour.
態度嫻雅 Refined manners and deportment.

慌 huāng (adj.)- Agitated; hurried; alarmed; apprehensive; nervous.
(v.)- Scare; alarm.
慌忙 Agitated; hurried; fluttered.
慌張 Abashed; alarmed.
慌亂 Disorder; in confusion.

慍 yùn (n.)- Suppressed anger; indignant feelings.
(adj.)- Indignant; angry.
慍色 Angry appearance.

慕 mù (v.)- Desire ardently; be fond of; esteem; admire; long for; wish for.
慕仰 Esteem; respect; admire.
慕想 Be fond of.
慕名利 Long for fame and fortune.
慕尼黑協定 Munich Agreement.

慘 cǎn (adj.)- Sorrowful; miserable; cruel; hardhearted; sad.
慘死 Die distressingly; meet with a tragic death.
慘狀 Wretchedness; sadness; a dreadful condition.
慘案 Tragical incident.
慘殺 Cruel massacres. Murder; slaughter.
慘敗 A disastrous defeat; a serious defeat.
慘痛 Pained in mind; deeply grieved.
慘酷 Cruel; hard-hearted.
慘劇 A tragedy; a tragic event.
慘淡經營 Take pains on the work; do business with little profit.

慚 cán Same as 慙.
(adj.)- Ashamed; mortified; blushful.
(v.)- Blush for; feel ashamed of.
慚愧 A feeling of shame; remorse; regret. Be ashamed.

慢 màn (n.)- Slow; sluggish; late; dilatory.
(v.)- Treat haughtily.
(adj.)- Leisurely; slowly. Negligently; carelessly.
慢行 Walk slowly; stroll; saunter.
慢性(醫) Chronic; lingering; deep-seated.
慢板 Slow time in music.
慢客 Be rude to a guest; impolite.
慢性病 A chronic disease.
慢手慢脚 Slow in movements.

慣 guàn (adj.)- Habitual; accustomed to; used to; familiar with.
(prep.)- In the habit of.
慣用 Usage.
慣例 Custom; usage; a precedent.
慣性 Inertia; habit.
慣用語 An idiom; a common expression.
慣性定律(物) Law of inertia.

慧 huì (n.)- Wisdom; sagacity; intellect.
(adj.)- Intelligent; bright; quick.
慧敏 Clever; sagacious; intelli-

gent.
慧眼 Mental perception; clear-sightedness; quick eyes.

慨 kǎi (n.)- Generous feeling.
(adj.)- Generous; elevated; honourable; hearty.
慨嘆 Deplore; lament; grieve.

慮 lǜ (n.)- Anxiety. Suspicion; doubt.
(adj.)- Anxious; suspicious. Thoughtful; doubtful.
(v.)- Be anxious; consider; care for; feel sad.
慮及 Have anticipated.
慮念 Think anxiously about; concern oneself about.
慮遠 Long foresight.

慶 qìng (n.)- Happiness; welfare; joy.
(adj.)- Good; joyful; blessed; lucky.
(v.)- Bless; congratulate. Reward.
慶幸 Be favoured by fortune; good luck.
慶祝 Celebrate.
慶賀 Congratulate; offer congratulation.
慶壽 Congratulate on a birthday.
慶祝會 A meeting in celebration of a happy event.
慶賀新年 Congratulate at the New Year. Happy New Year.

慰 wèi (v.)- Console; comfort.
慰唁 Condole.
慰問 Comfort; give compliment for.
慰勞 Soothe with kind words; comfort.
慰藉 Consolation.
慰勞金 A bonus; a gratuity.
慰勞品 Comfort gift.

慷 kāng (adj.)- Magnanimous; public-spirited; high-toned; generous.
慷慨 Noble; openhanded; public-spirited.
慷慨悲歌 Sing mournfully.

慾 yù (n.)- Appetite; passion; desire; violent desire; earnest longing.
(adj.)- Covetous; lascivious; lustful.
慾念 Carnal thoughts.
慾望 Desires.

憂 yōu (n.)- Sorrow; grief. Sickness; illness.
(adj.)- Sad; sorry; anxious; thoughtful; sorrowful.
(v.)- Sympathize with; grieve; think of with sorrow.
憂心 Anxiety.
憂色 Long faced.
憂忿 Sad and angry.
憂患 Distress; misery.
憂悶 Disappointed; cast-down; sorry; grieved; sorrow; spiritless.
憂傷 Sadness; grief.
憂愁 Sorrowful; melancholy; sad. Sadness; distress; bitterness.
憂慮 Be anxious; be concerned about.
憂鬱 Out of spirits; low-spirited.
憂慮不堪 Be buried in anxiety; be filled with grief.

憊 bèi (n.)- Fatigue; weakness; weariness.
(adj.)- Worn-out; tired; fatigued; exhausted; worn-out.
憊倦；疲憊 Tired; worn-out; fatigued; exhausted.

憎 zēng (adj.)- Hateful; abominable; loathsome.
(v.)- Hate; dislike; loathe.

憎恨；憎厭 Hate; dislike; detest.
憎嫌；憎惡 Disgust; have a hatred for.

**憐** (n.)- Pity; compassion; fellow feeling.
lián (v.)- Sympathize; pity; have charity for; commiserate.
憐惜 Love with compassion. Regard with pity.
憐愛 Be fond of; pity; regard.
憐憫 Sympathize; pity.
憐貧 Pity the poor.

**憑** (n.)- Proof; evidence; licence; certificate.
píng (v.)- Lean on; trust to; depend on; rely on; confide in.
憑此 Rely upon this.
憑空 Without proof; imagination.
憑單；憑照 A certificate; a voucher; a licence; a receipt; a bill.
憑據；憑證 Evidence; proof; guarantee.
憑良心 On one's conscience.
憑票入內 Admit by ticket.
憑票支領 At sight on demand.

**憔** (adj.)- Grieving; distressed and pining.
qiáo 憔悴 Becoming thin and haggard; in distress.

**憤** (n.)- Anger; vexation; illfeeling; resentment.
fèn (v.)- Resent; anger.
憤世 Look life upon its dark side.
憤恨 Angry.
憤怒 Indignant; filled with anger and vexation.
憤慨 Resentment; indignation.
憤發 Ardent; earnest; impetuous.
憤激 Become excited; become angry.

**憨** (adj.)- Foolish; silly; simple.
憨生 Silly.
hān 憨直 Simple minded.
憨笑 Simper; laugh in a silly manner.
憨態 Foolish; stupid-looking.

**憩** (v.)- Rest; take repose.
憩息 Take a rest; rest.
qì

**憫** (n.)- Grief; pity; sympathy.
(adj.)- Lamentable; concerned
mǐng for.
(v.)- Mourn; pity; sympathize; commiserate.
憫恤；憫測 Pity; compassionate.

**憲** (n.)- Law; constitution; an example; regulation.
xiàn (adj.)- Well-informed; intelligent.
(v.)- Follow.
憲兵 Gendarmes. Military police (MP).
憲法 A constitution; the constitution law.
憲章 Constitutional provisions; the charter of constitution.
憲法大綱 The principles of a constitution.

**憶** (v.)- Think; recall; recollect; remember; reflect; bear in mind.
yì 憶念；憶思 Reflect on; think of; bear in mind.
憶昔 Remember former times.
憶起 Recall; call up.

**憾** (n.)- Vexation; hatred; regret. Enmity.
hàn (adj.)- Regretful; hateful; vexed; grievous.

(v.)- Be dissatisfied at; hate; dislike; murmur.
憾事 A matter of regret.
憾恨 Deep remorse or regret; hatred.

懂 (v.)- Understand; know.
dǒng 懂得 Understand.
懂人情 Understand human nature.
懂情理 Have common sense.

懃 (adj.)- Zealous; earnest; eager.
qín 懃懃懇懇 Zealous; earnest.

懇 (adj.)- Sincere; frank; unfeigned.
kěn (v.)- Beg; solicit; entreat.
(adv.)- Truly; earnestly; eagerly.
懇切 Very urgent; importunate; earnest; zealous.
懇求 Beg; request earnestly; entreat; solicit.
懇談 A friendly talk; a chat.
懇請 Entreat; implore; beg earnestly.
懇親會 A friendly gathering; a social meeting.

懈 (adj.)- Idle; lazy. Careless; negligent.
xiè 懈怠；懈弛 Negligent; slack; inattentive; lax; sluggish.
懈惰 Lazy; idle; indolent; remiss.

應 (n.)- Influence; effect. Answer; response.
yīng (adj.)- Right; suitable; correspondent.
(v.)- Should; ought to; must. Answer; fulfill; response; reply.
(adv.)- Therefore; accordingly.
應允；應諾 Assent to; accord; comply with.
應付 Honour a draft. Face a situation; dealt with.
應用 Practical application. Apply to; put to practical use.
應合 Ought to.
應否 Whether it should be or not.
應當 Fitting; proper. What is due; worthy of.
應該 Ought to.
應酬 Social intercourse; social affairs; entertain.
應對 Reply; answer.
應戰 Accept a battle; take the glove; take up a challenge.
應變 Adapt oneself to circumstances.
應用品 Necessaries.
應用科學 Applied science.
應酬朋友 Entertain friends.
應對如流 His replies flowed like a stream.

懊 (v.)- Regret; angry; vexed.
ào 懊悔 Regret; reproach oneself.
懊喪 Disappointed; dissatisfied.
懊惱 Angry; vexed.

懍 (n.)- Fear; awe. Respect; apprehension.
lǐn (v.)- Respect; fear; be afraid of; heed; notice; attend to.
懍然 Startled; awestruck.
懍懍 Trembling with fear.

懨 (adj.)- Sickly; tired.
yān 懨懨一息 Scarcely a breath left; on the point of dying; on death bed.

懦 (adj.)- Timid; weak; cowardly; feeble.
nuò 懦夫 A coward; a sluggard.
懦弱 Without energy; feeble-minded; weak in mind; weak-

spirited.
懦庸 Vulgar and timid.

**懲** (n.)- A warning; a caution. Punishment; admonition.
chéng (v.)- Punish; reprove; repress.
懲戒 Discipline; punish; correct; warn against.
懲惡 Censure wrong-doing; reprove evil conduct.
懲罰 Chastise; punish; afflict a penalty.
懲辦從嚴 Deal with strictly.

**懶** Same as 嬾.
lǎn (adj.)- Lazy; indolent; disinclined; listless; idle; sluggish; inactive.
懶於 Averse to.
懶婦 A slut.
懶惰 Lazy; unwilling to work.
懶散 Heedless; indolent; sluggish.
懶漢 A lazy fellow; a sluggard.
懶洋洋 Reluctantly; in a slow and listless manner.
懶骨頭 Lazy bones.

**懷** (n.)- The bosom; the heart. The affections; breast; chest.
huái (v.)- Long for; dwell on. Think of; hold in mind.
懷中 In the bosom.
懷古 Meditate on ancient times; remember the past.
懷孕 Become pregnant; conceive.
懷念 Think of; remember with anxiety.
懷抱 Inclasp with arms; carry in the arms.
懷恨 Cherish resentment; bear ill will; cherish hatred.
懷想 Think upon.
懷鄉 Homesick; sick of home.
懷疑 Doubt; hesitate; suspect; suspicious; discredit; distrust.
懷舊 Think of one's old friends; retrospection.
懷鬼胎 Conceive mischief; scheme evil.
懷恨在心 Harbour resentment in one's bosom.

**懸** (adj.)- Hanging.
xuán (v.)- Hang up; suspend. Be anxious; concern.
(adv.)- Anxiously.
懸念 Bear in mind; think anxiously about. Anxiety.
懸空 Suspended in space—unfounded; suspend in nothing.
懸殊 Very different; unlike.
懸崖 An overhanging cliff; a precipice.
懸掛 Hang up.
懸樑 To commit suicide by hanging oneself.
懸賞 Offer a reward; promise a reward.
懸橋 Suspend bridge.
懸賞通緝 Wanted.

**懺** (n.)- Ritualistic worship among Buddhist.
chàn (v.)- Regret; feel sorry for; repent.
懺悔 Repent and reform; regret.
懺悔自新 Repent and reform one's conduct.

**懼** (n.)- Fear; apprehension; dread.
jù (adj.)- Apprehensive; afraid; fearful.
(v.)- Fear; dread; be afraid of.
懼內 Henpecked; afraid of one's wife.
懼怯 Timid; nervous; timorous; afraid of; cowardly.
懼怕 Fear; be afraid of; tremble.

**戀** (v.)- Attach to; to fall in love with; to be fond of.
liàn 戀人 Sweetheart.

戀主 Attached to one's master.
戀愛 Fall in love; love ardently.
戀歌 A love song; a love lyric.
戀愛自由 Freedom of love.
戀戀不捨 Unwilling to part.
戀戀之情 Be warmly attached to.

# 戈 部

**戈** gē (n.)- A lance; a spear; a javelin. Weapons. War.
戈壁沙漠(地) Gobi Desert.

**戊** wù (n.)- The fifth of the Ten Stems (天干).

**戌** xū (n.)- The eleventh of the Twelve Branches (地支).
戌月 The ninth month.
戌時 7 to 9 P.M.

**戎** róng (n.)- Weapons. Arm troops; soldiers.
(adj.)- Military; warlike. Great. Barbarous; savage; brutal.
戎伍 The ranks; the army.
戎兵；戎器 Weapons; arms.
戎裝 Clad in uniform.

**成** chéng (n.)- One tenth; tenths.
(adj.)- Entire; whole; full.
(v.)- Finish; accomplish; succeed; become. Bring about; complete.
成人 An adult; a person of full age; a grown-up.
成品 A product.
成分 Elements; essentials.
成功 Accomplishment; success; achievement. Succeed; carry out; fulfil.
成本 Cost of production.
成立 Accomplish. Establish; found.
成交 Close a bargain.
成名 Make a name; become famous.
成形 Take shape.
成事 Execute; acccomplish; compass a business.
成果 The result; the outcome.
成長 Growth; grow up; be brought up.
成家 Get married.
成效 Effect.
成婚；成親 Marry; be married.
成敗 Success and failure.
成單(商) An invoice.
成就 Bring about; success; achievement.
成都(地) Chengtu.
成羣 Form into groups. Flock; herd.
成語(文) An idiom; a set phrase.
成熟 Become ripe; ripen; mature.
成績 Merit gained; results; record.
成功者 A successful man.
成衣匠 A tailor; a dressmaker.
成績表 A list of student's records.
成本價格(商) Cost price.
成立大會 The inaugural meeting.
成吉斯汗(人) Genghis Khan.

**戒** jiè (n.)- A limit. Warning; instruction.
(v.)- Take precautions; warn; watch; against; guard against.
戒口 Be careful of one's diet.
戒心 Wary; cautious from.
戒忌 Avoid; beware of.
戒指 A finger ring; a circlet.
戒食 Fast.

戒酒 Abstain from drinking; on the wagon.
戒煙 Give up smoking.
戒備 Stand guard; take precautions.
戒賭 Break off gambling.
戒嚴 Declare martial law.
戒禁 Exhort; forbid.
戒嚴令 Martial law.

我
wǒ
(pron.)- I; me; my; mine; we; us; our.
(adj.)- My dear.
我的 My; mine.
我們；我輩 We; us.
我國 Our country.
我自己 I myself; my own.
我們的 Our; ours.
我們自己 Ourselves.

戔
jiān
戔戔 Small; narrow.

或
huò
(n.)- A certain man; some one; somebody.
(pron.)- Who?
(adj.)- Uncertain; some.
(adv.)- Perhaps; prechance; probably.
(conj.)- If; whether; either; or.
或人 A certain person; some one.
或可 Probably.
或否 Probably not.
或是；或者 Perhaps. It may be; probably so; likely.
或然 Probably.
或大或小 Either large or small.
或早或晚 Either early or late; sooner or later.
或來或往 Either coming or going; to and fro.
或彼或此 Either that or this.
或然或否 It may be so or not.

戚
qī
(n.)- Relations. Misery; anxiety.
(adj.)- Sorrowful; sad; dejected; melancholy.
(v.)- Pity; commiserate; mourn.
戚戚 Dejected; feel sad.
戚屬 Relatives; relatives by marriage.

截
jié
(v.)- Cut off; cut into pieces; stop.
截止 Close; stop; cut off.
截住 Stop; cut short; interrupt.
截角 Cut off a corner.
截阻 Obstruct.
截面 Section.
截剿 Bar the enemy's advance.
截斷 Sever; part off; cut asunder. (農) Chopping
截管器 Pipe cutter; tube cutter.
截長補短 Cut off from the long to supply the deficiency of the short.
截然不同 Entirely different.
截斷交通 Interrupt communications.

戰
zhàn
(n.)- War; battle; fight; contest.
(adj.)- Terrified; fearful; trembling.
(v.)- Fight; join battle; bear arms against.
戰士 Soldiers; warriors; combatant.
戰友 Comrade-in-arms.
戰功 Military merits (exploits); military achivement.
戰史 Military history.
戰犯 A war criminal.
戰守 Attack and defence.
戰死 Die in battle; death from action.
戰局 The situation of war.
戰役 War; campaign; warfare; battle; fighting.
戰法 Tactical method.
戰果 Success in battle; war result.
戰爭 Fight; wrangle; contest. A war;

a battle.
戰俘 Prisoner of war (POW).
戰後 Post-war; after the war.
戰陣 Line of battle.
戰區 The zone of warfare.
戰略 Stratagem.
戰船；戰艦 Battleships; men-of-war.
戰術 Tactics.
戰敗 Beaten; defeated.
戰勝 Victory; win a battle.
戰場 The battle field; battle front.
戰慄 Shiver; shudder; tremble.
戰歌 War song; battle cry.
戰備 War preparations.
戰線 The fighting line.
戰壕 Trenches; rifle pit.
戰利品 A trophy; spoils of war; prey.
戰敗國 A defeated (vanquished) country; the vanquished.
戰鬥力 Fighting strength or power.
戰鬥機 A fighting plane.
戰鬥艦 A battle-ship.
戰地記者 The war correspondents.
戰事新聞 War news.
戰爭行爲 An act of hostilities.
戰爭犯罪 A war crime.
戰時狀態 State of war; war-state; war conditions.
戰爭販子 War-monger.
戰爭影片 A war film.
戰無不勝 Win in every battle; invincible.
戰戰兢兢 In great fear.
戰鬥部隊 Combat troop.
戰鬥巡洋艦 Battle cruiser.

**戲** xì (n.)- A play. Amusement; game; fun; sport.
(v.)- Play; make fun of. Play a trick on.
戲本 A playbook; a drama.
戲曲 Drama; play.
戲弄 Make fun of; disturb; annoy; tease; play jokes upon.
戲法 Sleight of hand ; jugglery.
戲迷 A playgoer; a theatregoer.
戲場 A stage; a theatre.
戲院 A theatre; a playhouse.
戲臺 The stage.
戲劇 Plays; a dramatic performance.
戲嬉 Play; fun.
戲曲家 A dramatist; a playwright.
戲劇化 Dramatize.
戲劇界 The theatrical world; theatrical circles.

**戴** dài (v.)- Wear; bear; put on the head. Honour.
戴帽 Put on a cap.
戴眼鏡 Wear spectacles.

# 戶 部

**戶** hù (n.)- A door; a hole. A family. Population.
戶口 The population; the householders.
戶主 A householder; the head of a family.
戶外 In the open air; out of doors; under the open sky.
戶籍册 The register.
戶籍法 Census law.
戶口調查 Census-taking. Take a census.
戶外運動 Open-air (outdoor) exercise; sports.
戶曉家喻 Make known to the people.

戶口調查局 Census bureau.

**房** (n.)- A house; an apartment; a chamber; a room.
fáng 房子 A building; a room; a house.

房東 The owner of a house; landlord.
房契 Title deeds for houses; building licence.
房客 Tenant.
房屋 Houses; dwellings; buildings.
房租 Rent.
房產 Estate; house property.
房頂 Roof.
房簷 The eaves.
房屋稅 A house tax (duty).
房屋建築 Building construction.

**所** (n.)- A place; a building; an office.
suǒ (pron.)- What; that which.
(adv.)- Whereby; therefore.

所以 Wherefore; therefore.
所在 Whereabouts; the site; the position; the location.
所有 Possession.
所見 Observation; one's view (opinion).
所長 The head of a department.
所要 Necessary; requisite; required; needed.
所期 Expectation; anticipation.
所感 One's impression.
所載 Printed (published, reported).
所謂 As it is said; so-called.
所屬 Belong to; be attached to.
所以然 The cause; the reason.
所在地 The seat; the location.
所有權 Ownership; title; right of possession.
所得稅 The income tax.
所定地點 The appointed place.
所要時間 The time required.
所需金額 The amount needed (required); the necessary funds.
所有債權人 All creditors.

**扁** (n.)- A tablet; a signboard.
(adj.)- Flat; mean; small.
biǎn 扁平 Flat.
扁鼻 A flat nose.

扁擔 The flat stick; a carrying pole.
扁額 A tablet.
扁平足 A flat foot.
扁桃腺 Tonsil.
扁桃腺炎 Tonsillitis.

**扇** (n.)- A fan. The leaf of a door.
扇子 A fan; a folding fan.
shān 扇形 Fan-shaped; semicircular.
扇面 The face of a fan.

**扉** (n.)- A door with one leaf.
扉頁 Title-page of a book.
fēi

# 手 部

**手** (n.)- The arm; the hand.
(v.)- Handle; hold in the hand.
shǒu 手巾 A towel.
手工 Handicraft; handiwork; manual training.

手下 Under orders; under control. An adherent; a follower.
手巧 Skilful with the hand; dexterous; handy.
手印 A thumb-mark; finger prints.

手册 A note-book; a memo-book.
手快；手捷 Cleverness of hand. Quickly.
手抄 Manuscript; copy.
手杖 A walking stick.
手足 Brothers. Hands and feet; the limbs.
手車 Barrow; hand-cart.
手帕 Napkins; handkerchief.
手法 Technique; execution.
手斧 A hatchet; an axe.
手段 Means; measures; steps.
手指 The fingers.
手套 A pair of gloves.
手術 Surgical operations.
手球 A hand-ball; a small ball.
手掌 The palm of the hand.
手腕 Wrist. Ability; skill; talent.
手跡 Handwriting; autography.
手勢 Gestures.
手緊 In financial difficutly. Stingy; closefisted.
手製 Hand-made; home-made.
手簽 Autograph; hand signed.
手辣 Malicious; evil-minded.
手稿 Manuscript.
手錶 Wrist watch.
手臂 The arm.
手錘 Hand hammer.
手鎗 A pistol; a revolver.
手藝 Handicraft; manual arts.
手續 Process; procedure.
手鐲 Bracelets.
手工科 A manual training course.
手工業 Handicraft.
手印機 A hand-printing press.
手風琴 An accordion.
手術台 An operating-table.
手術室 An operating-room.
手術費 Charges for an operation.
手提包 A hand-bag (-satchel); a grip-sack.
手電筒 Electric torch; flash light.
手榴彈 A hand-grenade.
手術醫生 An operating surgeon.
手提行李 Hand-baggage.
手藝工人 Handicraftsman.
手搖抽水機 A hand pump.

**才** cái (n.)- Ability; gift; faculty; talent. A genius.
(adv.)- Just; now; then.
才子 A man of parts; a man of talent.
才能；才幹 Talent; capacity; ability; parts.
才智 Intelligence; talents; wisdom.
才學 Wit and learning; acquirement; accomplishments.
才德兼備 Virtuous and talented.
才貌雙全 Beautiful and talented.

**扒** bā (v.)- Scratch. Pull out.
扒手 A shoplifter; a pickpocket.
扒竊 Steal; purloin.

**打** dǒ (n.)- A blow; a stroke. A dozen.
(v.)- Beat; strike; fight; fetch; perform.
打印 Stamp.
打扮 Dress; do up; make-up.
打劫 Plunder; rob.
打胎 Feticide; the action of destroying a foetus.
打倒 Knock (strill) down; overthrow.
打破 Smash; break into pieces; crack.
打掃 Sweep up.
打敗 Defeat; beat.
打牌 Play cards.
打開 Break open; open.
打算 Calculate; reckon; estimate; plan; scheme.
打噎 Belch.
打樁 Drive piles.
打擊 A blow; a hit; a shook.

打獵 Go hunting.
打翻 Upset; overturn.
打聽 Make inquiry; detect; ascertain.
打攪 Trouble; bother.
打主意 Plan.
打包費 Package.
打字員 Typist.
打字機 Typewriter.
打耳光 Slap on the face.
打官司 Go to law; sue.
打勝仗 Win a victory; gain a battle.
打暗號 Signal; give hint.
打電報 Send a telegram to; cable.
打電話 Speak by telephone.
打拍子 Beat time.
打網球 Play tennis.
打算盤 Calculate; reckon on the abacus.
打樁機 Pile driver.
打稿子 Draft.
打鞦韆 Swing.
打噴嚏 Sneeze.
打鐵匠 A blacksmith.
打草驚蛇 Beat the grass and startle the snakes—frighten out of cover; cause undesired agitation.

托 tuō (v.)- Support with the hand; bear up; carry on the shoulder.
托詞 Pretend; pretext.
托盤 A tray.
托兒所 Nursery; nursery school.
托辣斯 A trust.

扛 káng (v.)- Raise; lift up; carry by two men.
扛檯 Carry on a pole.

扣 kòu (v.)- Strike; discount. Hook on; button; fasten. Knock against.
扣留 Detain. Arrest.
扣除 Deduct from; strike out; rebate.
扣門 Knock at the door.
扣問 Ask; inquire.
扣頭；折扣 Discount; rebate; allowance. Commission.
扣繫 Tie; fasten.

扭 niǔ (v.)- Turn round; twist; wry; grasp; seize.
扭打 Struggle.
扭傷 Sprain.
扭率 Coefficient of torsion.
扭結 Twist; grapple.
扭毆 Struggle; squabble.
扭轉 Twist about; turn over and over.

扮 bàn (n.)- Dress; ornament.
(v.)- Disguise oneself; adorn; dress up.
扮作 Dress up.
扮裝 Dress (make) up; impersonate.
扮戲；扮演 Act or play the part of; represent a character.

扯 chě (v.)- Pull. Haul. Tear.
扯上 Pull up; hoist.
扯下 Pull down; haul down.
扯平 Take an average.
扯拉 Pull; drag.
扯破 Tear.
扯開 Pull apart; tear open.
扯毀 Tear down and destroy.

扶 fú (v.)- Lend a hand; aid; assist.
扶手 Support by the hand.
扶住 Support.
扶助 Aid; succour; help; assist; stand by.
扶持 Uphold; support; sustain.
扶起 Assist in rising; help up.
扶植 Implantation. Plant.
扶養 Nourish; take care of; maintain; support.
扶助金 An allowance in aid.

扶養者 A supporter; a sustainer.

批 (n.)- A criticism; a judgment.
(v.)- Criticize. Reply officially.
pī Endorse.
批示 Publish a case; a proclamation.
批判 A verdict.
批准 Grant a petition; ratify; sanction.
批發 Sell by wholesale; wholesale.
批評 A criticism; a remark. Censure; criticize.
批銷 Write off; endorse as correct.
批駁 Reverse a judgment; a written defence.
批覆；批回 Reply officially.
批發處；批發店 Wholesale house.
批評家 A critic; a reviewer.
批准條約 Ratify a treaty.
批發商人 A wholesale dealer (merchant).
批發價目 Wholesale prices.

扼 (v.)- Grasp; clutch; seize.
扼守 Hold; command.
è 扼制 Control; hold.
扼要 Hold a strategical position.
扼殺 Strangulation; strangle one to death.
扼守要害 Have the command of. . .
扼住咽喉 Hold . . . throat; by the grip the throat of.

找 (v.)- Find; search; look for. Make up.
zhǎo 找尋 Find; seek; search.
找續 Change.
找頭 Balance . Change.
找竅門 To find a short cut.

承 (v.)- Undertake; take a charge. Acknowledge. Promise. Re-
chéng ceive. Succeed. Continue.
承允 Agree to; promise.
承受 Receive; inherit.
承前 Continued from. . . .
承接；承攬 Take in, as a job; contract for.
承當 Make oneself responsible for; abide the consequences.
承蒙 I am indebted to you for. . .
承認 Recognition; consent; approval; acknowledgement.
承辦 Undertake to manage, or put through any business.
承諾 Acceptance; consent; assent.
承繼 Succeed to; inherit.
承繼人 Inheritor; successor; heir.
承繼權 Right of succession.
承認獨立 Recognize the independence of a country.

技 (n.)- Art; skill; talent; ability.
(adj.)- Skilful; ingenious.
jì 技巧 Ingenious; skilful.
技能 Talent; ability.
技倆 Ability; talent; skill.
技師 Artists; experts; a mechanist; an engineer.
技術 Skill; art.
技擊 Boxing.
技藝 Arts; crafts; accomplishments.
技術專家 A technical expert.

抄 (v.)- Seize. Search. Copy out.
抄化 Solicit subscriptions.
chāo 抄本 Epitome; a copy-book.
抄沒 Confiscate.
抄附 Append a copy of.
抄案 Take down the evidence in the case.
抄家 Confiscate one's property by order of government.
抄給 Give a copy of.
抄稿 Make a fair copy; copy a draft.
抄錄；抄寫 Copy; transcribe.

抄襲 Plagiarize; copy; steal other's ideas.
抄寫 Copy book.
抄近路 Take a short cut.

把 bǒ (n.)- A handle. A bundle; a fagot.
(v.)- Grasp; hold; seize. Watch
把手 A handle; a grip.
把守 Guard; keep possession of.
把住 Retain; hold up.
把持 Control; monopolize.
把柄 Proof; evidence.
把舵 Steer; pilot.
把握 Take hold of; seize; chance of success.

抑 yǐ (v.)- Restrain; repress; rule; curb; stop; keep back.
(conj.)- Else; moreover; if; either. . . or; otherwise.
抑止 Check.
抑制 Keep down; control; restrain; supress; stop.
抑或 Or else; otherwise.
抑揚 Low and high, as musical notes.
抑鬱 Depressed; grieved; despondent; melancholy; downcast.

抓 zhuā (v.)- Scratch; tickle; tear with the claws. Seize; take; clutch; grab.
抓住 Seize with the claws; grasp with the talons or hands.
抓賊 Arrest a thief.
抓癢 Scratch an itchy place.

投 tǒu (v.)- Throw; cast; reject. Deliver present to.
投下 Throw (fling) down; drop.
投井 Jump into a well.
投水 Jump into water.
投交；投遞 Hand over to.
投生 Be born again.
投考 Participate in examination.
投身 Give oneself to.
投到 Attend; be present.
投帖 Send a card.
投河 Drown oneself.
投軍 Join the army; enlist; serve in the ranks.
投奔 Fly to for refuge.
投降；投誠 Surrender; lay down one's arms; capitulate.
投票 Cast a vote; vote by ballot; vote.
投書；投信 Send a letter. Post a letter.
投宿 Lodge; put up at.
投遞 Deliver; hand over.
投報 Report; inform; send in an application.
投資 Investment; invest money.
投獄 Throw into (put in) prison; imprison.
投彈 Drop a bomb; bomb.
投標 Tender for the supply of a certain line of goods at a competitive price. Bid.
投稿 Contribute to; write for.
投機 Fall in with one's views. Speculate. Speculation. Agree.
投親 Visit one's relatives.
投票者 A voter.
投票處 The polling place (station).
投票權 Suffrage; right of vote.
投資者 An investor.
投稿人 A contributor.
投票選舉 Elect by ballot.
投資信託 (商) Investment trust.
投稿報紙 Contribute an article to a newspaper.
投機分子 A time-serve; an opportunist.
投機市場 Speculation market.
投機主義 Opportunism; an expectant (a wait-and-see) policy.
投機商業 Speculation commerce.

**抖** (v.)- Tremble; shiver. Rouse.
dǒu 抖擻精神 Rouse one's spirits; stimulate.

**抗** (v.)- Raise with the hand. Oppose; resist.
kàng 抗拒 Resist; oppose. Resisting; opposing; violating.

抗敵 Resist the enemy; fight against the enemy.

抗論 Refute; repudiate.

抗衡 Struggle against; rival.

抗戰 Resistance; offer resistance.

抗議 Express opposition to; object to. A protest; an objection.

抗毒素 An antitoxin.

抗生素 Anti-biotic.

抗議書 Form of protest.

抗戰到底 Resist to the bitter end.

**折** (n.)- An act of a play.
(v.)- Snap in two. Deduct.
zhé Oppress. Cut short one's life. Lose.

折半 Reduce by half; break in the middle.

折合；折算 Calculate; conversion.

折回 Return halfway.

折扣 Discount.

折衷 Compromise.

折射 Refraction of light.

折減 Rebate.

折疊 Fold (double) up.

折價 Reduced rate.

折線(幾) A broken line.

折磨 Illtreat; afflict; gall; oppress.

折斷 Break asunder; snap short. Decide; determine.

折扣單(商) Bills discounted.

折扣價目 Reduced price.

折衷主義 Eclecticism.

折衷計劃 A compromise; a conciliatory measure.

折舊帳目(商) Depreciation account.

折舊準備金 Depreciation reserves.

**披** (adj.)- Dishevelled.
(v.)- Open; spread out; uncover.
pī Throw on.
披衣 Throw on clothes.

披肩 A shawl; a cape; a scarf.

披卷 Open a scroll or a book.

披屋 An out house.

披風 A woman's cloak.

披靡 Scatter.

披露 Announce; publish.

披星戴月 Travel by night.

披荊斬棘 Cut a way through brambles.

**抱** (n.)- The bosom; the heart.
(v.)- Hold in the arms; hug;
bào embrace.
抱住 Hold fast in the arms.

抱怨 Cherish ill will; bear malice; feel resentment; bear a grudge.

抱負 Aspiration; ambition.

抱病 Fall sick; be sick.

抱歉 Regret; feel sorry.

抱不平 Dissatisfied; indignant at.

抱頭痛哭 One embraces his head and weep bitterly.

**抵** (n.)- Pledge; security; mortgage. Substitute.
dǐ (v.)- Oppose; resist. Butt. Arrive at; withstand; reach.

抵任 Reach one's post.

抵充 Imputation.

抵扣 Deduct from.

抵抗 Resistance; defiance.

抵制 Boycott.

抵岸 Ashore.

抵押；抵質 Give something as a pledge or security.

抵消 Set-off; offset.

抵擋 Check; keep back; hinder.

抵禦 Antagonize; withstand; oppose; contend; prevent approach; resist.
抵賴 Repudiate.
抵觸 Butt; rush against; conflict (clash) with.
抵抗力 Resistance; resisting power.
抵押品 Collateral security; a mortgage; a pledge.
抵押借款 Loan on collateral security; lend money on mortgage (security).

抹 (v.)- Rub; wipe off; scrub; brush; dust; clean away.
mǒ 抹去 Wipe off; cancel; efface.
〔mò〕 抹布 A dish-cloth; a duster; a wiper.
抹枱 Wipe the table.
抹殺 Sweep away; exterminate.
抹粉 Make up the face.
抹乾 Wipe dry.
抹淚 Wipe away tears.

押 (v.)- Sign; stamp a seal. Guard; detain; put in jail. Press;
yā compel. Deposit; pledge; mortgage.
押抵；押借 Mortgage; pawn; pledge.
押契 A written security for a loan; a mortgage deed.
押品 Security.
押租 A deposit for renting a house.
押送；押解 Send in custody to; escort.
押款 Deposit money; earnest money. A mortgage loan.
押舖 Pawnshop.
押韻 Rime; rhyme.
押送費 Escort expense.
押滙票 Documentary bill.

抽 (v.)- Take out; draw. Levy; asses. Draw, as a lot. Bud;
chōu pull up.
抽水 Draw up water.
抽出；抽取 Draw or take out from a lot.
抽烟 Smoking.
抽屜 A drawer.
抽稅 Levy taxes.
抽筋(醫) Spasms; cramp; convulsion.
抽象 Abstraction.
抽絲 Reel silk.
抽籤 Draw lots.
抽油機 Oil pump.
抽水機 Water pump.
抽象名詞 Abstract noun.

拂 (n.)- A brush; a duster.
(v.)- Shake off; wipe; brush
fú away. Oppose; expel.
(adj.)- Perverse; obstinate.
拂拭 Dust; wipe away: brush away.
拂塵 Brush off the dust. A brush; a duster.
拂曉 At dawn; at daybreak; early in the morning.
拂袖而行 To walk away in anger.

拆 (v.)- Open. Destroy; pull down; break; demolish.
chāi 拆股 Dissolve partnership.
拆散 Disperse; scatter; break to pieces; break away.
拆開 Disclose; break apart; break open.
拆毀 Demolish; pull down; throw down.
拆房子 Pull down a house.

拇 (n.)- The thumb; the first toe.
拇指 The thumb.
mǔ 拇趾 The first toe; great toe.
拇指印 A thumb-print.

拈 (n.)- Take with the fingers; carry; handle; pick up.
niān 拈花 Pick a flower.

**拉** (v.)- Pull; drag; draw; bend.
la
拉入 Drag into.
拉上 Pull up.
拉下 Pull down.
拉手 Shake hands; seize the hand. A door-knob.
拉住 Hold fast.
拉回 Pull back.
拉車 Draw a cart; pull a cart.
拉起 Pull up.
拉緊 Draw tight; strain.
拉鋸 Pull a two-handed saw.
拉薩(地) Lhasa.
拉丁文 The Latin language.
拉丁民族 The Latin races.
拉丁美洲(地) Latin America.

**拋** (v.)- Fling; cast off; reject; throw; abandon.
pāo
拋家 Leave home.
拋球 Throw or pitch a ball; play ball.
拋開 Throw off.
拋棄 Abandon; reject; cast aside; throw away.
拋網 Throw (cast) a net.
拋擲 Fling; throw.
拋錨 Drop or cast anchor.
拋物線(幾) Parabola.
拋射體 Projectile.
拋棄兒女 Leave one's children.
拋頭露面 Expose oneself in public —said of women.

**拌** (v.)- Throw away; cast off. Mix.
bàn
拌勻 Mix properly and evenly.
拌嘴 Quarrel; wrangle; bickering.

**拍** (v.)- Pat; beat; clap; strike.
pāi
拍子 Time; tact.
拍手；拍掌 Clap the hands in applause.
拍肩 Pat at the shoulder.
拍板 Wooden clappers.
拍胸 Beat the breast.
拍照 Take photo.
拍電 Send a wire.
拍賣 Auction; be sold at auction; bring to hammar.
拍翼 Clap the wings.
拍拍子 Keep (beat, mark) time.
拍紙簿 Writing pad.
拍電報 To send a cable.
拍賣商 Auctioneer.
拍賣場 Auction room (house).
拍賣價額 Amount of bidding.
拍賣時最初之價格 Up-set-price.

**拐** (n.)- A staff; a stick.
guǎi
(v.)- Kidnap; decoy; entrap; deceive; swindle.
拐子 A kidnapper; a crimp; a swindler.
拐杖 An old man's staff.
拐帶；拐誘 Kidnap; seduce; decoy; abduct.
拐彎 Turn a corner.
拐騙 Decoy away.

**拒** (v.)- Resist; oppose; reject; withstand; refuse; prevent; stop; decline.
jù
拒卻 Decline.
拒捕 Resist arrest.
拒絕 Exclude; refuse; reject.
拒敵 Resist an enemy; keep an enemy at bay; defend.
拒絕付款 Dishonour for non-payment.
拒絕承諾(商) Dishonour for non-acceptance. Deny.

**拓** (v.)- Push by the hand. Develop; enlarge; open; break.
tuò
拓本 A facsimile.

拓殖 Colonize; colonization.

拔 bó (adj.)- Conspicuous.
(v.)- Pull up; extirpate; promote. Take by storm; root up; eradicate; draw off. Elevate.

拔刀 Draw a sword.
拔牙 Extract or pull out a tooth.
拔河 Tug-of-war.
拔根 Pull up roots; eradicate; up-root.
拔草 Weeds.
拔萃 A man of outstanding ability. Extraction; selection.
拔劍 Draw a sword.
拔取人才 Pick out men of talents.

拖 tuō (v.)- Pull; drag; draw. Delay.
拖欠 Owe one money for a long time; in debt.
拖延 Delay; out off; procrastinate.

拖車 A trailer; a wagon.
拖長 Lengthen.
拖後 Draw after.
拖船 A tugboat.
拖累 Involve; embroil; implicate; entangle.
拖鞋 Slippers.
拖輪 A steam-tug.
拖拉機 Tractor.
拖泥帶水 Be dragged through mud and water.

拘 jū (adj.)- Bigoted.
(v.)- Arrest; seize. Detain; restrain. Adhere to.
拘束 Restrain; restrict; uneasy.

拘拿 Seize; arrest.
拘留 Detain; keep in custody.
拘票 Warrant of arrest.
拘禁；拘管 Keep in custody; detain; confine.
拘禮 Be formal; adhere to ceremony.
拘留所 Lockup; guardroom; a house of detention.

拙 zhuō (adj.)- Stupid; unskilled; bad; foolish; poor.
拙劣 Poor; clumsy; unskilful; bungling.

拙作 My poor composition; my poor work.
拙笨 Stupid; clumsy.
拙筆 My bad hand-writing.

拚 pīn (v.)- Sweep; reject; cleanse; brush away.
拚命 Risk one's life; desperation.

拚除 Clear away; sweep.

抨 pēng 抨擊 Attack; criticise.

招 zhāo (n.)- A signboard; a placard. A target.
(v.)- Beckon; call; invite to come. Proclaim. Confess. Provoke.

招工 Advertise for labourers; take in workman.
招手 Beckon with the hand.
招生 Advertise for students.
招考 Entrance examination. Invite entries for the examination.
招兵 Enlist to recruit; levy soldiers.
招待 Wait upon; attend to.
招呼 Call to; hail; give notice.
招租 To let; to be let.
招集 Invite to come together.
招牌 A signboard.
招貼 Notices; handbills.
招尋 Seek for; look for; wanted.
招惹 Incur; provoke; expose oneself to.

招募 Enlist.
招認 Confess; acknowledge.
招待日 A day for reception.
招待券 A complimentary ticket.
招待室 A guest room; a reception room.
招待員 Usher; those appointed to receive visitors.
招待客人 Entertain guests.

拜 bài (v.)- Bow; worship; visit. Salute; respect.
拜年 Pay New Year's calls.
拜訪 Pay a visit to.
拜見 Call upon; pay one a visit or call.
拜神 Worship the gods.
拜師 Pay one's respect to a master before becoming his pupil.
拜託 Request; beg.
拜賀 Congratulate respectfully.
拜壽 Congratulate on one's birthday.
拜金者 A worshipper of Mammon.
拜物教徒 A fetishist.
拜火教徒 A fire-worshipper.
拜金主義 Worship of money; mammonism.

括 kuò (v.)- Inclose; contain; embrace; include; envelop.
括弧 Parentheses; round brackets (　); square brackets〔　〕; brace {　}.

拭 shì (v.)- Dust clearly; cleanse; wipe; erase.
拭目 Rub the eye.
拭垢 Wipe off the dirt.
拭桌 Wipe a table.
拭塵 Brush, wipe or sweep away dust.

拮 jié (adj.)- Occupied; labouring hard.
拮据 Embarrassed; perplexed. Money is short.

拯 zhěng (v.)- Rescue; pull out; lift up; raise; save; deliver.
拯救 Save or free from danger; deliver; rescue.
拯溺 Save the drowning.

拱 gǒng (n.)- Hands joining. An arch. A span.
(adj.)- Arched; curved.
(v.)- Salute by folding hands; encircle.
拱手 Salute with the hands folded.
拱起 Rise.
拱廊 Cloister.
拱道 Archway.
拱橋 Arch-bridge.

拳 quán (n.)- The fist.
(v.) Clasp; grasp in the hand; make a fist.
拳法；拳術 Pugilism; boxing; manly art.
拳頭 The fist.
拳教師 An instructor of boxing; boxer; a pugilist.

拷 kǎo (v.)- Put to the question; beat.
拷打 Beat and extort a confession; torture; flog.
拷貝 A copy.
拷訊 Try by torture.
拷問 Bring upon the carpet; put to the question.

拾 shí (adj.)- Ten; tenth.
(v.)- Pick up; collect; gather up; put to order; arrange.
拾去 Take away.
拾起 Pick up.
拾得 Find; pick up.
拾得者 The finder.

拿 Same as 拏.
(v.)- Seize; take; capture; lay hold on; arrest; grasp.
nó 拿手 Dexterous; expert.
拿出 Take out.
拿去 Take it away.
拿住 Grasp; seize.
拿來 Bring it here.
拿緝 Search and arrest.
拿定主意 Decide; make up the mind.

持 (v.)- Manage; direct; grasp; hold. Support; maintain; preserve.
chí 持久 Lasting; enduring.
持正 Upright.
持守 Keep fast; hold of; maintain.
持家 Take charge of a family; housekeeping.
持戟 Grasp the spear; take arms.
持續 Last; continue.
持久戰 A protracted war.
持票人 Bearer.
持械搶劫 Armed robbery.

指 (n.)- A finger.
(v.)- Teach. Command; denote; point out; indicate. Touch. Assign.
zhǐ
指引 Lead; direct; conduct; show the way.
指令 Instructions; an order.
指甲 Finger nails.
指示 Show; indicate; denote; instruct.
指名 Nominate; name.
指使 Instigate.
指定；指明 Designate; name; fix; appoint.
指南 Guide.
指紋 A finger-print.
指針 Index hand; indicator; compass-needle.
指教 Correct; point out the right way; give a man the straight tip.
指望 Hope for; desire; hope; expectation.
指揮 Command; point to; conduct; give order; lead; direct.
指責 Denounce; criticise.
指標(算) The index; target.
指數(算) Exponent; index number.
指導 Direct; advice; instruct; conduct; guide.
指環 A finger-ring.
指甲花(植) Broad Egyptian privet.
指示針 Pointer.
指示器 Indicator.
指南針 A compass.
指路標 A signpost; a finger post.
指揮官 A commander; an officer in command.
指揮棒(音) A baton.
指導員 A director.
指關節(解) Articulations of the fingers.
指手畫足 Gesticulate.
指定日期 Apointed day.
指數函數 An exponential function.
指樣定貨 Order by sample.
指示代名詞 A demonstrative pronoun.
指數方程式(算) Exponential equation.

挂 Same as 掛.
(v.)- Hang up; suspend.
guà

按 (v.)- Place the hand on; grasp; press down; cease; put down; stop. Try; examine.
àn
(prep.)- According to; in accordance with; by.
按下 Press down; not to mention.
按日 Every day; daily.
按月 Monthly; per month; every month.
按年 Per year; yearly.

按序 Follow the order; by order.
按法；按例 According to law; by law.
按脈 Feel the pulse.
按時 In season; at seasonable time.
按期 According to the fixed time.
按照 Act according to; in agreement with; comply with.
按鈴 Press on the bell.
按價（商）Nominal value.
按摩 Massage.
按額 According to number.
按日付 Daily installment.
按月付 Monthly installment.
按比例 Prorate.
按兵不動 Keep troops entrenched.
按步就班 Orderly; well behaved; keep rules.
按重量出售 Sale by weight.

拴 shuān (v.)- Fasten; tie up.

挑 tiāo (v.)- Carry on the shoulder with a pole; lift. Select; pick out; choose.
挑夫 A coolie; a porter; a bearer.
挑水 Carry buckets of water on shoulder.
挑事 Stir up trouble.
挑剔 Sort out and reject; find fault with.
挑唆 Set at variance; stir up; make mischief; excite to discord.
挑動 Sow strife; disturb; excite suspicion; excite.
挑開 Open; clear out; put aside.
挑撥 Set a variance.
挑戰 Challenge to battle; provoke a fight.
挑選 Pick out; select; choose.
挑釁 Aggress; provoke hostilities.
挑戰書 A challenge; a cartel.
挑戰行爲 Provocative action.

挖 wā (v.)- Excavate; dig out; hollow out; dredge; scoop.
挖井 Dig a well.
挖木 Excavate a piece of wood.
挖泥 Scoop out earth.
挖洞 Dig a hole; dig through.
挖破 Break up by scooping.
挖掘 Excavation.
挖泥機 Dredger; grab dredger.
挖鑿機 Excavator.
挖肉補瘡 Cut off some flesh to patch up an ulcer–silly work.

挨 āi (adj.)- Near; next to.
(v.)- Lean to. Delay. Be beaten; suffer.
挨打 Be beaten.
挨駡 Scolded.
挨次 In order.
挨飢受餓 Suffer cold and hunger.

挪 nuó (v.)- Move; transfer; remove.
挪用 Embezzle; misappropriate funds.
挪威（地）Norway.
挪動 Move.
挪開 Move away.
挪用公款罪 Embezzlement.

挫 cuò (n.)- Adversity.
(v.)- Break. Humiliate. Oppress. Adverse; obstruct; check.
挫折 Suffer a set-back; breakdown; be frustrated.
挫銳氣 Repress one's spirit; damp one's ardour.

振 zhèn (v.)- Rouse; stimulate; excite. Revive; move; stir up.
振作 Encourage; stimulate;

cheer.
振翅 Clap the wings.
振動 Shake; move. Vibration.
振救 Save from danger; rescue.
振幅 Amplitude of an oscillation (a vibration).
振奮 Exert oneself.
振興 Rouse; encourage; promote. Revive; refresh; flourish.
振翼 Flutter; spread the wings.
振動表 Vibroscope.
振動器(電) A vibrator; an oscillator.
振奮人心 Exciting; encouraging; to rouse people.
振興實業 Development of trade.

挺 (adj.)- Eminent; stiff and upright; straight; prominent.
tǐng (v.)- Thrust; pull up; straighten; stiffen; resolute.
挺出 Stretch out.
挺立 Stand straight up.
挺身 Straighten the body; put oneself forward.
挺胸 Thrust forward the chest.
挺進 Dash forward; go (advance) ahead of the rest.

挽 (v.)- Lead; draw. Restore; pull; conduct; turn over.
wǎn 挽回 Bring back; retrieve; recall; recover.
挽留 Retain; ask a friend to stay.
挽救 Save from disaster; rescue.
挽聯 Mourning scroll.
挽手同行 Walk together hand in hand.
挽回大局 Restore the general situation.

挾 (v.)- Clasp under the arm; clasp; pinch.
jiā 挾制 Coerce. Intimidate; control.
挾持 Grasp; intimidate.

捆 (n.)- Bundle; package.
(v.)- Bind; plait; tie up.
kǔn 捆住 Tied up.
捆縛 Bound; tied.

捉 (v.)- Lay hold of; grasp; catch; seize; apprehend; arrest.
zhuō 捉住 Catch hold of; grasp and hold fast.
捉弄 To fool; to make a sport of.
捉拿 Apprehend; arrest; seize; catch.
捉魚 Fish.
捉鳥 Catch birds.
捉迷藏 Blindman's buff; hide-and-seek.
捉襟見肘 To be in financial difficulty.

捍 (v.)- Defend; ward off; resist; gurad against; protect.
hàn 捍衛 To defend; protect.
捍禦 Guard against; resist an attack.

捏 Same as 揑 .
(v.)- Pick up or knead with
niē the fingers. Invent.
捏造 Insinuate against; fabricate; trump up; make up.
捏一把 Take a pinch.
捏土機(工) Pug.
捏造謠言 Manufacture rumours; tell long stories.

捐 (n.)- Subscription. Taxation; duty.
juān (v.)- Reject; renounce. Subscribe. Contribute.
捐款 Make a contribution to (toward).
捐募 Collect contributions.
捐稅 Tax.
捐錢 Contribute. Contribution.
捐稅局 Tax bureau.
捐助善舉 Subscribe money to a charity.

**捕** (v.)- Seize; catch; apprehend; arrest.
bǔ
捕房 A police station.
捕拿 Arrest; catch.
捕魚 Fishing.
捕獲 Capture; seizure.
捕差；捕役 Constables; police runners.
捕獸機 Trap.
捕鯨船 A whaling-vessel; a whaler.
捕獲物 A prize.
捕蠅紙 Fly paper.
捕蠅器 A fly trap.
捕風捉影 Catch the wind and grasp the shadow—invent a story.

**捧** (v.)- Hold up in both hands. Offer.
pěng
捧住 Grasp carefully; hold firmly.
捧場 Support; patronise.
捧持 Hold with both hands.
捧腹 Hold one's belly, as in laughing aloud.
捧讀 Hold up and read; read respectfully.
捧腹大笑 Hold (split) one's sides with laughter; be convulsed with laughter.

**捨** (v.)- Give alms; let go; give up; leave.
shě
捨去 Part with; give up.
捨身 Devote the person; give up one's life.
捨命 Give up life for other; sacrifice life.
捨棄 Forsake; abandon; give up.
捨不得 Cannot part with it; grudge.

**据** (adj.)- Embarrassed; restricted; hard up; in need of money.
jū
据法 According to the laws; legal.

**捲** (adj.)- Rolled up; spiral; curly.
(v.)- Roll up.
juǎn
捲入 Involve.
捲尺 A tape.
捲烟 Cigarette.
捲起 Roll up.
捲袖 Turn up one's sleeves.
捲髮 Curly hair.
捲心菜(植) Cabbage.
捲筒機(印) Rolling-press.
捲土重來 Make a strong effort to recover lost ground after a defeat.

**捶** (v.)- Beat with a staff; cudgel.
chuí
捶撻 Whip; beat.

**捷** (n.)- Victory.
(adj.)- Quick; prompt; active; clever; swift; rapid.
jié
(v.)- Gain a victory; accomplish; win.
捷徑 A compendious way; a short cut.
捷報 Announcements of successful examination, promotion, or victory; victory news.
捷克斯洛伐克(地) Czecho-slovakia.
捷克斯洛伐克人 Czech. Czekh.

**捻** (n.)- A pinch.
(v.)- Pinch up; nip with the fingers; twist.
niǎn
捻手 Snap the fingers.
捻絲 Shake out skeins of silk.

**掀** (v.)- Raise up; open; pull aside; hold high.
xiān
掀被 Throw off the coverlet.

**掃** (n.)- A broom.
(v.)- Sweep; clear away; wipe or rub with a broom.
sǎo

掃平 Put down rebellion.
掃帚；掃把 A broom; a sweeper.
掃除 Clear away; sweep away; dust.
掃射 Shoot; rake; sweep with fire.
掃墓 Visit the grave.
掃蕩 Sweep away; wipe out; annihilate; mop up.
掃興 Disappoint; spoil the fun; cast down; discourage.
掃帚星；彗星；孛星 A comet.
掃乾淨 Sweep clean.
掃雷艇 A mine-sweeper.
掃街夫 A scavenger; a sweeper.
掃蕩戰 Mopping warfare.
掃而空之 All swept away; clean up.
掃除文盲；掃盲 To eliminate illiteracy.

授 shðu (n.)- Grant; give; pay to; bestow; impart; confer. Teach.
授任 Be appointed to the post of.
授命 Sacrifice or give up one's life.
授受 To give and to receive.
授粉(植) Pollination.
授與 Give to.
授精(生) Fertilization.
授課 Teach; instruct; give lessons to.
授錢 Give money.
授職 Confer the rank of.
授權 Authorization.

掉 diðo (v.)- Move; fall; slip off. Change. Shake.
掉色 Lose colour; fade.
掉尾 Wag the tail.
掉換 Exchange.
掉頭 Return back; turn the head.

掌 zhǒng (n.)- Palm; sole. (v.)- Grasp. Manage; superintend; control.
掌故 Records of past events; historical and mythological episodes.
掌舵 A steersman; helmsman.
掌握 Have in the grasp; under control.
掌理 Manage; superinted; control.
掌管 Overseeing.
掌櫃 An accountant; a shop owner.
掌上珠 A pearl on the palm—a beloved daughter.
掌聲雷動 Thunders of applause; a storm of cheers (applause).

排 pái (n.)- A line; a row. A rank. (v.)- Push open. Arrange; place in order.
排水 Drainage.
排外 Anti-foreign.
排出 Eject; throw up.
排斥 Reject; expel; exclude; discard; renounce; reprobate.
排列 Arrange in order; set in array. (算) Permutation.
排字 Set up type; compose.
排泄 Excretion; discharge.
排長(陸) Lieutenant. Commander of a section.
排除 Reject.
排骨(生) Ribs; meat chops.
排球 Volley ball.
排筏 Rafts.
排隊 Fall in; line up.
排開 Spread out.
排置 Laying out.
排解 Interpose; mediate; intervene.
排擠 Expel; thrust out.
排戲 Arrange or rehearse.
排水口 Drainage outlet.
排水量 Displacement.
排水管 A discharge pipe; a drain pipe.
排字術 Typography.
排字盤 Composing stick.
排字機 Linotype.
排泄物 Discharges; excretions; excre-

ments; excreta.
排氣管 Air pump; exhauster.
排水噸數 Displacement tonnage.
排外思想 Anti-foreign ideas; an anti-foreign spirit.
排成兩行 Arranged in two rows.
排泄作用 Excretory process.
排泄系統(解) Excretory system.
排泄器官(解) Excretory organ.
排除萬難 Overcoming many difficulties; surmounting every obstacle.
排山倒海 To move mountains and drain seas.
排名不分先後 Co-starring.

掘 (v.)- Dig; hollow out; scoop; grub.
jué 掘井 Dig a well.
掘出 Dig out; unearth; excavate.
掘地 Dig the earth.
掘坑 Dig a pit.
掘金 Dig gold.
掘洞 Dig a hole.
掘穿 Dig through.
掘起 Dig up.
掘壕 Entrench.
掘鑿機(工) Digging machine; land dredge.

掙 (v.)- Get free from; make an effort; struggle.
zhèng 掙扎 Struggle hard.
〔zhēng〕 掙脫 Get rid of; get free from; get off.
掙錢 Earn money.

掛 (adj.)- Anxious.
(v.)- Hang up. Think of. Note; record; register.
guà 掛上 Hang up.
掛心；掛念 Feel anxious about; miss. Concern; think of.
掛名 Register one's name. Nominal.
掛冠 Resign office; retire.
掛帥 Be appointed generalissimo; to be the centre forward in a game of football.
掛號 Register.
掛圖 A scroll picture. A wall map.
掛燈 Hang up lanterns.
掛鐘 A wall-clock.
掛招牌 Hang up a signboard.
掛號信 Registered letter.
掛號處；登記處 A registry; a register office.
掛號費 Registration fee.
掛號信件 Registered letter; registered mail matter.

掠 (v.)- Rob; plunder. Graze.
lüè 掠取；掠奪 Rob; plunder; ravage; appropriate.
掠食 Seize food.
掠過 Sweep; go right by one.
掠誘 Kidnap.
掠奪品 Capture; spoil; loot; booty; prey; prize.

採 (v.)- Pick; collect; suck; pluck; gather; select; choose.
cǎi 採用 Adopt; appoint.
採伐 Falling of trees; deforestation; disforestation.
採果 Pluck fruits.
採花 Pluck flowers; gather (pick) flowers.
採納 Take; adopt; accept.
採茶 Gather tea leaves; collect tea leaves.
採訪 Spy out; make inquiries; investigate; inquire about.
採集 Gather; collect; make a collection of.
採蓮 Pick lotus.
採摘 Pluck; pick; gather.
採礦 Mining.

採藥 Gather medical herbs.
採石場 Quarry.
採訪員 A correspondent; a reporter; a newspaper reporter.
採用規則 Regulation of adoption.

**探** (n.)- Detective; spy.
(v.)- Search out; detect; find
tàn out; spy; investigate; examine; explore; test; try. Visit.
探員 Detective; a spy.
探長 Inspector.
探友 Pay a visit to a friend.
探出 Find out.
探求 Seek; search; look for.
探究 Investigate; examine.
探明 Detect; find out by inquiry; spy (smell) out.
探病 Inquire after a patient.
探索 Quest; search.
探討 Inquire about.
探悉 Find out; ascertain.
探望 Pay a visit to.
探問；探訪 Inquire about; have an interview with.
探試 Temptation; try.
探親 Visit one's relatives.
探險 Explore; exploration.
探照燈 A searchlight.
探險家 Adventurers; an explorer.
探險隊 Exploration party; expedition.

**掣** (v.)- Obstruct; embarrass; hinder. Pull.
chè 掣制 Restrain.
掣電 Quick as lightning.
掣動帶 Driving band.

**接** (v.)- Receive; accept. Connect; Associate with. Bound upon;
jiē join; unite.
接引 Guide; conduct.
接手 Take over the duties of another; take charge of.
接任 Take the seals of an office; take up duty.
接生(醫) Midwifery; deliver.
接合 Join; unite.
接收；接管 Receive; take over; re-occupy.
接尾；續尾 Append; attach at the end.
接吻 Kiss.
接見 Receive; allow one an interview.
接到 Receive; come to hand.
接受 Receive; accept; be in receipt of.
接近 Near to; close to; approaching.
接客 Receive guests.
接待 Receive and wait upon a guest; entertain; attend.
接班 Take a turn on duty.
接骨 Bone-setting.
接辦 Take over the management of.
接濟 Support; help; supply.
接觸 Contact; touch.
接力棒 Relay baton.
接棒區 Take-over zone.
接尾語 A suffix.
接班人 Successor.
接待室 A reception room; a drawing-room.
接線者 Operator.
接頭語 A prefix.
接觸面 An osculating plane.
接觸點 A point of contact.
接力賽跑 Relay race.
接觸作用(化) Catalysis; catalytic action.

**控** (v.)- Control; check; hold up; suppress.
kòng 控告 Charge; accuse; impeach.
控制 Control; overrule; rein in.
控訴 Appeal. An appeal to a higher court.
控訴人 Appellant.
控訴期間 The term of appeal.

**推** (v.)- Push; thrust. Give up; refuse; select.
tuī
推回 Push back.
推究 Examine; find out; investigate.
推拒 Push away; reject.
推後 Push backward.
推度；推想 Inference; deduction.
推前 Push forward.
推倒 Overthrow; upset; push down.
推拿 Massage.
推託 Elusion; make excuses.
推動 Push about.
推理 Inference; reasoning.
推銷 Sell; offer for sale.
推測 Conjecture; guess; suppose.
推進 Impulse; impel; propel.
推開 Push open; push away.
推想 Infer; suppose; conjecture.
推敲 Choice of diction; polish.
推算 Calculate; reckon; cast destinies.
推廣 Extend.
推墮 Push down.
推論 Infer; deduce; conclude.
推薦 Recommend.
推選 Elect.
推舉 Recommend.
推斷 Ratiocination; draw a conclusion.
推翻 Push over; overturn; overthrow; knock down.
推辭 Refuse; decline; plead an excuse.
推拉門；滑門 Slide door.
推銷員 A salesman.
推薦書 Letter of recommendation.
推廣商業 Extend trade and commerce.
推陳出新 To discard the old and create something new.
推定遺產承繼人 Expectant heir to property.

**掏** (v.)- Pull out; take out. Clean out.
tāo

**掩** (v.)- Cover; conceal; hide; screen; shade from view; close; shut.
yǎn
掩口 Cover the mouth with the hand.
掩卷 Close a book.
掩面 Hide the face; conceal the face.
掩門 Close or shut a door.
掩埋 Bury; cover up.
掩鼻 Stop the nose.
掩飾 Hide the error; conceal the faults; disguise.
掩蔽；遮掩 Screen; shelter; shade; conceal; cover up.
掩覆 Cover; muffle.
掩護 Protect; shelter; screen; covering.
掩護部隊 Screening force.

**措** (v.)- Put or set in order; arrange. Employ; place.
cuò
措手 Set about.
措施 Give out; publish; work; arrange.
措資 Raise money.
措詞 Wording.
措辦 Arrange; furnish; raise.
措手不及 Not in time with one's hand —as to save something from falling.

**揀** (v.)- Choose; pick out; select.
jiǎn
揀取 Pick out by preference.
揀派 Select and dispatch.
揀貨 Sort goods.
揀擇；揀選 Select; choose; pick out.
揀日子 Choose a day.
揀選錄用 Choose for employment.

**揉** (v.)- Bend; twist; curve. Rub; massage.
róu
揉目 Rub the eyes.
揉搓 Rumple in the hand.
揉碎 Twist and break into pieces.

揩 (v.)- Wipe; clean; brush.
kāi 揩巾 Napkin.
揩面 Wipe the face.
揩淨 Wipe clean.

描 (v.)- Trace; draw; design; outline; paint.
miáo 描字 Copy writing.
描寫 Sketch or copy; describe.
描摹 Copy exactly. Description.
描繪 Delineate; paint.

提 (v.)- Lift; carry; pull up. Mention. Suggest; raise; bring up.
tí 提及 Mention; bring to notice; suggest.
提包 Satchel.
提出 Hold out; put forward; bring up. Bring forward.
提示 Indicate.
提交 Hand over to the custody of.
提名 Nominate.
提究；提審 Bring up for trial.
提防 Guard against; watch against; take care of.
提供 Offer; tender; furnish.
提拔；提升 Raise; promote; lift.
提要 Essentials; outlines; a summary.
提前 Give precedence; give priority.
提倡 Advocate; introduce; bring forward.
提案 Propose; make a proposal; suggest.
提神 Refresh; take care.
提起 Bring forward.
提高 Raise; lift; elevate.
提桶 A bucket.
提單；提貨單 Bill of lading.
提款 Draw money—from a bank.
提琴 A fiddle; a violin.
提箱 A suitcase.
提醒 Remind; suggest; bring to mind.
提籃 A hand-basket.
提議 Propose; bring up a proposal.
提案人 A proposer; a sponsor.
提條件 Bring forward certain conditions.
提琴手 A fiddler; a violinist.
提心吊胆 Timidly; nervously.
提供担保 Offering for security.

插 (v.)- Put between; insert; thrust into; put in or among. Interfere.
chā 插入 Insert; put in; stick in; interpose; interject.
插咀 Interrupt—in speaking; meddle by words.
插手；插身 Have a hand in; meddle officiously.
插曲 Interlude.
插花 Put flower into a vase; arrange flowers.
插秧 Transplant young seedlings.
插旗 Stick in flags; plant a banner.
插圖 An illustration.

揖 (n.)- Folding the arms; a salutation.
yī (v.)- Salute; greet.
揖別 Say good-bye to; bid adieu (farewell) to.

揚 (v.)- Raise; lift; spread; publish abroad; make known; praise.
yáng 揚手 Raise the hand.
揚名 Spread one's name; extend one's fame; become famous.
揚帆 Hoist the sails; spread a sail; sail forward.
揚言 Proclaim; declare; profess.
揚塵 Raise a dust.
揚聲 Raise one's voice.
揚聲器 Loudspeakers.
揚子江(地) The Yangtze River.
揚眉吐氣 Emerge suddenly from a humble station into an honour-

able position.
揚揚得意 Self-satisfied; conceited.

換 (v.)- Change; exchange. Substitute; replace.
huàn 換衣 Change clothes.
換車 Change car.
換姓 Change one's surname.
換約 Ratify a treaty; exchange ratifications.
換班 Relieve guard.
換船 Trans-ship.
換替 By turns; alternately.
換新 Renew; change for new.
換銀；換錢 Change money; money exchange.
換言之 In other word; that is to say.

握 (n.)- A handful.
(v.)- Grasp; hold fast.
wò 握手 Shake hands; a handshake.
握緊 Grasp tightly.
握得政權 Come into power.

揭 (v.)- Lift up; take off; uncover; carry off. Make known; disclose; inform.
jiē 揭示 Post a notice; notify.
揭破 Disclose; lay bare.
揭起 Unglue.
揭開 Lift off the cover; uncover; strip off.
揭露 Uncover (a plot).
揭幕禮 Unveiling ceremony.
揭竿而起 Raise a rebellion.

揮 (v.)- Shake; wave; wag. Scatter; sway. Direct.
huī 揮手 Wave the hand.
揮汗 Wipe off perspiration.
揮拳 Fight with the fist.
揮發(化) Volatilization. Volatilize; evaporate.
揮霍 Spend money freely; profuse; lavish; squander.
揮淚 Wipe away tears.
揮發性 Volatility.
揮發油 Naphtha; volatile oil.
揮金如土 Spend one's money like water.

揪 (v.)- Grasp; pick up; seize.
jiū

援 (v.)- Help by the hand; assist; aid; save.
yuán 援兵；援軍 Reinforcements; relieving force.
援助 Help; assist; aid.
援救 Relieve; rescue; assist.
援助者 A supporter; a patron.

損 (n.)- Injury; ill luck; disadvantage; loss.
sǔn (adj.)- Injurious; harmful.
(v.)- Wound; injure. Spoil; damage; diminish; criticize.
損友 An injurious friend.
損失 Damage; loss.
損害 Injure; damage; loss.
損耗 Loss; damage.
損傷 Injure; harm; damage.
損壞 Damage; impair.
損毀信用 Injure the credit.
損壞貨物 Detrimental goods.

搏 (v.)- Spring upon. Seize. Fight.
搏取 Seize; catch hold of.
bó 搏擊 Strike; attack; fight.

搓 (v.)- Rub or roll between the hands or fingers.
cuō 搓手 Rub the hands together.
搓揉 Crumple up in the hand.

搔 (n.)- The nails.
(v.)- Scratch.
sāo 搔首 Scratch the head.
搔擾 Annoy; trouble.
搔癢 Scratch an itch.

搖 (adj.)- Shaking. Discomposed; agitated.
yáo (v.)- Move; waver; shake; sway.
搖手 Wave the hand; move the hand.
搖尾 Wag the tail.
搖床 A swinging cot; a cradle.
搖頭 Shake the head.
搖動 Shake; move; sway to and fro.
搖椅 A rocking chair.
搖鈴 Ring a bell.
搖擺 Walk with a conceited strut; swaggering; swaying to and fro.
搖櫓 Row the oar.
搖籃 A cradle.
搖搖欲墜 Shaking as if about to fall.
搖搖擺擺 Swaggering; proud bearing.

搗 (v.)- Beat; pound; hull. Attack.
搗米 Hull rice in a mortar.
dǎo 搗鬼 Play tricks.
搗亂 Throw into confusion; disturb.
搗毀 Smash; destroy.
搗亂分子 Agitators.

搜 (v.)- Search; inquire; examine.
搜出 Find out; discover.
sōu 搜查；搜索 Search; look for; seek.
搜票 A search warrant.
搜尋 Search; seek for; look for.
搜集 Collect; pile up.
搜檢；搜身 Search the person.
搜查令 A warrant.
搜索隊 A search party.
搜集證據 Collecting evidence.

搥 (v.)- Beat; pommel. Throw at.
chuí 搥石 Throw stones at; cast stones.
搥胸 Beat the breast.
搥鼓 Beat a drum.
搥鐘 Strike a bell.

搪 (v.)- Ward off; keep out.
搪瓷器皿 Enamel ware.
táng

搬 (v.)- Remove; transport.
搬入 Bring in; carry into.
bān 搬出 Take (carry) out.
搬移 Remove to another place; change abode.
搬運 Transport to another place; transfer.
搬運費 Porterage; transfer charge.
搬弄是非 Carry tales; make mischief.

搭 (v.)- Add to; hang. Build. Join. Take a passage, as on a
dā car or a boat.
搭車 Take a train.
搭客 Passengers.
搭乘 Go on board a ship; get on a plane; take a train.
搭配 Match.
搭載 Load; take in.
搭橋 Build a bridge.
搭載量 A loading (carrying) capacity.

搯 Same as 掏.
(v.)- Take out; pull out; clean
tāo out.
搯井 Clean out a well.
搯耳朵 Clean the ears.

搶 (v.)- Rob; plunder; take away by force.
qiǎng 搶先 Struggle to get first.

搶劫；搶奪 Rob; plunder.
搶匪 A robber.

搽 (v.)- Smear; paint on.
chá
搽粉 Powder the face.
搽藥 Spread a plaster; apply medicine.
搽脂抹粉 Powder and paint.

摔 (v.)- Throw; dash down. Cast at.
shuāi
摔交 Wrestle.
摔角 Wrestling.
摔倒 Thrown over; turns over.
摔角家 Wrestler.

摘 (v.)- Pick; pluck; take off; point out; select.
zhāi
摘果 Pick fruit.
摘取 Pick; nip off; pluck off.
摘要 An extract; an outline; an epitome. Summarize.
摘茶 Pick tea.
摘記 Summarize; sum up.
摘錄 Sum up; make an extract. A summary.

摟 (v.)- Drag or pull; embrace; hug.
lǒu
摟住 Hold fast in the arms.
摟抱 Throw the arms around; embrace; hug.

摧 (v.)- Destroy; break. Grieve.
cuī
摧辱 Humiliate; bring to disgrace.
摧殘 Despoil; destroy.

摩 (v.)- Feel; rub with the hand; polish.
mó
摩擦 Friction; rubbing. Chafe (rub) against. Be at strife.
摩天樓 A lofty building; a sky-scraper.
摩托車 Motor car; automobile.
摩洛哥（地） Morocco.
摩擦音 A fricative consonant.
摩擦係數 Coefficient of friction.
摩擦極限 Limit of friction.
摩擦發電機 Frictional electric machine.

摸 (v.)- Touch. Feel for; grope.
mō
摸索 Feel for; seek for; look for.
摸脈 Feel the pulse.
摸索而行 Grope one's way.

摹 (n.)- A pattern; a form; a copy.
mó
(v.)- Follow a pattern; imitate.
摹本 A facsimile; a copy from a tracing.
摹仿 Copy a pattern; imitate.
摹造 Imitate.

摺 (n.)- A paper folded up; a fold.
zhé
(v.)- Fold up; bend.
摺尺 A folding scale.
摺扇 A folding fan.
摺紙 Fold paper.
摺椅 A joint stool.
摺疊 Fold up.

撇 Same as 擎.
piē
(v.)- Reject; put away; brush away.
撇下 Desert; abandon; leave behind.
撇油 Skim off fat.
撇脫 Cast aside.
撇開 Cast off; set aside; put away; pay no attention to; forget.

撈 (v.)- Dredge for; drag out of the water.
lāo
撈泥 Dredge mud.

撈起 Drag or pull out of water; raise up by grappling.
撈魚 Scoop out fish.

**撐** Same as 撑.
(n.)- A leaning post; a prop.
chēng (v.)- Support; fill. Row; scull.
撐持 Support; prop up.
撐船 Pole or scull a boat; punting.
撐篙 Pole a boat.
撐竿跳 Pole vault.

**撒** (v.)- Scatter; disperse; set loose.
sā 撒手 Let go the hand; lose control of.
〔sǎ〕 撒布 Scatter; spread.
撒開 Spread out; scatter about.
撒種 Sow seeds.
撒網 Cast a net.
撒謊 Tell a lie.
撒哈拉沙漠(地) Sahara Desert.

**撓** (v.)- Vex; disturb; twist; bend; distort.
náo 撓敗 Beaten; defeated.
撓亂；撓擾 Throw into confusion.

**撕** (v.)- Tear; cut asunder; rend.
sī 撕破 Tear up.
撕票 Tear up the ticket. Kill one who is held for ransom by brigands.
撕開 Rip open; torn.
撕碎 Tear to pieces.

**擎** (v.)- Lift up.
qíng

**撞** (v.)- Strike; meet; collide.
撞見 Meet by chance.
zhuàng 撞倒 Knock down; upset.
撞着；相撞 Collide with; come into collision.
撞騙 Embezzle; swindle.
撞鐘 Strike a bell.
撞球戲；打彈子 Billiards.

**撤** (v.)- Remove; send away; reject; withdraw.
chè 撤回 Withdraw; retract; repeal; relinquish.
撤兵 Withdrawal of troops; evacuation.
撤退 Evacuate; withdraw.
撤廢 Abolish; remove; do away with; lift the ban.
撤銷 Cancel.
撤職 Fire; sack; dismiss.

**撥** (v.)- Get rid of; transfer. Distribute.
bō 撥正 Correct; revise.
撥交；撥給 Hand over to; appropriate to.
撥款 Appropriate a fund.
撥轉 Alter for the better; turn round.
撥雲見日 Scatter the clouds and see the sun—dissipate error.

**撫** (v.)- Hold. Quiet; comfort. Play a lute. Cherish; provide for.
fǔ 撫摸 Feel; touch; caress.
撫愛 Love; endear.
撫養；撫育 Bring up; foster; rear; nurture.
撫慰 Soothe; comfort.
撫卹金 A pension.

**播** (v.)- Sow; scatter. Publish; make known.
bō 播音 Broadcast.
播揚 Winnow; publish; spread a report.
播散 Scattered.
播種 Sow seeds.

**撮** (n.)- A handful; a pinch; a little quantity.
cuō (v.)- Take with the fingers; select from; gather up; pinch up a little.
撮合 Bring together; make a match; unite.
撮要 Make extracts; pick out the important points. Essentials; outlines.
撮要貨單 Abstract invoice.

**撰** (v.)- Compose; collect; edit; revise and publish; arrange.
zhuàn 撰文 Write an essay.
撰述 Narrate; record.
撰著者 The author; the writer.

**撲** (v.)- Whip; strike; brush away.
撲克 Poker.
pū 撲滅 Put out; stamp; wipe; exterminate.
撲鼻 Strike the nostrils—as a smell.

**撼** (v.)- Move; excite; stir up.
撼動 Shake; move.
hàn

**撾** (v.)- Beat; knock.
撾門 Knock at the door violently.
zhuā
撾鼓 Beat the drum; drum.

**擁** (v.)- Clasp; hug; crowd.
擁抱 Clasp; embrace; hug.
yōng 擁腫 Gnarled (said of a tree). Inflated; swollen.
擁擠 Crowd; jostle.
擁有 Possess.
擁護 Protect; defend; support; stand by; safeguard.
擁護者 A protector; a defender.
擁上前 To surge forward.

**擂** (v.)- Drum. Pound.
擂台 The platform for contest
léi in boxing.
擂鼓 Beat a drum.

**擄** (v.)- Capture prisoners. Plunder; seize.
lǔ 擄掠 Plunder; carry off.

**擅** (adj.)- Wilful; despotic; arbitrary.
shàn (v.)- Assume; presume.
擅自 Arbitrarily.
擅用 Use without permission; use on one's own account.
擅取 Take without permission.
擅長 Versed in; expert in; skilled in.
擅進 Enter without permission.

**擇** (v.)- Select; choose; pick out; prefer.
zé 擇尤 Select the best.
擇選；擇取 Choose; cull; pick out.

**擊** (v.)- Strike; knock; attack; rush against; kill.
jī 擊打 Beat; strike; attack.
擊沉 Sink; torpedo; send to the bottom.
擊破 Defeat; crush; blow up.
擊殺；擊斃 Kill; beat one to death; strike one to death.
擊退 Repulse; repel; drive back.
擊敗 Beat; defeat.
擊掌 Strike with the hand; clap the hands.
擊滅 Exterminate; destroy; annihilate.
擊落 Shoot (bring) down; strike (knock) down.
擊鼓 Strike a drum.
擊劍 Sword fight. Fencing.
擊劍者 A sword player; a gladiator;

a fencer.

**擋** Same as 攩.
(v.)- Defend. Impede; obstruct.
dǎng 擋住 Prevent.
擋風 Keep off the wind.
擋眼 Obstruct one's view.
擋路 Obstruct the road.
擋頭陣 The vanguard.
擋風玻璃 Windshield; windscreen.

**操** (v.)- Take in hand; keep; maintain; hold of. Manage.
cāo Drill.
操心 Anxious; concerned.
操行 Conduct; behaviour; deportment.
操兵 Drill troops.
操作 Do manual labour; work.
操場 A place of military exercise; parade ground; play ground.
操勞 Painstaking; toiling.
操練 Drill; exercise.
操縱 Control the action of; manage; operate.
操行分數 The conduct mark.
操勞過度 Overwork.

**擒** Same as 捦.
(v.)- Capture; take prisoner;
qín arrest; apprehend. Catch; hold of.
擒賊 Capture a thief or a rebel.
擒獲 Arrest; seize; catch; take.
擒賊擒王 In capturing rebels, first take the leader–pay heed to what is important.

**擔** Same as 担.
(n.)- A burden; a load. A picul.
dān (v.)- Carry on the shoulder.
(dàn) Bear; undertake.
擔子 A load; a burden.
擔心 Be anxious.
擔任 Undertake; take charge; take responsibility.
擔保 A guarantee; a security; a bail.
擔架 A stretcher; a litter.
擔負 Take responsibility.
擔當 Bear; assume responsibility.
擔憂 Bear sorrow; be grieved.
擔擱 Delay.
擔保人 Warranter; guarantor; surety.
擔保信 Letter of guarantee.
擔架兵 A stretcher-bearer.
擔心害怕 Anxious and alarmed.

**據** (n.)- Proof; evidence; witness.
(v.)- Occupy; maintain. Depend
jù on; rely on; base upon.
(prep.)- According to; in accordance with.
據此 In view of these facts.
據點 A stronghold.
據守 Guard; occupy; take forcible possession of.
據有 In possession of.
據說 It is said that . . . ; people say.
據實 Reply on facts; according to the facts.

**擠** (v.)- Crowd. Press upon. Push against; squeeze.
jǐ 擠出 Screw out; elbow out.
擠乳 Milk.
擠進 Make one's way by force; press in.
擠滿 Overcrowded.
擠提(存款) To run on a bank.
擠擁 Crowdy.

**擡** Same as 抬.
(v.)- Elevate; lift; praise; com-
tái mend.
擡扛 Carry on a pole.
擡價 Raise the price of.
擡頭 Raise one's head.
擡舉 Raise; promote; recommend.

擡高身價 Put a high value upon oneself.

擦 (n.)- A brush.
(v.)- Rub; brush; wipe; clean; erase.
cā
擦去 Wipe out; erase; rub off (out).
擦油 Varnish; oil; grease.
擦亮 Polish; rub bright.
擦淨 Rub clean.
擦乾 Wipe dry.
擦傷 An abrasion. Graze the skin.
擦鞋 Polish shoes; shoe shine.
擦牙 Brush the teeth.
擦牙粉 Tooth-powder.
擦地板 To scrub the floor.
擦鞋油 Shoe-polish.
擦字橡皮 Eraser.

擬 Same as 拟.
(adj.)- Like; similar to.
nǐ
(v.)- Estimate; consider; compare; guess; assume.
擬人 Personification.
擬定 Fix; determine; decide.
擬律(法) Draft law.
擬稿 Make a draft.
擬議 Decide after deliberation.

擱 (v.)- Lay by; put down. Hinder; delay; place on; obstruct; lay off.
gē
擱下 Put down; put aside.
擱住 Hold up; delay.
擱淺 Go ashore; run aground.
擱開 Put aside.
擱置 Put off; put away.
擱筆 Put down the pen; stop writing.

擰 (v.)- Twist; pull about.
擰干(乾) Spin dry; wring dry.
níng

擲 (v.)- Throw; cast; fling away; reject; Jump.
zhī
擲下 Throw down.
擲去；擲棄 Fling (throw) away; throw off; give up.
擲骰子；耍骰子 Play with dice.
擲鐵球 Put the shot.
擲鐵餅 Discus throw.

擴 (v.)- Expand; enlarge; extend; spread out; widen.
kuò
擴大 Magnification; magnify; enlarge; aggrandize.
擴充 Amplify; expand; extend; enlarge.
擴張 Extend; dilate; expand; develop.
擴音筒 A loud-speaker; a megaphone.
擴音機 A microphone.
擴眼界 Increase one's experience; enlarge the vision.
擴張營業 Expansion of business.
擴大戰爭 To extend a war.

擺 (n.)- A pendulum.
(v.)- Spread out; display; expose; place; exhibit. Arrange. Shake.
bǎi
擺手 Wave the hand.
擺布 Place; arrange in order. Do one some injury.
擺列 Array; exhibit; display.
擺弄 Play or meddle with.
擺脫 Get rid of; break away.
擺渡 Ferry across. A ferry.
擺動 Swing; oscillate.
擺設 Exhibit; decorate.
擺開 Spread out.
擺齊 Arrange evenly; place in order.
擺檯；鋪檯 Spread a table.
擺攤 Display on a stall.
擺架子 Make a great show; stand upon one's dignity.
擺酒席 Give a feast.
擺動器 Oscillator.

**擾** rǎo (v.)- Trouble; disturb; confuse; annoy.
擾亂 Disorder; disturbance; confusion.
擾亂人心 Agitation.
擾亂治安 Disturb the public peace.

**攀** pān (v.)- Grasp; drag. Climb up; creep up; clamber.
攀登 Climb; clamber; scramble up.
攀親 Engage; get into relationship.
攀緣植物(植) Climbing plants; clambers.

**攏** lǒng (v.)- Collect; assemble; gather. Draw near to; close up.
攏近 Draw near to.
攏總 All; the sum total.

**攔** lán (v.)- Stop; prevent; hinder; embarrass; obstruct; debar.
攔阻 Stop; obstruct; hinder; hedge up.
攔開 Separate; part.
攔路 Block up the road; stand in the way.
攔截 Hinder; cut off.
攔搶 Rob on the way.
攔路賊 Highwayman.

**攘** rǎng (v.)- Steal; snatch; seize. Reject.
攘災 Ward off calamity.
攘除 Reject; expel; cut off.

**攙** chān (v.)- Pierce. Support; sustain. Mix; mingle; blend.
攙扶 Support; uphold; help; assist.
攙假 Adulteration.
攙嘴 Interrupt in speaking.
攙雜 Mix up; blend.

**攜** xié (v.)- Carry; bring; take along. Lead by the hand. Connect.
攜手 Hand in hand; take by the hand.
攜去 Take away.
攜物 Carry things.
攜眷 Carry family along.
攜帶 Take along; bear; take.

**攝** shè (v.)- Control. Substitute; assist. Lift up; hold up; take.
攝石 The loadstone.
攝政 The regency.
攝取 Take; absorb.
攝影 Photograph; take a picture.
攝鐵 Magnet.
攝影者 A photographer.
攝影室 A studio.
攝影學 Photography.
攝影機 A camera.
攝影技師 A cameraman; a film-operator.
攝氏寒暑表 A Celsius (centigrade) thermometer.

**攢** zǎn (v.)- Collect; bring together.
攢聚 Collect together; assemble.

**攤** tān (n.)- A stall; a booth.
(v.)- Spread out; display. Divide equally; apportion; share.
攤分 Divide up share.
攤位 A street stall.
攤開 Open out; spread out. Unfold.
攤還 Amortization.

**攪** jiǎo (v.)- Stir up; disturb; annoy; confuse; excite; trouble.
攪勻 Mix evenly.
攪拌 Beat up; stir.
攪亂 Confuse; throw into disorder; disturb.

攪擾 Make trouble; create disturbance.
攪拌機 A blender.

攫 (v.)- Seize; grasp; snatch; catch; take hold of.
jué 攫取 Seize and carry off; snatch; take by force.
攫捕 Catch hold of; seize.
攫奪 Seize; snatch.

攬 (v.)- Grasp; hug; clutch.
lǎn 攬取 Seize up; grasp.
攬權 Grasp at authority; get the ascendancy; hold of power.

# 支 部

支 (n.)- A branch; descendants; tributary; posterity.
zhī (adj.)- Divergent; branched.
(v.)- Prop; support; assist; succour; hold up. Branch; seperate. Pay; draw out; receive in advance.
支付 Payment.
支出 Expenditure; disbursement. Pay; expend; disburse.
支吾 Confused and indistinct.
支局 A branch office.
支店 A branch store; an agency.
支取 Draw out.
支持 Hold up; bear up; support; maintain; carry through; sustain.
支柱 Support; brace.
支派 Branches; descendants; tribe; sect.
支借 Lend; receive in advance.
支流 A tributary; an affluent; a feeder stream.
支部 A branch; a subdivision.
支配 Assortment; allotment; disposition. Control; manage; govern; direct.
支票 Check; cheque.
支款 Draw out money.
支管 Branch pipe.
支撐 Hold up; prop.
支線 A branch line.
支錢 Draw money.
支配權 Control; management; supremacy.
支付日期 The due date.
支付滙款 Drafts payable.
支配階級 The ruling (governing) class.
支付代理人 Pay agent.

# 攴 部

收 (v.)- Receive; collect; gather; take in. Close; conclude. Harvest; reap. Arrest.
shōu 收入 Receipt; income.
收工 Stop work.
收口 (醫) A closure of a wound.
收支 Income and expenditure; revenue and expenditure.
收回 Receive again; get back; retrieve.
收成；收割；收穫 Harvest; reap; crop.
收兵 Withdraw (recall) troops.
收捐 Collect contributions.

收取 Collect.
收拾 Make ready; put in order; repair.
收容 Give shelter; harbour.
收效 Have result; reap; bear fruit.
收租 Collects rents.
收益 Profit; gains; proceeds.
收訖 Payment received.
收條 A receipt; acquittance.
收帳 Collect accounts.
收集 Gather; collect; call; bring together.
收稅 Collect taxes.
收場 Conclude; come to an end.
收禁；收監 Keep in confinement. Imprison; put in jail.
收賄 Take (accept) a bribe.
收管 Take charge.
收養 Adoption.
收斂 Gather in the harvest. Contraction; astringency.
收殮 Put in a coffin.
收縮 Shrink; contract.
收藏 Keep; store up.
收音機 Radio.
收容所 Asylum.
收帳人 Collector.
收稅員 A tax-collector (-gatherer); a revenue-officer.
收稅單 A duty-paid certificate.
收縮性 Contractibility.
收穫者 Reaper.
收藏家 A collector; a curio hunter.
收回紙幣 Call in bank notes.
收到日期 Date of receipt.
收拾行李 Pack up baggage.
收歸國有 Nationalization of property.

**攸** yōu (adj.)- Distant; far. Pleasant. (v.)- Start suddenly; find a home.
攸久 A long time.
攸然 Pleasantly.
攸遠 Far; distant.

**改** gǎi (v.)- Change; alter. Reform; correct.
改正 Set right; correct; amend.
改行 Change to another trade; take up another calling; change profession.
改良 Improve; make better; reform; mend.
改制 Change the system.
改建 Rebuilding; reconstruction.
改訂 Revise.
改革 Reformation; renovation.
改悔 Repent of; be penitent.
改組 Re-organize; re-shuffle.
改造 Rebuild; reconstruct; alter; reorganize.
改換 Change; put another in place of; exchange.
改期 Alter the date; postpone.
改嫁 Marry a second husband.
改善 Improve; better; amend; ameliorate.
改進 Progress; advance.
改裝 Disguise; change the style of dress.
改過 Mend or correct errors; reform.
改編 Reorganization; revision.
改選 Reelection. Elect anew; reelect.
改變 Alter; change.
改良社會 Reformation of society.
改良風俗 Reform manners and customs.
改良舊習 Reform a usage.
改過自新 Turn over a new leaf; become a new man.
改變態度 Change one's attitude.

**攻** gōng (v.)- Attack. Work at.
攻入 Incursion.
攻打 Fight; engage in battle; attack; fight against.
攻守 Offensive and defensive.
攻克 Overcome; conquer.

攻取 Capture a place; occupy by attack.
攻破 Carry by assault; break down.
攻書；攻讀 Study hard; study.
攻勢 Offensive.
攻擊 Attack; assault; fall upon; pitch into.
攻擊戰 An offensive war.

放 fàng (v.)- Set free; liberate; let off; let go. Put; settle; lay down. Scatter.
放下 Lay down; put down.
放大 Enlarge; magnify.
放工 Quit work; release from work.
放心 Make mind easy; ease oneself.
放手 Let go one's hand; loose one's hold.
放火 Set fire; commit arson.
放任 Laissez-faire. Do not interfere.
放免；釋放 Release; acquit; set free (at liberty).
放走 Let a culprit escape; release; let go.
放長 Prolong.
放牧 Pasture; graze; put (turn out) to grass.
放砲 Fire a cannon.
放射 Emission; radiation.
放假 Give a holiday; on holiday.
放晴 Clear up.
放寬；放鬆 Widen; loosen.
放棄 Abandon; renounce; give up; discard; desert.
放肆 Be disorderly and rude.
放哨 Post on sentry; stand guard.
放電(物) A discharge of electricity.
放債 Make loans to others; lend money on interest.
放槍 Fire; shoot.
放箭 Shoot an arrow.
放蕩；放浪 Wild; extravagant; set adrift; luxurious.
放學 Break up school; close the school.
放縱 Self-indulgence; licentious.
放聲 Give forth his voice; in a loud voice.
放鬆 Relax; loosen.
放大器 An amplifier.
放大鏡 Magnifying glass.
放火犯 An incendiary; an arsonist.
放風箏 Fly kites.
放射性 Radioactivity.
放學後 After school is over; after school hours.
放爆竹 Fire crackers.
放浪生活 A wandering (vagrant) life.

故 gù (n.)- Reason; cause.
(adj.)- Ancient; old; late; deceased.
(v.)- Die; pass away.
(adv.)- Formerly. Purposely. For this reason.
(conj.)- Therefore; for; because; so that; according to; as a consequence.
故人 Old friends.
故此 On this account; therefore.
故事 A story; a tale; a legend; a novel.
故意 Intentionally; on purpose.
故鄉 Native village; native place; motherland.
故障 A hindrance; an obstacle; a trouble.

政 zhèng (n.)- Government; administration laws; policy.
(v.)- Rule; regulate.
政局 Political situation.
政事 Politics; government affairs.
政府 The government.
政法 Politics and legislature.
政治 Politics.
政制 Government system.
政客 Politicians.

政界 The political world; political circles.
政務 Government business; political affairs.
政策 Policy; method of administration.
政論 Politics; political argument.
政黨 A political party.
政權 Political power; a regime.
政體 The system of government; a form of government.
政變 A change of government. A coup d'etat.
政治犯 A political offender; political prisoner.
政治局 The Politburo.
政治家 A politician; a statesman.
政治學 Political science.
政局危機 A political crisis.
政府公報 The Government Gazette.
政府當局 The government authorities.
政府機關 Government organ.
政治思想 Political ideas.
政治問題 A political question (issue).
政治運動 A political movement (campaign).
政治領袖 A political leader.
政治學家 A political scientist.
政治鬥爭 Political struggle.

效 (n.)- Effects; results; efficacy; efficiency; consequence.
xiào (adj.)- Efficacious; effective; effectual.
(v.)- Imitate; pattern after; copy. Serve; fulfil.
效力 Efficacy; validity. Render service.
效用 Utility; potency.
效忠 Loyal.
效法 Follow ancient examples; pattern after; follow in the step; imitate.
效果 Results; effects. Outcome.
效能 Potential.
效率 Efficiency.

敍 (v.)- Arrange in order. Converse; narrate. Chat.
xù 敍事 Narration; statement.
敍述 State; narrate.
敍談 Chat; converse.
敍舊 Talk over old times.
敍利亞(地) Syria.
敍事文 A description; a narrative.
敍事詩 A narrative (descriptive) poem; an epic poem.

敎 (n.)- An instruction; a doctrine; a precept. A religion.
jiào (v.)- Instruct; teach. Order; command.
敎士 A clergyman; preachers; pastors; priest.
敎父 A godfather.
敎友 Church members; fellow converts.
敎母 A godmother.
敎主 The founder of a religion.
敎材 Teaching stuff; materials for teaching.
敎育 Education; teaching; instruction; learning; culture.
敎室 Classroom.
敎派 Sect; denomination.
敎皇 Pope.
敎科 Course of instruction. Subjects.
敎徒 A believer; an adherent; church members.
敎員；敎習 An instructor; a teacher.
敎師 A pastor. A teacher; an instructor.
敎訓 Instructions; precepts; a lesson. Teach; instruct.
敎區 Parish.
敎理 A doctrine; a tenet.
敎堂 A chapel; a church; a cathedral.
敎授 The director of studies in a department; a professor.
敎會 An ecclesia; a church.
敎練 Drill; train; trainer; coach.
敎養 Educate and support; bring up.

敎壇 The platform; the pulpit.
敎導 Educate; teach; guide.
敎育局 Department of education.
敎育界 Educational circles.
敎育家 An educationalist.
敎育部 Ministry of Education.
敎科書 Textbooks.
敎務處 The instruction department.
敎育事業 Educational work.
敎育制度 System of education.
敎育部長 Minister of Education.
敎會學校 Missionary schools.
敎條主義 Doctrinairism.

敏 (adj.)- Active; prompt; clever. Quick; sharp; skilled in.
mǐn 敏捷 Quick motion; vigorous; active; agile.
敏感 Sensitiveness; susceptibility.
敏慧 Intelligent; sagacious.
敏銳 Acute.

救 (n.)- Deliverance; assistance.
(v.)- Save; relieve; assist; cure.
jiù 救火 Put out a fire.
救出 Help one out of; rescue.
救命 Save life. Help! help!
救星 A deliverer; a star of salvation.
救活 Save alive.
救國 Save the country.
救濟 Deliver the poor; relieve with money and food.
救護 Save and protect.
救火隊 Salvage corps. Fire brigade.
救火車 Fire engine.
救世主 The Saviour; the Redeemer; the Messiah.
救生帶 A life belt; a safety-belt.
救生圈 A life buoy.
救生船 A life-boat.
救生網 A safty-net; a life-saving net; a tramcar fender.
救助費 Salvage expenses.
救傷車 Ambulance.
救濟金 A relief fund; relief-money.
救濟會 A relief society.
救濟事業 Relief work; poor-relief work.

敦 (adj.)- Honest; sincere.
敦厚 Sincere and generous.
dūn

敗 (n.)- A defeat; a loss.
(adj.)- Fallen; spoiled.
bài (v.)- Defeat; destroy; spoil; ruin; rout; vanquish.
敗兵；殘兵 Defeated troops.
敗軍 A defeated (routed) army.
敗退 Defeat; retreat; lose the field.
敗將 Defeated general.
敗壞 Spoil; corrupt; destroy.
敗類 Bad characters; a bad class; scoundrels.
敗血病 Blood (septic) poisoning; septicaemia.
敗家子 A prodigal; a black sheep; a spend thrift.

敝 (adj.)- Bad; poor; unworthy.
bì

敞 (adj.)- Open; spacious.
chǎng

敢 (adj.)- Bold; daring.
(v.)- Dare; venture on.
gǎn 敢言 Speak boldly.
敢爲 Dare to do; bell the cat.
敢死隊 Dare-to-die corps; a suicide squad; a forlorn hope.
敢作敢爲 Not afraid to do; afraid of nothing; daring.
敢怒不敢言 Daring to be angry, but

not daring to show it in speech.
敢於鬥爭，敢於勝利 To be bold; to struggle and seize victory.

散 (n.)- A medicinal powder.
(adj.)- Separated; miscellaneous.
sàn (v.)- Scatter; break up; disperse. Distribute.
散工 Odd jobs; day labourers.
散文 Prose.
散布 Intersperse; scatter; spread.
散光 Diffused light.
散沙 Scattered sand.
散步 Take a walk; jaunt; promenade.
散場 Separate—as an audience.
散開 Spread; scatter; disperse.
散亂 Be despersed; be scattered about.
散會 Dismiss a meeting; close a conference.
散漫 Want of organization; orderless; diffuseness.
散播 Strew; broadcast; give currency to.
散熱 Refrigeration; disperse heat.
散課 Dismiss a class.
散髮 Dishevelled hair.
散文詩 A prose poem.
散光鏡 A diverging lens.
散熱器 Radiator.
散播傳單 Distribute handbills.

敬 (n.)- A present.
(adj.)- Honourable; reverent;
jìng respectful.
(v.)- Respect; honour.
敬老 Venerate the aged.
敬畏 In reverential fear of; awe.
敬愛 Venerate; reverence and love.
敬意 Respect; reverence; homage. Pay one's respect to; in honour of.
敬酒 Toast.
敬稱 A title of honour; an honorific.
敬慕 Admire; adore; revere.
敬請 Invite.
敬語 A term of respect; an honorific.
敬禮 Salute; pay respect to. Salutation; a bow; a salute.
敬啓者 I have the honour to inform you.

敲 (v.)- Pound; strike; knock; rap on.
qiāo 敲打 Beat; hammer at.
敲門 Knock at the door; rap; tap.
敲詐 Extort; blackmail.
敲鼓 Drum; beat a drum.
敲鐘 Strike a bell; knoll.
敲鑼 Beat the gong.
敲竹槓 Work a racket on. Blackmail.
敲擊樂器 Percussion instrument.

敵 (n.)- Enemy; opponent; antagonist; rival.
dí (v.)- Fight; match; withstand; oppose.
敵人 An enemy; a foe.
敵手 An opponent; a rival; a match.
敵兵；敵軍 The enemy's troops.
敵性 Enemy character.
敵視 Be hostile to; regard with hostility; show enmity towards.
敵對 Opposition; defiance.
敵機 An enemy aeroplane; a hostile plane.
敵營 The enemy's camp.
敵艦 The enemy's ship; the hostile fleet.

數 (n.)- A number; an account. A lot. Fate; destiny.
shù (adj.)- Several; few; some.
〔shǔ〕 (v.)- Count; reckon; number; calculate.
(adv.)- Often; frequently.
數日 Several days in succession.

數目 The amount; number; accounts.
數年 Several years.
數次 Several times.
數字 A figure; a numeral.
數百 Hundreds.
數倍 Several times more.
數量 Quantity; volume.
數學 Mathematics.
數錢 Count coin or cash.
數不清 Cannot be reckoned; cannot count them clearly.
數日來 For the last (past) few days.
數目字 Numerals; numeral characters.
數學表 Mathematical tables.
數學家 A mathematician.

整 zhěng (adj.)- Uniform; orderly. Whole. (v.)- Place evenly; set in order; regulate. Prepare; make ready. Repair.

整年 The whole year.
整夜 The whole night.
整理 Regulate; adjust; put in order.
整隊 Stand in row; form a line; line up.
整頓 Adjust or arrange; regulate.
整齊 In good order; well-regulated.
整數 An integer; an integral number.
整容術 Plastic surgery.
整流器(電) Rectifier.
整整齊齊 Regular; in good order; tidy.
整套設備 Complete set of equipment.

斂 liǎn (v.)- Collect. Concentrate. Shrink.

斃 bì (v.)- Die a violent death; kill. 斃命 Die; fall (drop) dead; perish.

# 文 部

文 wén (n.)- The written language; literature; a dispatch; a composition.
(adj.)- Elegant; refined; gentle; scholarly; classical. Civil.

文人 The literati; a man of letters.
文才 Literary talents; literary genius.
文化 Civilization; culture.
文件；文卷 Documents; papers; dispatches; letters.
文字 Written characters; writings.
文具 Stationery.
文官 A civil official.
文明 Civilization.
文物 Historical relics.
文法 Grammar; rules of composition.
文盲 Illiterate; ignorant.
文科 Arts course in college; department of literature; a literary course (department).
文庫 A collection of works; a library; a series.
文書 Official dispatches. A document. Correspondence.
文案；秘書 A secretary; a clerk.
文章 An essay; a literary composition.
文雅 Gentle; graceful; well-bred; elegant; gentleman-like.
文筆 Letters; the literary art.
文意 The meaning of a passage; the purport of a letter.
文豪 A great (master) writer; a literary giant (star).
文稿 A manuscript.

文典 Classics; grammar book.
文學 Literature.
文憑 Diploma; certificate.
文選 Anthology; selection of literary readings.
文藝 Literature; literary arts.
文獻 Literature on a subject; records.
文體 Style.
文具商 A stationer.
文學史 A history of literature.
文學家 A man of letters; a literary man; a literate.
文學院 The college of literature.
文化生活 A cultural (civilized) life.
文化運動 A cultural movement (campaign).
文化革命 Cultural revolution.
文化交流 Cultural exchange.
文化遺產 Cultural heritage.
文學藝術 Literature and art.
文字改革 Reform of Chinese characters.
文武全材 A man endowed with civil and military virtues.
文科大學 College of literature.
文學博士 Doctor of Literature (D.Lit).
文藝批評 Literary criticism.
文藝復興 Renaissance; the Revival of Learning.

斑 (n.)- Spots; mottles; speckles. (adj.)- Variegated; streaked; mottled.
bān
斑文 Mottled; streaked.
斑馬 Zebra or Mountain zebra.
斑鳩 The turtle dove.
斑點 A spot; a speck.
斑白者 A gray-headed old man.

# 斗 部

斗 (n.)- A measure of ten 升 or pints; a peck. A wine cup.
dǒu
斗篷 A blouse; mantle; cloak.
〔dǒu〕
斗笠 A wide rain hat.
斗胆 Great courage; audacity.

料 (n.)- Materials. Provender; grain. Glass.
liào
(v.)- Estimate; calculate; suppose; guess. Manage.
料理 Manage; arrange; put in order.
料想 Imagine; guess; consider.
料器 Glassware; imitation jade.

斜 (adj.)- Slanting; inclined; oblique; sidelong. Irregular.
xié
斜坡 A steep slope.
斜度 Gradient.
斜面 Inclined or oblique plane; a slanting surface.
斜紋 Transverse streaks.
斜路 Oblique ways.
斜陽 A setting sun; slanting sunbeams.
斜線 An oblique line.
斜邊 The hypotenuse.
斜紋布 Jean.
斜體字 Italics.

斟 (v.)- Pour out. Add to.
zhēn
斟酒 Pour wine.
斟酌 Consult about; discuss.
斟茶 Pour tea.

斡 (v.)- Revolve.
wò
斡旋 Arrange matters for; mediate.

# 斤 部

斤 jīn (n.)- A catty = 0.596816 kilogramme=1⅓ pound.
(adj.)- Minute.
斤斤 Minute.

斤兩 Catties and ounces; weight.

斤斤計較 Look after small trifling amounts.

斥 chì (v.)- Exclude. Blame; reprove. Point out.
斥候 Patrol; scout.
斥退 Dismiss; send away.

斥責 Reprove; reprimand; blame.

斧 fǔ (n.)- A hatchet; an axe.
(v.)- Split with a hatchet. Fell trees.
斧手 Axe man.

斧斤 A hatchet; an axe.

斧石(礦) Axinite.

斬 zhǎn (v.)- Kill; behead; slay.
斬首 Behead; execute; decapitate. Execution.
斬殺 Slay; put to the sword; kill.

斬草 Eradicate weeds.

斬新 Perfectly new and fresh; novel.

斬碎 Mince; cut fine.

斬草除根 Cut off the source of an evil.

斬釘截鐵 Determined; resolute; fixed.

斯 sī (v.)- Split with an axe; lop.
(adj.)- This; these; such.
斯文 Gentlemanly; scholarly; polished; elegant.

斯大林 Stalin.

斯巴達(地) Sparta.

斯文敗類 Polished scoundrels or rascals.

斯得哥爾摩(地) Stockholm.

斯干的納維亞半島(地) Scandinavian Peninsula.

新 xīn (adj.)- New; fresh; modern; recent.
(v.)- Renew; renovate; improve.
(adv.)- Newly; anew.

新人 A bride or bridegroom.

新手 A new (fresh) hand; a greenhorn inexperienced.

新任 Newly-appointed. A new incumbent.

新式 A new style; the latest fashion; new pattern; new shape; novelty.

新年 The new year.

新奇 Novelty.

新居 A new house; a new building.

新版 A new edition (publication).

新到 Newly arrived.

新近 Recently; of late.

新春 Early spring; new year.

新娘 Bride.

新書 New publication; new book.

新郎 Bridegroom.

新聞 News; intelligence.

新曆 The new (solar) calender.

新鮮 Fresh; new.

新舊 Old and new.

新疆(地) Sinkiang.

新大陸 The new world.

新月形 Crescent-shaped.

新世界 The New World.

新生代(地質) The Cainozoic (Caeno-

zoic) era.
新生活 A new life.
新加坡(地) Singapore.
新西蘭(地) New Zealand.
新局面 A new phase.
新政府 A new government.
新政策 New policy.
新紀元 A new era.
新紀錄 A new record.
新時代 A new age (era).
新發明 A new invention.
新聞紙 Newspaper.
新聞學 Journalism.
新聞界 The press.
新華社 Hsinhwa News Agency.
新德里(地) New Delhi.
新學期 New term.
新書目錄 A list of new publications.
新婚夫婦 A newly-married couple.
新婚旅行 A wedding trip; a honeymoon trip.
新陳代謝 Renewal.
新聞記者 A journalist; a reporter.
新聞記者席 The press-gallery; the reporters' gallery.
新聞通信社 A news-agency.

斷 duàn (v.)- Break off; cut off; sever. Interrupt. Decide.
斷水 Suspension of water-supply.
斷交 Sever friendship; cut off relation.
斷言 Assertion; declaration. Assert; affirm; say (state) positively.
斷乳 Wean.
斷定 Decide; settle; give judgment; conclude; judge; draw a conclusion.
斷面(橫,縱) A (cross, vertical) section.
斷氣 Breathe one's last; expire; yield up the life.
斷根 Cut off the roots.
斷除 Exterminate; get rid of; do away with.
斷崖 A precipice; a cliff; a bluff.
斷絕 Broken off; cut off; stop entirely; discontinue.
斷路 Block up the way.
斷開 Divide apart; break in two.
斷頭台 A guillotine; a scaffold.
斷續的 Intermittently; at intervals; off and on.
斷崖絕壁 A precipitous cliff.
斷然拒絕 Refuse flatly.
斷絕交通 Cut off communication.
斷絕邦交 Severance (rupture) of diplomatic relations.
斷絕關係 Absolve from all consequence.

# 方 部

方 fāng (n.)- A square. A region; a quarter. A direction.
(adj.)- Square; correct; regular.
(adv.)- Just then; now.
方丈 The abbot; a chief priest.
方寸 A square Chinese inch. The heart.
方尺 A square Chinese foot.
方今 The present time; nowadays.
方正 Good; upright; just; righteous.
方向;方位 Directions.
方式 An established form; a formula.
方形 Square.
方言 A dialect; a provincialism.
方法 A device; a method; a procedure;

a way; means.
方子 A prescription.
方便 Convenient; beneficial; good. General advantage.
方面 Square-faced. One side of; a region; a district.
方案 A plan; a scheme; a device.
方哩 A square mile.
方根(算) Square root.
方格 A copy slip.
方針 A policy; the aim; an object in view.
方陣 A square formation.
方凳 A square stool.
方磚 Square tiles for paving.
方檯 A square table.
方纔 A moment ago.
方程式 An equation.
方塊糖 Loaf-sugar; cube sugar.
方向指示器 A direction (traffic) indicator; a trafficator.

於 (prep.)- In; on; at; to; from; through.
yú (conj.)- Than.
於今 At present; now.
於左 As follows; on the left.
於此 Here; in this place.
於是 Then; thereupon; accordingly.
於後 Afterwards; as follows.

施 (v.)- Arrange; do; execute; use.
shī 施工 Construction. Employ labour.
施行 Carry out; carry into effect; put in force; enforce.
施洗 Baptize.
施肥 Fertilization.
施恩 Show kindness; do one a favour.
施救 Give help; save; extend relief.
施手術 Performing an operation.
施行手續 The process of any action; the procedure.

旁 (n.)- The side.
(adj.)- Lateral.
páng (prep.)- Near; by the side of; beside.
旁門 A side-door.
旁晚 Near evening.
旁路 A side-walk.
旁邊 By the side. The side.
旁證 Circumstantial evidence; a linesman in a football match.
旁聽 Attendance. Hear; listen to; attend.
旁觀 Look on by the side. Indifferent.
旁聽席 Seats for the public; the gallery.
旁觀者 An onlooker; a looker-on; a spectator; a bystander.
旁觀態度 Look on with indifference; stand by; remain a spectator.

旅 (n.)- A brigade; forces; a multitude. A company. A stranger.
lǚ A traveller.
(v.)- Travel; sojourn.
旅行 A travel; a trip; a tour; a journey.
旅居 Sojourn at; lodge in; stay temporarily at.
旅長 A brigadier general; a brigade commander.
旅客 A traveller; a passenger.
旅程 A journey; the distance travelled.
旅費 Travelling expenses.
旅大(地) Lüta.
旅館；逆旅 An inn; a hotel; a boarding house.
旅行票 Tourist ticket.
旅行社 A tourist bureau.
旅客船 Passenger steamer.
旅客機 A passenger aeroplane.
旅行支票 Traveller's cheque.
旅行日程 An itinerary.
旅行指南 A guide-book.
旅客列車 Passenger train.
旅行目的地 The destination.

旋 (v.)- Turn round; rotate; revolve. Return; come back.
xuán 旋風 A whirlwind; a cyclone; a hurricane.
旋渦 A whirlpool; an eddy.
旋暈 Giddy; dizzy.
旋盤 A turning lathe.
旋轉 Revolution; rotation. Turn round.
旋律 A melody.
旋螺 Spiral.
旋轉體 A solid of revolution.

旌 (n.)- A banner.
(v.)- Distinguish; illustrate; give
jīng honour to; show; manifest.
旌旗 Flags; banners.
旌旗如林 A forest of banners.

族 (n.)- A family; a tribe; a class; a clan.
zú (v.)- Collect or gather together.
族人 Clansmen; family folks.
族姓 Family name.
族居 Live together.
族長 The head of a clan; senior of a clan.
族譜 Genealogy of a clan; a genealogical table; a family tree.
族誼 Kindred relations.

旗 Same as 旂.
(n.)- A banner; a flag; a standard.
qí 旗手 An ensign; a standard-bearer; a flagman.
旗杆 A flagstaff.
旗號 A signal flag.
旗幟 Flags and streamers; banner; ensign.
旗幟鮮明 Show one's colours; make one's attitude (standpoint); unfurl one's banner.

# 无 部

无 Same as 無.
无妄之災 An unexpected calamity.
wú

既 (adj.)- All. Finished; ended; already; entirely.
jì (v.)- Finish; exhaust; complete.
(adv.)- Already. Entirely.
(conj.)- When. Since.
既久 For a long time.
既而 Afterwards; finally.
既往 Past; by gone.
既然 Since.
既然如此 Since it is so.

# 日 部

日 (n.)- The sun. A day. Daytime.
(adv.)- Daily.
rì 日下 Under the sun.
日工 A day-labourer.
日久 As time goes on; in process of time.

日子 Days; a number of days.
日中 The daytime; midday.
日日 Daily; day by day; day in, day out; day after day.
日出 Sunrise; sun-up.
日本(地) Japan.
日用 Daily expenses; daily necessities.
日刊 Daily publication (issue).
日光 Sunlight; sunbeam.
日來；近日 Recently; lately; in recent days.
日夜 Day and night.
日食；日蝕 The eclipse of the sun; a solar eclipse.
日常 Every day; always.
日校 Day school.
日息；日利 Daily interest; rate per day.
日班 Day shift.
日記 A diary.
日期 The fixed date; the date.
日報 A daily newspaper. A daily report (bulletin).
日程 The order of the day; a day's program.
日落 Sunset; sundown.
日曆 A calendar.
日戲 Matinee.
日薪 Daily wages; a day's wages.
日內瓦(地) Geneva.
日本人 A Japanese.
日用品 Essential goods; articles of daily use; necessaries; personal effects.
日光浴 Sun bath; insolation; siriasis.
日耳曼(地) Germany.
日以繼夜 Night and day; day and night.
日光浴室 A sun-room; a solarium.
日光療法 A sun-cure; heliotherapy.
日夜不息 No rest day or night.
日常生活 Everyday (daily) life.
日常事務 The daily routine.
日暮途窮 Having no home to go; at stake.
日積月累 Days and months multiplying.

**旦** dàn (n.)- The morning; day-break; dawn; day; daylight.
旦夕；旦暮 Morning and evening.
旦日 To-morrow.
旦旦；日日 Every day; day by day.

**旨** zhǐ (n.)- A decree; an order. Delicacy. Meaning; sense. Intention; purpose; idea; will.
(adj.)- Excellent; delicate; nice; fine; splendid.
旨言 Good advice.
旨酒 Excellent wine; sweet liquor.

**早** zǎo (n.)- Morning.
(adj.)- Early; previous.
(adv.)- Soon; presently; beforehand.
早市 Morning market.
早年 In previous years.
早春 Early spring.
早秋 Early autumn.
早晨 Early morning.
早些 Earlier.
早晏 Early and late.
早起 Rise early.
早婚 Early marriage.
早晚 Morning and evening. Sooner or later.
早熟 Early maturity; premature growth (ripeness, development); precocity.
早稻 Early rice.
早膳 Breakfast.
早眠早起 Keep good (regular, early) hours.
早知如此 If I had known this at first.

旬 (n.)- A period of ten days or ten years; a decade.
xún 旬日 Ten days.
旬刊 A magazine published three times a month.
旬年 A full year. Ten years.

旭 (n.)- The rising sun; the dawn.
旭日 The rising sun.
xù 旭日東升 The morning sun rises from the east.

旱 (n.)- Dry weather; drought. Dry land.
hàn (adj.)- Dry; arid; parched; rainless.
旱天 Dry weather.
旱地 Dry land.
旱災 Drought; continued dry weather.
旱船塢 Dry dock.

旺 (adj.)- Brilliant; glorious; prosperous; brightening; flourishing.
wàng 旺月 The best month of a year.
旺年 A prosperous year.
旺盛 Flourishing; vigorous; energetic.
旺運 Good fortune; lucky.

昂 (v.)- Raise; elevate; lift up; increase.
áng (adj.)- Grand; dignified; elevated; lofty; stately. High; dear; expensive.
昂首 Carry the head high; perk up one's head.
昂然 Proudly; haughtily; elatedly.
昂貴 Dear or high in price; costly.
昂藏 Dignified.

昆 (n.)- An elder brother. A multitude.
kūn (adj.)- Many; numerous.
昆蟲 Insects.
昆蟲學 Entomology.
昆蟲類 Insecta.
昆蟲採集 Insect-collecting.

昇 (adj.)- Peaceful; tranquil; quiet; calm.
shēng (v.)- Rise; ascend; elevate; come up.
昇格 Be raised to a higher rank (status).
昇級 Promotion. Be promoted; rise in rank.
昇起 Rise.
昇降 Ascend and decend. Rise and fall.
昇降機 An elevator; a lift.

昌 (adj.)- Glorious; prosperous; flourishing. Elegant; beautiful;
chāng splendid.
(v.)- Prosper; thrive; illuminate.
昌明 Bright; shining; splendid; illuminate.
昌盛 Flourishing; prosperous abundant.

明 (n.)- The dawn. Clearness; brilliance.
míng (adj.)- Bright; clear; intelligent. Plain; evident; apparent. Light; brilliant.
(v.)- Illustrate. Understand; know; explain.
明日；明天 To-morrow; the next day.
明月 The bright moon.
明文 An express statement (provision); a clear statement; definite instructions.
明白 Clear; open; simple; palpable; understand; comprehend; catch the idea; obvious.
明年 Next year.
明見 A clear view.
明亮 Brilliant; intelligent.

明星 The morning star. A film star.
明珠 Brilliant pearls.
明理 Maturity of reason. Understand reason.
明眸 A bright eye.
明媚 Bright and charming; bright and attractive.
明晰 Clear; distinct; perspicuous.
明朝 The Ming Dynasty (1368–1644 A.D.).
明暗 Light and darkness (shade); chiaroscuro.
明察 Clear discernment; keen insight.
明蝦 Prawn.
明確 Accurate; clear.
明辨 Clear discrimination. Explain clearly.
明瞭 Clear; distinct. Understand.
明證 A plain proof.
明顯 Visible; manifest; conspicuous; obvious; prominent.
明礬(化) Potassium alum.
明信片 Post card.
明眼人 A clear-sighted man.
明目張胆 Undaunted; fearlessly; openly.
明知故犯 Commit a crime on purpose; wilful offence.
明信回片 Return card.

昏 hūn (n.)- Twilight; evening; dusk.
(adj.)- Dark; dim; gloomy; obscure; indistinct. Confused. Unconscious.
(v.)- Faint.
昏夜 Dark night.
昏倒 Faint away; swoon; fall down senseless (in a swoon).
昏眩 Dizzy; giddy.
昏迷 Infatuate. Unconscious; insensible; stupefied.
昏黑 In the darkness of the night. Dusk.
昏亂 Confused; disordered; perplexed.
昏暈 Faint; become senseless.
昏暗 Dark; dim; gloomy; dusky.

易 yì (n.)- Change; alteration. Ease.
(adj.)- Easy. Indifferent to; inattentive; negligent; at ease; pleased.
(v.)- Change. Barter; exchange. Disregard.
易見 Obvious; conspicuous; easily seen.
易俗 Improve customs.
易怒 Prone to anger; passionate; temper.
易燃 Inflammable.
易換 Change.
易銷售的 Marketable.

昔 xī (n.)- A night.
(adj.)- Old; former; previous; ancient.
(adv.)- Formerly; in the past; long ago; before; of old; previously.
昔日；昔時 Formerly; in former days; aforetime; in the past.

星 xīng (n.)- A star; a planet. A spark. A dot.
星光 Starlight.
星辰 The stars.
星系 Planetary system.
星河(天) The Milky Way.
星座 A constellation.
星球(天) Stars; planets.
星期 Sunday. A week.
星期日 Sunday.
星期一 Monday.
星期二 Tuesday.
星期三 Wednesday.
星期四 Thursday.
星期五 Friday.
星期六 Saturday.

星期休業 Closed on Sunday.

映 (n.)- A reflection; an image.
yìng (adj.)- Shining; bright; clear; open; brilliant.
(v.)- Shine on; reflect; illumine.

映日 Clear daylight.
映眼 Dazzle the eyes.
映照 Shine.

春 (n.)- Spring; springtime. Prosperity.
chūn (adj.)- Vernal; glad; joyous. Obscene; amorous.

春分 The vernal equinox.
春色 Delightful view; spring scenery.
春天 Spring; primrose season; smiling year.
春光 Spring sunshine; vernal sunbeams.
春季 The spring season.
春秋 Spring and Autumn Annals. Age.
春風 Spring breeze. Pleasing countenance. Smile.
春耕 Spring plowing.
春假 Spring vacation.
春景 The spring scenery.
春節 The Spring Festival.
春曉 A spring morning.
春蠶 A spring silkworm.
春季用品 Spring articles.

昧 (adj.)- Dark; obscure; gloomy; dim. Stupid; dull; blunt.
mèi 昧良；昧心 Against conscience.

昨 (adv.)- Yesterday. Previously; formerly.
zuó 昨午 Yesterday noon.
昨天 Yesterday.

昨年 Last year.
昨夜 Last night.
昨晨 Yesterday morning.
昨晚 Last evening.

昭 (n.)- Brightness.
zhāo (adj.)- Bright; light; splendid. Manifested; distinct.
(v.)- Show forth; display; manifest; illuminate.

昭然 Intelligently.
昭著 Clear; evident; plain.
昭彰 Plainly shown; luminously manifested.
昭耀 Bright; light; luminous; brilliant.
昭然若揭 As plain as when the cover is taken off.

是 (adj.)- Right; correct. This.
shì (v.)- The verb to be; am; is, are, was, were.
(adv.)- Such; thus. Yes.

是日 On that day; this day.
是必 Certainly.
是否 Is it so or not?
是非 Right or wrong; justice.
是故 On this account; for this reason; hence.
是則是非則非 What is right is right, what is wrong is wrong.

時 (n.)- Time; season; hour; opportunity. Period. Occasion. Moment.
shí (adv.)- Always; constantly; often; from time to time.

時人 Contemporaries; the people of the day.
時日 The date and time.
時代 Age; period; epoch.
時局 The present situation.
時事 Current events.
時刻 Time; hour.
時宜 Well-timed; seasonable; appropriate.
時時 From time to time.
時常 Constantly; frequently; from time to time.

時速 Miles per hour (m.p.h.).
時期 Time; period.
時間 Interval; period.
時勢 State of affairs; present outlook or circumstances.
時態（文）Tense.
時機 Opportunity; chance; proper time.
時節 Occasion; time.
時興 Fashionable; in vogue.
時辰表 A watch.
時辰鐘 A clock.
時間表 Time card or table; schedule.
時代精神 The spirit of the times.
時事問題 Current topics.
時間恰好 Punctually; on time.
時髦人物 Men of fashion.
時髦女郎 A fashionable girl.
時機成熟 The opportunity was ripe.

晋 jìn (n.)- The province of Shansi. The Chin Dynasty.
(v.)- Increase; flourish. Proceed; forward; advance; go on. Promote.
晋級 Promotion.
晋朝 The Chin Dynasty (265–419 A.D.).

晏 yàn (n.)- A clear sky. Afternoon; evening.
(adj.)- Late. Quiet; peaceful; tardy.
晏起 Get up late.

晌 shǎng (n.)- Noon; midday; noontide.
(adv.)- At noon.
晌午 Noon; midday.

晚 wǎn (n.)- Evening; sunset; twilight; night time.
(adj.)- Late; behind.
(adv.)- Lately.
晚上 In the evening.
晚年 One's old age; the evening of one's life.
晚安 Good evening!
晚宴 A feast in the evening; an evening party.
晚婚 Marrying late; late marriage.
晚報 Evening paper.
晚飯；晚餐 The evening meal; supper.

晝 zhòu (n.)- Daytime; daylight.
晝夜 Day and night.
晝夜不息 Never ceasing, day nor night; work day and night.

晤 wù (adj.)- Bright; light; clear.
(v.)- Meet. Perceive. See; understand; comprehend.
晤會；晤面 A personal interview.
晤解 Perceive; understand.

晦 huì (adj.)- Obscure; dark; dim; foggy; misty. Unlucky; unfortunately.
晦明 Night and morning.
晦氣 Bad luck; ill-luck.
晦蒙；昏晦 Gloomy; dark; obscure.

晨 chén (n.)- Morning; dawn; day break.
晨夕；晨昏 Morning and evening.
晨安 Good morning.
晨星 The morning star. Few; scarce; rare.
晨間 In the morning.
晨操 Morning exercise.
晨昏顛倒 Topsy-turvy; turn night into day.

普 pǔ (adj.)- All; general; pervading. Great; universal; common.
(adv.)- Everywhere; in all directions; thoroughly.

普及 Make widely available; prevailing; widespread.
普通 General; universal. Generally; as a rule; common.
普選 General election.
普天下 The world over; throughout the world.
普及版 A popular (cheap) edition.
普通人 The average man; the common run.
普通科 The general course.
普遍的 Universal; general.
普遍性 Universality.
普及教育 Universal education.
普通名詞 Common noun.
普通知識 General knowledge; common sense.
普通教育 Elementary education; common (popular) education.
普通習慣 Common usage.
普通信用狀 General letter of credit.
普通教育文憑 General Certificate of Education (G.C.E.).

**景** (n.)- Light. A view; sight; scenery. Circumstances; situation; condition.
jǐng (v.)- Regard kindly; long for; admire; honour; respect.
景色；景緻 Scenery; a view; a landscape.
景仰 Idolize; adore; regard kindly; venerate; admire.
景況；景狀 Condition; circumstances; prospects.
景物 Spectacle; scenery and things.
景氣 Condition of trade (the market).
景象 Appearance; outlook; aspect.
景泰藍 Cloisonne enamel.

**晰** (adj.)- Clear; perspicuous; plain.
xī

**晴** (n.)- The fine weather; the clear sky.
qíng (v.)- Clear up.
(adj.)- Fine; clear.
晴天 Fine weather; a clear sky.
晴和 Fine and mild.
晴雨 Rain or shine; wet or fine.
晴雨表 A barometer; the mercury.
晴天霹靂 A bolt from the blue.

**晶** (n.)- Crystal.
(adj.)- Bright; pure; crystalline.
jīng 晶體 Crystal.
晶瑩 Brilliant; shining; lustrous.
晶糖 Crystallized sugar.
晶系(礦) Systems of crystallization.

**智** (n.)- Wisdom; knowledge; intelligence; sagacity; cleverness.
zhì (adj.)- Wise; sagacious; prudent; intellectual; clever; bright; sagacious.
(adv.)- Intellectually.
智力 Intellectuality; intellectual power; mind; intellect; wit.
智士；智者 A prudent man; a wise man.
智巧 Skill; ingenuity.
智利(地) Chile.
智育 Intellectual culture; mental training.
智勇 Brave and wise.
智能 Wisdom and ability; mental (intellectual) faculties.
智慧 Wisdom; intelligence; sagacity.
智謀 Shrewdness; cleverness; wisdom and resources.
智囊團 A brain trust.
智力商數(智商) Intelligence Quotient (I.Q.).
智力測驗 An intelligence test.
智勇兼備 Possession of sagacity and valour.

**晾** (v.)- Dry in the sun or air; hang in the wind to dry.
liàng 晾乾 Dry in the air.
晾開 Spread out to air.

**暇** (n.)- Leisure; freedom from work.
xiá (adj.)- Free; unemployed; disengaged.
暇時 Unemployed time; spare moment.

**暄** (n.)- The warmth of the sun.
(adj.)- Warm; genial.
xuān

**暈** (n.)- The halo of the moon or sun.
yùn (adj.)- Dizzy; giddy; obscure.
〔yūn〕 (v.)- Be giddy; faint.
暈車 Train sick.
暈船 Seasick.
暈倒 Fall down in a faint.

**暉** (n.)- A ray of the sun.
(adj.)- Bright; luminous.
huī

**暑** (n.)- The summer heat; hot weather.
shǔ 暑天 Dog days; hot weather.
暑伏 The hot season.
暑假 A summer vacation; summer holidays.
暑熱 Very hot; hot climate.
暑期學校 Summer school.

**暖** (adj.)- Warm; genial; mild; temperate.
nuǎn (v.)- Make warm or become warm.
暖手 Warm the hand.
暖衣 Warm the clothes.
暖和 Warm; genial.
暖風 A warm, gentle wind; genial breezes.
暖流 A warm current.
暖氣 Warm air. Warm weather.
暖壺 A warming pan; a thermos bottle.
暖氣裝置 A heating apparatus; a heater.

**暗** (adj.)- Dark; cloudy; gloomy; obscure. Private; hidden.
àn (adv.)- Secretly.
暗示 A hint; a suggestion.
暗中 Secretly; stealthily.
暗室 A dark room.
暗害 Secret injury.
暗殺 Assassination; murder.
暗探 A detective.
暗訪 A secret inquiry.
暗號 A secret sign; a password; a countersign.
暗算 Machination. Plot privately against others.
暗影 A shadow; a gloom.
暗碼 A cipher; a code.
暗礁 A reef; a sunken rock.
暗藏 Conceal.
暗射地圖 A blank (skeleton) map.

**暝** (n.)- Night.
(adj.)- Obscure; dark.
míng

**暢** (adj.)- Joyful; refreshing; happy; joyous; contented. Long.
chàng 暢快 Delightful; happy; pleasant; jovial.
暢敍 Have a pleasant talk or conversation.
暢流 Freely flowing.
暢飲 Drink with gusto.
暢談 Talk pleasantly.
暢銷 Active demand of commodities.
暢開胸襟 Unbosom oneself; open one's

heart.

暫 (n.)- A part of a day. A short time.
zàn (adv.)- Briefly; suddenly. Meanwhile; a short time.
暫住 Sojourn; lodge temporarily; a short (brief) stay.
暫別 Temporary separation.
暫借 A temporary loan.
暫時 For a while; temporarily; for a moment; a short time.
暫憩 Rest a while.
暫緩 Tarry; delay a little.
暫時停止 Suspension.

暮 (n.)- The evening. The end of a period of time.
mù 暮年 In old age.
暮色 Evening gloom (dusk); the shades of evening.
暮夜 Evening.
暮色蒼然 The shades of night fall.

暴 (n.)- A scorching heat.
(adj.)- Cruel; tyrannical; violent.
bào Sudden.
(v.)- Expose; dry in the sun. Injure.
暴力 Brute force; violence; coercion.
暴主；暴君 A tyrant; a despot.
暴行 Violence; riotous behaviour; an outrage.
暴利 Excessive profits; profiteering; usury.
暴卒 A sudden death.
暴雨 A squall; a heavy shower; a downpour.
暴怒 Very angry; in hot blood.
暴政 Tyrannical rule (government); tyranny; despotism.
暴虐 Tyranny; cruelty.
暴風 A violent wind; a storm; a tempest; a hurricane.
暴徒 Violent characters; rioters; a rowdy.
暴言 Violent (strong) language.
暴烈 Terrific; violent.
暴動 A riot; a disturbance; an uprising.
暴亂 Reign of terror.
暴富 An upstart; a parvenu.
暴飲 Excessive (heavy) drinking; carousal; drink heavily (hard).
暴躁 Hot-headed; hot tempered; hasty.
暴露 Exposed; left uncovered. Expose to view.
暴曬 Dry in the sun.
暴風雨 A storm; a gale; a typhoon; a tempest.
暴風雪 A snow-storm; a blizzard.
暴力行爲 An act of violence; terrorism.
暴風中心 The storm-centre; the eye of a storm.
暴風警報 A storm-warning.

暹 (v.)- Advance.
暹羅(地) Siam.
xiān 暹羅人 A Siamese.

暨 (prep.)- Together with.
(conj.)- And; also.
jì 暨今 Up to this present time; now.
暨及 And; together with.

曆 (n.)- Signs of the heavens; calendar.
lì (v.)- Calculate.
曆法 The system of determining the seasons and solar terms of a year.
曆書 A calendar; an almanac.

曇 (n.)- Black clouds over the sky.
曇華(植) Cannaindica; Indian
tán shot.

**曉** (n.)- The morning; dawn.
(adj.)- Bright; luminous. Perspicuous.
xiǎo (v.)- Understand; know. Make to understand.

曉示；曉諭 Tell plainly; issue a plain proclamation.
曉風 Early morning breezes.
曉得 Understand; comprehend.

**曖** (n.)- The sun obscured by clouds.
ài (adj.)- Obscure.
曖昧 Ambiguous; vague; equivocal. Secret matters.

**曙** (n.)- The light of the morning sun; the dawn.
shǔ (adj.)- Bright; clear; manifest.
曙日 In the morning.

曙光 The first streak of light; dawn; twilight.

**曚** (n.)- The sun below the horizon.
méng 曚昧 Dim; dull; stupid; ignorant.

曚曨 The dim light of early dawn.

**曝** (v.)- Sun; air; expose. Dry.
曝晒 Dry in the sun.
pù 曝露 Expose.
曝光不足 Under-exposed.

曝光過度 Over-exposed.

**曠** (n.)- A wilderness; a desert.
(adj.)- Vacant; desolate; wild.
kuàng Spacious; distant.
(v.)- Leave empty; neglect.

曠工 Neglect one's business.
曠日 Waste time.
曠野 A wilderness; a vast plain.
曠課 Absent from class without permission.
曠學 Neglect study.

**曬** Same as 晒.
(v.)- Dry in the sun.
shài 曬乾 Dried in the sun.
曬衣服 Sun clothes.

曬衣架 Clothes horse.
曬藍圖用紙 Blue print paper.

# 曰 部

**曰** (v.)- Speak; say; utter.
yuē

**曲** (n.)- Songs; lyrics; ballads. A bend.
qū (adj.)- Crooked; curved; winding. Injured. False.

曲尺 A carpenter's square.
曲折 Winding; curvature; bend.
曲直 Crooked and straight.
曲面(幾) A curved surface.
曲解 A wrong (biassed) interpretation. Misinterpret; pervert.
曲管 Bending tube.
曲線 A curved line.
曲調 A tune; a melody.
曲譜 Musical notes; a music book.
曲藝 Music and arts.
曲線美 The curve of beauty; a beautiful curve.
曲折變化 Ups and downs; vicissitudes.

**曳** yè
(v.)- Drag; draw; pull.
曳尾 Wag the tail.
曳船 A tow-boat.

**更** gēng 〔gèng〕
(n.)- A night watch. Change.
(v.)- Change; repair. Act for.
(adv.)- More; moreover; again.
更正 Correct; make right; rectify.
更多 Far more.
更名 Change one's name.
更好 Preferable. Much better.
更衣 Change clothes; go to stool.
更妙 So much the better.
更改 Change; alter.
更甚 Further; farther; still more.
更新 Reform an evil habit; begin a new course of life; renew; renovate.
更換 Replace; substitute.
更樓 A watchtower.
更衣室 Dressing room; toilet.

**書** shū
(n.)- A book; a letter. Handwriting; a written document.
(v.)- Write; compose.
書本 A book.
書目 Index to a book; a catalogue of books.
書包 A satchel for books; a school bag; a bookcase.
書件 Books; documents; papers.
書桌 Desk.
書名 Title of a book.
書店；書坊；書局 A book store; a bookseller's store; a book-shop.
書房 A study; a studio.
書法 Calligraphy; the art of penmanship.
書信；書札 A letter.
書架 A bookshelf; a bookstand.
書面 The cover of a book.
書頁 The leaf of a book.
書庫；藏書樓 A library.
書院 A college; a school.
書記 Clerks; copyists; writers.
書畫 Pictures and writings.
書寫 Write; inscribe.
書櫥 Bookcase.
書癖 Book-mindedness; love of books; bibliomania.
書癡 A bookworm; a student closely attached to books.
書簽 A label on books.
書籍 Books.
書生氣 The student character (temperament).
書法家 A good penman; a calligrapher.
書信夾 A letter-clip; a letter file.
書獃子 A bookworm.
書目提要 A bibliography.
書面記錄 Written statement.

**曹** cáo
(n.)- A company; a class. A judge.
曹達明礬(礦) Soda alum.
曹達硝石(礦) Nitre.

**曼** màn
(adj.)- Long; prolonged. Beautiful.
曼谷(地) Bangkok.

**曾** zēng 〔céng〕
(adj.)- Past. Done; finished.
(adv.)- Already; still; yet.
(conj.)- But; how.
曾孫 A great-grandson (grandchild).
曾經 Already.
曾祖父母 A great-grand father or mother.

**替** tì
(v.)- Substitute; change; supersede. Decline.
(prep.)- For; instead of; in place of.
替工 A substitute; take another's place

in work.

替代 Instead of; on behalf of; talk the place of; be substituted for.

替換 Substitute; change in order.

**最** (adv.)- Very; exceedingly; in the highest degree.
zuì 最上 Highest; best.
最下 Lowest; worst.

最大 The greatest; maximum.

最小 The smallest; least. Minimum.

最先 First of all; in the front rank; first.

最初 At the very beginning; the outset.

最近 Latest; most recent; newest.

最後 The last; the end.

最美 The most handsome.

最高 Highest; supreme.

最新 Newest; latest; recent.

最優；最佳 Best; finest; superior; supreme.

最壞 Worst; basest.

最難 The most difficult.

最上級 The highest class. (文) The superlative degree.

最下等 The lowest grade (class).

最可愛 Most dear; dearest.

最多數 The greatest number; the largest majority.

最前線 The advance line.

最高音 Soprano (女); alto (男).

最高價 Maximum price.

最高層 The uppermost stratum.

最小限度 The minimum.

最大限度 The maximum.

最不發達 Least developed.

最低工資 The lowest salary; minimum wages.

最低年齡 The minimum age.

最低價目 The lowest price.

最近消息 The latest information.

最後一人 To the last man.

最後一刻 At the last moment.

最後目的 The ultimate objective.

最後通牒 An ultimatum.

最後勝利 The final victory.

最高法院 The supreme court.

最高速度 The maximum velocity.

最高統帥 The supreme commander.

最高會議 The supreme council.

最新樣式 Latest style.

最小公倍數 A least common multiple (L. C. M.).

最大公約數 The greatest common divisor (measure); (G. C. M.); the highest common factor (H. C. F.).

最後五分鐘 The last five minutes.

最惠國待遇 The most favoured nation treatment.

最壞的打算 Prepare for the worst.

(n.)- An association; a society; a club; a union. A junction.
huì A meeting. An opportunity. A
[kuài] time. A procession.
(v.)- Assemble; meet together; associate. Be able. Should.

會心；會意 Understand; perceive; catch the idea; get the hint.

會合 Gather; assemble.

會考 Mass examination.

會見 Meet; have an interview with.

會所 Meeting house. Club room. Headquarters.

會社 A society; an association.

會長 The chairman of a society; the president of a club.

會客 Meet a guest.

會計 An accountant; a cashier; a treasurer.

會員 Members of a society. Membership.

會章 The regulations of a society.

會堂 An assembly-hall; a public hall.

會費 A membership fee; dues.

會場 An assembly-hall; a meeting-place.

會話 Conversation; dialogue.
會談 Have a talk with; confer with; have an interview with.
會館 A guild; a club.
會議 A conference; a convention.
會客室 A reception-room; a sitting-room.
會計師 An accountant.
會議室 A council-room (-chamber).
會議錄 The minutes; a minute-book.
會員名單 A list of members.
會員證章 A membership card; the badge of membership.
會議記錄 The minutes of a meeting.

# 月 部

月 (n.)- The moon. A moon or lunar month; a month.
yuè (adv.)- Monthly.
月月 Every month; month after month.
月刊 Monthly publication.
月球 The moon.
月光；月色 Moonlight; moonbeams.
月夜 A moonlit night.
月底；月尾 The end of a month.
月初 At the beginning of a month.
月信；月經 Menses; menstruation; the monthlies.
月圓 The full moon.
月臺 Platform.
月蝕 A lunar eclipse; an eclipse of the moon.
月餅 Moon cake.
月薪 A monthly salary (pay).
月份牌 A calendar.
月季花 The monthly rose.
月季票 Season ticket.
月臺票 Platform ticket.
月經不調 Menstrual irregularity.

有 (adj.)- Abundant; plentiful.
(v.)- Have; possess. Exist. Attain.
yǒu (conj.)- And; also.
有力 Powerful; influential.
有功 Meritorious; efficient.
有用 Useful; serviceable.
有名 Famous; noted; well-known; celebrated.
有孕 Pregnant.
有利 Profitable; paying; lucrative; advantageous.
有些 Somewhat; certain.
有毒 Poisonous; harmful; venomous.
有限 Limited; finite.
有害 Harmful; injurious; detrimental; noxious.
有時 Sometimes; at times; now and then.
有效 Remain in effect; be in force. Effective; valid; available.
有益 Useful; beneficial to; advantageous to; profitable.
有望 Hopeful; promising.
有理 Reasonable; rational.
有爲 Capable; able; efficient; of ability.
有意 Intentionally; purposely; deliberately; in the disposition.
有罪 Be guilty; be in the wrong. Guiltiness.
有餘 More than; over; above; upwards of.
有禮 Polite; courteous; civil; obliging.
有價值 Valuable.
有系統 Systematic.

有理式(算) A rational expression.
有意義 Significant.
有機物 Organic matter.
有趣味 Interesting; amusing.
有膽量 Having courage.
有史以來 Since the dawn of history; in history; on record.
有色人種 A coloured race.
有限公司 A limited company.
有條不紊 Everything in order and well arranged.
有效方法 An effective means.
有效期限 The time of effect; the term of validity.
有發言權 Have the right to speak.
有機化學 Organic chemistry.
有機礦物 Organic minerals.
有聲有色 A vivid description.
有識之士 A well-informed (an intelligent) person.
有機化合物 Orangic compound.
有志者事竟成 Where there's a will there's a way.
有其父必有其子 Like father, like son; he is a true son of his father.

**朋** (n.)- A friend; a companion; an associate.
péng (v.)- Associate; consort with.
朋友 A friend; an acquaintance; a companion.
朋黨 A junto; a cabal; a party; a clique.
朋友心腹 Bosom friend.
朋友往來 The intercourse of friends.

**服** (n.)- Clothes; dress; garment.
fú (v.)- Dress; put on. Serve; wait on. Take, as medicine.
〔fú〕 Yield; conquer. Submit; obey; subjugate.
服式 Costume; style of clothing.
服役 Render service to.
服侍 Serve; wait on.
服毒 Swallow poison purposely; commit suicide.
服從 Obey; accord with; submit to; be obedient to; lay under; give in.
服務 Perform the duties of one's office; serve.
服裝 Costume; dressing.
服藥 Take medicine.
服務年限 The term of office; the period of one's continual service.

**朔** (n.)- The 1st day of the month. The beginning. North.
shuò 朔風 The northern wind; a winter gale.
朔望 The 1st and 15th of the month.

**朗** (adj.)- Clear; bright.
朗月 A bright moon.
lǎng 朗吟 Recite; declaim.
朗朗 The sounds were clear and distinct.

**望** (n.)- Hope; expectation.
(v.)- Hope; expect; look forward to. Look at; look ,oversee; gaze at.
wàng
望見 See.
望遠 Take a distant view; look far away.
望遠鏡 A field glass; a telescope.

**朝** (n.)- Morning; dawn. Government; a dynasty.
cháo (prep.)- Toward.
〔zhāo〕 朝夕 Morning and evening; early and late.
朝代 A dynasty.
朝政 Imperial politics.
朝朝 Every morning.
朝鮮(地) Korea; Chosen.
朝三暮四 Tweedledum and tweedledee; imposture.

朝氣蓬勃 Young and vigorous.

期 (n.)- A set time; a fixed day. A period.
qī (v.)- Hope; expect; long for; wait for; Aim at.

期刊 Periodicals.
期內 Within a fixed time.
期待 Wait; expect; look forward to.
期限 A limit of time; a period; a term.
期票 A promissory note; time draft.
期望 Hope; anticipate with certainly. In expectation; long for.
期間 A term; a period; space of time.
期滿 At the expiration of the set time; the termination of term.
期限以內 Within a term.
期限以外 After a term.

朦 (n.)- The setting moon.
(adj.)- Dim; obscure.
méng 朦朧 The moon about to set. Dim; obscure; moon clouded over.

# 木 部

木 (n.)- A tree; wood; timber; lumber; log.
mù (adj.)- Wooden. Stiff; unpending. Dull.

木工 Timber work; carpentering.
木片 Chip.
木瓜(植) The quince; the papaya.
木匠 A carpenter.
木耳(植) A Jew's-ear; an edible fungus.
木板 Planks; boards.
木虱(動) A bed-bug; a wood-louse.
木版 Wood-engraving; block-printing; xylography.
木炭 Charcoal.
木星(天) Jupiter.
木柵 Stockade.
木屋 A wooden house.
木偶 A wooden image; a wooden idol.
木屑 Saw dust.
木屐 Wooden shoes; high clogs.
木料 Timber; lumber; wood.
木馬 A wooden horse.
木魚 "Wooden-fish," beating while chanting.
木場 A timber yard; a lumber-yard.
木棍 A club; a cudgel.
木棉 Kapok.
木琴 Xylophone.
木塞 Cork.
木製 Wooden; made of wood.
木箱 A wooden box.
木器 Woodenware.
木乃伊 Mummy.
木刻畫 A woodcut; a wood-block print.
木刻像 A wooden image (statue).
木炭紙 Charcoal-paper.
木偶戲 A puppet-show.
木已成舟 What is done can't be undone.

未 (adv.)- Not; not yet; not now. Never.
wèi 未完 Unfinished; incomplete.
未來 Future; the time to come.

未免 Unavoidable; inevitable.
未定 Undecided; unfixed.
未知 Unknown; uncertain.
未婚 Unmarried; single.
未曾 Not yet; never; at no time.
未詳 Unknown.

未亡人 A widow.
未知數 An unknown quantity.
未婚夫 Fiance.
未婚妻 Fiancee.
未婚女子 Spinster.
未婚男子 Bachelor.

末 (n.)- The tip; the end; the last. Powder; dust. The limbs.
mò (adv.)- Finally; at last; subsequently.
末日 The last day of the world. The judgment day; doomsday.
末年 Last year.
末尾 Final; at the last; terminal.
末後 At last; finally; subsequently.
末座 The last (lowest) seat; the humblest.
末路 The end (of a career, etc.).
末端 The end; the tip.

本 (n.)- Root. The origin; beginning; foundation; principal; cause; starting point. A copy.
běn (adj.)- Essential. Original; natural; proper; native; radical.
本分 Duty; obligation.
本文 The text; the body of a letter. The original text.
本日 This day; to-day.
本月 This month; instant.
本末 The beginning and end; the whole story. Primary and secondary matter.
本年 This year; the current year.
本地；本埠 Local; native.
本位 Standard; basis. Unit.
本利 Principal and interest.
本身 Oneself.
本來 Original.
本性 Nature. Natural disposition; the true (original) character.
本能 Instinct.
本國 One's native country; one's mother country.
本部 Headquarters.
本領 Ability; capacity.
本質 Essence; substance.
本錢 Capital; principal.
本生燈 Bunsen burner.
本地人 Natives of a place; aborigines.
本國語 Mother tongue.
本國製 Home-made; of home manufacture.
本來面目 The original expression; the natural form.
本草綱目 A Chinese Materia Medica.
本國商人 Home merchant.
本國價目 Home price.
本國製品 Domestic manufactures.
本該如此 Ought to be so.
本初子午線 The first (prime) meridian.

札 (n.)- A thin wooden tablet. A letter. A despatch.
zhá 札記 Sketches; notes-taking.

朱 (n.)- Red; vermilion.
(adj.)- Red; scarlet.
zhū 朱門 The gentry; the wealthy family.
朱砂 Cinnabar.
朱紅 Scarlet; red; vermilion.
朱櫻(櫨) Red cherry.

朵 Same as 朶.
(n.)- A cluster of flower; bud. The lobe of the ear.
duǒ 朵朵 A collection of flowers.

朽 (adj.)- Rotten; decayed. Useless. Worn-out; failing.
xiǔ (v.)- Decay; spoil.
朽木 A rotten tree.
朽壞 Spoiled; rotten; worthless; decayed.

杆 gān (n.)- The shaft of a spear. A pole.

杉 shān (n.)- A cryptomeria.
杉樹 Chinese fir; a cryptomeria.

李 lǐ (n.)- A plum; a prune. A surname.
李子(植) Plums.

杏 xìng (n.)- An apricot.
杏仁 Almonds; apricot kernels.
杏花 Apricot flower.
杏桃 A variety of plum.
杏仁茶 Almond tea; emulsion of almond.
杏仁餅 Apricot cakes.

材 cái (n.)- Materials. Timber; wood stuff. Ability; capacity.
材料 Materials; stuff.
材能 Capacity; ability.
材質 Natural abilities.

村 cūn Same as 邨.
(n.)- A village; a hamlet; a small town.
(adj.)- Rustic; vulgar.
村夫；村人 Villagers; a bumpkin; a boor.
村長 A village headman.
村俗 Rustic.
村莊 A village; a farm stead.
村鄉；村落 Country village.

杖 zhàng (n.)- A staff; a stick; a club; a cane; a crutch; the shaft of a lance.
(v.)- Beat; strike; bamboo. Lean on.
杖打；笞杖 Beat with the bamboo.

杜 dù (n.)- A kind of pear.
(v.)- Shut out; keep off. Impede; stop; shut up; restrict.
杜造；杜撰 Frabrication.
杜絕 Be stooped (blocked, cut off).
杜漸 Be precautions beforehand; caution against small matters.
杜鵑(動) A cuckoo.
杜鵑花(植) An azalea.

束 shù (n.)- A sheaf; a bundle; cluster.
(v.)- Control; keep in order. Tie in a bundle; restrain; bind with cords.
束手 Draw back one's hand; fold up the hands.
束住 Tie up.
束花 A bundle of flowers.
束腰 Bind on the girdle.
束緊 Bind fast.
束髮 Bag the hair; bundle up the hair.
束縛 Restriction; restraint; fetters; bind; tie; control; enchain; tie up or down.
束擱 Put away.
束身自愛 Practise discipline and self-respect.

杪 miǎo (n.)- The tip; the end. A small branch.
(adj.)- Small.
杪末 The very end.

杭 háng (v.)- Sail.
杭州(地) Hangchow.
杭綢 Silks from Hangchow.

杯 bēi (n.)- A cup; a glass; a goblet; a tumbler.
杯酒 A cup of wine.
杯筷 Cups and chopsticks.
杯盤 Cups and saucers.

東 (n.)- The east. A master; an employer.
dōng (adj.)- Eastern.
東方 The east; eastward.
東北 North east. The Northeastern Provinces.
東西 Articles; things. East and west.
東亞 Eastern Asia; the Far East.
東京(地) Tokyo, Japan.
東風 The east wind.
東南 Southeast.
東家 The landlord; the employer; the master; the host.
東經 The east longitude.
東方人 Orientals; Asiatics.
東半球 The eastern hemisphere.
東南亞 Southeast Asia.
東道主 A manager; a host; a caterer.
東西兩岸 Sea-route between east and west banks.
東西南北 From north and south, east and west; from all points of the compass; the cardinal points.
東奔西走 Busy oneself about.
東南偏北 Southeast by north.
東南偏南 Southeast by south.

杳 (adj.)- Obscure; dusk.
yǎo 杳冥 Dark; cloudy; indistinct.
杳遠 Distant and obscure.
杳然 Dissapear; gone.
杳無音訊 No news whatsoever.

杷 (n.)- A kind of rake without teeth, used to smooth seed-
pa plots.

松 (n.)- The pine tree; evergreen.
sōng 松子 Pine seeds; fir cones.
松林 A pine forest; a pinery.
松油 Pine-tree oil.
松柏 Pine and cypress.
松香；松脂 Colophony.
松針 Pine needles.
松鼠 The squirrel.
松樹 The pine tree.
松花江(地) The Songari River.
松花蛋 Preserved eggs.
松節油 Turpentine oil.

板 (n.)- A board; a plank; a plate; a slab; block for a book.
bǎn 板本 Edition.
板魚(動) The sole.
板凳 A wooden stool; a bench.
板壁 A wooden partition; a wooden wall; a board-fence.

枇 枇杷 The loquat.
pí

枉 (n.)- A wrong; a grievance; injustice.
wǎng (adj.)- Oppressed; wrong; bent down; distorted.
(v.)- Act crookedly. Do or suffer wrong.
(adv.)- In vain; no purpose.
枉費 Spend to no purpose; in vain.

析 (v.)- Distinguish; divide; split; analyze; discriminate.
xī

枕 (n.)- A pillow; a crossbar at the back of a carriage.
zhěn (v.)- Pillow; rest on.
枕木 A sleeper; wooden sleepers of a railroad.
枕衣；枕巾 A pillow-case; a pillow slip.
枕伴 A bedfellow; a bed mate.
枕梁(工) Bind rail.
枕頭 Pillow.
枕邊 In bed; by one's bedside.

# 林
lín

(n.)- A forest; a thicket; a wood; a grove. A company; a group; crowd; multitude.

林立 Numerous; a forest of masts or chimneys, etc.

林業 Forestry.

林蔭大道 A boulevard.

# 枚
méi

(n.)- The stalk of a shrub. One of anything. A piece.

(v.)- Number.

枚數 The number of.

枚舉 Count; number; enumerate.

# 果
guǒ

(n.)- A fruit. Results; effects; consequences.

(adj.)- Hardy; daring. Determined; resolute.

(v.)- Surpass; overcome; conclude; finish; complete.

(adv.)- Certainly; really; truly; indeed; surely; in fact.

果刀 A fruit-knife.

果仁 The kernel of a fruit.

果汁 Fruit juice; squash.

果皮 The pericarp or outer covering of the seed.

果品 Fruits of various kinds.

果商 Fruit dealer.

果敢 Courageous; brave; daring.

果然 Certainly; actually; verily; really.

果腹 Satisfied; full in eating.

果酸 Tartaric acid.

果實 A fruit; a nut; a berry.

果樹 Fruit trees.

果斷 Resolute; decisive; drastic.

果醬 Jam; jelly.

果攤 Fruit stall.

果子酒 A fruit-wine; a fruit-drink.

果子露 Syrup of fruit.

果子鹽 Fruit salt.

果樹園 An orchard; a fruit-garden.

果有其事 There was really this matter.

# 枝
zhī

(n.)- A branch; a bough; a twig.

(v.)- Branch. Scatter. Support; hold off.

枝梢 The tip of a branch.

枝路 A branch road.

枝幹 Trunk and branches.

枝葉 Leaves and branches. Offspring. Unnecessary particulars; digressions.

枝節 Troubles; hitches.

枝氣管炎 Bronchitis.

# 枯
kū

(n.)- A dead tree.

(adj.)- Decayed; dried up; arid; wilt.

枯死 Be withered (blighted).

枯枝 A dead (dry) branch.

枯草 Dried, withered grass.

枯乾 Dried and withered.

枯渴 Be parched dry; be dried up; be exhausted (drained).

枯魚 A fish dying out of water.

枯萎 Decay. Rot.

枯葉 Dead (dry) leaves.

枯樹 A dead (withered) tree.

# 柿
shì

(n.)- The persimmon.

柿餅 Dried persimmon.

# 柺
guǎi

(n.)- A staff or crutch for an old man; a stick.

柺杖 An old man's staff; a crutch.

# 架
jià

(n.)- A shelf; a framework; a stand; a rack.

(v.)- Support; put up.

架子 A shelf.

架起 Raise up.

架設 Construct; erect.

架橋 Construct (build) a bridge.

架子大 Putting on airs of greatness.

架電線 Wire laying.
架空鐵路 An overhead railway; an elevated railroad.
架設電話 Install a telephone; have a telephone installed.

枷 (n.)- A cangue or wooden pillory for criminals.
jiā

枸 (n.)- A kind of aspen.
gǒu
枸杞(植) Matrimony vine; lycium chinense.

柏 (n.)- The cypress; the cedar.
bó 〔bǎi〕
柏林(地) Berlin.
柏油 Pitch. Tar.
柏油路 Tarred road.

某 (pron.)- A certain person or thing.
mǒu
(adj.)- Certain.
某人 A certain person.
某日 A certain day.
某某 Mr. so-and-so.
某處 A certain place; somewhere.

柑 (n.)- Mandarin orange.
gān
柑皮 Orange peel.
柑核 Orange pips.

染 (v.)- Dye; colour made by dyeing; stain; contaminate.
rǎn
染布 Dye cloth.
染污 Soiled; dirtied; defiled; polluted.
染上 Take to addicted to.
染色 Dyed; coloured.
染廠 A dye-house; a dye-works.
染料 Dyestuffs; dyes.
染病 Be infected with disease.
染色業 The dye industry.
染色體(生) Chromosome.

柔 (adj.)- Soft; tender; mild; gentle; yielding; submissive.
róu
(v.)- Show kindness or tenderness; subdue by kindness.
柔和 Mild; gentle.
柔弱 Soft and weak; effeminate; enervate.
柔道 Judo.
柔軟 Soft; pliant; yielding.
柔順 Submissive; yielding; obedient; meek.
柔韌 Flexible; elastic.
柔語 Mild speech; soft word.
柔聲 A soft voice. Passive voice.
柔軟體操 Physical or gymnastic exercises; free gymnastics; callisthenics.

柘 柘榴 A pomegranate; the pomegranate tree.
zhè
柘榴石(礦) Garnet.

柚 (n.)- The pomelo. The reed of a loom.
yóu
柚子 The pomelo or shaddock.
柚木 Teak; Indian oak.

柞 (n.)- An oak tree.
zuò
柞蠶 Antheraea pernyi.

柢 (n.)-Root; foundation; base.
dǐ

查 (v.)- Examine; search; investigate.
chá
查出 Discover; find out; seek out.
查收 Examine and receive.
查究 Try; examine.
查核 Verify; compare.
查帳 Audit accounts.
查探 Find out by inquiries.

查問；查訊 Investigate; inquire.
查對 Check up.
查辦 Examine; inquire into; investigate and deal with accordingly.
查驗 Examine; scrutinize.
查帳員 An auditor.
查對無訛 Audited and found correct.
查根問底 Investigate thoroughly.

柩 (n.)- A coffin with a corpse in it.
jiù 柩車 A hearse.

柬 (n.)- A visiting card; a letter; a note.
jiǎn 柬帖 A visiting card.

柯 (n.)- A stalk or stem. The handle of an axe.
kē

柰 (n.)- The bullace; the greengage.
nài

柱 (n.)- A pillar; a support; a column.
zhù (v.)- Uphold; support; sustain.
柱石 The base of a pillar; a foundation-stone; a corner-stone.
柱狀 Columnar; pillar-shaped.
柱脚 Pedestal.
柱頭(植) Stigma. Abacus; capital of a pillar.

柳 (n.)- The willow tree.
liǔ 柳眉 A woman's crescent eyebrows.
柳條布 Stripped cotton cloths.

柴 (n.)- Brushwood; firewood.
chái 柴火 Fuel; wood.
柴炭 Charcoal.
柴堆 A stack of fuel.
柴米油鹽 Firewood, rice, oil and salt-necessities of life.

栅 (n.)- A palisade; a fence; a barrier; a stockade.
zhà 栅門 Barrier gate.
栅欄 A railing; a fence.

栓 (n.)- A peg; stopper.
shuān

栗 (n.)- The chestnut.
lì (adj.)- Reverential. Firm; solid; durable. Strict.
栗子 Chestnuts.
栗色 Chestnut colour; chestnut brown.
栗樹 The chestnut tree.
栗毛馬 A bay; a chestnut horse.

校 (n.)- A school. Wooden stocks. A military officer.
xiào [jiào] (v.)- Compare. Revise. Examine. Oppose.
校友 A schoolmate; an old boy.
校外 Outside the school.
校長 The head-master; the principal; the director; the president.
校舍 A school-house(-building).
校門 A school (college) gate.
校服 A school uniform.
校紀 School discipline.
校風 The tradition (moral) of a school.
校務 School affairs.
校尉 A colonel; a lieutenant.
校章 School regulations; school badge.
校對 Correct proofs; read proofs.
校旗 A school banner (flag).
校歌 A school (college)song.
校樣 A proof-sheet; proofs.
校醫 A school doctor (physician).

校友會 A students' association; an alumni association; an old boys' association.
校董會 Board of directors or trustees.
校對人 A proof reader; a corrector of the press.
校際運動大會 An inter-school athletic meet.

株 zhū (n.)- The trunk of a tree; a unit for trees, etc.
株幹 The trunk of a tree.

核 hé (n.)- The stone or kernel of a fruit.
(v.)- Examine; inquire into. Estimate; calculate.
核子 Nucleus.
核仁 The kernel of a fruit; nucleus.
核心 Nucleus; the core.
核明；核查 Investigate.
核計 Examine an account; find the amount.
核准 Grant after due consideration. Permission after considering.
核桃 The walnut.
核對 Compare; audit.
核算 Calculate; reckon.
核子彈 A nuclear bomb.
核爆炸 A nuclear explosion.
核武器 A nuclear weapon.
核子戰爭 Nuclear war.

根 gēn (n.)- Root. Base. Origin; cause.
根本 Root; base; foundation; source.
根由 Cause; origin.
根式(算) Surd root. Irrational expression.
根究 Inquire into cause.
根性 Nature; disposition; temper.
根治 Radical cure; cure a disease completely.
根莖；根塊 A root stock. A rhizome.
根絕 Root out; exterminate; eradicate.
根源 The origin; the source; the root.
根號(數) A radical sign. Root.
根數(數) A root; a radical.
根據 The base; the foundation; the ground. Occupy a firm footing; take root; base upon.
根本上 Fundamentally; basically.
根瘤菌(植) Tubercle bacteria.
根據地 A base of operations; a stronghold.
根本改革 Radical reform.
根本原理 The fundamental (primary) principle.
根本問題 A fundamental question.
根本解決 A radical solution.
根深柢固 Have a firm foundation.

格 gé (n.)- A pattern. A rule. A diagram. Lattice.
(v.)- Move; influence. Reform; change. Attack; resist. Research.
格子 Stripes; lines.
格外 Beyond measure; exceptional; extraordinary; unusual.
格式 A pattern; a model; an example.
格局 Deportment; bearing; style; manner.
格言 A maxim; a wise saying; a proverb.
格殺 Kill.
格調 Metre; tune; rhythm; style.
格陵蘭(地) Greenland.
格蘭姆 Gramme.
格格不入 Repulsive; incongruous.

栽 zāi (v.)- Plant; care for plants.
栽花 Plant flowers.
栽秧 Transplant rice.
栽培 Cultivate; patronize; care for.
栽種 Plant and sow.

栽樹 Plant trees.
栽種花卉 Floriculture.

**桂** (n.)- The cassia tree; the cinnamon tree. Laurel.
guì 桂月 The 8th month.
桂皮 Cassia bark; cinnamon.
桂林(地) Kueilin.
桂花 Osmanthus fragrance; fragrant flower.
桂圓 Dried longans.
桂冠詩人 A poet laureate.

**桃** (n.)- The peach.
桃李 Disciples; pupils.
táo 桃花 Peach blossoms.
桃紅 Pink; peach-coloured.
桃核 Peach stones.
桃仁 Peach kernels.
桃園 A peach garden.
桃源 Arcadia; a place for refuge.
桃樹 A peach tree.
桃醬 Peach jam.
桃色事件 A romantic affair; a love-affair.

**桅** (n.)- A mast.
桅尾 The mast-head.
wéi 桅杆 A mast.

**框** (n.)- A frame; a framework.
框子；框檔 A door frame; a
kuàng window sash.

**案** (n.)- A table. A case in law. A plan; a proposal.
àn (v.)- Examine; try.
案子 Law suit.
案由；案情 The circumstances of a legal case.
案件 A case in law.
案頭日曆 A desk calender.
案情相似 A similar case.

**桌** (n.)- A table; a desk; a stand.
桌子 A table.
zhuō 桌布 Table cloth.
桌面 The top of a table.
桌球 Billiards.

**桐** (n.)- Tung tree. Aleurites cordata.
tóng 桐油 Tung-oil; wood oil.
桐樹 The tung tree–Aleurites cordata.
桐油灰 Putty.

**桑** (n.)- The mulberry tree.
桑子；桑葚 Mulberries.
sāng 桑梓 One's native place.
桑葉 Mulberry leaves.
桑園 A mulberry orchard.
桑田滄海 The changing world.

**桔** (n.)- The small loose-skinned orange.
jú 桔餅 Dried orange flattened like a cake.

**栩** 栩栩 Pleased; well-pleased; lively.
xǔ

**桶** (n.)- A barrel; a cask; a bucket.
桶口 Top of a barrel.
tǒng 桶底 Bottom of a barrel.
桶蓋 Lid of a barrel.

**桿** (n.)- A pole; a post; a handle; a lever.
gān 桿形菌 Bacillus.

**梁** Same as 樑.
(n.)- A bridge. A beam. A dam.
liáng A seam in a cap.
梁木 Beams; timber.
梁柱 Beams and pillars.

**梅** méi (n.)- A plum tree.
梅花 The plum flower; the plumblossoms.
梅雨 The rain in the wet season.
梅毒 Syphilis; veneral disease (VD).
梅樹 A plum tree.
梅花鹿 The spotted deer.
梅雨季 The rainy (wet, pluvial) season.

**梓** zǐ (n.)- The catalpa.
梓鄉；梓里 One's native town.

**梗** gěng (n.)- A stem.
(adj.)- Thorny. Upright; erect. Strong; wilful; stubborn.
梗性 Obstinate in disposition.
梗概 An outline; a general idea; a summary.

**條** tiáo (n.)- A branch. A clause; an article. A law. A strip.
(adj.)- Long. Striped.
條文 The text of regulations.
條目 An item; an article.
條件 A condition; a term; a provision.
條例 Rules; laws; regulations; acts.
條約 A treaty; an agreement.
條紋 Stripes; streaks.
條理 Order; system; sequence. Method; plan. Reasonable; systematic.
條款 Clauses; articles; provisions.

**梟** xiāo (n.)- An owl.
(adj.)- Brave; wicked.
梟首 Exposure of a decapitated head.
梟雄 A wicked, vicious man with some influences and authorities.

**梢** shāo (n.)- A twig; a tree-top.
梢末 The extreme end of a thing.

**梧** wú 梧桐(植) The phoenix tree; Sterculia platanifolia.

**梨** lí Same as 棃.
(n.)- A pear.
梨子 A pear.
梨花 Pear blossoms.
梨園 A theatre; a playhouse.
梨樹 A pear tree.
梨園子弟 Actors.

**梭** suō (n.)- A shuttle.
(v.)- Go to and fro, like a shuttle.
梭子 A shuttle.
梭布 Cotton cloth.

**梯** tī (n.)- A ladder. Steps; stairs.
梯子 A ladder.
梯形(幾) Trapezoid; trapezium.
梯級 Stair steps.
梯氈 Stair carpet.

**械** xiè (n.)- Weapons; arms; fetters; stocks. Tools.
械鬥 Fight with weapons.

**梳** shū (n.)- A coarse comb.
(v.)- Comb.
梳洗 Comb and wash. Dress.
梳粧 Dress up; make one's toilet.
梳頭 Comb the hair.
梳粧臺 A toilet; a dressing table; a dresser.
梳粧具 Toilet-set.

**梵** fàn (n.)- Brahma. Pure and clean.
梵字 Sanskrit characters.
梵咒 Prayers and charms of Buddhists.
梵刹；梵宮 A Buddhist monastery.

梵國(地) India.
梵語 Sanskrit.
梵文學 Sanskrit literature.
梵蒂岡(地) Vatican.

棄 (adj.)- Wasteful.
qì (v.)- Reject; abandon; give up; forget; cast aside; desert.
棄世 Leave the world; die. Renounce the world.
棄去 Give up.
棄邪 Depart from evil; discard erroneous opinions.
棄逐 Expel; drive away.
棄業 Abandon one's property; leave one's occupation.
棄置 Cast away; neglect; throw aside.
棄養 The death of a parent.
棄職 Give up one's post.
棄權 Renounce a right; disclaim one's right; abstain from voting.
棄舊戀新 Reject the old and love the new.

棉 (n.)- The cotton plant; cotton.
mián 棉子 Cotton seed.
棉布 Cotton cloth.
棉衣 A wadded garment.
棉花 The cotton plant. Raw cotton; cotton wool.
棉被 A wadded coverlet.
棉袍 A wadded gown.
棉絮 Cotton rags; cotton fibers.
棉線 Cotton thread.
棉褲 Wadded trousers.
棉襖 A wadded jacket.
棉子油 Cotton-seed oil.
棉紗線 Cotton yarn.
棉花火藥 Gun cotton.

棋 Same as 棊，碁.
qí (n.)- The game of chess.
棋子 Chesses; chessmen.
棋布 Scattered about.
棋盤 A chessboard; a draught-board.
棋戰 Chess-game.
棋譜 A book on chess.
棋逢敵手 Diamond cuts diamond.

棍 (n.)- A stick; a truncheon, a quarterstaff; a club; a staff.
gùn A rascal.
棍子 A stick; a staff.
棍打 Strike with a stick; beat with a cudgel.
棍棒 A staff; a club; a cudgel. An Indian-club (體操用).
棍騙 Swindle; cheat; deceive.

棒 (n.)- A club; a stick; a cudgel; a staff.
bàng (v.)- Strike; beat; cudgel.
棒球 Baseball.
棒喝 A warning.

棗 (n.)- A chinese date tree; a jujube tree.
zǎo 棗子 Dates.
棗核 Date stones.
棗泥色 Date colour; a reddish brown.

棘 (n.)- A thorn; bramble; brier.
jí (adj.)- Troublesome. Earnest; prompt; urgent.
棘手 Troublesome; get pricked in the hand; in difficulty.
棘皮動物 Echinoderm.

棚 (n.)- A mat awning; a shed; a booth.
péng 棚匠 An awning maker.

棟 (n.)- A beam; a pillar; a post; a ridge-pole.
dòng 棟樑 Pillars and beams; important people.

棟樑之才 A man fit to be a pillar of the state.

棠 (n.)- The crab apple. The wild plum.
táng

棧 (n.)- A storehouse; a warehouse; a godown. A hotel; an inn.
zhàn
棧房；貨棧 An entrepot; a warehouse; a storehouse.
棧租 Storage; the price paid for storing; godown charge.
棧單 Warehouse entry (receipt).
棧道 A path in steep places made with boards or planks; a plank road.

森 (adj.)- Overgrown with trees. Dark; somber; abundant. Prosperous; luxuriant. Severe; strict.
sēn
森林 A forest; a wood; woods.
森陰 Dark; dim.
森嚴 Solemn; severe; strict.
森林地帶 A forest zone; woodland.

棲 Same as 栖.
qī
(n.)- A perch; a sleeping house; a place of residence or lodging.
(v.)- Roost; stay; rest; settle down; sleep on.
棲息 Rest.
棲身之所 A shelter.
棲身無所 No place to put oneself at.

棵 (n.)- A numerary adjunct for trees.
kē

棺 (n.)- A coffin; an inner coffin.
guān
棺木；棺材 A coffin.
棺殮 Coffin and grave clothes.
棺槨 Inner and outer coffin.

椅 (n.)- A chair; a seat; a couch.
yǐ
椅子 A chair.
椅背 The back of a chair.
椅墊 A cushion to a chair; chair-cushions.

植 (n.)- Trees; plants.
zhí
(v.)- Plant; set up; erect; lay down. Lean on.
植林 Afforestation.
植物 Plants; vegetables; vegetation.
植樹 Plant trees.
植物油 Vegetable oils.
植物界 The vegetable kingdom.
植物園 A botanical garden.
植物學 Botany.
植樹節 Arbor day; tree-planting day.
植物採集 Plant-collecting. Botanize; herborize.
植物化學 Phytochemistry.
植物標本 A botanical specimen.
植物學家 A botanist.
植樹運動 A tree-planting campaign.

椎 (n.)- A mallet; a club.
zhuī
(chuī)
(v.)- Strike; beat; knock.
椎子 Hammar.
椎骨 Vertebra.
椎鼓 Beat a drum.

椒 (n.)- Spice plants; pepper.
jiāo
(adj.)- Hot; peppery.
椒末 Ground-pepper.
椒粒 Pepper corn.

椰 (n.)- The cocoa-nut tree (palm).
yē
椰子(植) Cocoa-nut.
椰汁 The cocoa-nut milk.
椰肉 The cocoa-nut meat.
椰菜 Cauliflower.
椰乾 Copra.
椰子油 Cocoa-nut oil.
椰子樹 A cocoa-nut palm.

**椶** Same as 棕.
(n.)- The coir palm.
zōng 椶色 Dark brown.
椶墊 A coir mattress.
椶繩 Hemp-palm rope; palm-hair rope.
椶櫚 The palm tree.
椶色人種 The Brown Races.
椶色顏料 Brown oxid.

**楊** (n.)- The aspen; the poplar.
楊柳 The willow.
yáng 楊桃 Sweet carambola.
楊梅 The arbutus; strawberry tree.
楊柳腰 A willowy waist.

**楓** (n.)- The maple tree.
楓葉 Maple leaves.
fēng

**楔** (n.)- A side post. A wedge; a chock.
xiē 楔子 A prologue; a preface; an introduction. A wedge.
楔形 Wedge-shaped; cuneiform.
楔形文字 Cuneiform characters.

**楚** (adj.)- Sharp; keen. Painful. Clear; fresh; bright; clean;
chǔ orderly; distinct.
楚理 Put in order.
楚歌四面 Surrounded on all sides by foes.
楚楚可憐 Piteous.

**楞** (n.)- An edge. Angular.
楞角 Angles or sharp corners.
léng

**楠** Same as 枏.
(n.)- A machilus nanmu.
nán 楠木 A kind of fine yellow wood.
楠梓 A fine, grained hard wood.

**榆** (n.)- The elm tree.
yú

**楣** (n.)- The lintel of a door. The crossbeam.
méi

**楫** (n.)- A paddle; an oar.
楫師 A boatman.
jí

**業** (n.)- Occupation; profession; employment; vocation; calling.
yè Industry; business. Estate; property; patrimony. Merit.
(adv.)- Already.
業主 Owner of property or estate.
業務 Vocation; occupation; business; service; profession.
業經；業已 Already.
業餘 Amateur.
業精於勤 Efficiency comes from diligence.
業餘體校 Amateur Athletic School.
業餘田徑總會 Amateur Athletic Association.

**楮** (n.)- Paper. A paper mulberry.
楮片 Slips of paper.
chǔ 楮紙 Paper.

**極** (n.)- The extremity; the utmost degree. The poles of the earth;
jí end.
(v.)- Reach the end. Exhaust.
(adv.)- Very; extremely; exceedingly.
極力 With all one's strength; use extreme efforts.
極大 Greatest; maximum.

極小 Smallest; mere nothing; minimum.
極少 Next to nothing; very few.
極刑 Capital punishment.
極好 Very good.
極光 The aurora (polaris); the polar lights.
極多 Very many; numerous.
極冷 Cold as stone; intense cold.
極其 Exceedingly; very.
極度 The utter most; the extreme; the highest degree.
極品 The highest rank. The best quality; the best of the kind.
極限 The limit.
極高 Topmost.
極速 At full speed.
極圈 A polar circle.
極端 The extreme; the utmost.
極點 The extreme limit; the climax; the summit.
極權 Totalitarism.
極端派 An extremist; a zealot.
極爲興奮 Be extremely excited; be excited in the extreme.
極樂世界 The abode of the blessed; paradise; an Eden.

**楷** kǎi
(n.)- A model; a pattern.
楷書 The square style of Chinese character-writing.
楷模 A pattern or model.

**榕** róng
(n.)- The banyan tree.
榕城(地) A name for Foochow.
榕樹 Tree with aerial roots; banyan-tree.

**榜** bǎng
(n.)- A notice; an announcement; a placard.
榜示 Announce publicly. Make a public notification.
榜樣 A model; a pattern; an example.

**榨** zhà
Same as 搾.
(n.)- A press for extracting oil or juice.
(v.)- Express; squeeze.
榨汁 Squeeze the juice out of anything.
榨油 Press oil.
榨取 Exact; wring; extort; squeeze; exploit.
榨菜 A kind of preserved mustard.
榨牛乳 Milk a cow.
榨壓機(機) Squeezer.

**榮** róng
(n.)- Glory; honour; splendour; excellency; esteem.
(adj.)- Prosperous; glorious; renown; honourable.
(v.)- Honour; glorify; esteem.
榮光; 榮耀 Glorious; splendid.
榮辱 Honour and disgrace.
榮盛 Prosperous.
榮華 Glory and prosperity.
榮達 Advancement; fame and wealth; great distinction.
榮譽 Renowned; honorary.
榮華富貴 Honour and wealth.

**榴** liú
(n.)- The pomegranate.
榴槤 The durian.

**榻** tà
(n.)- A bed; a couch; a sofa; a divan.
榻墊 A coir-mat bedframe.

**槁** gǎo
(adj.)- Dry; rotten, as wood; withered.

**構** gòu
(v.)- Build; construct; compose; make; plot. Unite; copulate.
構成 Constitute; form; compose.

構思 Design; make a plan.
構造 Structure; construction; frame.
構成公式(化)Constitutional formula.

**槌** chuí (n.)- A mallet; a pestle; a beater; a bludgeon; a hammar; a club.
(v.)- Beat; strike.
槌鼓 Beat drum.
槌擊 Beat with a hammar.

**槍** qiāng (n.)- A spear; a lance. A gun; a rifle.
槍口 The muzzle of a rifle.
槍兵；槍手 A spearman.
槍身 The barrel of a rifle; a gun-barrel.
槍托 The stock of a gun.
槍法 Spear drill; the art of fighting with a spear.
槍柄 A spear-handle.
槍殺 Shoot dead (to death); execute by shooting.
槍眼 A loophole.
槍管 Bore.
槍彈 Cartridge.

**槐** huái (n.)- Locust tree; Sophora japonica.

**槓** gàng 槓杆 A lever.
槓杆作用 Leverage.

**概** gài (n.)- A summary; a condensed statement; general outline. Bearing; attitude.
(adj.)- General.
(v.)- Level; even; adjust; sum up.
(adv.)- Generally.
概念 A concept; a general idea.
概況 A general condition; an outlook.
概括 Sum up; summarize; generalize.
概要 An outline; a summary.
概略 A summary; an outline; the gist.
概論 A sketch; an outline; general remarks; introduction.
概觀 A general view; an outline.

**槳** jiǎng (n.)- An oar; a paddle.
槳手 An oarsman.

**槽** cáo (n.)- A trough; a channel; a groove; a trench; a ditch.

**樁** zhuāng (n.)- A stake; a pile; a stick; a club; a post.

**樂** lè [yuè] (n.)- Music; singing. Pleasure; delight; comfort; joy; ecstasy.
(adj.)- Happy; joyful; delightful; pleasant; cheerful; pleased.
(v.)- Rejoice; find pleasure in; enjoy; take pleasure; be pleased with.
樂土 A paradise. Heaven; fairyland.
樂曲 A tune; a musical piece.
樂師 Musicians.
樂善 Delight in doing good.
樂隊 A band; an orchestra.
樂園 A paradise; Eden; amusement park.
樂意 Willingly; voluntarily.
樂聞 Show willingness to listen.
樂章 A movement.
樂趣 Cheer; pleasant.
樂器 Musical instruments.
樂譜 A musical note; a score.
樂觀 Be optimistic about; look on the sunny side of things; hope for the best.
樂曲家 A musician.
樂觀派 Optimists.

**樑** See 梁.
liáng (n.)- A beam; a ridge.
樑木 Beams; timber.
樑架 Queen post truss; beam truss.
樑柱 Beams and pillars.
樑上君子 A burglar; astealer; a thief.

**樓** (n.)- An upper floor or story; a tower.
lóu 樓上 Upstairs.
樓下 Downstairs; ground-floor.
樓頂 Attic.
樓梯 A staircase.
樓閣 An upper chamber; a terrace.
樓臺 A stage for the theatrical exhibitions; tower.

**標** (n.)- A mark; a sign; a standard; a banner; a beacon; a signal;
biāo a flag. A warrant; a notice. A spear.
(adj.)- Pretty; fine; beautiful.
(v.)- Display; appear. Write; inscribe or insert in a book.
標本 A specimen; a sample.
標記 Marks.
標註 A top-note.
標準 A standard; a norm.
標榜 Publish the list—of successful candidates. Profess; declare.
標旗 A signal flag.
標語 A motto; a slogan; a watchword.
標價 Marked price.
標緻 Very pretty; very beautiful.
標題 A title; a heading.
標點 Punctuation.
標籤 A name-plate.
標準英語 The King's (Queen's) English; the standard English.
標準時間 The standard (universal, international) time; the Greenwich time.
標點符號 Punctuation marks.

**樞** (n.)- An axis; the center of motion; a pivot; a hinge.
shū 樞要 Important; chief; principal.
樞紐 Cardinal point; a hinge; a pivot.
樞密 State affairs.
樞密院 The Privy Council.
樞要之位 An important post.
樞機主教 Cardinal.

**樟** (n.)- The camphor tree.
樟木 Camphor-wood.
zhāng 樟腦 Camphor.
樟樹 The camphor tree; Cinnamomum camphora.
樟腦丸 Camphor balls; moth balls.
樟腦油 Camphor oil.
樟腦精 Spirit of camphor.
樟木箱 A camphor–wood chest.

**模** (n.)- A pattern; a model; a style. An illustration.
mó 模型 A pattern; a model; a mould.
模倣 Imitation. Follow the example of another.
模製 Reproduce; imitate.
模樣 A style; a fashion; a form; shape; looking; appearance.
模糊 Indistinct; blurred; obscure; dim.
模範 A model; a pattern; an example.
模特兒 Model.
模型地圖 A relief-map.
模型飛機 A model aeroplane.
模稜兩可 Ambiguous; two-sided.

**樣** (n.)- A kind; a manner; a way; a pattern; a model; an example.
yàng 樣本 A specimen copy; a standard type.
樣式 A pattern; a fashion; a model;

a style.
樣貨 Pattern; sample.
樣樣 Various; of all kinds.

樵 qiáo
(n.)- A woodcutter.
(v.)- Gather firewood; cut fuel.
樵子；樵夫 A woodcutter; a woodman.

樸 pǔ
Same as 朴.
(adj.)- Plain; simple.
樸素 Plain and unadorned.
樸實 Simple-minded; honest.

樹 shù
(n.)- A tree; a plant.
(v.)- Plant. Set up; erect.
樹木 Trees. Plant trees.
樹立 Set up; erect; raise; establish; found.
樹皮 Bark; rind; cortex.
樹汁 Sap.
樹林 Forests; woods; groves.
樹枝 Branches; boughs; twigs.
樹根 Roots.
樹脂 Resin.
樹陰 The shade of a tree.
樹幹 The trunk of a tree.
樹葉 Leaves.
樹膠 Gum; India rubber.

樺 huà
(n.)- A kind of birch found in Manchuria and Mongolia.
樺木 A birch-tree.

樽 zūn
(n.)- A wine jar; a cask; a barrel.
樽頸 Bottle neck.

橄 gǎn
(n.)- The Chinese olive.
橄欖 Olive.
橄欖色 Olive colour.
橄欖油 Olive oil.
橄欖枝 The olive branch.

橇 qiāo
(n.)- A sledge for mud or snow.

橋 qiáo
(n.)- A bridge.
橋工 Bridge work.
橋洞 The arches of a bridge.
橋脚；橋墩 A bridge pier; an abutment.
橋樑 Bridges; beams that span the distance between the piers.
橋牌 Bridge, a card game for four players.
橋頭堡 A bridge-head.

橘 jú
(n.)- A mandarin orange.
橘紅 Dried orange peel.
橘子水 Orange-ade.
橘紅色 Orange colour.

橙 chéng
(n.)- The common orange.
橙子 An orange.
橙汁；橙露 Orange-ade.
橙色 Orange colour.
橙醬 Marmalade.
橙皮 Orange peel.

機 jī
(n.)- The moving power. Opportunity. A machine; a loom.
(adj.)- Secret.
機匠 A mechanic.
機車 Locomotive.
機要 Important; essential.
機能 A faculty; a function.
機師 An artisan.
機密 Secrecy; a secret.
機械 A machine; an engine.
機敏 Quick; prompt; sharp; clever.
機智 A device; an artifice; a flash of wit.
機雷 A mechanical mine.
機會 An opportunity; a chance; an occasion.

機構 Mechanism; an enterprise; a corporation.
機製 Machine made.
機器 Machinery; a machine.
機關 An organ; an organization. The power in a machine.
機警 Sharp-witted; acute.
機帆船 A steam-and-sail-driven boat.
機車房 Engine house; running shed.
機械化 Mechanize.
機械的 Mechanical; automatic; machine-like.
機械師 Machanist.
機器人 A robot.
機關砲 A gatling-gun; a mitrailleuse.
機關槍 A machine gun; a quick firing gun.
機要秘書 Confidential secretary.
機械力學 Dynamics of machinery.
機密文件 Secret (confidential) documents.
機會主義 Opportunism.
機械工程 Mechanical engineering.
機械工業 Machine building.
機關槍手 A machine-gunner.
機械化部隊 A mechanized (motorized) unit.

橡 xiàng (n.)- The oak tree.
橡子；橡實 Acorns.
橡皮 India rubber.
橡膠 Rubber.
橡皮胎 Rubber tire.
橡皮球 Rubber ball.
橡皮圈 India rubber ring; rubber band.
橡皮膏 Adhesive plaster.
橡皮管 Rubber tubing.
橡膠樹 The gum tree; the rubber tree.

橢 tuǒ (adj.)- Elliptic.
橢圓 An ellipse; an elliptic.
橢圓形 Ellipse; oval form.

橫 héng (n.)- The width; the side; the flank.
(adj.)- Cross; horizontal; transverse. Unreasonable; perverse.
橫死 An unnatural (a violent) death; an untimely end.
橫行 Walk sideways. Unreasonable behavior; outrageous conduct.
橫臥 Lie down; recline; be recumbent.
橫門 A side door; a back door.
橫閂；橫木 A cross-bar.
橫紋 Cross lines; crossgrained.
橫梁 Crossbeams.
橫街 A by (side) street.
橫路 A crossway; a crossroad; sideway; by-way.
橫軸 Cross axis.
橫禍 An unexpected misfortune or calamity.
橫寫 Written in horizontal lines.
橫線 A transverse line; a horizontal line.
橫斷 Intersection; crossing. Traverse; run across.
橫紋木 Cross-grained wood.
橫紋肌(解) Striated (striped) muscles.
橫隔膜 The diaphragm; the midriff.
橫斷面 A transverse (cross) section.
橫行霸道 Act against reason; lawless.

檀 tán (n.)- A kind of hard wood like rosewood; the sandalwood.
檀香山 (地) Honolulu, Hawaii.
檀香木 Sandalwood.
檀香樹 Sandal tree.
檀香扇 Sandalwood fan.

檄 xí (n.)- A manifesto; a proclamation.
(v.)- Issue a manifesto.
檄文 A declaration; a manifesto.

**檐** Same as 簷.
yán (n.)- The eaves of a house.
檐下 Under the eaves.

**檢** (v.)- Examine. Compare. Arrange.
jiǎn 檢字 The index of a dictionary of Chinese characters.
檢定 Official approval (sanction); authorization.
檢查 Look up the records; examine; investigate.
檢疫 Quarantine; medical inspection.
檢閱 Look through; inspect; examine; review.
檢討 Make a self-criticism; review.
檢舉 Prosecution; round up.
檢點 Check; count over; arrange and take an account of.
檢驗 Examine; verify. Hold an inquest.
檢波器 A detector.
檢查官 An inspector; an examiner; a censor.
檢查處 An inspecting office.
檢察長 The chief public procurator; attorney general.
檢察官 Government prosecutor; public procurator.

**檔** (n.)- Shelves; archives.
dàng 檔案 Archives, files.

**檯** Same as 枱.
tái (n.)- A table; a stage.
檯布 Tablecloth.
檯面 The top of a table.
檯球 Ping-pong; table tennis.
檯椅 Tables and chairs.

**檳** (n.)- The betel nut; the areca nut.
bīng 檳榔 The areca nut; the betel nut.
檳榔嶼(地) Penang.

**檸** (n.)- The lemon.
níng 檸檬 The lemon.
檸檬水 Lemonade.
檸檬汁 Lomon juice.
檸檬色 Citrine.
檸檬油 Lemon-oil; the essence of lemon.
檸檬酸 Citric acid.
檸檬露 Lemon-squash.
檸檬冰水 Lemonade and ice.

**檻** (n.)- A railing; bars. A cage. A door-sill; threshold.
jiàn 檻車 A cart with a cage for prisoners.

**櫃** (n.)- A case; a press; a box; a drawer.
guì 櫃子 A cupboard.
櫃桶 A drawer.
櫃檯 A counter.

**榥** (n.)- A stool; bench.
dàng

**櫓** (n.)- A long oar. A watch-tower.
lǔ

**櫚** (n.)- A palm.
lú

**櫻** (n.)- The cherry.
yīng 櫻口；櫻脣 Cherry lips; small mouth.
櫻花 Cherry-blossoms (-flowers).
櫻紅 Light pink; cherry-coloured.
櫻桃 The cherry.

櫻桃樹 The cherry tree.

**欄** (n.)- A railing; a balustrade. A pen or inclosure for animals.
lán A column in newspaper.
欄杆 A balustrade; a hand rail; a railing.

**權** (n.)- A weight. Power; influence; authority. Inherent rights.
quán (adj.)- Influential. Temporary; exigency; circumstances.
(v.)- Weigh; balance.
權力 Power; authority.
權利 Rights; privileges.
權威 Authority; power; influence.
權益 Rights and interests; invested rights.
權勢 Influence; authority.
權衡 Weigh; deliberate; measure. Yard and weight.
權力之爭 A struggle for power.
權威的著作 An authoritative work.

**欖** (n.)- The Chinese olive.
欖仁 The seeds of olives.
lǎn 欖青 Olive green.
欖仁樹 Indian almond.

# 欠部

**欠** (n.)- A yawn; yawning.
(adj.)- Deficient; wanting; lacking.
qiàn (v.)- Owe; lack.
欠伸 Stretch when tired; yawn.
欠缺 Wanting; lacking; deficient.
欠單 A promissory note; an I. O. U; a debt note.
欠款 Debts; liabilities.
欠債 Debt; obligation; liability.
欠錢 Owe money; be in debt.
欠薪 Back pay.
欠資郵票 Postage due stamps.

**次** (n.)- A time. Order; position.
(adj.)- Second; next; secondary; inferior.
cì 次要 Less important.
次日 The next day; the following day.
次年 The next year.
次序；次第 Order; series; sequence.
次於 Inferior to; next in order to.
次長 A vice-minister; an under-secretary.
次貨 Articles of inferior quality.
次等 Second class.
次中音 Tenor.
次高音 Mezzo soprano.
次等貨 Second class goods; goods of second quality.

**欣** (n.)- Joy; delight; gladness.
(adj.)- Happy; joyful; merry; glad.
xīn 欣悉 Be glad to learn that.
欣喜 Happy; joyful; delightful.
欣然 Pleasingly; merrily; with a light heart.
欣慰 Perfectly satisfied; well satisfied.
欣賞 Enjoy (music, a show, etc).
欣賞(圖畫) Admire (a painting, etc).

**欲** (n.)- Desire; passion. Avarice; greed.
yù (v.)- Wish; desire; intend.
欲得 Be desirous of obtaining.

欲望 Expectation; wish; desire.

**欺** (v.)- Cheat; defraud; beguile; befool; insult; abuse.
qī
欺負 Humbug.
欺侮 Insult; abuse; maltreat.
欺凌 Insult; oppress; treat badly.
欺詐 Fraud; imposture; cheating; swindling.
欺騙 Deceive; cheat; swindle; defraud; trick.
欺人者 A deceiver.

**欽** (n.)- Look upon; respect.
(v.)- Respect; admire.
qīn
(adj.)- Imperial; respectful; reverent.
欽仰 Look up to.
欽佩 Heartily agree with; respect.
欽差 An ambassador; a high commissioner.
欽差大臣 An imperial commissioner; an ambassador; diplomatic envoy.

**款** Same as 欵.
(n.)- A kind. An article; a clause. A sum of money. A style.
kuǎn
(adj.)- Sincere; real; true. Empty.
(v.)- Treat well; entertain. Knock at. Reach.
(adv.)- Slowly.
款式 A style; a fashion; a pattern; a sample.
款待 Treat; entertain; give a warm reception.
款項 A sum of money.

**歇** (v.)- Stop a while; halt; quit. Exhaust.
xiē
歇涼 Rest and cool off.
歇息 Take rest; rest a while.
歇業 Stop business; close business.
歇斯底里 Hysteria.

**歉** (adj.)- Deficient; discontented. Ashamed; sorry.
qiàn
歉仄 Regretful.
歉收 A bad harvest; failure of crops.

**歌** (n.)- A song; a ballad.
(v.)- Sing; compose a song.
gē
歌手 A singer.
歌本 A song book.
歌曲 The tune of a song; a song.
歌唱 Sing; chant.
歌詞 The words of a song.
歌頌 Carol. Sing praises.
歌舞 Singing and dancing.
歌劇 An opera; an operette.
歌謠 Folk-songs; popular ballads.
歌劇場 An opera-house.
歌劇團 An opera company (troupe).

**歎** Same as 嘆.
(n.)- Grief; sorrow; sigh.
tàn
(v.)- Sigh; groan. Admire; applaud.
歎氣 Heave a sigh.
歎息 Sigh; moan.
歎惜 Sigh sorrowfully.
歎詞 Interjection.
歎賞 Praise highly; admire; extol; applaud.

**歐** (v.)- Vomit; retch.
歐人 Europeans.
ōu
歐化 Westernize; Europeanize; occidentalize.
歐亞(地) Eurasia.
歐洲(地) Europe.
歐美 Europe and America.
歐戰 The European War.
歐洲大陸 The European Continent.

歐羅巴的 European.

**歡** (adj.)- Jolly; cheerful; merry; pleased; happy.
huān (v.)- Rejoice; be pleased; be glad; delight.

歡心 Favour; goodwill.
歡呼 Cheer; shout with joy.
歡迎 Welcome; give a cordial welcome; receive with open-arms.
歡容 A pleasing face; a cheerful countenance.
歡笑 Laugh with joy.
歡送 Bid farewell; a good send-off.
歡喜 Great joy; delight; rejoice exceedingly.
歡樂 Happy; merry; glad; delightful.
歡呼中 Amid hearty cheers.
歡迎會 A reception; a welcome party.
歡迎辭 An address of welcome; a welcoming address.
歡送會 A farewell meeting; a send-off party.
歡迎參觀 Admission free.

# 止部

**止** (n.)- Deportment; behaviour; conduct.
zhǐ (v.)- Stop; cease; halt; remain; lodge at.
(adv.)- Only; but; simply.

止血 Stanch bleeding.
止步 Stand still; cease from walking. No admittance.
止住 Detain; stop.
止渴 Quench or allay thirst.
止痛 Stop or allay pain.
止癢 Stop itching; allay irritation.
止血藥 Styptics.
止咳藥 A cough medicine.
止痛藥 An anodyne; an antalgic; a balm.

**正** (adj.)- Principal. Legal. Proper; regular. Positive. Straight.
zhèng Exact.
(v.)- Correct; adjust. Govern.

正中 Just in the center.
正切(幾) A tangent.
正文 The text.
正月 January. The first month.
正午 Noon; midday.
正方 Square.
正好 Just all right.
正本 Authentic writing; original copy.
正北 Due north.
正直 Upright; honest; straight.
正門 The main entrance; the front gate.
正負 Positive and negative.
正派 Direct descent. Honest.
正是 Just so.
正面 The right side.
正值；正適 Just at the time of.
正副 The principal and the vice or secondary.
正常 Normal conditions; normalcy.
正割(幾) Secant.
正統 Legitimate; orthodox; traditional; lineal.
正視 Look straight at.
正號(算) Positive sign (+).
正楷 The square style of Chinese writing.
正當 Proper; exact; right; fitting; indispensable.

正義 Righteousness; justice.
正經 Moral; upright and honest.
正道 The right (righteous) road; the way of justice; the path of duty. The true religion.
正電(物) Positive electricity.
正誤 Set straight; adjust; correct an error.
正確 Precise; exact; right; accurate; true.
正數 A positive number.
正方形 A regular square.
正比例 Direct proportion (ratio).
正合時 Just in time.
正教授 A professor.
正規軍 A regular army.
正誤表 A table of errata.
正大光明 Open and impartial; upright and open-minded.
正式組織 The formal organization.
正面衝突 A head-on collision.
正當手續 Legitimate procedure.
正當行爲 A lawful act.
正當要求 Formal demand; fair claim.
正當理由 A just cause.
正義之戰 Fighting for a rightful cause; a righteous war.

此 (pron.)- This; these.
(adj.)- This; the; these.
cY 此人 This man; the said man.
此日 This day.
此外 Besides this; in addition to this; furthermore.
此生 This life.
此次 This time.
此刻 At this moment; now.
此事 This matter.
此後 Hereafter; from now on; henceforth.
此時 At present; for the time being.
此間；此處 This place; here.
此路不通 No thoroughfare.

步 (n.)- A step; a pace. A land measure at five feet. A fate.
bù (v.)- Walk; go on foot; step; march.
步伐 Measured steps. March.
步行 Go on foot; walk; pace; march.
步兵 Infantry; foot soldiers; grenadier.
步哨 Sentry; out guard.
步槍 Rifle.
步調 Pace; step.
步伐整齊 March in order; in fine array.
步步留心 Careful of every step.
步步高陞 Rise step by step.

武 (n.)- A footstep; a trace.
(adj.)- Military; martial; brave;
wǔ courageous; valiant.
武力 Military power (strength); force of arms.
武功 Military merits.
武昌(地) Wuchang.
武漢 Wuhan.
武官；武弁 Military officers; a service man.
武俠 Knightly; chivalrous.
武術；武藝 Military arts.
武備 Armaments; military preparations; the defence.
武裝 Armed; under arms.
武器 Military weapons; arms.
武斷 Decide arbitrarily.
武士道 The way of knighthood; chivalry; bushido.
武力干涉 Military (armed) intervention.
武裝暴動 Take up arms and make a riot.

歧 (adj.)- Forked; divergent; different.
qí 歧字 Synonyms.
歧異 Conflicting; divergent.
歧路 A fork in a road; diverging roads.

歧誤 A mistake.

歪 (adj.)- Awry; slanting; oblique; deflected. Wicked; bad; evil.
wāi (v.)- Crook; curve; bend; distort.

歪曲 Distort; distortion.
歪斜 Out of the straight.
歪路 Oblique road.
歪嘴 A wry mouth.

歲 Same as 嵗.
(n.)- A year. Age.
suì (adj.)- Yearly; annual.
(adv.)- Yearly.

歲杪；歲暮 The end of the year.
歲首 Beginning of a year.
歲數 Age.
歲月如流 Months and years run by as a current. Time flies.
歲月不留人 Time and tide wait for no man.

歷 (adj.)- Orderly; clearly; successive.
lì (v.)- Pass over; undergo; go through. Experience.

歷久 Long ago; for a long time.
歷代 Successive generations; generation after generation; from age to age.
歷史 History; annals.
歷年 Year after year; for many years.
歷法 Astronomy, calculations of the stars and times.
歷來 Heretofore; hitherto.
歷歷 Distinctly; vividly.
歷史家 Historians.
歷史小說 A historical novel.
歷史地理 Historical geography.
歷史眼光 In the light of history.
歷史的事件 A historical event.
歷史唯物論 Historical materialism.
歷史博物館 The historical museum.

歸 (v.)- Return; go back; send back; revert; restore. Belong.
guī Divide. Become loyal.
歸一 Unification; reduction to unity.

歸于 Attribute; ascribe; belong to.
歸天 Die.
歸化 Naturalize. Naturalization.
歸功 Give credit to.
歸咎 Blame; impute to; charge with; be down upon a person; lay at the door of.
歸家 Return home; come back.
歸納 Induce; conclude.
歸國 Return to one's own country.
歸宿 The final resting-place.
歸途 On one's way home (back).
歸程 Homeward.
歸期 The date of one's return.
歸還 Return; restore.
歸納法 The inductive method.
歸屬感 Identification.

# 歹 部

歹 (adj.)- Bad; wicked; malicious; evil; depraved; immoral.
dǎi 歹人 A bad man; a knave.
歹徒 Outlaws; rascals.

死 (n.)- Death; end; demise.
(adj.)- Dead. Lifeless; deadly.
sǐ (v.)- Die. come to an end; lose one's breath; perish; pass

away.
死人 A dead person; a corpse.
死亡 Die. Death; breathlessness; pass away.
死水 Stagnant water.
死囚 A criminal (convict) under sentence of death.
死光 Death ray.
死守 Hold fast till death: die in the last ditch; defend to the last.
死地 Place of execution; place of death.
死物 Inanimate objects; a lifeless thing.
死者 The dead; the deceased.
死刑 A death sentence, capital punishment.
死活 Life and death.
死屍 A corpse; a dead body.
死胎 A still-born child.
死海(地) Dead Sea.
死期 The time of death; the last hour.
死路 A dangerous road; road to death.
死難 Die for the country.
死黨 Sworn confederates.
死亡率 Death-rate; mortality.
死火山 An extinct volcano.
死硬派 The diehards.
死傷者 The dead and injured; the killed and wounded; casualties; losses.
死亡統計 Statistics of mortality.
死亡證書 A certificate of death; a death certificate.
死生與共 Live or die together; share each other's fate.
死裏逃生 A narrow escape.

歿 mò (n.)- Death.

殃 yāng (n.)- Misfortune; calamity; evil accident. Retribution.
(v.)- Punish. Injure.
殃及 Come upon, as calamity.
殃害 Injure.

殆 dài (adj.)- Dangerous; perilous. Near; imminent.
(v.)- Endanger; to be in danger.
(adv.)- About; nearly; only.

殉 xùn (v.)- Be buried with the dead; die for another.
殉國 Die for one's country.
殉情 Favouritism. Comply with people's honours; curry favour.
殉葬 Bury the living with the dead.
殉職 Die at one's post.
殉難 Suffer martyrdom; sacrifice one's life to.

殊 shū (adj.)- Different; unlike; special; distinguish.
(adv.)- Really; very; extremely. Somewhat; rather; truly.
殊甚 Extremely.
殊異;懸殊 Very different; unlike.
殊死戰 Fight to the death.
殊途同歸 Arrive at the same end by different means.

殍 piǎo (n.)- Starvation.
(v.)- Die of hunger; perish.

殖 zhí (v.)- Fatten; prosper; get rich. Produce. Cultivate; propagate; grow; flourish; thrive.
殖民 Colonize; plant a colony. Colonization; colonists.
殖民地 A colony; a settlement.
殖民政策 Colonial policy.

殘 cán (n.)- The remnant; the remainder.
(adj.)- Spoiled; useless. Oppres-

sive; cruel; savage. Withered; injured.
(v.)- Injure; destroy; mangle; kill; spoil; ruin; oppress; slay.
殘月 A waning moon; a morning moon.
殘年 Old age; declining years.
殘兵 Disabled (defeated) soldiers; remnant troops.
殘忍 Cruel. Cold-bloodness; inhumanity.
殘殺 Slaughter; butcher; massacre.
殘害 Injure; destroy.
殘缺 Deficient; broken; imperfect.
殘滓 Leftovers; remnants; leavings.
殘酷；殘暴 Cruelty; brutality; atrocity.
殘廢 Useless; decrepit; disabled.
殘餘 Remainder; remnant; leavings.
殘廢院 Asylum for the disabled.
殘暴行爲 A brutal act; brutalities.

殭 jiāng (adj.)- Dead but corrupted; stiff; rigid; stolid; hard.
殭屍 A rigid (stiff) corpse.
殭直 Stretched out stiffly.

殮 liàn (v.)- Dress a corpse for burial; shroud; encoffin; lay out.
殮服 Shroud.
殮埋 Shroud and bury.

殯 bìn (v.)- Carry to burial; encoffin a corpse; make a funeral; lay out a dead body.
殯葬 Inter; bury.
殯殮 Prepare a corpse for funeral; encoffin.
殯儀館 Funeral parlour.

殲 jiān (v.)- Destroy; kill.
殲滅 Exterminate; annihilate.
殲滅戰 Annihilating operation.

# 殳 部

段 duàn (n.)- A piece; a section; a part; a portion; part of any thing. A paragraph.
段落 A section; a paragraph. A conclusion; an end; a close; a stage.

殷 yīn (n.)- A dark-red colour; blood colour.
(adj.)- Flourishing; abundant; prosperous. Great; many.
(v.)- Regulate.
殷商 Prominent merchant.
殷勤 Diligent and attentive. Treat well; earnestly; assiduously; friendly.
殷實 Substantial; rich; well-to-do.

殺 shā (v.)- Kill; murder; put to death. Reduce; diminish.
(adv.)- Very; furiously.
殺死 Kill; put to death; slay; deprive of life; slaughter.
殺害 Murder; kill.
殺頭 Capital punishment; behead.
殺人犯 Homicide; murder.
殺菌藥 A sterilizer; a germicide.
殺蟲藥 An insecticide; an insect-powder.
殺人事件 A murder case.

殼 kó (n.)- Husk; seed coat; covering; shell; crust.
殼果類(植) Nut.

殿 (n.)- A palace; a hall.
(v.)- Establish.
diàn 殿宇 Temple buildings.
殿下 Your (His, Her) Royal Highness.
殿軍 The rearward of an army; the rearguard; a second runner-up.
殿閣 Pavilions; halls.

毀 (v.)- Break to pieces; destroy. Slander; defame; injure; harm.
huǐ 毀形 Deform; disfigure.
毀棄 Cast away; throw off.
毀滅 Destroy entirely; exterminate; demolish; smash; ravage; extirpate.
毀謗 Throw dirt or mud at.
毀壞 Destroy; spoil; ruin.

毅 (adj.)- Firm; magnanimous; resolute; constant; compact; unshaken.
yì 毅力 Grit; unwearied effort. Intrepidity; steadiness.
毅然 Bravely; courageously; firmly; resolutely.

毆 (v.) Beat; strike; fight; thrash.
ōu 毆打 Beat; fight. A scuffle; a fistic fight.
毆殺 Kill with blows; beat to death.
毆鬥 Fight.

# 毋 部

毋 (v.)- Don't.
(adv.)- Not.
wú 毋去 Don't go.
毋須 There is no necessity.
毋急急 Don't be in hurry.
毋庸介意 Let it pass; do not allow it to trouble you.

母 (n.)- A mother. A dame; a female.
mǔ 母子 Mother and son. Capital and interest.
母牛 Cow.
母后 The empress or queen; queen mother.
母羊 Ewe.
母乳 Mother's milk.
母狗 Bitch.
母音(文) A vowel sound.
母馬 Mare.
母校 A mother college; a mother school; one's alma mater.
母魚 Spawner.
母親 A mother; mamma.
母艦 A depot-ship; a mother-ship; a carrier.
母雞 Hen.
母體 The mother's body.
母性愛 Maternal love; mother's heart; maternity.
母螺絲(工) Nut.

每 (adj.)- Each; every.
(adv.)- Constantly; usually commonly; always.
měi (conj.)- Although.
每一 Every one.
每人 Every man; each person; everybody.
每天 Daily; every day; day by day.
每月 Every month; per month; monthly.

每年 Every year; yearly; annual; annually.
每件 Every article or thing.
每次 On each occasion; every time.
每每 Always; invariably; often; frequently.
每夜 Every night.
每屆 Each term.
每事 Everything.
每季 Quarterly.
每時 Each time.
每處 Everywhere.
每逢 On each occasion; every time. Whenever.
每週 Every week.
每二日 Every other day.
每人一個 One to each.
每況愈下 From bad to worse.

毒 (n.)- A poison; a bane; a venom; an injury; virus; harm.
dú (adj.)- Poisonous; harmful; malicious; cruel; virulent; hurtful.
(v.)- Poison; hate; be indignant against.
毒牙 A poison fang.
毒打 A cruel beating.
毒計 A malicious project; a wicked plan.
毒氣 Noxious vapour; poisonous gas.
毒害 Injure; do evil to others; injure by poisoning.
毒酒 Poisoned wine.
毒素 Toxin; ptomaine.
毒草 Noxious herbs; a poisonous plant (weed).
毒蛇 A venomous snake.
毒菌 Mildew.
毒腺 Poison-glands.
毒瘡 Malignant ulcer.
毒箭 Poisoned arrow.
毒罵 Call one a hard name.
毒蟲 Poisonous insects; vermin.
毒藥 Poison; poisonous drugs.
毒死人 Poison a person.
毒瓦斯 Asphyxiating (poison)gas.
毒氣彈 Poison-gas bombs.
毒氣戰爭 Poison gas warfare.

# 比 部

比 (n.)- An equalization. A comparison.
bǐ (v.)- Compare; collate. Classify; sort. Equal. Follow.
(adv.)-When.
比方 For instance.
比例(數) Ratio; proportion.
比武 Compare strength.
比重(物) Specific gravity.
比率 A ratio.
比喻 A parable; a metaphor; an illustration; an allegory.
比試 Compete with.
比照 According to.
比較 Compare.
比對 Pair; match.
比熱 Specific heat.
比鄰 Near neighbours.
比賽 Compete.
比目魚(動) A flatfish.
比利時(地) Belgium.
比例尺 A proportional scale.
比重計 A standard hydrometer; a densimeter; a stereometer.
比較級(文) The comparative degree.
比例中數 The mean proportional.

# 毛 部

**毛** (n.)- The hair of an animal; fur; feather.
máo (adj.)- Rough; coarse.
(v.)- Deprive of hair.

毛巾 Towel.
毛孔 Pores of the skin.
毛皮 Fur.
毛布；粗布 Sackcloth.
毛竹 A large variety of bamboo.
毛羽 Fur and feathers.
毛病 A fault; a flaw; a defect. Disease.
毛毯 Blanket.
毛筆；毛穎 A hair pen; a brush pen; Chinese pen.
毛髮 The hair.
毛氈 Carpet.
毛利 Gross profit.
毛鬃 Hog bristle.
毛襪 Worsted (woolen) socks.
毛玻璃 Ground glass.
毛細管(解) Capillary tubes.
毛絨線 Woolen yarn; worsted; Berlin wool.
毛織物 A woollen textile; stuff goods; woolen goods (cloth).
毛髮悚然 Hair standing on end; horror-stricken.
毛髮脫落；禿頭症 Alopecia.

**毧** (n.)- Fine, soft fur; felt.
róng (adj.)- Felt.
毧毡 Felt rugs.

**毫** (n.)- The down on plants; long, soft hair. Extremely light in weight.
háo
毫無 Not an ace. In no way.
毫髮 A minute thing.
毫釐 Very little. A mere fraction.

**毬**
qiú 毬板 A racket.

**毯** (n.)- Rugs; carpets. Blankets.
tǎn 毯子 A rug; a carpet.

**氈** (n.)- Felt; rugs; druggets.
zhān 氈匠 A felt maker.
氈帽 Felt hats or caps.
氈毯 Druggets and carpets.
氈鞋 Felt shoes.
氈褥 A felt mattress.

# 氏 部

**氏** (n.)- Family name. A family. A clan. A person.
shì 氏族 Clan.
氏族社會 Gens society.

**民** (n.)- The people; citizens; inhabitants; subjects; populace; mass.
mín
民心 Popular sentiments; the

minds of the people.
民主 Democracy.
民生 The livelihood of the people.
民兵;民丁 A militiaman; volunteers; citizen soldier.
民俗 Folk customs.
民政 Civil administration.
民軍 Militia.
民情 Popular feelings.
民族 Tribes; a race; the nation.
民衆 The people; the masses.
民間 Among the common people. Popular; civilian.
民歌 Ballad; folk songs.
民權 The people's rights; the civil right.
民主化 Democratize.
民主制 Democratic system.
民主國 A democratic state.
民主黨 The Democrats; a democratic party.
民主主義 Democracy; democratism.
民主政體 Democracy; government by the people.
民事法庭 A civil court.
民事案件 A civil case (suit, action).
民事訴訟 A civil action (procedure).
民族主義 The principle of nationalism.
民族平等 Racial equality.
民族自決 Racial self-determination.
民族問題 A problem of nationalities.
民族精神 The racial spirit.
民衆運動 Popular movement.
民間故事 Folk-tale.

**氓** méng (n.)- The people.

# 气 部

**气** qī Same as 氣. (n.)- Breath; air; steam; gas. Weather.

**氖** nǎi (n.)- Neon.
氖燈 Neon lamp.

**氟** fú (n.)- Fluorine.

**氣** qī (n.)- Air; steam; gas; vapour; atmosphere; mist; fume. Breath. Spirit. Temper. Influence. Smell. Weather; climate.
(v.)- Irritate; enrage.
氣力 Strength; energy.
氣化(物) Vaporization; evaporation.
氣孔 Breathing holes; a pore; (植) a stoma; (動) a stigma.
氣死 Grieve to death.
氣色 Colour; tint; shade.
氣味 Flavour; smell; odour; scent.
氣泡 A bubble.
氣息 Breath.
氣根(植) Aerial roots.
氣流 An air (aerial, atmospheric) current.
氣候 Climate; weather; temperature.
氣球 A balloon; an aerostat.
氣喘 Asthma; shortness of breath; panting.
氣圈 Atmosphere.
氣窗 Transom; air window.
氣惱 Rage; anger.

氣象 Appearance; bearing; looks. Weather; atmospheric phenomena.
氣絕 Exhausted; dead; breathless.
氣勢 Strength; spirit; animation.
氣溫 Atmospheric temperature.
氣概 Resolution; determination.
氣管 The windpipe; the trachea.
氣節 A strong character. Season.
氣魄 Spirit; overpowering influence.
氣質 Natural qualities; temperament; disposition.
氣壓 Atmospheric pressure.
氣體 Gas; vapour.
氣象圖 A weather map (chart).
氣象臺 Meteorological observatory.
氣量大 Generous; magnanimous.
氣量小 Narrow-minded.
氣壓表 A manometer; a barometer.
氣墊船 A hovercraft.
氣味相投 Be like minded; be of the same cast of mind.
氣候溫和 Mild climate.
氣管支炎 Bronchitis.

**氧** yǎng See 養. (n.)- Oxygen.

**氦** hài (n.)- Helium.

**氫** qīng See 輕. (n.)- Hydrogen.
氫彈 Hydrogen bomb.

**氬** yà (n.)- Argon.

**氮** dàn See 淡. (n.)- Nitrogen.

**氯** lǜ See 綠. (n.)- Chlorine.

# 水部

**水** shuǐ (n.)- Water; a flood. A stream. Liquid; fluid.Discount. (adj.)- Aqueous; aquatic; watery; liquid.
水力 Water power.
水土 Climate.
水分 Water; moisture; humidity.
水庫 A reservoir.
水塘 A pond; pool.
水牛 A buffalo.
水手 Sailors; seamen; crew; navigator.
水仙(植) Daffodil; narcissus.
水平；水準 Water-level.
水田 A paddy-field; a rice-field.
水母(動) A jelly-fish.
水池 A water-tank; a cistern; a basin.
水兵 Bluejackets; a marine soldier.
水利 Water beneficial to agriculture.
水災 An inundation; a flood; a deluge.
水車 Water-wheels.
水泥 Cement.
水泡 A bubble. A blister.
水芹(植) Water celery.
水柱 A water-column.
水流 Water current.
水星(天) Mercury.
水盆 Basin.
水缸 Earthen jar.

水面 The surface (level) of the water.
水氣 Moisture; dampness.
水根 Water root.
水草 An aquatic plant; a water-plant.
水桶 A water-bucket; a water-pail.
水袋 A water-bag.
水深 The depth of water.
水產 Marine products; aquatic products.
水蛇 Water snakes.
水漲 High tide.
水退 Low tide.
水莖(植) Water stem.
水晶 Crystal.
水痘(醫) Chicken-pox; varicella.
水菓 Fresh fruit.
水萍(植) Duckweed.
水路 The waterway; the watercourse.
水塔 Water tower.
水溝；溝渠 Drain; ditch; gutter.
水源 The source of a river; the headwaters.
水腫(醫) Dropsy; hydropsy; oedema.
水運 Water carriage; transportation by water.
水雷 A torpedo; a submarine mine.
水閘 A weir; a sluice. A dam; a canal lock; a flood-gate.
水管 Water pipe.
水銀 Mercury; quicksilver.
水槽 An aqueduct; a cistern; a gutter.
水稻(農) Rice.
水線 Water line.
水螅(動) Fresh-water polyp.
水險 Marine insurance.
水鴨(動) A teal; a water duck.
水龍 Fire-engine.
水壓 Hydraulic pressure; water pressure.
水獺(動) The common otter.
水邊 The waterside.
水警 Marine police.
水龍頭 Tap; cock.
水手裝 A seaman's uniform; a sailor blouse (suit, costume)( 兒童用 ).
水仙花(植) Narcissus.
水平面 A horizontal-plane; a level surface.
水平線 The horizontal line; the sea-line; the horizon.
水彩畫 Water colour painting.
水族館 An aquarium.
水晶石 Kryolite.
水晶宮 The crystal palace.
水雷艇 A torpedo-boat.
水蜜桃 A chingstone peach.
水蒸氣 Steam; aqueous vapour.
水銀柱 The column of mercury; barometric column.
水銀燈 A mercury lamp.
水壓機 Hydraulic press.
水上飛機 A hydroplane; a sea-plane; a water-plane.
水土不服 The climate does not agree; unused to a place.
水利工事 Embankment works; river embanking.
水災救濟 Flood relief.
水產公司 Marine products company.
水落石出 When the water ebbs, stone appear—saying the case is made clear.
水力起重機 Hydraulic crane.
水力發電機 Water motor; a hydroelectric machine.
水力發電廠 A hydro-electric power station (plant).
水上運動會 An aquatic sports meeting.
水產博覽會 Marine products exhibition.
水陸兩用機 An amphibian plane.
水陸兩棲類 The Amphibia.

**永** (adj.)- Perpetual; long; permanent; final; eternal; everlasting.
yǒng (v.)- Prolong.

(adv.)- Always; perpetually; forever.
永久 Eternity; permanence; everlasting; perpetual.
永不 Never.
永生 Eternal life; immortal.
永存 Perpetual existence. Everlasting.
永安 Perpetual repose; perpetual peace.
永固 Permanently fixed.
永别 A final separation; parting forever.
永遠 Eternally; perpetually; forever.
永壽 Long life; longevity.
永久中立 Permanent neutrality.
永久和平 A permanent or lasting peace.
永不分離 Inseparable; never to be separated.
永遠之計 A permanent plan; a far-reaching policy.

氾 fàn (n.)- Water overflowing; a flood.
(adj.)- Unsettled. Wide; extensive.
(v.)- Inundate; overflow; flood.
氾濫 Inundate; overflow; flood.

汀 tīng (n.)- A low, level bank along a river; a beach.
汀洲 An islet.

汁 zhī (n.)- Juice; liquor; gravy.
汁水 Juice; essence.
汁漿 Gravy; juice.

求 qiú (n.)- A request; a claim; a demand.
(v.)- Beg; ask; request. Look for; entreat; supplicate.
求乞 To beg for alms.
求友 Seek for a friendship.
求生 Sue for life; seek for life.
求見 Seek for an interview.
求利 Seek after gain.
求和；求成 Sue for peace; make overtures of reconciliation.
求情 Ask a favour; appeal to another's mercy.
求救 Ask for help.
求教 Ask advice of; ask for instruction.
求婚 Woo; sue for one's hand in marriage; propose to; court.
求愛 Make love to. Courtship.
求學 Seek for learning; study.
求婚者 A suitor; a wooer.
求人不如求己 Better depend on one's self than ask for help from others.

汎 fàn (n.)- High water; high tide.
(adj.)- Wide; universal; watery; wet.
(v.)- Float; be driven by winds and waves.
汎舟 Float a boat.
汎美 Pan-American.
汎愛 Universal love.

汐 xī (n.)- The evening tide; night tide.

汕 shàn (n.)- A basket for catching fish.
汕頭(地) Swatow.

汗 hàn (n.)- Sweat; perspiration.
(v.)- Sweat.
汗巾 A handkerchief; a towel.
汗衫 A shirt; underwear; a banian; a sweater.
汗珠 Beads of sweat.
汗疹 Lichen; hydroadenitis.
汗腺(解) Sweat gland.
汗顏 Blush with shame; feel ashamed of.
汗血錢 Money earned by the sweat of one's brow.

**汚** Same as汙.
wū (n.)- Stagnant water; dirt; impurity; foulness; stain.
(adj.)- Dirty; filthy; impure. Corrupt; mean; unclean.
(v.)- Insult; speak evil against. Defile; become dirty; stain.
汚水 Foul water; sewage; slops.
汚吏 Corrupt officials; covetous and mean officials.
汚物 Filth; dirt; dust.
汚染 Stain. (海港) Contaminate (the harbour, etc.) (空氣) Pollute (the air etc.)
汚辱 Insult; affront; dishonour; bring disgrace upon.
汚語 Dirty words.
汚穢 Dirty; foul; filthy; impurity.
汚點 A stain; a spot; a blemish; a taint; a blot; a blur.
汚衊 Abuse slanderously.

**汛** (n.)- High water. A military post.
xùn (v.)- Sprinkle. Guard.
汛地 Guard station.
汛兵 The police.

**汝** (pron.)- You; your; thou.
rǔ 汝曹；汝等 You, in plural number.

**汞** (n.)- Quicksilver; mercury.
gǒng 汞粉(化) Calomel.

**江** (n.)- A river.
jiāng 江口 An estuary; the mouth of a river.
江山 Rivers and mountains—the country; territory.
江水 River water.
江西(地) Kiangsi.
江河 Rivers.
江南(地) Kiangnan, south of the Yangtze River.
江浙(地) Kiangsu and Chekiang.
江湖 Rivers and lakes.
江蘇(地) Kiangsu.

**池** (n.)- A pond; a pool; a reservoir.
chí 池水 Pond water.
池塘 A pool; a pond.

**汪** (n.)- A vast expanse of water.
wāng (adj.)- Wide and deep; vast.
汪洋 The wide ocean; the open sea.

**汰** (adj.)- Excessive.
tài (v.)- Wash out; rinse; clean; cleanse; scour; correct; revise.
汰去 Purify.
汰侈 Too extravagant.

**汲** (v.)- Draw water. Draw forth; lead; drag.
jí 汲水 Draw water.
汲水桶 Bucket.
汲水機 A water-elevator.

**決** (v.)- Open out. Cut off; execute. Decide; settle; determine; resolve upon. Cleanse; purify; clear out. Pass sentence by.
jué (adv.)- Certainly; decidedly; no doubt; surely; undoubtly.
決口 A breach.
決心 Resolution; resolve; determination. Make up one's mind.
決不 Never; by no means; not for the life; on no account.
決定 Decide; determine; set down; fix; conclude; make a decision.
決要 Insist on. Determined to have.
決然 Certainly; determinately; decided-

ly; surely.
決非 Anything but; certainly not.
決裂 Destroy; ruin; breach; split; rupture; break up.
決算 Settlement of accounts.
決賽 Final contest.
決斷 Decide; determine. Judgment. Determination.
決議 Resolve; decide. A resolution.
決定權 The decisive power; the casting-vote.
決算表 Balance-sheet.
決議案 Closing bill; a resolution.
決鬥書 A letter of challenge; a cartel.

**汽** qì (n.)- Vapour; steam; gas.
汽化 Vaporization.
汽水 Aerated water.
汽車 A motor car; an automobile; motor vehicles.
汽油 Gasoline; petrol.
汽缸 Cylinder.
汽浴 Russian bath; Turkish bath.
汽船 A steamship; a steamboat; a steamer.
汽笛 A steam whistle; a siren; a hooter.
汽墊 Air cushion.
汽槍 Air gun; pop-gun.
汽鍋 Steam boiler.
汽車間 Garage.
汽油站 Gas station.
汽油彈 Napalm.
汽車司機 Chauffeur; driver.
汽車工廠 Auto plant.
汽車保險 Car insurance.
汽車餐廳 Drive-in (restaurant).
汽車速度表 An autometer; a speedometer.
汽機抽水器 Steam pump.

**沁** qìn (v.)- Soak into; penetrate.

**汾** fén (n.)- Name of a river in Shansi (山西).

**沃** wò (adj.)- Rich; fertile; fat; luxuriant.
沃土 Fertile soil; rich soil.
沃溉 Irrigate.
沃壤 A rich soil; rich tracts.
沃饒 Rich; fertile; fruitful; productive.

**沅** yuán (n.)- Name of a river in Hunan (湖南).

**沉** chén (adj.)- Deep; profound. Sunk. Ruined; depraved; destroyed. (v.)- Sink; submerge; drown; fall into; immerse; droop;
沉水 plunge; indulge.
沉吟 Sink in the water.
沉沒 Hesitate.
Sink; go down; be submerged; be lost in water; sink to the bot-
沉思 tom of a river.
Ponder; think deeply. A state of
沉重 mental absorption.
沉浮 Very heavy; sedate; grave; serious.
Floating up and down; bobbing
沉船 on the water.
沉冤 A shipwreck; a sunken ship.
沉痛 An unredressed wrong.
Acute pain; serious; pathetic; grave.
沉悶 Closeness; humdrum.
沉溺；沉迷 Infatuated; addicted to; confused; drowned.
沉着 Imperturbable; firm; calm; serene.
沉睡 Sound sleep.
沉醉 Intoxicated; dead drunk.
沉澱 Sedimentation.
沉靜 Silent; sedate; imperturbable; stillness.

沉默 Keep silent; hold one's tongue. Silence; reticence.
沉澱物 A precipitate; a sediment; a deposit.
沉迷不醒 Deeply infatuated in vice.

沌 dùn See 混沌. (adv.)- Confused; chaotic; turbid.

沐 mù (v.)- Wash; bathe. Receive favours.
沐浴 Wash the hair and the body; bathe.

沒 mò 〔méi〕 (adj.)- Gone. Exhausted. Sunk; dead.
(v.)- Die; perish. Sink; immerse; drown. Disappear; vanish. Exceed.
(adv.)- Not; no; never.
(prep.)- Without.
沒用 Useless.
沒收 Forfeiture; confiscation.
沒有 None; there is not..
沒法 No help; without remedy.
沒落 Ruin; fall; downfall.
沒趣 Uninteresting; unpleasant.
沒出息 Good for nothing.
沒奈何 No help for it; no alternative left.
沒精打彩 Dispirited and discouraged.
沒頭沒腦 Stupid; heedlessly; thoughtlessly.

沖 chōng (v.)- Rise high; shoot up. Wash with running water.
沖天 Rising (shooting up) to heaven; soaring; booming.
沖茶 Infuse tea.
沖破 Burst open.
沖撞 Offend in word.
沖照片 Developing, fixing and washing.
沖積土 Alluvial soil; alluvion; alluvium.
沖繩島(地) Okinawa.

沙 shā Same as 砂.
(n.)- Sand; pebbles. Reefs; sand banks; beaches. A desert.
沙土 Sandy soil.
沙布 Emery-cloth.
沙石 Sand stone; pebbles.
沙丘 A sand hill; a dune.
沙地 A sandy tract; the sands.
沙洲 A shoal; a sandbank.
沙眼(醫) Trachoma.
沙堆 Sand dunes.
沙梨(植) The sweet pear.
沙漠 A desert.
沙磚 Bath brick; sand brick.
沙糖 Brown sugar.
沙鍋 An earthenware cooking pot.
沙聲 Hoarse.
沙灘 A sand beach; the sands.
沙龍 Salon.
沙籠 Sarong, a strip of cloth worn as a skirt by Malays.
沙丁魚 Sardine.
沙皮紙 Sand paper.
沙發椅 A sofa; a couch; a lounge.
沙漏水 Filtered water.
沙勝越(地) Sarawak.
沙特阿拉伯(地) Saudi Arabia.

沛 pèi (adj.)- Abundant; plentiful. Sudden. Precipitate.
沛然下雨 Pour in torrents.

沫 mò (n.)- Foam; bubbles. Spittle; saliva; froth.

沮 jǔ (v.)- Stop; prohibit; destroy; squash; injure; ruin; spoil.
沮止 Stop.
沮喪 In low spirit; downcast.

**河** hó (n.)- A river; a canal; a stream; a brook.
河山 Territory.
河口 The mouth of a river; an estuary.
河內(地) Hanoi.
河水 River water.
河北(地) Hopei.
河床 River bed.
河系 River system.
河岸 River bank.
河底 River bottom; a river-bed.
河流 A river course; waterway.
河南(地) Honan.
河套 The Great Bend of the Yellow River.
河畔 The riverside; the side (bank) of a river.
河馬(動) The hippopotamus.
河堤 Canal bank; dyke.
河港 River port.
河豚(動) Globe fish.
河源 The source of a river.
河道 River course; stream.
河灣 A bend in a river.
河東獅 A shrew; a virago.
河道工程(工) River engineering.

**沸** fèi (v.)- Boil; bubble up.
沸水 Boiling water.
沸石(鑛) Zeolite.
沸溢 Boil over.
沸點 The boiling point.
沸騰 Boiling; ebullition; excitement; unrest.

**油** yóu (n.)- Oil; grease; fat. Paint.
(adj.)- Fat; oily; glossy. Glazed; easy; gilding; smooth.
油井 Oil-well.
油田 Oilfield.
油布 Oilcloth.
油門 Accelerator.
油印 Oleograph.
油汚 Smeared with oil; greasy; oil-stained.
油刷 Paint brush.
油味 Oily taste.
油店 Oil shop.
油氣 Oil; fat; grease.
油紙 Oiled paper.
油脂(化) Olein; grease.
油條；油炸檜 Fritters of twisted dough.
油渣 Oil cake.
油畫 An oil-paintings (colour); a picture in oils.
油菜(植) Rape.
油跡 Oil stains.
油滑 Slippery.
油煎 Fry in fat.
油膏 Ointment.
油漆 Paint; varnish.
油箱 Fuel tank.
油嘴 Oily-tongued; a flattery tongue.
油膩 Oily; fatty.
油豆腐 Fried bean-curd.
油頁岩 Oil-shale.
油畫家 An oil-painter.
油畫像 An oil portrait; a portrait in oils.
油漆匠 Painters.
油腔滑調 Glib, plausible speech.
油漆未乾 Wet paint; new varnish.
油鹽醬醋 Oil, salt, soy and vinegar—condiments.

**治** zhì (v.)- Govern; rule; manage; regulate; control. Punish. Heal; cure; remedy; treat.
治水 Regulate the waters; reduce the waters to order.
治安 Public order; public safety; security.
治家 Manage or rule a family.
治病 Cure illness; heal; remedy.

治國 Govern a state.
治理 Manage; put in order; rule over.
治產(法) Administering of property.
治喪 Attend to funeral rites; look after funerals.
治罪 Punish.
治療 Medical treatment; a surgical operation; cure.
治水工程 Embankment work; river embanking.
治外法權 Extraterritoriality.
治理家務 Housekeeping.
治國安民 Rule wisely.

**沼** zhǎo (n.)- A pond; a pool. A marsh; a bog.
沼地 A marshy (swampy) place; a bog-land.
沼氣 Methane; marsh gas.

**沽** gū (v.)- Buy; sell.
沽名釣譽 Fish for praise and reputation.

**沾** zhān (v.)- Moisten; wet. Tinge; stain. Be imbued with; be infected with. Receive benefits from. Add.
沾光 Gain some advantage from another; get through your grace.
沾染 Be imbued with; be affected by; be infected with.
沾濕 Damp; wet; moist.
沾沾自喜 In good spirits; feel happy about it; very much contented.
沾花惹草 Enticing and seductive.
沾染惡習 Corrupted by bad habits.

**沿** yàn [yán] (v.)- Follow; go along. Hand down; continue.
(prep.)- Along; by.
沿江 Along the river.
沿岸 Along the coast.
沿海 Along the sea-coast.
沿途；沿路 Along the way.
沿海漁業 Inshore fishery.

**況** kuàng (n.)- Condition; circumstance; situation.
(adv.)- Moreover; furthermore.
況且 Besides; moreover.

**泄** xiè (adj.)- Easy.
(v.)- Scatter; leak; disperse.
泄氣 Leakage.
泄痢(醫) Diarrhea.
泄漏 Disclose; leak out.
泄水閘 A flood-gate; a lock.
泄漏秘密 Divulge a secret; violate confidence.

**泗** qiú (v.)- Swim; float.
泗水 Swim.

**泉** quán (n.)- A spring; a fountain. Coin.
泉水 Spring water.
泉源 Source.

**泊** bō (n.)- A marshy lake.
(v.)- Anchor; touch at; moor; park (a car).
泊岸 Disembark.
泊船 Anchor a ship; moor a boat.
泊期 Lay days.
泊車 Park a car.

**泌** mì (v.)- Bubble out; secrete; excrete; gush forth.
泌尿管(解) Urinary passage.
泌尿器(解) Urinary organ.

**法** fǎ (n.)- Law; rules; regulations; code; statute. Ways; method; means.

(adj.)- Legal.
(v.)- Imitate; take as an example.
法人 A legal person; a juridical person.
法子；方法 Means; ways; method.
法文 The French language. (法) Text of law.
法令 Laws and ordinances.
法例 Precedent.
法定 Legal; authorized; prescribed by law.
法官 A judge; a judicial officer.
法典 Code; statue; canon.
法治 Government by law.
法律 Laws; statutes; code.
法院 Courts of justice.
法庭 Law court; forum; court of justice.
法郎 The *franc*, unit of money in France; Belgium and Switzerland.
法條 Articles of law.
法國；法蘭西(地) France.
法術 The black arts; magic.
法場 An execution ground.
法碼 Balance weight; standard weights.
法權 Legal right.
法律學 The science of law. Jurisprudence.
法蘭絨 Flannel.
法定年齡 Legal age.
法定期間 Legal time.
法定價格 Legal price.
法律問題 Legal question.
法律範圍 The sphere of the law.
法律顧問 A legal adviser; a juriconsult; counsel.
法西斯主義 Facism.
法定承繼人 The legal heir; the heir-at-law.

泛 fàn
(adj.)- Unguided; careless; vague; reckless.
(v.)- Float; drift; sail.
泛舟 Float a boat.
泛交 A superficial acquaintance.
泛論 A general remark.
泛濫 Overflow; inundation.

泡 pào
(n.)- Froth; a bubble; foam; a blister.
(v.)- Soak; dip.
泡沫 Bubbles; foam; froth.
泡茶 Make tea; infuse tea.
泡製 Decoction. Decoct, as medicine.
泡影 A glittering bubble–unreality.

波 bō
(n.)- Waves; surges; billows.
波狀 Wave form; undulation.
波長(物) Wave length.
波紋 Ripples; a water-ring.
波浪 Waves; surges; billows.
波動 A wave motion; undulation. Rise and fall; undulate. (幣值) Fluctuations.
波斯(地) Persia.
波濤 Waves; billows; surges.
波蘭(地) Poland.
波平浪靜 Calm waters.
波利維亞(地) Bolivia.
波羅的海(地) The Baltic Sea.
波羅密多 *Paramita*; moral and intellectual perfection.
波濤洶湧 Waves roaring; rough.
波茨坦宣言 The Potsdam Declaration.

泣 qì
(n.)- Weeping; lamentation.
(v.)- Weep silently; lament; shed tears.
泣別 Part weeping (in tears); tear oneself away from.
泣哭 Weep; cry.
泣訴 Tell with tears.
泣聲 A tearful voice; a cry.

泥 nǐ
(n.)- Mud; mire. Earth; soil; clay.
(adj.)- Muddy. Adhesive.

泥人；泥像 A clay image.
泥土 Mud; earth; soil.
泥地 A clay soil; a muddy place.
泥炭 Peat; turf.
泥屋 Mud house.
泥堆 Mound.
泥路 A muddy road.
泥漿 Mire.
泥磚；土磚 Sun-dried bricks.
泥濘 Muddiness; miriness.
泥鰍(動) The loach.
泥水匠 A mason; a brick-layer; a plasterer.

注 (v.)- Pour; infuse; soak. Fix the mind on; lend into. Record.
zhù Stake. Comment.
注入 Pour into; instil; inject.
注目 Fix the eyes upon; gaze at; watch; pay attention to.
注重 Concentrate on; lay stress upon.
注射 Injection; inject.
注視 Gaze steadily; observe closely; watch.
注意 Attend to; observe; watch; give attentive application; pay attention to.
注意力 The power of attention.
注音符號 Phonetic alphabet.
注射藥水 An injection; a clyster.
注意事項 Matters that demand special attention.
注意集中 Concentrate (accumulate) attention upon.

泮 (n.)- A bank; a shore. A pool before a study hall.
pàn (v.)- Scatter. Melt; break.
泮冰 Melt like ice.

泯 (v.)- Flow off; stop; put an end to.
mǐn 泯亂 Disorder; confusion.

泰 (adj.)- Large; great; extensive; grand; excellent; superior. Liberal; broadminded.
tài 泰山 Tai Shan, Shantung. Father-in-law.
泰平 Peace.
泰國(地) Thailand.
泰然 Calm and composed.

泱 (adj.)- Widespread; expansive; boundless.
yāng 泱泱 Vast and deep; expansive.

泳 (v.)- Dive; swim.
泳池 Swimming pool.
yǒng

洋 (n.)- The ocean.
(adj.)- Wide; vast; extensive.
yáng Foreign.
洋人 Foreigners.
洋化 Westernised.
洋文 Foreign language.
洋行 Foreign firms; hongs.
洋房 A foreign-style building.
洋服 Foreign clothes.
洋酒 Foreign drinks (liquors).
洋貨 Imported goods; foreign goods (articles).
洋琴 Piano. The butterfly harp.
洋葱(植) Onions.

洗 (v.)- Cleanse; purify. Bathe; wash; rinse.
xǐ 洗刷 Cover the defects of. Wash and brush.
洗淨 Wash clean; wash down.
洗塵 Entertain a returned friend.
洗熨 Wash and iron smooth.
洗澡 Bathe; take a bath.
洗頭 Shampoo.
洗濯；洗滌 Wash; cleanse.
洗禮 Receive baptism; be baptised.

Baptism.
洗衣板 A washboard.
洗衣桶 A washtub.
洗衣裳 Wash clothes.
洗衣機 A washing-machine.
洗面所 A lavatory; a wash-stand.
洗衣店 A laundry.
洗面架 A wash-stand.
洗面盆 A wash basin.
洗澡房 A bathroom.
洗澡盆 A bathing tub.
洗耳恭聽 Wash the ears and listen reverently; listen with reverent attention.
洗衣肥皂 Washing soap.
洗滌用藥 A wash; a lotion.

洛 luò (n.)- Name of a river in Honan (河南).
洛陽(地) Loyang.

洞 dòng (n.)- A hole. A cave.
洞穴 A cavern; a grotto.
洞察 Examine thoroughly; discern.
洞庭湖(地) The Tungting Lake in Hunan.
洞房花燭 Wedding festivities.
洞若觀火 As clear as looking at a fire.

津 jīn (n.)- A ferry; a ford. Saliva.
(v.)- Moisten; overflow.
津貼 Extra money; gratuity; allowance; subsidy. Help with money.
津津有味 Very interesting.

洪 hóng (n.)- Flood.
(adj.)- Great; extensive.
洪水 A deluge; a flood.
洪亮 Loud.
洪恩 Great benevolence (kindness, favour).
洪量 Magnanimity.
洪爐 A great furnace.
洪福齊天 Your vast happiness is as high as the sky.

洲 zhōu (n.)- A continent. An islet.
洲際導彈 Intercontinental (ballistic) missile.

洵 xún (adv.)- Really; truly.

洶 xiōng (n.)- The rush of water. Excitement; clamour; uproar.
洶動 Unquiet; excited.
洶湧 The forcible rush of water; the dashing of waves.

活 huó (n.)- Life; livelihood; living.
(adj.)- Living; lively; active; nimble; mobile; movable.
(v.)- Live.
(adv.)- Alive.
活力 Vital energy; vitality.
活用 Put to practical use; make practical application.
活字；鉛字 Movable types.
活命 Live on; survive.
活門；活塞 A valve; a piston.
活埋 Bury alive.
活捉 Catch alive.
活該 Serve you (him) right.
活現 Vivid; lifelike.
活動 Movable; active; versatile. Move actively; show activity.
活路 A thoroughfare; a way out of the difficulty.
活輪(機) Idle wheel.
活躍 Play an active part (important role); be active in politics.
活火山 An active volcano.

活字典 A walking dictionary (a very learned person).
活葉本 A loose-leaf notebook.
活版印刷 Printed with movable types.
活動影戲 Moving pictures; movie; cinematograph.
活動範圍 A sphere of activity (action).
活期存款 Current deposit.
活潑潑地 Extremely active and lively; vividly.
活龍活現 Make the matter real; genuine.

**洽** qià (v.)- Harmonize.
洽和 Harmonize; on good terms.
洽當 Proper; suitable; agreeable.

**派** pài (n.)- A branch. A sect; a school. A party.
(v.)- Appoint; send; depute. Distribute; allot.
派人 Send a person.
派系 Cliques.
派出 Send out; dispatch.
派兵 Dispatch soldiers.
派別 Sect; clan; party.
派定 Assign.
派遣 Dispatch; send; detach.
派出所 A branch station (office).
派代表 Send a representative.

**流** liú (n.)- A fluid. A stream. A class; a kind.
(adj.)- Flowing; drifting; moving; shifting.
(v.)- Flow; drift. Circulate; spread. Pass. Banish.
流入 Flow in. Inflow.
流水 Running water.
流出 Flow out. Outflow.
流去 Be swept away; be carried away.
流民 Vagrants; wandering people; tramps.
流汗 Perspire; sweat.
流血 Bleed. Bloodshed.
流行 Prevail; be wide-spread (prevalent). Popularity; prevalence; fashion; vogue.
流沙 Shifting sands; quick sand.
流言 A rumour; hearsay; a wild report.
流氓 Rascals; loafers; vagabonds.
流放 Banish; exile; expel; drive out.
流毒 Spread injury; bad influence.
流星 A meteor; a shooting-star. Strings and balls used by jugglers.
流涕；流淚 Shed tears.
流浪 Wandering about.
流涎 Slaver.
流域 A basin; a valley; the catchment area; the area drained by a river.
流動 Flow; run; circulate.
流產 Abnormal birth; miscarriage; abortion.
流通 Circulation; ventilation.
流落 Wander. Be detained in a place by poverty.
流傳 Hand down. Be made public; get abroad; spread.
流暢 Fluent; eloquent; flowing.
流彈 A stray bullet.
流質 Fluid; liquid; liquid food.
流離 Homeless; wandering.
流露 Disclose; unfold; reveal.
流水帳 Current account; journal.
流行病 An epidemic; a contagious disease.
流行歌 A popular song.
流浪者 A wanderer; a ranger.
流動性 Liquidity; fluidity.
流線型 The stream-line form (shape).
流亡政府 A government-in-exile.
流言蜚語 False (alarming) rumours.
流浪生活 A wandering (vagrant) life.
流通紙幣 Circulating notes.
流通貨幣 Money in circulation; cur-

rency.
流動人口 Floating population.
流動資本 Circulating (floating)capital.
流動資產 Current (floating) assets.
流質食物 Liquid food; a liquid diet.
流行性感冒 Influenza.

**浙** zhè (n.)- Name of a river in Chekiang (浙江).
浙江(省) Chekiang province.

**浚** juàn (v.)- Dig; deepen; dredge.
浚井 Dig a well.
浚掘 Dredge.

**浜** bāng (n.)- A ditch; a creek.

**浣** huàn (v.)- Bathe; wash; cleanse; purify.

**浦** pǔ (n.)- A river bank; the beach of a river.

**浩** hào (n.)- A vast expanse of water. (adj.)- Great; extensive; immense; vast.
浩大 Very great; extensive; vast.
浩劫 A great calamity.
浩然 Magnanimous; liberal of mind.
浩繁 Numerous.
浩浩蕩蕩 Exceedingly great.

**浪** làng (n.)- Waves; billows; surges. (adj.)- Profligate; dissolute. Wasteful.
浪子 A spendthrift; a prodigal; a dissolute person.
浪花 Spray.
浪遊 Wandering; roaming.
浪費 Reckless expenditure; waste; extravagance.
浪蕩 Dissipated; prodigal.
浪漫的 Romantic.
浪漫主義 Romanticism.

**浬** lǐ (n.)- A nautical mile; a knot.

**浮** fú (adj.)- Buoyant; light. Volatile; floating. Unsubstantial. Excessive.
(v.)- Float; drift. Overflow. Exceed.
浮力 Buoyancy.
浮出 Emerge; refloat; come to the surface.
浮沉 Floating and sinking; ups and downs; vicissitudes of life.
浮島 A floating island.
浮起 Float up; buoy up.
浮動 Float; be float; be unsettled; fluctuate.
浮屠 A pagoda.
浮華 Vanity; frivolity; idle show.
浮萍 Duckweed.
浮詞 High-sounding words.
浮雲 Floating clouds.
浮腫 Dropsical swelling.
浮誇 Be vain; high-flown; random talk.
浮遊 Waft; float; drift.
浮塵 Floating dust.
浮標 A buoy.
浮影 Floating shadows—visions.
浮橋 A pontoon (floating)bridge.
浮雕 Relief; embossed carving.
浮躁 Frivolous; hot-headed; rash; careless; thoughtless.
浮船塢 A floating dock.
浮碼頭 A floating pier.
浮遊水雷 A floating mine.
浮標燈號 Light buoy.

浴 (v.)- Bathe; wash; purify; cleanse.
yù 浴池 A bathing pond.
浴盆 A bath-tub.
浴室 A bath-room.
浴用肥皂 Bath-soap.
浴室用巾 A bath-towel.

海 (n.)- The sea; the ocean.
(adj.)- Marine; maritime.
hǎi 海上 On the sea; at sea.
海口 A port; a harbour. An estuary.
海中 In the sea; submarine.
海牙(地) Hague.
海內 Within the four seas; all over the country.
海水 Sea water.
海外 Beyond the sea; foreign countries; overseas; abroad.
海角 Promontory.
海里；浬 A nautical (sea) mile.
海岸 The sea shore; the coast.
海防 Coast-defence.
海拔 The sea-level; above the sea.
海底 The bottom of the sea the sea-bottom; the sea-bed.
海空 The sea and air.
海味 Marine delicacies.
海風 A sea breeze (wind).
海軍 The navy.
海面 The sea-surface; the sea-level; the sea.
海洋 The ocean.
海流 An ocean current; a tidal current.
海員 A seaman; a sailor; a mariner.
海狸 A castor; a beaver.
海峽 A strait; a channel.
海島 An island.
海帶 Seaweed.
海馬 A sea-horse; hippocampus.
海參 Sea slugs.
海產 Marine products.
海深 The depth of the sea.
海豹 A seal; a sea-leopard.
海陸 Both land and sea; on land and sea; afloat and ashore.
海鳥 A sea fowl (bird).
海盜 Sea robbers; pirates; corsairs; picaroons.
海港 A seaport.
海棠 Pyrus; Chinese flowering apple.
海象 Walrus.
海景 Sea view.
海程 A sea voyage.
海路 A sea-route.
海豚 A dolphin.
海圖 A sea chart.
海綿 A sponge.
海運 Transportation by sea.
海蜇；水母 Sea-blubber; jelly-fish.
海蝕 Erosion of the sea.
海嘯 A tidal wave.
海燕 Petrel.
海戰 A sea fight; a naval battle.
海鮮 Fresh fish from the sea; marine delicacies.
海濱；海邊 The seashore; the seaside.
海獺 A sea otter.
海霧 A sea-fog.
海關 A custom-house; the customs.
海藻 Seaweeds; marine plants.
海權 Sea power.
海鷗 A sea gull.
海鷹 A sea eagle.
海鹽 Sea salt.
海灣 A bay; a gulf.
海王星(天) Neptune.
海水浴 Sea bathing.
海岸線 Coast line.
海南島(地) Hainan Island.
海參威(地) Vladivostok.
海盜船 A pirate-ship.
海蜇皮 The dried skins of the blubber fish.
海運業 Shipping (marine transporta-

tion) business; carrying trade; mercantile marine.
海綿狀 Spongiform.
海綠色 Seagreen.
海龍王 The Chinese Neptune.
海關稅 Customs duties.
海上交通 Oversea communication.
海上封鎖 Sea blockade.
海上運送；海運 Carriage by sea.
海上霸權 The command of the seas.
海口稅關 Custom of port.
海水化淡 Desalt; desalinate; desalinize.
海外市場 Overseas market.
海外華僑 The overseas Chinese.
海市蜃樓 A mirage.
海底電報 A cablegram; a submarine telegram.
海底電線 A submarine cable.
海底隧道 An undersea tunnel.
海軍上校 Captain in the navy.
海軍上尉 Lieutenant commander in the navy.
海軍上將 Admiral.
海軍中校 Junior captain in the navy.
海軍中尉 Sublieutenant in the navy.
海軍中將 Vice admiral.
海軍少校 Commander in the navy.
海軍少尉 Midshipman in the navy.
海軍少將 Rear admiral.
海軍法庭 Court of admiralty.
海軍部長 The minister of navy; the First Lord of the Admiralty (英); the Secretary of Navy (美).
海軍學校 The naval college.
海洋氣候 Maritime (ocean) climate.
海水化淡廠 Desalination plant.
海峽殖民地(地) The Straits Settlements.

浸 jìn (v.)- Soak; saturate; immerse; sink into. Penetrate.
(adv.)- Gently; gradually.
浸水 Be flooded; be inundated; be deluged.
浸死 Drowned.
浸透 Soaked through.
浸潤 Permeate through; infiltrate into; soak gradually.
浸濕 Wet; drenched; saturated; soaked.
浸蝕作用 Erosion; erosive action.

消 xiāo (v.)- Melt; thaw; dissolve; consume; lessen; diminish; reduce. Exhaust. Disappear.
消化 Digest. Melt; thaw; dissolve.
消失 Disappear; vanish; dissipate; evaporate.
消毒 Disinfection; sterilization.
消息 Tidings; intelligence; information; report; news; rumours.
消耗 Waste; use up; exhaust.
消除 Remove; abolish.
消悶；解悶 Dissipate sorrows; get rid of dullness; alleviate grief.
消極 Negative; passive.
消費 Consumption; spending.
消愁 Dissipate grief.
消滅 Diminish; disappear; be extinguished.
消瘦 Lost flesh; thin.
消遣 Amusement; diversion. Employ time; fill up time; kill time.
消融 Melt away.
消化力 Digestive power.
消石灰(化) Slaked lime.
消防局 A fire-brigade station; a fire department.
消防員 A fireman; a fire-fighter.
消防隊 A fire bridgade.
消毒藥 A disinfectant; an antidote; a bactericide; a germicide.
消耗戰 A war of attrition.
消費力 Consuming power (capacity).
消費者 A consumer.
消費稅 A consumption tax; an excise.

消費品 Consumables.
消化不良 Impaired digestion; indigestion; dyspepsia.
消化良好 Eupepsia; eupepsy.
消化系統 Digestive system.
消防演習 A fire drill.
消毒棉花 Sterilized cotton.
消極行爲 Negative act.
消極抵抗 Passive resistance.
消極態度 A conservative attitude; act passively.
消費都市 A consuming (consumer) city.
消息靈通者 A well-informed person.

**涉** shè (v.)- Wade; pass through. Concern; involve.
涉水 Wade through water; cross water.
涉水鳥 A wading bird; a wader.
涉禽類 Grallatores.

**涌** yǒng (v.)- Bubble up; rise up; rush on; flow rapidly; gush out.
涌出 Gush out; spring; flow forth.
涌泉 A bubbling fountain; a bubbling spring.
涌進 Rush into.

**涎** xián (n.)- Saliva; slaver; spittle.
涎巾 Pinafore.
涎沫 Saliva; spittle; foam from mouth.
涎圍 A bib.

**涓** juān (n.)- A brook; a rivulet.
(adj.)- Pure; clear; clean.
(v.)- Select.

**涕** tì (n.)- Snivel; tears.
(v.)- Weep.
涕泣 Weep; shed tears.

**涖** lì Same as 蒞.
(v.)- Arrive at; come to.
涖任 Come into office; exercise official functions.
涖事 Attend to official duties.
涖治 Govern; rule; exercise government.

**涯** yá (n.)- A bank; a limit; a shore; a water line.

**液** yè (n.)- Juices; sap. Fluids; liquids.
液化 Liquefaction. Liquefy.
液體 Liquid; fluid.
液體燃料 Liquid fuel.
液體比重表(物) Areometer.

**涵** hán (adj.)- Marshy. Capacious; vast; grand.
(v.)- Submerge; immerse; soak. Contain; bear. Be indulgent.
涵畜 Contain; deep; abstruse.
涵養 Cherish; keep one's temper; be patient.

**涸** hé (adj.)- Dried; exhausted.
(v.)- Dry up.
涸竭 Dry up; run dry.

**涼** liáng (adj.)- Cool; cold; refresh.
涼水 Cold water.
涼快 Cool and refreshing.
涼亭 A pavilion; a bower; a resting place for travellers.
涼風 A refreshing (cool) breeze.
涼爽 Pleasant; refreshing; cool as a cucumber; cold and pleasant.
涼意 Coolness; the cool.
涼血動物 Cold-blooded creatures.

**淋** lín (v.)- Drip; pour; soak through; flow down.
淋巴(生) Lymph.

淋雨 Wet through rain.
淋病 Gonorrhoea; blennorrhoea.
淋濕 Wet through; drenched.
淋巴球 Lymph-corpuscles.
淋巴腺 A lymphatic gland.
淋巴腺炎 Lymphitis.
淋漓盡致 Thoroughly imbued with.

淑 shū (adj.)- Clear; pure. Virtuous. Fine; excellent; accomplished; blameless.
淑女 An accomplished lady; a virtuous woman.
淑秀 Virtuous; modest.

淒 qī (adj.)- Bleak; cold; shivering; freezing. Miserable; dull and cheerless; poor; lonely; afflicted.
淒風 Cold winds.
淒涼 Gloomy; solitary; desolate. Cheerless; lonely; afflicted.
淒風苦雨 Chilly wind and heavy rain.

淘 táo (v.)- Wash or clean; sift; weed out.
淘井 Clean out a well.
淘米 Wash rice; scour rice.
淘沙 Sift sand.
淘汰 Natural selection; select and reduce in number; weed out; wash out.
淘氣 Mischievous; irritated.
淘汰作用 Elimination.
淘汰競賽 Elimination contest.

淚 lèi (n.)- Tears; beads of sorrow.
淚珠 Teardrops.
淚眼 Washed or weeping eyes; tearful eyes; swimming eyes.
淚痕 Traces of weeping.
淚如雨下 Tears trickling down like rain.

淞 sōng (n.)- Name of a river in Kiangsu.

淡 dàn (adj.)- Tasteless; insipid; dull. Weak, as liquids. Light, in colour.
淡水 Fresh water.
淡色 A light colour.
淡味 Insipid taste.
淡泊 Content with little; frugal.
淡酒 Weak wine.
淡雅 Quiet and refined.
淡菜 Dried mussels.
淡飯 Poor food.
淡薄 Thin. Profitless; poor. Vapid. Diluted.
淡水魚 Fresh-water fish.
淡水湖 Fresh-water lake.
淡紅色 Pink; pale rose-colour.
淡褐色 Light-brown colour.

淤 yū (adj.)- Muddy; sedimentary.
(v.)- Block up.
淤血 Stagnant blood.
淤泥 Mire; filthy mud.
淤塞 Be blocked up.
淤積 Silt up.

淨 jìng (adj.)- Pure; neat; clean; undefiled.
(v.)- Cleanse; purify. Wash.
淨化 Purify; clarify.
淨水 Pure (clean) water.
淨重 The net weight; net load.
淨數 Net amount.

淩 líng Same as 凌.
(v.)- Insult; treat badly; maltreat. Exalt; advance. Cross; traverse.
淩空 Tower aloft; soaring.
淩辱 Insult; disgrace; put to shame; dis-

respect; dishonour; defile; abuse.
淩亂 In disorder; confused.
淩駕 Exceed; surpass; outdo.

淪 (n.)- An eddy; a ripple; a whirl in the water.
lún (adj.)- Submerged; engulfed; sunk. Lost; ruined; impoverished.
淪亡 Ruined; lost.
淪沒 Lost; ruined.
淪落 Ruin; degeneration. Sink into vicious courses; fall into misery; go to the bad.
淪陷 Occupied by enemy.
淪陷區 Occupied area.

淫 (adj.)- Dissolute; licentious; lewd; obscene; lustful. Immoral;
yín bad; vicious. Excessive.
(v.)- Debauch; commit adultery; fornicate; corrupted with lewdness.
淫女；淫婦 A wanton woman; a pert girl; a giglet or giglot.
淫邪 Immodesty; obscenity.
淫雨 Long continuous rain; excessive rain.
淫辱 Debauch.
淫畫 Obscene pictures.
淫逸 Luxurious ease.
淫意 Lewd idea; lascivious thoughts.
淫歌 Licentious songs.
淫詩 Obscene odes.
淫慾 Carnal passion; sexual desire; lust.
淫蕩 Debauched; lecherous.
淫穢；淫猥 Obscene; indecent; lewd.
淫辭 Licentious talk; lewd words.

淮 (n.)- Name of a river in Honan and Anhwei.
huái 淮河 The Huai River.

深 (adj.)- Deep. Intimate. Strong; intense. Long; profound; mys-
shēn terious.
(adv.)- Very; extremely.
深入 Penetrate; enter at great depth; go deep into.
深切 Intensely; earnestly; eagerly; in a friendly manner; kind-hearted.
深水 Deep water.
深色 Deep colour.
深究 Make a thorough investigation.
深坑 A deep pit.
深沉 Crafty; artful.
深刻 Deep; profound; cutting; penetrating; poignant.
深夜 Deep night; dead hours; midnight.
深信 Believe firmly; have faith in; full of confidence; in the fullness of one's heart.
深度 Depth.
深思 Deep thought; contemplation.
深紅 Dark red.
深恩 Great kindness; deep gratitude.
深海 A deep sea.
深耕(農) Deep plowing.
深情 Deep feeling; intimate feelings.
深淵；深潭 An abyss; a ravine.
深奧 Deep; profound; mysterious; very abstruse; abstract.
深感 Affect deeply.
深睡 Sound sleep.
深遠 Far distant; remote.
深憂 Deep sorrow.
深謀 Deep designs; profound designs.
深藍 Deep blue; dark blue.
深呼吸 A deep breath; deep breathing.
深不可測 Unfathomable.
深不見底 Bottomless.
深水炸彈 A deep-sea bomb.
深信不疑 Be profoundly convinced of.
深感於心 Make a deep impression.
深謀遠慮 Thoughtful and farseeing.

**淵** yuān (n.)- An eddy; a whirlpool.
(adj.)- Deep; profound.
淵博 Extensive; wide knowledge; profound in learning.
淵源 The source; the origin. Originate from; take its rise in.
淵遠 Very far distant.

**混** hùn (v.)- Mix; mingle; blend.
混入 Intermix; mix up with.
混水 Muddy water.
混合 Mix; mingle; compound.
混淆 Mix up; jumble; confuse.
混捏 Implicate others by false charges.
混亂 In confusion; in disorder; chaotic.
混戰 A confused conflict; a free fight.
混濁 Muddy; turbid; thick.
混合物(物) A mixture.
混合酒；鷄尾酒 Cocktail.
混血兒 A half-blood; a half-breed; a hybrid.
混凝土 Concrete.
混水摸魚 Fish in troubled waters.
混淆黑白 Mix the black and the white.
混亂世界 A troublesome world.

**清** qīng (adj.)- Pure; clean; clear; innocent; incorruptible. Transparent; distinct.
(v.)- Clear out; cleanse; purify.
清水 Clear (fresh)water.
清白 Pure; unspotted; fair; unblemished.
清早 At dawn; very early.
清明 The Ching Ming festival; tomb festival.
清油 Pure oil.
清秀 Handsome.
清香 Fragrant.
清泉 Clear springs.
清風 A cool (refreshing) breeze.
清晨 Early morning; dawn; day break.
清茶 Pure tea.
清高 Pure and exalted.
清賬 Clear off an account.
清涼 Pure and cool; refreshing.
清理 Settlement; clearance; arrangement.
清貧 Honest poverty; poor but untarnished.
清朝 The Ching Dynasty; Manchu Dynasty. (1644–1912 A. D.).
清單 A statement of accounts; a list.
清溪 A clear stream.
清楚 Clear; neat; tidy.
清閒 At calm retirement. Leisure; undisturbed.
清新 Fresh; new.
清潔 Clean; neat; pure.
清靜 Quiet; secluded; calm.
清醒 Get sober; come to one's sense.
清明節 Ching Ming Festival.
清眞教 Mohammedanism.
清道夫 Scavenger; street sweeper.
清白人家 Undefiled family.
清理賬目 Adjust an account.

**淹** yān (v.)- Soak; saturate; immerse; overflow. Stay long.
淹沒 Drown.
淹死 Drowned.

**淺** qiǎn (adj.)- Shallow; light; superficial. Easy; simple.
淺水 Shallow water.
淺色 A light colour; tint.
淺白 In plain word.
淺見 Small experience; a superficial view. Empty-headed; shallow brained.
淺陋 Vile; vulgar; mean.
淺窄 Insufficient; straitened; narrow-minded.
淺學 A smattering of (superficial) learning; slight knowledge.
淺薄 Shallow; superficial.

淺而易見 Simple and easily understood.

添 (adj.)- Additional; extra; more.
tiān (v.)- Increase; add to; annex; aggravate; raise; advance.
添丁 Add a son to a family.

添造 Construct.
添菜 Have more dishes.

渙 (adv.)- Wide scattered.
huàn 渙散 Be scattered (dispersed).

減 (v.)- Subtract; decrease; diminish; lessen; reduce; deduct.
jiǎn 減少 Diminish; lessen; decrease. Fall away off.

減去 Take away; deduct from; substract.
減半 Reduce to one half.
減刑 Commutation.
減收 Decrease in receipt.
減低 Lower.
減法 Subtraction.
減租 Reduce or lower rent.
減短 Shorten.
減罪 Extenuate a crime.
減稅 Reduction of taxes (duties); tax reduction.
減號 The sign of subtraction.
減輕 Extenuate; palliate; mitigate; diminish; relief; relax; ease.
減價 Reduce the price; come down in price; undersell; sale.
減肥 To reduce weight.
減省費用 Retrench the expenditure.
減價出售 Sell at reduced price; a reduction sale.

渝 (n.)- The name of a river in Szechwan ( 四川 ).
yú (v.)- Change.

渠 (n.)- A drain; a gutter; a ditch; water course.
qú

渡 (n.)- A ferry; a ford.
dù (v.)- Cross; ford; ferry; pass through.
(adv.)- Across.

渡江；渡河 Cross a river.
渡船 A ferry boat; a passage boat.
渡海 Cross the sea.
渡過 Pass; bridge over.

渣 (n.)- Sediment; refuse; grounds; residue; impurities; slag; dreg.
zhā 渣滓 Dregs; grounds; settlings; sediment.

渤 (n.)- An arm of the sea.
bó 渤海(地) Pohai; the Gulf of Hopei.

渥 渥太華(地) Ottawa, Canada.
wò

渦 (n.)- A whirlpool; an eddy.
wō 渦流 Circular current in a river.
渦輪 Turbine.
渦輪發電機 Turbine generator.

測 (adj.)- Pure; clear.
cè (v.)- Measure; survey. Guess; calculate; estimate.
測光 Measure the light.

測定 Measurement.
測度 Estimate; measure; calculate.
測量 Measure; survey; fathom.
測繪 Draw a map.
測驗 Tests.
測風向 Define the direction of the wind.
測望臺 Observation platform.

測量員 Surveyor.
測量隊 A surveying corps.
測量圖 A survey-map; a plan of survey.
測光錶 A light-meter; exposure-meter.
測量學 Surveying.
測繪所 Drawing survey office.
測天氣稀度表；氣壓表 Manometer.

港 gǎng (n.)- A port; a harbour; the entrance of a river; the mouth of a river.
港口 A harbour; a port. The entrance of a habour.
港內 Inside the harbour; in the port.
港外 Outside the port (harbour).
港務 Harbour (port) service.
港稅 Port dues.
港灣 Harbour.
港務局 Bureau of harbour.

渴 kě (adj.)- Thirsty; dry; parched. Desirous of; longing.
渴死 Dying of thirst.
渴念；渴想 Long for; think upon earnestly; anxious.
渴望 Eagerly expect; long (crave) for.

游 yóu See 遊.
(n.)- Recreation; stream; excursion; amusement.
(v.)- Travel; wander; roam; ramble. Swim; float; drift.
遊子 A son away from home; a wanderer.
游蕩 Wander.
游水 Swim; bathe.
游民 Wandering people; loafer.
游玩 Have an excursion; travel for pleasure.
游泳 Swim.
游客 Tourist.
游艇 Yacht; barge; motor-boat.
游歷 Travel.
游泳池 A swimming pool.
游泳衣 A swimming suit.
游擊隊 Guerrilla brigade; flying army.
游擊戰 Guerrilla (partisan) warfare.
游園會 Garden party.
游泳比賽 A swimming contest (race).

渾 hún (adj.)- Dirty; turbid; muddy; polluted. Mixed; confused; disordered; chaotic; blended. Whole; entire; complete.
渾圓 The universe.
渾身 The whole body.
渾濁 Dirty; foul; turbid.

湃 pài (n.)- The sound of waves.

湄 méi (n.)- The margin of a stream.
湄公河 Mekong River.
湄南河 Menan Chao Phraya.

湊 còu (v.)- Collect; gather. Hit on; meet.
湊巧 By chance. A fortunate coincidence.
湊合 Collect together; gather; assemble.
湊數 Make up the number; fill up the number.
湊熱鬧 Join in the fun; take part in the merry-making.

湍 tuān (n.)- Rushing of water; a torrent.

湖 hú (n.)- A lake; a sheet of water.
湖北(地) Hupeh.
湖南(地) Hunan.
湖畔；湖邊 The shores of a lake; the lake-side.
湖海 Lakes and seas.

湘 (n.)- Name of a river in Hunan.
xiāng 湘竹(植) The spotted bamboo.

湧 (v.)- Bubble up; gush forth.
yǒng

湮 (v.)- Fall into water; sink.
yān 湮沒 Be drowned; lost.
湮滅 Destroyed; disappeared.

湯 (n.)- Hot water; broth; soup.
tāng 湯匙 A soup spoon; a soup ladle.
湯碗 A soup basin.
湯圓 Dumplings.
湯麵 Noodles in soup.

渺 (adj.)- Vast; boundless distant.
miǎo 渺小 Tiny.
渺茫 Doubtful; remote.

源 (n.)- A source; a spring; the head of a river.
yuán 源泉 The source; the fountain head.
源頭 The source of a stream.
源源而來 Incessantly coming—of a stream of people.

準 (n.)- A water level; a plumb line; a standard; a scale; a criterion.
zhǔn (adj.)- Exact; true; right; proper.
準則 A rule; a law.
準時 On time; proper time.
準備 Prepare; get ready; arrange; fit up.
準繩 A plumb line; a marking line; a rule of conduct.
準決賽 Semi-final.
準備市 Reserve cities.

溝 (n.)- A ditch; a creek; a trench; a drain; a channel.
gōu 溝通 Understand each other; promote a mutual understanding.

溜 (adj.)- Smooth; glossy.
liū (v.)- Glide.
溜冰 Skating.
溜冰場 A skating-rink.
溜冰鞋 A pair of skates.

溢 (adj.)- Excessive; abundant.
yì (v.)- Overflow; spread around.
溢出 Flow out; run over; be in excess.
溢滿 Full; abundant.

溪 (n.)- A stream; a brook; a creek; a rivulet.
qī [xī] 溪水 Creek waters. A stream; a freshet.
溪谷 A den; a valley.
溪流 A mountain stream.

溫 (adj.)- Warm. Tepid; lukewarm. Temperate. Mild; gentle; kind; cordial; genial.
wēn (v.)- Warm; heat. Revise; review.
溫水 Warm water.
溫床 A hot-bed.
溫和 Mild; benign; gentle. Temperate; genial.
溫泉 A hot spring.
溫厚 Kind and generous.
溫度 Temperature.
溫柔 Gentle; mild; meek.
溫帶 The temperate zones.
溫室 A hot house; a greenhouse; a glasshouse; a conservatory.
溫書；溫課 Review the lessons.
溫情 A warm feeling.
溫習 Review; exercise; practice; study;

go over.
溫順 Meek; obedient.
溫暖 Warm.
溫度計 A thermometer.
溫泉浴場 Hot springs; a hot-bath resort.
溫帶地方 The temperate regions.
溫情主義 Paternalism.

**溯** sù (v.)- Go up a stream; trace up to a source.
溯源 Trace to the source; search out the origins.

**溶** róng (v.)- Dissolve; melt.
溶化 Dissolve.
溶液 A solution.
溶解 Dissolve; solve.
溶劑 Resolvent.
溶解度 Solubility.
溶解點 Melting point.
溶解溫度 Melting temperature.

**溺** nì (v.)- Sink; drown. Pass urine; make water. Addicted to; indulge in; fond of.
溺死；溺斃 Be drowned; die in water. Death from drowning.
溺愛 Blindly attached to; doting upon; drowned in love; excessive love of one's children.

**溼** shī Same as 濕.
(n.)- Low-lying grounds; muck land.
(adj.)- Wet; damp; moisten; humid.
溼布(醫) A stupe; a wet pack; a compress.
溼度 Humidity.
溼氣 Damp; moisture; humidity.
溼疹 Eczema.
溼透 Wet through.
溼電池 A galvanic battery.

**滂** pāng (n.)- Heavy rain.
滂沱大雨 A great rain; a heavy shower.

**滄** cāng (adj.)- Cold. Blue; green. Vast.
滄洲 The edge of water.
滄海 The deep blue sea.
滄溟 The ocean.
滄海一粟 Like a grain afloat on the ocean; a drop in the bucket.
滄海桑田 Great change of the circumstance or place.

**滅** miè (v.)- Destroy; overthrow; exterminate; extinguish; put out; suppress.
滅亡 Fall; be ruined; be destroyed; go out of existence.
滅火 Put out a fire; quench a fire.
滅裂 Careless; want of thoroughness.
滅跡 Destroy all the evidence.
滅絕 Exterminate; extinguish; put out.
滅種 Exterminate a race.
滅火器 A fire-extinguisher.

**滋** zī (adj.)- Rich; juicy; nutritive.
(v.)- Increase; rise high; produce to breed. Enrich.
滋生 Sprout; multiply.
滋味 Taste; flavour.
滋補 Strengthen. A tonic.
滋長 Breed.
滋潤 Fertilizer; enrich.
滋養 Nourish; invigorate; promote growth.
滋養品 Nourishment; nutriment; aliment.

**滌** dí (v.)- Cleanse; wash.
滌塵 Wash off the dust.

**滑** (adj.)- Smooth; slippery; glossy; polished.
huá 滑石 Soapstone; talc; steatite.
滑冰 Skate.
滑走 Glide; taxi; volplane.
滑翔 Slide.
滑梯 A slide.
滑倒 Slip down; lose one's footing.
滑動 Slip.
滑雪 Ski.
滑落 Slip off; slide down.
滑稽 A joke; a jest; humour; fun.
滑膩 Oily; greasy.
滑潤 Glossy; smooth.
滑冰鞋 A skate.
滑翔機 Glider.
滑潤油 Lubricator oil.
滑稽戲 Farce.

**滓** (n.)- Sediment; dregs.
zǐ

**滔** (n.)- Rushing water.
(v.)- Flow; overpass.
tāo 滔滔 In a large stream; in torrents; fluently.
滔滔辯論 Eloquently; flowingly; speak with great fluency.
滔天大罪 Deadly crimes.
滔滔不絕 Speak unceasingly.

**滬** (n.)- A name for Shanghai.
滬江(地) Another name for
hù Shanghai.

**滯** (adj.)- Indigestible; discordant; dilatory.
zhì (v.)- Obstruct; stop; impede.
滯下；痢疾 Dysentery.
滯住 Impeded; stopped.
滯食 Indigestion.
滯運 Bad fortune; adversity.

**滲** (v.)- Penetrate; soak; leak.
滲出 Exude; secrete; ooze out.
shèn 滲透 Permeate; spread itself. Percolation.
滲漏 Leak.
滲透性(物) Osmose; osmosis.
滲透作用 Osmotic action.

**滴** (n.)- A drop; dripping; a trickle.
(v.)- Drop; drip; ooze; trickle.
dī 滴下 Drip; fall in drops.
滴出 Drop out; drip out.
滴瓶 A dropping bottle.
滴管 Pipette; medicine dropper.

**滸** (n.)- The bank of a river.
hǔ

**滾** (n.)- Bubbling water.
(adj.)- Boiling; bubbling.
gǔn (v.)- Roll; boil.
滾水 Boiling water.
滾開 Begone! be off! get away; beat it! get out!
滾熱 Boiling hot.
滾動 Roll.
滾進 To roll into.
滾出 Get out of; hands off.

**滿** (n.)- Fullness.
(adj.)- Full; sufficient; enough.
mǎn Complete; whole; entire.
(v.)- Fill up; complete; abound.
滿分 Full marks.
滿月 A full moon. The month after childbirth.
滿地 All over the ground.
滿足 Satisfaction; contentment. Satisfy; have gratification; content oneself with.
滿身 The whole body.
滿杯 A full cup.

滿面 All over the face; the whole face.
滿座 Be full up (all full). "House Full"; "Full up".
滿期 The expiration of a term; maturity; complete one's term of service.
滿意 Satisfied; contented.
滿額 Full allowance.
滿心歡喜 Filled with joy.
滿面笑容 Beaming with delight; smiling all over.
滿腔熱血 Full of sympathetic feelings.

**漁** yú
(n.)- Fishing; fishery.
(v.)- Fish. Seize; search for; hunt for.
漁人；漁夫 A fisherman.
漁民 Fisherman.
漁舟 A fishing-boat (vessel).
漁村 A fishing village.
漁竿 A fishing-rod.
漁翁 An old fisherman.
漁場 A fishing ground.
漁業 Fishery.
漁業公司 Marine products company.

**漂** piǎo [piào]
(v.)- Float; drift; wander about.
漂白 Bleach; blanch.
漂布 Bleach cotton.
漂亮 Bright; good-looking; beautiful; handsome.
漂流 Drift about; be carried by the current; roam about without aim; float to and fro.
漂蕩；漂泊 Adrift; wandering about; without fixed abode.
漂白粉 Bleaching powder; chloride of lime.
漂洋過海 Cross the ocean.

**漆** qī
(n.)- The varnish or lacquer tree; paint.
(adj.)- Black.
(v.)- Paint; lacquer; varnish.
漆匠 Painter; varnisher.
漆黑 Jet-black; coal-black; raven.
漆器 Lacquered ware.
漆樹 The varnish tree; the lacquer tree.

**漏** lòu
(v.)- Leak; drip; disclose; let out; let slip; lose; omit.
漏斗 A funnel; a hopper.
漏稅 Leakage; smuggling.
漏洞 A loophole.
漏電 Leakage of electricity; electric leak.
漏網 Escape the net; evade punishment; escape from the meshes of the law.
漏斗形 Funnel-shaped; infundibular.
漏風聲 Disclose a secret.

**漑** gài
(v.)- Irrigate; water; wash.

**演** yǎn
(adj.)- Extensive; wide.
(v.)- Practise; exercise; perform; act; play.
演出 Play; perform; present.
演技 Acting; performance.
演奏 A musical performance; a recital.
演員 Actor; player.
演習 Exercise; practice.
演唱 Musical entertainment.
演說 An oration; a speech; an address. Give a lecture; make a speech.
演變 Developments.
演戲；演劇 Perform; act plays; act on the stage.
演講 Lecture; speak; address.
演繹 Deduction; deduce.
演說者 A speaker.
演說家 An orator.
演說稿 Notes on lecture.
演戲節目 A programme; a repertoire.

**漕** cáo (n.)- A canal; a channel. Transportation by water.
漕運 Transportation of rice in Grand Canal.

**漠** mò (n.)- A desert.
(adj.)- Indifferent; cool; careless.
漠視 Take no heed to; ignore; disregard; neglect.
漠然 In an indifferent manner; unconcerned; coolly; calmly; vaguely; obscurely.
漠不關心 Showing no concern; indifferent.

**漢** hàn (n.)- A man.
(adj.)- Chinese.
漢人 A Chinese.
漢口(地) Hankow.
漢文 Chinese.
漢字 A Chinese character (ideograph).
漢奸 A disaffected Chinese; a traitor; a spy.
漢城(地) Seoul, Korea.
漢堡(地) Hamburg.
漢朝 The Han Dynasty (206B.C.–220 A.D.).
漢譯 A Chinese translation (version).
漢英字典 Chinese-English dictionary.

**漣** lián (n.)- Flowing water.
漣漪 A ripple on water.

**漫** màn (adj.)- Diffused; spreading. Boundless; wild. Careless; reckless.
(v.)- Overflow; set loose.
漫延 Spread.
漫步 Strolling.
漫畫 A cartoon; a caricature; genre sketches.
漫遊 A tour; a pleasure trip. Make a tour; travel.
漫漫 Vast; boundless; far and wide; a long road.
漫談 A chat; desultory remarks (talks).
漫畫家 A caricaturist; a cartoonist.
漫不經心 Careless; heedless.
漫條斯理 An easy manner.

**漬** zì 漬痕 Stain; spot; marks of watering.

**漱** shù (v.)- Rinse; gargle.
漱口 Rinse the mouth.
漱口盂 Mouth washing cup.

**漲** zhǎng (v.)- Overflow; swell; expand; rise high.
漲落 Fluctuation.
漲價 Rise (advance) the price; appreciate; making up price.
漲潮 Flood-tide.

**漸** jiàn (v.)- Advance; flow; penetrate; reach; tinge; soak.
(adv.)- Gradually; by degrees; slowly; little by little.
漸次 Step by step; bit by bit.
漸減 Decrease gradually (by degrees).
漸漸 Gradually; by degrees; little by little.
漸增 Increase gradually (by degrees).
漸强音 Crescendo.

**漿** jiāng (n.)- A thick fluid; congee; sirup; starch; paste.
漿汁 Juice.
漿果 Berry.
漿洗 Wash and starch.
漿粉 Starch powder.
漿糊 Paste.
漿洗店 Laundry.

**潑** (v.)- Throw water out; spill; sprinkle.
pō 潑婦 A termagant; a virago; a shrew.
潑辣 Saucy; malignant; malicious.
潑瀉 Spill.
潑濺 Dash; spatter.

**潔** (adj.)- Clear; clean; limpid; pure; neat; tidy.
jié 潔白 Pure and white; spotless; stainless; pure.
潔淨 Clean; neat; tidy.
潔身自好 Keep one's self clean.

**潛** (v.)- Hide away. Pass through water; swim under water.
qián (adv.)- Secretly; stealthily; carefully.
潛入 Enter secretly; slip into.
潛水 Dive; submerge.
潛伏 Concealed; lie hidden.
潛逃 Run away secretly.
潛水員 A diver.
潛水艇 A submarine boat.
潛伏期 The period of incubation; the latent period.
潛望鏡 A periscope.
潛勢力 Potential (latent) energy.
潛意識 Subconsciousness.
潛心學問 Put one's soul into (devote oneself to) study.

**澗** (n.)- A brooklet; a torrent.
jiàn 澗流 A rapid; a torrent; a stream in valley.

**潤** (adj.)- Moist; glossy; shining; sleek.
rùn (v.)- Moisten; bedew. Enrich; fatten; benefit; increase.
潤飾 Touch-up.
潤滑 Smooth; slippery.
潤澤 Glossy; agreeable; enrich by favours.
潤滑油 Lubricating oil.

**潦** (adj.)- Negligent; careless.
liǎo (v.)- Flood; overflow; rain all times.
潦草 Scrawl negligently; scamp, as work; do a thing carelessly; scribble over.
潦倒 Unlucky; never getting a chance of good life.

**潭** (n.)- A deep pool; a big pond.
tán 潭水 Deep water.

**潮** (n.)- The tide.
(adj.)- Moist; damp; humid.
cháo 潮水 The tide; the tidal waters.
潮平 At high water.
潮汐 Morning and evening tides.
潮流 A tidal current; the current; the tide. Tendency; trend.
潮氣 Moisture.
潮漲 Flood tide. The tide is rising.
潮濕 Damp; moist.

**潰** (adj.)- Confused; defeated; scattered; dispersed; broken.
kuì (v.)- Rush, as water; be defeated; give way; collapse. Burst.
潰兵 Scattered troops.
潰敗 Defeated; beaten; destroyed; routed; dispersed; scattered.
潰瘍 Ulcer.
潰爛 Sore; inflamed; festered.

**潺** (n.)- The sound of flowing water.
chán 潺潺 The gurgling of water in flowing; murmuring water.

**澁** sè
Same as 澀.
(n.)- Rough; harsh. A harsh flavour.
澁味 Astringent taste; a harsh flavour.

**澄** chéng
(adj.)- Clear; pure; transparent.
澄清 Clear; clean; make clear.
澄清天下 Bring about peace in the country.

**澆** jiāo
(adj.)- Perfidious.
(v.)- Sprinkle; water; moisten; irrigate.
澆花 Sprinkle flowers.
澆灌 Irrigate; water.

**澈** chè
(adj.)- Clear.
(v.)- Search out.
澈白 Pure white.
澈底 Reach the bottom; go the last.
澈查 Make a thorough investigation; search out.

**澎** péng
(n.)- The noise of rushing water.
澎湃 The sound of rushing water; the noise of great wave; the roar of the angry sea.
澎湖列島(地) Pescadore Islands.

**澡** zǎo
(v.)- Bathe; wash; take a bath.
澡房 A bath; a bath room.
澡盆 A bathtub.
澡堂 A public bath; a bathing house.

**澤** zé
(n.)- A marsh; a bog. Favour; kindness.
澤地 Marshy place; a bog; a swamp.
澤國 The watery land; flooded region; a country submerged.

**澱** diàn
(n.)- Precipitation; dregs; sediment.
澱粉 Starch.

**澳** ào
(n.)- A bank; a bay; a harbour.
澳門(地) Macao.
澳洲；澳大利亞(地) Australia.

**激** jī
(adj.)- Indignant; vexed; enraged; irritated; agitated.
(v.)- Rouse; excite; stimulate; stir; encourage; rush against.
激昂 Passionate; spirited; vigorous. Be excited.
激流 A rapid stream; a torrent.
激怒 Enrage; anger; irritate or provoke.
激烈 Vehement; exasperated; intemperate; radical. With great violence.
激動 Terrible shock; great excitement. Be agitated; be stirred up; tremble terribly.
激發 Rouse to action.
激素 Excitant; stimulant.
激增 A sudden (remarkable) increase.
激勵 Encourage; urge.
激戰 A severe (bloody) battle; a desperate fight. Fight furiously.
激變 A violent (an unexpected) change.

**濁** zhuó
(adj.)- Muddy; foul; impure. Dull. Corrupt; degenerate.
濁水 Muddy water.
濁音 A sonant; a voiced sound.
濁流 A muddy (turbid) stream.

**濃** nóng
(adj.)- Thick; strong; heavy; rich; dense; dark.
濃厚 Thickly; densely; richly; heavily.
濃度 Thickness; consistency; density.

濃眉 Thick eyebrows.
濃烟 Dark smoke.
濃茶 Strong tea.
濃淡 Light and shade; tint; shading; strong and weak.
濃湯 Thick soup.
濃粧 Overdressed; a rich attire.
濃霧 A dense (thick) fog.
濃縮 Concentrated; condensed.
濃厚興趣 Intense interest.

濛 (n.)- Drizzling; fine rain.
(adj.)- Misty; foggy; obscure.
méng 濛濛細雨 Misty rain.

濟 (n.)- Success; completion; accomplishment.
jǐ (v.)- Help; aid; relieve. Cross a river; ferry. Complete.
濟民 Save the distressed masses.
濟災 Relieve a famine.
濟南(地) Tsinan.
濟善 Assist a good cause.
濟糧 Give alms of grain.

濠 (n.)- A moat; a ditch; a trench.
濠溝 Ditches; trenches.
háo

濤 (n.)- Large waves; surges; billows.
tāo 濤頭 A wave-crest.

濫 (v.)- Overflow; exceed.
濫支 Extravagant expenditure.
làn 濫用 Lavish; use recklessly; waste; misuse.
濫交 Form undesirable companionships.
濫刑 Excessive punishment; tortures.
濫食 Eat extravagantly.
濫造 Careless manufacture. Produce at random.
濫費 Wasteful. Make wasteful use of.
濫寫 Scribble.
濫用職權 Abuse official authority.

濱 (n.)- A shore; a beach; a bank; a coast; a brink.
bīn (v.)- Border; adjoin.

濺 (n.)- Swift current.
(v.)- Spatter; splash; sprinkle.
jiàn 濺泥 Be splashed with mud.

濾 (v.)- Filter; strain; purify.
濾紙 Filter paper.
lǜ 濾清 Filter; strain through cloth; percolate; leach.
濾水池 A settling pond; a depositing reservoir.
濾光鏡 A sunfilter.
濾乳器 A milk strainer.

瀆 (n.)- A gutter. A river.
(v.)- Trouble; annoy; profane;
dú defile; abuse.

瀉 (n.)- Diarrhoea.
(v.)- Let water off; clear the
xiè bowels; purge.
瀉吐 Purging and vomiting.
瀉肚 Have loose bowels.
瀉疾 A flux; a dysentery.
瀉藥 A purgative; a laxative; a cathartic; an aperient.
瀉鹽 Epsom salt; the sulphate of magnesia.

瀋 (n.)- Juice; gravy.
瀋陽(地) Shenyang.
shěn

瀑 (n.)- A cascade; a waterfall; falls; a cataract.
pù 瀑布 A cataract; a mountain

torrent; a waterfall.

**瀕** bīn (n.)- A bank; a brink; a shore; a beach.
瀕死 On the brink of death.
瀕臨 Near; to get near; close to.
瀕於破產 Be on the verge of bankruptcy.
瀕於滅亡 Imminent doom.

**瀝** lì (n.)- A drop.
(v.)- Trickle; drop; drain out.
瀝青 Bitumen; asphalt; pitch.
瀝青路 Asphalt pavement.

**瀟** xiāo (n.)- Sound of beating rain and wind.
(adj.)- Light; ethereal.
瀟瀟 The sound of the driving storm.
瀟灑 Light-hearted; unconventional.

**瀰** mí (v.)- Overflow; spread.
瀰漫 Diffuse; spread over; prevail; permeate.

**瀾** lán (n.)- Waves; swelling waters.
瀾漫 Overflow; an inundation.

**灌** guàn (v.)- Irrigate; water; discharge; pour; moisten. Give one's drink.
灌木 A shrub.
灌注 Flow into; pour into.
灌酒 Force one to drink.
灌腸 Intestinal injection; enema; clyster.
灌溉 Irrigation; watering.
灌醉 Make a man drunk; inebriate.
灌輸 Nourish; transmit; pour into.
灌腸器 A clyster-pipe; an enema-syringe.
灌輸知識 To introduce knowledge to.

**灘** tān (n.)- A rapid. A sand bank; a shoal; a shallow sand; a beach.
灘頭堡 Beach-head.

**灑** sǎ See洒.
(v.)- Sprinkle; scatter.
灑脫 Free and easy; graceful; with no trace of constraint.
灑淚 Shed tears.
灑水 Sprinkle.

**灣** wān (n.)- A winding shore; a bay; an anchorage; a harbour.
(v.)- Anchor; moor.
灣口 The mouth of a bay; the entrance to a bay.

# 火 部

**火** huǒ (n.)- Fire; flame.
(v.)- Burn; consume; fire.
火力 The power or force of fire; heating power; combustive force.
火山 A volcano.
火夫 A fire-man; a stoker.
火化；火葬 Cremate; consign to the flames; burn the dead. Cremation.
火水 Kerosene.
火石 Flint; firestone.
火坑 A fire pit. A state of misery.
火把；火炬 A link; a torch.
火災 A conflagration; calamity of fire.

火車 A railway train; a railway carriage.
火花 Sparks. Electric spark.
火性；火暴 Hot tempered; fiery.
火柴 A match.
火星 Mars. Flying sparks.
火海 A sea of fire.
火酒 An alcoholic liquor; spirits.
火氣 Temper; anger.
火速；火急 Very urgent; pressing.
火葬 Cremation. Cremate.
火鉗；火箸 A pair of fire-tongs.
火漆 Sealing-wax.
火腿 A ham.
火線(軍) Line of fire.
火箭 Rocket.
火燒 A fire. Outbreak of fire; catch fire.
火燄 Flame; blaze.
火險 Fire insurance.
火藥 Gunpowder; ammunition.
火爐 A stove.
火警 A fire-alarm.
火鷄(動) A turkey.
火山口 Crater.
火山灰(鑛) Volcanic ashes; lapilli.
火成岩 Eruptive rocks; igneous rocks.
火車站 Railway station.
火車頭 Locomotive.
火箭炮 A rocket-gun.
火藥庫 A powder magazine.
火力集中 Concentration of fire.
火山爆發 The eruption of a volcano.
火車時間表 A railway time-table.

## 灰
huī

(n.)- Ashes; cinder. Lime.
(adj.)- Gray. Disheartened; despaired.
灰土 Dust; dirt.

灰心 Disheartened; despaired; disappointed.
灰色 Ash-colour; drab; grey.
灰塵 Dust.
灰燼 Ashes.

## 灼
zhuó

(v.)- Burn; singe. Cauterize with moxa.
灼見 A clear view.
灼灼 Bright; dazzling; glorious.

灼熱 Heat; make red-hot.
灼爍 Luminous.

## 災
zāi

Same as 灾.
(n.)- A calamity; misfortune; danger; misery.
災民 Famine-striken people.

災病 A pestilence; a plague.
災區 Famine district.
災情 Famine conditions.
災禍；災殃 A calamity; a disaster; a misfortune.
災難 Calamities; sufferings; a disaster; a catastrophe.

## 灶
zào

(n.)- A stove; furnace.

## 炊
chuī

(v.)- Steam; boil; cook.
炊事 Cooking; cookery.
炊飯 Steam rice.
炊事員 A cook.

## 炎
yán

(n.)- A flame; a blaze.
(adj.)- Brilliant; glorious. Hot; burning; parched.
(v.)- Blaze; flare up.

炎日 Burning sun.
炎症 Inflammation.
炎夏；炎暑 Hot summer.
炎腫 Inflammation and swelling.
炎熱 Extreme (sweltering, blazing) heat.

## 炒
chǎo

(v.)- Fry; roast. Cook.
炒肉 Fry meat. Fried meat.
炒蛋 Omelet or omelette.
炒飯 Fried rice.

炕 (n.)- A brick bed warmed by fire.
kàng (v.)- Dry; toast.
炕床 A stove bed; hot bed.
炕旱 Very dry weather.

炙 (adj.)- Warm; hot.
(v.)- Roast flesh; broil; toast; heat.
zhì 炙手 Warm the hand at the fire.
炙乾 Dry by heating.

炫 (adj.)- Bright; luminous; blazing; shining.
xuàn (v.)- Dazzle. Make a show; display.
炫目 Dazzle the eyes.
炫耀 Illumine; make a show of.

炬 (n.)- A torch; a fire-brand; a torchlight.
jù

炭 (n.)- Charcoal; carbon.
炭化 Carbonization. Cabonize.
tàn 炭灰 Charcoal ashes.
炭氣 Carbonic gas.
炭筆 A charcoal pencil for drawing.
炭酸 Carbonic acid.
炭精 Pure carbon.
炭爐 A brazier.
炭化物 A carbide.
炭化器 A carburetter.
炭素紙；複寫紙 Carbon paper for manifolding.
炭筆畫 Charcoal drawings.
炭酸氣 Carbonic acid gas.
炭酸鹽 Carbonate.
炭酸鈉 Sodium carbonate.
炭酸鉀 Potassium carbonate.
炭化作用 Carbonization process.
炭水化合物 A carbohydrate.

炮 (n.)- A cannon; a gun. A fire cracker.
pào (v.)- Bake or roast.
炮火 Artillery fire; gun fire.
炮手 A gunner; a cannoneer.
炮台 A fort; a fortress; a battery.
炮竹 Firecrackers.
炮兵 An artillery. An artilleryman.
炮攻 Bombardment.
炮眼 An embrasure.
炮隊 A company of artillery.
炮煙 Smoke from a gun.
炮製 Decoction. Decoct, as medicine.
炮彈 A shell; a cannon-ball; a cannon shot; a projectile.
炮轟 Bombard; fire at; cannonade.
炮艦 A gunboat.

烔 (adj.)- Bright; clear.
烔烔 Glittering; glaring; gleaming. Clear; lucid.
jiǒng

炳 (adj.)- Bright; luminous; brilliant; perspicuous.
bǐng

炸 (adj.)- Explosive.
(v.)- Explode; burst; bomb.
zhá 炸裂 Explosion. Explode; split.
炸開 Blow up.
炸餅 A cake fried in oil.
炸彈 A bomb.
炸藥 Dynamite; guncotton; explosives; trinitrotoluene (TNT).
炸藥線 Blasting fuse.

烈 (n.)- Merit; exploit.
(adj.)- Fiery; burning; energetic;
liè violent; radical; explosive; exasperated.
烈士 A hero; a patriot; a martyr.
烈火 A very hot fire; a fierce fire; a blazing fire.

烈日 The hot sun.
烈風 A violent wind; a hurricane.
烈酒 Strong-wine.
烈暑 Very hot summer.
烈烈轟轟 Eminent and rigorous.

烏 (n.)- A crow.
(adj.)- Black; dark.
wū 烏木 Ebony.
烏有 Nothing; naught; none.
烏金 A term for coal.
烏魚 The black-fish.
烏棗；黑棗 Black dates.
烏賊(動) The cuttlefish.
烏鴉 A crow; a rook; a raven.
烏龜 A tortoise. Brothel proprietors; a cuckold.
烏干達(地) Uganda.
烏托邦 Nowhere; Utopia.
烏克蘭(地) Ukraine.
烏拉圭(地) Uruguay.
烏龍茶 Oolong tea.
烏蘭巴托(地) Ulhan-Bator.
烏魯木齊(地) Urumchi.

烘 (v.)- Bake; dry at a fire; roast; scorch; parch.
hōng 烘手 Warm the hands over a fire.
烘托 Convey an idea by implication; an inference.
烘烤 Roast; toast.
烘乾 Dry at the fire.
烘爐 A portable furnace; a stove; a bake pan.
烘乾衣服 Dry clothes over a fire.
烘火取暖 To warm oneself at a fire.

烙 (n.)- A branding iron.
(v.)- Burn; brand bake.
lào 烙印 A burning mark; a brand.
烙餅 A kind of thick, hard pancake.
烙鐵 A branding iron; an iron.
烙衣裳 Iron clothes.

烝 (v.)- Rise, as steam. Incest.
烝烝 Generous and great.
zhēng

烤 (n.)- Toast; warm; bake.
烤手 Warm the hands.
kǎo 烤餅 Bake a cake.
烤牛肉 Roast beef.
烤麵包 Toasted bread.

烹 (v.)- Boil; cook; decoct.
烹飪；烹調 Cooking.
pēng 烹飪法 Cookery.

烽 (n.)- A signal fire by which an enemy's approach can be
fēng watched.
烽煙；烽火 A beacon fire; a signal fire.

焉 (n.)- A final affirmative sign.
(adv.)- How? where?
yān 焉用 Needless.
焉有 How is there?
焉敢 How dare?

焚 (v.)- Burn; set on fire.
焚香 Burn incense.
fén 焚毀 Burn down.
焚燒 Fire; set fire.
焚化爐 An incinerator.
焚紙錢 Burn paper money to the dead.
焚書坑儒 Burn the books and bury the reactionary literati.

無 (adj.)- No; none; destitute of; wanting.
wú (adv.)- Not.
(prep.)- Without.
無人 No body.

無力 Powerlessness; impotency.
無比 Unequalled; matchless.
無他 Nothing else.
無用 Useless; futil; unavailing; unserviceable; incapable.
無名 Unknown; nameless; obscure.
無色 Colourless; achromatic.
無妨 There is no objection; it does not matter; harmless.
無形 Supernatural; invisible.
無私 Unselfish; selfless; disinterested.
無知 Foolish; ignorant.
無味 Insipid; uninteresting; prosaic. Tasteless; flat.
無奈 There is no alternative.
無定 Indefinite; indeterminate; uncertain.
無非 Nothing but; merely.
無故 Without cause; no reason.
無限 Infinite; immeasurable; unlimited.
無能 Incompetent; inefficient; incapable.
無家 Houseless; homeless.
無害 Harmless; innocuous; innoxious.
無恙 Well; in sound health; in good health.
無效 Ineffectual; invalid; of no effect; futile; resultless.
無須 Not necessary.
無恥 Shameless.
無益 Useless; of no use (benefit, advantage); unprofitable.
無幾 Shortly afterwards. Not much.
無情 Heartless; cold-hearted; unfeeling; inhuman; merciless.
無措 At a loss; without means.
無望 Hopeless.
無理 Unreasonable; unjust.
無處 Nowhere.
無期 Indefinite time.
無痛 Painless.
無辜 Innocent; guiltless.
無意 Unintentionally; without settled aim or purpose.
無罪 Innocent; guiltless.
無端 Without reason or cause.
無疑 Doubtless; certainly; no doubt; without question.
無誤 No mistake.
無敵 Matchless; unequalled.
無窮 Endless; infinite; eternal.
無數 Innumerable; countless; out of number; numberless.
無稽 Groundless.
無論 No matter; whatever may be the consequences.
無錢 Poor; out of pocket.
無雙 Unequalled; uncomparable.
無禮 Impolite; discourteous.
無賴 A rascal; a villain.
無疆 Illimitable; boundless.
無關 It does not concern.
無名氏 Anonymous.
無名指 The ring finger.
無奈何 Have no choice. There is no resource.
無定見 Lack of conviction; absence of definite opinion.
無定期 No fixed time.
無花果 The fig.
無政府 Anarchy.
無紀律 Indiscipline.
無神論 Atheism.
無差別 Without discrimination.
無秩序 Disorder; confusion.
無能力 Incompetency; incapability.
無條件 Unconditional; without reservation.
無條理 Illogical.
無責任 Free from duty; irresponsibility.
無產者 A man without property; a proletarian.
無勝負 A drawn game; a draw; a tie down.
無煙煤 Anthracite; hard coal; smoke-

less coal.
無意義 Meaningless; senseless; empty; absurd.
無意識 Unconsiousness; nonsense.
無經驗 Inexperience; want (lack) of experience.
無資格 Want of qualification; disqualification; disability.
無價值 Worthless.
無價寶 A priceless jewel.
無窮盡 Inexhaustible; endless; infinite.
無機物 An inorganic matter.
無線電 Radio.
無關係 Having no relation to; unrelated to (with); unconcerned in (with).
無證據 Lack of proof (evidence).
無上光榮 The highest (supreme) honour.
無中生有 Beget something out of nothing.
無名之輩 An insignificant person; a nobody.
無名英雄 An unknown hero.
無定向風 Fishtail wind.
無法可想 No way to arrange it.
無法無天 Reckless; lawless.
無神論者 An atheist.
無恥之徒 A shameless rascal.
無軌電車 Trolly tram.
無理取鬧 Make trouble out of nothing.
無產階級 The proletariat.
無期徒刑 Penal servitude for life; life imprisonment.
無稅港口；自由港 A freeport.
無話可說 Nothing to say in reply; speechless.
無價之寶 A priceless treasure.
無機化學 Inorganic chemistry.
無線電報 Wireless telegraph.
無線電話 A wireless telephone; a radiophone.
無線電視 Wireless television.
無線電台 A radio station.
無論如何 Under any circumstances; whatever might happen; however; anyhow; no matter how; in any case.
無濟於事 Of no help in the matter; useless; inadequate.
無政府主義 Anarchism.
無脊椎動物 An invertebrate animal.
無記名投票 Secret voting (ballot); open ballot.
無線電傳眞 Radio photo.
無機化合物 An inorganic compound.

焦 jiāo (adj.)- Scorched; vexed; burned; singed; dried up. Anxious; harassed; solicitous.
焦土 Be burnt to the ground; be reduced to ashes.
焦心；焦思 Worried; anxiety.
焦炭 Coke.
焦急 Urgent; pressing; burning.
焦黃 Bright yellow; sallow; auburn.
焦距 The focal length.
焦慮 Anxious; worry.
焦躁 Be impatient; fret; worried; hurried; feel restless (nervous).
焦點 A focus; a burning point.
焦氣味 A burning smell.
焦土政策 Scorched earth policy (tactics).

焰 yàn Same as 燄.
(n.)- Flame; blaze.
焰火 Fireworks.

然 rán (v.)- Burn.
(adv.)- Yes; so; thus; certainly; truly.
(conj.)- But; however; then; though; although.
然而 However; but; though; although; nevertheless; on the other hand.

然則 But; but then.
然後 Afterwards; then.

**煇** Same as 輝.
huī (adj.)- Bright; luminous.
煇光；煇煌 Brilliant; luminous; splendid.

**煌** (adj.)- Bright; luminous; glittering.
huáng

**煉** Same as 鍊.
liàn (v.)- Refine; melt; purify.
煉奶 Condensed milk.
煉糖 Refine sugar.
煉鋼 Refine steel.
煉鐵 Puddled iron; wrought iron.
煉糖廠 Sugar refinery.
煉鋼廠 Steel refinery.
煉鐵廠 Blooming mill.
煉鐵爐 A puddling furnace.

**煎** (v.)- Decoct; boil; cook; parch.
jiān 煎汁 Extract by boiling; prepare an infusion of.
煎炒 Fry.
煎魚 Fry fish.
煎湯 Heat broth.
煎熬 Fry in plenty of fat—long continued trouble or suffering.
煎餅 A very thin large pancake.
煎藥 A medical decoction; simmer drugs.

**煮** (v.)- Cook; boil; decoct; stew.
zhǔ 煮沸 Boil up.
煮菜 Cook food.
煮粥 Boil congee.
煮飯 Boil rice; prepare food.
煮熟 Boil until cooked; boiled thoroughly.
煮水壺 A tea-kettle.

**煙** Same as 烟.
yān (n.)- Smoke; vapour; mist. Cigarette; tobacco; opium.
煙斗 A pipe.
煙匣 A cigarette-case; a tobacco box.
煙囱；煙突 A stovepipe; a chimney; a smoke-stack; a funnel.
煙咀 A cigarette holder.
煙花 Fireworks.
煙袋 Tobacco pouch.
煙商 A tobacconist.
煙捲 Cigarettes.
煙絲；熟煙 Prepared tobacco.
煙葉 The tobacco plant; leaf-tobacco.
煙幕 A smoke screen; a veil (curtain) of smoke; camouflage.
煙塵 Smoke and dust.
煙灰缸 An ash-tray; an ash-pan.
煙筒嘴 The mouthpiece of a smoking pipe.
煙幕彈 Smoke bomb.
煙霧迷漫 Misty; beclouded.

**熙** (adj.)- Bright; glorious; light; harmonious; ample; extensive.
xī 熙熙攘攘 Coming and going in crowds.

**煤** (n.)- Coal; charcoal. Soot.
méi 煤田 Coal field.
煤灰 Coal ashes.
煤坑；煤窰 A coal-pit.
煤油 Petroleum; kerosene.
煤氣 Gas; coal-gas.
煤球 Coal-balls; a briquet.
煤渣 Cinders.
煤煙 Soot; smoke.
煤礦 A coal mine; a colliery.
煤油爐 A petroleum furnace.
煤氣表 A gasmeter.
煤氣管 Gas pipe; gas tube.
煤氣廠 Gas factory.
煤焦油；柏油 Coal tar.

煤礦業 Coal-mining.
煤氣中毒 Gas-poisoning.
煤氣公司 A gas company.
煤礦工人 A collier; a coal-miner.

煥 (adj.)- Bright; brilliant; lustrous; resplendent.
huàn 煥然一新 Brand-new.

煦 (adj.)- Warm; kind; gracious; genial.
xù (v.)- Heat. Be kind; warm.
煦日 A warm day.

照 (v.)- Enlighten; illumine; shine; light on. Patronize; look after.
zhào Accord with. Take photo.
照行 Sanction its adoption; act accordingly.
照收 Duly received.
照例 According to custom.
照明 Lighting; illumination.
照相 A photograph; a picture. Take a photo; portray.
照料 Look after; take care of.
照常 As usual.
照會 Inform officially; licence; communique.
照像 Take an image or a picture; photo.
照辦 Act accordingly.
照錄；照抄 Make a copy of.
照應 Oversee and take care of; patronize.
照舊 As of old; as usual.
照耀 Bright light, as from the sun.
照鏡 Look in a glass.
照顧 Pay attention to; take care of; look after. Buy of; patronize.
照明彈 A flare bomb; a light-ball.
照相術 Photography.
照相機 A camera.
照相館 Photographic studio.
照原價 At cost price.

煨 (v.)- Bake; stew; simmer. Burn in ashes.
wēi 煨肉 Stewed meat.
煨鷄 Chicken stew.
煨山芋 Bake potatoes.

煩 (n.)- Annoyance; trouble; vexation.
fán (adj.)- Grieved; sorry.
(v.)- Trouble. Ask; bother; annoy; vex.
煩交 Please deliver to.
煩惱 Worries; weight on one's mind; vex.
煩悶 Perplexed; annoyed; cumbrous; depressed; vexatious; in low spirit.
煩勞 Trouble one to do a thing.
煩碎；煩瑣 Troublesome; impertinent and vexing.
煩擾 Bother; annoy; disturb.
煩躁 Perplexed; distressed.
煩瑣哲學 Scholasticism; scholastic philosophy.

煞 (v.)- Stop.
(adv.)- Very extreamly.
shà (adj.)- Evil; noxious; deadly.

煽 (v.)- Excite; stir up. Blaze; fan a flame.
shān 煽動 Incite; instigate; agitate.
煽亂 Stir up revolt; instigate to rebellion; sedition.
煽動者 An agitator; an instigator.

熄 (v.)- Extinguish; quash; blaze out; obliterate; put out; destroy.
xī 熄滅 Extinguish; quench.
熄燈 Put out a lamp.
熄燈號 Lights out; taps.
熄燈時間 The hour for putting out lights.

熊 (n.)- A bear.
xióng 熊人；人熊 The brown bear.
熊掌；熊蹯 A bear's paw.
熊熊 Brilliant glare.
熊膽 Bear's gall, used as a medicine.

熏 Same as燻.
xūn (n.)- Smoke; fumes; vapour; smoke issuing from a fire.
(v.)- Smoke. Perfume. Heat.
熏肉 Bacon; smoked meat.
熏炙 Cauterize.
熏風 A warm southeast wind.
熏乾 Dry at the fire.
熏魚 Smoked fish.

熒 (n.)- Lights; shining.
yíng (adj.)- Bright; sparkling; brilliant.
(adv.)- Brightly.
熒火(動) Glow-worm.

熔 (v.)- Melt; fuse.
róng 熔岩 Lava.
熔解 Melt; smelt; fuse.
熔鑄 Lava.
熔礦爐 A smelting-furnace.

熟 (n.)- A crop.
shú (v.)- Ripe; mature. Cooked. Well-acquainted; mellow; familiar; intimate.
熟人 One who is familiar; an acquaintance.
熟手 An old hand; an experienced man; practised hand.
熟知 Have full knowledge of; be familiar (well acquainted) with.
熟食 Cooked food.
熟煙 Prepared tobacco.
熟記 Commit in memory.
熟悉 Well versed in; familiar with; conversant with.
熟習；熟練 Skilfulness; competence; be skilful in.
熟睡 Sleep soundly; sleep like a dog. A sound (deep) sleep.
熟慮 Consider carefully.
熟識 Be well acquainted.
熟讀 Read thoroughly; get by heart; have by heart; repeat by rote.
熟鐵 Wrought iron; manufactured iron.
熟石灰 Slaked lime.
熟能生巧 Practice makes perfect.
熟練技工 A skilled hand; a skilled labourer.

熨 (n.)- A flat-iron.
yùn (v.)- Iron.
熨斗 A flat-iron; a smoothing-iron.
熨衣服 Iron out clothes.

熬 (v.)- Boil; decoct; simmer; distil. Endure; bear.
áo 熬湯 Make soup.
熬痛 Endure pain.
熬粥 Make congee.
熬煎 Boil; fry; seethe.
熬藥 Decoct drugs.

熱 (n.)- Heat. Fever; warmth.
rè (adj.)- Hot; very warm. Warm-hearted; enthusiastic.
(v.)- Warm up; heat. Be excited.
熱水 Boiled water.
熱心 Enthusiastic; eager; fervent.
熱天 A hot day.
熱血 Hot-blooded.
熱門 Favourite.
熱狗 Hot dog.
熱度 Temperature.
熱風 A hot (burning) wind; a simoom.
熱病 A fever.
熱烈 Fervent; ardent; arduous; earnest.
熱帶 The torrid zone.

熱情 Passion; fervour; ardour.
熱量 The quantity of heat; calorie (calory).
熱愛 Love fervently (passionately); be madly in love with.
熱誠 Hearty; zealous; ardent; with heart and soul.
熱鬧 Busy; noisy; bustling; hubbub.
熱餅 Hot cake.
熱學 Thermotics.
熱心人 An earnest person; an enthusiast.
熱水壺 A hot-water pot; a thermos bottle (flask).
熱度表 Thermometer.
熱帶病 A tropical disease.
熱血動物 A warm-blooded animal.
熱帶地方 The tropics.
熱帶植物 A tropical plant.

熾 chī (n.)- Blaze of fire.
(adj.)- Splendid; illustrious.
熾烈 Blaze out; burst into flames.

燃 rán (v.)- Burn; fire; light; set on fire.
燃火 Light a fire.
燃料 Fuel.
燃燒 Burn; to be on fire. Combustion.
燃燒物 Combustibles; inflammable goods.
燃燒彈 An incendiary shell; a fire-bomb.
燃燒點 Point of combustion.

燄 yàn See 焰.
(n.)- A flame; a blaze.

燈 dēng Same as 灯.
(n.)- A lamp; a lantern; a light.
燈心 A lamp wick.
燈火 Lamplight.
燈光 The light of a lamp.
燈油 Lamp oil.
燈泡 Bulb.
燈船 A lightship.
燈塔 A lighthouse; a pharos; a beacon.
燈罩 A lamp shade.
燈頭 Burner.
燈謎 A riddle; a conundrum; an enigma.
燈籠 A lantern.
燈火管制 Blackout.
燈火輝煌 Brilliant lights.

燉 dùn (v.)- Boil; stew.
燉肉 Stew meat.
燉茶 Boil tea.
燉鷄 A steamed fowl.

燎 liáo (v.)- Burn; illuminate.
燎原 A great fire.

燐 lín (n.)- Phosphorus. A flitting light; jack-o-lantern.
燐火 Phosphorous light.
燐光 Phosphorescence.
燐素 Phosphorus; phosphor.
燐酸 Phosphoric acid.
燐化物 Phosphorate.
燐酸鈣 Calcium phosphate.
燐酸肥料 Phosphatic manure.

燒 shāo (n.)- Fever; heat. Roasting; baking.
(adj.)- Roasted. Fired.
(v.)- Burn. Bake.
燒死 Death by fire. Be burnt to death; lose one's life in the flames.
燒肉 Roast pork; broiled meat; grill.
燒杯 A beaker.
燒香 Incense-burning; incense-offering. Offer incense.

燒紅 Red-hot.
燒酒 Samhoo.
燒烤 Bake and roast.
燒焦 Scorch; sear.
燒燬 Destroy by burning; burn out; be burnt down.
燒傷 A burn.
燒飯 Cook rice.
燒窰 A kiln.
燒餅 Baked cakes.
燒石膏 Plaster of Paris.

燕 yàn (n.)- The swallow.
燕子 A swallow.
燕京(地) A name for Peking.
燕雀 Small birds.
燕麥 Oats.
燕窩 A sea-bird's nest; a swallow's nest.
燕尾服 An evening dress; a swallow-tailed coat; a dress-coat.

燙 tàng (v.)- Burn; scald. Iron. Heat by placing in hot water.
燙斗 A flatiron.
燙手 Scald the hand.
燙傷 Scald.
燙髮 Have a permanent wave; have one's hair permed.
燙衣服 Iron clothes.

營 yíng (n.)- An encampment; a camp; barracks. An army corps.
(v.)- Regulate; manage. Build. Plan; work; scheme.
營地 Barracks; a guard station.
營利 Money making. Be bent upon gain.
營房 Barracks.
營長 The commander of a battalion.
營救 Plan for help.
營帳 A camp; a soldier's tent.
營盤 A camp.
營造 Construct; build.
營業 Business; trade.
營養 Nourishment; nutrition.
營業日 Business day.
營業所 An office; a place of business.
營業部 The business (selling) department.
營業稅 Business tax.
營業費 Trade expenses.
營業主任 I/C business.
營業經理 An operating (business) manager.
營業時間 Business hours; office hours.
營業執照 A business (trade) licence.
營養不足 Malnutrition; insufficient (want of) nutrition; undernourishment.
營養良好 Well-fed; well-nourished.

燥 zào (adj.)- Dry; arid.
(v.)- Dry up; parch.
燥熱 Very hot; fiery.

燦 càn (adj.)- Bright; brilliant; glittering; shining; refulgent; resplendent.
燦爛 Bright; lustrous; luminous.

燧 suì (n.)- A flint. A signal fire. A torch.
燧石 A flint.

燬 huǐ (v.)- Destroy by fire.

燭 zhú Same as 烛.
(n.)- A candle; a light.
燭光 Candle - power; candle-light.
燭油 Candle oil.
燭芯 The candle-wick.
燭臺 A candlestick; a candle-stand.

**爆** (v.)- Crack; crackle. Burn; burst; explode; pop; blow up; scorch.
bào
爆竹 Firecrackers; a squib.

爆炸 Explode; burst; bomb; blow up.
爆裂 Cracked; blaze; blow up.
爆發 Explosion; burst; eruption.
爆炸力 Explosive power.
爆炸物 An explosive.

**爐** Same as 炉，鑪.
lú
(n.)- A stove; a fireplace; a hearth in the floor. A furnace; an oven.

爐灰 Ashes from a stove.
爐邊 The fire-side.
爐竈 A kitchen stove; a cook stove.

**爛** (adj.)- Bright; splendid. Broken; smashed.
làn
(v.)- Overcook; break; tear.
爛衣 Ragged garments.

爛紙 Waste paper.
爛熟 Overripe; attain complete maturity.
爛醉 Dead drunk.
爛漫 Luxuriant; in full splendour; in its glory.

# 爪 部

**爪** (n.)- A nail (人); a claw (禽獸); a hoof (牛馬); a talon (鳥).
zhǎo
爪牙 Claws and teeth; fangs. Private agents.

爪哇(地) Java.

**爬** (v.)- Scratch; creep; crawl; climb; clamber; scale.
pá
爬上 Climb up; creep up.
爬山 Climb up a hill.

爬出 Crawl out; creep out.
爬行 Crawl; creep; go on all fours.
爬蟲 A creeper; a reptile.
爬山家 A mountaineer.
爬蟲類 Reptilia.

**爭** (v.)- Contest; dispute; quarrel; struggle; debate; contend.
zhēng
爭功 Contend for merit.
爭先 Contend in a race; struggle to be first; strive to be the first (foremost).

爭吵 Quarrel; squabble; brawl; contest; feud; broil.
爭財 Strive for wealth.
爭權 Struggle for power.
爭氣 Determination; put forth effort.
爭勝 Strive for mastery; contend for victory.
爭雄 Struggle for supremacy.
爭奪 Snatch; seize by force.
爭論 Dispute; debate; rebut; quarrel; argue.
爭辯 Debate.
爭面子 Save one's face.
爭霸戰 A struggle for supremacy.
爭先恐後 Rush to the front.

**爲** (v.)-Do; perform; act; make; play the part of. Cause; effect.
wèi
(prep.)- For; because of; on account of.
(conj.)- For; because; on account of; for the sake of.

爲公 For the public interest.
爲止 As far as . . .

爲此 On this account.
爲何 For what reason? Why?
爲我 For myself; selfishness.
爲要 Be important; be emphasized.
爲首 Take the lead. The promoter.
爲國 For one's country.
爲期 As a limit of time.
爲憑；爲據 Serve as a proof.
爲證 As a witness.
爲難 Be in difficulty; in a dilemma.

爵 jué (n.)- A wine cup. Dignity; noble; rank.
爵士 Knight.
爵位 Peerage and court rank.
爵士音樂 Jazz music.

## 父 部

父 fù (n.)- A father. An elder.
(adj.)- Fatherly; paternal.
父子 Father and son.
父母 Father and mother; parents.
父老 Village elders; fathers; senior.
父親 Father; daddy; papa; pa.

爹 diē (n.)- Father.
爹爹 Daddy; papa.

爺 yé (n.)- A father. A gentleman; an old man.
爺爺 A grandfather. Your honour.

## 爻 部

爽 shuǎng (adj.)- Pleasant; light-hearted; happy; refreshed; delighted; healthy; agreeable. Clear.
(v.)- Fail; miss; change.
爽快 Pleasant; refreshing; enlivening.
爽身 In good health.
爽氣 Smart; vigorous.
爽朗 Open-minded.

爾 ěr Same as 尔，你.
(pron.)- You; your; thou.

## 爿 部

牀 chuáng Same as 床.
(n.)- A bed; a couch; a sofa.
牀位 A bedstead.
牀帳 Bed curtains; mosquito net.
牀墊 Mattress.
牀蝨；臭蟲 Bedbugs.
牀舖 Bedding; bedclothes.
牀單 A bed spread.

**牆** Same as 墻.
(n.)- A wall.
qiáng 牆脚 The foot of a wall.

牆壁 Walls. Partitions.
牆頭 The top of a wall.
牆磚 Wall brick.

# 片 部

**片** (n.)- A strip; a slice; a chip; a piece. A card.
piàn (v.)- Slice; divide.
片刻；片時 A short time; in a moment.
片段 Clauses and sentences; fragment.
片面 *Ex parte*; one side.
片言隻語 A single word or phrase.

**版** (n.)- A block for printing. A register; a schedule. An edition; a plank.
bǎn 版本 An edition; a printed book.
版稅 Royalty.
版圖 Territory; dominions.
版權 Copyright.
版權法 Copyright law.
版權所有 Ownership of copyright; copyright reserved; all rights reserved.

**牌** (n.)- A tablet; a signboard; a board. A shield. A warrant.
pái A permit. Playing cards.
牌子；牌號 A trade-mark; a brand.
牌坊 An honorific arch.
牌匾；招牌 A signboard.
牌照 A certificate; a commission.
牌樓 A triumphal arch or gateway; an honorary portal.

**牒** (n.)- Document; record; dispatch.
dié 牒文 An official dispatch.

**牘** (n.)- A note; a letter; a document.
dú

# 牙 部

**牙** (n.)- The teeth; a fang; a tusk. A broker.
yá 牙肉 The gums.
牙刷 A tooth-brush.
牙牀 An ivory bedstead. The jawbone.
牙垢 Tartar (impurities) on the teeth.
牙科 Dentistry.

牙根 The fang (root) of a tooth.
牙腔 Dental cavity.
牙痛 Have a toothache.
牙膏 Tooth paste; tooth-cream.
牙質 Dentine.
牙醫 A dentist.
牙關；牙骨 The jawbone.
牙籤 A toothpick.

# 牛 部

**牛** (n.)- An ox; a cow; a bull; cattles.
niú 牛皮 Ox-hide; cowhide.
牛奶；牛乳 Milk.

牛肉 Beef.
牛角 Cow's horns.
牛車 An ox-cart (- waggon).
牛油 Butter. Beef tallow.
牛排 Beef-steak.
牛酪 Cream.
牛圈 A cow pen; a cattle yard.
牛棚 A cow-shed (-house); a cattle-shed.
牛仔 Cowboy.
牛痘 Vaccine; cow-pox.
牛羣 Herd of cattle.
牛疫；牛瘟 Rinder-pest; cattle plague (disease).
牛皮膠 Cow's glue.
牛肉汁 Beef-tea.
牛肉乾 Dried beef.
牛油麵包 Bread and butter.
牛頭不對馬嘴 Things that do not agree; incongruous.

**牟** (v.)- Usurp; encroach. Low; bellow.
móu 牟利 Make profits in trade.

**牡** (n.)- The male of birds and animals.
mǔ 牡丹花 A tree peony.

**牢** (n.)- A jail; a prison. A pen; a stable for cattle.
láo (adj.)- Strong; firm; secure; solid.

牢犯 A prisoner.
牢固 Firm; solid.
牢記 Commit to memory.
牢獄 A prison; a gaol; a jail; a dungeon; a quod.
牢騷 Discontented; grumbling.
牢不可破 Impregnable; firm; secure.

**牧** (n.)- A shepherd; a cowboy.
(v.)- Pasture; look after; take
mù charge of.
牧人 Herdmen.

牧牛 Cattle-breeding.
牧羊 Sheep-farming.
牧師 A pastor; a Christian minister; a preacher; a clergyman.
牧馬 Horse-breeding.
牧畜 Stock-farming; cattle-breeding.
牧草 Grass; pasture; pasturage.
牧笛 A reed; a shepherd's pipe.
牧場 A pasture; a meadow; a stock-farm; a ranch.
牧童 A herd boy; a cowboy; a boy shepherd.
牧歌 A pastoral song; bucolics.
牧畜業 Pastoral industry.

**物** (n.)- A thing; an object; substance; matter; article; goods.
wù A creature.
物主 Possessor; owner.

物件 Thing; substance; article; goods.
物色 Find out; look for carefully; be on the lookout; search out.
物品 A thing; an article; goods.
物產 Produce of a country; products.
物理 Theory of matter; natural law.

物業 Property.
物資 Goods; commodities; materials.
物價 The price of commodities.
物質 Matter; substance.
物體 A physical body; a substance; an object.
物主權 Proprietary rights.
物理學 Physics.
物價表 A price list; a price catalogue.
物理化學 Chemicophysics; physical chemistry.
物理性質 Physical property.
物理現象 Physical phenomena.
物理學家 Physicist.
物理變化 Physical change.
物價下落 Fall in prices.
物價漲落 Fluctuating in price.
物質三態 Three states of matter.
物質名詞(文) A material noun.

牲 (n.)- An animal sacrifice; victims.
shēng (v.)- Sacrifice.
牲口 Domesticated animals.
牲畜 Livestock.

特 (adj.)- Special; prominent; single; distinguished; peculiar; particular.
tè (v.)- Stand forth; isolate.
(adv.)- Alone. Specially; particularly. Purposely.
特有 Peculiar; special.
特地 On purpose; designedly; specially.
特色 A salient (special) feature; a speciality; a characteristic.
特別 Special; particular; uncommon; extra.
特例 A special case (example); an exception.
特使 A special envoy.
特性；特質 Special character; a characteristic; a peculiarity.
特長 A strong point; a forte.
特約 A special contract. Make a special contract with.
特效 Special efficacy (virtue).
特殊 Special; particular.
特務 Spy; espionage; secret agent.
特赦 Special pardon; amnesty; act of grace.
特產 A special (unique) product; a speciality.
特設 Specially set up.
特徵 A characteristic; a special feature.
特意 On purpose.
特製 Special make (manufacture).
特價 A special (bargain) price.
特寫 Close-up.
特薦 Recommend specially.
特點 Trait; distinctive feature.
特權 Privileges; chartered rights; special powers; prerogative.
特派員 A specially-dispatched person; a delegate; a special correspondent.
特效藥 A specific medicine.
特許權；專利權 Patent right.
特等座 A special seat.
特價品 Articles for special sale; bargains.
特別快車 A special express train.
特別會議 Special meeting.
特惠待遇 Preferential treatment.
特權階級 Privileged class.

牽 (v.)- Pull; drag; haul. Connect with. Influence. Lead; induce; implicate.
qiān 牽引 Draw; drag; lead; tow.
牽制 Check; restrain; hamper.
牽涉 Be dragged into an affair; involved.
牽掛 Hold in suspense; in anxiety.
牽連 Embarrass; involve in trouble.
牽强 Forced; unnaturally; arbitrarily.

牽出 Pull out.
牽累 Be entangled with.
牽纏 Detain; be unwilling to let go.
牽牛花 The morning glory.

犀 (n.)- Rhinoceros.
(adj.)- Hard; sharp.
xī 犀牛 The rhinoceros.
犀利 Hard and sharp.
犀角 Rhinoceros horn.

犂 (n.)- A plough.
(v.)- Plough.
lí 犂刀；犂頭 A coulter; a ploughshare.
犂田；犂耕 Plough the field.

犧 (n.)- Victims for sacrifice.
犧牲 Sacrifice.
xī 犧牲者 A prey; a victim.
犧牲精神 The spirit of sacrifice.

# 犬 部

犬 (n.)- The dog; a hound; a bitch.
quǎn 犬牙；犬齒 A canine tooth; an eyetooth.
犬吠 Bark; yelp.

犯 (n.)- A criminal; an offender.
(v.)- Rush against; offend; violate; invade; transgress; commit; infringe; break; oppose.
fàn
犯人 A criminal; a jail-bird; a delinquent; a culprit; a prisoner.
犯法 Break the laws; violate the laws.
犯規 Break through a rule or custom; violate regulations; transgress the law.
犯罪 Commit or perpetrate a crime; incur punishment.
犯法者；犯罪者 An offender; a transgressor.
犯罪行爲 A culpable (criminal) act.

狀 (n.)- Form; appearance; shape; state; condition.
zhuàng 狀元 Highest graduate of the Hanlin Academy.
狀況 Circumstances; state of affairs.
狀態 Condition; state; situation.
狀貌 Manner; style.

狂 (adj.)- Mad; enthusiastic. Violent; cruel; outrageous.
kuáng (v.)- Become insane; go mad (crazy).
狂人 A madman; a lunatic.
狂犬 A mad (rabid) dog.
狂妄 Rowdy; disorderly.
狂言 Lying; nonsense; wild talk.
狂怒 Fury.
狂風 A strong gale.
狂笑 Laugh foolishly.
狂喊 Bawl.
狂喜 Frantic with joy; extreme (wild) joy.
狂想 Extravagant thoughts.
狂飲 Guzzle; greedy drinking.
狂暴 Outrageous; violent.
狂熱 Fanatical enthusiasm.
狂歡 Rapture; enchant; be in an ecstacy.
狂犬病 Hydrophobia; rabies; canine madness.
狂歡節 Carnival.
狂想曲 A fantasia; rhapsody.

狂風暴雨 Tempest.

狄 (n.)- Northern barbarians.
dí

狐 (n.)- A fox; a vixen.
hú 狐臭 The rank smell of the armpit; B.O. (body odour).
狐狸 A fox.
狐步舞 Fox trot.
狐羣狗黨 A set of rogues.

狗 (n.)- A dog; a bitch.
(adj.)- Petty; contemptible.
gǒu 狗吠 The bark of dog.
狗蚤 A flea.
狗展 Bench show; dog show.
狗熊 The black bear.
狗醫 Dog physician; veterinary surgeon for dogs.
狗竇 A doghole; a kennel.
狗癲；狗瘋 Rabies.
狗餅乾 Dog-biscuit.

狠 Same as 很.
(adj.)- Cruel; hard-hearted.
hěn (adv.)- Very; extremely.
狠心 Hard-hearted; cruel.
狠好 Very good.
狠毒 Cruel; malicious.

狡 (adj.)- Crafty; cunning; sly.
狡詐 Swindling; deceitful.
jiǎo 狡猾 Cunning; crafty; sly; wily; tricky.
狡辯 Quibble.
狡猾手段 A sharp practice; a trick; a chicanery.

狩 (n.)- Hunting. A hunting dog.
(v.)- Hunt.
shòu 狩獵 Hunt; hunting.

狸 Same as 貍.
(n.)- A fox; a wild cat.
lí 狸貓 A wild cat.

狹 (adj.)- Narrow; limited; confined; restricted.
xiá 狹小 Contracted and small.
狹窄 Narrow and close.
狹徑 A small path.
狹路 A lane.
狹量 Narrow-minded; ungenerous; meanspirited.
狹義 Narrow sense; technical sense; strict sense.
狹隘 Narrow; confined; limited.

狼 (n.)- The wolf.
(adj.)- Cruel; wolfish; fierce.
láng 狼心 Unmerciful; cruel. A brutal mind.
狼狗 A wolf-dog.
狼毒 Cruel; merciless; savage.
狼狽 In a helplessly dependent condition; in a confusion; in a panic.
狼藉 In disorder; scattered about.
狼心狗肺 Cruel and fierce disposition.
狼狽爲奸 Banded together, in collusion for seditious purposes.

猖 (n.)- A herd of animals fleeing.
猖狂 Mad; ungovernable; wild;
chāng unbridled.
猖獗 Powerful; strong, said of bandits; disturbing; notorious.

猙 猙獰 Hideous; ferocity.
zhēng

猛 (n.)- A fierce, violent dog.
(adj.)- Severe; violent; brave;
měng strong; fierce; cruel; savage. Resolute.

猛士 A brave man.
猛火 A blazing fire; raging flames.
猛攻 Make a desperate attack; a furious assault.
猛虎 A fierce tiger.
猛勇 Valorous; brave.
猛烈 Ferocious; fierce; violent.
猛將 A brave general; an intrepid general; a dauntless (fearless) leader.
猛擊 Attack vigorously (powerfully); a hard blow; an onslaught.
猛獸 A violent (wild) beast; a beast of prey.

猜 cāi (v.)- Guess. Suspect.
猜中 Guess right.
猜想 Guess; surmise; suppose; conjecture.
猜疑 Suspicion; distrust; mistrust.
猜謎 Guess riddles.
猜不中 Unable to guess correctly.

猥 wěi (adj.)- Low; rustic.
猥褻 Obscene; indecent; impure; nasty.

猩 xīng (n.)- A yellow haired ape.
猩紅 Scarlet red.
猩猩 Pongo.
猩紅熱 Scarlet fever.

猪 zhū Same as 豬.
(n.)- The pig; a hog.
猪肉 Pork.
猪油 Lard.
猪排 Pork ribs.
猪鬃 Hog's bristles.
猪肝色 Bister; liver-coloured.

猴 hóu (n.)- A monkey.
猴戲 The monkey show (play).
猴類 Quadrumana.

猶 yóu (n.)- A kind of monkey.
(adj.)- Like; similar; equal to.
(adv.)- Still; yet; even.
猶如 As if; just like.
猶豫；猶疑 Doubtful; hesitating; be in suspense.
猶太人 A Jew; a Hebrew.
猶太教 Judaism.
猶豫期間 The period of grace.

猾 hua (adj.)- Artful; cunning; wily.
猾頭 A knave. Treacherous; cunning.

猿 yuán Same as 猨.
(n.)- A gibbon; an ape.
猿猴 Apes; monkeys.

獃 dāi (adj.)- Foolish; silly; idiotic.
獃子 A simpleton; a fool.
獃笑 A silly laugh.
獃話 Nonsense.
獃頭獃腦 Looking like an idiot.

獄 yù (n.)- A prison; a jail. A criminal case. A trial at law.
獄中 In prison.
獄卒；獄吏 A turnkey; a gaoler; jailer.

獅 shī (n.)- A lion.
獅子 A lion; a lioness.
獅吼 The roar of a lion.
獅子狗 The lion dog, or a Pekinese dog.
獅身人面像 The Sphinx.

獨 dú Same as 独.
(adj.)- Solitary. Single. Only.
(adv.)- Alone; by oneself.
獨立 Stand alone; be independent. Independence; self-support.
獨自 By oneself; one's own.

獨身 Bachelorhood (男); spinsterhood (女); single blessedness; celibacy.
獨奏 A solo.
獨特 Peculiar; special; unique.
獨唱 A vocal solo. Sing a solo.
獨創 Original; creative.
獨裁 Autocracy; dictatorship.
獨木舟 A canoe.
獨木橋 A single-plank bridge.
獨立國 An independent state.
獨生子 The only begotten son.
獨唱者 A soloist.
獨奏會 A recital.
獨幕劇 An one-act play; sketch.
獨眼龍 A one-eyed hero.
獨裁者 A dictator; an autocrat.
獨立主義 Independency.
獨立宣言 The Declaration of Independence(美).
獨裁政治 Dictatorship; monocracy.

獰 nîng (adj.)- Ferocious; fierce.
獰笑 Hyena laugh.

獲 huò (v.)- Catch; seize; get; acquire.
獲犯 Arrest a criminal.
獲利 Make profit; get gain.
獲得 Come into possession; acquire; obtain.
獲勝 Gain a victory; achieve a victory.

獵 liè (n.)- The chase; hunting; field sports; shooting.
(v.)- Hunt wild animals; chase.
獵人 A hunter; a huntsman.
獵戶 Foresters; huntsmen.
獵犬 A pointer; a hunting dog; a hound.
獵奇 Curious and grotesque facts.
獵鎗 A hunting gun; a fowling-piece.
獵獵 Sound of the wind.
獵得物 Booty; plunder.

獸 shòu (n.)- An animal; a beast; a quadruped.
(adj.)- Brutal.
獸心 The heart of a beast; a brutal heart.
獸穴 A den; a lair.
獸皮 A hide; a skin; fur.
獸性 Animality; bestiality; beastliness.
獸醫 A veterinary surgeon; a vet.
獸類 Beasts; animals.
獸醫學 Veterinary science.

獺 tǎ (n.)- An otter.

獻 xiàn Same as 献.
(v.)- Offer up; present; dedicate.
獻上 Make a present of; offer Presentation.
獻身 Devote oneself to; self-sacrifice; devotion.
獻計；獻策 Give advice; lay a plan before one.
獻媚 Curry favour; flattery.
獻詞 Dedication.
獻醜 Expose one's defects.
獻禮 Offer present.

獾 huān (n.)- A boar; a badger.

# 玄 部

**玄** xuán (adj.)- Dark; black. Mysterious.
玄月 The ninth month.
玄妙；玄奧 Abstruse; profound; mysterious; occult; miraculous.
玄學 Metaphysics. Taoism.

**玆** zī (adj.)- This.
(adv.)- Here. Now; at present.
玆因 Now because of.
玆者 Now; at present.
玆查 It appears.

**率** shuài (n.)- A rate; an example. A guide.
(v.)- Lead; command. Follow; act in accordance with.
率兵 Lead troops.
率直 Simple and honest; frank; open-hearted.
率眞 Speak the truth.
率領 Conduct; lead.

# 玉 部

**玉** yù (n.)- A gem; jade; a precious stone.
(adj.)- Precious. Beautiful.
玉女 A pretty girl.
玉石 Jadestone.
玉米；玉蜀黍 Indian corn; maize.
玉器 Jade articles; jade ware.
玉簪 A jade hair pin.
玉璽 The imperial seal.
玉蘭 Yulan; a Chinese magnolia.

**王** wáng (n.)- A ruler; a king; a prince.
(adj.)- Royal; princely; regal.
王子 A prince.
王瓜 The cucumber.
王位 The throne; the crown.
王冠 A crown.
王宮；王府 The royal palace.
王國 A kingdom; a monarchy.
王朝 The dynasty.
王權 The king's authority; regality; royality; scepter.

**玩** wán (n.)- Toys; trinkets.
(v.)- Amuse with; play with; make sport of.
玩弄 Play with; make a plaything (toy) of.
玩物；玩具 Toys; playthings.
玩耍 Amuse with; make fun of; trifle with.
玩笑 Jest; joke.
玩賞 Enjoy; find pleasure in.
玩具店 A toy-shop.

**玫** méi (n.)- A sparkling red gem.
玫瑰花 The rose.
玫瑰紅 Rosy; rose-coloured.
玫瑰露 Rose juice.

**玲** líng (n.)- Tinkling of gem-pendants.
玲瓏 Bright as gems; elegant; fine and regular; splendid.

**玳** dài Same as 瑇.
(n.)- A tortoise shell.
玳瑁(動) Tortoise-shell turtle.

**玷** diàn (n.)- A stain; a defect.
(v.)- Strain; spot; blot.
玷汚 Deflower; debauch.

玷辱 Blot; disgrace; bring discredit on.

**玻** (n.)- Glass.
bō 玻璃 Glass.
玻璃片 Window glass; a pane.
玻璃匠 A glass blower; a glass worker.
玻璃杯 A glass cup; glass; a tumbler.
玻璃珠 Glass beads.
玻璃瓶 A glass bottle; a glass vase.
玻璃窗 A glass-window; a glazed window.
玻璃質 Glassy; vitreous.
玻璃器 Glass-ware.
玻璃砂紙 Glass paper.
玻璃製品 Glass works.

**珀** (n.)- Amber.
pò 珀末 Amber dust.

**珊** (n.)- Coral.
shān 珊珊 The tinkling of jake ornament.
珊瑚 Coral.
珊瑚石 Corallite.
珊瑚海(地) Coral Sea.
珊瑚島 A coral island; an atoll.
珊瑚礁 Coral reefs.
珊瑚蟲 A coral-polyp (-insect).
珊瑚藻 A coralline.

**珍** (n.)- Curiosities; a rarity.
zhēn (adj.)- Valuable. Rare. Delicious.
珍奇；珍異 Rare things; curious.
珍味 A dainty; a delicacy.
珍物 A gem; a precious thing.
珍重 Think much of; value highly.
珍珠 Pearls.
珍品 A rare (priceless) article; a curio.
珍貴 Precious; highly-prized.
珍愛；珍惜 Prize; love.
珍藏 Treasure up; preserve with care.
珍寶 Valuables; jewels; a treasure.
珍珠米 Maize; Indian corn.
珍珠紅 Pearl-red–liquor.
珍珠粉 Pearl sago.
珍珠港(地) Pearl Harbour.
珍禽異獸 Rare birds and beasts.

**珠** (n.)- A pearl; a bead.
zhū 珠淚 Tears like pearls.
珠算 Reckoning on an abacus; abacus calculation.
珠寶 Gems; jewelry.
珠鷄 Guinea fowl.
珠寶匠 A jeweller; a silversmith.
珠寶匣 A jewel case; a casket.
珠寶商 Jeweller.
珠圓玉潤 Rounded and smoothed like pearls and jade.

**班** (n.)- A class; a rank. A squad.
bān 班次 Rank; class.
班師 Withdraw troops after victory.
班頭 A manager; a chief; a headman.
班級 A class.

**現** (adj.)- Conspicuous; apparent. Plain.
xiàn (v.)- Manifest; display; come out; appear.
(adv.)- Now; at present. At once.
現今 At present; present time; now.
現代 The present age (time); modern times.
現任 The present post (office).
現在 At present; now.
現存 In stock; on hand.
現場 The spot; the field.
現成 Ready-made.

現有 Have on hand.
現役 Active service.
現狀 The present condition; the existing state of things.
現金 Ready money; cash in hand.
現買 Buy for cash; pay ready money for.
現象 Phenomena.
現價 Cash price; present price.
現賣 Sale on cash; cash sale.
現實 Actual; real.
現代化 Modernize.
現成品 Ready-made article.
現代文學 A contemporary literature.
現代生活 Present-day life.
現代作家 A contemporary writer.
現代思想 A modern idea; modernism.
現代精神 The spirit of the age.
現金交貨 Cash on delivery.
現實生活 Actual life.
現實主義 Realism.
現錢交易 Cash transaction (sale); no credit.
現在完成式(文) The present perfect tense.

球 (n.)- A ball; a sphere; a globe. A cluster.
qiú 球形 A spherical shape; spherical; globular.
球拍 Racket.
球門 The goal in football.
球面 The surface of a sphere; a spherical surface.
球場 A tennis court; a football (baseball) ground.
球隊 A football team.
球員 Player.
球迷 Fans.
球棒 Bat.
球會 Football club.
球證 A referee; an umpire; a judge.
球面幾何學 A spherical geometry.

琅 See 琳琅.
(n.)- A kind of jade.
láng 琅璫 A jingling or tinkling noise.

理 (n.)- Law; principle; doctrine; theory. Reason; cause.
lǐ (v.)- Arrange; regulate; manage.
理化 Physical chemistry.
理由 Ground; reason; cause.
理事 A director.
理性(哲) Reason.
理屈 Contrary to reason; wrong.
理科 College of sciences. Natural science.
理智 Intellect; intelligence.
理想 Theory; idea; ideal.
理會；理解 Understand; comprehend.
理論 Theory. Discuss.
理髮 Dress the hair; hair cutting.
理學 Metaphysics; moral science.
理事長；董事長 The chairman of a board of directors.
理事會 A board of directors.
理解力 The power to understand; the understanding. Perception.
理想的 Ideal.
理想家 Idealists; thinkers; theorists.
理髮匠 A barber; a hair dresser.
理髮店 A barber's shop; a tonsorial parlour; a hair-dressing room.
理所當然 Be but right; be natural; have good reason to . . . ; in accordance with what is right.
理直氣壯 Be in the right and confident.
理科大學；理科學院 The college of science.
理科博士 Doctor of Science (D. Sc.).
理科碩士 Master of Science (M. Sc.).
理科學士 Bachelor of Science (B. Sc.).
理論科學 Pure science.
理屈辭窮 To find oneself devoid of all

argument.
理論與實際 Theory and practice.

琉 liú (n.)- A precious stone.
(adj.)- Glazed; bright.
琉璃 An opaque, glass-like substance.
琉璃瓦 Glazed tiles.
琉球羣島(地) Ryukyu Islands.

琢 zhuó (v.)- Work on gem; polish; carve; cut.
琢句 Sentence formation; compose and polished phrases.
琢磨 Polish; cut. Study with diligence.

琥 hǔ 琥珀；虎魄 Amber.
琥珀珠 Amber beads.

琳 lín (n.)- A gem.
琳琅 Tinkling of gems. Valuables.

琴 qín (n.)- The Chinese lute with seven or five strings; piano; organ.

琵 pí (n.)- A musical instrument; the four-stringed guitar.
琵琶 A Chinese guitar.

琶 pa See 琵琶.
(n.)- A guitar.

琺 fà 琺瑯 Enamel.
琺瑯搪瓷器皿 Enamelware.

瑕 xiá (n.)- Error; fault; defect; spot; stain; imperfection.
瑕疵 A weak point; a defect.

瑙 nǎo See 瑪瑙.
(n.)- Agate; cornelian.

瑚 hú See 珊瑚.
(n.)- A vessel used to contain grain in the imperial sacrifices. Coral.

瑜 yú (n.)- The lustre of gems. Excellence; virtues.
瑜伽 Yoga.

瑞 ruì (n.)- A happy omen. A jade tablet.
(adj.)- Lucky; felicious; auspicious; favourable; opportune; fortunate.
瑞士(地) Switzerland.
瑞典(地) Sweden.
瑞雪 Seasonable snow.
瑞士人 A Swiss.
瑞典人 A Swede.

瑟 sè (n.)- A kind of harp or lute.
(adj.)- Many. Harsh. Neat.
瑟瑟 The soughing of wind.
瑟縮 Numbed and stiff from cold.

瑣 suǒ Same as 璅.
(adj.)- Trifling; minute; insignificant; microscopic; inconsequential.
瑣事 A trivial matter; a trifle.
瑣屑 Unimportant; insignificant; small.
瑣碎 Trifling.
瑣聞 Rumour; gossip; tittle-tattle.

瑤 yáo (n.)- A beautiful stone or gem; a green jasper; a precious jade.
瑤函 Your letter; your esteemed favour.

**瑩** yǐng (n.)- A coloured stone.
(adj.)- Bright; shining; transparent; brilliant; pure.
瑩潔 Pure; clear.

**瑪** mǎ (n.)- Cornelian; agate.
瑪瑙；紅瑪瑙 Cornelian.
瑪瑙珠 Cornelian beads.

**瑰** guī (n.)- A kind of jasper.
(adj.)- Extraordinary; admirable.
瑰瑋；瑰奇 Extraordinary; preeminent.
瑰麗 Beautiful.

**璃** lí See 玻璃.
(n.)- Glass; a glassy substance.

**璧** bì (n.)- A jade.
璧趙 Return a thing to its rightful owner.
璧謝 Return a present with thanks.

**環** huán (n.)- A ring; a bracelet; a circlet.
(v.)- Surround; enclose; encircle; encompass; environ; go around.
環生 Spring up on every side.
環行 Go around; encircle.
環狀 Loop; annular; circular; cricoid.
環旋 Revolve; go around.
環球 Round the whole world.
環遊 Travel around; tour.
環境 Environment; surrounding.
環節(動) A segment.
環繞 Environ; encircle; encompass; surround.
環球旅行 Round the world trip.
環節動物 The Annulata.

**瓊** qióng (n.)- A jade.
(adj.)- Excellent; beautiful.
瓊筵 A banquet.

# 瓜 部

**瓜** guā (n.)- Gourds; cucumbers; melons.
瓜子 Watermelon seeds.
瓜代 Substitute.
瓜果 Fruits.
瓜秧 Melon sprouts.
瓜葛 Related; connected. Complications; involved in relatives.
瓜分 Partition; separate; divide.
瓜子臉 An oval face.

**瓢** piáo (n.)- A gourd used for a ladle.

**瓣** bàn (n.)- Petal of a flower. The carpels of an orange; the segments.
瓣膜 The valves of the heart.

# 瓦 部

**瓦** wǎ (n.)- A tile; Pottery; earthenware.
瓦匠 A tiler; a tilemaker.
瓦房 A tile-roofed house.

瓦面 Roof.
瓦瓶 A goglet.
瓦斯 Gas.
瓦解 Disintegrate; collapse; disperse; crush; separate.
瓦窰 A tile kiln.
瓦器 Earthenware; pottery.
瓦礫 Broken pottery and tiling; rubbles; bits of tile and stone.
瓦罐 An earthen jar.

**瓷** cí (n.)- Chinaware; porcelain; china; crockery.
瓷土；高嶺土 Kaolin; porcelainclay.

瓷瓶 A porcelain vase.
瓷器 Chinaware; crockery; porcelain.

**瓶** píng (n.)- A bottle; a flask; a jar; a vase; a jug; a pitcher.
瓶塞 A cork; a stopper.

瓶蓋 Lid of a bottle.
瓶頸 A bottle neck.

**甄** zhēn (v.)- To separate; differentiate.
甄別試 An adaptation test.

**甎** zhuān Same as 磚 .
(n.)- A square flat tile; a brick.
甎瓦 Bricks and tiles.
甎匠 A bricklayer.

甎茶 Brick-tea.
甎窰 A brick-kiln.
甎牆 A brick wall.
甎造房屋 A brick house; a house in brick.

**甌** ōu (n.)- A bowl; a cup.

**甕** wèng (n.)- An earthen jar.
甕缸 A jar for wine or water.
甕中捉鼈 Catch a turtle in a jar—no escape.

# 甘 部

**甘** gān (n.)- Sweetness.
(adj.)- Sweet; delicious. Pleasant; refreshing. Willing; voluntary.

甘心 Willing; contented; pleased.
甘味 Sweet taste; sweetness.
甘油 Glycerine.
甘泉 Fresh spring.
甘苦 Sweet and bitter. Prosperity and adversity.
甘草 Liquorice.
甘肅(地) Kansu.
甘美 Delicacies; luscious.
甘蔗 Sugar-cane.
甘蕉 Banana.
甘霖 Sweet or timely rain; seasonably rain.
甘藍 Cabbage.
甘願 Willing.
甘藷 Sweet potato.
甘露 Genial dews; honey dew.
甘蔗糖 Cane sugar.
甘拜下風 Play second fiddle to; be subordinate to.

**甚** (adj.)- What? who?
(adv.)- Very; too; extremely;
shén exceedingly; excessively.
甚大 Very big; huge; very large.

甚少 Very few; hardly any.
甚早 Very early.
甚多 A large part or number; a great deal; very much; very many.
甚至 At the worst; in extreme cases of some subject already mentioned; even that.
甚而 So much so that. . . .
甚好 Very good.
甚遠 Very far.
甚麼 What?
甚麼人 Who is it? Who is he?
甚麼事 What's the matter?
甚麼話 What talk! Bosh!

**甜** (n.)- Sweet taste; sweetness.
(adj.)- Savoury; agreeable;
tián sweet.
甜瓜 Sweet melons.

甜味 Sweet.
甜香 Sweet perfume.
甜脆 Sweet and crisp.
甜菜 A sugar beet.
甜睡 A sweet sleep; a sound sleep.
甜蜜 Sweet; sweet honey.
甜橙 Sweet orange.
甜如蜜 Sweet like honey; as sweet as honey.
甜言蜜語 Sweet honeyed words; flattery.

# 生 部

**生** (n.)- Life. Birth. Means of living; livelihood; vitality.
shēng (adj.)- Living. Unacquainted. Raw; unripe.
(v.)- Bear; bring forth; produce. Live. Arise; beget; grow.

生人 A mortal; a living person. A stranger.
生手 A raw hand; a novice; a beginner; a greenhorn.
生日 A birthday.
生水 Unboiled water.
生平 Habitually; the whole life; lifelong.
生母 A real (true) mother; one's mother.
生死 Life and death; alive or dead.
生成 Become; grow to. Innate.
生字 New words; unfamiliar characters.
生存 Existence; life; being; living; exist; live; come to being; keep alive.
生命 Life.
生油 Peanut oil.
生物 A living thing; an animal; a creature.
生育 Beget; get; give birth to; generate.
生長 Growth; grow up.
生前 Before death.
生客 A stranger.
生活；生計 Livelihood; occupation; living; life; way of life; subsist; get (earn) one's living.
生息 Bear interest.
生根 Take root.
生氣 Become angry. Breath of life; vitality; vigour.
生動 Life-like; lively; vivid.
生涯 Occupation; living; career.
生產 Bear; bring forth; produce; give birth to. Production; birth; bearing; child-birth.

生魚 Fresh fish; raw fish.
生菜 Lettuce; salad.
生意 Business; trade.
生疑 Throw doubt upon; raise a question.
生瘡 Get an ulcer; break out in sores.
生養 Rear; bring up.
生銹 Rust; get rusty.
生薑 Green ginger.
生鐵 Pig iron; cast iron.
生石灰 Quicklime.
生命線 A lifeline.
生物界 The animals and plants; all living beings; the biological world.
生物學 Biology.
生活費 The cost of living.
生產力 Productive power (capacity); productivity.
生產物 Products; produce.
生產者 A producer; a manufacturer.
生產費 Productive cost; cost of production.
生理學 Physiology.
生殖器 Generative (reproductive, sexual) organs; genitals.
生髮油 Hair-tonic.
生年月日 The date of birth.
生物學家 Biologist; naturalist.
生活方式 A mode of life.
生活狀態 The condition of life; living conditions.
生活指數 Cost of living index.
生活程度 The standard of living.
生活問題 The problem of living (existing).
生氣蓬勃 Full of life (vitality); vigorous.
生產過剩 Over production; excessive production.
生產關係 Relationship of production.
生殖細胞 A reproductive cell; a sex-cell; a gamete.
生活必需品 The vital goods (commodities); the necessities (necessaries) of life.

**產** chǎn (n.)- Birth; confinement. An estate; property. Productions; resources.
(v.)- Produce; yield. Breed; be confined; become a mother; bear; bring forth.
產戶；產門 The vagina.
產生 Bear a child; give birth to; produce; generate. Production; generation; bearing; breeding; creation.
產品 Products.
產地 The place of production; the habitat; the home.
產房 A lying-in room; a maternity room.
產科 Obstetrics.
產婦 A lying-in woman; a parturient female.
產業 A property; possessions; a patrimony; an estate.
產卵期 The spawning-time; the breeding season.
產科醫生 An obstetrician; an obstetrix (女).
產科醫院 A lying-in (maternity) hospital.

**甥** shēng (n.)- The sister's children; a son-in-law; nephew.
甥女 Sister's daugher. A niece.

# 用 部

用 yǒng (n.)- Expenditure; expense. Use. Employment; outlay.
(adj.)- Useful; available.
(v.)- Use; employ; make use of; spend.
(prep.)- By; with; from; because of.

用人 Employ others. Servants.
用手 By hand.
用心；用意 Give one's attention; exercise the mind closely; take care of. Attentiveness.
用功 Study diligently; work hard.
用去 Use up; expend.
用完 Used up; work up; finish.
用具 Instrument; tool.
用武 Use violence.
用法 The direction for use; directions.
用途 Usage; appropriation.
用處 Use; usefulness.
用意 Purpose.
用飯 Take a meal.
用盡 Exhaust; use up; consume by using; play out.
用錢 Spend money.
用不慣 Not accustomed to use.
用途廣大 Be of great use; have varied use; be very useful.
用盡方法 Employ all means; try every possible means; leave no stone unturned.

甫 fǔ (n.)- The first name of a person.
(adj.)- Great; large. Fine. Numerous; good.
(v.)- Begin.
(adv.)- Just now; a short time ago; immediately; after.

甫田 A large, wide field.
甫初 At first; a beginning.

# 田部

田 tián (n.)- Cultivated ground; fields; arable land.
(v.)- Plant; cultivate; plow. Hunt.

田地 Field; farm. State of things; condition.
田租 Rent for fields.
田產 Estate; land property.
田野 Fields.
田園 Fields and gardens; rural fields.
田賦；田稅 The land tax.
田鼠 The mole; the field mouse.
田賽 Field events.
田螺 A pond-snail; a mud-snail.
田鷄 The edible frog.
田徑賽 Track and field sports.
田園詩 An idyl; pastoral poems.

由 yóu (n.)-Way. Means. Source; origin. Reason; motive; cause.
(v.)- Follow. Permit; let. Pass through.
(prep.)- By; from; through. Because of.

由於 Arising from; caused by; resulting from; because of.
由來 The origin; the source; a cause.
由衷 Heartily; sincerely.
由來已久 It has been so for some time.
由淺入深 From shallow to profound.

甲 jiǎ (n.)- The first of the Ten Stems (天干). An open bud. A cuirass. An armour. The finger nails; claw; shell.

(adj.)- First; foremost.
甲板 The deck of a ship.
甲殼 A shell; a carapace.
甲魚 Turtles; green turtle.
甲等 First class; first grade.
甲蟲 A beetle.
甲狀腺 The thyroid gland.
甲於天下 Surpassing the whole world.

申 (v.)- Extend; prolong. Report. Give orders. Explain; state.
shēn 申告(法) Complaint. State; report.
申明 Explain clearly.
申述 State carefully.
申冤 Redress a grievance.
申詳 Report in detail.
申請 Request a superior; apply; demand.
申辯 Defend.
申請人 An applicant.
申請書 A written application.
申請護照 An application for a passport.

男 (n.)- A man; a male. A son.
男人 A husband. A man.
nán 男女 Men and women. Boys and girls.
男生 A boy student; a schoolboy.
男巫 A wizard.
男性 The male; the stronger sex; the masculine nature.
男裝 Male attire.
男爵 A baron.
男厠 Gentleman's lavatory; men's toilet; gent's room.
男子漢 Manlike; a hero.

界 (n.)- A frontier; a boundary; a limit. A line. A world.
jiè (v.)- Limit; border on.
界尺 A ruler for ruling lines.
界限 A limitation.
界址 The border line.
界線 A boundary line; a limit; a margin.

畏 (n.)- Fear; awe; deep reverence; terror.
wèi (adj.)- Dreadful; afraid.
(v.)- Fear; dread; be afraid of.
畏羞 Bashful; shy; sensitive to shame.
畏罪 Fear punishment.
畏縮 Exhibit fear; shrinking; fear and draw back; flinch. Hesitating; timid.
畏難 Dread or difficulties.
畏懼 Fear; dread; be afraid of; tremble with fear.
畏日眼 Day blindness.
畏夜眼；夜盲 Night blindness.

畔 (n.)- A boundary path; a sidewalk; a bank.
pàn (v.)- Leave. Resist; rebel.
畔岸 A bank; a boundary.

留 Same as 畱.
(v.)- Detain; keep; leave behind; remain; delay; retain; stay; save; reserve.
liú
留心 Bear in mind; pay attention to.
留任 Keep in office; remain (continue) in office.
留住 Keep; stay.
留難 Make things difficult for someone.
留神 Be on the lookout; pay attention to.
留級 Degrade; leave in the same class without promotion.
留宿 Lodge a person; ask one to lodge over the night.
留意 Pay attention to; take notice of; give heed to.
留學 Study abroad.

留戀 Unwilling to leave.
留學生 Students studying abroad; returned students.
留聲機 Phonograph; talking machine.

畚 bĕn
畚箕 A dust-basket.

畜 chù
(n.)- Domestic animals.
(v.)- Feed; nourish; domesticate. Raise; retain.
畜生 A beast; a brute.
畜牧 Rear or raise, as domestic animals; pasture; graze.
畜養 Feed; rear; raise.
畜類 Brute; animals.
畜牧場 A stock farm; a ranch; a pasture-ground.

畝 mŭ
(n.)- A Chinese acre; a *mou* or *mow*.

畢 bĭ
(n.)- A small bird net.
(adj.)- Ended; terminated.
(v.)- Finish; close; complete; terminate.
(adv.)- Entirely; all; totally.
畢生 Whole lifetime; lifelong.
畢竟 After all; at last; finally.
畢業 Graduate. Finish at school.
畢業生 A graduate.
畢業文憑 A certficate of graduation; a diploma.
畢業考試 A graduation examination.
畢業典禮 The graduation ceremony; the commencement day.
畢業論文 A graduation thesis.

略 luè
(n.)- An outline; a sketch. A path; a course. A summary.
(adj.)- Scarce; sharp.
(adv.)- Slightly; rather; a little; somewhat.
略可 Perhaps it will do; slightly possible.
略去 Omit; leave out.
略有 Only a few.
略同 Much alike; very similar.
略傳 A brief history of one's life; a short biography.
略圖 Sketch.
略言之 In a word; be short (brief).

番 fān
(n.)- Barbarians; savages; aborigines. A turn; a time.
(v.)- Repeat; duplicate.
番茄 The tomato.
番椒 Green pepper; capsicum.
番號 A number.
番薯 Potato.
番石榴 Guava.

畫 huà
(n.)- A drawing; a painting; a picture. A mark. A stroke.
(v.)- Draw; paint. Map. Lay a plan.
畫工；畫匠 A painter.
畫分 Define; mark off.
畫册 A picture book (album).
畫布 Canvas.
畫具 Artist's materials.
畫板 A drawing board.
畫法 The art of drawing (painting).
畫室 A studio; an *atelier*.
畫師；畫家 An artist; a painter.
畫展 An art exhibition; an exhibition of pictures.
畫筆 Paint-brushes.
畫報 Illustrated news; a pictorial; a graphic.
畫像 Paint a portrait. A portrait; a likeness.
畫題 The subject of a painting; a theme; a motif.

**異** yì (n.)- A difference.
(adj.)- Different. Unusual. Foreign; distinct; unlike.
(v.)- Divide; differ; vary; separate. Wonder. Oppose.

異日 Another day.
異同 Difference.
異性 The opposite (other) sex.
異常 Unusual; extraordinary; uncommon; abnormal.
異教 Paganism; heresy; heathenism.
異鄉；異地 A strange land.
異樣 Strange; queer; fantastic; grotesque.
異議 Objection; protest; dissent. Demurrer (法).
異於此 Different from this.
異教徒 A pagan; a heretic; a heathen.
異口同聲 With one voice (accord); unanimously; in chorus.
異想天開 Stretch of imagination; flight of fancy; fantastic.

**當** dāng (adj.)- Suitable; adequate; just; proper; fitting.
(prep.)- During; at the time of; in the course of.
(conj.)- When; as soon as; while.

當下 Just now; presently.
當中 In the midst.
當今；當茲 At present; now.
當心 Beware; take care.
當日 On that day; in those days. The said day; during that day.
當地 On the spot; this place.
當兵 Be a soldier; bear arms. In active military service; serve in the rank.
當作 Represent; replace. Regard or consider as.
當局；當道 The authorities; the person responsible for the matter.
當初 At first; at the beginning.
當面 Face to face; in the presence of.
當值 Be on duty; keep watch.
當眞 Really. In good earnest. Take it as true.
當時 At that time; in those days; then.
當場 On the spot; at once.
當票 A pawn ticket.
當衆 In the presence of all.
當街 In the street; abroad.
當然 Naturally; as a matter of course.
當舖 A pawnbroker; pawn shop.
當選 Be elected.
當頭 Right ahead; overhead. A pledge.
當權 Exercise power (authority).
當選者 An elected person; a successful candidate.
當心扒手 Beware of pickpockets.

**畸** jī (adj.)- Irregular; oblique; strange; overplus; odds and ends.
畸人 An extraordinary man; quaint; eccentric persons.

畸形 Malformation; deformity.
畸形發展 Uneven development.

**疆** jiāng (n.)- A boundary; a limit; frontier; termination.
(v.)- Draw a limit.
疆界 A border; the frontier.

疆域 Territory.
疆場 A battle field.

**疊** dié (v.)- Fold up; overlap.

# 疋 部

**疋** pǐ
(n.)- A piece; a bale; a roll.
疋頭 Piece goods.

**疏** shū
Same as 疎.
(n.)- Memorial; petition.
(adj.)- Wide apart. Remiss; negligent; careless. Coarse.
(v.)- Divide; partition off. Clear out. Discard. Spread. Manage.
疏忽 Careless; negligent; remiss; unwary; unwatchful; off one's guard.
疏遠 Distant—make a stranger of. Distant.
疏漏 Careless; heedless; negligent.
疏隔 Alienation.
疏濬 Dredge a river.
疏闊 Having not met for a long time.
疏散人口 To evacuate.

**疑** yí
(n.)- Suspicion; doubt; mistrust.
(adj.)- Doubtful; hesitating; suspicious.
(v.)- Doubt; suspect. Guess. Dislike.
疑心 Suspicion.
疑犯 A culprit.
疑兇 An alleged murderer.
疑問 A question or query.
疑惑 In doubt of; suspicious; mistrust; doubt about.
疑點 A doubtful point; a question.
疑難 Mysterious matter; knotty problem.
疑心病 Hypochondria.
疑問符號 An interrogation mark; a question mark.
疑惑不決 Suspicious and irresolute.
疑問代名詞 An interrogative pronoun.

# 疒 部

**疔** dīng
(n.)- A pimple; a boil; a venereal ulcer.
疔瘡 Boils; ulcers; sores; buboes.

**疝** shàn
(n.)- Rupture; hernia; stricture; swelling of the testicles.
疝氣；小腸疝氣 Rupture; hernia.
疝痛 Colic.

**疙** gē
(n.)- A pimple; sore.
疙瘩 A pimple; wart.

**疣** yóu
(n.)- A tumor; a wart; a small, hard excrescence on the skin.
疣腫 A tumor; a wart.

**疤** bā
(n.)- A scar; a cicatrix.
疤痕 A scar; a cicatrix.

**疥** jiè
(n.)- The itch.
疥瘡 Itch sores.
疥癬 Ringworm; itch.

**疫** yì
(n.)- A pestilence; a plague; an epidemic; a prevalent disease.
疫症 An epidemic; a pestilence.
疫癘 A plague.

**疲** pí
(n.)- Fatigue; loss of strength; exhaustion; weariness.
(adj.)- Tired; worn out; weary; wearisome; tiresome.

(v.)- Be exhausted; grow weary; be tired; get tired.
疲乏 Worn out; tired out.
疲倦 Fatigued; worn out.
疲勞 Fatigue; weariness.
疲於奔命 Wearied of running errands; be tired with restless exertion and anxiety.
疲勞過度 Over-fatigued.

疳 gān (n.)- A disease of children. Sores; ulcers.
疳黃；黃疸 Jaundice.

疴 kē (n.)- Disease; pain; ailment; sickness; illness.
疴痢 Dysentery.
疴嘔 Diarrhoea and vomiting.

疵 cī (n.)- A blemish; a fault; a flaw; a mole; a defect.

疹 zhěn (n.)- A rash or eruption; pimples; pustules; small pox.
疹子 A rash; measles.
疹熱症；猩紅熱 Scarlet fever.

症 zhèng (n.)- Disease; ailments.
症候 A disease; a malady; symptoms of a disease.

疼 téng (n.)- Ache; soreness; pain; rawness; pang. Affection.
(adj.)- Sore; painful.
(v.)- Ache; sting; tingle; pain.
疼痛 Pain; ache.
疼愛 Dote on; love passionately; very fond of.

疽 jū (n.)- A carbuncle; an abscess; an ulcer; a cancer.
疽癰 Carbuncle.

疾 jí (n.)- Illness; disease; ailment; sickness. Quickness; haste.
(adj.)- Quick; prompt; fast; hasty; rapid.
(v.)- Envy; hate; dislike; loath.
疾呼 Calling out; shouting.
疾苦 Grievance; suffering; sufferance.
疾病 Ailment; illness; disease; sickness.
疾速 In great haste; quick.
疾病潛伏期 The period of incubation.

病 bìng (n.)- Sickness; illness; disease. Affliction; misery.
(adj.)- Ill; sick; out of order.
(v.)- Worry; dislike; damage; distress; afflict; catch a disease.
病人 A patient; an invalid; a sick person.
病牀 A sick bed.
病狀 Condition of illness (a patient).
病故；病沒 Die of illness; natural death; succumb to a disease; die in one's bed.
病毒 Virus; disease germs.
病重 Very ill.
病症 Symptoms (the nature) of a disease.
病假 Sick leave; an absence on account of illness.
病痛 The pain (torment) of a disease.
病菌 A disease germ; a virus.
病源；病根 The cause (origin, germ) of a disease.
病癒 Cured; convalescent. Recover from sickness; get well; recovered.
病徵；病象 Indication; symptom.
病魔 The horrors; demon of ill health; curse of a disease; malady.
病理學 Pathology.
病復發 A relapse.
病源菌 A disease germ; a bacillus.
病牀日記 A sick-bed record; the nurse's report.

病從口入 Diseases contracted by the mouth.

痊 (adj.)- Cured; convalescent; get well; be cured.
quán (v.)- Recover from sickness.
(adv.)- Well.
痊癒；痊可 Recover; cured; convalescent.

痔 (n.)- Piles; an ulcer of the anus.
痔漏 Anal fistula.
zhì 痔瘡 Sores in the rectum; bleeding piles; a posterior ulcer.

痕 (n.)- A scar. A mark; a trace. A stain; a spot.
hén 痕跡 Marks; traces; vestiges.

痘 (n.)- Smallpox; cowpox.
痘子 Smallpox.
dòu 痘疤 Scabs.
痘疹 Smallpox pustule.
痘漿；痘苗 Vaccine virus.

痙 (n.)- Convulsions; fits.
痙攣 Fits; convulsive contractions.
jìng

痛 (n.)- Pain; acute feeling; affliction; disease; ache; painfulness; trouble.
tòng (adj.)- Agonizing; painful; sore.
(v.)- Complain of a pain; be painful; grieve.
(adv.)- Sorely; extremely; bitterly; severely.
痛心 Be grieved at heart; cut one to the heart; heart-broken.
痛打；痛毆 Beat soundly; severe blow; sound thrashing. Strike hard.
痛快 Extreme joy; delightful.
痛苦 Bitter suffering; acute pain; pang; misery.
痛恨 Bitter hatred; great regret; hate bitterly; virulent.
痛哭 Weep bitterly; moan; lament; bewailing.
痛惜 Great sorrow; deep regret.
痛處 A sore (tender) place (spot).
痛責 Scotch blessing.
痛楚 Pain; in pain.
痛飲 Drink deeply or profusely; revels riotous drinking; deep drinking.
痛愛 Burn with passion. Love deeply.
痛罵 Scold bitterly; condemn; denounce; abuse; inveigh against; taunt; rail at; blow up; give one's fits; scold severely; scold bitterly.
痛改前非 Reform with a keen sense of error.
痛定思痛 Recall past pains.

痞 (n.)- Constipation; dyspepsia; a stoppage.
pǐ 痞症；痞塊 A swelling of the stomach from constipation.
痞匪；痞棍 Rebels; marauders; bandits.

痢 (n.)- A disorder of the bowels; a purging; a flux.
lì 痢疾 Dysentery; diarrhoea.

痣 (n.)- Spots on the body; moles; heat spot.
zhì 痣記 Characteristic marks upon a person's body; birthmarks.

痧 (n.)- Cholera; colic.
痧藥丸 Cholera pills.
shā

痰 (n.)- Phlegm; expectoration; mucus; sputum.
tán 痰盂 A spittoon; a spitbox; a

cuspidor.
痰涎 Phlegm; spittle.
痰症；痨病 Phthisis.

**痱** (n.)- Prickly heat; pimple; an eruption.
fèi 痱子；痱瘡 Prickly heat; miliaria.

**痳** (n.)- Measles. Numbness; paralysis.
má 痳子 Pockmarks.
痳木 Numb.
痳疹 The measles.
痳瘋 Leprosy; spotted leprosy.
痳痹 Paralysed; benumbed; numb. Paralysis.
痳醉 Anaesthetize; narcotize; render insensible; drug.
痳藥；痳醉劑 An anaesthetic; a narcotic; an opiate.
痳瘋醫院 A lazaretto; a leprosery.
痳瘋病人 Leper.

**痼** 痼癖 A deeply-rooted habit; a bad habit.
gù

**瘀** (n.)- Effusion; accumulation of blood.
yū 瘀血 The effused blood.
瘀傷 A contusive bruise.
瘀膿 Effuse pus.

**瘁** (n.)- Toil. Disease.
(adj.)- Distressed; wearied;
cuì wornout; careworn.

**瘋** (n.)- Paralysis; insanity; lunacy.
(adj.)- Mad; insane; lunatic; wild
fēng deranged; palsied.
瘋子；瘋人 A madman; a maniac; a lunatic.
瘋狗 A mad dog.
瘋傻 Stupid.
瘋話 Gibberish.
瘋癱 Paralysis; palsy.
瘋癲 Mental derangement; lunacy; insanity.
瘋人院 A lunatic asylum; an insane hospital; a madhouse; a bedlam.
瘋犬病；恐水病 Dog-bite; rabies; hydrophobia.

**瘌** (adj.)- Bald.
瘌痢 Bald from skin disease;
là smooth-headed; scald-head.

**瘟** (n.)- Plague; pestilence; epidemic.
wēn 瘟疫 Plague; epidemic; pestilence; contagion; infection.
瘟神 The god of plague.
瘟疹 Scarlet fever.
瘟疫流行 Widespread epidemics.

**瘠** (adj.)- Lean; barren.
瘠土 Barren soil.
jí

**瘡** (n.)- An ulcer; an abscess; a sore; a wound; a boil; an
chuāng eruption.
瘡疤；瘡瘢 The scab of a sore; the scar of a boil.
瘡症 Ulcers; boils.
瘡痍 Calamity; plagues; distress.
瘡癤 A rash; a swelling.

**瘤** (n.)- A tumor; a wen; a swelling; a lump; a hunch.
liú

**瘦** (n.)- Lankness; leanness; thinness; tire.
shòu (adj.)- Lean; meager; thin. Poor;

barren; skinny.
(v.)- Become thin; lose flesh.
瘦田；瘦地 Sterile soil; unproductive land.
瘦肉 Lean meat.
瘦削；瘦小 Thin; lean.
瘦弱 Emaciated; withered; thin.
瘦臂 A thin (slender) arm.
瘦骨嶙峋 Scraggy.

瘧 nüè (n.)- A remittent fever; ague influenza; malaria.
瘧疾 Intermittent or remittent fevers; malaria.
瘧蚊 Malaria mosquito; anopheles.

瘴 zhàng (n.)- Malaria; pestilential vapours; miasma; epidemic.
瘴氣病 Paludism; malaria.
瘴熱症 Fever occasioned by malaria.

療 liáo (n.)- Recuperation; restoration.
(v.)- Heal; cure; restore; treat; remedy.
療法 A method of treatment; means of remedy.
療病；療治 Treat; cure. Medical treatment.
療養 Medical treatment; be under medical treatment.
療養院 A convalescent hospital; an infirmary; a sanatorium.

癆 láo (n.)- A consumption; tuberculosis; wasting away from toil or anxiety; decay.
癆咳 Consumptive cough.
癆病；癆瘵 Phthisis; consumption.

癇 xián (n.)- Fits; convulsions; epilepsy.
(adj.)- Mad.
癇病 Epilepsy; convulsions.

癌 ái (n.)- A cancer. A gangrenous evil; a deep-rooted source of strife.
癌腫 A cancerous swelling.

癖 pǐ (n.)- A weakness. A vicious appetite; a habit; a craving; a hobby; an inordinate fancy.
癖好 Eccentricity; a craving disposition; a propensity.

癒 yù (adj.)- Healed; recovered.

癟 biē (adj.)- Shrivelled up; empty.
癟三 A skinny rascal.
癟羅痧 Cholera.

癡 chī Same as 痴.
(n.)- Folly; foolishness; stupidity.
(adj.)- Stupid; foolish; idiotic; simple; silly; crazy; dull.
癡人 A simpleton; an idiot; a fool.
癡心 Vain thoughts; reverie.
癡呆；癡獃 Silly; foolish; doltish.
癡迷 Besotted; stupefied.
癡笑 Simper; horse laugh; ceaseless giggling.
癡情 Infatuation; blind love.
癡想 Vain thoughts; lost in thought.
癡漢 A dolt; a fool.
癡蠢 Dull; stupid.
癡呆症；白癡 Dementia; imbecility.

癤 jiē 癤子 A pimple; a small sore; a little boil.

癢 yǎng Same as 痒.
(n.)- Itch.
(adj.)- Itching; itchy.

(v.)- Itch.

**癧** (n.)- Scrofula; struma.
lì 癧瘡 Swelling on the neck.

**癩** (n.)- Skin disease; impetigo; leprosy; scabies.
lài (adj.)- Leprous.
癩狗 A mangy dog.

癩者 A leper; a leprous patient.
癩病 Leprosy; lepra.
癩痢 A scabby head.
癩癬 Ringworm; a spreading scab.
癩蝦蟆 The toad.
癩蝦蟆想吃天鵝肉 The toad thought to partake of the meat of the swan —vain hopes; foolish imaginings.

**癬** (n.)- Ringworm; tetter.
xuǎn 癬瘡 Tetter.

**癰** (n.)- A carbuncle; an ulcer; an abscess.
yōng 癰疽 A carbuncle.
癰瘡 An abscess.

**癱** (n.)- Paralysis; palsy; numbness.
tān 癱子 A paralytic.
癱手 Paralysis of an arm.
癱病；瘋癱 Paralysis; stiffness of the limbs.

癱脚 A paralytic effection of the legs; leg stiffness.

**癲** (n.)- Madness; insanity; convulsions; mania.
diān (adj.)- Crazy; mad; infatuated; insane.

癲死 Die of madness.
癲狂；瘋癲 Raving mad; delirious.
癲狗 A mad dog.
癲癇 Epilepsy.
癲癇病人 An epileptic.

# 癶 部

**登** (v.)- Ascend; mount; step up; go up; start. Approach.
dēng 登山 Ascend a mountain.
登岸；上岸 Disembark; land; go ashore.

登記 Register; enroll; make an entry. Enrolment; registration; enlist.
登高 Ascend heights—as is done on the 9th day of the 9th month.
登陸 Land. Journey overland.
登場 Appearance; come upon the stage.
登報 Put it in a newspaper; insert an advertisement in a newspaper.
登臺 Go up on the platform; take up a high position; appear on the stage.
登樓 Go up stairs.
登記處 A register office; a registry.
登記稅 Registration tax.
登記費 A registration fee.
登記簿 A register book.
登陸艇 Landing craft.
登門答謝 Go to the house and return thanks.
登記商標 Registered trade mark.
登陸部隊 Landing force.

**發** (adj.)- Prosperous; vigorous.
fā (v.)- Send forth; give out; discharge; dispatch. Issue; promulgate. Utter. Start; set out.

發火；發怒 Become angry.
發生 Begin to grow; bud; break out; happen; take place.
發刊 Publish; issue.
發令 Give a command; issue order.
發光 Radiate; emit light. Luminous; shine; enlighten.
發回；發還 Return; send back.
發行 Sell wholesale. Publish. Distribute; put in circulation.
發見 Discover; find out; light upon.
發冷 Aguish; shiver.
發言；發語 Speak; utter; break silence.
發誓 Swear.
發抖 Shiver; shudder; tremble.
發作 Break out; develop into.
發狂 Become mad; became insane (crazy); lose one's senses.
發炎 Become inflammed.
發明 Invent; publish an original idea. Invention.
發育 Grow; develop.
發芽；發苗 Sprout; bud; germinate.
發表 Reveal; show forth; notify; publish; make public; explain fully; announce; reveal.
發紅 Become red; blush.
發音 Pronunciation.
發信 Dispatch (send) a message (letter).
發射 Shoot; fire a gun; discharge a gun; shoot a rifle.
發財 Make money; become rich; grow rich; prosper by becoming wealthy.
發展 Extend; expand; develop.
發砲 Fire; fire off a gun.
發病 Get sick; fall ill.
發笑 Bring about laugh.
發送 Send out; dispatch; forward.
發起 Promote; originate; start.
發條 Spring; coiled spring.
發動 Start move; put in motion; set on foot; press the button.
發售；發賣 Begin to sell; offer for sale; put on sale.
發問 Question.
發掘 Unearth; excavate; dig up.
發現 Come to light; manifest; appear; burst into view; become manifest; discover; appear; turn up; lay bare; crop out.
發款 Distribute payments.
發票 A bill of sales; an invoice.
發貨 Send goods.
發揚 Make known; exalt; raise; promote.
發射(火箭) To launch (a rocket).
發散 Dissipate, as a cold; emit; send forth; give out.
發脹 Swell up.
發揮 Explicate; make clear. Work out in full; display.
發慌 Be agitated; lose presence of mind.
發電 Generate electricity.
發達 Prosper; rise in distinction; develop; make progress.
發福 Be in good health; grow fat.
發瘋 Go mad.
發酵 Ferment.
發霉 Get moldy; grow mildewed.
發燒；發熱 Get hot; be feverish; have an attack of fever.
發覺 Come to light; be discovered (disclosed, detected, exposed, found out).
發刊辭 A prologue; a forward.
發光體 A luminant body.
發行所 Place of sale or publication; sales office; a publishing house.
發行者 A publisher.
發牢騷 Be discontented; grumble.
發言人 A spokesman.
發言權 A voice; the right to speak.
發明家 An inventor.
發起人 A founder; a promoter.

發射體 Projectile; missile.
發假誓 Tell lies in a court of law.
發動力 Motive power (force).
發動機 An engine; a motor.
發祥地 The cradle-land.
發脾氣 Be out of temper.
發電機 A dynamo; an electromotor.
發酵粉 Baking powder.
發生衝突 Cause a clash; arouse opposition.
發動羣衆 To mobilize (arouse) the masses.
發展壯大 To grow and progress.
發生變態 Metamorphosis of development.
發行價格 The issue par; the issue price.
發冷發熱 Remittent fever.
發表意見 To express an opinion; to deliver one's opinion (on, about).
發表宣言 To issue a manifesto.
發育不良 Be under-grown.
發育良好 Be well-grown.
發音符號 Phonetic signs (symbols).
發音器官 The vocal organs.
發動戰爭 To launch a war.
發揚光大 Bring to light; glorify.

# 白 部

白 (adj.)- White; snowy. Bright; clear; fair. Plain.
bói (v.)- Make clear; express; say.
(adv.)- Freely; in vain; gratuitously; gratis.
白人 A white man.
白水 Plain water.
白天 The day; daytime.
白玉 White jade.
白瓜 A white musk-melon.
白色 White.
白金 Platinum.
白銀 Silver.
白俄 A White Russian.
白食 A free meal.
白浪；白波 White-caps; white horses; white foaming waves.
白宮 The White House, the official residence, at Washington, of the President of the U.S.A.
白粉 Chalk; whiting.
白紙 White paper. Blank paper.
白帶(醫) Leukorrhoea; the whites.
白淨 A fair and clear complexion.
白晝 Broad daylight; in open day.
白喉(醫) Diphtheria.
白菓 A ginkgo-nut.
白菜 Cabbage.
白雲 A white (fleecy) cloud.
白煙 White smoke.
白楊 An aspen; a white poplar; an abele.
白旗 A white flag; a flag of truce.
白熊 A white (polar) bear.
白種 The white race.
白髮 White hair; grey hair.
白糖 White (refined) sugar.
白鴿 Domestic pigeons.
白癡 An idiot; an imbecile; a born fool.
白蟻 A white ant; a termite.
白礬 Alum.
白鐵 Galvanized iron; tin-plates.
白蠟 White wax.
白刃戰；白兵戰 Hand-to-hand fighting (struggle); a close combat.
白內障(醫) Cataract.
白日夢 Day dreaming.

白皮書 A white paper; a white-book.
白血病(醫) Leukemia.
白血球 The white blood-corpuscle; a leucocyte.
白雲石 Dolomite.
白雲母 Muscovite; white mica.
白瑪瑙 Chalcedony.
白頭翁；白髮老人 A white-haired old man.
白手起家 Rise in life by one's own efforts.
白令海峽(地) Bering Strait.
白俄羅斯(地) White Russia; Byelorussia.
白葡萄酒 White wine; sherry.
白髮蒼蒼 Hair streaked with grey.
白蘭地酒 Brandy.

## 百
bǎi
(n.)- A hundred.
(adj.)- Many; numerous.
百分 One-hundred points; a full-mark.
百年 A hundred years; a century.
百姓 The common people.
百倍 Centuple; hundredfold.
百萬 A million.
百分比；百分率 Percentage.
百日咳(醫) Pertussis; whooping cough.
百合花 Lily.
百貨店 The stores; a department store.
百葉窗 Venetian shutter.
百靈鳥 The Mongolian lark.
百分之一 One per cent.
百分之百 One hundred per cent.
百年大計 A far-sighted policy.
百年紀念 A centennial anniversary; a centenary.
百折不撓 An indomitable spirit (will); tenacity of purpose.
百科全書 An encyclopedia.
百發百中 Hitting the mark every time; never miss the mark.
百菓饅頭 Stuffed pudding.
百萬富翁 A millionaire.
百戰百勝 Win battle after battle; be ever victorious.
百聞不如一見 Seeing is believing.
百尺竿頭更進一步 Make still greater progress; take one more step forward.

## 皁
zào
Same as 皂.
(n.)- Police runners; lictors; underlings. Soap. Stable.
(adj.)- Black; dark.
皁白 Black and white; bad and good.
皁白不分 Not to distinguish black from white–indiscriminating.

## 的
dí
(n.)- The bull's-eye of a target; an aim; a mark.
(adj.)- Evident; actual; true.
(adv.)- Clearly; evidently.
的當 Properly; satisfactorily.
的確 Real; genuine; actual; in fact; in truth; in reality.
的士 Taxi.
的士司機 Taxi-driver.
的是夠格 Discotheque.

## 皆
jiē
(adj.)- All.
(adv.)- Altogether.
皆因 All due to.
皆知 Known to all; well-known; famous.

## 皇
huáng
(n.)- A sovereign; a ruler.
(adj.)- Imperial. Admirable. Excellent. Supreme. Great; magnificent.
皇上 The emperor.
皇天；皇天上帝 Almighty God. Heaven.
皇后 The empress.
皇位 The Throne.
皇帝 An emperor; a sovereign.

皇宮 The Imperial Palace.
皇陵 The imperial catatombs; the imperial tombs.
皇太子 The heir apparent; the crown prince.
皇太后 The Empress Dowager.

**皎** jiǒo (n.)- The bright moon.
(adj.)- Clear; splendid; pure.
皎日 Bright daylight.
皎潔 Pure and clean.

**皓** hào (adj.)- White; bright.
皓月 A brilliant moon.
皓首 A white head; old age.

**皖** wǎn (n.)- The Province of Anhwei.

**皙** xī (adj.)- White; clear; fair.

# 皮 部

**皮** pí (n.)- A wrapper; a covering. The skin; a hide; pelt; leather; fur; bark; peel; rind. A surface.
(v.)- Cover, as skin does.
皮包 Wrapping of packages; small handbag or valise.
皮衣 A leather (fur) garment; a furcoat.
皮匠 A tanner; a cobbler; a shoe maker.
皮夾 A leathern portfolio; a wallet.
皮革 Hides; leather.
皮相 Superficial.
皮帶 A leather belt; belting for machinery.
皮球 A ball.
皮蛋 Preserved eggs.
皮袋 A leather purse or bag.
皮靴 Leather boots.
皮箱 A leather box.
皮鞋 Leather shoes.
皮層 Dermal cortex.
皮膚 The skin.
皮襖 A fur coat.
皮膚炎 Dermatitis.
皮膚科 Dermatology.
皮膚病 A skin (cutaneous) disease.
皮下注射 Subcutaneous (hypodermic) injection.
皮開肉綻 Effects of a severe thrashing.
皮膜組織(解) Epithelial tissue.
皮膚感覺 Cutaneous sensation.
皮篷汽車；敞篷汽車 A touring car.
皮膚科醫生 A dermatologist.

**皺** zhòu (n.)- Wrinkles; furrows; folds; creases; rumples.
(adj.)- Shrivelled; shrunken.
(v.)- Frown; shrink.
皺皮 A shrivelled skin.
皺眉 Knit the brows; frown.
皺面 A wrinkled face; a lined face.
皺紙 Crumpled paper.
皺紋 Wrinkles.
皺痕 Marks of crinkling.

# 皿 部

**盂** yú
(n.)- A large cup; a basin.
盂鉢 Basins and bowls.
盂蘭盆會 Buddhist festival of the dead; the Feast of Lanterns.

**盆** pén
(n.)- A tub; a pot; a dish; a jar.
盆地 A basin; a valley.
盆栽 A plant grown in pot; a pot-growing plant.
盆景 A tray-landscape; a miniature (mimic) landscape laid out on a tray.

**盃** bēi
See 杯.
(n.)- A cup; a wine-cup.

**盈** yíng
(n.)- Abundance; surplus.
(adj.)- Full; abundant; replenished.
(v.)- Exceed. Fill.
盈盈 Lovely; gracious; fascinating; attractive.
盈溢 Overflowing; superabundant.
盈滿 Become full; be filled; abound with.
盈餘 An overplus; gain; profit.
盈虧 Gain and loss.

**盅** zhōng
(n.)- A covered cup; bowl.

**益** yì
(n.)- Advantage; profit.
(adj.)- Beneficial; profitable; gainful.
(v.)- Add; increase. Benefit.
益友 Beneficial friends.
益多 More and more.
益處 Advantage; benefit.
益鳥 Useful birds; beneficial birds.
益蟲 Beneficial (useful) insects.

**盎** àng
(n.)- A basin or dish. Abundant.
盎斯 Ounce, a unit of weight.

**盒** hé
(n.)- A box; a carton; a casket.
盒子 A small box; a carton.
盒子槍 A mauser.

**盔** kuī
(n.)- A helmet.
盔甲 Armour; helmet and coat of mail.

**盛** shèng
(adj.)- Full; abundant; luxuriant; prosperous; flourishing; grand; excellent; developing.
(v.)- Put into a vessel; contain; receive.
盛大 Grand; splendid.
盛年 Prime of life; early manhood; youth.
盛名 Noted; well-known; a great reputation.
盛況 Prosperity; a bloom.
盛宴 A grand feast (entertainment).
盛酒 Fill with wine.
盛夏 The middle (height) of summer; mid-summer; dog-days.
盛衰 Prosperity and adversity; ups and downs; rise and fall; prosperity and decline.
盛情 Abundant kindness; great favour.
盛開 In full bloom or blossom, as flowers.
盛筵 A sumptuous feast.
盛會 A splendid meeting.
盛意 Good intentions; good will.
盛裝 Gayly dressed; in fine dress; full dress.
盛舉 A festivity; a gala; a grand occasion; a great deed; excellent enterprise.
盛禮 Profuse of politeness. A grand ceremony.

盛氣凌人 Put on airs and insult others.

**盜** (n.)- A robber; a thief; a burglar; a bandit; a pirate; a plunderer; a highwayman.
dào (v.)- Steal; rob; plunder.

盜用 Stealing; peculation.
盜寇；盜匪 Rebels; bandits; brigands.
盜賊 A robber; a thief; a burglar.
盜竊 Steal; rob; purloin; pilfer.

**盟** (n.)- An oath; a covenant; a contract; a league.
méng (v.)- Swear; take an oath. Make a treaty.

盟主 Lord of covenants; suzerain power ; the chief of a confederacy.
盟約 A promise; a pledge; a covenant; a pact; a compact.
盟國 States bound to one another by covenant; allied states.
盟兄弟 Sworn brothers.

**盞** (n.)- A shallow cup; a teacup; a cup.
zhǎn

**盡** (n.)- The utmost; the last.
jǐn (adj.)- All; exhausted; finished; completed.
(v.)- Finish; fulfill; come to an end; terminate.
(adv.)- Fully; wholly; extremely. All gone.

盡力 With might and main; with all one's strength; do the utmost; make every effort; do one's best; endeavour.
盡忠 Perfectly loyal.
盡殺 Exterminate; annihilate.
盡責 Fulfill the duties of one's office.
盡量 Utmost; fully; to the full extent.
盡瘁 Serve to the end; work hard for; devote oneself to.
盡頭 The very end; the extremity.
盡義務 Fulfill obligations.
盡忠報國 Loyalty and patriotism.

**監** (n.)- A prison; a jail.
jiān (v.)- Examine carefully; oversee. Take charge of; supervise.
監工 Oversee work; superintend work. A foreman; a head contractor; a supervisor.

監犯 A prisoner; a jail bird.
監守 Have in custody; keep watch.
監考 Examine; inspect; invigilate.
監房 A cell; a cage; a ward; a quod.
監視 Police surveillance; look over.
監督 Overseer; a superintendent; a director.
監禁 Put in prison; confine. Imprisonment; detention.
監察 Superintendence; inspection; survey.
監獄 A prison; a gaol.
監考人 An invigilator.
監視人 An inspector; a superintendent; a guard.
監察員 Inspector.
監護人 A guardian.
監守自盜 Embezzlement.

**盤** (n.)- A dish; a basin; a tray; a vessel.
pán (v.)- Coil up; twist; wind.
盤上 Wind up; coil up.

盤曲 Coil up.
盤谷；曼谷(地) Bangkok.
盤問；盤詰 Question closely; interrogate.
盤旋；盤繞 Wind around; rotate.
盤川 Travelling expenses.
盤算 Calculate; consider.
盤踞 Hold a strong position.

**盥** (v.)- Wash.
guàn
盥沐；盥洗 Wash; bathe.
盥盆 A wash basin.
盥洗室 A lavatory; a wash-room.

**盧** (n.)- A hound.
lú
(adj.)- Black.
盧比 Rupee—the standard monetary unit of India.
盧布 Rouble—the monetary unit in the U.S.S.R.
盧森堡(地) Luxemburg.

**盪** (n.)- A tub for bathing.
dàng
(adj.)- Moved; agitated.
(v.)- Move. Row. Cleanse.
盪滌 Cleanse.

# 目 部

**目** (n.)- The eyes. A director; a cheif or head. A list. An article; an item.
mù
(v.)- Look upon; eye. Designate.

目的 An aim; an object; an end; a purpose.
目送 Follow with the eyes; watch.
目測 Measure with the eye.
目標 A mark; a target; an objective; an aim.
目錄 A catalogue; a table of contents.
目擊 Witness.
目的地 The destination.
目擊者 An eyewitness; a witness.
目中無人 Supercilious; contemptuous.
目不轉睛 A fixed gaze.
目不識丁 Illiterate.
目光無神 Dull eyes; lacking lustre.
目前形勢 As things stand now; under the existing circumstances.
目瞪口呆 Dumbfounded.

**盲** (adj.)- Blind. Dark. Indiscriminate.
máng
盲人 A blind person; the blind.
盲目 Blindness.

盲動 Act recklessly; go it blind.
盲從 Follow blindly; blind adherence.
盲腸 The caecum; the blind gut.
盲點；盲斑 Blind spot.
盲人院 Blind asylum.
盲腸炎(醫) Appendicitis; caecitis; typhlitis.
盲目飛行 Blind flying; instrument flying.
盲人文字 Braille.
盲人學校 A school for the blind.

**直** (adj.)- Straight. Direct. Perpendicular; vertical. Erect; upright; honest. Exact; sincere; outspoken.
zhí
(v.)- Straighten; go direct; proceed.
(adv.)- Exactly; directly; just; straight-forward; merely.

直上 Go straight-upward.
直下 Fall straight down.
直立 Stand on end; stand erect (up).
直至 Until; direct to; heading to.
直向 Facing; straight-toward.
直角 A right angle.
直言 Be outspoken; make a clean breast of; speak frankly.
直射 Direct rays of the sun. Direct

(frontal) fire.
直徑 The diameter.
直爽 Frank; outspoken.
直接 At first hand; from original sources: direct.
直視 Look straight at: look one in the face; stare; face squarely.
直達 Reach directly.
直腸 The rectum.
直線 A straight line; an air-line.
直諫 Direct admonition (reproof); remonstrance.
直覺 Intuition; immediate perception.
直譯 A literal translation; a verbatim (word-for-word) translation.
直轄 Immediate (direct) control.
直觀 Direct view. Intuition.
直立面 A vertical (perpendicular) plane.
直角形；長方形 A rectangle.
直角柱(幾) A right prism.
直角板 A set square.
直角線 A vertical line; a perpendicular.
直射砲 A direct-firing gun.
直達車 A thorough train.
直系親族 Lineal relatives (consanguinity).
直接交易 Direct transaction.
直接原因 An immediate cause.
直接傳染 Direct contagion.
直接影響 Direct effect.
直達客車 A through passenger-train.
直角三角形 A right-angled triangle.
直流發電機 A direct-current dynamo.
直布羅陀海峽(地) Strait of Gibraltar.

相 xiāng (n.)- Appearance; countenance; looking.
(adj.)- Mutual; correlative; reciprocal.
(v.)- Inspect; select; examine. Look at. Help; aid; assist.
(adv.)- Mutually; reciprocally.

相仇 Be enemies.
相反 Contrary; exactly the opposite; opposed to each other; opposition; inversion.
相比 Compare with.
相友 Mutual friendship.
相互 Mutual; reciprocal.
相片 A photograph; a picture.
相打 Fight together; fight hand to hand; combat; exchange blow.
相同 Identical; similar; like.
相似 Alike; similar; coincide with; resemble; look like.
相交 Have dealings with; associate with; intercourse.
相好 On good terms. Intimate; friendly.
相助；相援 Mutual help; helping each otehr; assist.
相伴 A companion; a mate. Accompany; go along with.
相見 Meet; see; have an interview.
相近 Adjoining; near to; not very distant; close by.
相迎 Welcome; meet.
相依 Interdependent; mutually dependent.
相爭 Quarrel; compete.
相看 Look at each other.
相信 Believe; trust.
相思 Think of one another as lovers.
相配 Correspond; match.
相救 Mutual relief.
相符 Agreeing; corresponding.
相處 Live together.
相距 Distant from.
相等 Similar; equal; corresponding; no better than.
相傳 Hand down; transmit. Be current-ly.
相會 Meet together; fall in.
相當 Suitable; fit; proper; appropriate; adequate; corresponding.
相遇；相逢 Meet with a friend; come

in contact with; encounter; come across.
相對 Relatively. Oppose.
相聚 Meet together; assemble.
相撞 Clash; collide; jostle.
相談 Talk with; converse to; confer with.
相罵 Mutual reviling and recriminations; quarrel.
相貌 Countenance; appearance.
相聲 Comic monologue.
相離 Separated from; apart.
相贈 Make a present to.
相識 Acquaintance. Know each other.
相勸 Warn; caution.
相繼 Consecutively; one following another; one after another.
相戀；相愛 Mutually attached; be in love with each other.
相思病 Lovesickness. Languish for love.
相對的 Relative.
相對論 Theory of relativity.
相互作用 Reciprocal action.
相互扶助 Mutual aid.
相互關係 Correlation; reciprocity; mutual (reciprocal) relation.
相親相愛 Be mutually attached; be in love with; love each other; mutual love.

**盼** pàn
(n.)- A beautiful, bright eye.
(v.)- Gaze at; glance at. Long for.
盼望 Hope for; long for; look forward to.

**盾** dùn
(n.)- A buckler; a shield. Guilder, silver coin used in Holland.
盾牌 A shield.

**省** shěng
(n.)- A province.
(adj.)- Frugal; saving; economical.
(v.)- Save; diminish; reduce; abridge. Visit. Examine; consider; reflect on; look back.
省力 Save strength.
省分；省區 A province.
省長 Provincial governor.
省事 Save trouble.
省城；省會 The provincial capital.
省悟 Be aroused to.
省時 Save time.
省料 Save material.
省略 Abridgement; omission.
省費 Save expense; avoid heavy expenses.
省儉 Thrifty; frugal; sparing.
省親 Pay a visit to one's parents.
省錢 Save money; lay by money; economize.
省政府 The provincial government.
省吃儉用 Very frugal.
省略符號 Ellipsis (–, . . .).

**眇** miǎo
(adj.)- Blind of one eye. Minute; subtle.
眇小 Small; minute; trifling.

**眈** dān
See 耽.
(v.)- Dote on.
眈眈 Look at someone fiercely.

**眉** méi
(n.)- The eyebrows.
眉毛 The eyebrows.
眉目 Eyebrows and eyes; the face. Idea.
眉來眼去 Exchanging glances.
眉目清秀 Handsome; beautiful; pretty.
眉開眼笑 A beaming countenance.

**看** kān (kàn)
(v.)- Look at; see. Look after; take care of; regard carefully; observe; guard; watch over; attend. Practice. Visit.
看出 Find out.

看守 Protect; guard; keep watch.
看作 Regard as; consider of.
看更 Look after the night watch.
看法 According to one's point of view.
看重 Respect; esteem; regard as important.
看家 Look after a house.
看書 Read; look over books.
看病 Attend to a patient. Take care of an invalid. See a doctor.
看望 Visit.
看輕 Look down upon; make light of.
看過 Overlook; let pass.
看飽；看厭 Be tired of seeing (looking at); have seen enough of.
看慣 Get used to seeing; become familiar to.
看戲 See a performance; go to a theater.
看顧 Look after; care for.
看護 Nurse; tend; take care of; pay attention to; look after.
看不見 Disappear from sight; be lost to sight.
看守人 A keeper; a warden.
看機會 Watch for an opportunity.
看電視 Watch television.
看電影 See a film.
看醫生 Consult a doctor.

眞 zhēn Same as 真.
(n.)- Truth. A likeness or portrait; reality; genuineness. Divinity.
(adj.)- True; actual; real; genuine; unfeigned. Sincere; faithful; true-hearted.
眞心 True-hearted; sincere.
眞正 True; genuine; authentic.
眞材 Good stuff; real talent; one possessing useful qualities.
眞空 A vacuum.
眞相 The real appearance; the true state; the real facts.
眞情 Real sentiment; true feelings. The facts of the case.
眞理 Truth; orthodox principles; gospel.
眞意 Real intention (motive).
眞愛 True love.
眞話 The truth.
眞誠 Sincerity.
眞僞 Truth or falsehood; truth.
眞像(光) Real image.
眞實 True; real; actual; sincere.
眞摯 Earnest; sincere.
眞確 Absolutely true; authentic; actual.
眞空管 A vacuum tube.
眞面目 One's true character.
眞美善 Truth, beauty, and fineness.
眞心朋友 True-hearted friend.
眞珠光澤 Pearly.

眠 mián (v.)- Lie down. Sleep; close the eyes; doze.
眠臥 Lie down to sleep.

眩 xuàn (adj.)- Confused; mistaken; dazzled; confounding; giddy.
(v.)- Grow dizzy (giddy).
眩惑 Be at a loss; be perplexed (puzzled).
眩暈 Vertigo; giddiness.
眩耀 Dazzle.

眶 kuàng (n.)- The socket of the eye.

眸 móu 眸子 The pupil of the eye.

眷 juàn (n.)- Family. Relatives.
(v.)- Love; be fond of. Care for. Look backward.

眷念；眷顧 Regard with affection; look after.
眷屬；家眷 One's family.
眷戀 Affectionate adherence. Be attached to; set one's affections on.

眺 (n.)- Gaze at; look at eagerly; stare at; glance or peep at.
tiào 眺望 Gaze at; look at from afar.

眼 (n.)- The eye. A hole; an opening; an orifice.
yǎn 眼力 Sharpness of sight. Visual power; perception; foresight.
眼中 In one's eyes.
眼孔；眼眶 The eye-socket; an eye-hole.
眼毛 Eyelashes.
眼皮；眼瞼 The eyelids.
眼白 White of an eye.
眼光 Foresee. Vision; outlook.
眼花 Dim of sight; eyesight blurred.
眼前 Before one's eyes; at present.
眼科 Ophthalmology.
眼紅 Covetous eye.
眼界 The range of vision; the field of view; prospect.
眼病 An eye-affection (-disease); an ophthalmic disease; ophthalmia.
眼淚 Tears.
眼球；眼珠 An eye-ball.
眼痛 An eye-sore; pain in the eyes.
眼跳 The eye twitching.
眼暈 Dizzy; giddy.
眼線 A detective. An informer; a talebearer; a spy.
眼瞳 Pupil.
眼藥 Eye medicine; eye-water (-lotion, wash).
眼簾 The iris of the eye.
眼鏡 Spectacles; glasses.
眼中釘 A nail in the eye—a person who is a thorn in the flesh.
眼膏藥 Eyesalve.
眼鏡店 An optician; a spectacle-maker.
眼鏡盒 A spectacle case.
眼科醫生 An oculist; an ophthalmologist; an eye-doctor.
眼科醫院 An ophthalmic hospital.

衆 Same as 衆.
zhòng (n.)- A multitude; a majority. The people; crowd; group; throng.
(adj.)- Many; much; numerous; abundant.
衆人 Everyone; the multitude; the crowd; all the people.
衆多 Numerous; very many; abundant.
衆望 Confidence of the people.
衆意 Public opinion.
衆論；衆議 General consultation. Public opinion.
衆議員 A member of Parliament (M.P.).
衆議院 The House of Representatives. The House of Commons.
衆志成城 Union is strength; unanimity of purpose is like a fenced city.

着 Same as 著.
zhuó

睏 (v.)- Sleep; doze; sleepy.
kùn 睏倦 Tired and sleepy.
睏着了 Fall into sleep.

睛 (n.)- The pupil of the eye; the eyeball.
jīng 睛珠；水晶體 The crystalline lens.

睜 (v.)- Look at angrily. Open the eyes.
zhēng 睜眼 Open the eyes.

**睡** shuì (v.)- Sleep; slumber; repose.
睡衣 Nightshirt; nightdress; sleeping garment; pajamas.
睡床 Bed.
睡車；臥車 Sleeping-car; sleeper.
睡眠 Sleep; go to sleep; fall asleep; slumber.
睡椅 A sofa; a settee; a lounging chair.
睡熟 Sleep soundly.
睡醒 Awaken; wake up.
睡藥；催眠藥 Narcotic; soporific; sleeping draft (drug, potion).
睡午覺 Take a siesta.
睡眠不足 Insufficient sleep; want of sleep.
睡眠時間 Hours of sleep; sleeping hours.

**督** dū (n.)- An overseer; a superintendent.
(v.)- Direct; superintend; lead; command; rule; oversee; watch; supervise; look after. Reprove.
督促 Press; urge; importune.
督察 An inspector; a supervisor. Superintend; supervise.
督辦 Directory general; managing director. Supervise; oversee.
督學官 An inspector of schools; a school-inspector.

**睦** mù (adj.)- Harmonious; friendly; affectionate; neighbourly; conciliated.
(v.)- Keep peace with; intimate with; harmonize.
睦誼 Friendly feeling.
睦鄰 Friendly neighbours.
睦鄰政策 A good neighbour policy.

**睪** gāo Same as 睾.
(n.)- The testicles.
睪丸(解) The testicles.
睪丸炎 Orchitis.

**睫** jié (n.)- The eyelashes.
睫毛 The eyelashes.

**睬** cǎi (v.)- Greet; pay attention to.

**睹** dǔ Same as 覩.
(v.)- See; look at.

**瞄** miáo (v.)- Take aim.
瞄準 Aim at; take sight; lay a gun.
瞄準器 A sight.

**瞋** chēn (v.)- Stare at scornfully; glare at angrily; be angry at.
瞋視 Glare at in anger. An angry stare.

**瞌** kē (adj.)- Sleepy from fatigue.
瞌睡 Doze.

**瞎** xiā (adj.)- Blind. At random; reckless; careless; rude.
(adv.)- Carelessly; recklessly; at random.
瞎子 A blind man.
瞎走 Go blindly on.
瞎話 Lie; falsehood.
瞎說 Nonsense; talk recklessly.

**瞑** míng (v.)- Close the eye.
瞑目 Close the eyes; die.
瞑眩 Confuse; make dizzy.
瞑想 Meditate on; contemplate; muse on (over).
瞑瞑 Blinded; indistinct.

**瞞** (v.)- Deceive; conceal the truth; cheat.
mán 瞞過 Hide the truth of.
瞞騙；欺瞞 Deceive; cheat; impose upon; defraud.
瞞稅 To evade tax.
瞞心 To act against one's conscience.

**瞥** (v.)- Glance at; catch a glimpse of.
piē 瞥見；瞥眼 Catch a glimpse of; glance at; peep.

**瞪** (v.)- Stare at.
dèng 瞪目 Staring in anger.

**瞬** (v.)- Glance; blink; wink; twinkle with the eye.
shùn 瞬時 At an instant.
瞬息之間 In the twinkling of an eye; in a moment.

**瞭** (n.)- Clearness of sight; bright eye.
liǎo 瞭望 Take a distant view; look from afar.
瞭然 Clearly; plainly; fully understand.
瞭望臺 A belvedere; a lookout station; a watch tower.
瞭如指掌 Be as clear as day light; be as plain as the nose on one's face.

**瞰** (v.)- Watch; spy. Look down.
kàn 瞰視 Look down; command a view.

**瞳** (n.)- The pupil of the eyes.
tóng 瞳孔膜 Pupillary membrane.

**瞧** (v.)- Look at; glance at; see.
qiáo

**瞻** (v.)- Look up. Regard respectfully; reverence.
zhān 瞻仰 Look up with respect; admire.
瞻望 Look up to; gaze at; expect.
瞻前顧後 Circumspect.

**矇** (adj.)- Dim-sighted; blind. Ignorant; untaught.
méng 矇昧 Ignorant.
矇朧 Dim; misty.

**矗** (adj.)- Upright. Eminent.
(v.)- Rise up high.
chù 矗然 Straight; upright.
矗立 Stand high up.
矗立雲表 Sticking up into the clouds.

**矚** (v.)- Gaze at earnestly.
zhǔ 矚目 Stare at; look eagerly.

# 矛 部

**矛** (n.)- A spear; a lance.
máo 矛盾 Spears and shields—contradiction; inconsistency.
矛戟 Lance and spears.
矛頭 A spearhead.
矛槍 Spears and javelins.
矛盾尖銳化 Sharpening of contradiction.

矜 jīn (n.)- The handle of a spear.
(adj.)- Careful. Conceited. Distressed.
(v.)- Pity; have sympathy with; commiserate. Value. Respect.

Boast; speak highly of.
矜持 Solemn; austere.
矜恤；矜憐 Sympathize. Have pity on.
矜惜 Pity; sympathize.
矜貴 Precious; valuable.

# 矢 部

矢 shǐ (n.)- An arrow; a dart.
(v.)- Vow; take an oath. Resolve.
矢誓 Take an oath; swear.
矢如雨下 Shower of arrows.

矣 yǐ A final particle to denote perfect tense.

知 zhī (n.)- An intimate friend. Wisdom; knowledge; learning.
(v.)- Know; perceive; recognize; understand. Distinguish.
知心；知音 An intimate or bosom friend.
知交 Intimacy.
知名 Well-known; noted; celebrated; prominent.
知足 Be content; be satisfied.
知情 Know the real facts.
知悉 Be fully acquainted with; understand; know well; be aware of.
知羞；知恥 Feel ashamed.
知道 Know; recognize; understand.
知錯 Know, or acknowledge one's wrongs; know one's fault's.
知識 Knowledge; information; learning.
知覺 Sensation; perception; consciousness.
知更鳥(動) Robin.
知識界 Intellectual circles.
知人善任 Use a man according to his ability.
知己朋友 Very intimate friends.
知名之士 Well-known (noted) persons; notables.
知識分子 The intellectuals; the intelligentsia.
知識技能 Knowledge and skill.
知覺神經 Sensory nerves.

矩 jǔ (n.)- A carpenter's square. A law; a rule. A pattern.
矩形 A rectangle; rectangular.

短 duǎn (n.)- Defect; shortcomings.
(adj.)- Short; brief; contracted. Lacking; wanting; needing; deficient. Dwarfish.
(v.)- Shorten; come short; be short of; be in debt to.
短刀；短劍 A short sword; a dagger.
短小 Short and little.
短文 Short essay.
短衣；短衫 A jacket; a short dress.
短見 A short-sighted view. Shallow knowledge. Suicide.
短命；短折 A short life. Die young.
短波 A short wave-length.
短促 Transient.
短針 The short-hand; the hour-hand.
短音 A short sound.
短缺 A deficency; in defect.

短少 Be less than. Few; not many.
短處 A defect; a shortcoming; a weak point; a demerit.
短跑 A dash.
短期 A short-term; a short-period.
短視 Short-sighted.
短路 A short cut; short circuit.
短槍 A musket.
短篇 A short piece; a sketch.
短襪 A sock.
短時間 A short space of time.
短距離 A short distance (range); a close range.
短小精悍 Short in stature and alert.
短篇小說 A novelette; a short story.
短篇文章 A short composition.
短距離選手 A sprinter; a sprint-runner.
短距離賽跑 A short-distance race; a sprint-race; a dash.

矮 (n.)- Dwarf.
ǎi (adj.)- Short in stature. Diminutive; low.
矮子 A dwarf; a pigmy.
矮小 Undersized; dwarfish; diminutive.
矮屋 A low house.
矮胖 A short fat man.
矮櫈 A low stool.

矯 (adj.)- Martial; strong; robust; vigorous.
jiǎo (v.)- Straighten; correct; rectify; revise. Bend; twist. Falsify; misrepresent.
矯正 Rectify; correct; reform; set right; cure; remedy.
矯健 Vigorous; brave; valiant.
矯飾 Pretend.
矯正惡習 Cure one of bad habits.

# 石 部

石 (n.)- Stone; rock. A picul.
shí (adj.)- Hard. Barren.
石人；石像 A stone figure; a statue.
石子 Pebbles.
石女 A barren woman.
石匠 A stonemason; a stone-cutter.
石灰 Lime; calcium oxide.
石油 Petroleum.
石板 A slate.
石柱 A stone pillar.
石英(礦) Quartz.
石炭 Coal.
石屋 A stone house.
石洞 Rock cave.
石堆 A heap of stones.
石崖 A cliff.
石筍 Stalagmite.
石階 Stone-steps.
石路 A stone-paved road.
石塊 A stone; a pebble (小); a boulder (大).
石膏 Gypsum; plaster of Paris.
石綿；石絨 Asbestos.
石榴 Pomegranate.
石墨(礦) Graphite; black lead.
石器 Stone-ware.
石橋 A stone bridge.
石礦 A stone-pit; a quarry.
石蠟 Paraffin wax.
石鹽 Rock salt.
石灰水 Lime water.
石灰坑 Lime pit.
石灰粉 Lime powder.
石灰窰 Lime-kiln.
石灰質 Calcareous.

石英岩(礦) Quartzite; quartz-rock.
石斑魚 Spotted grouper.
石膏像 A plaster-bust (figure).
石綿片 Asbestos sheet.
石鍾乳(礦) Stalactites.
石器時代 The stone age.
石灰混凝土 Lime concrete.

**矽** xī (n.)- Silicon (Si).
矽岩 Quartzite.
矽酸 Silicic acid.
矽酸鹽 Silicates.
矽氟化氫 Hydrogen silico-fluoride.

**砂** shā See 沙.
(n.)- Sand; gravel.
砂土 Sandy soil.
砂布 Emery cloth.
砂紙 Emery paper; sand-paper.
砂粒 Gravel.
砂塵 Dust.
砂糖 Powdered sugar.
砂礫 Gravel; gritstone.
砂鐵 Iron-sand.
砂灘 A sandy beach; the sands.
砂囊 A gizzard.
砂濾器 A filter.
砂礫土 Sandy gravel soil.
砂質石灰土 Sandy lime soil.

**砌** qī (n.)- A stone step.
(v.)- Lay; pave.
砌路 Pave the road.
砌牆 Build a wall.

**砍** kǎn (n.)- A mortar or small vase.
(v.)- Cut; chop; cut off.
砍下 Cut down.
砍伐 Fell a tree.
砍開 Split open.
砍落 Cut down.
砍傷 Wound by cutting.
砍頭 Behead.
砍斷 Cut in two.

**砒** pī (n.)- Arsenic.
砒酸 Arsenic acid.
砒霜 Arsenic.

**砥** dǐ (n.)- A whetstone.
砥柱中流 A rock in the Yellow River in Honan—unmovable under great stresses.

**砧** zhēn Same as 碪.
(n.)- A block; an anvil.
砧木(農) Stock for propagation.
砧板 A chopping board.

**破** pò (adj.)- Broken. Ruined; destroyed.
(v.)- Break; ruin. Defeat. Discover; expose.
破片 A fragment; a splinter.
破布 Rag.
破屋 A ruined house.
破除 Break away; do away with.
破船 Ship-wreck; wreck.
破浪 Cut the sea.
破案 Clear up a case; find out offenders.
破財 Lose money (property).
破產 Bankruptcy; insolvency.
破裂 Be broken off; end in a rupture.
破費 Spend; waste.
破碎 Break to pieces; smash; crush.
破綻 A fault revealed; the weak point or defect; an inconsistency; a breach.
破曉 Daybreak; dawn.
破舊 Old and shabby; torn; ragged; worn-out.
破壞；毀壞 Break down; destroy; devastate; demolish; wreck.
破天荒 Unprecedented; unparalleled.

破紀錄 Break (beat, smash) the record.
破產者 A bankrupt; an insolvent.
破落戶 A decayed family.
破傷風 Tetanus; lockjaw.
破冰船 An ice-breaker; an ice-boat.
破口大罵 Abuse freely.
破竹之勢 With irresistible force; overcoming all obstacles; easy as splitting open a bamboo.
破舊立新 Discard the old and create something new.
破除迷信 Break down superstitions.

**硃** zhū (n.)- Vermilion.
硃砂 Cinnabar.
硃紅漆 Vermilion paint.
硃砂橘 The mandarin orange.

**研** yán See硯.
(n.)- An inkstone.
(v.)- Rub; grind; powder. Study; examine; search into carefully.
研究 Make a study of; make researches in; investigate thoroughly.
研細 Grind fine.
研碎 Grind to pieces.
研墨 Rub ink on an inkstone.
研究所 A research laboratory; a research institute.
研究院 A post-graduate institute attached to a university.
研究材料 Materials for research.

**硝** xiāo (n.)- Nitre; saltpeter.
硝石 Nitre; saltpeter.
硝煙 Powder smoke.
硝酸 Nitric acid.
硝酸鈉 Sodium nitrate.
硝酸鉀 Potassium nitrate.
硝酸鉛 Lead nitrate.
硝酸銀 Silver nitrate; caustic silver.
硝酸銅 Cupric nitrate.
硝酸鹽 Nitrate.
硝鏹水 Nitric acid.
硝化作用 Nitrification.
硝化甘油 Nitroglycerine.
硝酸銀溶液 Silver-bath.

**硫** liú (n.)- Sulphur (S); brimstone.
硫化 Sulphuration. Sulphurate sulphurize.
硫黃 Brimstone; sulphur.
硫酸 Sulphuric acid; oil of vitriol.
硫化物 A sulphide; a sulphuret.
硫化鋅 Zinc sulphide.
硫化鐵 Iron sulphide.
硫黃泉 Sulphur-spring.
硫酸鈣 Calcium sulphate.
硫酸銀 Silver sulphate.
硫酸銅 Sulphate of copper; blue vitriol.
硫酸鋅 Sulphate of zinc.
硫酸鐵 Sulphate of iron.
硫酸鹽 A sulphate.

**硬** yìng (adj.)- Hard; firm; strong.
硬化 Harden; be hardened; stiffen; become callous.
硬水(化) Hard water.
硬心 Hard-hearted.
硬皮 Hard skin.
硬性(物) Hardness.
硬度 Degree of hardness.
硬殼 A shell.
硬貨；硬幣 Hard money; metallic currency; coins.
硬石膏 Anhydrite.
硬殼蟲 A beetle.

**硯** yàn (n.)- An ink slab; an ink-stone.
硯池 The hollow for water on an inkstone.
硯盒 An ink-stone case.

**硼** péng (n.)- Boron (B).
硼砂 Borax.
硼酸 Boric acid.

硼酸鹽 Borate.

碇 dǐng (n.)- A stone anchor.
碇泊 Anchoring; anchorage; mooring.
碇泊港 Roadstead port.
碇泊費 Anchorage-dues; anchorage.

碉 diāo (n.)- Stone house. Pill-boxes.
碉堡 Pill-boxes.

碌 lù (adj.)- Rough; uneven. Toilsome; laborious.
碌碌 Ordinary; common.

碎 suì (n.)- Small pieces; fragments; odds and ends.
(adj.)- Broken. Petty. Troublesome.
(v.)- Break to pieces; smash; crush.
碎片 A broken piece; a splinter.
碎銀 Small changes.
碎石子 Broken stone.
碎石路 Macadam.
碎石機 Stone breaker.

碑 bēi (n.)- A monument; a large stone tablet.
碑文 An epitaph.
碑帖 Rubbings or prints from tablets.

碘 diǎn (n.)- Iodine.
碘化 Iodize.
碘酒 Tincture of iodine.
碘素 Iodine.
碘化物 Iodide.

碗 wǎn Same as 盌，椀.
(n.)- A bowl; a flat basin.
碗碟 Bowls and plates.
碗碟櫃 A cupboard.

碟 dié (n.)- A small dish; a plate.
碟子 A plate; a saucer.
碟架 A plate rack.

碧 bì (n.)- Green and blue jade.
(adj.)- Green; blue.
碧玉 Green jade; jasper.
碧血 Dark blood.
碧空；碧落 The blue sky.
碧海 The blue sea.
碧綠 Bright green.

碩 shuò (adj.)- Ripe; full. Eminent; great.
碩士 Wise men. Master of arts or science (M.A. or M.Sc.).
碩學 A man of great learning; a profound scholar.
碩大無朋 Great and peerless.

碳 tàn See 炭.
(n.)- Carbon.

確 què (adj.)- Hard. True; reliable.
(adv.)- Really; certainly; indeed.
確切 True to fact; exact.
確立 Establish; settle; fix; secure.
確知 Be fully assured of.
確定 Be decided (fixed, settled).
確信 Believe confidently; have strong confidence. A reliable news or information.
確認 Certify; confirm.
確實 Certain; sure; undoubted.
確據 Reliable evidence; sure proof.
確證 Infallible proofs; conclusive evidence. Prove positively; give convincing proofs of.
確實性 Certainly; reliability.

碼 mǎ
(n.)-Numerals; numbers; A yard.
碼尺 A yard stick; a yard measure.
碼頭 A jetty; a wharf.
碼頭脚夫；碼頭工人 A long-shore man.

碾 niǎn
(n.)- A stone roller.
(v.)- Roll; triturate.
碾米 Husk rice.
碾房 A mill for husking grain.
碾碎 Pulverize; grind to powder.
碾米廠 A rice hulling mill.
碾米機 A hulling machine.

磁 cí
(n.)- Chinaware; porcelain; crockery. A magnet.
磁力 Magnetism; magnetic force.
磁化 Magnetization.
磁石 A magnet.
磁性 Magnetism.
磁針 A magnetic needle.
磁場 The magnetic field.
磁極 The magnetic poles.
磁器；瓷器 Porcelain; chinaware.
磁鐵 Magnetic iron.
磁力線 Line of magnetic force.
磁極性 Magnetic polarity.
磁電鈴 Magnetic bell.
磁鐵鑛 Magnetite.

磅 bàng
(n.)- A pound (lb.).
磅秤 Scale; weight measure.
磅礴 Vast, as space. Filling up everywhere.

磋 cuō
(v.)- Rub; work at; correct carefully.
磋商 Negotiate; consult with; confer with; discuss.

磐 pán
(n.)- A large rock; a foundation stone.
磐牙 League together, as bandits.
磐石 A rock; a crag.

磕 kē
(v.)- Hit against. Strike stones together.
磕頭 Kotow.

磧 qì
(n.)- Rocks awash at low tide. Desert.

磨 mó [mò]
(n.)- A mill. Trial.
(v.)- Grind; powder; sharpen. Afflict.
磨刀 Sharpen a knife (sword).
磨牙 Grind the teeth.
磨石 A whetstone.
磨去 Rub off (out).
磨坊 A mill.
磨利 Grind sharp; sharpen by grinding.
磨損 Fray.
磨滅 Defacement; obliteration. Rub out; wear out; be defaced.
磨床 Grinding machine.
磨鍊 Work at; practise. Discipline diligently. Go under trial; improve one's ability.
磨難；磨折 Sufferings; tribulations.
磨麵 Grind flour.
磨刀石 A grindstone; a whetstone; cutter grinder.

磬 qìng
(n.)- Musical instruments made of stone; musical stones.
(adj.)- Empty; exhausted.

礁 jiāo
(n.)-Half-tide rocks.
礁石 A hidden or sunken rock.
礁標 Beacon.

磽 qiāo
(n.)- A stony or arid soil.
磽地 Arid land.
磽脊 Thin; poor.

**磷** lín
Same as 燐.
(n.)- Phosphorus.
磷肥 Phosphate fertilizer.
磷酸 Phosphoric acid.

**礎** chǔ
(n.)- The plinth; the base; the foundation.

**礙** ài
Same as 碍.
(n.)- Obstruction; hindrance; block; objection.
(v.)- Be obstructed; impede.
礙事 Obstruct; be in the way.
礙眼 Not pleasing to the eye.

**礦** kuàng
Same as 鑛.
(n.)- A mine; the ore of metal.
礦山 A mine.
礦工 A miner; a mine-worker.
礦井 The shaft of the mine; a pit.
礦石 The ore.
礦物 A mineral.
礦油 Mineral oil.
礦泉 A mineral spring.
礦區 A mine-lot; a mining area.
礦務 Mining affairs.
礦產 Minerals.
礦業 Mining industry.
礦泉水 Mineral water.
礦物界 The mineral kingdom.
礦務局 The bureau of mines; the mining control office.
礦石收音機 A crystal radio set.
礦石分離器 An ore-separator.

**礫** lì
(n.)- Small stones; gravels.
礫土 Gravel soil.
礫質黏土 Gravel clay.

**礬** fán
(n.)- Alum.
礬土 Alumina.
礬石 Aluminite.

**礮** pào
Same as 砲；炮.
(n.)- A cannon; a gun.
礮火 A gun-fire; artillery-fire.
礮手 A gunner; a cannoneer.
礮兵 Artillery. An artilleryman.
礮攻 Bombardment; bombard.
礮船；礮艦 A gunboat.
礮臺 A fort; a battery.
礮彈 A cannon-ball; a cannon shot; a projectile; a shell.
礮擊 Bombard; fire at; cannonade; shell; batter.

**礱** lóng
(n.)- A wooden mill.
礱坊 A mill.

# 示 部

**示** shì
(n.)- A notice; a proclamation. A manifestation; a sign.
(v.)- Declare; proclaim; exhibit.
示知 Let know; inform; notify.
示威 Showing of power or influence; hold a demonstration.
示弱 Show weakness.
示衆 Make known to the public.
示敬 Show respect to.
示意 Make known one's wishes.
示警 Warn.
示範法 The method of teaching by example.
示威運動 A demonstration.

社 (n.)- A society; a company. A village.
shè 社交 Social intercourse.
社長 President of a society; director of a company. A village elder.
社會 Society; community.
社團 A corporation; an association.
社廟 A temple.
社論 A leading article; an editorial.
社學；鄉學 A village school.
社壇 An altar.
社會化 Socialize.
社會性 Sociality; social nature.
社會學 Sociology.
社會主義 Socialism.
社會地位 One's social position.
社會改革 Social reform.
社會事業 Social work; public welfare work.
社會制度 Social system.
社會服務 Social service: welfare work.
社會科學 Social science.
社會問題 A social problem (question).
社會教育 Social education.
社會現象 A social phenomenon (phase).
社會風氣 Social convention.
社會名流 Noted public figures; socialite.
社會的分工 Social division of labour.
社會經濟學 Social economics.
社會主義國家 A socialistic country.
社會主義覺悟 Socialist consciousness.
社會主義道德 Socialist morality.

祀 (n.)- A year. A sacrifice.
(v.)- Sacrifice; offer sacrifices
sì to gods or evil spirits.
祀天 The sacrifice to Heaven.
祀神 Make offerings to the gods.
祀祖 Sacrifice to ancestors.
祀上帝 Sacrifice to God.

祇 (adv.)- Only; but.
zhǐ

祈 (v.)- Offer a sacrifice; pray to the gods. Beg.
qí 祈求 Beseech; implore; entreat.
祈望 Hope; expect; trust that.
祈願 Pray; make supplication.
祈禱 A prayer; devotions. Pray.
祈禱文 A written prayer.
祈禱者 A prayer.
祈禱會 A prayer-meeting.
祈禱上帝 Pray to god.

祐 (v.)- Protect; defend.
yòu

祕 Same as 秘.
(adj.)- Secret; mysterious; super-natural; divine; private.
mì (v.)- Keep secret; hide; conceal.
祕方 A prescription of medicine kept secret; nostrums.
祕本 Rare books.
祕書 A secretary.
祕密 A secret; secrecy.
祕訣 An enigma; a dark saying; a secret.
祕結 Costiveness; constipation; one's bowels do not move.
祕魯(地) Peru.
祕書長 Chief secretary; secretary general.
祕書處 Secretariat.
祕密文件 Secret dispatches; confidential documents.
祕密會議 A secret conference.

祖 (n.)- A forefather. A grandfather.
zǔ 祖父 Grandfather.

祖母 Grandmother.
祖先 An ancestor; a progenitor; a forefather.
祖宗 Ancestors; forefathers; ancestry.
祖孫 Ancestor and posterity.
祖國；故國 The fatherland; one's mother country.
祖傳 Hereditary; received from one's ancestors.
祖父母 Grandparents.

祝 zhù (n.)- Greeting; congratulation. (v.)- Bless; pray; ask for blessing.
祝杯 A toast. Drink a toast; drink in honour of.
祝捷 Celebration of a victory.
祝詞 A congratulatory address; greetings.
祝賀 Congratulate; felicitate; hail.
祝壽；祝嘏 Congratulate on one's birthday.
祝福 Pray for blessings.

神 shén (n.)- Spirits; gods. Appearance; expression. (adj.)- Divine; spiritual; supernatural; wonderful.
神父 The "Father" in a Catholic Church.
神戶(地) Kobe.
神交 Spiritual communication.
神妙 Wonderful; mysterious.
神奇 Supernatural; miraculous.
神悟 Mysterious intelligence.
神秘 Mysterious.
神氣 Appearance; expression; air; look.
神鬼 Gods and demons.
神情；神態 Air; manner; bearing.
神童 A wise boy; a prodigy; an infant genius.
神聖 Holy; sacred.
神經 Nerves; nervous.
神話 A myth; mythology.
神廟 Temple of the gods.
神權 Divine right; divine power.
神經系 The nervous system.
神經病 A nervous disease; neuropathy; neurosis; mental disease.
神經痛 Neuralgia.
神經質 Nervous temperament.
神經衰弱 Neurasthenia; nerves prostration (debility).
神經細胞 Nerve cells.
神經組織 Nervous tissue.
神經過敏 Nervous; oversensitive; jumpy; nervy.
神魂顛倒 His mind confused.
神聖不可侵犯 Sacred and inviolable.

祟 suì (n.)- Calamities. An evil spirit; an evil influence.

祠 cí (n.)- A temple.
祠堂 The ancestral hall; a family temple.

祥 xiáng (n.)- Happiness; felicity. Good luck. A lucky sign.
祥兆 An auspicious omen.
祥瑞；吉祥 Felicitous; auspicious.

票 piào (n.)- A warrant. A ticket. A bill. A certificate; a document. A bank note. A coupon.
票子 A cash note; a ticket; a bill. A warrant (法).
票房 Ticket office; booking office.
票根 The counterfoil of a note, ticket, or a check.
票滙 Remittance by draft.
票數 Number of vote.
票據 Certificate; bill.
票額 Sum due on bill.

**祭** (n.)- A sacrifice; an offering.
jì (v.)- Worship; sacrifice to the gods of ancestors.
祭文 An address of consecration; a written prayer; a funeral address.
祭司 A priest; an overseer of sacrifices.
祭祀；祭奉 Offer sacrifices.
祭典 Sacred rites.
祭品 Sacrificial articles or offerings.
祭祖 Sacrifice to ancestors; services to the memory of one's ancestors.
祭壇 An altar for sacrifices.
祭禮 Sacrificial rites.

**禁** (n.)- Prohibition; restriction; an interdict; a ban.
jìn (v.)- Forbid; prohibit; prevent; keep off; restrain.
禁止 Prohibit; forbid; interdict; put an end to; stop.
禁令 A prohibition order; an interdict; a ban; an embargo.
禁地 Forbidden ground; forbidden land.
禁忌 Taboo. Contraindication (醫).
禁押 Imprison.
禁例 Prohibitory laws.
禁食 Fast.
禁書 A prohibited book.
禁絕 Expel; exclude.
禁運 An embargo. Prohibit the transportation of.
禁慾 Ascetic practice.
禁賭 Prohibit gambling.
禁止出口 Lay an embargo.
禁止吸烟 No Smoking.
禁止泊車 No parking.
禁止停車 No standing.
禁止吐痰 No spitting.
禁止入內 No admittance.
禁止通行 No thoroughfare.
禁止期限 Period of prohibition.

**禍** (n.)- Disaster; misfortune; misery; adversity; evil; calamity;
huò injury.
(v.)- Send down calamities; injure; harm.
禍首 A ringleader; cause of trouble.
禍害 Injury; damage.
禍根 The seeds of misfortune; a root of evil.
禍患 Misfortune; calamity; catastrophe.
禍亂 Disturbance.
禍難 A disaster; a calamity.
禍不單行 Misfortunes never come in single.

**禎** (adj.)- Lucky; auspicious.
禎祥 A lucky omen.
zhēn

**福** (n.)- Happiness; good fortune; felicity; prosperity.
fú (v.)- Render happy; bless.
福人 A felicitous person; a lucky man.
福州(地) Foochow.
福利 Happiness and blessing; welfare.
福星 A felicitous star; a lucky star.
福建(地) Fukien.
福氣 Good luck; divine favours.
福壽 Happiness and longevity.
福音堂 Chapel; gospel hall.
福利事業 Welfare work.

**禦** (v.)- Withstand; oppose; stop; hinder; resist; prevent.
yù 禦寒 Keep out the cold.
禦敵 Resist enemy; withstand enemy.
禦防線 A defend line.

**禧** (n.)- Blessings; good luck; joy; favour.
xǐ (adj.)- Happy; auspicious.

**禪** (n.)- Contemplation; meditation; abstraction; deep thought.
chán (v.)- Resign or abdicate the throne.

禪林；禪廟 Buddhist temples.
禪師 A term of respect for Buddhist priests.
禪讓 Abdicate.

**禮** (n.)- Ceremony; worship. Presents. Politeness.
lǐ (v.)- Salute; bow; make a bow.
禮物 A present; a gift.

禮金；聘禮 Betrothal money. An honorarium; a consideration; an emolument.
禮服 Full dress; evening dress; ceremonial (formal) dress; a dress coat (suit).
禮拜 Worship; devotion; service.
禮砲 A salute of guns; an artillery salute.
禮堂 An auditorium; hall of assembly in schools.
禮儀 Rules of ceremony; courtesy.
禮節 Courtesy; decorum; etiquette; propriety; manners.
禮貌 Politeness; good manners; civility.
禮拜日 Sunday.
禮拜一 Monday.
禮拜二 Tuesday.
禮拜三 Wednesday.
禮拜四 Thursday.
禮拜五 Friday.
禮拜六 Saturday.
禮拜堂 A church; a chapel; a house of worship.
禮輕意重 The present is a trifle, but the intention is weighty.

**禱** (n.)- Prayer; supplication; grace.
dǎo (v.)- Pray; offer prayers; supplicate; invoke.
禱文 A form of prayer.

禱告 Pray; say grace.
禱告會 A prayer-meeting.

# 内 部

**禽** (n.)- Birds; the feathered tribe.
qín 禽獸 Birds and beasts; animals.
禽獸之行 Beastly conduct; incestuous.

# 禾 部

**禾** (n.)- Growing grain; corn; crops.
hé 禾叉 Pitchfork.
禾苗 Growing rice.
禾稈 The straw of grain.

禾黍 Millet.
禾稼 Crops in general.
禾穗 An ear.
禾蟲 A harvest grub.

禾本科(植)　Gramineae.

禿 (n.)- A scald head; a bald head.
tū (adj.)- Bald; bare; hairless.
禿山 A bleak or barren hill.

禿子；禿頭　A bald head.
禿筆 Blunt pencil; blunt writing brush.
禿髮症 Alopecia; alopecy.

秀 (adj.)- Prosperous; luxuriant. Beautiful; accomplished; cultivated; elegant; fair; handsome; pretty.
xiù

秀才 A graduate of the first degree or bachelor of arts.
秀氣 Elegant manners; fine manner.
秀雅 Elegant; refined; graceful; comely.
秀麗 Handsome; beautiful; fair.

私 (adj.)- Private; secret; partial; illegal; contraband; prejudicial; personal; selfish.
sī (v.)- Favour; act selfishly; keep secret; prejudice.

私人 Personal; private.
私心 A selfish motive; private interest.
私立 Private.
私有 Private ownership (possession).
私自 Privately; clandestinely; arbitrarily.
私刑 Lynch law; lynching; mob law; illegal punishment.
私利 Private (personal) gain (profit); self-interest.
私奔 Elope; runaway.
私事 Private (personal) affairs; a private matter.
私信 A private (personal) letter.
私室 Private room.
私逃 Abscond.
私販 Smuggler.
私處 Private parts; the privates.
私訪 Make private inquiries.
私通 Adultery.
私運；私帶 Smuggle.
私塾 A private school.
私營 A private enterprise. Private-owned.
私生子 An illegitimate child; a bastard; a natural child; a love child.
私生活 One's private (home) life.
私人秘書 Private secretary.
私人資格 In one's personal capacity.
私立銀行 Private bank.
私立學校 Private school.
私有財產 Private property.
私有權力 Private right.

秉 (adj.)- Decided; maintained.
bǐng (v.)- Hold; maintain. Uphold; grasp; seize; be in charge of.
秉直；秉正　Adhere to correct principles.

秉權 Wield power.
秉公辦理　Act with justice.

秋 (n.)- Autumn.
秋千；鞦韆 A swing.
qiū 秋天；秋季 Autumn; the fall.
秋石；尿素 Urea.

秋收 The autumn harvest; crop.
秋色 Autumnal tints (scenery).
秋波 Bewitching eyes; soft glance.
秋毫 The least bit.
秋蟬 The autumn cicada which hums in the evenings.
秋海棠(植)　The begonia; the elephant's-ear.

科 (n.)- A department; a course; a section. A grade.
kē 科目 Subject of a study; curriculum; a course; a branch; a genus.

科長 Head of a department; chief of a

section.
科學 Science.
科學化 Scientification.
科學性 Scientific nature.
科學界 The scientific world.
科學家 A scientist.
科學方法 Scientific methods.
科學知識 Scientific knowledge.
科學研究 Scientific research or investigation.
科學實驗 Scientific experiments.
科學管理法 Scientific management.

秒 miǎo (n.)- A second. A little.
秒針 The second hand of a clock or watch.

秕 bǐ Same as 粃.
(n.)- Blasted or withered grain; unripe grain.
秕糠 Husks; chaff. Refuse.

租 zū (n.)- Rent. Tax.
(v.)- Lease; rent.
租房 Rent or let a house.
租契 A deed of lease; title-deed.
租界 A settlement; a concession.
租借 Lease; hold land by (on) lease.
租雇 Charter, as a ship; hire.
租稅 Tax; excise; rent.
租金 Rent.
租戶 A tenant.

秤 chèng (n.)- A steelyard; a balance; a weighing scale.
(v.)- Weigh.
秤手 Balancer.
秤杆 The beam of a steelyard.
秤星 The brass marks on a steelyard.
秤鈎 The hook at the end of a steelyard.
秤錘 The weight used with a steelyard.

秦 qín (n.)- Name of a feudal state, existed from (879-221 B. C.), which later unified the whole country and put it under the reign of the Chin Dynasty (221-209 B. C.).

秧 yāng (n.)- Young plant; seedling; shoots; fry.
秧田 Field where rice is sown and kept for transplanting; seed bed.
秧苗 Paddy sprouts.

秩 zhì (n.)- Rank. Order.
(adj.)- Orderly.
(v.)- Dispose in order.
(adv.)- Regularly.
秩序；秩次 Series; sequence; order.
秩序單 A program.
秩序混亂 Be in disorder; be out of order.

移 yí (v.)- Remove; shift. Send; transmit; convey; emigrate; change; displace; transpose; transfer.
移民 Emigrate; an emigrant (移出). Immigrate; an immigrant (移入).
移居；移遷 Change residence.
移近 Move or draw near.
移送；移交 Forward; hand over; deliver.
移動 Remove from place to place.
移植 Transplant.
移開 Move to one side.
移民局 Immigration Department.
移民政策 Emigration policy.
移風易俗 Reform a society.

稀 xī (adj.)- Few; rare; scarce. Thin; loose; sparse.
稀少 Little; few; scarce; rare.

稀釋 Dilute.
稀罕 Curious; rare.
稀疏 Scattered; sparse.
稀飯 Gruel; congee; porridge.
稀薄 Watery; thin; diluted; sparse.
稀淡液(化) Dilution.
稀硫酸 Dilute sulphuric acid.
稀硝酸 Dilute nitric acid.
稀鹽酸 Diluted hydrochloric acid.

稅 (n.)- A tax; a duty; a toll; a rate.
shuì (v.)- Impose a tax on; levy or lay a tax on.
稅收 Tax yields; tax revenues.
稅局 A revenue office.
稅捐 Duties and other taxes.
稅單 A duty-paid certificate; a transit pass for imports.
稅銀；稅金 A tax; a duty; money paid as taxes, duties, etc.
稅額 The legal revenue of a place. The amount of a tax.
稅務署 A taxation (revenue) office.

稈 (n.)- The stalk of grain; straw; culm.
gǎn 稈箒 A straw broom; a besom.

程 (n.)- A rule; a pattern; a schedule; a formula. A limit. A journey.
chéng (v.)- Measure; estimate.
程式 A pattern; a formula; a grade.
程序 Order; sequence. Formalities; procedure.
程度 Standard; stage; grade.
程途 A journey.
程度問題 A question of degree.

稍 (adj.)- Small; little.
shāo (adv.)- Gradually; slightly; some-what; rather.
稍好 Rather good; a little better.
稍微 Slightly; somewhat.
稍濃 A little too thick; rather strong.
稍有更動 Little change.

稚 Same as 穉.
zhì (adj.)- Tender; young; delicate; small; immature.
稚氣 Childish; youthful temper; the innocence of childhood.

稜 (n.)- A corner; an angle; an edge.
léng 稜光 Diffracted light.
稜角 An angle; a corner.
稜鏡(物) A prism.
稜錐體(幾) A pyramid.

稟 Same as 禀
bǐng (n.)- Endowment; nature; disposition. A report; a petition.
(v.)- Report to a superior; petition; solicit; request.
稟安 Pay one's respects.
稟告；稟控 Accuse; charge.
稟求；稟請 Apply for; solicit.
稟見 Apply for an interview.
稟命 Ask for orders.

稠 (adj.)- Dense; crowded; thick.
chóu 稠密 Crowded; close together.

種 (n.)- A seed. A species; a kind; a class.
zhǒng (v.)- Plant; sow; cultivate.
〔zhòng〕 種子 Seeds.
種田；種地 Till fields; cultivate the soil.
種花 Cultivate flowers.
種族 A race; a tribe.
種植 Plant trees; plant.
種菜 Plant vegetables.

種種 In great variety; various kinds; all sorts.
種稻 Plant rice.
種類 A kind; a class; a species; a variety.
種牛痘 Vaccinate; inoculate with vaccine (virus). Be vaccinated; take vaccination.
種子植物 Spermatophyta.
種痘證書 A vaccination certificate.
種種手段 All methods; by every means.
種族歧視 Racial discrimination.
種族主義 Racialism; racism.

稱 (n.)- A name; an appellation. A steelyard.
chēng (adj.)- Suitable; fit.
(v.)- Call; name. Praise; commend; state; express. Talk about; remark; say. Weigh; estimate.
(adv.)- Proper.
稱心；稱意 Agreeable.
稱呼；稱謂 Call; name; style; designation.
稱許；稱道 Commend; bestow praises; approve; compliment; esteem; value; honour.
稱揚 Praise; speak in high terms of.
稱獎 Praise; extol.
稱號 A designation; an appellation; a title.
稱謝 Thank.
稱職 Be qualified for the post.
稱霸 Be counted a dominant power.
稱讚；稱譽 Praise; commend; admire; speak highly of; extol to the skies.

稷 (n.)- Millet.
jì 稷子；黍稷 Varieties of millet.

稻 (n.)- Paddy; rice.
dào 稻田 Rice field; paddy field.
稻草 Rice straw, for fuel, etc.
稻穗 Ears of rice.
稻穀 Unhusked rice.
稻草人 A straw figure (effigy); a man (Jack) of straw; a scarecrow.
稻草褥 Paillasse.

稼 (n.)- Grain; farming.
jià (v.)- Farm; plant; sow grain; cultivate.

稽 (v.)- Delay; investigate; examine.
jī 稽考 Investigate; examine.
稽查 Inspect; search for; examine.
稽核 Audit.
稽核員 Auditor.

稿 (n.)- The stalk of grain; straw. A sketch; a proof; a manuscript.
gǎo 稿子 A rough draft; a first copy; MS (MSS).
稿紙 Manuscripts.
稿費 Copy money.

穀 (n.)- Cereals; corn; grain. Salary; emolument.
gǔ (adj.)- Lucky; happy; favourable.
穀子 Spiked millet.
穀倉 A barn; a granary; a bin.
穀粒 Grain.
穀場；禾場 A thrashing floor; a corn floor.
穀殼 Chaff; husks of corn.
穀種 Seed.
穀穗 Ear of corn.
穀蟲 A weevil.

糠 See 糠.
kāng (n.)- The husks of grain; bran; chaff.

穅秕 Husk; chaff; bran.

**穆** (adj.)- Solemn; profound; majestic; reverent.
mù (v.)- Revere; admire; respect; honour.

穆然 In deep meditation; in deep respect.

穆罕默德(宗) Mohammed (570-632 A. D. ), the great Arabian prophet who founded the Islam (religion).

**積** (n.)- The product. The area.
jī (v.)- Accumulate; board; store up; amass; collect; gather; assemble; bring together; hoard; pile up; heap up; gather together.

積分 Total marks. Integral calculus.
積水 Accumlated water.
積匪 An old offender; an old bandit.
積書 Collect books.
積極 Positive; enthusiastic.
積習 A long-standing practice or abuse; inveterate habit.
積雪 Accumulated snow.
積蓄 Save; store up; accumulate.
積數(算) The product.
積分法 Integration.
積分學 An integral calculus.
積勞成疾 Fall sick from overwork.

**穎** Same as 穎.
yǐng (n.)- The awn of grain. A sharp point of an awl. A pen head.
(adj.)- Preeminent; distinguished; bright; clever; eminent.

穎果(植) Caryopsis.
穎悟；穎慧 Clever; sharp.

**穗** (n.)- An ear or spike of grain; the flower of grasses.
suì 穗子 An ear of grain.

**穢** (n.)- Weeds growing among grain; dirt; disgrace.
huì (adj.)- Dirty; filthy; mean; obscene; unclean; indecent; detestable; foul.

穢土 The foul world; the corruptions of the world.
穢汚 Dirty; foul; filthy.
穢名 An evil reputation.
穢言 The dirty word; indecent talk; foul language.
穢物 Filth.
穢氣 Foul air.

**穩** (n.)- Rest; repose.
wěn (adj.)- Firm; immovable; safe; secure; steady.
穩妥；穩當 Stable; safe; steady; secure. Appropriate; reasonable; moderate.

穩定 Secure; stable.
穩固 Firm; fixed; strong.
穩重 Sedate; serious; grave.
穩健 Sound; moderate; firm and steady.
穩睡 Sleep soundly.
穩健派 The moderates.

**穫** (n.)- Reaping; harvest.
huò (v.)- Crop; harvest; reap.

# 穴 部

穴 xué (n.)- A cave; a den; a grotto. A hole; an opening. A sinus in the body.

穴居 Dwell in a cave. Cave dwelling.

穴道 A sinus in the body. An underground channel.

究 jiū (n.)- An examination. Consequence; conclusion.

(v.)- Examine; investigate; contrive; put to the test; search out.

(adv.)- After all; at last; finally.

究治 Inquire and punish; investigate and award punishment accordingly.

究竟 After all; in the end; finally.

究其根源 Search to the bottom; examine to the utmost.

穹 qióng (adj.)- Lofty; deep; empty; spacious; eminent; high and vast.

穹窿 A dome; a vault.

空 kōng (n.)- The sky; the air; heaven.

(adj.)- Empty; vacant. Leisure. Exhausted.

(v.)- Be above the world; exhaust; become empty.

(adv.)- In vain; to no purpose; fruitlessly.

空中 In the air; the sky.

空手 An empty-hand; bare hands.

空心 Nothing in the mind. Vacuous; hollow; empty.

空白 Blank space; unfilled space; marginal space.

空位 A vacant (an unoccupied) seat.

空地 An open area; vacant ground; waste land; outside.

空軍 An air force; a flying corps; an aerial fleet.

空氣 Air; atmosphere.

空缺 Vacancy; a vacant position.

空虛 Emptiness; vacancy; vacuum.

空間 Space; room.

空閒；空暇 Unoccupied; free at leisure.

空想 Imagination; fantasy. Imagine; wish for.

空腹 An empty stomach (belly); hunger.

空運 Air lift; air transport.

空隙 A vacant space; a aperture; a crevice; a gap.

空戰 An aerial fight (combat); an air warfare; a battle in the air; a dogfight.

空曠 Vast; boundless.

空襲 An air-raid.

空手道 Karate.

空口無憑 Speak without evidence.

空中堡壘 Flying fortress.

空中樓閣 Castles in the air; visionary projects.

空白單子 A blank form.

空空如也 As if entirely empty.

空前絕後 Unprecedented; unexampled; record-breaking.

空軍基地 An air-base.

空氣調節 Air conditioning.

空間觀念 Space idea.

空頭支票 Rubber check; protest check; false check; empty promise.

空襲警報 An air-raid alarm (warning); an alert.

空對空飛彈 Air-to-air missiles.

穿 chuān (v.)- Bore through; pierce through; dig; perforate; chisel; penetrate. Put on; wear; dress. Thread; string.

穿入 Enter; dig; penetrate; pierce.

穿孔 Punch; perforate; pierce.

穿衣 Wear; put on; dress.

穿洞 Make a hole.
穿珠 String beads or pearls.
穿針 Thread a needle.
穿透 Penetrate; pierce through.
穿着 Clothings.
穿鞋 Put on (wear) shoes.
穿山甲 (動) A scaly ant-eater.
穿衣鏡 A dressing glass.

突 tū (adj.)- Prominent; point.
(v.)- Rush out. Run against; collide with. Offend.
(adv.)- Abruptly; suddenly; unexpectedly; precipitously.

突出 Jut (stand) out; protrude; project; fly out.
突破 Break through.
突圍 Break away from a siege.
突牙 Projecting teeth.
突起 A protuberance; a projection. Stand out; project; protrude.
突厥 Turks.
突然 Suddenly; abruptly; all of a sudden; all at once; unexpectedly.
突擊 Rush upon; make a sudden attack upon; make a clash; attack suddenly.
突擊隊 A storming party; shock-troops.
突如其來 Arrived unexpectedly. Sudden outbreak.
突破紀錄 Break the record.
突破難關 Surmount obstacles.
突發事件 An unforeseen event (occurrence).

窄 zhǎi (adj.)-Narrow; contracted; tight; strait; limited; compressed.
窄小 Narrow and small.
窄巷 A narrow lane.

窄狹 Confined; closely hemmed in; cramped in space.
窄量 Narrow minded.
窄道 A narrow path.
窄軌鐵路 A narrow gauge railway.

窈 yǎo (adj.)- Profound; deep. Secluded; obsecure; Tranquil; retired.
窈寂 Retired.

窈窕 Modest and refined; charming; attractive beautiful.
窈窕淑女 The modest, retiring young lady.

窒 zhì (v.)- Stop; obstruct.
窒息 Smother; suffocate; choke off. Asphyxiation; suffocation.

窕 tiǎo (adj.)- Elegant; refined.

窖 jiào (n.)- A vault; a cellar; a pit.
窖藏 Stored in a cellar.

窗 chuāng Same as 窓，牕.
(n.)- A window; a skylight.
窗友；同窗 Fellow students; schoolmates.

窗戶 A window.
窗帘 A window-curtain.
窗格 A window-sash.
窗框 A window-frame.
窗臺；窗檻 A window sill.
窗簾 A window-shade; a window-screen; a blind.
窗欄 Window bar.
窗門玻璃 A window-pane.

窘 jiǒng (adj.)- Afflicted; embarrassed; distressed; pressed; poverty.
(v.)- Persecute; distress; harass; trouble; compress; straitened.

窘迫 Miserably poor; poverty-stricken; hard life.

**窟** kū (n.)- A cave; a hole; a furrow; a cellar; a pit; an opening; a den.
窟穴 A hole; an opening.

**窠** kē (n.)- A nest; a hole; a den.
窠臼 Old form; conventionalism.

**窩** wō (n.)- A hole; a nest; a den; a house.
(v.)- Receive secretly; harbour.
窩藏 Harbour.

**窪** wā (n.)- A pit; a swamp; a hollow.
(adj.)- Hollow; low.
窪田；窪地 Marsh land.

**窮** qióng (n.)- Poverty. Extremity; termination; exhaustion.
(adj.)- Exhausted; straitened; poor; needy; wanting.
(v.)- Investigate; search out. Exhaust. Go to extremes.
窮人 The poor; a poor man.
窮乏；窮苦 Poverty; need; want; lack; distress; necessity; difficulty; miserable; wretched.
窮困 In straits; without resource.
窮究 Examine thoroughly; investigate to the bottom.
窮追 Push to extremes; drive to the wall; pursue everywhere.
窮途 Striatened circumstances; distressing conditions.
窮兇極惡 Extremely violent and wicked.
窮鄉僻壤 Poor or remote villages; places in obscurity.

**窰** yáo Same as 窯，窑.
(n.)- A brick furnace; a kiln; a pottery.
窰子 A brothel.

**窺** kuī (v.)- Watch; peep; pry; spy.
窺佔 Encroach on.
窺見 Spy; observe.
窺知 Know; perceive.
窺探 Spy; detect; pry.
窺測 Spy and fathom with the mind; make observations.
窺察 Ferret out; look into; pry into.
窺聽 Listen stealthily.

**竄** cuàn (v.)- Flee; escape; hide; run away. Correct.
竄改 Change; revise; correct.
竄逃 Sneak off; skulk off; escape.
竄竊 Steal; pilfer.

**竅** qiào (n.)- An opening; a channel; a hollow; a pore.
竅門 Short-cuts; secrets.

**竇** dòu (n.)- A hole; a burrow; a drain.
竇路 A narrow path; a gorge.

**竈** zào Same as 灶.
(n.)- A cook-stove; a kitchen; a kitchen-furnace.
竈間 A kitchen.
竈頭 A cook-stove; a kitchen range.

**竊** qiè Same as 窃.
(n.)- A thief; a burglar.
(adj.)-Privately; secretly; stolen.
(v.)- Steal; usurp; assume; pilfer; snatch.
(adv.)- Privately; stealthily; secretly.
竊取 Steal; pilfer; take without permission.

竊案 A case of theft.
竊笑 Feel silent contempt for; laugh secretly; laugh in one's sleeves.
竊盜 A pilferer; a thief; a burglar. Steal; rob.
竊賊 A thief; a burglar.
竊窺；竊視 Peep stealthily; steal a glance.
竊聽 Overhear; eavesdrop; listen secretly.

# 立 部

**立** (adj.)- Established; fixed; upright.
lì (v.)- Stand up; erect; set up; fix; make stand; establish; draw up.
(adv.)- Just now; immediately; at once; instantly.
立方(算) Cube.
立冬 The beginning of winter.
立功 Establish one's merit; perform meritorious services; win one's way.
立正(軍) Attention! Draw oneself up.
立志 Resolve; form a purpose; make up one's mind; determination; decide.
立刻；即刻 Immediately; instantly; instantaneously; in a second; directly; at once.
立法 Make laws; legislate; enactment; law making; making of law.
立春 The beginning of spring.
立秋 The beginning of autumn.
立約 Conclude a treaty (agreement); make a covenant; sign a contract; make agreement.
立夏 The beginning of summer.
立案 Register; put on record in a government office.
立起 Stand up; rise; rise to one's feet.
立場 Position; ground; footing; situation; standpoint; point of view.
立會 Found a society.
立碑 Erect a monument.
立憲 Establishment of a constitution.
立體 A solid body.
立方寸 A cubic inch.
立方尺 A cubic foot.
立方根(算) The cube root.
立方體(算) A cube.
立合同 Draw a contract.
立法局 The Legislative Council.
立陶宛(地) Lithuania.
立脚點 A footing; a foothold.
立體感 Cubic effect.
立體聲 Stereo; stereophonic.
立憲制度 The constitutional system.
立憲國家 A constitutional country (state).
立體幾何 Solid geometry.
立體電影 A three dimensional (3D) film.

**站** (n.)- A stage of a journey; a station.
zhàn (v.)- Stand up. Stop; halt.
站立 Stand up.
站住 Stand still; stop.
站長 Station master.
站崗 Be at post; stand sentry.
站開 Stand away; stand off.
站穩 Stand firmly.
站不穩 Not strong enough to stand.

**竟** jìng (n.)- The end; the utmost; the extremity.
(adj.)- At an end; whole; all; endless.
(v.)- Finish; go to the end; examine thoroughly; exhaust; go through to the end; accomplish.
(adv.)- At last; after all; finally; then; in the long run; only.
竟有 Actually could be.
竟然 After all.
竟敢 Actually dare to.

**章** zhāng (n.)- An essay; a section; a chapter. A seal; a stamp. An article. An item. A memorial. A piece of music. Rules; statutes; regulation.
(adj.)- Clear; beautiful; variegated; elegant.
(v.)- Exhibit; show.
章句 Sections and paragraphs; chapters and verses.
章魚 An octopus.
章程 Regulations; rules; by-laws.
章節 Chapters and sections.
章句法 Syntax.
章程草稿 A draft of the regulations.

**竣** jùn (adj.)- Complete; done.
(v.)- Stand still; complete a task; make perfect; perfect.
竣工；竣事 Finish work; be completed. Completion.

**童** tóng (n.)- A boy; a lad; a child; a kid; a virgin; a youngster.
(adj.)- Childish. Young; juvenile; boyish; youthful.
童子 A lad; a youth; a child; a young boy.
童工 Child labour.
童年 In boyhood; in childhood; youthful age.
童話 A tale for children; a nursery tale; a fairy-tale; a juvenile story.
童裝 Boy's dress.
童謠 A children's song; a nursery rhyme (song).
童子軍 The boy scouts.
童話劇 A juvenile play.
童養媳 A girl, for reasons of poverty, is brought up in the home of her fiance.

**竭** jié (adj.)- Exhausted; finished; wanting.
(v.)- Exhaust; use up; consume; finish.
竭力 Do one's best or utmost; exert oneself.
竭盡 Energy quite gone; exhausted.

**端** duān (n.)- A piece; a kind; an end; a beginning; an extremity.
(adj.)- Proper; direct; modest; decent; regular; sober; grave.
端午；端陽 The 5th day of the 5th month. The Dragon-Boat Festival; the Tuen Ng Festival.
端正 Orderly; neat; proper; just; upright.
端容 A grave countenance; a sober mien.
端莊 Grave; solemn; dignified.
端詳 Explicitly; minutely; in minute detail; giving full particulars.
端飯 Bring in the food.

**競** jìng (n.)- Bout; contest.
(v.)- Compete; emulate; contend; struggle; rival; strive.
競技 Games; athletics.
競走 Run a race.
競爭 Vie; compete; emulate; contest; contend with; measure swords

with. Contention; competition; rivalry; emulation.
競馬；賽馬 Horse-racing.
競賽 Competition; contest; race.
競選 Election contest.
競技場 Arena; prize ring; circus.
競爭者 A competitor; a rival; a rival candidate.

# 竹 部

**竹** zhú (n.)- The bamboo. Musical instruments made of bamboo.
竹林 A bamboo grove.
竹竿 A bamboo-pole.
竹筍 Bamboo shoots.
竹筒 A bamboo tube.
竹園 Bamboo plantation.
竹箒 A bamboo-broom.
竹箭 Bamboo arrow.
竹器 Bamboo ware.
竹簾 A bamboo screen.
竹籃 A bamboo basket.
竹籬 A bamboo fence.
竹籮 A hamper.
竹葉青 A kind of liquor.

**竺** zhú (n.)- A kind of bamboo. India.
竺經 The Buddhist scriptures.

**竿** gān (n.)- A pole; a bamboo stick; the stem of bamboo; a rod; a cane.
竿頭日進 Make still greater progress.

**笆** bā (n.)- A bamboo fence; a hedge.

**笑** xiào (n.)- A smile; a laugh; a sneer.
(v.)- Smile; laugh; ridicule.
笑柄 A laughing-stock; a butt of ridicule.
笑容；笑臉 A laughing face; a smiling face.
笑納 Receive with a smile—please accept this trifle present.
笑話 A joke; a funny (humorous) story.
笑聲 The sound of laughter; a peal of laughter.
笑面虎 A smiling tiger—treacherous.
笑眯眯 Laughing till one's eyes are dim.
笑嘻嘻 Titter; giggle.

**笙** shēng (n.)- Chinese mouth organ.
笙簧 A reed organ.

**笛** dí (n.)- A fife; a flute; a whistle.
笛子 A flute; a fife; a pipe.

**笞** chī (n.)- A whip; a rod.
(v.)- Beat with the bamboo; flog; beat; whip.
笞背 Lash on the back.

**笠** lì (n.)- A basket-shaped hat; a rain hat made of bamboo splinters.

**符** fú (n.)- A spell; a charm.
(v.)- Correspond with; agree with; coincide.

符合 Agree with; correspond with; coincide with; tally with.
符咒 Amulets; charms; spells.
符號 A symbol; a sign; a cypher; a mark.

笨 bèn (adj.)- Awkward; clumsy. Stupid; foolish; silly.
笨人 A dolt; a stupid.
笨重 Heavy; clumsy; ponderous; cumbersome.
笨漢 An awkward, clumsy fellow; a simpleton.

第 dì (n.)- A series; a class; a gradation; a degree.
第一 The first (1st); the best.
第二 The second (2nd); the next.
第三 The third (3rd).
第宅 A dwelling-house.
第一千 The thousandth.
第一天 On the first day.
第一手 First-hand.
第一代 The first generation.
第一百 The hundredth.
第一次 For the first time.
第一件 In the first place.
第一列；第一排 The first row (line).
第一位 The first rank.
第一步 The first step; the very start; the beginning.
第一流 The first class (rank, rate).
第一等 The first-rate; No.1 ; A1.
第一課 The first lesson; lesson the first; lesson one.
第三者 The third party; the third person; a bystander.
第六感 The sixth sense.
第一(二,三)人稱 The first (second, third) person.
第一印象 The first impression.
第一要緊 Of the first importance.
第一國際 The First International.
第二國際 The Second International.
第二世界 The Second World.
第三世界 The Third World.
第三國際 The Third International.
第五縱隊 The fifth column.
第一期付款 The first instalment.
第一(二,三)期梅毒 Primary (secondary, tertiary) syphilis.
第一個五年計劃 The first five-year plan.

笳 jiā (n.)- A whistle made of reed, without holes for fingering. A kind of flageolet; a bugle.

筆 bǐ (n.)- A pen; a pencil; a writing brush. Penmanship; hand-writing.
(v.)- Write; compose.
筆尖 A pen-point; a nib.
筆名 A pen-name; pseudonym.
筆法 A penmanship; pencraft.
筆直 Straight as a pencil.
筆者 The writer; the author.
筆削 Correct; revise; touch up.
筆記 A note; jottings. Take notes of; take down.
筆套 A sheath to protect the brush.
筆盒 A pen box.
筆桿 A pen-holder.
筆跡 Handwriting.
筆試 Written examination.
筆算 Calculate with figures; ciphering.
筆墨 Pen and ink; writing materials; stationery.
筆記簿 A note-book.

等 děng (n.)- A class; a rank; a grade; a kind; a sort.
(v.)- Wait for; await; compare; equal; class.
(adj.)- Equal to; same as; similar

to.
等於 Be equal to.
等分 Divide equally; divide into equal parts.
等式(算) Equation. An equality.
等角 Equal angles.
等待 Wait for.
等級 Rank; steps; grade; class; order.
等等 And so forth; and so on; etc., etc.
等量 The same quantity; an equivalent.
等號(算) Sign of equality.
等價 Equivalence; equivalency.
等邊 Equal sides.
等距離 Equidistance; equal distance.
等閒視之 To treat casually.
等角三角形 An equiangular triangle.
等邊三角形 An equilateral triangle.

筋 (n.)- A sinew; a muscle; a tendon.
jīn 筋斗；觔斗 Head over heels; a fall; a somersault.
筋骨 Bones and sinews.
筋肉學；肌學 Myology.
筋疲力盡 Utterly exhausted.

筍 Same as 笋.
sǔn (n.)- A bamboo-shoot; a bamboo sprout. A dovetail.
筍乾 Dried bamboo shoots.
筍頭；榫頭 A dovetail; a tenon.

筏 (n.)- A bamboo raft.
fá 筏渡 A ferryboat.

筐 (n.)- A basket without a cover.
kuāng 筐子；籮筐 A large open basket.

筒 (n.)- A pipe; a tube; a hollow bamboo. A case.
tǒng

答 (n.)- A reply; an answer; a response; a solution.
dā (v.)- Reply; answer; respond to.
答案 An answer.
答數(算) Answer.
答應 Assent; respond; consent.
答謝 Return thanks.
答禮 Make return presents or salutations.
答覆 Answer; respond.
答辭 An address in reply (response).
答辯 An explanation; a defence.

策 (n.)- A book; a composition. A plan; a scheme; a plot. Policy.
cè (v.)- Whip; switch. Scheme; contrive; make a plot.
策略 Strategy; a plan; a device; a scheme.
策勵 Urge on; impel; incite; stimulate.
策源地 A base of operations.
策馬前進 Whip the horse and proceed.

筲 (n.)- A basket; a bucket.
shāo 筲箕 A basket for holding cooked rice; a bamboo basket.

筵 (n.)- A mat. A feast; a dinner; a banquet.
yán 筵席 A feast; a banquet.

筷 (n.)- Chopsticks.
kuài

箋 Same as 牋.
jiān (n.)- A letter. Note paper; letter paper; writing pad.
箋札 A letter.

箍 (n.)- A hoop; a belt; a fillet; a circlet.
gū (v.)- Hoop; draw tight.

箍桶 Put a hoop on a bucket.

箏 (n.)- A kite.
zhēng

箒 (n.)- A broom; a scrubbing brush.
zhǒu

箔 (n.)- A leaf; sheet.
箔紙；錫箔 Tin-foil.
bó

箕 (n.)- A winnowing basket; a sieve; a grain fan. A dustpan.
jī 箕帚 Dustpan and broom.

算 (n.)- Calculation; a plan; a scheme.
suàn (v.)- Reckon; calculate; estimate; count.
算式 Mathematical formula.
算命 Tell fortunes; calculate destinies.
算淸 Clear up an account.
算賬 Make up accounts; reckon accounts.
算術 Arithmetic.
算盤 The Chinese abacus or counting board.
算錯 Miscalculate; miscount.
算命先生 A fortune teller; a calculator of destinies.

箝 (v.)- Gag; lock; fasten; clasp; pinch; forbid.
qián 箝制 Force submission.

管 (n.)- A tube; pipe.
(v.)- To govern; control; look
guǎn after.
管束 Restrain; restrict; keep under restraint; govern.
管事 A manager. A steward; a butler.
管狀 Tubular; tubulous.
管家 A steward; a butler.
管理 Manage; administer; take charge of; control; supervise; superintend.
管賬 A bookkeeper; an accountant.
管教 Teach; instruct.
管家婦 A housewife; a house-keeper.
管理人 A superintendent; an administrator; a manager.
管理處 Administration department.
管理權 Right of management.
管轄區 The district of jurisdiction; the competent sphere.
管弦樂隊 An orchestra.

箭 (n.)- An arrow; a slender bamboo.
jiàn 箭竹 An arrow-bamboo.
箭杆 The shaft of an arrow.
箭翎 The feather on an arrow.
箭靶 A target, for archery.
箭豬 The porcupine.
箭頭 The point or head of an arrow.

箱 (n.)- A box; a trunk; a chest.
箱子 A box; a trunk; a coffer.
xiāng

箴 (n.)- A probe; a needle.
(v.)- Warn; exhort. Pierce.
zhēn 箴言 Warning words; admonitions.

節 (n.)- A knot; a joint. A section; a paragraph. A season; a festi-
jié val.
(v.)- Regulate; restrict; economize; retrench.
節目 Programme. Divisions; section; paragraph.
節拍 The rhythm or time of music.
節制 To control.

節育 Birth control.
節度 Rules; moderation.
節奏 Harmony. Beat time.
節約 Save; spare; economize.
節食 Cut one's normal diet.
節期；節日 Festival; holiday.
節減 Curtail; cut down; economize.
節儉 Frugal; thrifty. Spare; economize.
節衣縮食 Economy in clothing and food.
節足動物 An arthropod; the arthropoda.
節省時間 Save time.
節省費用 Save expenses.

範 fàn (n.)- A pattern; a standard; a model. Usage; law; rule.
範例 Example; model.
範圍 Limit; scope; sphere; range.
範疇(哲) A category.
範圍以外 Beyond the limit of. . . ; out of the sphere of. . . ; beyond the scope of. . . .
範圍廣大 Enlarge the scope; be of a wide range; be extensive.

篆 zhuàn (n.)- The seal character of the Chinese writing. A seal of office. A name.
篆字；篆文 Seal character.
篆刻 Engrave seal-characters.

篇 piān (n.)- A leaf or page of a book. A chapter; a section; an article.
篇目 Heading.
篇段 A paragraph.
篇章 Sections and chapters.
篇幅 A chapter; a section.

篋 qiè (n.)- A trunk; a satchel; a case; a chest.
篋衍 A bamboo box.

篙 gāo (n.)- A bamboo pole.
篙子 A boat-pole.

篡 cuàn (v.)- Rebel against a sovereign and take the throne; usurp.
篡位 Usurp the throne.
篡奪 Usurp; seize upon.

篤 dǔ (adj.)- Sincere; true.
(adv.)- Largely; very; greatly.
篤信 Earnest belief; believe truly.
篤厚 Honest; straightforward.
篤愛 Warm-hearted affection.
篤學 Diligent at study; studiousness.
篤於情誼 Be true to one's friends; be of a cordial nature.

篦 bì Same as 箆，篦.
(n.)- A fine-toothed comb.
(v.)- Comb.
篦髮 Comb the hair.

篩 shāi (n.)- A sieve.
(v.)- Sift; strain.
篩子 A sieve; a bolter.
篩米 Sift rice.
篩管(植) Sieve vessel; sieve tube.

築 zhù (v.)- Construct; build; raise.
築造 Build; construct.
築堤 Raise a dyke or an embankment.
築路 Build a road.
築壩 Raise embankments.
築碼頭 Construct a wharf or jetty.
築港工程 Harbour work.
築路工事 Road work.

篷 péng (n.)- A covering; the awning of a boat. A sail. A shelter; a tent.

篷布；帆布 Canvas.
篷帆 Sail; sailcloth.
篷車 Covered wagon.

**篾** (n.)- Splints for baskets; bamboo skin.
miè 篾席 A mat made of bamboo.

**簇** (v.)- Crowd together.
簇生 Grow together; crop up.
cù 簇新 Brand-new.
簇聚 Crowd together.
簇擁前來 Press on in a crowd.

**簍** 簍子 A basket; a hamper.
lǒu

**簡** (n.)- A slip of bamboo for writing on. Documents; a letter;
jiǎn a note.
(adj.)- Simple; brief; terse; laconic.
(v.)- Arrange; appoint; choose; examine. Treat with contempt.
簡札 A letter; correspondence.
簡縮 Abridged.
簡式(算) A simple expression.
簡明 Concise.
簡直 Concisely; directly; to the point; without circumlocution.
簡易 Brief and easy; simplicity.
簡便 Simple; handy; convenient.
簡要 Reduce into a compendium. The synopsis; a sketch; a summary.
簡略 Simple; brief; concise.
簡單 Brief; simple; plain.
簡短 Brief.
簡潔 Laconic; pithy; concise.
簡練 Choose and study thoroughly.
簡易化 Simplification.
簡筆字 A simplified character; a simpler substitute.
簡便方法 A simple and easy way.
簡單生活 A simple life.
簡單明瞭 Short (brief) and to the point; plain and simple.

**簧** (n.)- The spring (in a mechanical device).
huáng 簧管 Saxophone.
簧樂器 The reeds; reed instruments.

**簪** (n.)- A flat hairpin; a clasp.
(v.)- Stick in the hair.
zān 簪子 A hairpin; a bodkin.

**簫** (n.)- A flute; a wind instrument of music; a pipe.
xiāo

**簷** (n.)- The eaves of a house. The brim of a hat.
yán 簷口；屋簷 The eaves.

**簸** (n.)- A winnowing fan.
(v.)- Winnow.
bǒ 簸籮 An open basket for grain.

**簽** (n.)- A bamboo slip; a label.
(v.)- Sign; subscribe; indorse.
qiān 簽名 Signature.
簽署 Subscribe; sign.
簽證 Visa.
簽到簿 Attendance book.
簽訂合同 Sign a contract or agreement.

**簾** (n.)- A screen; a bamboo-blind.
lián 簾幕 A curtain; a hanging-screen.

**簿** (n.)- An account book; a register; a tablet; an exercise book.
bù (v.)- Record; register.

簿册 Registers; lists.
簿記 Bookkeeping.
簿記員 A book-keeper; a ledger clerk.
簿記學 Bookkeeping.
簿記學校 Bookkeeping school.

籃 (n.)- A basket.
lán 籃球 Basket ball.
籃球隊 A basket-ball team.

籌 (n.)- A tally; a ticket; a lot.
chóu (v.)- Calculate; count. Deliberate; plan; scheme.
籌備 Prepare for; plan and prepare.
籌款 Procure money; raise funds.
籌碼 A counter; a medium of exchange.
籌辦 Settle; arrange; consider about.
籌備委員 Committee of arrangements.
籌備會議 Meeting for making arrangements.

籍 (n.)- A record; list; a register. A book. One's native place.
jí (v.)- Be registered.
籍貫 One's native place; domicile of origin.

籐 (n.)- Cane. Rattan.
téng 籐蓆 A rattan mat.
籐竿；沙籐 Rattans.
籐條 A rattan whip.
籐牌 A cane shield.
籐椅 A rattan (cane) chair.
籐鞭 A rattan scourge.
籐傢具 Rattan furniture.

籠 (n.)- A cage; a basket.
lǒng 籠括 Contain; embody.
籠罩 Cover; include all; close in.
籠頭 A halter.

籤 Same as 籖；簽.
qiān (n.)- A slip of bamboo, a tag.
(adj.)- Sharp.
籤條 A label; a tag.
籤票 A warrant.

籬 (n.)- A bamboo fence; a hedge.
lí 籬笆 A bamboo fence.

籮 (n.)- A basket; crate.
luó

# 米 部

米 (n.)- Rice. Metre.
mǐ 米市 The rice market.
米色 Straw colour; rice colour.
米囤 A rice bin.
米店 A rice shop.
米粉 Rice flour.
米湯 Congee. Flattering words.
米粥 Congee; rice gruel.
米飯 Cooked (boiled) rice.
米糧 Provisions.
米丘林學說 Michurinism.

籽 (n.)- Seeds.
zǐ

粉 (n.)- Flour; powder. Cosmetic.
fěn (v.)- Whitewash; whiten. Pulverize; grind to powder.

粉末 Powder; dust.
粉刺 Grog blossoms; pus thorns.
粉紅 Flesh-coloured; pink.
粉盒 A puff-box.
粉筆 Chalk.
粉絲；粉條 Vermicelli.
粉碎 Be ground to powder; smashed to pieces; crush.
粉飾 Adorn; gloss over; make up; embellish; paint and powder.
粉撲 A puff; a powder-puff.
粉瘤 A tumor.
粉蝶 The white butterfly.
粉刷匠 A plasterer.

粒 lì (n.)- A grain; a granule; a kernel; a drop; a pill.
粒狀 Granular; grain-like.

粕 pò (n.)- Refuse; residuum; lees; dregs; sediment of liquor.

粗 cū Same as 麤.
(adj.)- Thick. Rough; coarse; vulgar. Rustic. Uncleaned.
粗人 A boor.
粗大 Coarse and large-sized; gross.
粗布 Coarse cloth.
粗壯 Robust.
粗石 Rubble.
粗劣 Crude; coarse; inferior.
粗俗；粗野 Vulgar.
粗陋 Coarse-looking.
粗略 Roughly; in a cursory way.
粗笨 Crude; coarse; rude; artless.
粗貨 A coarse article.
粗話 Obscene language.
粗暴 Rough; rude; violent; wild.
粗魯 Rough.
粗糙 Coarse; rough.
粗躁 A careless manner.
粗麻布 Coarse linen.
粗製品 A crude (coarse) article; an article of inferior make.
粗枝大葉 Coarse branches and large leaves—roughly finished.
粗茶淡飯 Coarse, homely fare.
粗斜紋布 Drills.

粟 sù (n.)- Millet.
粟米 Indian corn; maize.
粟米粉 Indian-corn meal.

粵 yuè (n.)- The provinces of Kwangtung and Kwangsi.
粵省(地) The province of Kwangtung.
粵語 Cantonese.
粵人 A Cantonese.
粵漢鐵路 The Canton-Hankow Railway.

粥 zhōu (n.)- Congee; rice gruel; porridge.

粧 zhuāng Same as 妝.
(v.)- Adorn oneself; beautify.
粧扮 Dress up; adorn.
粧奩；嫁妝 A bride's trousseau; a marriage portion; a dowry.
粧飾 Adorn; ornament.
粧臺 A dressing table; a dresser.

粱 liáng (n.)- Millet.
粱米；高粱 Sorghum; kaoliang.

粳 jīng Same as 秔.
粳米 Rice which is not glutinous.

粹 cuì (adj.)- Unmixed; pure; essence.
粹白 Perfectly white.

**精** (n.)- Cleaned rice. Essence. Sperm. Spirit. An apparition.
jīng (adj.)- Skilful; skilled; versed; expert. Fine; delicate; choice.

精力 Spirit and energy; vigour.
精工 Skilled workmen. Fine workmanship.
精巧 Clever; skilful; dexterous; adroit; elaborate.
精肉 Prime pieces of meat.
精利 Sharp.
精兵 The flower; the pick; efficient troops; trained troops.
精壯 Well-trained and muscular.
精明 Smart; clever.
精美 Refined; exquisite.
精悍 Dauntless.
精神 Soul; spirit; mind; will; mental energy; vigour.
精密 Precise; minute; detailed.
精液 Semen; sperm.
精細 Fine; delicate; minute; precision.
精通 Be versed in; practised in; acquainted with; have a thorough knowledge of.
精華 The essence of; the flower of.
精製 Refine; clarify.
精確 Accuracy; precision.
精銳 Well-trained and brave, as soldiers.
精緻 Fine; pretty; beautiful; delicate; minute.
精選 Careful selection.
精鍊 Refining; tempering.
精蟲 A spermatozoon.
精讀 Careful (intensive) reading; perusal.
精髓 Essence; quintessence.
精神病 A mental disease.
精裝本 De luxe edition.
精力旺盛 Energetic; vigorous; of great energy; full of vitality.
精明强幹 Skilled and capable.
精神生活 Spiritual (inner) life.
精神衰弱 Mental weakness (debility); feeble-mindedness.
精神分裂 Schizophrenia.
精神病者 A mentally-deranged person; a lunatic; a mental patient.
精神病院 A mental hospital.
精神病學 Psychopathology; psychopathy.
精神煥發 In good spirits; elation.
精銳部隊 Picked troops.

**糉** Same as 粽.
zǒng (n.)- Rice dumplings.

**糊** (n.)- Paste; starch.
hú (adj.)- Sticky.
(v.)- Paste up; stick together.
糊塗 Blundering; foolish. Blurred; muddled; stupidly; silly.

**糕** (n.)- Cakes; pastry.
gāo 糕點 Cakes and pastry.
糕餅店 Pastry shop.

**糖** (n.)- Sugar; candy; sweetmeats.
táng 糖分 Percentage of sugar.
糖汁 Molasses; syrup.
糖衣 A sugar coat.

糖果 Sweetmeats; preserves confection.
糖精 Saccharin.
糖薑 Preserved ginger.
糖醬 Jam.
糖尿病 Diabetes; melituria.
糖果店 A confectionery.
糖衣藥片 A sugar-coated tablet.

**糜** (n.)- Rice gruel; porridge.
mí (v.)- Rotten; corrupted.
糜爛 In utter ruin; decompose; ulcerate; putrefy.

糜爛生活 A life abandoned to pleasure,

debauchery, etc.

糞 (n.)- Ordure; dung; filth; manure; night-soil.
fèn 糞坑；糞池 A manure pit.
糞便 Excrement; night-soil.
糞肥 Manure.
糞廁 A privy; a latrine.
糞箕 A dustpan.
糞壤 Manure; refuse.

糟 (n.)- Sediment; dregs; settlings; wine-lees.
zāo (adj.)- Spoiled; ruined.
糟粕 Distiller's grains; dregs; lees.
糟肉 Picked meat.
糟糕 A dreg cake–unlucky. Too bad! What a mess!
糟蹋 Waste or spoil things.

糠 (n.)- Rice-bran.
kāng 糠秕 Rice-bran.

糧 Same as 粮.
liáng (n.)- Grain; provisions; rations. Taxes.
糧食 Provisions; food.
糧草；糧秣 Provisions and fodder.
糧餉；軍糧 Rations for the army.
糧米行市 Market-price of grain.

糯 (n.)- Glutinous rice.
nuò 糯米 Glutinous rice.
糯米酒 A sweet wine made from glutinous rice; rice wine.

糰 (n.)- Round cakes; dumpling.
tuán 糰子 A small dough cake.

# 糸 部

系 (n.)- A connecting link; a connection. Line; lineage. A system.
xì 系統 A system. Lineage; descent.
系主任 Head of a college department.
系統的 Systematically.

糾 (v.)- Collect; associate. Correct.
jiū 糾正 Correct errors; bring one's shortcomings to light.
糾合 Collect or gather together; rally; muster.
糾紛 Entanglement; complication; imbroglio.
糾察 Examine; investigate.
糾纏 Tangle; involve.
糾察隊 Picket; investigators; inspectors.

紀 (n.)- A period; A century. Rules; laws. A servant.
jì (v.)- Arrange. Record.
紀元 The first year of a new era.
紀念 Commemorate; keep in memory.
紀事 Make a note, or memorandum.
紀律 Written rules; regulations. Discipline; regularity.
紀錄 A record; minutes. Write down.
紀元前；公元前 B.C. (Before Christ).
紀元後；公元後 A.D. (Anno Domini).
紀念日 An anniversary; a commemoration day.
紀念刊 A memorial issue.

紀念物 A token of remembrance; a souvenir.
紀念章 Commemoration medal.
紀念碑 A monument.
紀念會 A memorial service; a commemorative gathering. Celebration; jubilee.
紀錄者 A recorder.
紀錄簿 A register.
紀念郵票 A memorial stamp.
紀念郵戳 A commemoration (memorial) postmark.
紀錄打破者 A record-breaker.
紀錄保持者 A record-holder.

約 yuē (n.)- A bond; a treaty; an agreement; a convention; an appointment.
(adj.)- Brief; condensed; poor; straitened.
(v.)- Bind. Restrict. Agree with; appoint. Moderate; economize.
(adv.)- Nearly; about.
約束 Restrain; restrict; hold; limit; bond.
約定 Agree to; engage by agreement; make an arrangement.
約會 Arrange to meet. Engagement.
約請 Invite.
約二十歲 About 20 years old.
約定時間 The appointed time.
約定期限 Stipulated time.

紅 hóng (n.)- A red colour; vermilion.
(adj.)- Rosy; red; scarlet.Lucky. Influencial.
紅木 Redwood.
紅日 The morning sun.
紅玉(鑛) Cornelian; ruby; carbuncle.
紅色 Red; vermilion; crimson; rosy.
紅利 Dividend; bonus.
紅豆 Scarlet bean.
紅花；紅藍(植) Safflower.
紅海(地) The Red Sea.
紅茶 Black tea.
紅疹 Rubella; German measles.
紅梅 A red plum.
紅棗 Red dates.
紅斑(醫) Erythema.
紅旗 Red flag.
紅種 Red Indians; the Red Race.
紅顏 Rosy-cheeked; pretty. A ruddy countenance; youthful.
紅十字 Red Cross.
紅血球 Red corpuscle.
紅利賬 Bonus account.
紅珊瑚 Red coral.
紅寶石 Ruby.
紅鐵鑛 Hematite.
紅蘿蔔 Carrots; radishes.
紅鸞星 A lucky star.
紅領巾 Red scarf (tie).
紅與專 Red and expert.
紅十字會 The Red Cross Society.
紅衣主教 Cardinal.

紆 yū (adj.)- Bent. Depressed; sad.
紆迴 Winding; crooked; circuitous; indirect.

紈 wán (n.)- White silk.
紈袴子弟 A fop; play-boy.

紊 wěn (adj.)- Confused; ravelled; disordered; disarranged; chaotic.
紊亂 Confused; out of order.

紋 wén (n.)- The pattern; marks; traces; ripple; lines.
紋身 Tattoo.
紋銀 Pure silver; sycee.

納 nà (v.)- Present; offer; give; pay; hand up. Take; accept; receive; adopt; insert; enter; admit.

納妾；納寵 Take a concubine.
納涼 Take an airing; take fresh air.
納款 Submit and pay tribute.
納稅 Pay duties; pay taxes.
納稅人 A taxpayer; a tax-bearer; a ratepayer.
納粹黨 Nazi, the National Socialist Party in Germany, founded by A. Hitler.
納稅日期 The tax-day.

紐 (n.)- A cord; a ribbon. A knot; a button.
niǔ (v.)- Tie.
紐約（地）New York.
紐西蘭；新西蘭（地） New Zealand.
紐芬蘭（地）Newfoundland.

純 (adj.)- Pure; clean; honest; sincere. Uniform. Simple. Fine.
chún (adv.)- Entirely; wholly.
純正 Upright; honest.
純色 Pure colour; of one colour.
純金 Pure or solid gold.
純厚 Sincere; honest.
純品 Fine quality.
純眞 Pure; genuine; unsophisticated.
純素；純白 Pure (immaculate, spotless) white.
純淨 Pure; unmixed.
純粹 Pure; genuine; unadulterated.
純銅 Pure or solid copper.
純潔 Fine; pure; chaste.
純質 Unadulterated substance.
純文學 Pure literature; *belles-lettres.*
純羊毛衫 All-wool sweater.
純潔之愛 Pure love.

紗 (n.)- Yarn; thread; gauze; thin silk.
shā 紗窗 A gauze window.
紗廠 A cotton mill.
紗線 Spun yarn; cotton thread.
紗錠 A spindle.

紙 Same as 帋.
(n.)- Paper.
zhǐ 紙片 A piece (slip) of paper. Card.
紙包 A paper parcel (package).
紙板 Card-board.
紙屑 Waste-paper; paper-scraps.
紙盒 A paper box; a carton.
紙傘 Paper umbrellas; kittisols.
紙牌 Playing cards.
紙鳶 Kites.
紙幣 Paper money; bank notes.
紙老虎 A paper tiger.
紙上談兵 A Paper plan.

級 (n.)- A step. A story. A grade; a rank; a degree; a class. A
jí decapitated head.
級長 The monitor of a class.
級任教師 The teacher in charge of a class.

紛 (adj.)- Confused; disorderly. Numerous.
fēn 紛爭 A dispute; a trouble; difficulties.
紛歧 A branch; side issues. A misunderstanding; in disorder diverging.
紛紛 Confusedly; in disorder; pellmell.
紛紜；紛繁 Numerous; prolific.
紛亂 Be in disorder (confusion); be confused; intricate.
紛紛四散 Dispersed in all directions.

素 (n.)- Pure white silk. Vegetable food.
sù (adj.)- White; pure. Simple; plain; not coloured or variegated.

(adv.)- Usually; formerly; generally.
素向 Usually; habitually.
素材 Material; a subject material.
素性 Habit; temperament.
素服 White clothes. Mourning garments.
素食 A vegetable diet.
素描 A rough sketch; a *dessin.*
素菜 Vegetarian diet.
素質 Predisposition; nature; makings.
素養 Culture; cultivation; elementary knowledge; accomplishment.
素食者 A vegetarian.

紡 fǎng (v.)- Reel; spin.
紡車 A spinning wheel; a cocoon reel.
紡紗 Spin cotton into yarn.
紡錠 A spindle.
紡織 Spinning and weaving.
紡紗廠 A spinning mill.
紡紗機 A jenny.
紡棉花 Spin cotton.
紡錘形 Spindle-shaped; fusiform.
紡織娘(動) A kind of grasshopper.
紡織機 Spinning machine; weaving machine.
紡紗工人 A spinner; a spinning operative.
紡織工業 Textile industry.
紡織公司 A weaving company.

索 suǒ (n.)- A rope; a cord.
(adj.)- Exhausted; isolated; scattered; solitary.
(v.)- Bind; fasten; cord; tie up. Demand; search; collect; ask for; inquire.
索引 An index.
索究 Search.
索性 Make up one's mind. May as well.
索取；索討 Demand; extort.
索價；開價 The asking rate; state the price.
索賠；索償 Claim damages; or indemnity.
索橋 Cable suspension bridge.

紫 zǐ (n.)- A dark brown colour; purple.
紫色；紫紅 A purple colour; amethyst colour.
紫荊(植) Judas tree.
紫菜(植) Laver; purple seaweed.
紫藤(植) Wistaria.
紫丁香(植) Purple lilac.
紫外線 Ultra-violet rays.
紫羅蘭(植) The violet.

紮 zā (n.)- A bundle.
(v.)- Tie; fasten; bind.
紮脚 Bind the feet.
紮綁；紮縛 Tie up; bind together.
紮緊 Bind up tight.
紮營 Station the army; quarter the troops; set a camp.

累 lèi 〔lěi〕 (n.)- Trouble.
(v.)- Accumulate. Involve; trouble; entangle; implicate.
(adv.)- Repeatedly; often.
累人 Implicate others.
累月 Month after month; month by month.
累積 Accumulate.
累贅；累墜 Troublesome; unmanageable. Worrying; harassing.

細 xì (adj.)- Fine; tender; slender; small. Minute; little; thin. Delicate.
(adv.)- Carefully; minutely; closely; little.
細小 Petty; trifling; little; tiny.

細心 Attentive; careful; prudent; heedful.
細末 Powder.
細巧 Fine and skilful, as opposed to rough and clumsy.
細目 Details; particulars; items.
細長 Long and slender; lanky.
細雨 A fine rain; a drizzle; a mizzle.
細胞 Cells.
細密 Close; delicate; fine; minute; exact.
細賬 A detailed account.
細菌 Bacteria; germs.
細微 Fine; minute; tiny.
細腰 A slender waist.
細嫩 Small and delicate.
細緻 Beautiful; fine; pretty.
細胞核 Cell nucleus.
細胞液 Cell sap.
細胞膜 The cell-wall (-membrane).
細胞質 Cytoplasm.
細胞體 Cell-body.
細菌戰 Bacterial (germ) warfare.
細心注意 With great carefulness; with the utmost care.
細胞分裂 Cell-division.
細斜紋布 Jeans.

紳 (n.)- The gentleman; the *literati*; gentry.
shēn 紳士 A gentleman.
紳商 Gentry and merchants; a wealthy merchant.

紹 (v.)- Connect; join; bring together. Continue; succeed.
shào 紹酒 Shaohing wine; Chinese beer.

終 (n.)- The end; close; conclusion. Death.
zhōng (adj.)- Whole; all; entire.
(v.)- Last; die; finish; pass away; conclude; bring to the end.
(adv.)- Finally; at last; at length; at the end.
終日 The whole day; all day long; throughout the day.
終年 Through the whole year.
終生 The whole lifetime.
終始 Throughout; all along; all the way; from first to last; from start to finish.
終夜 Throughout the night; whole night.
終站 Terminal station.
終結 An end; a close; a conclusion.
終止 End.
終點 The terminus; the terminal point; the end.
終止符 A full stop; a period.
終日終夜 Day and night.
終身大事 The great affair of a lifetime-marriage, of a woman.
終身不忘 Never-to-be-forgotten.
終身事業 One's life work.
終身監禁 Life imprisonment.

紘 (n.)- The string of a musical instrument.
xián 紘子 Fiddle.
紘線 A chord; a string; catgut.
紘樂 String music.
紘樂隊 A string-band.
紘樂器 A stringed musical instrument; the strings.
紘樂四重奏 A string-quartet.

組 (n.)- Tassels; fringe. A girdle; a tape. A group; a team.
zǔ (v.)- Organize; arrange.
組合 An association; a union. Form a partnership; unite with.
組成 Form; compose; constitute.
組長 A monitor.
組織 Form; organize; constitute.

Organization; system; formation. Tissue.
組曲 A suite.
組織化 Systematization.
組織部 The department of organization.
組織內閣 Form (organize) a ministry (cabinet).

絆 (v.)- Trip over; entangle; stumble.
bàn 絆倒 Trip and fall; stumble.

結 (n.)- A knot; a button; a tie; a joint.
jié (v.)- Tie; knot; wind up; unite. Connect. Consolidate; close.
結石(醫) A caculus.
結他 A guitar.
結合 Join or unite together; combine.
結冰 Freeze; be frozen over.
結交 Contract friendship; make friend; associate.
結伴 Form companionships.
結局 End; conclusion; outcome; result; upshot final stroke; consequence.
結尾 End; close; conclusion; termination.
結束 Wind up; close; put to an end.
結果 Outcome; result; effect; consequence; end; fruit; crop; harvest. Bear fruit.
結核 A tubercle.
結婚 Marriage; wedding. Marry; be married; get married.
結賬 Pay up or settle-an-account.
結淸 Settled; all paid.
結晶 Crystallize. Crystallization; a crystal.
結盟 Ally by treaty.
結腸(解) The colon.
結構 Construction; structure; framework.
結綵 Festoon.
結實 Firm; durable; lasting. Bear fruit; fructify.
結論 A conclusion.
結核病(醫) Tuberculosis (Tb).
結晶體 A crystal; a crystalloid.
結婚典禮 A marriage ceremony; a wedding; nuptials.
結婚指環 A wedding-ring.
結婚禮物 A wedding present (gift).
結婚證書 Marriage certificate.
結義兄弟 Sworn brothers.
結締組織(解) Connective tissue.
結婚紀念日 A wedding anniversary.

絕 (n.)- A verse; a poem.
(adj.)- Discontinued; interrupted; cut off.
jué (v.)- Discontinue; stop; cease; end; die. Sever; seperate; cut off; break off.
(adv.)- Extremely; greatly; very; most.
絕交 Sever intercourse; break off friendship with.
絕妙 Most admirable; exquisite.
絕佳 Beautiful beyond description; superb; extremely picturesque.
絕命 The end of life; death. Die.
絕食 Fast; abstain from food; eat nothing; starve oneself.
絕望 Blast hopes; hopeless; desperate.
絕頂 The summit; the height; the highest point.
絕路 Impasse. Cut off a retreat.
絕跡 Vanish; cease.
絕滅 Be extirpated (exterminated); become extinct; die out.
絕對 Absolute; positive; unconditional.
絕種 Exterminate a race.
絕緣 Severing of relations. Isolate; insulation (電).
絕育 Sterilised.

絕版書 An out-of-print book.
絕對值(數) Absolute value.
絕緣體 An insulator.
絕好機會 A golden (the rarest) opportunity.
絕對溫度 Absolute temperature.
絕對零度 Absolute zero.
絕對濕度 Absolute humidity.

條 (n.)- A sash; a band; a cord.
tāo 條蟲 A cestoid; a tapeworm.

絞 (v.)- Wrap; strangle; twist; twine; wreathe; wind together.
jiǒo 絞死 Strangle one to death.
絞刑 Hanged to death.
絞緊 Twist tight.
絞盤 A windlass; a capstan.
絞刑架 The scaffold.

絡 (v.)- Be connected. Continue.
luò 絡繹不絕 Unbroken; continuous.

給 (n.)- Present.
(adj.)- Sufficient; content.
gěi (v.)- Give; present; issue; offer; supply; provide.
給與 Furnish; grant; supply.
給發 Issue; grant; distribute; give.
給照 Grant a pass or certificate.
給還 Hand back; refund.
給賞 Give rewards.
給水管 A water-pipe.

絨 (n.)- Silk floss; wool; velvet; woolen cloth.
rǒng 絨毛 Wool; down; knitting wool; nap.
絨布 Flannel.
絨衫 Wollen sweater.
絨線 Woolen yarn.
絨氈 Blankets.

絮 (n.)- The catkins of the willow; cotton; wadding.
xǜ (adj.)- Talkative; gossiping; chattering. Silky; wooly and fluffy.
絮被 A wadded quilt.
絮煩；絮聒 Chatter; talkative; bother.
絮語 Chattering.
絮絮不休 Nagging without stop.

統 (n.)- A beginning; origin. A hint; a clue. A leader. A system.
tǒng (adj.)- Total; whole; entire.
(v.)- Gather into one. Rule; govern; control; command.
統一 Make all alike; render uniform. Centralization; concentrate.
統治 Govern; rule over.
統制 Control; regulate.
統括 Recapitulation; summary.
統帥 A generalissimo; a supreme commander.
統率 Command; lead.
統治者 The sovereign; the ruler.
統治權 The supreme power; sovereignty.
統計局 Bureau of statistics.
統計學 Statistics.
統一陣線 United national front.
統一祖國 National unification; unification of the motherland.
統治階級 The ruling class; the governing class.

絲 (n.)- Silk; thread. Satin; pongee.
(adj.)- Small; minute.
sī 絲瓜(植) The loofah gourd.
絲帶 Silk sashes; silk ribbons.
絲毫 The least number or quantity.
絲綿 Silk batting.
絲線 Silk thread, for sewing.

絲緞 Silk and satin.
絲襪 Silk stockings.
絲織物 Silk stuff; silk goods.
絲毫無誤 Without error; exact; no difference at all; exactly right.
絲綢衣服 Silk garments.

絹 (n.)- A kind of thin silk; lustring; silk taffeta.
juàn 絹子；手絹 A silk handkerchief.
絹扇 A gauze fan.

綁 (v.)- Tie; bind; take up; fasten together.
bǎng 綁住 Bind up; be bound up.
綁票 Capture a person for ransom by bandits; to kidnap.

綏 (n.)- A banner; a flag.
(adj.)- Quiet; peaceful; calm.
suí 綏定；綏靖 Pacify; restore peace; peaceful; quiet.

綑 (v.)- Bind; cord.
綑綁 Bind.
kǔn

經 (n.)- Classics; proper course; standard; law.
jīng (v.)- Manage; control; regulate. Pass through.
(adv.)- Already; past; then.
經心 Take care; be careful; attentive.
經手 Pass through the hands; manage; take charge of.
經文 Classical text.
經水；月經 The menses; the monthly courses.
經典 The scripture; a sacred book.
經度 Longitude.
經界 The division of the land into fields.
經紀 A broker; an agent.
經理 Manage; administer. A manager.
經常 Ordinary.
經商 Trade; carry on business.
經期 The time of menses; period of menstruation.
經痛 Painful menstruation.
經費 An outlay; expenses; expenditure.
經過 Pass; go by; elapse. Pass through; go by way of.
經歷 A career; one's past life; a record; experience.
經營 Build; construct. Plan; design. Manage; regulate.
經濟 Economic; practise economy.
經驗 Experience.
經緯度 Degrees of longitude and latitude.
經濟學 Economics; political economy.
經濟生活 Economic life.
經濟困難 Financial difficulties; economic straitness.
經濟侵略 Economic penetration.
經濟封鎖 Economic blockade.
經濟建設 Economic reconstruction.
經濟蕭條 Economic depression.
經濟學家 An economist; a political economist.
經驗豐富 Have wide experience.

綜 (v.)- Arrange; collect; sum up.
綜合 Synthesis; consolidation.
zōng Synthesize; put together.
綜括 Sum up; summary. Summarization.
綜合法 Synthetic methods.
綜合大學 A university.

綠 (adj.)- Green.
綠玉 An emerald.
lü 綠豆 Green lentils.
綠洲 An oasis.
綠肥(農) Green manure.

綠草 Green grass.
綠茶 Green tea.
綠氣(化) Chlorine.
綠葉 Green leaves.
綠酸(化) Chlorous acid.
綠蔭 A green shade; the shade of trees.
綠樹 Green trees.
綠化運動 A tree-planting campaign.

綢 chōu (n.)- Light silk; pongee.
綢衣 Silk garments.
綢緞 Silk piece goods; silk and satin.
綢繆 Close union, as married life.
綢緞莊 The mercer's shop; a silk store.

維 wéi (n.)- Fiber.
(v.)- Tie; connect; hold together; maintain; keep up; hold.
(adv.)- Only; but.
維持 Aid; keep up; maintain; support; sustain; preserve; stand; bear out.
維新 Reform; modernize.
維繫 Fasten together; connect with.
維也納(地) Vienna.
維他命 Vitamin.
維持秩序 Maintain order.

綱 gāng (n.)- Laws. General principle. The subject.
(v.)- Regulate; control.
綱目 A general outline; the main points. A heading; an item.
綱要 A summary; an outline.
綱領 General idea; essential points.

網 wǎng (n.)- A web; a net. A network of railways, telegraphic wires.
網索 Netting.
網球 Tennis.
網袋 A reticule.
網魚 Net fish.
網膜(解) The retina.
網球拍 A racket.
網球場 A tennis court—a lawn court or a hard court.
網膜炎 Retinitis.
網球比賽 A tennis match (tournament).
網球選手 A tennis player; a net star.

綴 zhuì (v.)- Sew together; bind; patch; mend.
綴文 Compose.
綴合 Bind together; fasten; file; sew together.

綵 cǎi (n.)- Coloured silk.
綵旗 Coloured silk flag.
綵綢 Coloured silk.

綸 guān (n.)- Silken threads. Fishing-line.

綺 qǐ (n.)- A kind of open-worked, variegated silk.
(adj.)- Fine; choice.
綺年 Young; youthful.
綺夢 A pleasant dream.
綺艷；綺麗 Pretty; beautiful; lovely; fine.

綻 zhàn (n.)- A seam which has come unsewn.
(v.)- Split; rip open.

綽 chuò (adj.)- Ample; spacious; wide; generous.
綽號 A nickname.
綽綽 Easy and free.

綾 líng (n.)- Silk damask.
綾羅 Silk gauze.

**綿** (n.)- Floss silk.
(adj.)- Soft; downy; weak. Lasting; prolonged; extended.
miɑ́n 綿力；綿薄 Delicate; weak.

綿羊 A wool sheep.
綿絮 Floss silk.
綿綿 Continuously; without a break; ceaselessly.
綿綢 Coarse pongee.
綿綿絮語 Endless talking.

**緊** (adj.)- Important; pressing; urgent.
jǐn (v.)- Bind tightly.
緊抱 Clinge; embrace; cuddle.

緊要 Urgent; important; essential.
緊急 Urgent; pressing; imminent; exigent.
緊密 Secret; tight.
緊張 Tension; strain; seriousness.
緊握 Grip; clench; grasp firmly.
緊隨 Follow closely after; come after.
緊急事件 An urgent affair; an emergency.
緊急命令 An urgent order.
緊急問題 An urgent (a burning) question; a matter of urgency.
緊急警報 Urgent alarm.
緊張局勢 A tense situation.

**緋** (adj.)- Dark red; vermilion.
緋紅 Deep red; dark red.
fēi

**緒** (n.)- A hint; a clue; the beginning.
xù (v.)- Connect; succeed.
緒言；緒論 An introduction; a preface; a foreword.

**緘** (n.)- A letter; a note.
(v.)- Seal up; close; bind up.
jiān 緘札 A letter.

緘口無言 Keep the mouth shut and say nothing.

**線** Same as 綫.
(n.)- A trace. A cord; a line;
xiɑ̀n a thread; a wire; a filament.
線人；眼線 A spy. A guide.

線索 A clue.
線條 A stripe; a streak.
線路 A trackway; a railway line; a route.
線速度(物) Linear velocity.
線加速度(物) Linear acceleration.

**緝** (v.)- Pursue; search; catch; come after. Twist a cord; spin.
jī 緝究 Bring to justice.
緝私 Seize smuggled goods. Preventive service.

緝捕 Search and arrest.
緝盜 Capture robbers.
緝私船 Revenue cruisers.

**緞** (n.)- Heavy silk; satin.
緞子 Satin.
duɑ̀n 緞帶；綢帶 Ribbon.

**締** (n.)- A close connection. A knot.
dì (v.)- Bind; join; connect; contract.

締約 Conclude a treaty.
締結 Conclude; betrothed; engaged.
締造國家 Build up a nation.

**緣** (n.)- A cause; a reason. A connection; a relationship.
yuɑ́n (v.)- Climb. Follow.
(conj.)- Since; because; on account of.

緣分 Affinity.
緣故；緣因 Cause; reason.
緣起 Origin; beginning.

**編** (v.)- To compile; knit.
biān
編入 Enroll; enlist.
編成 Organize; form; make up.
編制 Organization; formation; composition.
編訂 Revise and correct.
編結 Tie; bind.
編號 Number; classify.
編輯 Edit; compile.
編造(謠言) To fabricate (a story).
編譯 Edit and translate.
編輯長 Editor-in-chief.
編輯者 An editor; a compiler.
編輯部 The editing department.
編輯人員 Member of the editorial staff.

**緩** (adj.)- Slow; loose; sluggish; dilatory.
huǎn
(v.)- Delay; make slow; slow down; slacken; retard.
(adv.)- Gradually; slowly; gently.
緩刑 Reprieve. Suspension of sentence; probation.
緩步 Walk slowly. Snail pace.
緩和 Mollify; moderate; soften; temper.
緩急 Slow and fast. Emergency; urgency.
緩慢 Laxity; slackness.
緩下劑；輕瀉藥 A laxative; an aperient.
緩和局勢 Relieve the situation.
緩衝地帶 A buffer zone.

**緬** (n.)- Fine silk thread.
miǎn
(v.)- Remember; think of.
緬甸(地) Burma.
緬懷 Think; think of or upon.
緬甸人 A Burmese.

**緯** (n.)- The woof; the cross-threads. Parallels of latitude.
wěi
緯度 Degrees of latitude.
緯線 Cross-thread; woof; weft. Parallels of latitude.
緯度圈 Circle of latitude.

**緲** (adj.)- Minute. Distant. Indistinct.
miǎo
(adv.)- Far.

**練** (n.)- Experience; practise; training. A piece of silk.
liàn
(v.)- Practise; drill; train. Select; boil raw silk and soften it.
練兵 Military drill; parade. Drill troops.
練武 Military practice; drilling.
練習 Practise; exercise; train; drill; rehearse.
練習所 A training school.
練習簿 Exercise book.
練習純熟 Well-trained.
練習排演 Rehearse a play.
練習體操 Physical training.

**縈** (v.)- Wind around; reel; entwine; coil.
yíng
縈繞 Bind round; encompass.
縈繞於懷 Always remembering; unforgetful.

**縉** (n.)- Red silk.
jìn
縉紳 Gentry; gentlemen; men of rank.

**縊** (v.)- Hang; strangle.
yì

**縐** (n.)- Crape.
zhòu
縐紗 Crape.
縐綢 Crape silk.

**縛** (v.)- Tie up; bind; fasten.
fù
縛緊 Tie tightly.
縛住手足 Bind hand and foot.

縣 (n.)- A district; a county.
(v.)- Hang; be suspended.
xiàn 縣令；縣長 A district magistrate.
縣城 The city of a district.

緻 (adj.)- Delicate; soft.
zhì

縫 (n.)- A seam. A crack; a fissure.
(v.)- Sew; stitch. Mend; patch.
féng 縫口 Join a seam; sew a rent.
縫衣 Hem or stitch clothes; make garments.
縫合 Sew (stitch) together; stitch up.
縫紉 Stitch.
縫針 A needle.
縫補 Mend and pitch.
縫線 Sewing thread.
縫衣機 Sewing machine.

縮 (v.)- Draw back; withdraw. Shorten; shrink; shrivel; contract; wrinkle.
suō 縮小 Reduce; retrench; curtail; cut down; contract.
縮尺 Reduced scale; scale.
縮手 Refuse to give any help; pull in the hand.
縮回 Draw back; retract.
縮短 Shorten; shrink up.
縮寫 Abbreviate; abridge; abbreviation.
縮成一團 Huddle oneself up; curl oneself up.

縱 (adj.)- Perpendicular; vertical; straight; longitudinal.
zòng (v.)- Allow. Overlook. Let go.
(conj.)- Although; even if; though.
縱火 Fire on; arson.
縱使 Even if.
縱容 Connive at; tolerate.
縱隊 A column; a file.
縱橫 Vertically and horizontally; lengthwise and crosswise; in all directions.
縱橫密佈 Close network.
縱斷面圖 Profile.

縷 (n.)-Hempen or silken threads.
(v.)- State in detail.
lǚ

總 (n.)- A supervisor; a controller; a manager. A tuft of hair.
zǒng (adj.)- Whole; all; general.
(v.)- Bring together and tie up; unite. Sum up; collect. Control; supervise; manage.
總之 In a word; in short; in conclusion.
總共 The whole; the total; all.
總名；總稱 A generic (general) name.
總表 A general table.
總局；總行 Head office; headquarters.
總長 The chief; the chancellor; a cabinet minister.
總括 A summary; summarization. Sum up; summarize.
總計 The total; the total amount. Sum up; total; count up. Amount to; make a total of.
總理 The premier; the prime minister; the chief minister; the chancellor.
總務 General affairs (business).
總統 The president.
總裁 Director general.
總結 General recapitulation; summary.
總會 General assembly; general office. A club.
總督 Viceroy or governor general.
總監 A superintendent-general; an inspector-general.
總管 A superintendent; a general over-

seer.
總數 The total amount (number); the sum.
總賬 General ledger.
總額 The total amount; the sum total.
總人口 The total population.
總司令 A commander-in-chief.
總代表 Chief delegate.
總收入 The total income; gross receipts.
總批發 Sole agency.
總指揮 The high command.
總參謀 Chief of staff.
總動員 General mobilization.
總商會 General chamber of commerce.
總統府 The president's office.
總經理 General manager.
總領事 A consul general.
總編輯 Editor-in-chief.
總工程師 Chief engineer.
總代理人 General agent.
總司令部 The general headquarters.
總領事館 A consulate-general.

績 jī (n.)- Merit; meritorious deeds; distinguished services.
績分 School marks.

繁 fán (adj.)- Many; much; numerous; abundant; multitudinous.
繁多 Multitudinous; numerous.
繁忙 Busy; pressure of business.
繁茂 Thick (luxuriant) growth; luxuriance. Grow thick (in abundance).
繁盛 Prosperity; flourish.
繁殖 Breed; increase.
繁華 Show; pomp; display; gaiety.
繁榮 Prosperity.
繁瑣 Troubled by petty cares; vexatious.
繁雜 Complexity; complication.
繁簡 Complexity and simplicity.
繁分數(算) Complex fraction.
繁華世界 This vain world—Vanity Fair.

繃 bēng Same as 綳.
(v.)- Tie; fasten; bind.
繃帶 A bandage.

繅 sāo 繅絲 Reel silk.
繅繭 Reel silk off co-coons.

織 zhī (v.)- Weave.
織工 A weaver.
織女 A girl weaver.
織布 Weave into cloth.
織補 Darn.
織女星 Vega; Wega; Alpha Lyra.
織布廠 A factory for cloth making.
織布機 A loom.

繕 shàn (v.)- Mend; repair. Copy; write out.
繕修；繕治 Make ready; prepare.
繕鈔 Copy; transcribe.
繕寫 Write out.

繙 fān Same as 翻.
(v.)- Interpret; translate.
繙譯 Translation; interpretation.
繙譯員 A translator; an interpreter.

繞 rào (v.)- Wind round; surround; coil up; circulate. Inclose; entangle; involve.
繞行；繞路 Revolve; go round about.
繞過 Wind round, as a path; by-pass.

繩 shéng (n.)- A cord; a strand; a string; a rope. A marking-line.
繩子 A rope; a cord; a twine.
繩索；繩纜 Ropes; cordage;

riggings.
繩縛 Bind with a rope; rope; cord up.

繪 (v.)- Draw; paint; sketch; make a picture.
huì 繪畫 Pictures; paintings. Make a picture.
繪圖 Draw a picture.
繪圖尺 Plotting scale.
繪圖板 Drawing board.
繪圖室 Drawing office (room).
繪圖員 Draftsman.
繪圖器；縮圖器 Pantograph.
繪圖器具 Drawing instrument.

繫 (v.)- Bind; tie up, as with a rope; secure; attach.
xì 繫船 Moor a boat; fasten a boat.
繫馬 Tie up a horse; fasten a horse.

繭 (n.)- A cocoon. Blistered and rough skin.
jiǎn 繭絲 A silken thread.
繭蛹 Pupae.

韁 (n.)- A bridle; reins; halter; straps of a bridle.
jiāng 韁繩 The reins.

繳 (v.)- Bind. Hand over; deliver; send in; pay.
jiǎo 繳交 Deliver up; hand over.
繳呈 Submit to a superior.
繳卷 Hand in one's examination paper.
繳納 Pay over, as taxes.
繳械 Disarm; hand over weapons.
繳稅 Pay taxes.
繳還 Return; repay.

繡 Same as 綉.
(v.)-Embroider; embellish; variegate.
xiù
繡衣 An embroidered dress.
繡花；刺繡 Embroider.
繡球(植) The snowball.
繡錦 Embroidered silk.

辮 (n.)- A queue.
(v.)- Plait; braid; intertwine.
biàn 辮子 A queue; a cue; a pigtail.

繼 (v.)- Continue; succeed; follow after.
jì 繼父(母) Step-father (mother).
繼位 Succeed to the throne.
繼承 Succeed to; inherit.
繼室 A second wife.
繼續 Continue; go on with; keep on.
繼承人 A successor; an inheritor.
繼承權 Right of succession (inheritance).
繼續有效 Continuous effects or results.

繽 繽紛 Mixed colours; in confusion.
bīn

纂 (v.)- Edit; compose; compile; write.
zuǎn 纂訂 Revise and prepare for publication.

續 (v.)- Continue; connect; keep on; follow.
xù 續約 A supplementary treaty or agreement.
續假 Extend leave.
續增 Add to; supplement.
續稿 Next (remaining) manuscripts.
續篇 A sequel; a continuation; a supplementary (second) volume.

纍 (n.)- A large rope. An armour holder.
léi (v.)- Join; bind; tie; pile on;

place up.
纍纍 Piled one upon another; in heaps.

纏 (v.)- Wrap round; envelop; implicate; fold together. Tie
chán around.
纏緊 Bind tightly; tightly bound.
纏綿 Bound up with; protracted; inextricable; prolonged.
纏繞 Twist round and round; inclasp; encircle; twine; entangle.
纏擾 Annoy; incommode; vex.

纔 (conj.)- Just now; then; in that case.
cái 纔好 Then and only then it is all right.
纔來；纔到 Just arrived.
纔是 That is it; very well.

纖 (n.)- Fine silk.
(adj.)- Small; fine; slender;
xiān minute. Hairy; delicate.
纖毛 Cilia; ciliation.
纖小 Tiny; slender.
纖細 Taper; fine; minute; delicate.
纖維 Fibre.
纖纖 Slender; delicate; fine.
纖維質(植) Cellulose; fibre; filament.
纖維工業 Textile manufacture; fibre industry.
纖維組織 Fibrous issue; fibration.

纜 (n.)- A stern-cable (hawser); a rope; a cable; a cord.
lǎn 纜索 Cordage; thick ropes.
纜車鐵道 Cable railway.

# 缶 部

缸 (n.)- An earthen vessel; a jar.
gāng

缺 (adj.)- Insufficient; wanting; short; imperfect.
quē (v.)- Lack; want; need.
缺口 An opening or breach.
缺乏 Shortage.
缺席 Absence; non-attendance. Default of appearance (法).
缺唇 Harelip.
缺望 Disappointed; hopeless.
缺陷 A defect; a fault; an imperfection. Deformity(身體).
缺點 A defect; a flaw; a blemish; a weak point; a shortcoming.
缺乏資本 Lack of capital.
缺席判決 Judgment by default.

罄 (n.)- A jar; a vessel. An ancient musical instrument.
qìng (adj.)- Empty; exhausted; stern.
(adv.)- Entirely; all.

罌 (n.)- An earthenware; a jar; a pot; a vase.
yīng 罌粟(植) The opium poppy.

罐 (n.)- A jar; a pitcher; a bottle; a can; a pot; a tin.
guàn 罐頭 Tins; cans.
罐頭工廠 A cannery; a packing plant.
罐頭牛肉 Canned beef.
罐頭食物 Canned (tinned) food.

# 网 部

**罔** (adj.)- No; none.
(v.)- Deceive; cheat.
wǎng (adv.)- Without.
(prop.)- None.

罔兩；魍魎 Spirits; the spirits of the water.

**罕** (adj.)- Few; rare; scarce.
(adv.)- Scarcely; seldom; infrequently.
hǎn
罕有 Rare; scarce; seldom.

罕見 Seldom seen.
罕聞 Rarely heard.

**罩** (n.)- A basket; a cover; a veil; a shade.
zhào (v.)- Catch; protect; cover over; surround.

罩子 A cover; a shade.
罩衫 A cloak. An overcoat.
罩面布 A veil.

**罪** (n.)- A crime; a sin; a wrong; a fault; an offence.
zuì (v.)- Punish; condemn.
罪人；罪犯 A criminal; a delinquent; an offender; a malefactor.

罪名 A crime; an offence; the charge.
罪刑 Penalty.
罪狀 Guilt; the nature of a crime.
罪案 A criminal case.
罪惡 A sin (宗教); a crime (法律); an offence; a transgression.
罪過 Transgressions; crime; sin; wrong.
罪魁 The chief in the crime; a ring leader.
罪孽 Sin; iniquity.
罪惡滔天 Sins reaching to heaven.
罪孽深重 A great, deep-rooted fault.

**置** (v.)- Put aside; arrange; place; lay out; establish; employ;
zhì settle; set up. Buy.
置用 Buy for use.

置立 Establish; set up.
置產；置業 Buy an estate.

**罰** Same as 罸.
(n.)- Fine; penalty; punishment.
fá (v.)- Punish; fine; forfeit; mulct.
罰分 A black mark.

罰款 A fine; a forfeit; a penalty; an amercement. Impose a fine; punish by a fine.
罰罪 Punish the criminal.

**署** (n.)- A public office; a tribunal; a court.
shǔ (v.)- Sign; write; place; arrange. Appoint to an office.

署名 Signature. Sign one's name to; affix one's signature to.
署長 Director.

**罷** (v.)- Stop; cease; discontinue; dismiss.
bà 罷工 A strike; a walk-out.
罷手 Stop; cease.

罷市 Stoppage of trade; suspension of business.
罷免 Dismiss; discharge.
罷課 A school strike.
罷職；罷官 Resign office; be dismissed

from office.
罷工風潮 Trouble of strikes.

罵 (v.)-Scold; rail at; curse; reprove; abuse; revile; rebuke.
mà 罵人語 Abusive language; terms of abuse.
罵不絕口 Curse without ceasing.

罹 (n.)- Sorrow; grief.
(v.)- Undergo; suffer; incur; be a victim of.
lí 罹難 Killed in a disaster.

羅 (v.)- Spread out; gather together; arrange; set out in order.
luó 羅列 Arrange or set out in order.
羅馬(地) Rome.
羅針 A compass needle.
羅傘 A state silk umbrella carried in processions.
羅漢 The Arhans; the disciples of Buddha.
羅網 Nets for catching birds and fish.
羅盤 A compass.
羅馬人 A Roman.
羅馬字 The Roman letters; the Roman alphabet.
羅馬教 The Roman Catholic Church; Roman Catholicism; Romanism.
羅曼史 A romance; a romantic affair; a love-affair (story).
羅馬尼亞(地) Rumania.
羅馬帝國 The Roman Empire.
羅馬教皇 The Pope; the Supreme Pontiff.
羅馬教會 The Roman Catholic Church.
羅曼蒂克 Romantic.

羈 (v.)- Restrain; control. Detain.
羈押；羈禁 Detain; keep in custody.
jī 羈留 Detain; seize.
羈絆 A yoke; fetters; bonds. Be fettered; tied; fastened.

# 羊 部

羊 (n.)- A sheep; a goat; a ram; a ewe; a lamb.
yáng 羊毛 Wool; fleece.
羊皮 Sheepskin; goat-skin.
羊肉 Mutton.
羊角 A ram's horn.
羊脂 Suet.
羊羔 A lamb.
羊圈 A sheepfold; a pen for sheep.
羊羣 A flock of sheep.
羊腿 A leg of mutton; gigot.
羊毛衫 A knitted sweater.
羊皮紙 Parchment.
羊癎瘋(醫) Epilepsy.
羊腸小徑 A winding pass.

美 (n.)- Beauty.
(adj.)- Admirable; handsome; good; beautiful; goodlooking; nice; fine; lovely; excellent.
měi
美人；美女 A beauty; a belle; a beautiful (pretty) woman (lady, girl).
美化 Beautification. Beautify; embellish.
美妙 Admirable; excellent; delicate.

美味 Delicious; a good flavour.
美洲(地) America.
美酒 Fine wine; excellent wine.
美術 The fine arts; art.
美景 A beautiful scene; a fine view.
美感 The sense of beauty.
美滿 On the best of terms with; satisfied; perfect.
美態 Elegance of form.
美德 Excellent virtue; mental grace; a noble character; a good trait.
美學；美育 Aesthetics.
美貌 A beautiful (handsome) face; handsome features; personal attractions (charms).
美醜 Beauty and ugliness; personal appearance.
美譽 Good name; reputation.
美麗 Beautiful; handsome; pretty; fair; bonny.
美觀 Fine appearance; stylish looking.
美容院 A beauty-parlour; a culture saloon.
美容術 Beauty culture; the art of beauty; cosmetics.
美術品 Works of art; an object of art.
美術家 An artist.
美術館 An art museum (gallery).
美聯社 Associated Press (A. P.).
美術學校 An art school.
美國國旗 The Stars and Stripes.
美術展覽會 An art exhibition.
美利堅合衆國；美國(地) The United States of America (U.S.A.).

## 羔
gāo

(n.)- A kid; a lamb.
羔羊 A kid; a lamb.

## 羚
líng

羚羊 An antelope; a gazelle; chamois.

## 羞
xiū

(n.)- Dainties; savory food. Shame.
(adj.)- Ashamed; bashful.
(v.)- Feel ashamed; blush.
羞怯 Bashful and nervous.
羞恥 Shame.
羞辱 Insult; disgrace; cause shame.
羞愧；慚愧 Shamefaced; bashful.
羞人答答 Be shy (bashful); feel abashed.
羞得面紅過耳 Blushing to the ears.

## 羢
róng

(n.)- Fine wool.

## 羨
xiàn

(v.)- Desire; praise; esteem; speak highly of. Surpass; admire; long for.
羨慕 Be very desirous of; long for; admire.

## 羣
qún

Same as 群.
(n.)- A group; a crowd; a company; a multitude; a flock; a herd. Society; the community.
(v.)- Crowd; throng; group; flock together.
羣居 Reside or exist in large numbers; live gregariously together.
羣島 An archipelago; a group of islands.
羣衆 Masses; a crowd; mob.
羣集；羣聚 Swarm; gather in great numbers.
羣學；社會學 Sociology.
羣衆運動 Mass movement.
羣策羣力 United strength and wisdom.
羣起而攻之 All rise and attack him.

## 義
yì

(n.)- Meaning; senses; signification. Justice; reason; righteousness.
(adj.)- Right; proper. Loyal;

fair; faithful; reasonable; just; patriotic; dutiful; righteous. Common; public.
義士 A man of high principles; a knight; a patriot.
義子 An adopted son; a foster-child.
義軍；義師 A righteous army.
義勇 Courage; heroism; manliness.
義氣 Sense of justice (honour); self-sacrificing spirit; chivalry.
義務 An obligation; a duty.
義大利；意大利(地) Italy.
義和團 The Boxers.
義勇兵 A volunteer.
義勇軍 A volunteer army.
義務教育 Compulsory education.

羸 léi (adj.)- Lean; thin; feeble; worn out. Entangled.
羸弱 Feeble.

羹 gēng (n.)- Soup; broth.
羹匙；調羹 A spoon; a ladle.
羹湯 Soup.

# 羽 部

羽 yǔ (n.)- Birds. Wings; feathers; plumes.
羽毛 Feathers; plumes.
羽扇 Feather fans.
羽綢(緞) Bombazine; imitation camlets.
羽翼 Wings; helps; adherents.
羽黨 Supporters.
羽毛球 Badminton shuttlecock.
羽毛球拍 Badminton rackets.

翁 wēng (n.)- Father. Father-in-law. An old man; a venerable man. The feathers on the neck.

翅 chì (n.)- A fin. A wing.
翅膀 The wings.

翌 yì (n.)- To-morrow; next day.
翌日 To-morrow; the next day; the following day.
翌年 Next year.
翌晨 To-morrow morning; the next morning.

翎 líng (n.)- A plume; a feather; a wing. Feather on an arrow.
翎扇 Feather fans.

習 xí (n.)- A continued flight. A custom; a usage; a habit.
(adj.)- Intimate; familiar; accustomed. Expert; skilled.
(v.)- Learn; practise.
習字 Writing; penmanship. Learn handwriting.
習俗 Customs; usages.
習氣 A habit; a propensity.
習慣 A habit; practice. Accustomed to.
習作 Exercise; practise.
習題 An exercise.
習用語 Idiomatic phrase.
習字帖 A copy (writing) book.
習慣法 The consuetudinary (customary) law.
習慣成自然 Habit is a second nature.

翔 xiáng (v.)- Soar; hover over. Detailed.
翔空 Wheel around in the air.

翠 (n.)- Green pyroxene; chrysoprase. The kingfisher.
. cuì (adj.)- Bluish-green.
翠玉 A variety of jade.
翠竹 Emerald bamboo.
翠色 Deep green; kingfisher blue.
翠碧鳥；翡翠 The kingfisher.

翡 (n.)- A kingfisher.
翡翠(動) The small turquoise
fěi kingfisher.
翡翠玉 Chrysoprase; green pyroxene; malachite.

翦 See 剪.
(v.)- Cut with shears or scissors;
jiǎn shear; clip down; cut off; kill or extirpate.
翦刀 A pair of scissors.
翦枝 Prune (trim) a tree.
翦徑 Highwaymen.
翦碎 Cut into pieces.
翦髮 To have a haircut.

翩 (v.)- Flutter; fly about; hover; flap the wings.
piān 翩翩；翩躚 Moving about swiftly; fluttering.
翩翻 Fly in the air; flutter.
翩翩少年 A beau; a man of dress; a dandy.

翰 (n.)- Red plumage. A white horse. A pen.
hàn (adj.)- Literary.

翱 Same as 翶.
(v.)- Soar like a bird.
áo 翱翔 Wheel in the air; soar; roam.

翹 (n.)- Long tail-feather. A kind of head-dress.
qiáo (adj.)- High; eminent; lofty; elevated.
(v.)- Raise; elevate; lift up.
翹首 Raise the head.
翹翹 High; dangerous.

翻 (v.)- Turn over; upset. Fly to and fro; flutter about.
fān 翻印；翻版 Reprint; infringe a copyright.
翻車 Water wheels.
翻案 Reversing a judgement.
翻閱 Turn over the leaves of a book and read it.
翻臉 Change countenance; get angry.
翻轉 Turned round; wrong side up.
翻譯 Translation. A translator. An interpreter.
翻觔斗 Somersault.
翻譯本 A translation; a version.
翻印本 Pirated copies.
翻譯權 Right of translation.

翼 (n.)- The wings. The flanks or wings of an army.
yì (v.)- Assist; aid; protect. Brood over; shelter; defend.
翼助 Help; assist.
翼翼 Very careful and reverent.

耀 Same as 燿.
(adj.)- Glorious; brightly; brilliant; lustrous; shining.
yào (v.)- Shine; illumine.
耀眼 Dazzle the eyes.

# 老 部

**老** (adj.)- Old; aged. Venerable. Skilled; expert; accustomed.
lǎo (v.)- Grow old.
老人 The aged; the old; an old man.
老大 The eldest.
老手 An old hand; an adept; experienced.
老友 An old friend; an intimate friend; buddy!
老幼；老少 Young and old; youth and age.
老年 Old age; grey hair; evening of life; advancing age; declining years.
老早 Very early.
老伴 An old chum. A wife.
老虎 A tiger.
老酒 Old wine.
老師 An instructor; a professor; a teacher.
老弱 The old and the weak; old and infirm.
老婆 A wife. An aged woman; a dame.
老將 A veteran general.
老爺 An old gentleman.
老闆 The boss; shop-owner; proprietor.
老鼠 A rat; a mouse.
老僕 An old servant.
老實 Simple; honest; good-tempered.
老樣 Old fashion.
老練 Practised in; skilled in; experienced; good hand at.
老撾；寮國（地） Laos.
老人院 An asylum for old man.
老人家 An aged person—a title of respect.
老主顧 Regular customer; old customer; an old client.
老花眼；遠視眼 Presbyopia; long-sightedness.
老生常談 The platitudes of an old scholar.
老當益壯 Enjoy a green old age.

**考** Same as 攷.
kǎo (v.)- Examine; test; question.
考中 Pass the examination.
考生 A participant in an examination.
考妣 Deceased father and mother.
考究 Enquire into; look over; investigate.
考取 Examine and take out.
考官 Examiners.
考卷 Examination paper.
考查 Examine; test; scrutinize; look into.
考期 Date of examination.
考試 Examination.
考察 Investigate into; examine.
考據 Collation.
考慮 Deliberate; consider; take into consideration; think over.
考證 Verification. Proof.
考驗 Make trial of; examine; test.
考古學 Archaeology.
考古學家 An archaeologist.
考試及格 Pass an examination.
考試失敗 Fail in examinations.

**者** (pron.)- It; which; that; one who; that which; who; what;
zhě this.

# 而 部

**而** (conj.)- And; also. But; and yet; nevertheless; as; still; then.
ér 而已 That is all; nothing more–a final phrase.
而今 The present time; now.
而且 Furthermore; moreover; besides; in addition; still; else.
而況 With still stronger reason; still more; furthermore.
而後 Afterwards; henceforth; after that; then.

**耍** (v.)- Play; trifle; gamble.
shuǎ 耍弄 Play (toy) with; make a plaything of.
耍戲法 Do tricks; juggle.

**耐** (adj.)- Patient.
nài (v.)- Endure; bear; suffer; last; forbear.
耐久 Durable; lasting. Last a long time.
耐心 Patience.
耐冷；耐寒 Bear the cold.
耐性 A patient disposition.
耐苦 Hardy; bear suffering.
耐勞 Endure hardships.
耐煩 Stand the trouble; be patient.
耐熱 Heat-proof; heat-resisting.
耐用 To last long; lasting long.
耐久力 Durability; endurance.
耐不久 Cannot last long.
耐不住 Cannot bear it.

# 耒 部

**耕** Same as 畊.
gēng (v.)- Till; plough; cultivate.
耕夫 A farmer; a plough man.
耕牛 An ox trained to the plow.
耕田 Plough the fields.
耕地 Arable land; a cultivated field.
耕作 Cultivation; farming; farm work. Till; plough; cultivate.
耕耘 Cultivation. Work on the farm.
耕種 Plow and sow; hoe up and sow seeds.

**耗** (n.)- News; tidings; information; messages.
hào (v.)- Waste; spend; squander consume. Diminish; destroy; render void; injure; hurt.
耗子 A rat.
耗費 Squander; waste; consume.
耗損 Destroy; waste.

**耘** (v.)- Weed; remove grass and other plants from the field; root up.
yún 耘田 Weed a field.
耘草 Root up weeds.
耘耘 Numerous; confused.

**耙** (n.)- A rake; a drag; a harrow.
bà 耙子；犂耙 A harrow; a rake.
耙地 Rake the ground; harrow.

**耡** Same as 鋤.
chú (n.)- A hoe.
(v.)- Till; hoe.
耡地 Hoe the ground.
耡草 Weed.
耡頭 A hoe.

**耦** (n.)- A pair; a mate; a couple.
ǒu (v.)- Pair; match.
耦語 Whisper to each other.

# 耳 部

**耳** ěr (n.)- The ear; the organ of hearing. A handle, that which is at the side.
(adv.)- Only, a final particle.

耳目 Ears and eyes; the senses.
耳朶 The ears.
耳炎（醫）Otitis: inflammation of the ear.
耳垢 Earwax; cerumen.
耳挖 An earpick.
耳科 Otology.
耳殼 The concha; the auricle.
耳痛 Ear-ache; otalgia; otalgy.
耳筒 Ear-trumpet.
耳語 Whisper.
耳機 Receiver.
耳環；耳圈 An ear-ring.
耳聾 Deaf; hard of hearing.
耳邊風 A mere rumour; a matter of no concern.
耳科醫生 An otologist; an aurist; an ear specialist.
耳聞目見 Hear with ears and see with eyes. What one hears and what one sees.
耳鼻咽喉科 Otorhinolaryngology.
耳鼻咽喉科醫生 An otorhinolaryngologist.
耳鼻咽喉科醫院 A nose, ears, and throat hospital.

**耶** yē An interrogative particle—used at the end of a phrase, clause or sentence.
耶穌 Jesus.

耶和華 Jehovah.
耶穌教 Christianity; the Christian religion (faith).
耶穌會 The Society of Jesus.
耶路撒冷（地）Jerusalem.
耶穌教徒 A Christian.
耶穌聖誕 Christmas.
耶穌復活日 Easter.

**耽** dān See 躭.
(n.)- Pendent ears.
(v.)- Be addicated to; indulge in.

耽樂 Sunk in pleasure.
耽誤 Hinder; impede; delay.

**耿** gěng (adj.)- Bright; upright; sincere.
耿直 Upright; honest.
耿耿不寐 Disquieted and unable to sleep.

**聆** líng (v.)- Hear; pay attention to; listen; apprehend.
聆悉 Learn; hear.
聆教 Hear one's instructions.

**聊** liáo (n.)- A ringing in the ears.
(v.)- Depend on; rest on.
(adv.)- Carelessly; merely; anyhow; perhaps; then.

聊生 Something on which to live.
聊以謀生 With a view to make a living.
聊勝於無 Only better than nothing.

**聖** shèng (n.)- A sage.
(adj.)- Holy; sacred; reverend; divine.
聖人 A sage; a wise man. A

saint.
聖母 The Holy mother; Our Lady.
聖城 The Holy City.
聖徒 A saint; an apostle; the disciples.
聖堂 A temple; a sanctuary.
聖經 The Bible.
聖詩 A sacred song; a hymn.
聖像 Sacred effigies; images; idols.
聖潔 Holy; pure.
聖諭；聖旨 An imperial decree.
聖母像 A Madonna.
聖誕卡 A Christmas card.
聖誕節 Christmas Day; Xmas.
聖誕樹 A Christmas tree.
聖經文學 Biblical literature.
聖誕前夜 Christmas eve.
聖誕禮物 A Christmas present.

聘 (v.)- Enquire; pay a visit. To appoint employ; betroth.
pìn 聘金 Money paid at a betrothal.
聘書 Contract for employment.
聘請 Engage—as a teacher.
聘賢 Engage worthy men.
聘禮 The presents for a betrothal.

聚 (n.)- A hamlet; a village. A meeting.
jù (v.)- Assemble; gather; collect.
聚居 Dwell together.
聚集 Gather; assemble.
聚會 Gather together; hold a meeting.
聚餐 Dine (lunch) together.
聚積 Accumulate; amass.
聚光點 A focus.
聚光鏡 A condensing lens.
聚餐會 A dinner party.
聚精會神 Concentration of attention and energy.

聞 (n.)- Fame; reputation; knowledge.
wén (adj.)- Noted; famous.
(v.)- Hear; inform; report; smell.
聞人 A celebrity; a man of note.
聞及 Hear about.
聞名 Well-known. Famous.
聞知 Learn about; ascertain; hear of; be informed of.
聞名四方 Make known throughout the whole country.
聞所未聞 Hear that which one has never heard before.

聯 Same as 联.
(n.)- A couplet; a scroll.
lián (adj.)- Connective; allied; jointed
(v.)- Make alliance with; join; incorporate; unite; combine; connect. Continue; keep on.
聯句 A couplet.
聯合 Union; unification. Combine; unite; join.
聯邦 Federal states.
聯軍 The allies; the allied (army); the combined forces.
聯絡 Jointed to; in fellowship with; be friendly with; relate; contact; communicate.
聯想 Association of ideas.
聯盟 A league; a union; a federation. Form an alliance; league; ally.
聯合國 The United Nations Organization (UNO); UN.
聯絡官 A liaison officer.
聯合王國 The United Kingdom (U.K.).
聯合企業 Associated enterprise.
聯合戰線 A united front.
聯合政府 A coalition government.
聯合聲明 Joint statement.
聯邦政府 The federal government.
聯立方程式 Simultaneous equation.
聯合國大會 General Assembly of the United Nations.
聯合國憲章 The United Nations Char-

ter (U.N.C.).

聯合國安全理事會 United Nations Security Council (UNSC).

聯合國善後救濟總署 The United Nations Relief and Rehabilitation Administration (UNRRA).

聯合國教育科學文化組織 The United Nations Educational, Scientific and Cultural Organization (UNESCO).

聰 cōng (n.)- Cleverness; wisdom. The faculty of hearing.
(adj.)- Quick at hearing; wise; clever; sharpwitted; keen.

聰明；聰慧 Intelligent; acute; discerning; wise; clever.

聰明正直 Wise and upright.

聲 shēng (n.)- A sound; noise; tones; a voice. Reputation; fame; celebrity. Music; harmony; tone in music.
(v.)- Make known; state; declare.

聲名；聲望 Reputation; popularity; good name; fame; honoured; prestige.

聲明 A declaration; an announcement. Declare; announce; make a statement.

聲音 A tone; a sound; a voice.

聲浪 Sound waves.

聲帶 The vocal cords.

聲討 Declare or publish some one's crime. Denounce.

聲援 Encourage; shout encouragement; support.

聲量 Volume of one's voice.

聲勢 Display; majesty; influence.

聲稱 State verbally; declare.

聲樂 Vocal music.

聲調 A tone; a voice; a key.

聲響 A sound.

聲明書 A public statement.

聲樂家 A vocalist; a singer.

聳 sǒng (adj.)- High; elevated; lofty.
(v.)- Urge; raise up; stimulate; incite; stir up; egg on; excite; agitate; rouse to action.

聳肩 High shoulders. Shrug one's shoulders.

聳起 Stick up; emit; rise out of suddenly.

聳動 Egg on; stir up; incite; startle; exciting.

聳人聽聞 Arrest one's attention; create a great sensation.

職 zhí (n.)- Duty; trade; business; occupation; position; service; function; office; title.
(v.)- Manage; direct; take charge of.

職工 A workman; an artisan; an operative.

職位 Office; post; appointment.

職員 An officer; a functionary; the staff.

職責 One's duty and responsibility.

職業 An occupation; a vocation; a profession; an employment; a calling.

職權 Authority; official power; competence.

職工會 A trade-union; a labour union; a workmen's association.

職業病 An occupational disease.

職業選手 A professional player.

職工聯合會 A trade union; a workmen's association.

職業介紹所 A labour exchange; an employment agency.

聽 tīng Same as 聽.
(v.)- Hear; obey; listen to. Allow; grant; comply.

聽見 Heard.
聽候 Wait.
聽從 Comply; obey; heed; agree with; give into.
聽衆 Audience; attendance; hearers.
聽筒 Receiving set.
聽診 Auscultate; stethoscope.
聽話 Listen to advice.
聽察 Try and find out by listening.
聽說 Hearsay. Hear of . . . .
聽熟 Become familiar with one's voice (the sound).
聽講 Attend a lecture.
聽覺 The sense of hearing; the auditory sense.
聽診器 A stethoscope.
聽話器 Earphone.
聽覺力 The power of hearing.
聽天由命 Submit to Providence.
聽覺神經 The auditory (acoustic) nerve.

**聾** lóng (n.)- Deafness.
(adj.)- Deaf; hard of hearing.
聾人；聾子 A deaf man; the deaf.
聾啞 Deaf and dumb.
聾啞者 A deaf-mute.
聾啞學校 A school for the deaf and dumb; a deaf and dumb school.

# 聿 部

**肄** yì (v.)- Practise; learn. Labour.
肄業 Learn a profession or trade; study.

**肆** sì (adj.)- Four. Reckless; unrestrained.
(v.)- Let go; set forth. Be at ease. Display. Arrange.
肆力 Exert one's strength.
肆行 Give oneself over to vice.
肆意 Recklessly; unscrupulously.
肆口大罵 Abuse one outrageously.
肆行無忌；肆無忌憚 Care for nobody; act outrageously.

**肅** sù (adj.)- Respectful; reverential; majestic; solemn.
(v.)- Advance.
肅立 Stand in an attitude of reverence.
肅清 Suppress or put down a revolt; tranquillized.
肅復 Reply respectfully.
肅然 Reverentially.
肅敬 Respectful.
肅肅 Solemnly; in solemn silence.
肅靜 An awed silence.

**肇** zhào (v.)- Begin; found. Devise.
(adv.)- At first; at the beginning; for the first time.
肇始 Begin; commence. The beginning; the start.
肇興；肇造 Found.
肇釁；肇事 Stir up trouble; create a disturbance.

# 肉 部

**肉** (n.)- Flesh; meat. The pulp fruit.
ròu 肉丸 Meat balls.
肉汁 Meat juice; gravy; broth.
肉體 The body.
肉食 Meat (flesh) diet; flesh foods.
肉桂(植) Cinnamon.
肉眼 The naked eyes.
肉搏 Hand to hand fighting.
肉慾 Sexual desires; carnal appetite.
肉瘤 A tumor; a sarcoma.
肉鬆 Force-meat.
肉類 Flesh; meat.
肉食鳥 A bird of prey.
肉食獸 Carnivorous animals; a beast of prey; Carnivora.

**肋** (n.)- The ribs.
lē 肋骨 The ribs.
肋膜 The pleura.
肋間膜 Intercostal muscles.
肋膜炎 Pleurisy; pleuritis.

**肌** (n.)- Flesh; muscles.
jī 肌肉 Muscle.
肌骨 Flesh and bones.
肌節 Myotome.
肌膚 Flesh; skin.
肌纖維 Muscle fibres.
肌肉組織 Muscular tissue.

**肖** (adj.)- Alike; similar.
(v.)- Resemble; be like.
xiào 肖子 A worthy son.
肖像 A portrait; a likeness.

**肘** (n.)- The elbow.
zhǒu 肘關節 Elbow joint.

**肚** (n.)- The belly; the abdomen; the stomach.
dǔ 肚皮 The skin of the stomach; the abdomen.
肚痛 Bellyache; have a pain in the bowels.
肚脹 A swelled belly; dropsy.
肚飽 A full stomach.
肚餓 Feel (get) hungry.
肚瀉；下痢 Diarrhoea.
肚臍 The navel.

**肛** (n.)- The anus.
gāng 肛門 The anus; the fundament; the rectum.

**肝** (n.)- The liver.
gān 肝油；魚肝油 Cod-liver-oil.
肝蛭 Liver fluke.
肝癌 Carcinoma hepatitis.
肝臟 The liver.
肝臟病 Liver trouble.

**股** (n.)- The thigh. A division; a share in a concern. A part; a portion. A band.
gǔ 股份 A share in business.
股東 A shareholder; a stockholder.
股息 Dividend.
股票 A share (stock) certificate.
股份公司 A joint stock company.
股東大會 A general meeting of shareholders.
股票市價 Stock quotations (prices).
股票行市 The stock market.
股票掮客；股票經紀人 A share broker; a jobber.
股票跌價 Derogation.
股票買賣 Deal in stocks (shares).
股票讓渡 Assignment of share.
股票交易所 A stock-exchange; a bourse; a stock house.

**肢** (n.)- The limbs or members.
zhī 肢骨 Bones of the limbs.
肢體 Limbs and trunk; the

members of the body.

肥 (adj.)- Fat; fleshy. Oily; fertile. Abundant; rich.
féi 肥土 Fertile soil; rich soil.
肥大 Excessive fatness; corpulence.
肥肉 Fat meat.
肥皂 Soap.
肥壯 Stout and strong. Fat, as animals.
肥沃；肥饒 Fertile; productive; rich.
肥美 Plump.
肥胖；肥滿 Corpulence; fatness. Grow corpulent.
肥料 Manure; fertilizer.
肥瘦；肥瘠 Fat and lean; fertile and barren.
肥膩 Fattery; greasy; oily.
肥田粉 Powder fertilizer.
肥皂水 Soapsuds.
肥皂泡 Soap-bubbles.
肥皂盒 A soap-container.
肥皂廠 A soap-factory (-works).

肩 (n.)- The shoulder.
(adj.)- Competent to; firm.
jiān (v.)- Take upon; sustain; shoulder.
肩巾 A scarf; a cymar; a shawl.
肩挑；肩荷 Carry (bear) on the shoulder.
肩章 A shoulder-strap; an epaulette.
肩胛骨 The shoulder blade; the scapula.
肩並肩 Side by side; to stand shoulder to shoulder with.
肩負重任 Bear great responsibilities.

肯 (adj.)- Voluntary; willing.
(v.)- Consent to; agree to.
kěn Be willing.
肯定 Affirm; acknowledge. Affirmation.
肯定的 Affirmative.

肱 (n.)- The upper part; the arm, particularly.
gōng 肱骨 Humerus.
肱臂 The arm.

育 (v.)- Bear children; give birth; educate.
yù 育才 Bring up men of talent.
育嬰堂 A foundling hospital; an orphanage.

肺 (n.)- The lungs.
肺炎 Pneumonia; lung fever; the
fèi inflammation of the lungs.
肺病 A lung-disease; consumption.
肺葉 Lobe of the lungs.
肺臟 The lungs.
肺活量 The capacity of the lungs; breathing capacity.
肺氣腫（醫）Emphysema of the lungs.
肺結核 Pulmonary tuberculosis; phthisis.
肺癆病者 A consumptive patient.

胃 (n.)- The stomach.
胃口 The appetite.
wèi 胃炎；胃加答兒 Gastritis; catarrh of the stomach.
胃病 A stomach trouble; dyspepsia.
胃液 Gastric juice.
胃痛 Stomach-ache; a pain in the stomach.
胃癌 Cancer in the stomach.
胃下垂 Gastroptosis; falling of the stomach.
胃潰瘍 Gastric ulcer.
胃酸過多症 Pyrosis; water-brash; an acid stomach.

背 (n.)- The back; the rear.
(v.)- Turn the back. Disobey;
bèi turn against; violate; break

a promise. Bear; carry on the back. Repeat; recite. Leave; abandon.
背心 A vest; a waistcoat.
背泳 The back stroke.
背後 Behind the back; the rear.
背約 Break a treaty or promise; breach of contract.
背叛 Revolt; rebel.
背面；背部 The rear; the back.
背書 Recite from memory.
背景 Background; backing; support.
背棄 Reject; desert.
背誦 Repeat by heart.
背離 Be estranged (alienated); disobey.
背囊 A pack; a knapsack.
背對背 Back to back.

胎 tāi (n.)- A fetus. The pregnant womb.
胎生 Viviparity; born from within the body.
胎兒 A fetus; an unborn baby.
胎胞 The womb.
胎盤 The placenta.
胎生動物 Viviparous animals.

胖 pàng (adj.)- Stout; fleshy; fat.
胖子 A fat fellow.

胚 pēi (n.)- A germ; an embryo.
胚乳（植）Albumen; endosperm.
胚芽 An embryo bud.
胚胎 A pregnant womb; an embryo. Have its origin in; arise from.
胚盤 A germinal disc.

胞 bāo (n.)- The womb; the placenta. A bladder. Born of the same parents.
胞兄弟 Brothers by the same father.
胞子植物 Sporophyte.

胡 hú (n.)- The northern tribes.
(adj.)- Reckless.
(adv.)- How? Why? Blindly; foolishly.
胡瓜 The cucumber.
胡同 A lane.
胡桃 A walnut.
胡麻 Sesame.
胡琴 A fiddle; a stringed instrument of music.
胡椒 Pepper.
胡說 Talk incoherently; talk nonsense.
胡鬧 Make a row; create disturbance.
胡麻子 Linseed.
胡羅蔔 A carrot.
胡思亂想 Stupid thoughts; vain imaginings.
胡說八道 Nonsense; random talk.

胥 xū (v.)- Help; wait for.
(adv.)- Mutually; altogether; all.
胥吏 A clerk; a writer in an office.
胥役 Police; constables; runners.

胭 yān Same as 臙.
(n.)- Cosmetics; rouge.
胭脂 Cosmetic; rouge; lip-stick.

胯 kuà (n.)- The thigh; the groin.
胯下 The crotch between the legs.

胰 yí (n.)- The pancreas.
胰臟 The pancreas.
胰島素 Insulin.

胳 gē (n.)- The armpit.
胳膊 The arm.

**胸** (n.)- The breast; the bosom; the chest; the thorax.
xiōng 胸中 In the breast; in the bosom.
胸衣 Corsets.
胸泳 A breast-stroke.
胸部 The breast; the chest.
胸痛 A pain in the chest.
胸膛 The chest; the thorax.
胸膜 The pleura.
胸膜炎；肋膜炎 Pleurisy.
胸襟開闊 Generous; liberal-minded; broad-minded.

**能** (n.)- Ability; talent; skill.
(adj.)- Skilful; capable; able.
néng (v.)- Can be; be able.
能人；能手 A capable man; an efficient hand; an all work man.
能力 Faculty; ability; power to perform.
能夠 Possible.
能文 Skilled in writing.
能言 Eloquence; fluency.
能員 A capable official.
能做 Able to do.
能量（物）Energy.
能幹 Competency of talent.
能動的 Active.

**脂** (n.)- The fat of animals; tallows; grease. The gum or sap of trees. Cosmetics.
zhī 脂肪 Fat; grease; lard （猪）; suet （牛羊）.
脂膏 Fat wealth.
脂肪腺 The sebaceous glands.
脂肪組織 Adipose tissue.
脂肪質食物 Fatty foods.

**脅** (n.)- The ribs; the sides; the flanks.
xié (v.)- Intimidate; threaten; menace; reprimand.
脅生 Born from the ribs.
脅迫 Terrify or threaten by one's power. Threaten; menace; make threats against.
脅迫者 An intimidator; a blackmailer.

**脆** Same as 脃.
(adj.)- Crisp; brittle; fragile.
cuì 脆弱 Brittle and friable.

**脈** Same as 脉.
(n.)- The veins; the arteries;
mài the pulse.
脈弱 One has feeble pulses.
脈訣 The secret of the pulse.
脈絡 Coherence; logical-connection.
脈搏 Pulse; pulsation.
脈管 A blood vessel.
脈息微弱 A weak pulse.
脈搏停止 The pulse ceases to beat.

**脊** (n.)- The backbone; vertebrae; the back. The spine. A ridge,
jǐ as of a roof or of a mountain.
脊柱 The spinal column; the vertebral column; the backbone.
脊骨 The backbone; the spine.
脊梁 Vertebral column.
脊髓 The spinal cord (marrow).
脊椎骨 The vertebra.
脊髓炎 Myelitis.
脊髓病 A spinal complaint (disease).
脊椎動物 A vertebrata.

**脛** (n.)- The shank; the shin; the leg.
jìng 脛骨 The shinbone.

**脣** Same as 唇.
(n.)- The lips.
chún 脣舌 Eloquence; verbal contention; plausible speech.

脣音 A labial.
脣膏 Lip-stick.
脣鼻音 Labionasal.
脣亡齒寒 The lips being gone, the teeth are cold—mutually dependent.
脣紅齒白 Rosy lips and pearly teeth—pretty.
脣齒之邦 States that mutually depend on each other.

脩 xiū See 修.
(n.)- Dried meat. The salary; tuition.
(adj.)- Distant; long.
(v.)- Prepare; regulate; cultivate.
脩治 Get to rights; govern.
脩金；束脩 Tuition; school fee. Salary.
脩飾 Adorn; make up.

脫 tuō (v.)- Take off; drop off; strip; cast off; abandon. Omit. Renounce. Escape from; free from.
(conj.)- If; supposing; in case.
脫下 Take off.
脫手 Disengage one's hand. Sell out.
脫水(化) Dehydration.
脫去 Throw off; take off; pull off.
脫衣 Take off one's clothes; undress; disrobe; divest of clothing.
脫肛 Proctocele; prolapse of the anus.
脫臼；脫節 Be dislocated; be put out of joint.
脫免 Escape; avoid.
脫班 Not up to schedule—as a train.
脫退 Withdraw from; secede from; leave.
脫逃 Escape; get free (off); make one's escape.
脫掉 Renounced; left off.
脫帽 Uncover; take off a cap or hat. Hats off!
脫除 Get rid of; remove.
脫殼 Cast the shell. Exuviae.
脫罪 Exonerate a person from blame.
脫稿 Complete a manuscript; a manuscript be completed.
脫險 Removed from danger; be out of danger.
脫離 Rid self of; escape from; cut oneself off from; get rid of.
脫脂乳 Skim milk.
脫脂棉 Absorbent cotton.
脫身之計 A plan of escape.
脫離關係 Sever one's connection with; break away from.

脯 fǔ (n.)- Dried meat; jerked meat. Dried fruit.
脯資 Travelling expenses.
脯鮓品 Preserved meats.

脹 zhàng (n.)- Swelling of the stomach.
(adj.)- Dropsical.
(v.)- Swell up; grow big; swell, as the belly.
脹氣 Flatulence.
脹滿 Swelled out with dropsy; fully inflated.

脾 pí (n.)- The spleen. The temper; disposition.
脾胃 Digestion.
脾氣 Disposition; temper; nature.
脾虛 A weak stomach.
脾臟 The spleen.

腋 yè (n.)- The armpits. The part under the forelegs of animals.
腋下 Under the arms; the armpits; the axilla.
腋毛 Hair of the armpit.
腋臭；狐臭 Tetter of the armpits; B.O. (body odour.)

腎 (n.)- The kidney. The testicle.
shèn
腎石 A renal calculus.
腎囊；陰囊(解) The scrotum.
腎臟；內腎 The kidney.
腎盂炎 Pyelitis.
腎臟炎 Nephritis; inflammation of the kidneys.

腐 (adj.)- Rotten; corrupt; spoiled; old.
fǔ
(v.)- Decay; rot; putrefy; go bad; corrupt.
腐化 Deterioration; decomposition.
腐朽 Decayed; rotten.
腐乳 Soured bean-curd.
腐敗 Putrid; spoilt; corrupt; decayed.
腐蝕 Corrosion. Corrode; rot.
腐爛 Putrefy; be rotten; rot; decompose.
腐蝕劑 A caustic; a corrosive agent.
腐化分子 Corrupt element.
腐蝕作用 Corrosive action.

腑 (n.)- The bowels; the viscera; the entrails.
fǔ

腔 (n.)- The breast. A hollow cavity. A tune; an accent of voice. A singing tone.
qiāng
腔調 A tune. A way of acting.
腔腸動物 Coelenterate.

腕 (n.)- The wrist; a flexible joint.
wàn
腕力 Strength of wrist; physical force.
腕骨 The wrist bones; the carpus.
腕足類 Brachiopoda.

腥 (n.)- Measly flesh.
xīng
(adj.)- Offensive to the smell; stinking, as the smell of raw fish; fishy; rank; rancid.
腥味 A bad flavour; an evil, frowzy smell.
腥氣 A fishy smell.

腦 (n.)- The brain.
nǎo
腦力 Mental power.
腦炎 Encephalitis; brain fever.
腦海 The brain.
腦袋 The head.
腦殼；腦蓋 The skull; the brainpan.
腦中風 Apoplexy.
腦出血；腦溢血 Cerebral haemorrhage; an apoplectic stroke.
腦充血 Congestion of the brain; cerebral hyperemia.
腦貧血 Cerebral anaemia.
腦膜炎 Meningitis.
腦震盪 Concussion of the brain.
腦力勞動 Mental labour.
腦神經衰弱 Nervous debility.

腫 (adj.)- Inflated; swollen.
zhǒng
(v.)- Swell; tumefy.
腫起 Swell up.
腫痛 Swollen and painful.
腫瘤 A tumor.

腭 (n.)- The palate.
è
腭腺 Palate glands.

腮 Same as 顋.
sāi
(n.)- The cheek; the lower part of the face.
腮腺；耳下腺 Parotid gland.
腮腺炎；耳下腺炎 Parotitis.

腰 (n.)- The loins; the waist. The kidneys.
yāo
腰子 The kidneys.
腰帶 A girdle; a sash.
腰斬(足球賽) Blow off a game of

football.
腰痛 Lumbago.
腰鼓 Side drum.

**腳** Same as 脚.
(n.)- The foot; a leg; a paw.
jiǎo The bottom or base.
腳力 A messenger. Influence.
腳心；腳板 The sole of a foot.
腳本 A drama; a play; a playbook.
腳色 Actors.
腳步 A pace; a step.
腳盆 A foot-tub.
腳趾 A toe.
腳痛(醫) Podalgia. Be foot-sore; have a sore foot.
腳跡；腳印 Footsteps; footprints.
腳跟 The heel.
腳步快 Quick; swift; light-(swift-) footed.
腳步重 Have heavy feet.
腳步慢 Slow-footed.
腳步輕 Have light feet; be light of step.
腳氣病 Beriberi.
腳踏車 Bicycles.
腳踏實地 Plant the feet on solid ground—get a footing.

**腴** (adj.)- Rich; fertile; fat; fruitful.
yú 腴壤 Fertile soil; fertile land.

**腸** (n.)- The intestines; the bowels.
腸炎；腸加答兒 Enteritis; the
cháng inflammation of the intestines; intestinal (bowel) catarrh.
腸病 Enteropathy.
腸臟 Tripes.

**腹** (n.)- The belly; the abdomen.
腹心 Devoted; confidential;
fù faithful; trustworthy.
腹部 The abdominal region; the abdomen.
腹飢 Feel hungry.
腹腔 Abdominal cavity.
腹痛 Bellyache; colic. Have a pain in the bowels.
腹瀉 Diarrhea. Have loose bowels.
腹膜炎 Peritonitis.
腹心朋友 A bosom friend.

**腺** (n.)- A gland.
腺病 Adenosis; scrofula.
xiàn 腺細胞 Gland cells.

**腿** (n.)- The thighs; the legs.
腿骨 Femur; leg bones; thigh
tuǐ bones.

**膀** (n.)- The arms. The loins; the bladder.
páng 膀子 The arm or shoulder.
膀胱 The bladder.
膀胱炎 Inflammation of the bladder; cystitis.

**膈**
gé 膈膜 The diaphragm.

**膊**
bó (n.)- The arm. Dried meat.

**膏** (n.)- Fat; grease; ointment; oil; favours; lard.
gāo (adj.)- Rich; fertile.
(v.)- Fatten; enrich.
膏藥 An ointment; a plaster.
膏壤 Rich soil.

**膚** (n.)- The skin; the surface.
膚淺 Skin-deep; superficial; shal-
fū low.

**膛** táng (n.)- The breast. The swelling belly of a jar; the capacity of a vessel. The barrel of a gun.

**膜** mó (n.)- The membrane; a film.

**膝** xī (n.)- The knee; the lap.
膝下 At one's feet; under the care of one's parents.
膝蓋 The knee-cap.
膝蓋骨 The knee-cap (knee-pan); patella.
膝關節 The knee joint.

**膠** jiāo (n.)- Glue; gum, cement.
(adj.)- Sticky; glutinous.
(v.)- Glue; cohere or adhere; stick.
膠卷 Film.
膠水；膠汁 Glue; size.
膠漆 Glue and varnish.
膠樹；橡皮樹 Gum-tree.
膠囊 A capsule.
膠質物 Jelly.

**膨** péng (adj.)- Swollen.
膨脹 Expansion; swelling. Blow up; expand; swell.
膨脹率 The rate of expansion.
膨脹係數 The coefficient of expansion.

**膩** nì (adj.)- Greasy; fat. Oily; glossy; unctuous.
膩煩 Sick of; tired of; disgusted.
膩滯 Indigestion.

**膳** shàn (n.)- Provisions; viands; victuals; fare; savoury food; delicacies.
膳夫 A king's butler; a cook.
膳食 Meal; victual.
膳宿 Food and lodging.
膳費 Fees for board.

**膺** yīng (n.)- Breast.
(v.)- Bear; sustain; receive; undertake.
膺選 Elected.

**膽** dǎn Same as 胆.
(n.)- The gall, said to be the seat of courage. Courage; bravery; daring.
膽力；膽量 Courage; pluck.
膽大 Courageous; daring; bold; brave.
膽小；膽怯 Cowardly; timid; chicken-hearted; fearful.
膽石 A bile-stone; a gall-stone.
膽壯 Brave; fearless.
膽敢 Dare; venture; make bold.
膽戰；膽寒 Tremble with fear.
膽囊 The gall bladder.
膽石病 Chololithiasis.
膽大心細 Brave but cautious.
膽大包天 Be as bold as a lion.
膽戰心驚 Terror-stricken; in terror.

**膾** kuài (n.)- Minced meat or fish.
膾炙 Minced and roasted.

**膿** nóng (n.)- Pus; purulent matter.
膿水 Pus; matter; purulent discharge.
膿血 Bloody pus.
膿胞 Pustules filled with pus.
膿潰 Suppurating freely.
膿瘡；膿腫 An abscess; a pimple; a boil.

**臀** tún (n.)- The buckocks; the seat; the lower side; the bottom; the rump.

臀部 The buttocks; the hip.

**臂** bì (n.)- The forearm; the arm.
臂章 An arm-badge; a brassard.
臂膊 The arm.

**臆** yì (n.)- The breast; the heart. The thoughts; the feelings.
臆度；臆測 A guess; a supposition. Suppose; make a guess; conjecture.
臆斷 An arbitrary judgment.

**臉** liǎn (n.)- The face; the cheek.
臉色 Expression; complexion; colour; countenance.
臉紅 With a blush.
臉厚 Shameless; brazen-faced.
臉盆 A washing basin.
臉嫩 Timid; inexperience; fresh.

**臌** gǔ (adj.)- Dropsical swelling; bloated; bulging.
臌脹 Swollen; puffed out.

**臍** qí (n.)- The navel; the umbilicus.
臍帶 The umbilical cord; the naval-string.
臍部 The umbilical region.

**臘** là (n.)- The winter sacrifice. Dried and salted meats.
臘月 The 12th month.
臘肉 Salted meat.
臘腸 Sausage.
臘鴨 Dried salt ducks.

**臟** zàng (n.)- The entrails; the viscera; the inner parts of the animal body.
臟腑 Entrails; the intestines.

# 臣 部

**臣** chén (n.)- An attendant; a vassal.
臣子 A minister of state; courtiers.
臣民 Subjects.
臣僕 Servants and slaves.

**臥** wò Same as 卧.
(v.)- Lie down. Repose; rest. Sleep; slumber; take a nap; go to bed.
臥車 A sleeping-car; a sleeper; a pullman.
臥房；臥室 A bedroom; a bedchamber.
臥具 Bedding.
臥牀；臥榻 Lie on a bed. A couch; a bed.
臥倒 Lie down.
臥病在床 Be confined to bed; be ill (sick).

**臨** lín (v.)- Approach; descend; look down; attend; reach; visit.
(prep.)- On the point of; near to; during; about; at; on; whilst.
(conj.)-While.
臨行；臨別 On the point of departure; about to start; on leaving.
臨危 Get into danger; at the juncture of crisis.
臨近 Impending; imminent. Drawing near to; be just before one.
臨到 Approach.

臨夜 At nightfall.
臨帖 Copy plates; imitate a copy-slip.
臨急；臨忙 In a hurry.
臨盆 Parturition; to give birth to a child.
臨海 Seaside.
臨時 Offhand; at a moment's notice. Provisional; temporarily.
臨診 Examine diseases.
臨終；臨死 About to die; approach death; draw toward one's end; come to an end.
臨睡 Before going to sleep; at bedtime.
臨牀實習 Bedside and clinical training.
臨時大會 An extraordinary general meeting.
臨時主席 Temporary chairman.
臨時政府 A provisional government.
臨時雇工 Temporary employment. A temporary employee; an extra hand.

# 自 部

**自** zɪ (pron.)- Oneself; self.
(adv.)- Naturally; spontaneously. Personally; privately.
(prep.)- From; since; hence.
自大；自命不凡 Aggrandize; proud; self-important; conceited.
自己 Self; oneself; ego.
自今 Henceforth; hereafter; from this time forward.
自立 Independent. Support oneself.
自由 Freedom; liberty. Be free; be at ease; feel at home.
自主 Autonomous; independent.
自此 Henceforth; from this place.
自在 Ease; free and easy; unrestricted.
自我 Self; ego.
自卑 Humble oneself; self abased.
自投 Give oneself up.
自私 Selfish.
自制 Self-control; self-restraint; self-command.
自信 Self-confidence.
自後 Henceforth; hereafter.
自首(法) Self-denunciation; self-surrender.
自負 Vainity; egotism; self-importance.
自恃 Self-confident.
自悟 Come to one's senses; self-consciousness.
自尊 Self-respect (esteem); self-importance.
自殺；自盡；自裁 Commit suicide; self-destruction.
自修 Teach oneself; study by oneself.
自動 Automatic motion; voluntary.
自從 From . . . ; ever since . . . .
自備 Self-support; make provision for oneself.
自然 Of course; naturally; certainly.
自費 At one's own expense; self-supported.
自給 Self-support; self-supply. Support (provide for) oneself.
自傳 An autobiography; one's life story.
自愛 Self-respect. Take care of oneself.
自滅 Self ruin (destruction, annihilation).
自發 Spontaneously; voluntarily; on one's own initiative.
自滿；自足 Vain; self-confident; self-sufficient; haughty; conceited;

complacency.
自稱 Call (style) oneself; pretend to be ····(文) The first person.
自製；自造 Made by oneself; home-made.
自衛 Self-preservation; self-defence; self-protection.
自豪；自誇 Boast of; be proud of; plume oneself on.
自謙 Modesty; self-abasement.
自轉(天) Rotation.
自覺 Self-awakening; self-consciousness.
自讚 Self-praise; self-applause; praise oneself.
自主國 Sovereign state; independent state.
自主權 Right of autonomy; free-will; right of self-government.
自行車 Bicycle.
自由港 A free port.
自治權 Right of self-government; autonomy.
自來水 Water supply. Running water.
自助餐 Buffet dinner.
自動式 Automatic; self operating (acting).
自動梯 Moving staircase; escalator.
自然界 Nature; the natural world.
自以爲是 Self-approbation.
自古及今 From ancient time till now; in all ages.
自由主義 Liberalism.
自由自在 Comfortable; contented; easygoing; free and easy (unrestricted).
自由投票 A free vote.
自由結婚 Freedom of choice in marriage; free marriage.
自由貿易 Free trade.
自由發行 Free issue.
自由職業 Liberal profession.
自由競爭 Free (open) competition.
自由戀愛 Free love.
自力更生 To push forward by one's efforts.
自我犧牲 Self-sacrifice.
自作主張 To deside all by oneself.
自吹自擂 Self-advertisement.
自即日起 As from today.
自我批評 Self-criticism.
自言自語 Soliloquize.
自來水筆 Fountain pen.
自來水費 Water-rate.
自來水管 A water-pipe.
自來水廠 Waterworks.
自命不凡 Pride oneself on being uncommon; self possessed.
自始至終 From beginning to end; from top to bottom; all along.
自相矛盾 Self-contradiction.
自告奮勇 To volunteer one's service.
自食其力 Live by one's own exertions; help oneself.
自修時間 Study hours.
自覺自願 Voluntarily and consciously.
自動步槍 Automatic rifle.
自動電話 An automatic telephone; a dial telephone.
自給自足 Self-sufficiency.
自然科學 Natural science.
自尋煩惱 Bring trouble upon oneself.
自費留學 Studied abroad at one's own expense.
自暴自棄 Desperation; self-abandonment. Abandon oneself to despair.
自取滅亡 To count one's own doom.
自發罷工 Wildcat strike.
自動電話機 Automatic telephone.
自動打字機 Automatic typewriter.
自給自足政策 A self-supporting and self-sufficient policy.

臭 chòu (n.)- A strong smell; a stench; odour; scent.
(adj.)- Rank; stinking; strong-scented; rancid.

臭名 A foul reputation.
臭氣 A bad (strong) smell; an offensive odour.
臭蟲 Bedbugs.
臭化物 A bromide.
臭藥水 Carbolic acid.
臭味相投 Men of similar nature or tastes.
臭氣觸鼻 Strong-scent irritates the nose.

# 至 部

至 zhì (n.)- The end; the extreme.
(adj.)- Best; greatest; very; extremely; the most.
(v.)- Go to; arrive at (in); reach; come to.
(prep.)- To; at; up to; till.
至上 Highest; supreme.
至少 At least; least.
至今 Until now; up to the present time.
至此 Come here.
至死 To the bitter end; to the very last; until death; even to dying.
至多 Maximum; at most.
至於 With regard to; as to; come to; with respect to.
至要；至重 Of the greatest importance; most important; essential.
至理 Self-evident truths; axioms.
至善 The highest (supreme) good.
至極 The most; at best; to the utmost degree; very extreme.
至惡 Most wicked.
至禱 Most earnest desire.
至理名言 Axiom. A golden saying.
至上命令（哲） Categorical imperative.
至關緊要 Of the utmost importance.

致 zhì (n.)- Aim; end.
(v.)- Originate; render; induce; reach; go to. Attain. Transmit; convey; send. Sacrifice. Resign; retire from office. Invite. Make.
致力 Devote oneself to.
致知 Utilize one's knowledge.
致命；致身 Devote one's life; risk life.
致函；致書 Send a letter to; write to.
致祥 Bring about good luck.
致賀 Convey congratulations.
致意 Inform; pay regards.
致敬 Show deep respect.
致謝 Convey thanks.
致辭 To deliver a speech.
致命症 A fatal (mortal) disease.
致命處 A fatal spot.
致命傷 A mortal (fatal) wound; a fatal (death) blow.

臺 tái (n.)- A tower; a terrace; a stage; a platform; a stand; an observatory.
臺地 A table-land.
臺階 Steps. Stair-cases.
臺灣；台灣(地) Taiwan.
臺柱 Mainstay; pillar of support.

# 臼 部

**臼** jiù
(n.)- A mortar; a bowl.
臼齒 A molar teeth; the molars.

**臾** yú
(n.)- A moment; a little while; an instant; a very short time.

**舁** yú
(v.)- Lift up; raise up; carry.
舁舉 Raise up; lift up; offer up.
舁轎 Lift up a sedan-chair; carry a sedan-chair.

**舀** yǎo
(v.)- Ladle; bale out.
舀水 Bail out water.

**舂** chūn
(v.)- Pound grain; ram down.
舂米 Hull rice; pound rice.

**舅** jiù
(n.)- A father-in-law. Maternal uncles. Brothers-in-law.
舅父 A maternal uncle.
舅公 Father of husband.
舅母 An aunt; wife of mother's brother.
舅姑 A husband's parent.

**與** yǔ
Same as 与.
(n.)- Company.
(adj.)- Friendly.
(v.)- Give; transfer; submit.
(prep.)- With; by.
(conj.)- And; not less than; as well as.
與及 Together with.
與人不同 Unlike others.
與共命運 Share one's fortune; throw in one's lot with another.

**興** xīng
(n.)- A passion; delight.
(adj.)- Prosperous; flourishing; rising. Joyful.
(v.)- Rise; arise; get up; lift; elevate; raise. Start; originate. Found. Prosper; rise to power. Promote.
興工 Commence work.
興旺 Prosperous; flourishing; in good circumstances; successful.
興致 Leisure and ease; spirit.
興起 Rise into prominence.
興盛 Get ahead in business; get forward; prosper; flourish; prosperous.
興趣 Interest; pleasure; curiosity.
興奮 Excitement; stimulation. Be excited (stimulated); become hot.
興辦 Put into effective operation.
興奮劑 A stimulant.
興高采烈 Full of beans; in high spirits.

**舉** jǔ
(n.)- Matter; affair; event.
(adj.)- Whole; all.
(v.)- Raise up; lift up; uphold; hold up; elevate. Appoint; begin. Praise; recommend.
舉人 A graduate of the second degree.
舉手 Raising the hand.
舉止 Carriage; gait; deportment; manner.
舉行 Begin; carry out; hold; take place.
舉重 Weight lifting.
舉例 For example.
舉薦 To recommend.
舉步 Lift the feet; start.
舉杯 Raise the cup; lift the cup.
舉動 Actions; movement; behaviour.
舉國 The whole country.
舉辦 Deal with; put into operation.
舉止大方 Rectitude of character.
舉止端詳 The upright conduct.
舉手表決 Vote by raising the hand; show of hands.
舉世聞名 To be known; to all the

world.

**舊** (n.)- Friendship; acquaintance. (adj.)- Old; ancient. Worn; second-hand.
jiù
舊友 An old friend.

舊年 Last year; the past year; in former years.
舊式 Old fashioned; obsolete; antiquated; old styled.
舊事 Past events; things past.
舊例 A usage; an old custom.
舊居 One's old house; one's former residence.
舊案 An old-standing case.
舊情 Old affection.
舊教 The Catholic Church; Romanism.
舊傳 A legend runs that.
舊聞 Old news; an old story.
舊稿 An old manuscript (writing).
舊金山(地) San Francisco.
舊思想 Old ideas (thoughts); an obsolete (out-of-date) idea.
舊教徒 A Catholic.
舊病復發 Relapse; recurrence.
舊約聖經 The Old Testament.
舊誼重溫 Brush up one's acquaintance with; renew one's old friendship with.
舊石器時代 The paleolithic age.

# 舌　部

**舌** (n.)- The tongue. A clapper.
shé
舌尖 The tip of the tongue.
舌苔 Fur on the tongue. The tongue is coated with fur.

舌音 Lingual sounds.
舌根；舌本 The root of the tongue.
舌鈍 Mumbling; be inarticulate; be unable to speak distinctly; lisp.
舌戰 Wordy warfare; a heated discussion; a verbal fencing. Bandy words with; have a wordy war.

**舍** (n.)- A cottage; a hut; a lodge; a residence.
shè
(adj.)- Humble.
(v.)- Dwell; lodge; rest in. Set aside.

舍下；寒舍 My humble home; my poor residence.
舍利子 Sacred relics of Buddha.
舍己從人 Yield one's wishes to those of another.

**舐** (v.)- Lick; lap.
shì
舐盡 Lick up.

**舒** (adj.)- Comfortable exhilarated; leisurely; at ease.
shū
(v.)- Spread out; stretch out; open.

舒伸 Stretch out.
舒服；舒適 In good health; comfortable.
舒展 Open; expand; spread out.
舒散 Relax.
舒暢 In good spirit; cheerful; pleasant.

**舖** Same as 鋪.
pù
(n.)- A shop; a store; a place of business.
舖子 A shop.

舖主 A shopkeeper.
舖東 The owner of a shop.
舖夥 Shop assistants.

# 廾 部

舞 wǔ (n.)- Dancing.
(v.)- Dance; flutter about; brandish; fence; make posture.
舞刀；舞劍 Brandish a sword; sword-play.

舞女 Dancer; dancing girl; cabaret girl.
舞曲 A dance-music.
舞伴 Dancing partner.
舞動 Brandish; prance.
舞廳 A dancing hall; a ball-room.
舞會 A ball; a dancing party.
舞臺 A theatrical stage.
舞弊 Corruptions.
舞劇 A dance-drama.
舞蹈 Dance; gesticulate—for joy.
舞蹈家 Dancer.
舞台效果 Stage-effect.
舞台照明 Stage illumination (lighting).
舞台裝置 Stage-setting; stage-arrangement; *mise en scene*.
舞台監督 Stage management. A stage director (manager).

# 舟 部

舟 zhōu (n.)- A boat; a vessel; a ship; a junk.
舟車 Ships and cars.
舟師 Fleet.

舟山羣島(地) Chusan Islands.

舢 shān 舢板 A sampan; a small boat.

航 hóng (n.)- A boat; a large vessel; a square boat; a scow.
(v.)- Navigate; sail.
航行 Navigate; sail; cruise.

航空 Aerial navigation; flying; aviation.
航船 A passenger boat.
航海 Navigation; seafaring.
航程 The passage (run) of a ship.
航路；航綫 Marine routes; sea routes; fairway; course; line.
航業 Shipping.
航空學 Aeronautics.
航海家 Navigator.
航海圖 A chart.
航空公司 An air company.
航空母艦 An aircraft (aeroplane) carrier; a seaplane carrier.
航空地圖 An aero-map; an aerial chart.
航空信件 Air mail.
航空部長 The Air Minister; the Secretary of State for Air (英).
航空基地 An air base.
航空路線 An air-line (-route); an airway.
航空運輸 Aerial freight service; air transportation.
航空學校 An aviation school.
航海日誌 A log-book; a ship's log.
航海條例 Navigation Act.
航路浮標 A fairway buoy.

航路標識 A beacon.

般 (n.)- A sort; a class; a kind.
(v.)- Transport; withdraw.
bān

舵 (n.)- A helm; a rudder.
舵手 A helmsman; a steersman.
duǒ A coxswain (小舟).
舵把；舵柄 A tiller; a yoke.
舵尾 The lower portion of a rudder.
舵車；舵輪 A steering-wheel.

舶 (n.)- An ocean vessel; a large ship.
bó 舶來品 Imported goods; a foreign-made article.

舷 (n.)- The side of a ship; the bulwarks; the gunwale.
xián 舷門 A gangway.
舷側 A ship's side.
舷燈 A side-light.

船 (n.)- A boat; a junk; a vessel; a ship.
chuán 船夫 Sailors; boatmen; crew.
船主 A ship-owner.
船尾 The stern of a ship.
船身 The hull.
船長 A captain; a master mariner; a master of a ship.
船底 The ship's bottom.
船客 A passenger.
船面 The deck.
船員 Mariners; the crew; a seaman.
船桅 The mast.
船舶；船隻 Ships; vessels.
船票 A passage ticket.
船塢 A dock.
船暈 Seasickness.
船廠 A dockyard.
船艙 A hold; a cabin.
船失事 Shipwreck.
船長室 A captain's cabin.
船舶業 The shipping industry (business).
船塢費 Dockage.
船運貨 Shipment.
船務公司 A shipping company.
船運信件 Ship letter.

艇 (n.)- A small boat; a punt; a skiff.
tǐng 艇長 The coxswain.

艋 (n.)- A small boat; a junk; a long boat.
měng

艘 (n.)- A boat; a junk; a vessel. Auxiliary numeral for counting ships.
sōu

艙 (n.)- The cabins; the hold of a ship.
cāng 艙位 A cabin; the stowage of a vessel; the carrying capacity of a vessel; ship's hold.
艙底 At the bottom of the hold.
艙房 Cabins.
艙面；艙板 The deck.

艣 Same as 櫓，艪.
(n.)- An oar; a scull.
lǔ

艦 (n.)- A war vessel; a man-of-war; a warship.
jiàn 艦長 The commander of a warship; the captain.
艦隊 A fleet; a squadron.
艦旗 An ensign.
艦尾砲 A stern-chaser.
艦長室 The captain's cabin; the cabin.
艦首砲 A bow-gun; a bow-chaser.

艦隊司令 Captain of a squadron.

艦隊根據地 A fleet base.

# 艮 部

**艮** (adj.)- Good; virtuous. Loyal; obedient. Gentle. Beautiful. Skilful.
liáng (adv.)- Very; quite; indeed; really.

艮日 A good day; a lucky (an auspicious) day.
艮友 A good (true) friend.
艮心 Conscience; secret soul.
艮田 Fertile fields.
艮好 Good; successful; favourable; hopeful.
艮言 Wholesome advice.
艮辰；艮時 An auspicious occasion; a luckly hour; a seasonable time.
艮夜 A clear night. Late at night.
艮妻 A virtuous wife.
艮師 A good teacher.
艮馬 A gentle horse; a fine steed.
艮港 A fine harbour.
艮策 An excellent device; a good plan (scheme).
艮善 Good; virtuous.
艮種 A fine breed; a thoroughbred.
艮緣 A happy union; a good match.
艮質 Good quality.
艮醫 A skilful doctor; a good physician.
艮藥 An efficacious (a good) medicine.
艮心內疚 Feel the prick of conscience; feel a guilty (bad) conscience.
艮朋益友 Worthy friends.
艮妻賢母 A good wife and wise mother.
艮好的開端 A good beginning.

**艱** (adj.)- Difficult; hard; distressful. Sorrowful; troublesome.
jiān 艱苦；艱辛 Distress; hardship.
艱險；艱危 Difficult and dangerous.

艱難 Difficult; hard; trouble; distressing.
艱難困苦 Hardships and privations.
艱苦樸素 Hard-working and plain-living.
艱苦卓絕 To overcome untold difficulties with surpassing bravery.

# 色 部

**色** (n.)- Colour; hue. Looks; appearances. Beauty. Lewdness; lust. Kind; sort; quality.
sè 色盲 Colour blindness.

色相 Form and substance; aspect and reality. Sex appeal.
色彩 Colour; lustre.
色情 Sexual passion; carnal desire.
色慾 Concupiscence; lust; sexual desire (appetite).
色調 Tone.
色盲者 A colour-blind person.

色色俱全 Every sort is kept in stock.
色彩富麗 Be full of colours; be colourful.

艷 Same as 豔
yàn (adj.)- Beautiful; captivating; plump; voluptuous.

艷粧 Handsomely dressed.
艷陽 Fine weather.
艷聞 A love-affair; a romance.
艷慕 Admire; desire.
艷麗 Beautiful; glorious; charming.
艷色動人 Beauty excites men; attractive.

# 艸 部

艾 (adj.)- Old; fifty years old.
ài (v.)- Nourish. End; cease; finish.
艾灸 Cauterize with moxa.
艾灸法(醫) Moxibustion.

芋 (n.)- The taro and other edible tubers.
yù 芋頭 The taro; a sweet potato.

芒 (n.)- The awn or beard of grains. The sharp point of
máng grass. A ray of light.
芒果 Mango.
芒硝；硫酸鈉 Glauber's salt; sodium sulphate.

芙 (n.)- The hibiscus.
fú 芙蓉 Hibiscus.
芙蓉面 A pretty face.

芝 (n.)- The name of a fragrant herb; a species of fungus.
zhī 芝宇；芝顏 Your pleasant face.
芝麻 Sesame.
芝麻油 Sesame oil.

芟 (v.)- Mow; cut down.
shān 芟割；芟薙 Cut down; mow grass.
芟草除根 Mow grass and pull up the root.

芥 (n.)- The mustard.
jiè (adj.)- Trifling; petty; small.
芥末；芥粉 Ground mustard.
芥菜 The mustard plant.
芥末瓶 A mustard-pot.
芥藍菜 A coarse vegetable like a cabbage or Brassica.

芬 (n.)- Sweet-smelling.
fēn (adj.)- Numerous.
芬芳 Odoriferous; fragrant.
芬蘭(地) Finland.
芬蘭人 The Finns.
芬蘭語 The Finnish.

芭 (n.)- A fragrant plant. The banana plant; Musa Basjoo.
bā 芭蕉；香蕉 A banana.
芭蕉扇 A palm-leaf fan.

花 (n.)- A flower; a blossom.
huā (adj.)- Variegated; flowered ornamented.
(v.)- Spend; expend; lay out.
花王 A gardener; a florist.
花名 A nickname.
花卉 Flowers; flowering plants.
花布 Coloured cotton cloth.

花生 Peanut; groundnut.
花束 A bunch of flowers; a nosegay; a bouquet.
花芽；花蕾 A flower-bud.
花店 A flower-seller; a florist's shop.
花房 A greenhouse.
花炮；炮竹 Fire-works.
花架 A flower stand.
花盆 A flowerpot.
花粉 Pollen.
花紋 The figures on textures.
花瓶 A flower-vase.
花圈 A wreath; a garland.
花椒(植) Cayenne pepper; red pepper.
花費 Expenditure; spend.
花會 Flower show. A kind of gambling.
花園 A garden.
花貌；花容 Pretty-faced.
花邊 Lace.
花瓣 The petals of a flower; a flower-leaf.
花轎 A bridal sedan-chair.
花籃 A flower basket.
花柳病 Venereal disease; syphilis.
花崗石 Granite.
花露水 Cologne water; florida water; lavender water.
花言巧語 Figures of speech; exaggeration.
花花公子 A beau; a profligate; a debauchee; a playboy.
花花綠綠 Gay; many-coloured.
花容憔悴 A decay of beauty.
花燭之夜 The wedding-night.

芳 fāng (adj.)- Odoriferous; fragrant; sweet-scented; aromatic. Virtuous.
芳名 A good reputation; your honoured name.
芳年 A lady's age.
芳香；芬芳 Odoriferous; fragrant; sweet-smelling; aromatic.
芳氣 Sweet smell.
芳香劑 An aromatic.

芷 zhǐ (n.)- A fragrant bitter plant, used as a carminative; angelica anomala.
芷蕙 Fragrant plants.

芸 yún (n.)- Rue; a fragrant plant; a species of rue. A deep colour.
(adj.)- Deep yellow.
芸夫 A farmer.
芸芸 Numerous; many.
芸芸衆生 The people.

芹 qín (n.)- Celery; parsley.
芹菜 Celery.

芻 chú (n.)- Hay; straw; fodder.
(v.)- Cut grass.
芻言 Rustic speech.
芻豢 Animals fed on grass and grain.
芻蕘之見 My humble opinion.

芽 yá (n.)- A bud; a shoot; a sprout.
芽茶 New tea.
芽菜 Bean sprout.
芽葉 Leaf bud.
芽胞植物 Sporophyte.

苑 yuàn (n.)- A park; a garden.

苒 rǎn 苒苒 Luxuriant; dense.

苔 tái (n.)- Moss; lichen; fungi.
苔菜 A species of algae; an edible sea-weed; laver.

苔蘚植物 Bryophyta.

**苕** (n.) - Name of a plant.
tiáo 苕帚 A broom.
苕苕 Tall; high.

**苗** (n.)- Sprouts; a seedling. Descendant. Name of a tribe.
miáo 苗圃 A nursery.
苗條 Slender and graceful.

苗族 The Miao tribe in China.

**苛** (adj.)- Troublesome; petty; trifling; severe; harsh.
kē 苛刻 Very harsh; cruel.
苛性 Caustic.

苛求 To expect (ask for) too much; critical.

苛責 Rebuke; reprove; call to account.

苛稅 A heavy tax; heavy taxation.

苛酷 Severe; harsh; cruel.

苛性鈉 Caustic soda.

苛性鉀 Caustic potash.

苛捐雜稅 Extortive levies and miscellaneous taxes.

苛政猛於虎 An oppressive government is more brutal than a tiger.

**苞** (n.)- The bract.
(adj.)- Firm; enduring.
bāo 苞苴 Wrap up. Bribes.
苞稂 Bushy grasses.

**苟** (adj.)- Careless.
(adv.)- Roughly; improperly;
gǒu merely; simply.
(conj.)- If; at all.

苟且 Careless; remiss; cursory; rash. Inconsiderate; thoughtless.

苟安 Take improper ease; snatch a moment of ease.

苟活 A careless and dishonourable life.

苟簡 Insignificant.

苟能如此 If it can be thus.

**苣** (n.)- Plants like endive, lettuce, etc.
jù

**若** (pron.)- You.
(v.)- Conform; follow; be like;
ruò be in sympathy with; approve. Suppose.
(conj.)- And; as if; as to; as long as; if.

若干 A certain amount. How much?

若是 If; if so.

若不然 If not so; if otherwise.

**苦** (n.)- Misery; suffering. Bitterness.
kǔ (adj.)- Bitter. Painful. Troublesome; hard; poor; miserable.

苦力 A coolie.

苦工 Hard toil (labour); penal servitude; drudgery.

苦瓜 The bitter gourd.

苦味 A bitter taste; bitterness.

苦命 A miserable lot. Unfortunate; ill-fated.

苦笑 A grin; a bitter (sardonic) smile. Smile bitterly; force a smile.

苦處 A hardship.

苦悶 Agony; anguish; feel suffocating.

苦惱 Trouble; annoyance; suffering; worry.

苦痛 Pain; agony.

苦楚 Distress; torture.

苦學 Study hard.

苦戰 Fight desperately; a hard (severe) fight; a desperate battle.

苦藥 A bitter medicine (pill).

苦難 Calamity; hardship; pain; affliction.

苦樂相共 Share one's joys and sorrows; share one's fortunes.

苧 zhù
苧麻 China grass; ramie.
苧麻衣服 Linen garments.

英 yīng (adj.)- Superior; flourishing; brave; heroic; bright; noble.
英才 Superior talents; a genius.
英寸 Inch.
英文；英語 English; the English language.
英尺 Foot.
英里 Mile.
英明 Clever; shrewd; talented.
英俊 Showing the freshness of youth; good-looking; handsome.
英姿 A gallant figure.
英國(地) England; Great Britain; the United Kingdom of Great Britain and Northern Ireland.
英畝 Acre.
英雄 A hero.
英鎊 A pound (£1); pound sterling.
英文信 A letter in English.
英格蘭(地) England.
英國人 An Englishman; a Britisher; John Bull; the English; the British (總稱).
英屬地 A British dominion; British territory; a Crown Colony.
英聯邦 British Commonwealth (of Nations).
英文文法 English grammar.
英文教師 A teacher of English.
英文報紙 A newspaper in English; an English paper.
英文漢譯 Translation from English into Chinese.
英勇就義 To die with one's head high.
英雄主義 Heroism.
英勇奮鬥 Heroic struggle.
英文學系 The department of English (the English language and literature).
英文學校 An English school.
英文翻譯 An English translation (rendering).
英文讀本 An English reader.
英倫海峽(地) English Channel.
英國文學 English literature.
英語國家 The English-speaking world (countries).
英語學會 An English-speaking society.
英雄無用武之地 To be an able person with no scope for displaying his abilities.

茁 zhuó (n.)- The budding of plants; the growth of animals; manner of grass while sprouting.
茁壯 Vigorous; strong.

茂 mào (adj.)- Luxuriant; flourishing; elegant. Abundant; exuberant. Fine.
茂才 Fine, varied talents.
茂生 Grow luxuriantly.
茂盛 Abundant; luxuriant.
茂密 A rank growth.

范 fàn (n.)- Plants; grass.

茄 qié (n.)- The egg-plant.
茄子 The egg-plant; an egg-apple.

茅 máo (n.)- Reeds; rushes; cough grass.
茅屋；茅舍 A thatched hut; a cottage.
茅柴 Poor fuel.
茅草 Reeds; thatch.

茉 mò (n.)- The white jasmine.
茉莉花 White jasmine flowers.

**苯** běn (n.)- Benzene.

**茗** míng (n.)- The tea plant.
茗坊 A tea house (shop).

**荔** lì (n.)- A kind of rush. The litchi.
荔枝(植) The litchi. Sweet-sop.

**茜** qiàn (n.)- Rubia.
茜草 Rubia; madder.

**茨** cí (n.)- A thorny plant.
(v.)- Accumulate.
茨菰；慈姑(植) Arrowhead.

**茫** máng (adj.)- Vague; vast; expansive.
茫茫 Far and wide; boundless.
茫茫大海 The boundless ocean.

**茭** jiāo (n.)- An aquatic grass.
茭白 An aquatic grass, the stalks of which are edible.

**茲** zī (adj.)- This.
(adv.)- Now; here; still; more; thus.
茲因 Now because of . . .
茲定 It is now determined.
茲者 Now; at present; at this time.
茲查 It appears that; as; since.

**茴** huí (n.)- Fennel; anise.
茴香 Anise; fennel.
茴香酒；茴香精 Anisette.

**茵** yīn (n.)- A mat; a cushion.
茵草 Tender grass.
茵蔯(植) Wormwood.

**茶** chá (n.)- Tea; a tea plant; tea-leaves.
茶市 Tea market.
茶花；山茶花 The camellia.
茶具 A tea service; a tea-set.
茶室 A tea-room (-house).
茶盃 A teacup.
茶商 A tea dealer; a tea merchant.
茶晶 Tea stone; cairngorm stone; smoky quartz.
茶壺 A teapot; a tea-kettle.
茶會 A tea-party.
茶園 A tea-garden; a tea plantation. A theatre.
茶葉 Tea leaves.
茶餅 Tea cake.
茶館；茶店 A tea shop; a tea-stall.
茶錢 Tea-money; a tip.
茶點 A light meal; dainties served with tea.
茶話會 A tea party; an informal gathering.
茶水部 A canteen.
茶褐色 Light brown colour.

**茸** róng (n.)- Luxuriant growth of plants.
茸片 Deer's horn shavings.
茸生 Grow luxuriantly.
茸線；絨線 Flossy silk for embroidery.

**茹** rú (n.)- Madder. Roots which are connected.
(v.)- Eat. Reckon; calculate.
茹葷 Eat meat.

**荆** jīng (n.)- A thorn; a bramble.
荆棘 Thorny; annoying.

**草** cǎo (n.)- Plants; weeds; herbs; grass; straw. A rough copy; original draft. Running-hand writing.
(adj.)- Careless; rough.

(adv.)- Hastily; hurriedly; carelessly.
草人 A man of straw; a scarecrow.
草木 Plants and trees; plants.
草字 The running hand. My humble style.
草地 A meadow; a lawn; pastures.
草色 Dark green; sap-green.
草約 Draft treaty; provisional contract.
草原 A grassy plain; a prairie (北美); a steppe (俄國).
草根 Root of a plant.
草蓆 A straw-mat.
草案 Draft copy of a document; a draft.
草紙 Toilet-paper. Cap paper; coarse paper.
草草 Carelessly; in haste.
草莓 Strawberry.
草棚 A thatched hut; a shed.
草創 Originate; start. A rough beginning.
草帽 Straw hats.
草寫 Scrawl; write in the running hand.
草鞋 Straw sandals.
草稿 A rough draft; a manuscript.
草藥 Medicinal herbs.
草黃色 Straw-coloured.
草本植物 Herbs.
草草了事 Do business carelessly; heedless.

荏 (n.)- A large oily bean.
rěn (adj.)- Gentle; kind-hearted. Soft; weak.
荏弱 Soft and weak.

荒 (n.)- Famine. A wilderness. Frontier tribes.
huāng (adj.)- Wild; uncultivated; unproductive; waste; barren.
(v.)- Be desolate; be laid waste; neglect; put aside.
荒田；荒地 Barren land; waste land; uncultivated land.
荒年 A year of drought; a lean or barren year.
荒村 A deserted village.
荒涼 Devastated; deserted; desolate; bleak.
荒唐 Exaggerated; incoherent; boastful; idle; frivolous; incredible; untrustworthy; unreliable.
荒島 Barren island.
荒野 A wilderness; desert (desolate) land.
荒淫 Dissipated; porfligate.
荒廢 Go to ruin; be devastated; be laid waste.
荒謬 Absurd; irrational.
荒於嬉 Neglected for pleasure.
荒淫之樂 Sensual joys; dissipation.

荳 Same as 豆.
dòu (n.)- Bean; peas; pulse; legume.
荳芽 Bean sprout.
荳豉 Soy.
荳莢 Bean-pod.
荳蔻 Cardamon; nutmeg.
荳腐 Bean-curd.
荳漿 Bean-curd jelly.
荳餅 Bean cake.
荳瓣 The halves of a bean.
荳腐乾 Dried cakes of bean-curd.

荷 (n.)- The lotus or water lily.
hé (v.)- Carry on the shoulder; bear; sustain. Be obliged; be indebted to.
荷包 A purse or pouch.
荷池 A lotus pond.
荷花 The lotus; the water lily.
荷負 Carry; sustain; be adequate to; be competent.
荷葉 Lotus leaves.
荷蘭(地) Holland; the Netherlands.

荷蘭人 A Dutchman; a Hollander.
荷蘭文 Dutch; the Dutch language.
荷蘭水 Soda water or aerated water.
荷爾蒙 Hormone.
荷槍實彈 Carrying loaded rifles—ready for emergencies.

**荼** tú
(n.)- Sow thistle; weed; a bitter edible plant.
荼草 Bitter grass.

**莉** lì
(n.)- The white jasmine.

**莊** zhuāng
(n.)- A countryseat; a country; a hamlet; a village. A farmstead. A depot. A store; a shop.
(adj.)- Sedate; stern; grave; severe; solemn; serious.
莊丁 Farm labourers; country servants.
莊戶 Farmers; peasants.
莊重 Solemn; sublime; grand; impressive.
莊園 A manor.
莊嚴 Stately; solemn; austere; splendid; imposing; severe; rigorous; grave; stern.
莊稼漢 Husbandmen; field labourers.

**莖** jīng
(n.)- A stem; the stalk.
莖針(植) Stem thorn; branch thorn.

**莘** shēn
(n.)- A marshy plant.
莘莘 Numerous.
莘莘學子 A great number of outstanding students.

**荸** bí
荸薺 Water chestnut.

**莠** yǒu
(n.)- Weeds; tares; injurous weed.
(adj.)- Vicious; bad; mischievous; wicked.
莠言自口 Evil words come from the mouth.

**莢** jiá
(n.)- Pods of leguminous plants.

**莧** xiàn
(n.)- Amaranth.
莧菜 Amaranth.

**莩** fú
Same as 殍.
(n.)- The white pellicle lining; the culms of a water-plant. Starved to death.

**莫** mò
(adj.)- Extensive; great.
(adv.)- Do not; have not; must not.
莫大 Greatest; very great.
莫不 Perhaps; probably.
莫怪 Do not take offence.
莫說 Do not say; not to mention.
莫爲 Do not do it.
莫斯科(地) Moscow.
莫明其妙 Very strange; very mysterious and abstruse.
莫逆之交 A bosom (close) friend.

**莽** mǎng
(n.)- A jungle; undergrowth; herbs; shrubs; wooded swamp.
(adj.)- Rough; rustic; reckless; rude; rural.
莽莽 Deep and long, as grass.
莽撞；鹵莽 Rough; rude; reckless.

**菁** qīng
(n.)- The flower of the leek.
菁菁 Luxuriant.

菅 (n.)- The stem of grasses.
jiān

菇 (n.)- A mushroom; a fungus.
gū

菉 (n.)- A kind of grass. A reed.
(adj.)- Green.
lù 菉豆 A kind of lentil—green peas.
菉荳芽 Lentil sprouts used as vegetable.

菊 (n.)- The Chinese aster; the chrysanthemum.
jú 菊花 A chrysanthemum.
菊花茶 Infusion made from dried flowers of the chrysanthemum.

菌 (n.)- The mushroom; a fungus. Mildew; bacteria; germs.
jùn 菌毒 Musbroom-poison.
菌類 The fungi.
菌類學 Mycology.
菌藻植物 Thallophyte.

菓 Same as 果.
(n.)- Fruit; berries; nuts.
guǒ 菓子 Fruit.
菓仁 A kernel.
菓汁 Fruit juice; squash.
菓園 An orchard.
菓實 A fruit.
菓樹 A fruit-tree.
菓醬 Jam.
菓攤 Fruit stalls; fruit stand.
菓子酒 A fruit-wine (-drink).

菘 (n.)- A variety of cabbage.
菘藍 Dyers woad.
sōng

菜 (n.)- Vegetables; greens; edible herbs. Food; dishes.
cài 菜刀 A cook's chopper.
菜油 Cabbage oil; rape-seed oil.
菜肴 A side-dish; food eaten along with rice.
菜場 Market.
菜單 A menu; a bill of fare.
菜園 A vegetable garden; a kitchen-garden.
菜蔬 Vegetables.
菜館 Restaurant.
菜攤 A green stall.

菠 (n.)- Spinach.
菠菜 Spinach; spinage.
bō

菩 (n.)- A fragrant herb; a sacred tree of the Buddhists.
pú 菩提 Salvation; enlightenment; spiritual awakening.
菩薩；菩提薩埵 A Bodhisattva; gods.
菩提樹 A linden tree; a bo-tree; a lime tree.

華 (n.)- China. Glory. Flower; beauty; powder; essence.
huá (adj.)- Flowery; showy; variegated; splendid; elegant; gay; brilliant; beautiful; pompous. Glory; bright; charming; shining.
華山(地) Hwashan, the "Sacred Mountain of the West."
華沙(地) Warsaw.
華美；華麗 Showy; gorgeous; gaudy; pompous; beautiful; splendid; grand.
華夏；諸夏 China.
華商 Chinese merchants.
華貴 Honourable.
華僑 Chinese emigrants; Chinese overseas.

華盛頓(地) Washington.
華爾街(地) Wall Street, the American financial centre.
華爾滋舞 Waltz.
華而不實 Flashy (and) without substance.
華氏寒暑表 A Fahrenheit thermometer (F. or Fahr.).

菱 líng (n.)- A water chestnut; a water caltrop.
菱角(植) The water chestnuts; water caltrop.
菱形 A lozenge; a rhomb. Diamond-shaped; rhombic; lozenged.
菱粉 Flour made from the water chestnuts.
菱花鏡 A toilet looking-glass; a mirror.
菱鐵鑛 Siderite; spathic iron.
菱形六面體(鑛) Rhombohedron.

菲 fēi (n.)- A kind of plant having a turnip-like root.
菲林 Film.
菲律賓人 A Filipino ( 男 ); a Filipina ( 女 ); the Philippines (總稱).
菲律賓羣島(地) The Philippine Islands; the Philippines.

菴 ān (n.)- A hut; a cottage. A nunnery; a monastery; an abbey; a small temple.
菴堂 A Buddhist shrine; a nunnery.

菸 yān (n.)- Tobacco-plant.
菸鹼；尼古丁 Nicotine.

菽 shū (n.)- Beans; peas; pulse; leguminous plants.
菽乳 Bean-curd.
菽麥 Bean and wheat.

萃 cuì (n.)- A crowd; a herd; a collection.
(adj.)- Grassy; thick.
(v.)- Collect together; assemble.
萃集 Collect together.
萃於一堂 Brought together in one hall.

蓖 bì (n.)- A raincoat. The castor-oil plant.
蓖蔴(植) The castor-oil plant.
蓖蔴油 Castor oil.

萌 méng (n.)- A bud; a shoot; a sprout; the budding of plants.
(v.)- Bud; shoot forth; germinate; sprout.
萌生 Numerous; like sprouting grasses.
萌芽 Bud; germinate; sprout.
萌芽時代 Initial stages; period of growth and development.

萍 píng (n.)- Duckweed; floating plants.
萍浮 Drifting about; wandering.
萍水相逢 An unexpected meeting of friends abroad.

萎 wěi (v.)- Wither; fade; droop away.
萎謝 Fading; limp.
萎縮 Wither away; decline; shrink; atrophy.
萎黃病(醫) Chlorosis.

萬 wàn (n.)- Ten thousand. A myriad; a large number.
(adj.)- Ten thousand. All; many; numerous.
萬一 One chance in a thousand; ten thousand to one. If by any chance; should there be.
萬古 Perpetuity; for ever.
萬有；萬物 All things; the creation.

萬事 Everything; all things.
萬卷 A ten thousand volumes; many books.
萬倍 Ten thousand-fold.
萬般 All; every; various.
萬能 Almighty; omnipotent.
萬歲 A term for the emperor; cheers. Hip, hip, hurrah! "Long live . . .".
萬萬 Ten thousand of myriads; innumerable.
萬難 Many obstacles; all difficulties.
萬年青(植) Evergreen. Rhodea japonica.
萬花筒 A kaleidoscope.
萬不得已 If you absolutely cannot help it; cannot on any account.
萬分之一 10,000 to one.
萬有之主 Lord of all.
萬里長城 The Great Wall.
萬衆一心 All of one heart.
萬萬不可 Must not on any account; under no circumstances.
萬國發音符號 International phonetic symbol.
萬國郵政同盟 The Universal Postal Union.
萬國標準時間 The universal standard time.

萱 xuān
(n.)- Day lily.
萱草 Day lily.

落 luò
(n.)- A village; a hamlet; a gathering place.
(adj.)- Fallen; descending.
(v.)- Fall; drop; descend; set, as the sun; decline; fail.
落下 Fall down; descend; drop down; come (go) down.
落日 The setting sun.
落地 Fall to the ground. Be born.
落成 The completion of a building.
落車 Descend from a car.
落空 The effort has failed; come to nought.
落後 Fall behind; fall into the rear; lag behind.
落第 Fail in an examination; get plucked.
落筆 Put pen to paper; write.
落旗；下旗 Haul down the flag.
落葉 Fallen leaves.
落網 Be caught in a net; fall into the clutches (meshes) of the law.
落價 The price has fallen.
落選 Defeat in an election; failure.
落成禮 An inauguration ceremony; the formal opening of a building.
落花生(植) A peanut; a ground-nut.
落入陷井 To fall into a trap.
落花流水 Flower falling and streams flowing; all scattered.
落英繽紛 Falling blossoms flying about like snow-flakes.
落後地區 The backward territory.
落落大方 Generous; magnanimous.

葆 bǎo
(n.)- Luxuriant foliage.
(v.)- Nature. Conceal.

葉 yè
(n.)- A leaf. A page; a sheet. A period.
葉片；葉身 A blade; a lamina.
葉芽 The leaf-bud.
葉茂 Leafy; tufted.
葉落 Leafless; bare; naked.
葉綠素 Chlorophyll; leaf-green.
葉落歸根 The leaves fall and return to the root—everything returns to its original.

著 zhù
Same as 着.
(n.)- A composition; a literary production.

(adj.)- Clear; conspicuous; famous; well-known; prominent; bright; obvious.
(v.)- Edit; write; display; manifest; compose. Wear; put on; fix; dress; have on. Play, as at chess; touch; attach to; stick to.
著名 Famous. Become known(famous).
著者 A writer; an author.
著述；著作；著書 Write; edit.
著棋 Play at chess.
著作家 An author; a writer.
著作權 Copyright.
著眼點 The point aimed at.
著著進步 Make steady progress.

葡 pú (n.)- The vine; a grape.
葡萄(植) Grapes.
葡萄牙(地) Portugal.
葡萄酒 Grape wine; red wine; claret ( 紅 ); white wine; sherry; hock ( 白 ).
葡萄乾 Raisins.
葡萄園 A vine yard; a vine-garden; a grapery.
葡萄糖(化) Glucose; grape sugar.
葡萄牙人 Portuguese.
葡萄狀球菌 Staphylococcus.

董 dǒng (n.)- Direct; govern. Correct.
董事 A manager; a director.
董事長 Chairman of directors.
董事會 Committee meeting; board of directors.

葦 wěi (n.)- Reed; rush.
葦草(植) Reed.
葦蓆 Reed mats; mat of rushes.

胡 hú (n.)- The bottle gourd.
胡蘆(植) A gourd; a calabash; a bottle-gourd; a cucurbit.
胡蘆科(植) Cucurbitaceae.

葬 zàng (v.)- Bury; inter; consign to the grave.
葬地 Burial ground.
葬禮 A burial service; funeral rites (ceremonies).

葱 cōng (n.)- An onion; a stone-leek.
葱花 Chopped onions.
葱頭 Onions.

葵 kuí (n.)- The sunflower.
葵花 The holly-hock.
葵扇 Palm-leaf fan.

葷 hūn (n.)- Meat diet; flesh food.
葷素 Meat food and vegetable food.
葷菜 A meat diet; animal food.

葺 qì (n.)- Reeds; thatches.
(v.)- Repair; mend. Thatch; roof with straw.
葺補；修葺 Mend; repair.

蒂 dì Same as 蔕
(n.)- The stem or stalk of a flower; a base; a peduncle or footstalk of a flower or fruit.
蒂固 A firm support.

蒙 méng (adj.)- Young. Ignorant; stupid; dull. Obscure.
(v.)- Deceive; cajole; humbug; cheat. Cover; conceal; screen; hide. Receive; get; suffer; sustain.
蒙上 Deceive superiors.
蒙古(地) Mongolia.
蒙昧 Dull; stupid; ignorant; unenlightened.
蒙蔽 Hidden; obscured; screen.
蒙眼 To blind-fold.
蒙太奇 Montage; putting together; make-up.

蒙古人 A Mongol; a Mongolian.
蒙汗藥 Chloroform.
蒙昧無知 Stupid and ignorant.

**蒜** suàn (n.)- Garlic.
蒜頭(植) Garlic bulbs.

**蒲** pú (n.)- A kind of rush from which mats, bags, etc., are made.
蒲席；蒲墊 A mattress; rush mats for kneeling on.
蒲扇 A rush-leaf fan.
蒲公英(植) The dandelion.

**蒸** zhēng (n.)- Steam; vapour.
(v.)- Steam; cook by steam.
蒸氣 Vapour; steam.
蒸發 Evaporation. Evaporate.
蒸溜 Distillation. Distil; extract by heat.
蒸飯 Steam rice.
蒸糕 Steamed cake.
蒸鍋 A steam-kettle.
蒸籠 A basket or sieve for steaming food.
蒸汽機 Steam engine.
蒸氣浴 Steam-bath; vapour-bath.
蒸溜水 Distilled water.
蒸溜器 A still; an alembic.
蒸汽鍋爐 A steam boiler.
蒸蒸日上 Advance very quickly.

**蒞** lì Same as 莅, 涖.
(v.)- Arrive at; attend; go to.
蒞任 Come into office; accept office.
蒞臨 Be present.

**蓖** bì (n.)- The castor-oil plant.
蓖麻油；草蓖油 Castor oil.

**蒼** cāng (adj.)- Deep-green; azure; blue; the azure of the sky. Grey; hoary.
蒼天 The blue sky.
蒼生 The people.
蒼白 Pale; pallid; livid.
蒼老 An old person; a hoary old man.
蒼茫 A vast expanse.
蒼翠 Verdant green.
蒼蠅 Flies.

**蓄** xù (v.)- Deposit; save up; lay up in store; accumulate. Bring up; foster.
蓄養 Foster; rear; bring up.
蓄積 Accumulate; lay by; hoard; store up.
蓄水池 Reservoir.
蓄音器 A phonograph; a gramophone.
蓄電池 An accumulator; a storage battery.
蓄電器 An electric condenser.
蓄熱爐 Regenerator.

**蓆** xí Same as 席.
(n.)- A mat; a straw-mat.
蓆子 Matting; mats.

**蓋** gài Same as 葢.
(n.)- A covering; a lid; a roof; a top. An umbrella.
(v.)- Roof; cover. Hide; screen. Overtop. Seal.
蓋上；蓋起 Put on the cover.
蓋印；蓋戳 Affix a seal; stamp.
蓋屋 Erect a building; build a house.
蓋造 Construct; build.
蓋被 A coverlet. Cover with a quilt.
蓋印支票 Marked cheque.

**蓓** bèi 蓓蕾 Flower buds.

蓬 (n.)- A species of raspberry growing among hemp.
péng (adj.)- Overgrown; tangled.
蓬鬆 Dishevelled.
蓬萊仙境 Fairy-land.

蓮 (n.)- The lotus; the water lily.
蓮子 Lotus seeds.
lián 蓮花 The lotus flower or water lily.
蓮塘 A lotus pond.
蓮葉 Lotus leaves.
蓮蓬；蓮房 The seed-case of the lotus.
蓮藕 A lotus-root.

蔻 (n.)- Cardamom seeds.
蔻仁 Nutmeg.
kòu

蔑 (v.)- Despise; disdain. Disregard; neglect.
miè 蔑視 Despise; make little of; hold in contempt; slight.

蔓 (n.)- A creeping plant.
(adj.)- Spreading; climbing.
màn (v.)- Creep, as a plant; tangle; spread out.
蔓延 Be wide spread; diffusive; creep.

蔗 (n.)- The sugar cane.
蔗渣 Cane residue; *bagasse*.
zhè 蔗汁 Sugar-cane juice.
蔗水 Diluted sugar-cane juice.
蔗糖 Cane-sugar.

蔚 (adj.)- Luxuriant; prosperous.
蔚藍天 A clear, deep blue sky.
wèi

蔟 (n.)- A twisted bunch of straw on which silk-worms spin.
cù 蔟新 Bland-new.

蔭 (n.)- The shade of a tree; a shadow; a covert.
yìn 蔭處 A shady place; in the shade; under the shade of a tree.

蔬 (n.)- Vegetables; greens.
蔬菜 Vegetables.
shū

蔽 (v.)- Keep out of view; conceal; darken; shelter; screen;
bì hide; shade; cover up.
蔽目 Shade the eyes; blind fold.
蔽塞 Screen; close up; conceal.
蔽風雨 Shelter from the wind and rain.

蕁 (n.)- Nettle.
蕁麻(植) Nettle; Urtica thun-
qián bergiana.
蕁麻症(醫) Nettle-rash; urticaria.

蕃 (adj.)- Luxuriant; flourishing; numerous; plentiful; plenty.
fán (v.)- Increase; multiply; breed; produce.
蕃盛 Abundant; plentiful.
蕃庶 A numerous population.
蕃國；藩邦 The feudatory states.

蕉 (n.)- The plantain or banana.
蕉子；芭蕉(植) Plantains or
jiāo bananas.
蕉扇 A palm-leaf fan.

蕊 Same as 蘂.
(n.)- Stamens or pistils of
ruǐ a flower. Buds; unopened flowers.
蕊心 Stamens and pistils.

蕎 (n.)- Buck wheat.
蕎麥 Buck wheat.
qiáo 蕎麥麵 Buckwheat vermicelli.

蕓 (n.)- Rape.
蕓薹；油菜(植) Rape.
yún

蕙 (n.)- A kind of orchid.
蕙蘭 A fragrant species of orchid, having many flowers on one stalk.
huì

蕨 (n.)- Bracken.
蕨粉 Starch prepared from the roots of the bracken, used as food.
jué

蕩 (adj.)- Unsettled; reckless; licentious; extensive.
dàng (v.)- Subvert; upset; overturn; wash. Squander; waste; consume. Move; shift.
蕩子 A profligate; a prodigal; a scapegrace; a rake; a rakehell.
蕩婦 A whore; a harlot; a dissolute woman.
蕩寇 Destroy rebels.
蕩產 Squander one's property; dilapidated fortune.
蕩漾 The rippling of water.
蕩槳 Paddle.

蕪 (adj.)- Confused; mixed up; weeded; neglected; waste.
wú 蕪湖(地) Wuhu, Anhwei.
蕪菁 Turnip.

薄 (adj.)- Thin; weak; poor; dilute. Slight.
bó (v.)- Reach; extend; reduce; diminish. Treat coldly.
薄片 Slice.
薄皮 A thin skin; a film.
薄呢 Serge.
薄弱 Weak; feeble; fragile; frail; sickly; ailing.
薄荷(植) Peppermint.
薄情；薄倖 Feelingless; heartlessness; ungrategful; no sense of gratitude; destitute of right feeling; jilt.
薄產 A small estate.
薄視 Slight; look down upon; despise.
薄膜 A membrane.
薄暮 The evening; twilight; towards dark; near sunset.
薄如紙 As thin as paper.
薄荷油 Peppermint oil.
薄荷腦 Menthol.
薄情之人 A cold-hearted person.

蕾 (n.)- A flower bud.
lěi

薇 (n.)- The name of a fern.
wēi

薑 (n.)- Ginger.
薑水 Ginger pop (ale, beer).
jiāng 薑末 Ground ginger.
薑黃 Turmeric.
薑黃紙(化) Turmeric-paper.

薔 (n.)- A rose; a thorny plant.
薔薇(植) Rose.
qiáng 薔薇花 The Chinese rose; the rose of China.
薔薇科(植) Rosaceae.
薔薇疹；紅疹(醫) Roseola; rose-rash.

薦 (n.)- The feeding grass. A straw mat.
jiàn (v.)- Introduce; recommend.

Present; offer; honour; worship.
(adv.)- Repeatedly.
薦人 Recommend a person.
薦任 Recommend for an appointment.
薦拔 Raise to dignity.
薦書；薦信 A letter of introduction (recommendation).

薪 (n.)- Fuel; firewood. Salary; payment.
xīn 薪水；薪金 Salary; earning.
薪水階級 Salariat.
薪金生活者 Wage-earner; wage-worker.

蕭 (n.)- A specie of artemisia.
(adj.)- Lonely; desolate. Troublesome; annoying.
xiāo 蕭條 Desolate; solitary; lonely; gloomy; dreary.
蕭瑟 Bleak; dreary.
蕭蕭 The neighing of the horses. Whistling of strong winds.

薯 Same as 藷.
(n.)- Tubers; potatoes.
shǔ 薯仔；荷蘭薯 Irish potato; white potato.
薯粉 Sweet-potato flour.
薯蕷；山藥(植) The Chinese yam.

薰 (adj.)- Warm; mild.
(v.)- Perfume; embalm; burn; cauterize; becloud.
xūn 薰沐 Bathe; disinfect.
薰陶 Training; education. Cultivate; culture.
薰香滿室 A house is full of fragrance.

藉 (n.)- A mat; a soft pad; a cushion.
jiè (adj.)- Confused; disordered.
藉口；藉端 A good cause for complaint; a pretext. Take advantage of.
藉此 Hereby; by means of.
藉詞 On the plea; give as an excuse.
藉故推託 Make excuse under some pretext.

藍 (n.)- The indigo plant; blue colour.
lán (adj.)- Blue.
藍布 Blue cloth.
藍色 A blue colour; blue.
藍青 Indigo blue.
藍菜(植) Cabbage.
藍圖 A blue-print.
藍靛 Indigo.
藍皮書 Blue book.
藍花荳 Broad beans.
藍銅鑛(鑛) Azurite.
藍寶石 The sapphire.

藏 (n.)- A storehouse; a warehouse; a receptacle; a storage. Wealth.
cáng (v.)- Hide away; conceal; harbour. Store; accumulate; hoard.
藏身 Hide oneself.
藏庫；藏府 An armoury; a government store house.
藏置 Put up.
藏積 Reserve.
藏身之地 A hiding-place.
藏書目錄 A library catalogue.
藏置貨物 Goods in deposit.

藐 (adj.)- Petty; contemptible; slight; small; minute.
miǎo (v.)- Slight; despise; disregard; treat with contempt; disdain; look down.
藐小 Small; petty; insignificant; trifling.
藐視 Treat with contempt; slight; set at

naught; disdain; treat lightly; look down upon; despise.

藐視一切 Despise everything.

**藕** ǒu (n.)- The lotus root; the root stock of the lotus.
藕粉 Lotus root starch; arrowroot.

藕斷絲連 The lotus-root breaks, but the fibres hold together—the affection remains.

**藝** yì (n.)- Art. Ability; accomplishment; skill.
(adj.)- Skilled; expert.
(v.)- Plant. Discriminate.

藝人 A public (professional) performer (entertainer); an artist.
藝術 Art; fine arts.
藝徒 An apprentice.
藝術品 A work of art; an object of art.
藝術界 The world of art.
藝術家 An artist.
藝徒學校 School for apprentices.

**藤** téng (n.)- Creeping plants; climbing plants; vines; wistaria; rattan.
藤蓆 Rattan mat.
藤條 Split rattans.

藤絲 Rattan shavings.
藤椅 A cane chair.

**藥** yào Same as 葯.
(n.)- Medicinal herbs; drugs; medicines; a remedy; a tonic (補藥); a specific (特效藥).
(v.)- Administer medicine. Remedy; cure; heal.

藥丸 Pills.
藥片 Medical tablets.
藥水 Liquid medicine; a lotion.
藥方 A prescription; a medical recipe.
藥材；藥料 Drugs; medicines; medical stuffs.
藥性 The nature of a drug.
藥物 Medicines.
藥味 Taste of medicine.
藥房 A dispensary; a drug store; a pharmacy.
藥品 Medicines; drugs; chemicals.
藥瓶 A phial; a medicine bottle.
藥草 Medicinal herbs.
藥膏 Ointment.
藥箱 A medicine-chest.
藥物學 Pharmacology; the science of medicines.
藥劑師 A pharmacist.
藥劑學 Pharmacy.
藥用肥皂 Medicated soap.
藥物治療 Pharmacotherapy; medical treatment.
藥科學校 A school of pharmacy; a pharmaceutical school.
藥學博士 A doctor of pharmacology.

**藩** fān (n.)- A fence; a hedge. A boundary; the frontier; an enclosure. A colony; a settlement.
藩邦；藩屬 A feudatory state.

藩域 The frontier.
藩牆 Inclosing wall.
藩籬 A bamboo fence; a barrier.

**藹** ǎi (adj.)- Friendly.
藹然可親 Friendly; lovable.

**藻** zǎo (n.)- Several kinds of aquatic grasses; aquatic plants; an alga; a water weed.
(adj.)- Elegant; splendid; graceful.

藻井 A ceiling.
藻飾 Embellished; decorated.
藻類(植) Algae.

**藿** huò (n.)- Leaves of pulse or beans.
藿香(植) Betony.

**蘆** lú (n.)- Common reed.
蘆柴 Rush faggots.
蘆根 Reed roots.
蘆蓆 Rush mats.
蘆葦(植) Rushes; reeds.

**蘇** sū (v.)- Revive; come to life again; recover; cheer up; brighten. Gather grass.
蘇丹(地) Sudan.
蘇打(化) Soda.
蘇生 Revive; come to life again; rise from the dead.
蘇州(地) Soochow.
蘇息 Rest; recuperate.
蘇葉；紫蘇 Perilla nankinensis.
蘇聯(地) The Soviet Union.
蘇醒 Revive; awaken.
蘇打水 Soda-water.
蘇格蘭(地) Scotland.
蘇維埃 Soviet.
蘇門答臘(地) Sumatra.
蘇彝士運河(地) The Suez Canal.
蘇維埃社會主義共和國聯盟(地) The Union of Soviet Socialist Republics (U.S.S.R.)

**蘊** yùn (adj.)- Mysterious; secret.
(v.)- Collect; heap; store up; bind together; accumulate; hoard.
蘊藏 Hoard; collect.
蘊釀 Brew; foment; bring on; stir up.
蘊積如山 Piled up as a hill.

**蘋** píng (n.)- Duckweeds; floating plants.
蘋果(植) The apple.
蘋果汁 Apple juice.
蘋果酒 Cider.

**蘚** xiǎn (n.)- Moss; lichen.
蘚類(植) The musci; mosses.

**蘭** lán (n.)- An orchid.
蘭州(地) Lanchow.
蘭花(植) Orchids.
蘭質蕙心 A refined nature.

**蘸** zhàn (v.)- Dip into; plunge; sink in.
蘸筆 Dip a brush in ink.
蘸濕 Soak in.

**蘿** luó (n.)- Ivy; vine; creeping plant.
蘿蔔(植) The garden radish.

# 虍 部

**虎** hǔ (n.)- A tiger; a tigress.
虎口 A tiger's mouth. A place of danger.
虎穴 Tiger's den.
虎政 Tyrannical government.
虎將 A brave general.
虎嘯 A tiger's roar.
虎鬚 Tiger's whiskers.
虎列拉(醫) Cholera.
虎睛石；虎眼石(鑽) Tiger-eye.
虎穴龍潭 Tiger's den and dragon's lair—a very dangerous place.
虎狼之性 A savage, wolfish disposition.

**虐** nüè (adj.)- Harsh; fierce; tyrannical; barbarous; cruel; severe; despotic; oppressive.
(v.)- Oppress; maltreat; treat with cruelty.

虐待 Maltreat; give hard measure; bear a heavy hand on; illtreat; treat with cruelty.

虐政 Oppressive government; tyranny; maladministration.

**虔** qián (v.)- Act with reverence; be respectful.
(adj.)- Devout; sincere; pious. 虔心 With pious wishes; reverently.

虔求；虔禱 Pray devoutly.

虔誠 Sincere and devout.

**處** chǔ (n.)- A place; a state; a region; a location; position; condition. A department; an office.
(v.)- Be at; rest; live; be in a state of; dwell; stay. Deal; treat; place; set; put; meet out; manage; dispose of.

處女；處子 A maiden; a virgin.

處分 Official punishment. Manage; deal with; dispose of.

處方 Write a prescription; prescribe.

處死 Punish with death.

處刑(法) Condemn; sentence; be punished.

處身 Conduct oneself; carry oneself.

處家 Manage the affairs of a family.

處理 Treat; get along; manipulate; bear through; transact.

處處 Everywhere; in all places; here and there.

處罰 Punish according to law; impose (inflict) a punishment.

處女航 A maiden voyage.

處女膜 The hymen; the maiden-head.

處理能力 Capacity of management.

**虛** xū (n.)- Vacancy; hollow; emptiness.
(adj.)- Empty; deceptive; fallacious; false; unreal; unsubstantial; untrue; airy; visionary. Humble; modest. Weak.

虛心 An empty mind; a humble mind.

虛字 A grammatical particle.

虛度 Fool away; idle away time; pass the years in vain.

虛弱 Weak; infirm. (醫) Adynamia.

虛報 A false report; a fabrication.

虛想 Imagination; fancy; conceive; dream.

虛僞 False; sham; unreal.

虛榮 Vanity; vainglory; display.

虛數(算) Imaginary number.

虛線 Imaginary line; dotted line.

虛驚 A false terror; a false alarm.

虛榮心 Vanity; love of display; petty pride.

虛度光陰 Waste time.

虛張聲勢 A false show of power (influence). Bluff; make a show of power; make a display.

虛無縹緲 Utterly visionary; no reality whatever; utterly void.

**虜** lǔ (n.)- A prisoner of war; a slave; a captive.
(v.)- Seize; capture prisoners. 虜掠 Capture; take captive; plunder; seize.

**虞** yú (adj.)- Prepared; ready; vigilant. Delightful; joyful; pleasant.
(v.)- Expect; be anxious about. Reckon; extimate; provide against.

虞人 A forester.

虞候 Attendants.

虞美人(植) Corn poppy.

**號** hào (n.)- A sign; a mark; a signal; a designation. A title; a name; an appellation; a denomination. A shop; a firm; a concern. A number.
(v.)- Name; style; call; shout; roar. Cry; weep; bewail.

號叫 Roar; yell.
號外 An extra; a special issue.
號召 Summon; command.
號角 A trumpet or horn.
號呼 Shout out; cry out with a loud voice.
號稱 Call; name; designation; is said to be.
號數 A register number.
號碼 A number; a mark; a sign.
號令全國 Hold sway over the whole land.

**虧** kuī (n.)- Failure. Deficiency; diminution; loss. Defect. The waning of the moon.
(adj.)- Waning; decreasing; declining.
(v.)- Injure. Fail; lose; wane.
(prep.)- Owing to; in consequence of.

虧心 Discreditable; ungrateful; apprehension; a bad conscience.
虧本 Loss of capital. Fail in business.
虧空 Deficit; bankruptcy; a total failure.
虧得；幸虧 Fortunately.
虧損 Injure; injury.
虧心事 Things which conscience condemns; a discreditable affair.
虧損不少 Lose a great deal.
虧損淨數 Balance; net loss.
虧空公款 To embezzle or misappropriate funds.

# 虫 部

**虯** qiú Same as 虬.
(n.)- A young dragon.

**虱** shī Same as 蝨.
(n.)- Lice; bugs; fleas.
虱子 A louse.
虱卵 Nit.

**虹** hóng (n.)- Rainbow.
虹霓 The rainbow.
虹吸管(物) Siphon.

**虻** méng Same as 蝱.
(n.)- A horse-fly; a gad-fly.

**蚊** wén (n.)- Mosquitoes; gnats.
蚊子；蚊蟲 A mosquito.
蚊咬 Be bitten (stung) by a mosquito.

蚊叫 Gnats buzz.
蚊香 Mosquito incense.
蚊帳 A mosquito net (curtain).
蚊式艇；魚雷艇 Mosquito boat.

**蚌** bàng (n.)- Mussels; oysters.
蚌珠 A pearl from the oyster.
蚌蛤(動) A clam or mussel.

**蚓** yǐn (n.)- The earthworm.

蚜 yá (n.)- A louse.
蚜蟲 The antcow; the aphis.

蚤 zǎo (n.)- The flea.
(adj.)- Early.

蚧 jiè (n.)- A redspotted lizard.

蚪 dǒu (n.)- A tadpole.

蚯 qiū (n.)- The earthworm.
蚯蚓 The earthworm.

蚱 zhà (n.)- A species of locust.
蚱蜢 A grasshopper.

蛀 zhù (n.)- Insects which eat books or clothes.
(v.)- Eat or bore.
蛀牙 A decayed tooth.
蛀蟲 A bristetail; a moth.
蛀爛 Spoiled by insects; moth-eaten.
蛀蟲丸 Moth-ball.
蛀米大蟲 A useless person.

蛆 qū (n.)- Maggots.
蛆蟲 A maggot; a grub.

蛇 shé (n.)- A snake; a serpent.
(adj.)- Serpentine; snaky.
蛇皮 Snake's skin.
蛇形 Snaky; serpentine.
蛇蛻 The slough (cast skin) of a snake.
蛇類 Ophidia.
蛇頭瘡(醫) Whitlow.

蛋 dàn (n.)- The egg.
(adj.)- Oval-shaped.
蛋白；蛋清 The white of an egg; albumen.
蛋形 Egg-shaped.
蛋黃 The yolk of an egg.
蛋殼 An egg-shell.
蛋白石(礦) Opal.
蛋白質 Albumin; protein.
蛋白質食物 Albuminous food.

蛔 huí 蛔蟲 A round worm; an ascarid; an intestinal worm.

蛙 wā (n.)- A frog; a bull frog.
蛙泳 The breast stroke.
蛙鳴 The frog croaks.

蛛 zhū (n.)- The spider.
蛛絲 A spider's thread.
蛛網 The spider's web; a cobweb.

蛟 jiāo (n.)- A scaly dragon.
蛟龍 The flood-dragon—supposed to be the cause of landslides.
蛟龍得水 The flood-dragon gets to water—getting a good opportunity.

蛤 gé (n.)- An edible clam.
蛤蚧 A red spotted lizard.
蛤蚌 Oysters.
蛤蜊 A clam.
蛤蟆 The frog.

蛭 zhì (n.)- The leech.
蛭類 The Hirudinea.

**蛹** yǒng
(n.)- A pupa; a chrysalis.

**蛺** jiá
(n.)- A butterfly.
蛺蝶 A butterfly.

**蛻** tuì
(v.)- Slough off the skin; cast off skin.
蛻殼 Cast-off skins.
蛻變(物) Disintegration.

**蛾** é
(n.)- A moth.
蛾眉 Pretty (crescent) eyebrows.
蛾眉月；新月 The crescent moon.

**蜀** shǔ
(n.)- A caterpillar. Szechuan.
(adj.)- Single; isolated.

**蜂** fēng
(n.)- A bee (蜜蜂); wasp (黃蜂); a hornet (馬蜂).
蜂王 The queen bee.
蜂房；蜂巢 A beehive; a hornet's nest; the honey comb.
蜂蜜 Honey.
蜂囊 Honey-bag.
蜂擁而上 Press forward in swarms.

**蜃** shèn
(n.)- A huge clam. A sacrificial vessel. A marine monster.

**蜆** xiǎn
(n.)- Basket mussel; clams.
蜆肉 Mussels or clams without shells; clam-flesh.
蜆蚧 Raw clams seasoned.

**蜇** zhé
(n.)- The jelly-fish.

**蜈** wú
(n.)- A centipede.
蜈蚣；百足 A centipede.

**蜉** fú
(n.)- May-fly.
蜉蝣 May-fly.

**蜘** zhī
(n.)- A spider.
蜘蛛 The spider.
蜘蛛絲 A spider's thread.
蜘蛛網 A spider's web.
蜘蛛類(動) Arachnida.
蜘蛛結網 A spider spins its web.

**蜜** mì
(n.)- Honey.
(adj.)- Sweet.
蜜月 The honey-moon.
蜜柑；蜜橘 Sweet oranges from Swatow.
蜜棗 Honey dates.
蜜蜂 A honeybee; a bee.
蜜語 Sweet talk; honeyed words.
蜜糖 Honey.
蜜餞；蜜煎 Confections; sweetmeats; preserves.
蜜月旅行 A honey-moon trip.

**蜢** měng
(n.)- A small grasshopper or locust.

**蜣** qiāng
(n.)- Dung beetle.
蜣螂 The dung beetle.

**蜥** xī
(n.)- A species of lizard.
蜥蜴 The elegant skink.

**蜻** qīng
(n.)- A dragon-fly.
蜻蜓 A dragon-fly.

**蜿** wǎn (v.)- Crawl; creep.
蜿蜒 Winding; meandering; the wriggling motion of a snake.

**蝌** kē (n.)- The tadople.
蝌蚪 The tadpole.

**蝎** xiē (n.)- A grub which bores into trees and destroys them; lizard.
蝎虎 Gecko.

**蝕** shí (n.)- Eclipse. Erosion.
(v.)- Eat away; be moth-eaten or worm-eaten.
蝕本 Lose capital; fail in business.
蝕損 Damage; injure; diminish by encroachment.

**蝗** huáng (n.)- The locust.
蝗蟲 Chinese migratory locust.

**蝙** biān (n.)- A bat.
蝙蝠 A bat.

**蝟** wèi (n.)- The hedgehog.
蝟鼠 The hedgehog.
蝟縮 Curl up as a hedgehog.

**蝠** fú (n.)- The bat.

**蝦** xiā (n.)- A shrimp; a lobster; a prawn.
蝦仁 The flesh of shrimps (prawns).
蝦米 Dried shrimps without shells.
蝦蟆 A toad; a frog.
蝦醬 Shrimp paste.
蝦膏 Roe.

**蝴** hú (n.)- A butterfly.
蝴蝶 A butterfly.
蝴蝶結 A rosette; a bow-tie.

**蝶** dié (n.)- A butterfly.
蝶鉸關節；樞紐關節(解) Hinge joint.

**蝸** wō (n.)- A snail.
蝸牛 A snail.
蝸居；蝸舍 My humble abode; my narrow residence.

**螂** láng (n.)- A mantis; a praying-mantis; a dung-beetle.

**蟛** péng (n.)- A crab.
蟛蟹 The swimming crab; the hairy-clawed crab.

**融** róng (n.)- Vapour rising up.
(adj.)- Intelligent; clear; bright.
(v.)- Melt; dissolve; thaw. Compromise. Harmonize.
融化 Dissolve; melt.
融洽 Come to mutual understanding; be on good terms.
融解 Fusion. Melt by heat; fuse.
融融 Happy; joyful; cheerful.
融解熱 Heat of fusion.
融解點 Melting point.
融通票據 An accommodation paper (bill, note); a negotiable note.
融會貫通 Well versed in; understand thoroughly.

**螞** mǎ (n.)- A leech. An ant.
螞蟥 A leech.
螞蟻 Ants.

**螟** (n.)- A small insect which destroys rice plant; a grain insect.
míng
螟蟲 A larva of a pearl moth.

**螢** (n.)- A glowworm; a firefly; luminous insect of any kind.
yíng
螢石(礦) Fluor-spar; fluorite.
螢光(物) The glow of a firefly. Fluorescence.
螢火蟲 A firefly; a glowworm.
螢光燈 A fluorescent lamp.
螢光鏡 Fluoroscope.
螢光體 A fluorescent body.

**螯** (n.)- The nippers, claws, or pincers of a crab.
máo

**螳** (n.)- A mantis.
táng
螳螂 A mantis; a praying-mantis.

**螺** (n.)- A spiral univalve shell; a conch.
luó
(adj.)- Spiral; screwlike.
螺旋；螺絲 A screw; a spiral.
螺殼 Univalve shells; conch-shells.
螺旋形 Spiral; helical.
螺旋體(幾) Helicoid.
螺旋鑽 An auger.
螺絲紋 Thread.
螺絲釘 Screw nail.
螺旋鑽 A screw-driver; a wrench.
螺旋樓梯；盤梯 Spiral (screw) stairs.
螺絲彈簧 Spiral spring.
螺旋起重機 A lifting-screw; a screw-jack.
螺旋機汽船 Screw-steamer.

**螻** (n.)- A mole-cricket.
lóu
螻蛄 A mole-cricket.
螻蟈 A small green frog.
螻蟻；螻螘 Ant.

**蟀** (n.)- A cricket.
shuài

**蟄** (v.)- Hibernate; become torpid; dormant; hide; rest in a quiet.
zhé
蟄伏 Hibernate; lie concealed; conceal oneself.
蟄居 Keep indoors; live in seclusion; confine oneself in one's home.

**蟆** (n.)- A frog; a toad.
ma

**蟋** (n.)- A cricket.
xī
蟋蟀 A cricket.
蟋蟀相鬥 Cricket fighting.

**蟑** (n.)- A cockroach.
zhāng
蟑螂；蜚蠊 A cockroach.

**蟒** (n.)- A serpent; a python; a boa-constrictor.
mǎng
蟒蛇 A python.
蟒龍 A terrible dragon; a monster.

**蟠** (v.)- Coil round; wind into a ring; curl up.
pán
(adj.)- Curling; encircling.
蟠屈 Coil like a snake.
蟠據 Occupy; encroach upon.
蟠繞 Coil around; curl up; encircle; spirally.

**蟥** (n.)- The horse-leech.
huáng

**蟬** (n.)- The cicada, or broad locust.
chán 蟬蛻；蟬衣 The exuviae of the cicada.
蟬噪；蟬鳴 The chirp of the cicada.
蟬聯 Continuous; connected.

**蟲** (n.)- An insect; a worm; a caterpillar; a larva; a vermin.
chóng 蟲災 Plague of locusts.
蟲蛀 Worm-eaten.
蟲害 Damage done by insects; insect damage; blight.
蟲鳴 The chirp of insects.

**蟮** (n.)- The earth-worm.
shan

**蟶** (n.)- Mussels; clams.
蟶子 The razor clam.
chēng

**蟹** (n.)- A crab.
蟹螯 The claws or pincers of a crab.
xiè

**蟻** (n.)- The ant.
蟻垤；蟻封；蟻冢 An ant-hill.
yǐ 蟻酸(化) Formic acid.

**蟾** (n.)- A striped toad.
蟾宮 The moon.
chán 蟾酥 A juice from the warts of a toad-used for medicine.
蟾蜍(動) The toad.

**蠅** (n.)- A fly.
蠅卵 Fly-blow.
yíng 蠅屎點 A flyspeck.
蠅頭小字 Very small characters.
蠅頭微利 Petty profits.

**蠍** (n.)- A scorpion.
蠍子 A scorpion.
xiē

**蠔** (n.)- An oyster.
蠔油 Oyster sauce.
háo 蠔豉 Dried oysters.

**蠕** (n.)- The crawling or wriggling of worms.
rú (v.)- Wriggle, as a worm; crawl slowly.
蠕行 Creep, as insects.
蠕動 Wriggling; squirming. Wriggle, as a worm.
蠕形動物 Vermes.

**蠟** (n.)- Wax; paraffin; bees-wax.
(adj.)- Glazed; waxy.
là 蠟石 Yellow quartz; steatite; wax stone.
蠟紙 Glazed paper; wax paper.
蠟梅 The winter-sweet; the calycanthus praecox.
蠟像 Waxwork; a waxen statue.
蠟製 Waxen; wax.
蠟線 Wax thread.
蠟燭 A candle.
蠟燭臺 A candlestick.

**蠡** (n.)- A wood-boring insect. A calabash; a gourd.
lǐ

**蠢** (adj.)- Stupid; foolish; sluggish; silly; dull.
chǔn 蠢才 A blockhead.
蠢笨；蠢鈍 Stupid; foolish; clumsy; awkward.

**蠣** (n.)- An oyster.
蠣鷸(動) Oyster catcher.
lì

**蠱** (n.)- Worms in the belly. The husk of grain. A poison.
gǔ (v.)- Deceive; beguile; entice; allure.
蠱惑 Allure; cozen; impose upon; beguile; delude.
蠱惑多端 Cunning.

**蠶** Same as 蚕.
cán (n.)- The silkworm; a caterpillar.
蠶豆(植) The horse beans; the broad beans.
蠶食 Encroach upon; gnaw–as a silk worm; gain on; encroach stealthily; gradual encroachment; aggression; nibble; eat away.
蠶絲 Silk-thread; filature (raw) silk.
蠶蛾 A silkworm moth.
蠶蛹 The chrysalis of the silkworm; pupa of the silkworm.
蠶繭 The cocoon of the silkworm.

**蠹** Same as 蠧.
dù (n.)- Grubs in the wood; worms in books, clothes, etc.
(adj.)-Decaying; rotten; worm-eaten.
(v.)- Waste; embezzle.
蠹吏 Extortionate officials; rapacious underlings.
蠹蟲 Hairy caterpillars.
蠹國害民 Prey upon one's country and injure the people.

**蠻** (n.)- The southern barbarians.
mán (adj.)- Savage; wild; rude; brutal; barbarous.
蠻力 Brute force; huge strength.
蠻性 A barbarous disposition.
蠻族 Barbarous tribes.
蠻橫 An outrage; an atrocity; savage deed; a brutality.
蠻好 Very good; excellent.
蠻不講理 Savage and absurd.

# 血 部

**血** (n.)- Blood.
xuè 血汗 Blood and sweat.
血肉 Flesh and blood.
血色 The colour of blood; scarlet.
血型 Blood type.
血庫 Blood bank.
血崩；月經過多 Menorrhagia.
血淚 Tears of blood; bitter tears.
血清 Serum.
血液 Blood.
血球 A blood-corpuscle.
血統；血胤 Lineage; a family line; descent; blood relationship.
血痢 Bloody-flux.
血跡；血痕 Blood stains.
血腥 Sanguinary; bloody.
血管 Blood vessels; arteries and veins.
血漿；血汁 Blood plasma.
血戰 A bloody fight; severe battle; bloody war; war to the knife (death).
血壓 Blood-pressure.
血虧；貧血 Exsanguinity; an(a)emia.
血壓計 A sphygmomanometer.
血紅素；血質 Haematin.
血過多；充血 Hyperaemia.
血壓低 Low blood pressure.
血壓高 High blood pressure.
血液循環 Circulation of the blood.

血液檢查 A blood test; haematoscopy. Examine the blood.
血管破裂 Rupture of a blood-vessel.
血緣關係 Relationship; kinship; consanguinity.

衆 (n.)- A multitude; a crowd; a group; the masses.
zhòng (adj.)- All; many; multitudinous; numerous; abundant.
衆生 All living things; mankind.
衆多 A great many.
衆議院 The House of Representatives; the House of Commons; the Lower House.
衆議院議長 The President of the House of Representatives; the Speaker of the House of Commons.
衆議院議員 A member of the House of Representatives; a member of Parliament (M.P.); a congressman.

# 行部

行 (n.)- A path; a road. Conduct; actions. A store; a wholesale
háng store. A row; a line; a series.
〔xíng〕 (v.)- Walk; step; travel; go; leave; be off. Move. Circulate; prevail. Do; act; conduct.
行人 A passer-by; a wayfarer.
行伍 Ranks of an army; military ranks.
行列 A parade; a procession; a line; a row.
行刑；用刑 Apply punishment; punish; execution.
行李；行裝 Luggage; baggage.
行走 Walk; pace; tread.
行事 Act.
行長 Manager.
行刺 Assassinate.
行政 Administration.
行星 A planet.
行軍 March.
行動 An action; a movement. Act; move; take action; behave.
行旅 A traveller.
行情；行市 The current price; rate of exchange.
行爲 An act; an action; a deed.
行程 A distance; a journey; a march.
行善 Practise good deeds.
行進 March; advance; proceed.
行賄 Bribe; corrupt.
行當；行業 A man's business or occupation.
行禮 Perform a ceremony; salute; carry out ceremonies.
行醫 Practise as a doctor.
行人道 Pavement; side walk; footpath.
行李車 Baggage car; luggage van.
行李房 Baggage-room.
行政法 Administrative law.
行政官 Administrative official; executives.
行政區 An administrative district.
行政權 Administrative power; executive authority.
行人隧道 A subway; an underpass.
行李收據 Baggage receipt.
行李運輸 Luggage traffic.
行使權利 Exercise one's rights.
行政法院 Administrative court.
行政命令 Administrative order.
行政處分 Administrative disposition.

行政規則 Regulation of administration.
行政機關 An administrative organ.
行爲不端 Misconduct.
行車時間表 Railway time-table.

衍 (adj.)- Abundant; fertile; rich; fruitful. Superfluous.
yǎn (v.)- Overflow; flood; extend; amplify; spread out; enlarge.
衍沃 Rich, fertile lands.

衒 (v.)- Expose; show off; make a display; boast.
xuàn

術 (n.)- A device; an art. A way; a plan; a method. An artifice;
shù a trick; a mystery.
術士 A juggler; a conjurer; a magician.
術策 A stratagem; an artifice.
術語 A technical term.
術語學 Terminology.

街 (n.)- A street; an avenue; a road; a passage; a thoroughfare.
jiē A small marketplace.
街上 In the street; in the market.
街市 Streets and markets.
街坊 Neighbours; a neighbourhood.
街卒；清道夫 A scavenger.
街燈 A street-lamp (-light).
街談巷議 Street gossips; the common talk; rumour.

衙 (n.)- A government office; an official residence; a yamen.
yá 衙吏 Yamen clerks.
衙門 A court; a yamen; a government office; a civil or military court.

衝 (v.)- Rush against; collide; move toward. Be in front of; con-
chōng front; face.
衝突 Collide with; run against; come into collision with; clash into (against, upon); conflict with.
衝倒 Throw down by collision; upset by collision; overthrow.
衝動 An impulse; an impetus.
衝鋒 Break through an enemy's lines; charge with bayonets.
衝擊 Strike against; impinge upon.
衝鋒隊 Storm troops.

衞 Same as 衛.
(n.)- A military station; a
wèi garrison.
(v.)- Escort; guard; defend; protect; convoy.
衞生 Sanitation; hygiene.
衞兵；衞隊 Guard corps; bodyguards.
衞星 A satellite.
衞護 Protect.
衞生局 The Sanitary Bureau.
衞國家 Protect the country.
衞生知識 Hygienic knowledge.
衞生設備 Health facilities.
衞生學家 A hygienist.
衞星國家 Satellites; satellite countries.
衞生試驗所 A hygienic laboratory.

衡 (n.)- A balance; a pair of scales. A railing. The yoke
héng of an ox.
(adj.)- Transverse; crosswise.
(v.)- Weigh; in the balance; measure. Calcuate; judge consider; adjust.
衡山（地）A mountain in Hunan, one of the five Sacred Mountains.
衡行；横行 Be rampant; be at large.
衡量 Measure; weigh; estimate; calculate.

# 衣 部

**衣** yī (n.)- Clothes; coat; dress; apparel; garment; attire. Husk; covering.
(v.)- Wear; put on clothes.

衣匠 Tailor; dressmaker.
衣刷 A clothes-brush.
衣服；衣裳 Clothes; garments; dress; apparel; habiliment.
衣架 A clothes-horse; a clothes-rack.
衣料 Material for clothing; clothing stuff; drapery.
衣廚 A wardrobe; a clothes-press.
衣領 Collar.
衣襟 Lapel of a coat.
衣帽間 Cloakroom.
衣衫襤褸 Ragged dress.
衣冠整齊 In full dress.

**表** biǎo (n.)- The carriage of a person. A signal; a memorial; a list. A table; a meter; a watch; a timepiece. Outside; exterior.
(adj.)- External; exterior; superficial.
(v.)- Make known; manifest; show; exhibit; express. Represent; designate.

表示 Show; manifest; express; make known.
表白；表明 Express; state clearly; designate.
表皮 The cuticle; the epidermis.
表面 The surface; the external appearance; the outside; the face.
表格 Table; list.
表現 Manifest; express; give expression to.
表情 Expression of emotion.
表嫂 A cousin's wife.
表彰 Commend officially.
表演 Perform; exhibit; play; show.
表兄弟 Sons of paternal or maternal aunt.
表姊妹 Daughters of paternal or maternal aunt.
表決權 Right to vote.
表姑母 Father's elder female cousins of different surname.
表姪女 Cousin's daughters.
表面化 Come to the front; become conspicuous.
表示敬意 In honour of.
表示滿意 Express oneself satisfied; express one's satisfaction.
表示慶賀 Offer one's congratulations.
表示態度 To define one's attitude.
表示支持 To give support for (to).
表示關懷 To express concern.
表面張力(物) Surface tension.
表現主義 Expressionism.
表裏如一 Outside and inside the same; sincere.

**衫** shān (v.)- A shirt; a jacket; a robe; a gown.

**衰** shuāi (n.)- Mourning dress.
(adj.)- Weak; limping; declining; decaying; growing old; fading; wearing away.
(v.)- Decrease; decline; decay; fall off(away).

衰亡 Ruin; destruction.

衰老 Old and feeble; decayed; worn out.
衰弱 Be weakened; grow weak; become feeble.
衰退 Decline, decay; fall off; sink.
衰敗 Failing; worn out. Be in a state of decline or decay; decrease.
衰落 Descend ;run low; languish; decay; crumble.
衰頹 Decline; retrogression.
衰弱症 A wasting disease.

衷 zhōng (n.)- The heart; the mind. Goodness; sincerity. Rectitude; righteousness; justice. Inner garments; under-clothes.
衷誠 Sincere.
衷心 One's inmost heart.
衷情 One's inmost feelings; one's true heart.
衷懷 The mind; the bosom; the feelings.

衾 qīn (n.)- A large quilt; a coverlet; bedclothes.
衾裯 A quilt; bed-clothes.

袂 mèi (n.)- The sleeve of a robe.

袋 dài (n.)- A bag; a sack; a pouch. A pocket; a purse.
袋鼠(動) The kangaroo.

袍 páo (n.)- A robe; a gown; a long garment; a mantle; a frock-coat.
袍褂 Robe and jacket.

袖 xiù (n.)- A sleeve.
袖口 A cuff; a wristband; the mouth of a sleeve.
袖章 Badge.
袖鈕 A sleeve button.
袖珍本 A pocketbook; a pocket edition; a hand book.
袖手旁觀 Look on with folded arms; remain indifferent (idle) spectator.
袖珍辭典 A pocket (vest) dictionary.

被 bèi (n.)- Bedclothes; a coverlet; a quilt.
(v.)- Cover; be subjected to; be charged with; be acted upon.
被告 The defendant(民事); the accused (刑事).
被胎 A cotton quilt without a cover.
被辱 Be put to shame; be subjected to insult; be insulted.
被殺 Be killed.
被害 Be injured; be damaged; suffer from.
被動 Passive. Be influenced upon; moved by some one or thing.
被單 A bed sheet; a bedspread.
被搶 Be robbed.
被逼 Be forced or compelled.
被褥 Bedding; coverlet; mattress.
被加數 A summand.
被乘數 The multiplicand.
被除數 The dividend.
被害者(法) The injured party. A sufferer; a victim.
被減數 A minuend.
被動語態 Passive voice.
被統治者(法) The governed; the ruled.
被選舉人 Person to be elected.
被壓迫階級 An oppressed class; the oppressed.

袴 kù Same as 褲.
(n.)- Trousers; breeches; drawers; pants.
袴子 Trousers.

袴帶 The string to fasten trousers round the waist; a belt.
袴腰 A waistbelt.
袴腿 The legs of trousers.
袴襠 The seat of trousers.

**袷** qiā
Same as 裌.
(adj.)- Double; lined.
袷衫 A lined(double)garment.

**裁** cái
(v.)- Cut out; trim. Reduce; cut off; diminish. Regulate; plan; moderate. Decide; determine upon.
裁人；裁員 Cut down the number of persons employed.
裁衣 Cut out clothes.
裁判 Judgment; trial. Judge; decide; a judge; a referee.
裁兵 Disarmament.Reduce the number of troops.
裁紙 Cut paper.
裁剪 Cut out. Plan; arrange.
裁縫 A tailor; a tailoress (女); a dress-maker; a seamstress. Sew; do needlework.
裁決書(法) A written verdict (judgment).
裁判官 A judge; a justice.
裁判長 The presiding (chief) judge.
裁判所 A law court; a court of justice.
裁判權 Jurisdiction; judicial right.
裁軍會議 Disarmament conference.
裁縫學校 A school of needlework; a sewing-school.

**裂** liè
(v.)- Crack; split; break; rip open; rend; tear; sever.
裂口 A rent; a crack; a slit; a chink.
裂紋 Cleavage.
裂痕 Fissure; chasm.
裂片 Splinter.
裂開 Split open; burst.
裂縫 A crack; a rent; a breach.
裂爲兩半 Be split in two; be rent asunder.

**裊** niǎo
(adj.)- Curling up, as smoke.

**裏** lǐ
Same as 裡.
(n.)- A lining.
(adj.)- Inside; internal; inner.
(adv.)- In.
(prep.)- Within; in.
裏子；夾裏 A lining.
裏外 Inside and outside; within and without.
裏衣 A shirt; an underwear.
裏面；裏頭 Interior; inside; within.
裏海(地) The Caspian Sea.

**裔** yì
(n.)- A frontier; edge; boundary. Posterity; off-spring; descendants. The skirt of a robe.
裔夷 Frontier tribes.

**裕** yù
(adj.)- Rich; wealthy; abundant. Generous; liberal.
裕足 Sufficient; enough; ample; well off; abundant.
裕政 A liberal government.
裕國 Enrich the country; enrich the state.

**裘** qiú
(n.)- Fur garments. Fur.

**裙** qún
(n.)- The skirt of a lady's dress; a petticoat.
裙釵 Women; ladies.
裙邊 Hem of a petticoat.

**補** (n.)- Supplement; replenishment.
bǔ (v.)- Make up; repair; mend; patch. Help; aid. Fill up; fill a vacancy.
補充 Supplement; fill up; replenish.
補血 Increase the blood.
補考 Supplementary examination.
補足 Make up; make good a deficiency; supply; render full.
補身 Build up the body; recruit the vital powers.
補角(幾) A supplementary angle.
補助 Help; assist; support; subsidize.
補弦(幾) A supplementary chord.
補救 Rectify shortcomings and reform abuses.
補發 Issue; pay.
補給 A supply to meet a deficit. Supply (cover) the want.
補綴 Darn; patch.
補網 Mend nets.
補綻 Patch; mend.
補領 Receive anew—as a document, salary, overdue, etc.
補課 Make up one's lessons; fill up the hour.
補償；賠償 Compensate (indemnify) a person for his loss.
補藥 Tonic; a bracing medicine; restoratives.
補衣服 Mend clothes.
補足語 A complement.
補助金 A subsidy; a grant-in-aid.
補鞋匠 A cobbler.
補其不足 Make up the deficit.
補其所短 Remedy (make up) a defect.
補習學校 A supplementary school; a continuation school.

**裝** (n.)- Baggage; luggage. Ornament; dressing.
zhuāng (v.)- Adorn; dress; make up. Pretend; sham. Pack; load.
裝扮 Dress up; disguise.
裝束 Dress up. A style of dress.
裝卸 Load and unload a cargo.
裝訂 Bind into a book; the binding.
裝修 Decorate, as dwellings; fittings; fixture.
裝船 Shipment; load a ship (boat).
裝配 Fixture.
裝貨 Pack goods; load goods.
裝備 Outfit; equipment. Fit out; equip.
裝置 Equipment; installation. Equip with; install; arrange.
裝載 Pack; stow; load; contain.
裝運 Load and transport; ship.
裝滿 Fill up; packed full.
裝飾 Ornament; adorn; decorate; embellish.
裝箱 Pack a box; packing.
裝燈 Install electric lights.
裝鎗 Load a gun.
裝甲師 Armoured division.
裝甲車 An armoured car.
裝飾品 An ornamental article; ornaments.
裝腔作勢 Affected coyness.
裝置電話 Install a telephone.
裝飾美術 Decorative art.
裝模作樣 Affection; assume airs.

**裨** (n.)- Advantage; benefit.
bī (adj.)- Small; inferior; subordinate; petty. Beneficial; advantageous; profitable.
(v.)- Assist; aid; benefit. Do good to; supply; furnish.
裨海 The high seas.
裨益 Advantage. Do one good; be beneficial to; be advantageous for.

**裳** (n.)- Clothes; skirts; petticoats; garments, especially the lower
shang ones.

祼 (adj.)- Naked; bare; unclothed; uncoverd; nude; unprotected.
luǒ (v.)- Unclothe; stripe.
祼足 Barefooted.
祼麥 The rye.
祼體 Nakedness; nudity.

裹 (v.)- Wrap; pack up; envelop; wind around; bundle up.
guǒ 裹肚 A stomacher; a band for the belly.
裹脚 Bind the feet.
裹傷；裹創 Bind up a wound.
裹頭巾 A turban.
裹足不前 Stop; not daring to advance.

製 (n.)- Make; manufacture.
(v.)- Make; manufacture; produce; turn out. Regulate; put up; compound, as drugs.
zhì
製成 Ready-made.
製作 Manufacture; produce; make.
製法 A method (process) of manufacture; a recipe.
製品 Manufactured goods; manufactures; products.
製造 Make; manufacture.
製圖 Draw (draft) a plan. Draughtsmanship; cartography.
製冰廠 An ice-manufactory.
製造力 Producing (manufacturing) capacity.
製造家 A manufacturer.
製造廠 A manufactory; a factory; a mill.
製煉廠 Refinery.
製圖板 A drawing-board; a trestle-board.
製圖者 A draughtsman; a cartographer.
製圖室 A drafting (drawing) room.
製鞋廠 A shoe factory.
製鋼廠 A steel-foundry.
製錶人 A watch-maker.
製藥師 A pharmacist.
製圖機械 A drawing (draughtsman's) instrument.
製造鋼鐵廠 Iron and steel works.

褂 (n.)- An outer jacket; a coat.
guà

複 (n.)- Double things.
(adj.)- Double; compound.
fù (v.)- Reiterate; repeat.
複句 A complex sentence.
複述 Rehearse.
複習 Review.
複製 Reproduction. Reproduce; duplicate.
複寫 Copy; reproduce.
複數 The plural number.
複雜 Complexity; complication.
複合語 A compound word.
複名數 Compound numbers.
複印機 A mimeograph; a duplicator.
複製品 A reproduction; a replica.
複寫紙 Copying-paper; carbon paper.
複化合物 Double compound.
複合名詞 A compound noun.
複合關稅 Compound duty.
複式會計 Double account system.
複數名詞 A plural noun.

褊 (adj.)- Narrow; small; petty. Narrow-minded; mean.
biǎn 褊小 Narrow; small; contracted; mean; incapacious; narrow-minded.
褊窄 Cramped; traitened; small.
褊淺 Shallow; petty; limited.

褐 (n.)- Coarse cloth. Poor people.
(adj.)- Brown.
hè 褐色 Brown.
褐炭 Brown coal; lignite.

褐鐵礦 Limonite; brown hematite.

褥 (n.)- A thick, stuffed mat; a mattress; a cushion; beddings.
rù 褥單 A sheet.
褥墊 A mattress; a cushion.

褪 (v.)- Take off. Fade; discolour. Draw back.
tuì 褪色 Fade; discolour.
褪色劑 Ink eradicator.

褫 (v.)- Disrobe; strip off; deprive off; discharge; put an end to.
chǐ 褫衣 Undress.
褫奪 Deprivation.
褫職 Discharge; dismiss from office.
褫奪公權(法) Deprivation of civil rights.

褶 (n.)- A fold. A double garment; a lined coat.
zhě 褶裥 Embroidered pleats in a robe.
褶曲山 Fold mountain.

褻 (n.)- Under-clothes.
(adj.)- Dirty; filthy. Acquainted
xiè or familiar with. Indecent.
(v.)- Treat irreverently; dishonour; profane.
褻服 Under-clothes.
褻器 A chamber-utensil.

褒 Same as 襃.
(v.)- Praise; admire; extol; com-
bāo mend.
褒貶 Praise and censure.
褒獎；褒美 Praise; admire.

襄 (v.)- Help; assist; complete.
襄同 Take part in; assist.
xiāng 襄理 An assistant manager.
襄贊其事 Help on an achievement.

襖 (n.)- A short garment; a coat; a jacket.
ǎo

襟 (n.)- The lapel of a coat. The bosom.
jīn 襟要 An important point.
襟懷 The feelings.
襟兄弟 Brothers-in-law; the husband of wife's sister.

襤 (adj.)- Ragged; tattered; shabby.
襤褸 Tattered clothes; ragged;
lán threadbare; shabby.

襪 Same as 袜
(n.)- Stockings; socks; hoses.
wà 襪筒 The tube of a stocking, often used as a pocket.
襪廠 Hosiery.

襯 (n.)- Inner garments; underclothes.
chèn (v.)- Lie beneath; assist; be the back-ground of.
襯衣 An underwear; an undershirt.
襯色 Add colour to; adorn the person.
襯衫 A shirt.
襯袴 Drawers.
襯裙 A petticoat; underskirt.

襲 (n.)- A suit of clothes.
(adj.)-Double; reapeated. Here-
xí ditary.
(v.)- Inherit; succeed to. Invade; assault; attack stealthily; take by surprise. Plagiarize.
襲營 Attack a camp.
襲擊 Attack; charge; assault; storm; raid.
襲其後路 Take the enemy in the rear.

# 襾 部

**西** ㄒㄧ (n.)- The west.
(adj.)- Western; foreign; European.
西人；西洋人 Men from the west; occidentals; westerners; foreigners; Europeans.
西方 West.
西北 Northwest.
西瓜 Water-melon.
西式 European (foreign) style.
西米 Sago.
西洋 The Occident; the West; the Western countries.
西南 Southwest.
西風 The west wind; zephyr.
西貢(地) Saigon.
西部 The western part; the west.
西湖(地) West Lake in Hangchow.
西菜；洋菜 European (foreign) cookery (cooking).
西裝；西服 Western dress.
西歐 Western (west) Europe.
西嶽(地) The Western Sacred Mountain, i.e.華山 in Shensi.
西藏(地) Tibet.
西北風 A northwesterly wind; a northwester.
西半球(地) Western hemisphere.
西瓜子 Water-melon seeds.
西南風 A southwester; a southwesterly wind.
西洋化 Be Westernized (Europeanized).
西班牙(地) Spain.
西式建築 A foreign-style building.
西式傢具 Foreign-style furniture (upholstery).
西伯利亞(地) Siberia.
西班牙人 A Spaniard; the Spanish.
西班牙文 The Spanish language; Spanish.
西歐國家 West European countries.
西印度羣島(地) The West Indies.

**要** yào (adj.)- Important; necessary; essential.
(v.)- Desire; want; require; ask for; demand. Claim; force.
(adv.)- Must.
要人 A notable; a man of note; a prominent man; a keyman.
要之 Sum up; in a word; in short; in a few words.
要目 Principal items; essence; element.
要件 An important matter; a requisite.
要旨；要義 Essence; the main point.
要求 Demand; claim; require. A claim; a demand.
要是 If; supposing; should it be that . . .
要害 A strategic position; a stronghold; a fortress.
要素 An essential element; an important factor.
要港 An important port.
要塞 A fortress; a fortification.
要道 Important doctrine. An important road.
要領 The point; the pith; the gist.
要點 The gist; the main (essential) point.
要職 An important post; a responsible position; a high place.
要目索引 An index of principal topics.
要求條件 Conditions of claim.
要求會見 Ask for an interview.

要求說明 Call for an explanation.
要求數額 The sum of claim; the amount demanded.
要即付款 Payable on demand.

覆 fù (v.)- Overthrow; overturn; upset. Reply; respond. Defeat. Shelter; cover.
覆核 To check.
覆言 Repeat in words.
覆沒 Sunk; lost; routed.
覆函；覆信 A reply; an answer.
覆滅 Downfall; ruin; destruction; collapse.
覆試 Re-examination; a further examination.
覆蓋 Cover over.
覆審 Re-examine a case.

# 見 部

見 jiàn (n.)- A glance; an opinion; a sight; an interview; a view; a mind.
(v.)- See; appear; view; perceive; meet with; come out; manifest; show; look.
見到 Come in sight.
見怪 Take offence.
見面 Have an interview with.
見效 Produce effect; it is efficacious, as medicine.
見笑 Be laughed at.
見習 An apprentice; a novice.
見解 An opinion; a point of view.
見聞 Experience; knowledge; observation. See and hear.
見諒 Be excused.
見禮 Salute.
見識 Experience; knowledge.
見習生 An apprentice; a novice.
見票即付 Payable at sight.
見習軍官 A cadet; a student officer.
見解不同 Hold a different view (opinion); differ (disagree) in opinion.
見聞廣博 Be well-informed; have wide experience.
見機而作 Act as occassion serves.
見識甚淺 Shallow knowledge.
見識高超 Be far-sighted; have lofty ideas.

規 guī (n.)- A pair of compass. Law; rule; regulation. Usage.
(v.)- Describe a circle. Advise; dissuade; admonish. Regulate; plan; contrive; design.
規例 Regulations; rules; by-laws.
規定 Define; regulate; fix; provide; prescribe by rule.
規則 Regulations; rules.
規律 Order; discipline; rules.
規矩 The compasses and square. Usage; custom. Law; regulation.
規模 A pattern; a rule; a model. Scale; scope.
規範 Standard; model.
規勸 Advise; counsel; admonish; advise; dissuade.
規模宏大 On a large (grand, gigantic) scale.

覓 mì (v.)- Look after; search for; seek.
覓人 Look for a person.
覓食 Seek food.
覓路 Seek the right road.

覔據 Seek for proofs or evidence.

視 (v.)- Look at; inspect. Regard; show; see.
shì 視力 Eyesight; visual power; vision.
視爲 Regard as; look upon as; make account of; esteem.
視察 Visit; see; inspect; examine.
視線 The line of vision.
視點 The visual point; the point of vision.
視覺 The sense of sight.
視神經 The optic nerve.
視察員 An inspector; a committee of inspection.
視學官 A school-inspector.
視力檢查 A test of vision.
視財如命 Regard wealth as one's life.
視覺器官 An organ of vision.
視力檢查器 Optometer.

覩 Same as 睹.
(n.)- Look at; observe; witness; see; gaze at.
dǔ 覩此情形 In view of these circumstances.

親 (n.)- Parents; a relation or relative; kindred; relationship;
qīn affinity; a kinsman.
(adj.)- Near; close; intimate; dear. Personal; self.
(v.)- Love; approach.
親切 Having intimate connections. Kindness; goodness.
親友 Relatives and friends.
親手 Of one's own hand.
親近；親密 Close; intimate; familiar.
親信 Trusted.
親家 Relatives by marriage.
親眷 Near relatives.
親眼 With one's own eyes.
親戚；親屬 Consanguinity by marriage; relatives; kindred.
親善 Amity; comity; goodwill; friendly relations (terms).
親筆 One's own handwriting; an autograph. Written by one's own hand.
親愛 Dear; beloved; love dearly or intimately; affection; love.
親誼 Affinity; appetence; friendliness.
親熱 Cordial; on good close; intimate.
親暱 Familiar; intimate.
親嘴 Kiss.
親臨 Visit personally.
親兄弟 Blood brother.
親筆信 An autograph letter.
親眼目睹 Seen with one's own eyes.
親密朋友 A close (an intimate) friend.
親族關係 Relationship; kinship.

覬 (v.)- Covet; long for; desire.
覬望 Ardent longings.
jì 覬覦 Have an eye to (for); have sinister designs upon; watch secretly.

覯 Same as 遘, 逅.
(v.)- See; meet.
gòu 覯見 Meet with.

覺 (adj.)- Straightforward. Intelligent; conscious.
jué (v.)- Feel; understand; awake; arouse; enlighten; find; be discovered; be brought to light; perceive; be conscious of.
覺冷 Feel cold.
覺悟 Be aroused; become aware of; notice; understand; comprehend.
覺得 Perceive; know; be conscious of.
覺痛 Feel pain.
覺察 Keep an eye on; understand.
覺醒 Awake from; be disillusioned.

覽 (v.)- Inspect; look at; view; observe; read.
lǎn 覽勝 Visit places noted for scenery.

觀 (n.)- A view; a sight; an observatory; spectacle; a look-out.
guān A Taoist temple.
(v.)- Look at; see; view; inspect; display.
觀光 Go sightseeing; see the sights of.
觀玩；觀賞 Enjoy; view; appreciate.
觀念 Idea; concept.
觀看 Behold; inspect.
觀望 Look on; hesitate; watch.
觀衆 Spectators; bystanders; onlookers; the audience.
觀測 Observation.
觀察 Survey. Observe; watch closely.
觀劇；觀戲 Playgoing; theatre-going. Go to theatre; attend a theatre.
觀點 A point of view; a standpoint; a viewpoint.
觀光團 A tourist party.
觀念論 Idealism.
觀察力 The power of observation.
觀察點 A point of view.
觀念作用 Ideation.
觀客滿座 A full house.
觀音菩薩 The Goddess of Mercy.
觀賞植物 An ornamental (a garden) plant.
觀望的態度 An attitude of wait and see.

# 角 部

角 (n.)- A horn. A trumpet. A corner; a nook; a quarter. An
jiǎo angle. A cape. A piece of small silver coin; a dime. A goblet.
角力 Contest in strength; wrestling.
角色 Actors.
角度 An angle.
角逐 Compete for mastery; vie with.
角膜 The cornea of the eye.
角膜炎 Keratitis.
角質層 Horny layer.

觔 (n.)- A catty.
jīn 觔斗 A somersault.

解 Same as 鮮.
(n.)- Opinion; view.
jiě (v.)- Explain; understand. Get rid off. Loosen; untie; undo; cut apart. Break up; scatter; disperse; solve. Interpret. Take off; strip; remove. Relieve; alleviate.
解手 Wash one's hand; go to W.C.
解危 Deliver from peril.
解衣 Take off one's clothes.
解任 Release from office (one's duties).
解決 Settlement; solution.
解事 Have a clear apprehension of.
解放 Discharge; release; liberate; emancipate; set free.
解約 Cancel (dissolve) a contract.
解除 Cancel; rescind; release. Disarm; dismantle.
解剖 Dissection; anatomization. Analysis. Dissect; anatomize; analyse.
解疼 Alleviate pain.
解散 Scatter; disperse; dissolve; loosen;

disband.
解答 A solution. Solve; answer.
解渴 Quench thirst; slake.
解開 Untie. Settle up—as quarrels.
解悶；解憂 Dissipate sorrow; assuage grief; alleviate sorrow.
解雇 Discharge; dismiss; send out; turn away.
解圍 Raise a siege.
解說 Explain; illustrate.
解釋 Explanation; interpretation. Make more clear; explain; expound; construe; interpret.
解放者 An emancipator.
解剖刀 A dissecting knife; a scalpel.
解剖室 A dissecting room.
解剖學 Anatomy.
解款單 Cash remittance note.
解暑湯 A cooling drink.
解決方法 A solution.
解析幾何 Analytical geometry.
解除武裝 Disarmament; dismantlement.
解除契約 Rescission (cancellation) of a contract.
解除警報 Call off the air-raid warning.
解釋錯誤 Misinterpret; put a wrong interpretation upon.

觸 chù (v.)- Butt; gore; strike against; hit; dash against; oppose. Excite, offend. Stimulate; come in contact with; touch.
觸手 A tentacle.
觸犯 Offend; affront.
觸角 An antenna; a feeler.
觸怒 Incure one's anger; give offence to one.
觸動 Excite; stir up; provoke.
觸礁 Strike a hidden rock.
觸覺 The sense of touch; the tactile sense.
觸景生情 The circumstances excited his feelings—as of joy or sorrow.
觸覺器官 The organ of touch or feeling.

# 言 部

言 yán (n.)- A word; a character; a speech; a language.
(v.)- Say; talk; address; speak; mean.
言行 Words and deeds (actions); speech and conduct.
言詞 Words; speech.
言語 Speech; conversation; language.
言論 Discourse; speech; discussion.
言行錄 Record of one's acts; a biography.
言語學 Philology; science of language.
言論家 Speaker; editor.
言行一致 Act up to what one says. One's words are in keeping with one's deeds.
言過其實 Exaggerate; overstate; pull the long bow.
言論自由 Freedom of the press; liberty of speech; free speech.
言盡於此 I have no more to say.
言歸正傳 Return to the point (one's subject); return from the digression.

訂 dìng (n.)- Arrange; adjust; fix; settle. Examine. Compare. Edit.
訂立 Draw up; fix on.

訂正 Revise; correct; amend.
訂約 Conclude a treaty.
訂婚 Engage; betroth. Engagement; betrothal.
訂期 Fix a date; set a time; make an appointment.
訂報 Subscribe for a newspaper.
訂正版 Revised edition.
訂貨單 Bills to order; order sheet; small order.
訂貨單式 Order form.

訃 fù (n.)- An announcement of death; an obituary; a notice of death.
(v.)- Announce a death.
訃聞；訃告 Obituary notice.

計 jì (n.)- A plan; a scheme; a device; a plot; a trick.
(v.)- Plan; calculate; count.
計劃 A plan; a scheme. Make a plan; project; design.
計量 Estimate; measure.
計策 A plan; a stratagem; a project; a scheme.
計較 Discuss minutely; dispute; go into a matter.
計算 Calculate; reckon; count; compute; cast in the mind.
計謀 A plan; a stratagem; a contrivance. Take measure; plot.
計劃人 A designer; a projector.
計算尺 A slide (sliding) rule.
計算機 A calculating machine; calculator.
計上心來 Come across one's mind.
計劃生產 Planned production.
計算項目 Title of account.

訊 xùn (n.)- Trial; judicial examination. Tiding; news.
(v.)- Interrogate; examine judicially; hear a case; inquire; try.
訊究 Investigate thoroughly.
訊問 Examine; interrogate; question.
訊辦 Hear and deal with a case.
訊問處 Inquiry office.
訊問日期 Fixed day of hearing.

訌 hòng (v.)- Quarrel; make trouble; be disorganized.
訌亂 In disorder; rebellious.

討 tǎo (v.)- Beg; demand; dun; ask for. Search.
討伐 Punish; make war on; conquer. Subjugation; suppression.
討好 Toady; commend to another's good will; get advantage from; ingratiate oneself with.
討債 Dun for debts.
討飯 A beggar. Beg for food.
討厭 Incur dislike; annoying; disagreeable.
討論 Debate; discuss; hold a debate.
討錢 Ask for money.
討饒 Seek forgiveness.
討論案 A subject for debate.
討人歡喜 Seek the favour of others.
討論終結 Close the debate (discussion).

訓 xùn (n.)- Advice; instruction; counsel. Training.
(v.)- Teach; instruct; give lesson in.
訓令 An official order; an instruction.
訓育 Discipline; moral education.
訓話 A lecture; a sermon; admonition.
訓練 Drill; train; discipline.
訓導 A district instructor. Teach and guide.
訓練營 A training camp.
訓誨諄諄 Line upon line; precept upon precept; reiterated warnings.

**訕** (v.)- Abuse; speak evil of; libel; revile.
shàn
訕言 Slanders; backbiting.
訕笑 Mock at; laugh at.

**訖** (adj.)- Finished; ended; done; clear.
qì
(v.)- Come to an end; finish; complete; clear off or settle, as an account.
(prep.)- Up to; till; until.
訖今 Up to the present; until now.

**託** (v.)- Charge with; entrust to; commission; rely on; request; ask. Pretext; pretend.
tuō
託信 Entrust; trust one with something.
託故；推託 Give a pretext; make an excuse of.
託送 Send by; send under the care of.
託寄 Commission one to send.
託買 Ask a person to buy; on commission.
託管 Trustee; trusteeship.
託福 Many thanks; much obliged; it is kind of you.
託兒所 A public nursery; a creche.
託人辦事 Engage another to manage affairs.
託運貨品 Consignment.
託辣斯組織 A trust system.

**記** (n.)- A record; a narration; a history. A mark; a sign. Recollection.
jì
(v.)- Remember; call to mind; bear in mind. Record; register; give an account of; write (note) down.
記功 Record merits.
記名 Record the name of; make a list of names; put down one's name to.
記念 Bear in mind; keep in memory.
記性 The memory.
記者 A reporter; a correspondent; a journalist.
記述 Describe; give an account of.
記得；記起 Remember; come to remembrance; call to memory.
記賬 Charge it in account; keep account; make an entry in.
記過 Give a demerit mark.
記載 Put down in record; make record of.
記號 A mark; a sign; a symbol.
記憶 Remember; bear in mind.
記錄 Record; minutes. Write down.
記事簿 Note book; pocket-book.
記者席 A press-gallery (會場); a press-box (戲院); a press-stand (運動場).
記賬員 A book-keeper.
記憶力 Remembrance; memory.
記錄片 A documentary film.
記名投票 A signed vote (ballot).
記號及號數 Marks and numbers.
記憶力減退 Failure of memory.

**訛** Same as 譌.
é
(adj.)- False; erroneous; wrong.
(v.)- Lie; extort; defraud; black mail.
訛言 A lie; a false report.
訛詐 Extort; blackmail; swindle; cheat.
訛傳 Misinformation; wrong information; false rumour.
訛騙 To cheat; swindle.

**訝** (v.)- Express surprise; wonder at; suspect; doubt.
yà

**訟** (n.)- Litigation; contention.
sòng
(v.)- Bring a complaint or suit against; demand justice;

accuse.
訟事 Litigation; law suits.
訟庭 The law court.
訟詞 An indictment.

訣 (n.)- A craft; a rule; a mystery; a trick, as in legerdemain.
jué (v.)- Bid farewell; take leave.
訣竅 The secret; the knack of a thing.
訣別詞 Parting words.

訥 (v.)- Speak cautiously; stammer; stutter.
nè 訥口；訥訥 Stutter; stammer.
訥澀 Difficult in speech.

訪 (v.)- Visit; Inquire about; search for.
fǎng 訪友 Call on a friend; visit an acquaintance.
訪查 Search; find out.
訪問 Inquire of. Pay a visit to; call on a person.
訪尋 Look for; search for.
訪親 Inquire about one's relatives.
訪問記 An interview.
訪問團 A mission.

設 (v.)- Establish; set up; found; form; arrange; devise.
shè (conj.)- If; supposing that; in case of.
設立 Establish; erect; set up; found.
設法 Devise means; scheme; plan.
設計 Take measure; lay out a plan; plot; draw up a plan; design.
設宴；設席 Give an entertainment; make a feast.
設備 Equipment; arrangement; accommodation; facilities.
設想 Suppose; imagine.
設置 Establish; institute; found; set up.
設網；張網 Set a decoy net.
設計者 A designer.
設計圖 A plan.
設立政府 Set up a government.
設立學校 Found (establish) a school.
設備不全 Poorly-equipped.
設備完全 Well-equipped.

許 (v.)- Permit; allow. Promise; consent; approve.
xǔ (adv.)- About.
許久 A long time.
許可 Permission; permit. Admit; allow.
許多 A great many.
許配；許婚 Betroth; affiance.
許諾 Permit; consent to; approve of.
許可證 A licence; a charter.

訴 Same as 愬.
(v.)- Tell; inform; state. Plead;
sù lay a plaint; accuse.
訴苦 State one's wrongs; tell one's grievance; make complaint.
訴訟 A suit; a lawsuit; a case. Sue a person for libel; bring a lawsuit; go to law.
訴冤 State one's case in such a way as to escape punishment.
訴稱 State in detail.
訴訟人 A plaintiff; a suitor.
訴冤人；原告 A complainant; an informer.
訴於警察 Complain to the police.

訶 (v.)- Blame.
訶責 Blame; reprimand.
hē 訶護 Protect; screen; shield.

診 (v.)- Look at; examine disease; see a doctor; feel the pulse;
zhěn diagnose.
診治 Cure.
診所 A doctor's office; a clinic.

診費 A physician's fee; a medical fee.
診斷 Examine; diagnose; make a diagnosis of.
診病證 A consultation ticket.
診療室 A consulting (consultation) room.

註 (n.)- Note; explanation; commentary remarks.
zhù (v.)- Explain; annotate; write notes on; define; record; register; endorse; sign.
註册 Enter in a register; enroll; registration; register.
註定 Explain; define.
註明 Explain clearly and fully in writing.
註解 Explanatory notes; annotation.
註銷 Cancel; write off.
註釋 Explain; annotate; illustrate the meaning of.
註册費；登記費 A registration fee.
註册商標 A registered trade-mark.
註册執照 Certificate of registration.

詁 (n.)- Explanation; commentary; an explanatory note.
gǔ (v.)- Explain; note; comment.

詆 (v.)- Defame; slander; abuse.
dǐ 詆譭 Slander; defame; calumniate; backbite.

詈 (v.)- Abuse; scold; curse; rail at.
lì 詈罵 Blackguard; abuse; revile in scurrilous language; scold, revile; rail at; swear at.

詐 (adj.)- Cunning; false; fraudulent; deceitful; erroneous.
zhà (v.)- Deceive; cheat; lie.
詐取 Obtain by fraud; swindle; defraud.
詐哭 Crocodile tears.
詐病 Feign sickness.
詐術 Juggle.
詐欺 Fraud; imposture; cheating; swindling.
詐睡 Pretend to sleep.

詔 (n.) An edict; an imperial mandate; a decree.
zhào (v.)- Announce; proclaim. Instruct; encourage; advise.
詔命；詔令 An imperial decree (edict).

評 (n.)- Criticism; a running commentary.
píng (v.)- Discuss; arrange; comment; criticize; review.
評估 Estimate a value; adjudicate, as price.
評判 Review; criticize; judge; adjudicate.
評理 Discuss; settle.
評價 Appraise; estimate; value; assess.
評論 Discuss; debate; make observations; argue about. A comment; a review.
評斷 Decide; arbitrate.
評判員 A judge; an umpire.
評論家 A critic; a reviewer.
評判得失 Critically decide the merits and demerits of a case.

詛 (v.)- Curse; imprecate.
zǔ 詛呪 Curse; imprecate; execrate.
詛罵 Curse; rail at; revile; cursing and railing.

詞 (n.)- An expression; a word; a phrase. A poem; a versed essay.
cí 詞句 Wording; text; phrases and

sentences.
詞曲 Ballads, songs.
詞律 Rules of metrical composition.
詞性 The parts of speech.
詞意 Meaning; import; drift; gist.
詞藻 Ornate terms; rhetorical embellishment; figurative expressions.
詞不達意 The sentence does not fully convey the idea.

詠 yǒng Same as 咏.
(v.)- Sing; hum; chant; compose poetry.
詠詩 Chant verses.
詠歌 Compose; recite.
詠嘆 Sigh; admire.
詠景詩 An idyl.
詠懷詩 A lyric poem.

詢 xún (v.)- Ask about; deliberate. Investigate; inquire; consult with.
詢悉 Make full investigations.
詢訪 Make inquiries; investigate.
詢問 Ask; inquire of; interrogate.

詣 yì (v.)- Go to; reach; repair to; visit.
詣謁 Pay a visit.

試 shì (n.)- A trial; a test; an attempt.
(v.)- Try; make a try; test; make an attempt. Examine.
試用 Make a trial of: put to trial; employ or use on trial; on probation—of an official.
試卷 Examination paper.
試看 Take a look at.
試映 Give (hold) a pre-view.
試航 A trial trip.
試想 Think; consider.
試嘗 Sample; taste.
試演 Give a demonstration of; give a trial performance of.
試題 Questions for examination.
試驗 Try; test; examine; make an experiment.
試金石 A lydian stone; a touchstone.
試驗紙 Test paper; litmus paper.
試驗室 A laboratory.
試用期限 Period of probation.

詩 shī (n.)- Poetry; a verse; hymn; poem; an ode.
詩人 A poet; a poetess (女); a bard.
詩文 Poems and essays. Prose and poetry.
詩集 Poetical works; a collection of poems.
詩聖 A great (an eminent) poet.
詩經 The Book of Odes.
詩歌 Odes and songs.
詩劇 A verse drama.
詩選 An anthology.
詩韻 The rhyme of the verse.
詩中有畫,畫中有詩 Poems depicted pictures and pictures contained poems.

詫 chà (v.)- Wonder at; brag; be astonished.
詫異 Be surprised; be amazed; be astonished at.

詭 guǐ (adj.)- Odd; strange; peculiar. False; deceptive; cunning.
(v.)- Deceive; cheat; feign; defraud.
詭計 An artful device; a crafty design; a trick.
詭詐 Treacherous; guile; fraudulent.
詭辯 Quibble; prevaricate. Sophistry; casuistry.
詭辯家 A sophist.
詭計多端 Full of schemes and tricks.
詭辯學派 Sophism.

**詰** jié (v.)- Interrogate; ask. Examine. Punish. Prohibit.
詰責 Reprimand; rebuke; censure.
詰問 Cross-question (examine); question closely; inquire authoritatively; demand an explanation.
詰問口供 Take depositions.

**話** huà (n.)- Speech; talk; conversation; words; sayings.
(v.)- Talk; tell; narrate; conversate; speak.
話別 Bid farewell; bid adieu; say goodbye.
話題 A topic for conversation; a subject of talk.
話不投機 Talk not to the point; irrelevant remarks.
話中有話 Something hidden in one's speech.

**該** gāi (adj.)- Proper; fit. Necessary. The; this.
(v.)- Ought; should. Belong to. Owe.
該人 The said person.
該死 Deserving death; ought to die.
該犯 The said prisoner.
該處 The place in question.
該死的 Confound it! Damn it!

**詳** xiáng (n.)- Particulars; details.
(adv.)- Carefully; minutely; fully.
(v.)- Consider carefully; study; examine.
詳告 Tell minutely.
詳述 Detailed statement. Describe in full; explain in detail; give full details.
詳細 Part by part; by particulars; in detail.
詳問 Ask for details; inquire into fully.
詳解 Explain clearly; minute explanation.
詳閱 Read carefully.
詳細圖；部分圖 Detail drawing.
詳細情形 Situation in detail; ins and outs.
詳細說明 Detail; enter into particulars; enter into detail.
詳細價單；詳細價目表 Detailed price list.

**詼** huī (v.)- Joke; ridicule; jest.
詼笑 Make fun of; make sport of.
詼諧 Joke; jest.

**誅** zhū (v.)- Punish. Kill; put to death. Clear away. Claim; demand.
誅死 Kill; execute; put to death.
誅求 Demand booty; exact; squeeze.
誅滅 Exterminate utterly.
誅罰 Punish.
誅暴 Put the violent to death.

**誇** kuā (adj.)- Big; ample; wide; proud.
(v.)- Take pride in; be proud of; boast; vaunt; brag; exaggerate.
誇大 Exaggerate; magnify; overstate.
誇張 Brag; talk big; sound one's own praise; exaggerate.
誇獎；誇讚 Praise; extol.
誇耀 Make a display of; show off.
誇誇其談 Boastfulness; a big screed full of bombast; bragging.

**誌** zhì (n.)- Annals; history; record.
(v.)- Remember; keep in mind. Record; write down.
誌念 Keep in memory; bear in

mind.
誌哀 Express one's grief.
誌銘 Carve an inscription on stone.

認 (v.)- Acknowledge; recognize; promise; admit; accept.
rèn 認可 Give sanction; grant a permit. Sanction; approval.
認字 Recognize characters.
認作 Take as.
認眞 Be earnest in doing; in earnest; take it seriously.
認捐 Subscribe.
認許 Authorize; recognize; acknowledge; sanction; approve.
認爲 Deem; consider.
認罪 Confess a crime; apologize; confess sin; make a clean breast of.
認領 Establish the identity of.
認實 Confess the truth.
認輸 Yield the victory; acknowledge defeat; give in.
認錯 Admit one's fault; confess a fault.
認識 Know; recognize; take knowledge of; be acquainted with.
認不清 Unable to recognize clearly.
認可證 Certificate. License.
認識論 Epistemology; the theory of cognition.
認眞辦事 Give conscientious attention to the business.
認識不足 Lack of understanding.

誑 (n.)- A lie; a falsehood.
(v.)- Deceive; impose upon; lie; cheat; mislead.
kuáng 誑言 Lies; falsehood.

誓 (n.)- An oath; a vow.
(v.)- Take an oath; make a vow; swear; pledge.
shì 誓言 An oath; a vow; a pledge.
誓願 Make a vow.
誓效忠誠 Swear allegiance.

誕 (n.)- A birthday.
(v.)- Boast; brag. Bear baby.
dàn Deceive. Be wide apart.
誕日; 誕辰 A birthday.
誕生 Birth; give birth to; bear.

誘 (v.)- Lead; guide. Allure; tempt; entice; seduce.
you 誘引 Induce; attract.
誘出 Decoy out; entice away (out); lure away.
誘拐 Abduction; kidnapping. Kidnap; carry off.
誘食 Tempt to eat.
誘姦 Entice into adultery; seduce.
誘惑 Temptation; allurement. Tempt to evil; beguile; seduce; allure; fascinate; attract; entice; captivate.
誘陷 Decoy; betray; lure; delude.
誘敵 Draw out an enemy; make a diversion, as in war.
誘導 Lead; guide; induce; influence.
誘勸 Persuade.

語 (n.)- Language; phrases; words; conversation; discourse; sentence; speech; expressions;
yǔ statement.
(v.)- Talk; converse; speak. Tell; inform.
語句 Words and phrases.
語言 Language; words; speech.
語法 Grammar; phraseology.
語音 Enunciation.
語氣 Wording; address; diction; one's tone; mood.
語源 The derivation (origin) of a word.
語彙 A vocabulary; a glossary.
語態 Articulation; voice.

語調 A tone of voice.
語言學 Philology. Linguistics.
語音學 Phonetics.
語源學 Etymology.
語體文 Writings in the spoken style; vernacular literature.
語言學者 Philologist.

**誠** chéng (adj.)- Sincere; honest; guileless; truth.
(adv.)- Really; truly; indeed; certainly; in fact.
誠心; 誠意 Sincerity; faith; singleness of heart. Heartily; earnestness; cordiality; from the bottom of one's heart.
誠然 In reality; indeed; in fact; in truth; certainly; quite; exactly.
誠實 Honest; sincere; truthful; faithful; frankhearted; open as day.
誠懇 Honest; cordial.

**誡** jiè (n.)- A rule of conduct; a commandment; a precept; order; injunction.
(v.)- Warn; prohibit; admonish; caution against.
誡律 A commandment.

**誣** wū (v.)- Make a false accusation; charge (accuse) falsely.
誣告 Accuse wrongfully; charge falsely; make a false accusation.
誣陷; 誣賴 Implicate falsely; involve others by false charges.
誣謗 Malign; speak evil of; slander.
誣衊 Caluminate; slander.

**誤** wù Same as 悮 .
(n.)- A mistake; a fault; an error; a blunder.
(adj.)- Fallacious; erroneous; wrong; faulty; mistaken.
(v.)- Mistake; fail; delay; commit a fault.
誤用 Misuse.
誤印 A misprint; a printer's error.
誤字 A wrong word; a clerical error.
誤事 Spoil an affair.
誤時 Let the right moment pass; be behind time.
誤會 Misunderstand; misapprehend or misjudge.
誤解 Mistake; misunderstand; misinterpret.
誤了終身 Bring evil upon one's whole life; make a failure of one's life.
誤入歧途 Unwittingly to take a side track; degenerate; corrupt.

**誥** gào (v.)- Order; announce; command.
誥誡 Enjoin solemnly.

**誦** sòng (v.)- Hum over; sing; recite; read loudly; intone; chant.
誦經 Chant the liturgy.
誦詩 Recite poetry; chant poems.
誦讀 Read aloud; hum over; go over; chant.

**誨** huì (n.)- Counsel; advice; instruction; information.
(v.)-Teach; instruct. Admonish; advise; educate.
誨淫 Induce men to wantonness.
誨人不倦 Never tired of teaching others; teach without weariness.

**說** shuō (n.)- Words; speech; sayings.
(v.)- Talk; speak; tell; say; narrate; explain; persuade.
說服 Convince; bring round.
說到 Mention; speak of.
說明 Explain; clear up; expound; show;

explanation.
說法 A way of speaking; an idiom.
說謊 Preach Buddhism.
說話 Speak; talk; converse.
Tell lies; falsify.
說人情 Appeal to a person on behalf of another.
說明書 An explanation; an explanatory statement.
說相聲 Mimic sounds and voices—as showmen; cross-talk.
說笑話 Jest; joke; tell jokes.
說人是非 Backbite.
說來話長 It is a long story to tell.
說明理由 Tell (explain) the reason.
說得有理 Speak to the point.

誰 shuí (pro.)- Who? Whom? Which? Whose? Anyone.
誰的 Whose?
誰家 Whose family? of what family?
誰能 Who can?
誰想；誰料 Who thinks so? Who would have thought?

課 kè (n.)- An example; an exercise; a lesson. Taxes. A section; a division.
課文 An essay; a lesson.
課本 A text book.
課桌 Desk.
課室 Classroom.
課程 Lessons; course of study; a curriculum.
課題 A subject; a theme.
課程表 Schedule.
課外活動 Extra-curricula activities.
課稅繁重 Heavy taxes.

誼 yì (n.)- Friendship; relations; goodness.
(adj.)- Right; proper.
(v.)- Discuss; deliberate.
誼厚；誼篤 Deep friendship.
誼同手足 Brotherly relationship.

誹 fěi (v.)- Slander; backbite; defame; abuse; calumniate.
誹謗 Speak evil of; censure; abuse; slander; backbite; defame.
誹議 Malicious talk.
誹謗者 A slanderer; a libeller.
誹謗行爲 A libel action.

調 diào [tiáo] (n.)- A tune; a note.
(v.)- Mix; stir up; harmonize; adjust; regulate; blend; compromise; temper.
調子 Tune; pitch; key; tone; note.
調皮 Artful; cunning.
調兵 Move troops.
調味 Season; flavour; adjust the various tastes in eatables.
調和 Harmony; concord. Mix; blend. Make peace. Harmonize sounds; tune up in tune—as instruments.
調查 Investigate; examine; search for; find out; look over; beat over. Investigation; examination.
調動 Transfer.
調理 Arrange—as a business; heal; repair.
調換 Exchange; change.
調經 Regulate the menses.
調解 Come to an agreement.
調節 Regulate; adjust; control; modulate.
調整 Regulate; adjust; put (set) in order.
調劑 Arrange; temper; compensate; mingle in proportion.
調戲 Dally with; insult a female.
調遷 To transfer to another post.
調羹 A spoon. Season soups.

調子低 Low-pitched; in a low key.
調子高 High-pitched; in a high key.
調色板 A palette.
調味品 Seasoning; dressing material; condiments; spices.
調査員 An inspector; an investigator.
調和爭端 Mediate a dispute.
調査戶口 Take a census.
調整物價 Regulation (adjustment) of prices.

諂 (v.)- Flatter; toady; cajole; curry favour; fawn upon; wheedle; praise falsely.
chǎn
諂言 Flattering words; flattery.
諂笑 Flatter and giggle; laugh and joke with, in order to please.
諂媚 Flatter; fawn on. Flattery; blandishment.
諂態 Flattering manner.

諄 (v.)- Teach carefully; impress upon.
zhūn (adv.)- Carefully; earnestly. Repeatedly; emphatically.
諄諄 Unwearied in teaching. Earnestly; emphatically; patiently.
諄囑 Repeat one's orders.

談 (n.)- A conversation; a talk; a chat; a discourse.
tán (v.)- Chat; talk; converse; discuss.
談及 Talk about; touch on.
談心 Familiar talk; hearty talk.
談天 Talk about everything.
談判 Negotiation; parley. Negotiate; confer; talk over.
談笑 Laugh and talk. Converse pleasantly.
談起 Talk of.
談話 Talk (converse, chat) with; have a talk; confabulate; hold a conversation; engage in conversation.
談論 Talk over; discuss; argue; discourse; converse.
談話會 A conversazione; an informal meeting.
談天說地 Talk all kinds of subjects.
談吐風生 Light, bright, interesting talk.

諉 (v.)- Implicate. Shirk; evade. Lay the blame on others.
wěi 諉託 Shift on to someone else.
諉過 Put the blame upon others.
諉爲不知 Pretend not to know.

請 (v.)- Invite; engage. Request; please; beg; ask permission.
qǐng Send for.
請示 Ask for instruction.
請進 Please come in.
請安 Present one's compliments; give one's best regards.
請坐 Please sit down; take your seat.
請求 Ask; beg; request; apply; pray; make a request.
請帖；請柬 An invitation card; a letter of invitation.
請客 Invite guests; give a feast.
請假 Ask for leave; petition for furlough.
請宴；請酒 Invite to a banquet.
請問 Ask civilly; request. May I ask you?
請教 May I ask you ? Ask for instruction. Will you kindly tell me ? Take counsel; take advice with; consult.
請罪 Apologize; ask for pardon; confess a fault.
請醫 Send for a doctor; call in a doctor.
請用菜 Please help yourself.
請願書 A written petition.
請假期間 The period for which leave of

absence is asked.

諍 (v.)- Argue; expostulate with; urge reason to; remonstrate with.
zhèng

諒 (adj.)- Sincere; faithful.
liàng
(v.)- Excuse; pardon; have faith in; believe. Suppose; guess.
(adv.)- Probably.

諒之 Excuse; make allowance for.
諒解 Understand; come to an agreement. Good understanding.
諒必如此 I think it must be so.

論 (n.)- An essay; a thesis; a composition; a treatise; a discussion; an argument.
lùn
(v.)- Discourse; talk about; consider; discuss; debate; criticize; regard; consult; argue.

論及 Talk or speak about; inasmuch as; in regard to; with reference to.
論文 Talk on literary subject. An essay; a thesis; a theme; a treatise; an article.
論定 Decide after discussion; settle.
論述 Treat of; state.
論壇 The world of criticism.
論據 Data; ground of proof; the basis of an argument.
論戰 A debate (disputation); a verbal clash (combat); wordy warfare.
論點 The point (purport) of an argument; the point at issue; the gist of the contention.
論斷 Infer; conclude; judge; draw an inference; make a conclusion.
論證 Demonstration. Prove the truth; demonstrate.
論辯 Debate; discuss.
論理學 Logic.
論理學家 A logician.

諛 (n.)- Flattery; adulation.
yú
(v.)- Flatter; praise; blarney.
諛色 A toadying expression.
諛言 Flattery.

諜 (n.)- A spy; a traitor.
dié
(v.)- Spy; play the traitor; reconnoiter.
諜探；間諜 A spy; a secret agent.

諜諜；喋喋 Talkative.

諠 (v.)- Bawl. Forget.
xuān
(adj.)- Noisy.
諠傳 Spread reports.
諠譁 Uproar; hubbub; clamour. Noisy; clamorous.

諦 (n.)- Buddhist term for the Truth.
dì
(v.)- Examine; make researches; discriminate.

諦視 Scrutinize; examine closely; look into.

諧 (adj.)- Harmonious; agreeing; accordant.
xié
諧和 Bring into harmony; keep chime with.

諧音 Chime; harmony in music.

諫 (n.)- An advice; a counsel; an expostulation.
jiàn
(v.)- Remonstrate; admonish; advise; reprove.

諫止；諫阻 Urge one to desist from evil.
諫勸 Advise; counsel.

諭 (n.)- An edict; an order; a command.
yù
(v.)- Order; command; proclaim. Instruct; advice; signify.

Know; understand.
諭示；諭告 Notify by proclamation.
諭令 Order.
諭禁 Prohibit publicly; issue orders for the stoppage of.
諭遵 Order obedience to.

諮 Same as 咨.
zī (v.)- Confer; consult.
諮問；諮詢 Consult; inquire of; ask advice; take advice.
諮詢委員 A consulative committee.
諮詢機關 An advisory organ.

諱 (n.)- A name after death; one's posthumous name.
huì 諱言 Forbidden talk; not to be mentioned.
諱法 Rules for applying names to deceased persons.
諱疾忌醫 Conceal the disease and avoid the doctor.

諳 (v.)- Fully acquainted with; versed in. Learn by heart; commit to memory.
ān 諳曉；諳悉 Have a good knowledge of.

諷 (n.)- Irony; satire.
fěng (v.)- Satirize; ridicule; hint at; allude to. Recite; rehearse.
諷味 Enjoy a book; relish.
諷刺 A pointed gibe; a satire; a squib. Ridicule; satirize.
諷語 Irony; satire.
諷刺畫 A caricature; a cartoon.

諸 (adj.)- All; many; every; whole; numerous; several.
zhū (prep.)- To; in; at; on; from.
諸色 All classes; all sorts; all kinds.
諸多 Many.
諸位；列位 You; sirs; gentlemen.
諸侯 The feudal princes; the feudal lords.
諸等數；複名數 A compound number.
諸子百家 All classes of authors or philosophers.
諸如此類 All are similar to this.

諺 (n.)- A proverb; a common saying; a maxim.
yàn 諺語 Proverbial phrase.

諾 (v.)- Promise; consent; assent. Respond; give one's word; answer a call.
nuò (adv.)- Yes.
諾言 A promise.
諾貝爾獎金 Nobel Prizes.

謀 (n.)- A plan; a device; a scheme.
(v.)- Plot; scheme; plan; devise.
móu Consult; deliberate; ponder.
謀士 A schemer; a strategist; a tactician; a counsellor.
謀生 Contrive to get a livelihood; plan to get a living; earn a living; work for one's living.
謀臣 A clever adviser; a counsellor; a strategist.
謀事 Plan; devise; desire a job; devise how to act.
謀害 Plot against; plan mischief; plot to injure; brew mischief.
謀殺 Premeditated homicide (murder); plot a murder.
謀殺事件 A murder case.

謁 (v.)- See or visit a superior; call upon; inform.
yè 謁見 Visit a superior: have an audience; interview.

**謂** wèi (n.)- Meaning.
(v.)- Address; speak of; say; tell; call; name.

**謄** téng (v.)- Copy; transcribe.
謄本 A transcript; a copy.
謄清 Make a fair copy; copy clearly.
謄寫；謄錄 Copy; transcribe; reproduce copies; press-copy.
謄寫板 A mimeograph; a manifolder.
謄寫員；書記 Copier.
謄寫機 Duplicating machine.

**謊** huǎng Same as 詤
(v.)- Make wild statement; lie; mis-state.
*謊言 Falsehoods; lies.
謊騙 Cheat; impose on.

**謎** mí 謎語 A riddle; a conundrum; a puzzle; an enigma.

**謗** bàng (v.)- Slander; backbite; defame; detract; speak against.
謗譭 Speak against; slander; vilify; detract.
謗譭者 Detractor; slanderer.

**謙** qiān (n.)- Humility.
(v.)- Be humble; humble oneself; be modest; be unassuming.
謙虛；謙遜 Humble; modest. Be modest (humble); condescend; depreciate oneself.
謙辭 Modest wording.
謙讓 Yield. Unobtrusive; courteousness.
謙恭持己 Hold oneself with modesty.

**講** jiǎng (v.)- Talk over; speak; discourse on; discuss; converse; explain; preach. Negotiate for peace.
講究 Be particular about. Splendid; elegant; careful.
講和 Negotiate peace; settle a matter peacefully.
講明 Explain a matter clearly; clearly stated.
講述 Describe; address.
講座 A chair.
講師 A lecturer.
講義 A transcript of lectures.
講經 Give a sermon.
講解 Give the sense.
講話 Talk; speak.
講演 A lecture; an address.
講價 Haggle over prices.
講故事 Tell stories.
講笑話 Tell funny stories; break a jest.
講習所 A training school.
講演會 A lecture-meeting.

**謝** xié (v.)- Thank; express gratitude. Refuse; reject; decline.
謝帖 A card of thanks.
謝信 A letter of thanks.
謝萎 To fade.
謝恩 Acknowledge a favour; give thanks for favour; return thanks for kindness received.
謝罪 Offer an apology; confess one's faults; apologize; beg pardon.
謝絕 Decline; cut off or sever intercourse with; decline seeing; break off intercourse with; refuse; reject utterly.
謝答 Return thanks.
謝意 Appreciation; gratitude; thanks.
謝辭 An address of thanks.
謝絕參觀 No visitors allowed. "No Admittance".

**謠** yáo (n.)- A rustic ditty; a street song; a ballad. A rumor; hearsay; a false report.

謠言 A rumour; wild stories; unfounded reports.
謠傳 It is rumoured that. . . ; rumour has it that. . . .
謠歌 A rustic ditty; a country ballad.

**謦** qǐng (v.)- Cough.
謦欬 Tone of voice.

**謨** mó (n.)- Well-organized plans; a plan; a scheme.

**謫** zhé (n.)- A fault; an error.
(v.)- Blame; scold; reproach; condemn; exile. Punish; banish.
謫奸 Condemn wicked deeds.
謫降 Degraded in office.
謫罰 Punish by fine.

**謬** miù (n.)- An error; a mistake; a blunder.
(adj.)- Fallacious; misleading; untrue; erroneous; absurd; wild.
謬傳 A false report.
謬誤 An error; a blunder; a mistake.
謬說 Nonsense; fallacious discourse.
謬論 A fallacy; a mistaken argument.

**謳** ōu (n.)- Local ditties.
(v.)- Sing; chant.
謳吟 Sing songs.
謳歌 Local ditties. Sing ballads.

**謹** jǐn (adj.)- Careful; cautious; vigilant; prudent; discreet.
(v.)- Heed; watch; be on guard; be cautious; be discreet.
(adv.)- Carefully; attentively.
謹守 Guard carefully; watch over.
謹防 Be on one's guard against.
謹言 Speak carefully. Bridle one's tongue; weigh one's words.
謹愼 Cautious; careful; watchful; heedful. Take every caution against; be circumspect; be discreet.
謹聽 Listen with attention; be attentive to; be all attention.
謹防假冒 Beware of counterfeits.

**謾** màn (v.)- Deceive; cheat; mislead. Insult. Tell a lie.
謾言 A lie; exaggrated talks.
謾罵 Abuse.

**譁** huá Same as 嘩.
(n.)- Clamour; noise; hubbub; tumult.
(adj.)- Noisy; clamorous; turbulent.
(v.)- Make a great noise; bawl; shout; vociferate.
譁笑 Noisy laughter.
譁鬧 Clamour; make noise.
譁衆取寵 To impress people by claptrap.

**證** zhèng Same as 証.
(n.)- Evidence; proof; testimony.
(v.)- Give proof of; prove; testify.
證人 A witness.
證明 Prove; certify; testify; confirm; verify; give proof of.
證券 A bill; a bond; securities.
證書 A certificate; a diploma.
證實 Prove it to be true; confirm; corroborate; ascertain; verify.
證據 Proof; evidence; testimony; verification; warrant; certificate.
證人席 A witness-box (-stand).
證明書 A voucher; a certificate.
證婚人 Witness in wedding.
證券市場 The securities market.

證券保險 Title insurance.
證據文件 Written testimony; documentary evidence.
證據不足 Insufficiency of evidence.
證券交易所 A stock exchange.

譏 (v.)- Ridicule; mock at; jeer; satirize; joke; slander. Inspect; examine.
jī
譏笑；譏刺 Ridicule; mock at; jeer; fleer; flout at; deride; sneer at; satirize.
譏諷 Satirize; ridicule; jeer.

譖 (n.)- Defamation.
(v.)- Slander; vilify; discredit; defame.
zèn
譖言 Slander.
譖譏 Injure by slanders.

識 (n.)- Knowledge; learning; insight.
shí
(adj.)- Acquainted with; versed in.
(v.)- Understand; know well; distinguish. Recognize; be acquainted with; remember.
識字 Be able to read; literate.
識別 Distinguish; discern; discriminate.
識破 Detect; see through; be fully aware of; find out.
識貨 Know the quality of goods.
識見廣博者 A man with breadth of view and understanding; a man of broad vision.

譙 (v.)- Blame; scold; ridicule.
譙責 Blame; scold.
qiáo

譚 (n.)- Extravagant.
(v.)- Boast; talk.
tán

譜 (n.)- A register; a record; a family genealogical list; a record of clans.
pǔ
(v.)- Arrange in order; set a song to music.
譜錄 Scientific repertories and similar works.
譜成歌曲 Compose (write) music to a song; set a song to music.

譟 (n.)- The noise of a crowd; disturbance; clamour; uproar.
zào
(v.)- Disturb; make a noise.
譟鬧 Hubbub; uproar.

警 (n.)- Police.
(v.)- Warn; notify; caution; call attention; admonish; make aware; give notice of danger.
jǐng
警犬 A police dog; a patrol dog.
警司 A (police) lieutenant.
警長 An inspector.
警告 Warning; caution; admonition. Give notice of alarm; give notice of danger; give warning.
警戒 Watch for; guard against. Warn; caution against; take precautions against.
警官 A police officer.
警惕 Caution; admonition.
警備 Defend; guard; stand guard.
警報 An alarm; a warning.
警察 The police.
警衛 Guard; be on guard.
警醒 Awake and be alert; arouse; stir.
警戒色 A warning colour.
警戒線 Lines of operation; a cordon.
警察局；警察署 The police station; the police board.
警察廳 Metropolitan police board; police bureau.
警察總局 The police headquarters.

警務處長 The commissioner of police.
警察行政 Police administrations.
警察署長 Chief of a police station.

譫 譫語 Delirium; incoherent talk.
zhān

譬 (n.)- A simile; a metaphor; an allegory; a fable; a parable.
pì (v.)- Compare; suppose; illustrate; liken.
譬如 For example; may be compared with; for instance.
譬喻 Comparison; illustration; metaphor. For instance; illustrate; compare to; use a simile (metaphor).

譯 (v.)- Explain. Translate; interpret; render.
yì 譯文 A translation; a version.
譯音 Transliteration.
譯員 A translator; an interpreter.
譯爲中文 Translate it into Chinese.
譯密碼電報 Decode a telegram.

議 (n.)- Articles of agreement; a proposal; discussion; deliberation; consultation.
yì (v.)- Discuss; consider; talk about.
議決 Resolve; pass a vote of; decide.
議定 Decide; agree; settled after deliberation; come to terms.
議長 The speaker; the chairman.
議員 Members of parliament; legislator; assembly man.
議案 A bill; proposal for discussion.
議院；議會 The House; the Chamber; the Parliament; the Congress.
議程 Programme.
議論 Discuss; argue; debate.
議決案 A resolution.
議決權 The right or voting; a vote.
議事廳 A public hall; a council office; an assembly hall.
議事日程 The order of the day; the agenda.
議會政治 Parliamentary government (politics).
議會領袖 Parliamentary chief; floor leader (美).
議會黨團 Parliamentary groups.
議會解散 Dissolve the House.
議論風生 Argue with great heat; engage in an animated discussion.
議會候選人 A carpet bagger.

譴 (v.)- Reprimand; scold.
qiǎn 譴責 Reprimand; blame; censure.

護 (v.)- Protect; guard; defend; escort; help; save; aid.
hù 護兵 A body-guard; an escort.
護送 Send under guard; convoy; escort.
護照 A passport.
護士 A nurse.
護理 To nurse.
護衞；保護 Protect; defend; guard; escort.
護國安民 Guard the state and pacify the people.

譽 (n.)- Fame; reputation; honour; praise.
yù (v.)- Praise; eulogize; flatter; admire; extol; commend; laud.
譽美 Commend goodness.
譽望 A good reputation.

讀 (v.)- Read; study; recite; learn; peruse.
dú 讀文 Read essays.

讀本 A reader; a reading-book.
讀法 The way of reading.
讀物 Reading matter; books.
讀者 A reader.
讀音 Pronunciation.
讀書 Study; reading.
讀報 Read a newspaper.
讀書人 A scholar; the literati.
讀音統一 Unification of the language.
讀音朗然 Read loudly.
讀錯一行 Miss a line.

**變** biàn (n.)- A change; an alternation; transformation. An emergency; an insurrection.
(adj.)- Versatile; changeable.
(v.)- Change; reform; transform. Modify; vary; make different; alter.
變心 Change one's mind; alter one's views.
變化 Change; transformation; evolution.
變成 Become; change into; be converted into; turn to.
變色 Change of colour; change countenance; fade; become discoloured.
變形 Deformation; transformation; transfiguration.
變法 Reform.
變相 Change appearance; change form; changeable; versatile.
變故 Calamity; misfortune; changes.
變革 A change; a revolution.
變動 Change; alteration; variation; fluctuation.
變換 Change; convert.
變量（數） Variable quantity.
變態 An anomaly; abnormality.
變價；變賣 Turn into money; sell; dispose by sale.
變遷 Change; alter; under many changes.
變調（樂） A variation. Change the tune.
變質 Change in quality; degeneration.
變壞 Change for the worse; spoiled; go bad.
變流器 A current-transformer; a converter.
變壓器 A transformer.
變成事實 To come true.
變節分子 Turncoat; backslider; apostate.
變態心理 Abnormal mentality.

**讎** chóu Same as 讐.
(n.)- An enemy; a foe; a rival.
讎人；讎敵 An enemy; a foe; an opponent.
讎隙 A breach; a quarrel.

**讒** chán (v.)- Slander; accuse; defame; misrepresent; detract; speak against; report maliciously.
讒人 A traducer; a slanderer; a calumniator.
讒害 Injure by misrepresentation.
讒謗 Slander; backbite; calumniate; talk scandal; libel.
讒言惹禍 Calumny brings trouble.

**讓** ràng (adj.)- Humble; retiring; courteous; polite; yielding; modest.
(v.)- Yield; resign; give up; cede; surrender. Reprove.
讓位 Abdicate; give up a seat; give away.
讓步 Give in; yield a step; concede; make a concession.
讓座 Invite to take a seat.
讓與 Transfer; cede to; yield; surrender.
讓路 Yield the path; make way; give way.
讓權 Yield one's right.
讓與價格 Transfer price.

**讙** huān
Same as 歡.
(n.)- Good news; clamour; noise; voice of joy.
(v.)- Bawl; stimulate by cheering words.
讙鬧 Clamour; hubbub.
讙囂 Acclamations; shoutings.

**讚** zàn
(n.)- Eulogium; admiration; commendation; eulogy.
(v.)- Praise; eulogize; admire; commend; extol; speak highly of.
讚文 A written eulogium.
讚美；稱讚 Praise; adore; extol; admire; commend.
讚揚 Praise; commend.
讚頌 Sing the praise of.
讚賞 Be appreciated.
讚美詩 A hymn; a psalm.
讚嘆不已 Praising and admiring unceasingly.

# 谷 部

**谷** gǔ
(n.)- A valley; a ravine; a gorge; a dale.
谷口 A gorge.
谷穴(生) The hollow behind the ankle.
谷底 The bottom of a ravine (gorge).

**谿** xī
(n.)- A brook; a rivulet; a current.
谿谷 A valley.
谿刻；刻薄 Mean and petty; stingy.

**豁** huō
(n.)- An open valley.
(adj.)- Wide; open.
(v.)- Split open; break. Expand. Release; remit. Understand.
豁免 Release; remit; exempt from.
豁除 Remove.
豁開 Frank; open.
豁然 Openly; evidently; suddenly.

# 豆 部

**豆** dòu
(n.)- Beans; peas; legumes.
豆沙 Bean cream.
豆油 Bean oil.
豆芽 Bean sprout.
豆莢 Bean pods.
豆腐 Bean curd.
豆蔻(植) Nutmegs; cardamoms.
豆漿 Juice from beans.
豆餅 Bean-cake.
豆醬 Bean sauce.
豆科植物 Legume.

**豈** qǐ
(adv.)- An interrogative particle. How?
豈可 How can it be?
豈敢 How dare I?—A self-depreciatory term.
豈能 How can he do it?
豈有此理 There is no such rule! There is no such principle!

**豉** chǐ (n.)- Salted beans, used as condiments.
豉油 Soy.

**豌** wān (n.)- Peas.
豌豆 Peas; the garden pea; pisum sativum.

**豎** shù Same as 竪.
(adj.)- Upright; perpendicular; vertical. A perpendicular stroke in writing.
(v.)- Set up; stand upright.
豎立 Raise; establish; stand erect.
豎直 Perpendicular; upright.
豎起 Set up; raise.
豎琴 A harp.
豎井礦 Shaft mine.

**豐** fēng (adj.)- Abundant; plentiful; copious; luxuriant; fruitful.
豐年 An abundant year; years of good crop.
豐收；豐稔 An abundant (bumper) harvest; a good harvest.
豐足 Abundant; prosperous; sufficient.
豐厚 Plentiful; sumptuous.
豐美 Luxuriant; abundant.
豐盛 Abundant; prosperous.
豐裕 Rich; wealthy; well-to-do.
豐富 Rich; wealthy; plentiful.
豐滿 Well-developed; buxom.
豐壤；豐腴 Fertile land.
豐饒 Fertile; rich.
豐富多彩 To show colour and variety.
豐衣足食 Ample clothing and sufficient food; well-fed and well-clothed.
豐盛酒席 Splendid banquet.
豐碩的果實 Rich fruits.

**豔** yàn Same as 艷，艶.
(adj.)- Beautiful; handsome; pretty; charming; fascinating. Seductive. Plump.
(v.)- Admire; desire.
豔粧 Beautifully dressed; handsomely dressed.
豔慕；豔羡 Admire; long for; desire.
豔麗 Beautiful; glorious; charming.
豔色動人 Beauty excites men; fascinating.

# 豕 部

**豕** shǐ (n.)- A pig; a hog; a swine.
豕心 A greedy mind.
豕肉 Pork.
豕牢；豕圈 A pigsty; a pig-pen.
豕油 Lard.
豕鬃 Pig's bristles.

**豚** tún (n.)- A sucking pig; a porker; a shoal.
豚尾 A cue; a pigtail.
豚蹄 Pig's pettitoes.

**象** xiàng (n.)- An elephant. An image; a resemblance. Phenomena.
象牙 Elephant's tusks. Ivory.
象皮 India-rubber; eraser; elephant's skin—used as a medicine.
象棋 The game of chess.
象徵 A symbol.
象鼻 Trunk.
象闕 The palace.
象牙扇 An ivory fan.
象徵派 The symbolist school.

象牙之塔 The tower of ivory.
象牙彫刻 Ivory carving.
象形文字 Hieroglyph.
象徵主義 Symbolism.

豢 huàn (v.)- Feed; rear; tend. Bait; bribe; befriend.
豢養 Rear; nourish; bring up.

豪 háo (adj.)- Eminent; superior; heroic; martial; brave. Extravagant.
豪雨 A heavy rain; a downpour; a cloudburst.
豪門 A wealthy and powerful family.
豪豬（動）A porcupine.
豪强 Violent; overbearing.
豪華 Luxurious; magnificent.
豪富 A millionaire.
豪傑 A hero; a great man.
豪語 Big talk; bombast. Brag.
豪邁 Undaunted; lofty; exalted; dauntless; of unfaltering courage; large-hearted.
豪華生活 Live in magnificent style; live like a lord.

豫 yù Same as 預.
(adj.)- Easy; contented; peaceful; pleased; happy; satisfied. Ready; prepared. The province of Honan.
(v.)- Prepare; prearrange; get ready.
(adv.)- Already; beforehand; previously.
豫付 Pay in advance.
豫兆 A presage; a portent.
豫先 Beforehand.
豫防 Be prepared against; keep (ward) off; guard against; take preventive measures.
豫告 Notify beforehand. A previous notice (warning).
豫言 Prophecy. Predict; foretell; forecast; prophesy.
豫科 A preparatory course.
豫料；豫期 Estimate; forecast; foresee.
豫習 Prepare lessons.
豫備 Prepare; make ready; arrange beforehand; prearrange.
豫測 Estimate; forecast.
豫報 Forecast; predict.
豫感 Premonition; preperception; presentiment; foreboding.
豫算 An estimate; a budget.
豫演 A rehearsal; a preliminary exercise.
豫選 Provisional selection (election); pre-election; nomination. Pre-elect; nominate; elect provisionally.
豫言家 A prophet.
豫備金 Appropriate money.
豫備品 Spare stores.
豫備軍 A reserve army.
豫算表 A budget.
豫防注射 Preventive inoculation.
豫防傳染 Prevent infection.

豬 zhū Same as 猪.
(n.)- The pig; the hog; the swine; a boar; a sow.
豬肉 Pork.
豬油 Lard; pork-fat.
豬鬃 Hog's bristles.
豬欄 Pigsty.
豬籠草 Pitcher plant.

# 豸 部

豹 (n.)- A leopard; a panther; a species of wild cat.
bào 豹略 Clever strategy.
豹眼 Look fierce.

豺 (n.)- A wild dog; the jackal.
(adj.)- Wolfish; wicked; cruel.
chái 豺狠 The jackal and wolf; cruel and avaricious persons.

貂 (a.)- The sable; the marten.
貂毛 Sable hair.
diāo 貂皮 Sable skins; sable fur.

貉 Same as 狢.
(n.)- The badger. A tribe of
hé savages.
貉道 The principles of savages.

貌 (n.)- Face; countenance; looking; appearance; figure; visage;
mào complexion; form; manner.
貌似 Seem; look like.
貌美 A beautiful face.
貌合心離 Apparently of one accord, but divided in heart.
貌似强大 To appear to be powerful; outwardly strong.

貍 Same as 狸.
(n.)- The wild cat; the fox;
lí the raccoon; a striped cat.
貍貓；山貓 A striped cat; a wild cat.

貓 Same as 猫
(n.)- The cat; a kitten.
māo 貓睛石 A cat's-eye.
貓頭鷹(動) The horned-owl.

貔 (n.)- The white fox.
貔貅(動) A kind of animal like
pí a tiger. A brave and courageous soldier.

貛 (n.)- The badger.
huān

# 貝 部

貝 (n.)- A shell; cowrie. Money; valuables; ancient; coin.
bèi (adj.)- Precious; valuable.
貝母(植) A fritellaria.
貝殼 A shell.
貝加爾湖(地) Baikal Lake.

貞 (adj.)- Pure; virtuous; uncorrupted; chaste; refined.
zhēn 貞女 A virgin.
貞木 A hard wood.
貞正 Pure and upright; firm in the right.
貞婦 A chaste widow who will not marry again.
貞淑 Chaste; pure.
貞操 Virtue; constancy; faithfulness.
貞潔 Chaste; pure, as a virgin.

負 (adj.)- Ungrateful; negative.
(v.)- Carry on the back; bear.
fù Be defeated. Turn the back on; offend; be ungrateful. Rely on; depend on; trust to; be in debt; owe. Fail; lose. Disregard; disappoint.

負心 Ungrateful; heartless.
負重 Bear a heavy burden.
負氣 Be in a bad temper; harbour ill feelings; proud and peevish.
負責 Take (shoulder) the responsibility of; bear the blame for.
負債 Get (fall) into debt. Be in debt; owe money.
負傷 Be wounded; be injured; get hurt; sustain an injury.
負號(算) A minus sign; a negative sign.
負數 A negative number.
負擔 A burden; a charge; a responsibility. Bear; sustain.
負義忘恩 Ungrateful.

財 (n.)- Property; wealth; valuables; money; riches.
cái (adj.)- Rich.
財力 Financial ability; resources; the power of wealth.
財主 A wealthy man; a capitalist; a rich fellow.
財帛 Riches; wealth; valuables.
財物 Property; effects.
財政 Finance.
財產 Property; estate.
財團 A foundation; a consortium; a financial group.
財政部 Ministry of finance; the Exchequer (英).
財政學 The science of finance.
財政年度 Fiscal year.
財政困難 Financial (pecuniary) embarrassments (difficulties).
財政計劃 A financial programme.
財政部長 Minister of finance.
財產繼承 Succession to a property.

貢 (n.)- Tribute; homage paid. Revenue.
gòng (v.)- Offer as a tribute. Submit.
貢品 Articles of tribute—of the best quality.
貢獻 An offering; a contribution. Make a contribution; render services.

貧 (n.)- Poverty; indigence; penury.
pín (adj.)- Poor; impoverished; destitute; needy.
貧人；貧民 A poor man; poor people; paupers.
貧苦 Poor and miserable; poverty and distress.
貧富 The poor and the rich; wealth and poverty; people of every condition.
貧農 Poor peasant.
貧賤 In humble circumstances; poor and humble.
貧民窟 The slums; the slum quarters; a poor district.
貧血症(醫) Anaemia.
貧病相連 Poverty and sickness are closely associated.

貨 (n.)- Goods; merchandise; commodities; wares; cargo. Wealth;
huò money.
貨主 The owner of goods; the vender.
貨色 Stock in trade.
貨車 A goods-wagon; a freight-car; a truck; a freight-train; a goods-train.
貨物 Goods; wares; merchandise; commodities; articles.
貨倉；貨棧 A warehouse; a godown; a freight house; a storehouse.
貨船 A freight vessel; a cargo-boat; a tramp.
貨單 A manifest; an invoice; list of goods.
貨價 The price of goods.

貨幣 Money; a coin; metal currency.
貨樣 Samples of goods; specimen.
貨艙 The hold of a vessel.
貨攤 A Stall.
貨箱船 Containership.
貨到付款 Cash on delivery (C.O.D.).
貨到通告 Advice of arrival.
貨品標號 Quality mark.
貨眞價實 Genuine goods and real (not nominal) price.
貨物陳列室 Show room.

販 fàn (n.)- A peddler.
(v.)- Buy and sell; deal; carry about for sale; traffic.
販夫 A peddler; a hawker.
販貨 Trade.
販賣 Sell; deal (trade) in; peddle.
販賣人口 Deal in human beings.
販賣佣金 Selling commission.
販賣契約 Selling contract.

貪 tān (adj.)- Greedy; desirous; covetous.
(v.)- Covet; be greedy for; be covetous of; wish for what is unlawful.
貪心 A greedy mind; covetousness.
貪官 A corrupt official.
貪玩 Fond of play.
貪食 Gluttonous; voracious. Devour.
貪財 Greedy of money; covetous for wealth.
貪汚 Corruption; graft; corrupt.
貪婪 Avaricious; greedy; covetous.
貪睡 Be fond of sleep.
貪慾 Avarice; rapacity; covetousness; greediness.
貪樂 Covet pleasure.
貪心不足 Very covetous; insatiable.
貪生怕死 Clinging of life.
貪官汚吏 Corrupt officials.
貪汚腐化 Corrupt and degenerate.

貫 guàn (n.)- A measure.
(v.)- Go in series; string; run a thread into; connect. Penetrate; through; implicate; pierce.
貫串 Thread together; connect.
貫穿 Pierce (run) through; penetrate.
貫通 Have a thorough understanding; go through.
貫徹 Accomplish; carry through.
貫徹主張 Carry one's point; accomplish one's object; fulfil.

責 zé (n.)- Duty; responsibility; charge; liability.
(v.)- Ask for; demand. Reprove; punish; blame; reproach; charge with; be responsible; lay a weight on.
責任 Duty; responsibility; liability; obligation; charge.
責問 Put to the question.
責備 Rebuke; reprimand; blame; reprove.
責罰 Punish; chastise; inflict punishment on a person.
責罵 Abuse; rail at; blame; reproach.
責難 Censure; criticize; find fault with.
責任觀念 Sense of responsibility.

貯 zhù (v.)- Store up; hoard; put up; keep.
貯存 Store up; save up; have in store; hoard; deposit.
貯金 Savings. Save (lay by) money; deposit.
貯備 Lay in; prepare for; have a reserve.
貯蓄 Save; store up.
貯藏 Preserve; store; lay by; garner; conserve.
貯水池 A storage-reservior; a tank; a cistern.
貯備金 Reserve funds.
貯藏物 Stocks; reserves.

貯藏室 A storehouse; a storeroom.
貯蓄存款 Savings deposit.
貯蓄銀行 A savings-bank.
貯蓄存款摺 A deposit pass-book.

**貳** (adj.)- Double; two. Second; assistant. Doubtful.
èr (v.)- Be changeable; doubt.
貳心 Disloyal; harbour a treacherous intention.
貳言 Different opinion; conflicting views.

**貴** (adj.)- Noble; honourable; dignified; high. Valuable; precious;
guì Dear; costly; expensive. Your.
貴賓 Guest of honour.
貴土；貴處 Your honourable home district.
貴州(地) Kweichow.
貴姓 What is your name? Your honourable name?
貴重 Precious; valuable; priceless.
貴族 The nobility; the peerage. A nobleman; a peer.
貴國 Your nation; your state.
貴陽(地) Kweiyang.
貴賤 Dear and cheap. Noble and base; dignified and mean; patricians and plebeians.
貴金屬 Precious (noble) metals.
貴重品 Precious things; a valuable article; valuables.
貴婦人 A lady of rank; a noblewoman.
貴族院；上議院 The House of Peers. The House of Lords; the Upper House.
貴賓席 Seats reserved for distinguished visitors. A distinguished visitors' gallery.
貴賓室 A state room.
貴賤之分 Distinction between high and low degree.

**貶** (v.)- Lower; humiliate; disgrace; degrade; bring down.
biǎn 貶值 Devaluation.
貶評 Pass adverse judgment.
貶詞 An expression of censure.
貶價 Bring the price lower.
貶黜；貶謫 Degrade from office; degradation.

**買** (v.)- Buy; purchase.
買入 Buy; purchase.
mǎi 買主 The buyer or purchaser; customer.
買物 Shopping; a purchase.
買貨 Purchase goods.
買價 A purchase price.
買賣 Buying and selling; purchase and sell. Trade; business; bargain.
買辦 A compradore.
買賣契約 Contract of sale.
買入分錄賬；進貨分錄賬 Purchase journal.
買入報告單 Purchase report.
買辦封建制度 Comprador-fuedal system.
買辦大資產階級 Big comprador bourgeoisie.

**貸** (v.)- Lend on interest; borrow. Release. Pardon; forgive.
dài 貸入 Borrow; ask for a loan.
貸方；付項 The creditor side.
貸主；債主 The creditor; the lender.
貸金 A loan; money lent.
貸給 Credit.
貸借財產 Loan property.
貸借對照表 Balance sheet.

**費** (n.)- Expenses; expenditure; outlay; cost; charge; fees.
fèi (v.)- Spend; waste; consume; expend; use; lavish.
費力 Put oneself to trouble; difficult;

laborious; use effort.
費心 Exhaust one's mind; thanks for the trouble you have taken.
費事 Vexatious; fussy; troublesome.
費時 Waste time.
費神 Effort of mind; mental fatigue. Thank you for your trouble.
費錢 Spend money; waste money; expensive; spend money lavishly.
費材料 Waste material.
費唇舌 Waste one's breath.
費用有限 Limited expenditure.
費用浩繁 Much expenses.
費盡心機 Spend much labour and care.

貼 (n.)- Subsidy; aid.
tiē (adj.)- Adjacent; attached to; in touch; in contact.
(v.)- Stick up; paste; make up. Supply.
貼心 Intimate; attached to; fellow-feeling.
貼耳 Incline the ear; be ready to listen to.
貼近 Attached to; adjacent; keep close to; contiguous; near.
貼紙；仿單 Label.
貼畫 Stick up a picture.
貼補 Subsidize; make up a deficiency; make up what is wanting; help—as by money.
貼錢 Pay up money; give monetary assistance.
貼廣告 Post bill.
貼膏藥 Stick on a medicated plaster.
貼心貼意 Amiable and obliging.

貽 (v.)- Give; present; confer; send. Hand down; bequeath; leave.
yí Cause. Commit.
貽害 Cause injury; cause evil.
貽誤 Cause any delay to business; throw a hinderance in the way of; mislead; commit error.
貽贈 Give to; present with; make a parting present; leave to.
貽累國家 Involve the State; entail damage to the State.
貽誤後人 Mislead posterity.

貿 (v.)- Barter; trade; exchange; carry on commerce.
mào 貿易 Barter; trade; exchange of goods; commerce.
貿易風 Trade-winds.
貿易港 A trading port; a commercial port.
貿貿然 Stupidly; unintelligently.
貿易中心 Commercial center.
貿易公司 Trading company; trading corporation.
貿易自由 Free trade.

賀 (v.)- Congratulate; felicitate; celebrate; greet.
hè 賀年 New-year's greetings. Congratulate on the New Year; wish a Happy New Year.
賀帖 Congratulatory cards.
賀喜；慶賀 Congratulate; felicitate.
賀壽 Birthday greetings. Congratulate on one's birthday.
賀儀；賀禮 Congratulatory presents.
賀年片 A New-year's greeting card (note).
賀爾蒙 Hormone.

賂 (v.)- Give present as a bribe; bribe.
lù

賃 (v.)- Rent; lease; charter; hire.
賃租 Rent; hire; lease.
lìn 賃房子 Rent a house.
賃租人 Hirer.

賃租金 Rent; the charge for hire.
賃租價 The value of a lease.
賃租權 A lease; the right of lease.

**賄** huī
(n.)- Money; riches; wealth. Bribes.
(v.)- Bribe.
賄買 Buy off (over); bribe; suborn.
賄賂 A bribe. Bribe; corrupt; oil (grease) one's hand.

**資** zī
(n.)- Wealth; property. Capital; stock; money.
(v.)- Avail of. Trust to. Help; aid; depend on; supply.
資力 Funds; means; capital.
資本；資金 Capital; funds; money.
資助 Help; aid. Assistance.
資財；資產 Property; wealth; riches; assets.
資料 Materials; data.
資格 Qualification; competency; eligibility; capacity.
資源 Resources.
資本家 A capitalist.
資本論 "Capital" (Das Kapital).
資本主義 Capitalism.
資產階級 Bourgeoisie.
資格證明書 A certificate of qualification; qualifications.
資本主義社會 Capitalist society.
資本主義時代 Period of capitalism.
資本主義國家 Capitalistic nations.
資本帝國主義 Capitalistic imperialism; imperialistic capitalism.
資產階級革命 Bourgeois revolution.
資本主義經濟制度 The capitalistic economic system.

**賈** gǔ
(n.)- A shopman; a resident merchant; a trade.
(v.)- Purchase; traffic; buy; sell.

**賊** zéi
(n.)- A robber; a thief; a pickpocket; a bandit. A rebel. A term of abuse.
(v.)- Injure; harm; plunder; kill.
賊性 Ungrateful; given to the thieving; thievish propensity.
賊首 A rebel chief; leader of robbers; a head thief.
賊匪 Rebels; bandits; brigands.
賊害；殘賊 Damage; injure; ruin.
賊巢 A resort of robbers; the enemy's camp.
賊盜 Robbers; brigands; rebels.
賊黨 Gang of thieves; band of rebels.

**賑** zhèn
(n.)- Relief.
(adj.)- Rich; wealthy; affluent.
(v.)- Give alms; relieve; assist; supply.
賑災 Relieve famine or other distress.
賑貧 Relieve the poor. Poor relief.
賑款 Relief funds.
賑濟 Alms-giving; giving relief; poor relief; charity. Give alms or relief; subscribe money for relief.
賑濟局 A charitable institution.
賑濟金 An alms; a relief fund.

**賒** shē
(v.)- Trade on credit; buy or sell on account.
賒欠 On credit; on trust. Buy on credit.
賒貨 Buy goods on trust; get credit for goods.
賒買 Credit purchasing. Buy on credit.
賒賬 Give credit to. Account of credit sales.
賒賣 Credit sale.

**賓** bīn
(n.)- A visitor; a guest.
賓主 Guest and host. Secondary and principal.

賓位 The guest's seat. Predicate.
賓客 A visitor; a guest.
賓格（文）Objective case.
賓朋滿座 Guests and friends filled up the room.

賜 (n.)- Reward.
(v.)- Confer upon an inferior;
cì bestow; grant; give.
賜祭 Honour the spirit of some deceased person.
賜恩 Bestow favours; give grace.
賜宴 An imperial banquet. Grant a banquet; bestow a banquet.
賜教 Condescend to teach; give an opinion.
賜贈 Bestow; confer upon; grant to.
賜福 Bestow grace upon; confer happiness; bless.

賞 (n.)- A reward; a prize.
(v.)- Reward; grant; bestow;
shǎng confer. Praise; commend. Enjoy; take pleasure in.
賞月 Enjoy the moonlight.
賞光 Favour with one's presence; honour with your presence.
賞金 A prize money; a purse.
賞賜 A reward. Bestow gifts; give a reward.
賞善罰惡 Reward the good and punish the wicked.

賠 (v.)- Compensate; pay back; indemnify; pay for; recom-
péi pense.
賠本 Get less than the capital invested; lose one's outlay.
賠款 An indemnity; a compensation; damages.
賠罪 Make an apology; apologize.
賠補 Compensate; make up a deficiency.
賠償；賠還 Recompense; make reparation for. Compensation.
賠禮 Make apologies; do something to appease another.
賠償金 An indemnity; reparations.
賠償名譽 Indemnity for defamation.
賠償損失 Compensate for the lose; make up for the loss.
賠償費用 Cover the cost (expenses).
賠償及津貼 Remedy and allowance.

賢 (adj.)- Moral; worthy; gentle; good; virtuous. Able; wise;
xián sagacious; talented.
賢人 A worthy man; a virtuous man; a wise man.
賢女；淑女 A virtuous woman.
賢母 A wise mother.
賢明 Wise; intelligent; judicious; sagacious.
賢妻 A good wife.
賢能 Superior abilities; good and able.
賢愚 Wise and foolish—all classes.
賢慧 Virtuous and sagacious.
賢德 Exalted virtue; high moral character.

賣 (v.)- Sell. Betray. Cheat. Show off.
mài 賣卜 Fortune-telling; divination.
賣力 Hire out for odd jobs; labour.
賣方 Vendor.
賣友 Betray one's friend.
賣主 The seller; the vendor.
賣完 Be sold out; go out of stock.
賣身 Sell oneself as a slave; become a prostitute.
賣唱 Sing along the streets for a living.
賣淫 Earn money on the streets; make a prostitute of herself.
賣貨 Sell goods.
賣國 Betray one's country; forsake

one's flag.
賣價 The selling price; the sale-price.
賣酒店 Tap-house.
賣票所 A booking office; a ticket office.
賣貨人 A salesman; a saleswoman.
賣貨單 A bill of sale.
賣國賊 A traitor; a betrayer.
賣弄風情 Flirtation; coquetry.
賣國求榮 To seek after glory by selling out one's own country.
賣國條約 Treasonable treaties.
賣國集團 Traitorous clique.
賣買契約 A bargain; a contract of sale; a sale-contract.

賤 jiàn (adj.)- Mean; low; worthless; cheap; poor; humble; base.
(v.)- Depreciate; disregard; despise; look down upon; slight; undervalue; disparage.
賤物；賤貨 Cheap and common things; inferior goods.
賤鄙 Base; low.
賤價 Low-priced; cheap.
賤賣 Cheap sale.
賤骨頭 A loafer; a worthless fellow.

賦 fù (n.)- Land tax. A long poem; one kind of poetical composition.
(v.)- Give; endow; bestow on. Spread out. Tax; levy; exact.
賦予 Give.
賦稅 Taxes.
賦詩 Compose a poem; write verses.
賦予……權力 To endow one with power; empower; to invest with power.

質 zhī (n.)- Substance; stuff; material; nature; matter; disposition; quality; elements; constitution. A pledge.
(adj.)- Essential; real; unadorned.
(v.)- Confront; cross-examine; question; ask. Check; pawn; pledge.
質子(物) Proton. A hostage, as a king's son.
質地；品質 Natural disposition; constitution; quality.
質料 Material.
質問 Question; ask one a question on (about).
質量(物) Mass; quality.
質實 Simple and sincere.
質樸 Simple and honest; plain; simple; unpolished; unadorned.
質權(法) Right of pledge.
質言之 In fact; in a word; in short.
質量不變律 The law of the constancy of mass.

賬 zhàng (n.)- An account; a bill; a claim.
賬目 Accounts.
賬員 A treasurer; a clerk; a counter.
賬單 A bill; an invoice.
賬項 Entries of accounts; items.
賬檯 A counter in a shop.
賬簿 Account books.

賭 dǔ (n.)- Gambling; betting.
(v.)- Lay a wager; gamble; stake; make a bet; risk.
賭友 A gambling companion.
賭咒 Take an oath; vow.
賭氣 Get in a rage and insist on doing something regardless of the consequences; for spite.
賭徒；賭棍 A gambler; a gamester.
賭彩 Try for a prize.
賭博 Gambling; a gambling game. Play for money; gamble; wager; stake.
賭館；賭場 A gambling-house (-place).

賭錢 Gamble for money.
賭輸 Lose in gambling or betting; gamble away.
賭賽馬 Bet on a horse; have a wager on a horse.

賴 (v.)- Depend on; rely on; trust to; lean on. Disclaim; disavow;
lài ignore. Deny; repudiate. Benefit.
賴人 Rely on some-body; depend on (upon) others.
賴婚；退婚 Break of promise; repudiate a marriage contract.
賴債 Repudiate a debt.
賴得乾淨 Deny all; repudiate the whole thing.
賴着不走 To be still hanging on there and refuse to clear out.

賺 (v.)- Make money; gain; earn; make profit. Cheat; deceive.
zhuàn 賺利 Interest accruing.
賺食 Earn a livelihood.
賺錢 Make money; earn money.

賻 (v.)- Present money at a funeral; send a funeral present.
fù 賻儀 A funeral gift; present of money for funeral expenses.
賻贈 Help with money; give pecuniary assistance.

購 (v.)- Purchase; buy; hire.
購物；購貨 Purchase merchan-
gòu dise.
購料 Buy material.
購買 Buy; purchase.
購買力 Purchasing power.
購買者 A purchaser; a buyer.
購買處 Place of purchase.
購入原價 Buying cost.
購入費用 Buying expenses.
購貨合同 Buying contract.
購買代理人 Buying agent.

賽 (v.)- Recompense. Compete; rival; strive; emulate; race; con-
sài test; struggle; contend for.
賽船 A regatta; a boat race. Row a race; row in a boat-race.
賽狗 A dog-race; dog racing.
賽馬 A horse-race; horse-racing.
賽球 Football contest.
賽跑 A foot-race; a running-race. Run a race.
賽會 An exhibition. An idolatrous procession in which the gods are carried.
賽過 Surpass; excel.
賽狗場 A canidrome; a dog-racing course.
賽馬場 The turf.
賽馬會 A horse-race club; a jockey club.
賽跑人 A runner; a sprinter ( 短距離 ).
賽跑場 The track; the course.
賽璐珞 Celluloid.

贄 (n.)- Gifts to superiors; offerings of ceremony; the gift
zhì given, by one person to another at their first interview.
贄見 Visit with a present.
贄見禮 Present made when calling.

贅 (n.)- An excrescence. Repetition; tautology; an useless ap-
zhuì pendage; prolixity.
(adj.)- Useless; superfluous.
(v.)- Repeat. Connect; hang on; append.
贅言；贅語 Superfluous words; redundancy; a lengthy remark.
贅筆 Add a post-script.
贅詞 Pleonasm.

**贈** (v.)- Present; give a gift; bestow; confer a title.
zèng 贈別 Give a present at parting.
贈言 Give an advice; send a word to.
贈券 Gift coupon; compliment ticket.
贈品 A present; a gift.
贈送 Present a thing to one; make a present (gift) of a thing.
贈款人 A donor; a giver.
贈以博士學位 Confer a doctor's degree on one.

**贊** Same as 贇.
zàn (v.)- Assist; second; help. Praise; admire; commend. Inform. Agree.
贊同 Concur with a person in an opinion; approve; support.
贊成 Support; approval; approbation; seconding.
贊助 Assist; help; support; patronize; second; back up.
贊美 Praise; adore; extol.
贊揚 Praise; commend; acclaim; extol.
贊賞 Praise; admire.
贊成者 A supporter; a seconder.
贊助者 A supporter; a sponsor.
贊美詩 Canticle; hymn; chant.
贊成與反對 Pro and con.

**贋** (adj.)- False; counterfeit; sham; spurious.
yàn 贋本 The false edition; a spurious copy.
贋造紙幣；僞鈔 Counterfeit paper-money; a false bank-note.
贋造貨幣；僞幣 False or counterfeit coin; counterfeit money.

**贍** (adj.)- Rich; wealthy; abundant; sufficient.
shàn (v.)- Give assistance; supply; aid; be sufficient for.
贍助 Assist with money; help the poor.
贍貧 Meet the needs of the poor.
贍補 Supply deficiencies.
贍養 Support.
贍養費(法) Alimony.

**贏** (n.)- Gain; profit; surplus; abundance; overplus.
yíng (v.)- Win; beat; excel; gain; be in excess; achieve. Bear; carry.
贏利 Gain; profit.
贏餘 A surplus; an excess; abundance.

**贓** Same as 賍.
zāng (n.)- Stolen goods; booty; plunder; bribes; prizes.
(v.)- Receive bribe.
贓官 A corrupt official.
贓物 Stolen articles (goods); pilfered property.

**贖** (v.)- Ransom; redeem; pay a fine; atone for.
shú 贖刑 Punishment redeemable by money.
贖回 Redeem back; ransom.
贖身 Ransom (redeem) oneself.
贖款 Ransom.
贖罪 Atone for (expiate) one's sin (crime). Expiation; redemption.

**贛** 贛省(地) Kiangsi Province.
gàn

# 赤 部

**赤** chī (n.)- An infant.
(adj.)- Red. Bare; naked. Destitute; poor; barren.
赤日 The red sun.
赤心 A true heart; sincerity.
赤字 A red letter; red figures.
赤足 Barefooted.
赤身 Naked; bare; in one's buff.
赤豆 Kidney-bean.
赤貧 Extreme (abject) poverty; destitution; penury.
赤痢 Dysentery.
赤誠 Sincerity; singleness of heart.
赤道 The equator.
赤銅 An alloy of copper, antimony and gold.
赤膽 Pure-hearted; brave.
赤外線 Infra-red rays; ultra-red rays.
赤血球 A red blood-corpuscle.
赤裸裸 Naked; bare; nude; in buff.
赤瑪瑙 Jacinth.
赤銅礦 Cuprite.
赤鐵礦 Hematite.
赤手空拳 Empty-handed; unarmed.
赤日當空 The hot sun overhead.
赤足而行 Walk with bare feet (in one's bare feet).
赤身露體 Stark naked; strip to the buff.
赤貧生活 Earn a bare living.
赤裸裸地暴露 To lay bare.

**赦** shè (n.)- Pardon.
(v.)- Pardon; excuse; forgive; remit; let off; set free.
赦免 Forgive; remit; let off; excuse; pass by.
赦書 An absolution; a letter of pardon.

**赧** nǎn (adj.)- Shameful.
(v.)- Blush; turn red; colour.
赧愧 Ashamed.
赧顏 Blushing.

**赫** hè (adj.)- Red; hot; fiery. Awe; angry. Bright; luminous; glorious.
(v.)- Frighten; be angry at.
赫然大怒 Burst into a passion; fly into a rage; flare up; bluster oneself into anger.
赫赫有名 Having a great reputation.

# 走 部

**走** zǒu (v.)- Walk; dash; gallop; run; hasten; proceed; go; flee.
走入 Walk in; enter.
走上 Run up; go up.
走下 Go down; run down.
走出 Walk out; go out; run out.
走私 Smuggle.
走味；變味 Lose flavour.
走狗 A hound; a sporting dog; a servile dependent; running dog.
走風 let out a secret.
走向 To head for (towards); to move towards.
走動 Move; begin to walk.
走開 Get out of the way! —as to a crowd stopping the road; run away; make off.
走路 Walk; travel.
走廊 A veranda; a corridor.
走遍 Travel everywhere.
走運 Have a good luck.
走漏 Disclose.

走錯 Take the wrong road; go astray.
走馬燈 A revolving lantern.
走讀生 Day student.
走投無路 There is no way getting out of it; there is no escape.
走馬看花 Give a hurried glance.
走漏消息 Let out a secret; the secret is out.
走上絕路 To head towards disaster; to head for one's doom.
走讀學校 A day-school.

赳 jiū (adj.)- Valiant.
赳赳武夫 A gallant soldier.

赴 fù (v.)- Go, as to a place; proceed; attend, as a meeting.
赴任 Take up the duties of a post; proceed to one's post; leave for one's new post.
赴告；訃告 Obituary notice.
赴席；赴宴 Attend a feast; go to a feast.
赴約 Engage to meet one; go to an engagement.
赴會 Attend a meeting.
赴試；赴考 Go to an examination.
赴墟；趁墟 Go to market.
赴湯蹈火 Go through fire and water for another.
赴……途中 On one's way to.

赶 gǎn Same as 趕.
(v.)- Chase; pursue; drive; run after. Hasten to a place; hurry.
赶上 Overtake; catch up.
赶車 Drive a cart.
赶逐 Overtake.

起 qǐ (v.)- Stand up; erect; put up. Get up; rise; raise; lift up. Begin; originate; start; commence; build up.
起火 Catch (take) fire.
起立 Stand up; rise on one's feet.
起伏 Ups and downs; undulation. Rise and fall; undulate.
起早 Get early in the morning.
起色 Improvement; recover from one's illness. Rise in value.
起身 Rise; get up.
起牀 Rise; get up; leave one's bed.
起初；起首 In the beginning; at the commencement; at first.
起碼 Begin with; at least.
起跑 To start.
起貨 Unload goods; discharge cargo.
起程；起行 Start on a journey; set out.
起訴 Sue one in court; prosecute.
起義 Start a revolution.
起價 Raise the price; advance the price.
起稿；起草 Prepare a statement; make a draft; draw up.
起錨 Weigh anchor.
起點 A starting-point.
起重機 A crane; a jack; a derrick.

趁 chèn (v.)- Avail oneself; come up behind; follow. Take advantage of; embark; engage.
趁早 Seize the first opportunity; start early.
趁船 Embark a ship.
趁時候 Make use of the times; take advantage of the chance.
趁機會 To take the opportunity.

超 chāo (v.)- Leap over; stride. Go before. Surpass; excel; promote; stepover; overcome; rise above; exceed.
超人 A superman.
超凡 Unusual; out of common.
超出 Exceed.
超級 Superior.

超然 Free from the cares, temptations or business of the world; make (keep) aloof from.
超等 First-class; best grade; super class.
超過 Overrun; transpass; exceed; be in excess of.
超羣 Above the average; pre-eminence; transcendent; distinct.
超音波 Supersonic waves.
超短波 Ultra-short waves.
超高速度 Ultra-high speed.
超級大國 A superpower.
超級市場 A supermarket.
超音速飛機 A supersonic aircraft.
超高速公路 A superhighway.

越 yuè (v.)- Over pass; exceed; overstep. Fall.
越南(地) Vietnam.
越界；越境 Cross a frontier (border); encroach on another's territory.
越軌 Out of the usual rut.
越級 Skip a grade.
越獄 Break prison.
越來越 More and more.
越早越好 The sooner the better.
越快越好 The faster the better.

趙 zhào (n.)- A surname. Ancient feudal state.
(v.)- Hasten to; visit.

趣 qù (adj.)- Interesting; amusing; pleasant.
(v.)- Hasten; advance quickly; urge; hurry on.
趣味 An agreeable favour; taste; interest.
趣事 An interesting matter.
趣味相同 Identity of tastes.
趣味無窮 Very interesting.

趨 qū Same as 趋.
(v.)- Run; walk quickly; hasten forwards.
趨向 A trend; a turn; a drift; a tendency. Long for.
趨候 Wait upon.
趨勢 Tendency; trend.
趨蹌 Run quickly.

# 足 部

足 zú (n.)- The foot. The base.
(adj.)- Enough; sufficient. Full; pure, of silver.
(v.)- Full.
足底 The sole.
足趾 The toes.
足球 Football; soccer.
足夠 Enough.
足痛 A pain in the foot; a footsore.
足跡 A trace; a footprint; a footmark.
足踢 Kick.
足球員 A football player; a footballer; a soccer.
足球隊 A football team.
足球賽 Football match.
足球迷 Football-fans.
足足兩年 Two full years.
足智多謀 Wise and full of stratagems.
足踏縫衣機 A treadle sewing machine.

趾 zhǐ (n.)- The toes. A hoof.
趾甲 Toe nail.
趾關節(解) Articulations of

the toes.
趾高氣揚 Step high and look proud.

跋 (n.)- The heel. The epilogue of a book.
bá (v.)- Travel; walk; step on; walk through the grass.
跋涉 Travel (go) about; traverse.
跋扈 Be arrogant; domineer over; be rampant.
跋山涉水 To travel over land and water.

跌 (v.)- Slip or fall over; stumble; take a false step.
diē 跌下 Fall down.
跌倒 Slip; fall; stumble over; take a false step.
跌傷 Injured by a fall.
跌價；折價 Depreciate; fall in price.
跌打醫生 A bone-setter.

跑 (v.)- Run; gallop; race.
跑馬 Horse-racing; the turf.
pǎo Ride a race.
跑道 A runway.
跑冰 Skate.
跑冰場 A skating-rink.
跑冰鞋 Skates.
跑狗場 A dog-racing course.
跑馬場 A race course; the turf.

跖 (n.)- The sole of the foot.
zhí

跗 (n.)- The top part of the foot.
跗骨(解) Tarsale.
fū

跚 (v.)- Limp.
shān

跛 (adj.)- Lame; crippled.
(v.)- Walk lame. Be partial;
bǒ lean to.
跛子 A lame (crippled) person; a cripple.
跛脚 Lame; limping; crippled.

距 (n.)- A bird's spur. Distance.
(adj.)- Distant.
jù 距離 Distance. A difference; a gap.
距躍 Leap over.

跟 (n.)- The heel. The end.
(v.)- Follow; imitate.
gēn 跟班 An official's servant; a valet.
跟隨 Follow; go with; accompany.
跟蹤 Trace one's footsteps; follow a clue.
跟上 To keep up with.
跟以往一樣 As . . . as ever.

跡 Same as 迹，蹟.
(n.)- A trace; a footmark; a
jī track; clue; mark left. A site. A print; a stain.
(v.)- Trace; follow up; by tracks.
跡象 Marks; traces; vestiges.

跺 (v.)- Stamp (the feet).
跺脚 To stamp one's feet.
duò

跣 (adj.)- Barefooted.
跣足 Barefooted.
xiǎn

跨 (v.)- Straddle; ride; bestride; pass over; step over; cross;
kuà encroach upon.
跨步 Straddle.
跨海 Cross the sea.

跨越 Pass over; excel; surpass.
跨欄賽 The hurdle-race.

跪 (n.)- Kneel; drop (go down) on one's knees.
guì 跪下 Kneel down; fall upon one's knees.
跪拜 Bow and kneel to; adore by kneeling.
跪謝 Give thanks on one's knees. Humble thanks.

路 (n.)- A road; a path; a route; a way; a line; a street; an avenue.
lù 路上 In the way; on the road; on a journey.
路口 The entrance to a road or street.
路面 Road-surface.
路旁 The roadside; the wayside.
路基 Road bed.
路程 A journey; a distance to be covered.
路費 Travelling expenses; passage fee.
路標 Guide post.
路線 Route; line.
路燈 Street lamps.
路透社 Reuters.
路不通行 No throughfare; close to traffic.
路透新聞社 The Reuter News Agency.

跳 (v.)- Jump; hop about. Leap; spring; skip; flee; dance.
tiào 跳上 Jump up; leap to one's feet.
跳下 Jump down.
跳虱；跳蝨 A flea.
跳河 Jump into the river.
跳板 The gangway plank; a springboard.
跳高 The high jump.
跳動 Move.
跳傘 Parachute; bail out.
跳過 Leap (jump) over.
跳遠 The long (broad) jump.
跳舞 A dance; dancing.
跳盪 Jump about.
跳繩 Rope-skipping. Jump the rope.
跳躍 Spring up; jump up.
跳舞場 A dancing hall.
跳舞會 Dancing party. Give a ball.
跳傘塔 A parachute tower.
跳出火坑 Escaped from grave danger.

跼 (v.)- Lean forward; bent down; crouch; stoop. Narrow; limited.
jú 跼蹐 Crouch; stoop; be bent up within; be confined.
跼促不安 Uneasy; constrained.

跟 (v.)- Hop.
liáng 跟蹌 Stagger; totter.

踊 Same as踴.
yǒng (v.)- Leap; jump.
踊躍 Jump about for joy; enthusiastic.

踏 (v.)- Step upon; tread on; trample; stamp; plant the feet; walk.
tà 踏平 Level by treading down.
踏死 Trample to death; crush under the feet.
踏板 A treadle.
踏破 Break by stepping on.
踏碎 Trample to pieces; tread under foot; crush.
踏脚板 A foot-iron (-plate); a carriage-step.

踐 (v.)- Walk; step; trample on; tread upon.
jiàn 踐約 Keep an appointment or

an agreement; not to break one's promise; fulfil one's promise.

踐踏 Trample under foot; tread on; trample (stamp) down.

踝 huái (n.)- The ankle; the heel.
踝跟 The heel.
踝關節(解) Ankle joint.

踞 jù (v.)- Crouch; squat.
踞坐 Crouch; squat down; sit on.

踢 tī (v.)- Kick; give a kick.
踢球 Play football.
踢出去 Kick out.

踰 yú Same as 逾.
(v.)- Exceed; overpass; go beyond; pass over.
踰限 Exceed the limit; go beyond bounds.

踰時 Pass the scheduled time.

踰期 Exceed the time-limit.

踰越界限 Go beyond the limits; go out of bounds.

踰越權限 Exceed one's authority.

踱 duó (v.)- Walk; step.
踱來踱去 Walking backwards and forwards.

踵 zhǒng (n.)- The heel.
(v.)- Follow; reach.
踵見 Call frequently.
踵門 Visit; go in person; call at one's home.

踵接 On the heels of; one after another; in rapid succession.

踵跡 Follow some one's steps or instructions.

踵謝 Thank in person.

蹀 dié (v.)- Stamp; tread.
蹀蹀 Stepping lightly.

蹁 pián (v.)- Walk lamely; limp.
蹁躚 Fluttering.

蹂 róu (v.)- Tread; trample on.
蹂躪 The devastation of troops. Oppressive exactions; ruin; lay waste; ravage.

蹂躪人權 Trample upon human rights.

蹄 tí (n.)- A hoof.
蹄子 A hoof.
蹄鐵 A horseshoe.

蹈 dǎo (v.)- Tread on; stamp; trample; step on. Fulfill.
蹈襲 Copy; plagiarize.
蹈虎尾 Tread on the tail of a tiger-dangerous.

蹉 cuō (v.)- Slip; mis-step; stumble.
蹉跎光陰 Waste time.

蹊 xī (n.)- Foot path.

蹌 qiàng (v.)- Move; run.

蹍 niǎn (v.)- Stamp; tread.

蹐 jí (v.)- Walk with short steps.

**蹙** (adj.)- Urgent. Cramped; wrinkled; contracted; grieved; troubled.
cù
(v.)- Press upon; impel; urge. Contract; wrinkle; retract; hasten.
蹙近 Press upon closely.

**蹠** (n.)- Foot; sole of a foot.
zhí
(v.)- Tread; step; pass into. Follow after; stamp.
蹠骨(解) Metatarsus.

**蹣** (v.)- Walk lamely. Pass over; get over.
pán
蹣跚 Walk lamely.
蹣跚不前 Wobble; totter.

**蹤** Same as 踪.
zōng
(n.)- A trace; a footstep; a footprint.
(v.)- Imitate; follow.
蹤跡 Traces; footsteps.
蹤影 A vestige; a clue; a sign.
蹤跡不明 Cover one's traces; leave no trace behind; disappear.
蹤跡可疑 Suspicious; questionable.

**蹩** (v.)- Limp.
bié
蹩脚 Far from good.
蹩脚英語 Broken English.

**蹲** (v.)- Crouch; squat; sit on the heals. Assemble.
dūn
蹲踞 Crouch down.

**蹶** (v.)- Stumble; slip; fall. Excite; move.
juě
蹶然而起 Spring (start) up; rouse oneself to action.

**蹺** (v.)- Raise the foot; lift the foot high.
qiāo
蹺蹺板 A seesaw.

**蹻** (n.)- Sandals.
juē
(v.)- Lift the foot high.
蹻蹻 Martial bearing; strong.

**蹼** (n.)- Webbed feet of waterfowl.
pǔ
蹼足 Webbed feet of waterfowl.

**躁** (adj.)- Hasty; rash; harassed in mind; passionate; fierce; angry; cruel.
zào
躁急 Hasty; quick-tempered; impatient.
躁動 Noisy; bustling.
躁暴 Cruel; rash; harsh; hot tempered.

**躅** (n.)- A trace.
zhú
(v.)- Walk slowly; limp.

**躇** (adj.)- Irresolute; undecided.
chú
(v.)- Hesitate; waver.

**躉** (n.)- A whole number; overplus.
dǔn
(v.)- Store.
躉貨 Goods stored up.
躉賣 Sell wholesale.

**躊** (adj.)- Undecided.
chóu
(v.)- Hesitate.
躊躇 Hesitation; irresolute.
躊躇滿志 Exceedingly gratified.

**躍** (v.)- Leap; spring; jump; skip.
yuè
躍起 Spring to one's feet; spring up from one's bed.
躍進 To leap forward.

**躚** Same as 蹮.
xiān
(adj.)- Inconsistent; changeable.

(v.)- Wobble.

**躡** (v.)- Step on; follow the heels.
躡履 Wear shoes.
niè 躡足不前 Not to proceed.

躡手躡脚 To walk stealthily.

**躪** (v.)- Tread; run over; ravage; ruin; destroy; lay waste.
lìn

# 身 部

**身** (n.)- The body; the trunk. The person. The hull. One
shēn self; a lifetime.
身分 Position.
身世 Personal history.
身材；身軀 Stature; height.
身長 Rather tall; height of the body.
身故；身亡 Die; pass away.
身段 Figure. Attitude; posture.
身邊 By the side of a person.
身體 The person; the body; the trunk.
身分證 An identification card; an identity card.
身敗名裂 Down and out.
身體檢查 Physical examination.

**躭** Same as 耽.
(v.)- Delay; loiter; hinder; ob-
dān struct.

躭悞 Hinder by neglect; retard.
躭擱 Delay; procrastinate.

**躲** (v.)- Hide away; conceal; shun; avoid; secrete; withdraw.
duǒ 躲開 Avoid; escape; hide from; withdraw.
躲閃 Dodge out of sight.
躲避；躲匿 Hide; escape from; evade.

**躺** (v.)- Lie down; lie stretched out; recline.
tǎng 躺下；躺臥 Lie down; recline.
躺平 Lie flat.
躺椅 A long chair; an easy chair.

**軀** (n.)- The body.
軀幹 The trunk.
qū 軀體；肉軀 The physical body.

# 車 部

**車** (n.)- A carriage; a vehicle; a car; a cart; a barrow; a wagon.
chē (v.)- Turn over.
車夫 A cartman; a coachman; a carter; a driver.
車長 A guard; a conductor.
車房 A car-shed; a car-house; a garage.

車牀 A turner's lathe.
車胎 Tire.
車站 A railway station.
車票 Ticket.
車廂 A carriage.
車軸 The axle.
車價；車費 Cartage; car-fare; car hire.

車輪 A wheel.
車輛 Cars; vehicles; trucks.
車輻 Spoke.
車頭 Locomotive.
車馬費 Carriage; cartage.
車輛執照稅 Car license duty.

軋 (n.)- A creaking, crushing sound.
zhá (v.)- Grind; crush; press.
軋碎 Crushed to pieces.
軋棉機 A cotton gin.
軋棉花廠 A gin mill.

軌 (n.)- The space between the two wheels of a cart; a rut; a track. Law; rules. An orbit.
guǐ 軌跡(數) A locus.
軌道 A track; a railway line; a tramway. (天) An orbit.

軍 (n.)- An army; troops; soldiers.
軍人；軍士 A soldier; a military man.
jūn 軍火 Ammunition; munitions of war.
軍令 Military command; war orders.
軍民 The military and people.
軍事；軍務 Military affairs.
軍官 Military officers.
軍服 Military uniform; regimentals.
軍政 Military administration.
軍校 Military academy.
軍械；軍器 Arms; weapons.
軍港 A naval port (station).
軍隊 An army; troops; forces; a corps.
軍閥 The militarists; the military clique (clan); a war lord.
軍機 A military plane.
軍營 A military camp; an encampment.
軍醫 An army surgeon; a naval surgeon.
軍艦 A man-of-war; warships; battleships.
軍權 Military power.
軍火庫 Powder magazine.
軍事化 Militarize.
軍器廠；兵工廠 An arsenal.
軍用飛機 A military plane; a warplane.
軍司令部 The general headquarters of an army.
軍事目標 Military objective.
軍事行動 Military action (operations).
軍事封鎖 Military blockade.
軍事訓練 Military training.
軍閥主義 Warlordism
軍校學生 Cadet.
軍國主義 Militarism.

軒 (n.)- A kind of carriage. A porch; a balcony; a small room;
xuān a studio.
軒昂 High-spirited; grand; dignified.
軒豁 Open and bright.

軔 (n.)- A catch; a skid; an impediment.
rèn (v.)- Skid a wheel; stop.

軟 Same as 輭.
(adj.)- Soft; mild; gentle; flexi-
ruǎn ble; weak; infirm; tender; yielding; pliable; maleable.
軟木 Cork.
軟化 Soften; yield to; become conciliatory.
軟片 Film.
軟性 Soft; yielding.
軟骨(解) Cartilage.
軟弱 Weak; feeble; sickly.
軟嫩 Soft and tender.
軟膏 An unguent; an ointment; a salve.
軟心腸 Soft hearted.
軟骨病 Rachitis.
軟脚病 Beri-beri.

軟體動物 The Mollusca; a mollusc.

軸 (n.)- An axis; an axle; a pivot; a shaft. A roll; a scroll.
zhóu
軸子 A roller for scrolls.
軸承 Bearing.

較 (adj.)- Rather; more; comparatively; somewhat.
jiào (v.)- Compare; contrast; compete; match; contest; contend.
較早 Earlier; sooner.
較量 Compare; compared with; test.
較準 Correct; adjust to standard.
較對；校對 Compare; compare with an original; proof reading.
較好 Better.
較貴 More expensive.

載 (n.)- A year. A cargo; a load.
(v.)- Contain; transport; convey;
zài carry; fill up; load; bear. Record; write down. Insert in. Begin.
載客 Take passengers on board; take on passengers.
載重 Weight.
載貨 Carry goods; load goods. A ship's cargo; a freight; a shipment.
載運 Transport; convey.
載滿 Fully loaded.
載重量 Carrying capacity.
載貨港 Port of loading.
載登廣告 Put an advertisement in.

輓 (v.)- Pull a carriage; draw a hearse.
wǎn
輓聯 Funeral scrolls.

輔 (n.)- Poles attached to the sides of cart. The jawbone.
fǔ (v.)- Help; assist; aid; second; support.
輔佐；輔助 Help; assist; aid.
輔衞 Protect.
輔導 Lead; guide.

輕 (n.)- Hydrogen.
(adj.)- Light; portable; unim-
qīng portant. Easy. Young; low.
(v.)- Mitigate; lessen; slight; regard lightly.
(adv.)- Lightly; gently.
輕巧 Light; agile; handy.
輕快 Light; light-hearted; cheerful; active;nimble; swift.
輕狂 Frivolous; dissipated; giddy.
輕易 Easy; lightly.
輕信 Ready credence; credulity. Be credulous; believe lightly; give ready credence to.
輕便 Handy; convenient; portable.
輕風 A gentle (soft, light) breeze (wind).
輕重 Light and heavy. Weight.
輕捷 Light and fast.
輕涼 Pleasantly cool; airy.
輕視 Make light (little) of; slight; neglect; ignore.
輕傷 A slight wound (injury).
輕微 Slight; not serious; unimportant; trifling; frivolous; inconsiderable.
輕蔑 Despise; disdain; slight off.
輕鬆 Light and free; relaxed; loose.
輕工業 Light industry.
輕化物 Hydride.
輕金屬 Light metals.
輕音樂 Light music.
輕氣球 A balloon.
輕氣彈 Hydrogen bomb; H-bomb.
輕信人言 Believe in other's words too easily.
輕機關槍 A light machine-gun.

輛 (n.)- A numeration for wheeled vehicles.
liàng

輝 Same as 煇.
huī (adj.)- Bright; brilliant; shining; glowing; gleaming; lustrous.
輝石 (礦) Pyroxene.
輝煌 Brilliant; glorious.

輟 (v.)- Stop; cease; end; suspend; rest.
chuò 輟工 Cease work.

輦 (n.)- The imperial carriage.
(v.)- Transport; bring by car.
niǎn 輦下 The metropolis; the capital.

輩 (n.)- A row of carriages. A generation. A class; a series;
bèi a sort; a kind. A company.
輩分；輩數 The position of the generation in a series.
輩出 Come out in succession; appear (come forth) in great numbers; numerous.

輪 (n.)- A wheel; a disk; a ring. A revolution; a circle; a circuit;
lún a gear.
(v.)- Turn; rotate; go around.
輪座 Wheel seat.
輪流 In turn; in rotation; by turns.
輪船 A steamer.
輪軸 Axis of wheel.
輪廓 An outline; the border lines; the contourlines.
輪盤 A wheel.
輪輻 Arms of wheel; spokes of a wheel.
輪流值日 Serve in turn.
輪廓地圖 An outline (a blank) map.

輯 (v.)- Compile; collect; compose. Make everything agreeable;
jí gather harmoniously together; reconcile; soothe.
輯要 An abstract; a synopsis; an outline.
輯錄 Compile; edit.

輳 (n.)- The hub of a wheel.
(v.)- Concentrate; collect to-
còu gether.
輳合 Converge.

輸 (v.)- Transport; convey. Lose; be defeated.
shū 輸了 Lose—as a wager, game, etc.
輸入 Import; introduce.
輸出 Export.
輸血 Transfusion. Transfuse blood.
輸送 Transport.
輸錢 Lose money.
輸入品 Imports; Imported articles (goods).
輸入港 An import port.
輸出入；進出口 Exports and imports.
輸出品 Exports.
輸出港 An export port.
輸出稅 Export duty.
輸卵管 (解) Oviduct.
輸精管 (解) Deferent duct.
輸入貿易 Import trade.

輻 (n.)- The spokes of a wheel.
輻射 Radiation. Radiate.
fú 輻射線 A radial ray.
輻射現象 Radio-activity.

輾 (v.)- Grate; squeak; turn half round; roll over on the side.
zhǎn 輾子 Roller.
輾轉 Turn over and over again; circulate; revolve; back and forth.

輿 (n.)- A carriage. A sedan-chair. The earth.
yú (v.)- Sustain; bear; hold.

輿人 A cartwright.
輿論 Public opinion.
輿論調查 A survey of public opinion.

**轄** xiá (n.)- The linchpin of a wheel. (v.)- Govern; regulate; control; rule.
轄地 Dominion.
轄管 Manage; control; have competence over.

**轅** yuán (n.)- The shafts of a cart or carriage. The outer entrance of a yamen.
轅木 The shafts.
轅門 The outer entrance of a yamen.

**轆** lù (n.)- Wheel and axle. A roller; a pulley.
轆轆 The rumbling of carriages.

**轉** zhuǎn (v.)- Turn round; revolve; rotate. Change; alter. Move; shift. Transport; transmit. Return.
轉化 Change; transformation. (化) Inversion.
轉向 Turn the head to; shift; change the direction.
轉回 Turn back; returned.
轉交；轉送 Turn over; transfer; forward; hand over.
轉身 Turn the body; turn round.
轉致；轉交 Send on; care of.
轉動 Move round.
轉載 Reproduce; reprint.
轉運 Transport.
轉調 Modulate.
轉學 Change one's school; transfer to another school.
轉機 A turning point; a crisis.
轉變 Mutation; changefulness; vicissitudes.
轉讓 Transfer.
轉彎；轉角 Turn a corner; go round the corner.
轉捩點 A turning point.
轉瞬眼 In the twinkling of an eye.
轉運港 Transit port.
轉運公司 Express company; transport company.
轉彎抹角 Turn a corner.

**轎** jiào (n.)- A sedan-chair; a palanquin.
轎子 A sedan chair.
轎車 A sedan car.

**轍** zhé (n.)- The track of a wheel; a rut.

**轟** hōng (v.)- Blow up; blast; explode; bombard.
轟炸 Bomb; attack with bombs.
轟擊 Bombard.
轟動 Exciting.
轟炸機 A bomber; a bombing plane.
轟轟烈烈 Grand; imposing.

# 辛 部

**辛** xīn (n.)- The 8th of the Ten Celestial Stems (天干). (adj.)- Acrid; hard; hot; pungent; sad; suffering; toilsome.
辛苦 Toilsome; tired; suffering; hardship; toil; pains.

辛勤 Industrious; diligent.
辛酸 Hardships; bitter sufferings; misery.
辛亥革命 The *Hsin-hai* Year Revolution (1911).
辛苦從事 To labour over. To take great pains over.
辛勤的努力 Devoted labours.

**辜** (n.)- A crime; a fault; guilt.
gū
辜負 Be ungrateful; ingratitude.
辜恩 Ungrateful for kindness.

**辟** (n.)- Laws; rules. The Emperor; a sovereign or prince.
pì
(v.)- Punish; put to death. Beat the breast. Avoid. Summon to court.
辟名 Merely nominal; false; pretended.

**辣** Same as 辢.
là
(adj.)- Acrid; hot; pungent. Severe.
辣手 Violent hand; cruel; harsh in treatment; rough handling.
辣味 Pungent; peppery taste.
辣椒(植) Capsicum.
辣詞 Sharp words.

**辦** (v.)- Manage; do; work; attend to; provide.
bàn
辦公 Transact business; do office work.
辦事 Transact business; manage an affair.
辦法 The way of managing an affair; plan; means.
辦酒 Prepare a feast.
辦理 Take in hand; transact; management.
辦公處 An office.
辦喜事 Manage a wedding; prepare for a happy occasion.
辦公時間 Office hour; business hour.
辦事章程 By-laws.

**辨** (v.)- Distinguish between; discriminate.
biàn
辨白 Explanation.
辨色 Distinguish colours.
辨別 Distinguish between; discriminate.
辨明 Distinguish clearly.
辨認 Recognize; distinguish.
辨明是非 Distinguish between right and wrong.

**辭** Same as 辞.
cí
(n.)- Words; an expression; a phrase. A speech. Instructions.
(v.)- Decline; excuse.Resign. Take leave of; depart.
辭世 Die; pass away.
辭句 Expression.
辭別；告辭 Take leave of; bid farewell; say good-bye.
辭典 A dictionary; a lexicon.
辭退 Turn away; leave a post; discharge.
辭彙 Vocabulary.
辭謝 Decline with thanks.
辭職 To resign; leave (retire from) office.
辭藻 Elegant, ornate style of literature.

**辯** (v.)- Argue; debate; dispute; discuss.
biàn
辯明 Explain clearly.
辯駁 Argue; criticize; contradict; contest in argument.
辯論 Discuss; debate; moot; argue.
辯護 Speak in defense of; defend; justify; vindicate.
辯證法 Dialectics.
辯論會 A debating society.
辯護士 A lawyer; a barrister.
辯證法唯物論 Dialectic materialism.

# 辰 部

**辰** chén (n.)- A day; a star; a time. Morning.
辰月 The 3rd month of a lunar year.
辰時 The time from 7 to 9 A.M.

**辱** rǔ (n.)- Disgrace.
(v.)- Insult; dishonour; abuse; dispise.
辱知 Enjoy (be favoured with) the friendship (patronage) of ... .
辱罵 Revile; insult; abuse.

**農** nóng (n.)- Agriculture; farming; husbandry; a peasantry.
(v.)- Till the soil; cultivate the ground; farm.
農民 Peasantry; peasants; farmers; the agricultural people.
農奴 A serf; a bondsman.
農村 A farm-village; village.
農具 An agricultural implement; a farming tool.
農場 A farm; a farmstead; a plantation.
農業 Agricultural industry; farming.
農林部 Ministry of Agriculture and Forestry.
農產物 Agricultural products; farm produce; crops.
農學家 Agriculturalist.
農業國 An agricultural country.
農民階級 The peasant class.
農奴制度 The system of serfdom.
農民暴動 An agrarian rising (riot); a peasants' uprising.
農科大學 An agricultural college.
農業合作社 Agricultural Co-operative Society.

# 辵 部

**迂** yū (adj.)- Far; distant; wide.
(v.)- Pervert; distort.
迂久 For long; a long time.
迂回 Take a roundabout (circuitous) route (way); make a detour.
迂緩 Slow; dilatory.
迂回線 A loop-line.

**迄** qì (v.)- Till; until; up to; reach to; extend to.
(adv.)- Finally; at last; after all; at length; till now.
迄今 Up to the present; even till now.
迄竟 After all; at last.

**迅** xùn (adj.)- Quick; swift; rapid; fast; speedy; prompt.
迅即 Immediately; at once.
迅速 Rapid; quick; swift; fast; speedy.
迅雷 A sudden peal of thunder; a thunderclap.
迅如脫兔 With the swiftness of a hare

in flight; with wonderful swiftness.

迎 (v.)- Meet; welcome; receive. 迎合 Ingratiate (tune) oneself
yíng with; cater to; curry favour with.

迎春 Welcome the spring; welcome the New Year.

迎接 Go out to receive; welcome; give a reception to.

迎春花 The winter jasmine.

迎刃而解 It splits as it meets the edge of the knife–like splitting bamboo, easily done.

迎頭痛擊 Strike back at a frontal assault.

近 (adj.)- Near; close; familiar; approximative.
jìn (v.)- Draw near; approach.
(adv.)- Recently; soon; close by; near by.

近世；近代 The modern age; the present time; recent times.

近年 In recent years; of late years.

近狀；近況 Recent circumstances; the present condition.

近東 The Near East.

近來；近日 Recently; lately; in these days.

近便 Near; convenient; handy.

近郊 The suburbs; the outskirts of a town; suburban districts.

近時 Of late; recently; nowadays.

近密 Intimate; familiar.

近傍 Neighbouring; adjacent; near-by.

近道 Near to the right way; a nearer way; a short cut.

近隣 The neighbourhood.

近親 A near relation (relative).

近似值 Approximate value.

近似數 Approximate quantity.

近視者 A near-(short-) sighted person; a myope.

近視眼 Near (short) sight; near-(short-) sightedness; myopia.

近代思想 Modern ideas.

近海漁業 Inshore (home-waters) fishery.

近朱者赤近墨者黑 He who touches pitch shall be defiled therewith.

返 (v.)- Return; go back; come back.
fǎn 返家 Return; home.
返程 A return journey.

返魂 Revival; a come-back.

返老還童 Second youth.

迢 (adj.)- Remote; distant.
迢迢 Distant.
tiáo

迤 Same as 迆.
(adj.)- Extending; sloping.
yǐ (v.)- Walk crookedly.
迤東 Toward the east.

迤迤 Continuous; extending.

迥 Same as 逈.
(adj.)- Far-off; distant; remote.
jiǒng 迥迥 Far-off; distant.
迥不相同 Quite different; utterly unlike; not in the least alike.

迨 (v.)- Come up to; reach; catch up.
dài (conj.)- Till; until; when.
迨今 Until now.

迨後 Till; afterwards; subsequently.

迫 (adj.)- Embarrassed. Narrow; crowded. Pressing; imminent.
pò (v.)- Compel; urge; press upon; force.

迫使 Force; enforce.
迫切 Urgent; pressing.
迫近 Be imminent; draw near; be just before one.
迫害 Persecute; oppress; hunt down.
迫脅 Coerce; intimidate.
迫擊砲 A trench-mortar.
迫於飢餓 Be pressed by hunger; be on the verge of starvation.
迫不及待 Keen on; hurriedly.
迫切要求 A pressing demand.

迭 (v.)- Alternate; change.
(adv.)- Alternately; reciprocally;
dié by turns.
迭用 Alternate use of; use in rotation.

逑 (v.)- Narrate; tell; detail; state. Compile.
shù 逑說 Give a detailed account.
逑懷 Recollection; reminiscence ; relate (reveal) one's thoughts and feelings.

迴 (adj.)- Crooked; winding.
(v.)- Curve; return; go back;
huí revolve; rotate.
迴翔 Wheel in the air; soar; roam.
迴憶 Recall; remember; recollect.
迴環；迴繞 Surround; enclose.
迴避 Withdraw from the presence of a superior; retire aside; shirk; evade; keep away from; avoid; stand back.
迴轉 Revolve; rotate; gyrate; turn.
迴轉門 A revolving door.

迷 (adj.)- Infatuated; stupefied; intoxicated; mad after.
mí (v.)- Confuse. Deceive; beguile; go astray; get lost. Bewitch; enchant; fascinate.
迷人 Charming.
迷失 Be at a lose; be in two minds.
迷信 Superstition; bigotry.
迷途 The path of error; go astray; lose one's way; in error.
迷惑 Bewildered; fascinated; bewitched; deluded; beguiled; confused; be at a loss; be perplexed.
迷路 Lose one's way; get lost; be thrown off track; go astray.
迷信者 A superstitious person.
迷於女色 Be enamoured of a woman; fall a victim to her charms.

追 (v.)- Chase; run after; give pursuit; trace out. Overtake.
zhuī Sue for. Escort. Recall; reflect on.
追及 Overtake; catch up with.
追求 Hunt; pursue; seek after; chase.
追究 Investigate thoroughly; search to the bottom; cross-examine; press one hard.
追悔 Feel remorse; regret.
追討；追債 Dun for debt.
追悼 Mourn for; lament for.
追想 Reflect; recall the past; reminiscent.
追踪 Follow a trail; pursue a clue.
追認 Ratification; confirmation.
追趕 Follow after; pursue; run after.
追慕 Revere (cherish) the memory of.
追憶 Remember; recollect; look back upon; retrospect.
追隨 Follow; follow in one's wake.
追悼會 A memorial service (meeting).
追悼辭 A memorial address.

退 (v.)- Decline; withdraw; draw back; retreat; retire; abate;
tuì subside; yield; give ground; send away.

退化 Degeneration; devolution.
退伍 Leave the army; retire from service.
退回 Retreat; shut out—as cargo.
退色 Fade—of colours.
退步 Fall backward; retrograde; deteriorate. Retrogression; deterioration.
退後 Draw back; go astern.
退租 Throw up a lease.
退堂；退庭 Leave the bench or court.
退潮 The ebb tide; low water.
退學 Leave (give up) school; be dismissed (expelled) from school.
退休 Retire (from office).
退還 Return unaccepted.
退隱 Retire from business; live in retirement (seclusion).
退職 Resign (leave) an office; retire from office (service).
退讓 Yield; give way; modesty.
退熱藥 Anti-pyretics.
退休金 Pension.
退伍軍人 Ex-service men.
退職年齡 Disqualifying age; age limits.
退還支票 Returned cheque.
退還訂貨 Returned order.

送 sòng (v.)- Present; send; forward; despatch; see one off. Accompany; escort.
送上 Send to a superior.
送行；送別 See a person off—as a friend on a journey. Farewell; send-off.
送交 Hand over to; forward to.
送回；送還 Send back; return.
送信 Send a letter or a message.
送禮 Send a present; give a gift.
送殯；送喪 Attend a funeral.
送別會 A farewell meeting; a send-off dinner party.
送花圈 Send a wreath.
送貨單 Certified invoice.
送舊迎新 Speed the old and welcome the new.

逃 táo (v.)- Run away; escape; get off; take flight; flee; abscond.
逃亡 Run off; decamp; flee; run away.
逃出 Run away; flee; fly; get off.
逃犯 An escaped criminal.
逃走；逃遁 Run away; flee; escape.
逃兵；逃軍 A deserter.
逃命；逃生 Run for life; fly for one's life.
逃荒 Flee from famine districts.
逃脫 Cast off; escape; get clear off.
逃避 Shirk; avoid; sneak off; hide; skulk; keep out of sight.
逃稅 Tax evasion.
逃學 Play truant.
逃難 Take refuge; flee from calamity; run away from trouble.
逃亡者 A fugitive; a runaway; an absconder; a deserter.
逃出虎口 Escape with hare life; escape from the jaws of death.
逃亡地主 Runaway landlords.
逃避兵役者 A slacker; a skirker; a dodger.

逆 nì (adj.)- Rebellious; seditious. Disobedient. Contrary.
(v.)- Oppose; disobey; go against; encounter. Receive. Calculate.
逆行 Move backward; reverse; run counter to; retrogress.
逆知 Know beforehand.
逆命 Disobey orders; bid defiance.
逆風 A contrary wind. Against the wind.
逆流 An adverse tide; a counter-current. Back water; up stream.

逆電流 Counter current.
逆耳忠言 Good advice is unpleasant to the ear.
逆旅主人 A host; a landlord.

逍 xiāo (v.)- Ramble; roam; saunter.
逍遙 At ease; rambling; wandering about.
逍遙自在 Free and unrestrained.

透 tòu (v.)- Pass through; comprehend; penetrate; understand.
(adv.)- Thoroughly; fully.
透支 Overdraft. Overdraw.
透光 Be transparent; let the light pass through; pervious to light.
透明 Transparent; lucid; clear.
透風 Let the wind through.
透氣 Let the air in or out; pervious —— as an ill-fitting cork or cover.
透視 Clairvoyance; second sight. Perceive by second sight.
透過 Penetrate; pass through.
透徹 Permeate; thoroughly; to the back bone.
透熱 Pervious to heat.
透濕 Wet through.
透明體 A transparent body.
透視圖 Perspective.
透視畫法 Perspective drawing.
透漏秘密 Divulge (leak out) a secret.

逐 zhú (v.)- Drive out; expel; send away. Pursue; run after; struggle.
逐一 In detail; minutely. One by one.
逐日 Day by day; daily.
逐次 One by one; one after another.
逐年 Year by year; annually.
逐條 Article by article; from point to point; item by item.
逐漸 By degrees; gradually; little by little; step by step; inch by inch.
逐出本境 Expatriate; deportation.
逐字翻譯 A word-for-word (verbatim) translation.

途 tú Same as 塗.
(n.)- A road; a way.
途中；途次 On the road (way); half-way.
途徑 A way; a path.
途程 A road; a journey.

逕 jìng Same as 徑.
(n.)- A path.
(v.)- Pass by; approach.
逕路 A path; a course.
逕啓者 I beg to inform you—opening phrase in correspondence.

逗 dòu (v.)- Stay; delay; tarry; loiter; tempt; excite.
逗留 Stay; loiter; tarry.
逗點 A punctuation mark; a comma.

這 zhè Same as 这.
(adj.)- This.
(adv.)- Here. Now.
這地 Here.
這些 These.
這個 This; this one.
這時 Now; at the present time.
這般 Such; of such kind; like this.
這等 This kind; such.
這裏 Here; in this place.
這樣 In this way; thus; such.

通 tōng (adj.)- General; complete; thorough. Pervious; pervading. Clear.
(v.)- Go through; perceive; succeed. Communicate with; circulate.

通史 A general history.
通令 Communicate orders.
通用 In common use; in general use.
通行 Prevailing; current; general; all-round.
通告 A notice; an announcement.
通車 Through train; non-stop train. A railway begins operation.
通例 Usage; custom; the rule.
通知 Notify; inform; give notice of.
通俗 Common; general; ordinary.
通信 Communicate by letters; correspond with. Correspondence; news.
通紅 Blush; red through and through.
通宵 Throughout the night. Whole night.
通航 Navigation; communication by sea.
通氣 Ventilation; airing.
通牒 A note; a report; a notification.
通過 Pass by (through, over); get through; be carried, as a motion.
通稱 A common (popular) name. Commonly called. . . .
通讀 Read through; peruse; look over.
通分母(數) A common denominator.
通用語 Current words.
通行稅 Toll on transit; a travelling tax; passage duties.
通行證 Safe-conduct pass; a pass.
通行權 Right of way; passage.
通知書 A notice.
通訊社 A news agency.
通訊員 A correspondent; a reporter.
通訊錄 Address-book.
通俗化 Popularize.
通用貨幣 Current coins; currency.
通俗小說 A popular novel.
通俗文學 Popular (light) literature.
通商條約 A commercial treaty; a treaty of commerce.
通貨膨脹 Inflation; excess supply of money.

逝 shì (v.)- Pass away; depart; die.
逝世 Die; pass away.

速 sù (adj.)- Hasty; quick; speedy; rapid; swift.
(adv.)- Hurriedly; fast; speedily.
速成 Rapid completion; quick mastery.
速決 Immediate decision.
速度 Velocity; speed; rapidity. (音) Tempo.
速記 Short-hand; stenography. Take down in short-hand.
速成法 A quick-mastery method; a royal road; a short cut.
速度快 Fast; rapid; high-speed.
速度慢 Slow in speed; slow-paced.
速記員 A stenographer; a shorthand writer.
速凍法 Quick-freezing.

逞 chěng (v.)- Exhaust. Free from; do as one likes; be pleased with.
逞勇 Heroic; brave.
逞威 Resume on power to intimidate others; play the tyrant.
逞强 Be violent; intimidate; make vigorous efforts.

造 zào (v.)- Make; do; build; create. Institute. Accomplish. Go to; prepare.
造反 Rebel; revolt.
造成 Compose; constitute. Complete; build up; finish.
造物 Make out; create things; prepare.
造船 Ship-building.
造詣 Attainment.
造幣 Coin money. Coinage; mintage.
造謠 Spread rumours; invent false re-

ports.
造句法 Construction of sentences; syntax.
造船廠 A shipyard; a ship-building yard; a dockyard; a navy yard.
造船業 The ship-building industry.
造紙廠 Paper manufactory.
造謠生事 Cause trouble by false stories.

逢 féng (v.)- Meet; come across (upon); fall in with; happen.
逢吉 Meet with good fortune.
逢迎 Meet; receive—as a guest. Curry favour with; cater to.
逢雨 Be caught in a rain; be overtaken by a shower.

連 lián (adj.)- Continuous; connected; successive.
(v.)- Bound upon; connect; unite; include; continue; ally; join; combine.
(conj.)- And; even; also.
連合 Connected; joined; banded together.
連忙 Without delay; at once.
連年 For successive years; for several years; year after year.
連夜 Night after night; every night.
連長 The captain; a company commander.
連接 Connect; attach.
連累 Be implicated (involved) in a crime.
連任 Re-appointed to office; re-elected.
連結 Connect; joint; combine.
連絡 Keep in touch with; make connection.
連貫 Coherent; linked up together.
連登；連載 Publish serially in a paper.
連隊 A company.
連綿 Continuous; uninterrupted; consecutive.
連鎖法(數) The chain-rule.
連絡機關 A liaison organ (agency).
連載小說 A serial novel.
連戰連勝 Win victory after victory.
連鎖反應 A chain reaction.

逮 dài (v.)- Reach. Chase; seize.
逮今 Until now.
逮捕 Arrest; apprehand.
逮捕狀 A warrant of arrest.

週 zhōu (n.)- A week. A revolution.
(v.)- Revolve; go round; return.
週末 The week-end.
週刊 Weekly publication.
週年 An anniversary; a whole year.
週期 A period; a periodic time.
週報 A weekly paper (magazine).
週期性 Periodicity.
週期表 Periodic table.
週年紀念 An anniversary.

進 jìn (n.)- Advance; progress; promotion. Income.
(v.)- Advance; go forward; Proceed; make progress; come; go in; enter; offer; present; promote.
進口 Import.
進去 Go in.
進出 Ins and outs. Incomings and outgoings.
進行 Proceed; advance; make progress.
進攻；進擊 Advance on; make an attack upon; assault.
進步 Progress; improvement; advancement.
進呈；進獻 Offer; present.
進來 Come in.
進食 Take a meal.
進修 Advance in culture.
進口商 An importer; an import trader.
進口貨 Imports; imported articles

(goods).
進化論 Evolutionism; the theory of evolution.
進行曲 A marching song.
進步的 Progressive.
進香客 A pilgrim; a palmer.
進一步 Further.
進出口商 Import and export merchant.
進退兩難 A dilemma.
進一步闡明 To set forth in further detail.
進口准許書 Import permit.

逸 (n.)- Extravagance; leisure; ease; idleness.
yì (v.)- Exceed. Retire. Run; get away; get off; escape; deviate; turn away. Set free.
逸才 Talents above the average.
逸士 A recluse; a hermit.
逸走 Run away; escape.
逸樂 Pleasure; enjoyment.

逼 (adj.)- Compelled; forced. Urgent.
bī (v.)- Press upon; force; oppress; harass; approach; draw near. Reduce; straits.
逼近 Crowd on; draw near.
逼迫 Press; compel; urge on. Be hard up; destitute.
逼眞 True. True to life; real.
逼嫁 Force a woman to marry.

遁 (v.)- Hide away; escape; conceal oneself; vanish. Retire.
dùn 遁去 Run away; flee; take to flight; escape.
遁逃；遁走 Flee; abscond; run away (off); take to flight; take refuge in.
遁辭 An excuse; an evasive answer; subterfuges.

遂 (v.)- Comply with; proceed to; follow; complete.
suì (adv.)- Thereupon; presently; then; subsequently.
遂心；遂意 According to one's fancy. Attain one's end; agreeable to one's wish.
遂行 Execute; carry out; carry into execution.
遂志 Carry out one's purpose.
遂願 Achieve (accomplish) one's purpose.

遄 (v.)- Hurry; go to and fro rapidly.
chuán (adv.)- Hastily; quickly.
遄行；遄往 Go quickly.

遇 (v.)- Meet. Happen; occur. Entertain.
yù 遇見 Happen to meet; meet with.
遇敵 Encounter the enemy.
遇險 Meet with dangers; in danger.
遇難 Meet with misfortunes; encounter difficulties.
遇暴風 Run into a storm.
遇難者 A victim.

遊 (adj.)- Wandering; travelling.
(v.)- Ramble; roam; rove; travel;
yóu saunter; wander.
遊行 Parade.
遊侶；遊伴 A companion in amusement; a playmate.
遊客 A holiday-maker; a sightseer; a tripper.
遊船 A pleasure-boat; a yacht.
遊記 Travel.
遊樂 Pleasure; amusement.
遊歷 Travel about; make a tour.
遊戲 Play; sport; a game.
遊覽 Go sightseeing; see the sights of.

An excursion; a pleasure-trip.
遊戲場 A place of amusement; a pleasure ground; a playground.
遊擊隊 A flying column; a flying squadron.
遊擊戰 Guerilla (partisan) warfare.
遊藝會 A social assembly. Public entertainment.
遊行示威 Hold a demonstration.
遊牧人民 Nomads; nomadic people.
遊客指南 A guidebook; an itinerary.
遊學海外 Go abroad for study.
遊歷世界 A trip (tour) round the world; a round-the-world trip.
遊戲時間 Play time; a recreation hour.

運 yùn (n.)- A turn or revolution of destiny. A circuit or period of time.
(v.)- Turn round; revolve. Transport; convey; carry.
運入 Import.
運出 Export.
運用 Employ; use; apply; put into practice.
運行 Revolve.
運往 Carry to; export.
運河 A canal.
運氣 Luck; fortune.
運動 Motion; movement.
運費 Cost of transport; freight; carriage.
運輸 Traffic; transport; transportation; conveyance.
運動衣 Sports shirts.
運動界；體育界 The sporting world.
運動員 A sportsman; an athlete.
運動場 A playground; a gymnasium; a stadium.
運動會 An athletic meet; a field day; a field meet.
運輸業 Carrying trade; freight trade.
運載火箭 Carrier rocket.
運輸公司 Transporting company; carriers.
運氣不佳 Have no luck; luck goes (fortunate runs) against one.
運氣轉好 Come to luck; luck turns in one's favour; fortune begins to smile on one.
運動器官 Organs of locomotion.

遍 biàn Same as 徧.
(n.)- A time. A tune.
(adj.)- Entire; whole.
(v.)- Go round.
(adv.)- Everywhere.
遍地；遍處 Everywhere; every place.
遍世界 All over the world; all the world over.
遍體鱗傷 One's whole body was wounded seriously.

過 guò (n.)- An error; a fault; a mistake.
(v.)- Pass; cross; go by; march. Pass through; exceed. Commit a fault; make a mistake.
(prep.)- Over; above; beyond.
過大 In excess; with exaggeration.
過小 Too little; too small.
過份 Excessive; overmuch; more than deserved.
過失 A fault; an error; a blunder.
過去 The past. Pass by; be past.
過世 Deceased; dead.
過年 Pass the New Year.
過多 Too much; too many; superabundance; excess.
過門 Marry — of girls.
過後 Afterwards; finally; next in order.
過重 Overweight.
過時 Behind times; past time.
過量 Beyond measure.
過期 Pass the limit of time. Beyond the fixed time; overdue.

過程 Process.
過剩 Surplus; excess.
過境 Cross the frontier.
過慮 Too anxious.
過磅 Weigh; be weighed.
過節 Pass a festival; spend the time of a festival.
過錯 An error; a mistake.
過關 Pass a custom's station.
過去之事 Past events.
過去分詞 A past participle.
過渡時代 A transitional stage (period).
過意不去 Feel ill at ease; your goodness makes me uneasy.

遏 è (v.)- Stop; check; cut off; prevent; curb.
遏止 Stop; cease.
遏制 Put down; repress.

遐 xiá (adj.)- Long-enduring. Distant; remote. Advanced in years.
(v.)- Abandon.
(adv.)- Far off.
遐邇皆知 Everybody far and near knows it.

遑 huáng (n.)- Leisure; vacant time.
(adj.)- Pressed; urged.
遑遑；皇皇 Disturbed and vacillating in mind.

道 dào (n.)- A road; a path; the right way. The truth; principle; a doctrine. Religion. A circuit. A word.
(v.)- Speak; tell. Govern; lead.
道士 Toaist priests.
道伴 A fellow-traveller; a travelling companion.
道具 Sets; settings; scenes; property.
道破 Give expression to; expound the secret of.
道術 Magical arts.
道教 Taoism.
道理 Right principle; doctrine; reason; truth.
道喜；道賀 Congratulate upon.
道路 A highway; a road; a thoroughfare; a way.
道義 Reason and right; sense of right honour; morality.
道歉 Apologize.
道德 Morality; virtue.
道學 The study of rules; ethics; moral philosophy.
道謝 Express thanks.
道德心 Moral spirit (sense); morality.
道聽途說 Tell on the road what you have heard by the way; gossip.
道德品質 Moral charactet; moral trait.

達 dó (n.)- A lamb.
(adj.)- Permeable. Suitable. Intelligent; successful in life; prominent.
(v.)- Reach; arrive at. Succeed. Perceive. Extend to. Inform; notify. Pass through.
達旦 Until daylight.
達成 Accomplish.
達到 Reach; arrive at (in); get to.
達意 Make one's meaning clear; to the point.
達目的 Obtain the object sought for.
達官貴人 Exalted personages; dignitaries.
達爾文主義 Darwinism.

違 wéi (v.)- Oppose; disobey; depart from; disregard; offend against; be different from.
違反 Infringe; break; violate; act contrary to; disobey.
違犯 Infringe; offend against; transgress; violate; act contrary to;

defy.
違抗 Disobey; rebel.
違言 Unreasonable word; contradictory. Be on bad terms.
違例 Exceptional; unprecedented; contrary to all precedent.
違法 Infract the laws. Illegal; unlawful.
違背 Disobey; act in opposition to.
違約 Breach of promise (contract); infract the treaty; contrary to terms.
違禁 Offend against contraband regulations; do what is forbidden.
違禁品 Prohibited goods; contraband goods.
違背人道 Be contrary to (a crime against) humanity; be inhuman.

遙 yáo (adj.)- Distant; remote; far.
遙夜 A long night.
遙望 Take a distant view.
遙遠 Very remote; far-off; in the distance; a good way off.

遜 xùn (adj.)- Complaisant; yielding; humble.
(v.)- Be humble; be modest; yield; withdraw; be obedient.
遜位 Abdicate; give up a position.
遜讓；退遜 Give up to others; yield.

遞 dì (v.)- Transmit; hand to; pass over; forward; change; substitute; present.
遞代 Instead of; substituted for; take the place of.
遞送 Forward; send; convey.
遞給；遞與 Give to; hand to.
遞減 Successive diminution; decrease in order; retard.
遞增；遞加 Successive increase; increase in order (by degrees); accelerate.
遞解出境 To deport; deportation.

遠 yuǎn (adj.)- Distant, in time or place; far.
(v.)- Keep away.
遠大 Vast; grand; far-reaching.
遠方 A great distance; a distant place; a remote place.
遠行 Travel far; take a long journey.
遠足 An excursion; a trip; an outing. Go on an excursion.
遠志 Far-reaching ambition.
遠見 See from a distance; behold from afar. Farsighted.
遠東 The Far East.
遠征 An expedition; an invasion.
遠視 Long-sighted.
遠望 Have a sight of from a distance; a distant view; a perspective.
遠處 A distant place.
遠景 A distant view; a perspective; a vista.
遠隔 Remote; far; far-off; distant.
遠親 A distant relative.
遠離 Keep at a distance. Far separated from.
遠征隊 An expedition; a visiting team.
遠視眼 Hypermetropia; long-sightedness.
遠大志向 A great ambition; a grand ideal.
遠程火箭 Long-range rocket.
遠程射擊 Long-range fire.
遠程導彈 Long-range guided missile.
遠大計劃 A grand (far-reaching) scheme.

遡 sù Same as 溯，泝.
(v.)- Go back; go up; go against; trace to the source.
(adv.)- Formerly; long ago.
遡自 Since then; it appears that ever since. . . .

遡流 Go against the current; row up a stream; come up the river.

**遣** (v.)- Send; banish; drive away. Order; dispatch.
qiǎn 遣回 Send back.
遣使 Send an envoy or messenger.
遣派 Send; despatch.
遣逐 Expel; drive away.
遣散費 Dismissal compensation.

**遨** (v.)- Ramble; travel for pleasure.
áo 遨遊 Travel without aim.

**適** (adj.)- Comfortable; at ease; agreeable.
shì (v.)- Go to; reach; proceed. Marry (of women). Happen; occur; suit; fall in with; hit off.
(adv.)- Suddenly; just now; only.
適于 Good for; be fit for; be suited to.
適口 Palatable.
適用 Sufficient for use; answer the purpose; apply; hold on; applicable.
適合 Accommodation; fittness; adaptation. Suit; meet; fit; be in conformity with; conform to; be adapted for (to).
適宜 Fit; agree; suit. Suitable; agreeable.
適度 Moderate; temperate; within measure.
適當 Appropriate; proper; well; suitable.
適應 Adjustment; adaptation. Adjust; fit; suit.
適用條例 Applicable rules.
適者生存 Survival of the fittest.
適當職業 A suitable calling.
適應環境 Adaptation to environment.

**遭** (n.)- A time; a turn.
(v.)- Meet with; encounter;
zāo happen; come across.
遭殃 Meet with calamity.
遭害 Meet with disaster.
遭遇；遭逢 Meet with; occurance; incur; happen; undergo; experience; chance.
遭難；遇禍 Meet with an accident (a disaster); be in distress.
遭盜劫 Be robbed.
遭遇不幸 Meet with misfortune.
遭到死亡 To meet (one's) death.
遭到挫敗 To suffer setbacks.

**遮** (v.)- Cover; protect; hide from view; shad; conceal; screen;
zhē shut off.
遮庇 Protect.
遮陽 An awning; a shade from the sun.
遮滅 Eclipse.
遮蓋 Cover it over; cloak; lay over.
遮蔽 Hide; conceal; cover.
遮蔭 Shade; shelter.
遮蔽物 A cover; a shelter.

**遲** (adj.)- Slow; late; delayed; behind in time.
chí 遲了 It is late; too late.
遲延 Delay; be retarded. Postponement; procrastination.
遲到 Be behind time; be late for school, dinner, etc. Late in attending.
遲鈍 Dull-witted; dull; sluggish; comprehend; blunt.
遲疑 Hesitate; vacillate; be in doubts; irresolute; slow and suspicious.
遲遲 Slowly; easy-going.
遲到者 A late comer.
遲早之間 Sooner or later.
遲疑不決 Hesitation; indecision. Hesitate.

**遵** zūn (v.)- Follow; honour; obey; conform to; comply with; adopt.
(adv.)- Accordingly.

遵守 Keep; observe; follow; abide by; obey.
遵行 Carry out obediently.
遵法 Obey the laws.
遵命；遵令 Obey a command.
遵循；遵照 Act in accordance with.
遵守條約 Observe the treaties.

**遷** qiān (v.)- Move; remove; transfer. Promoted. Change; shift; transpose.
遷居；遷移 Change one's house; move one's abode.

遷就 Make a compromise; accommodate; obliging.
遷都 Transfer of the capital.
遷移新居 Move into a new house.

**選** xuǎn (n.)- Choice; selection.
(v.)- Choose; select; pick out; elect.
選手 A player; a champion; a team.

選出 Pick out; select; elect.
選民 The elect. Electorate.
選定 Elected.
選拔 Select; pick (single) out; choose.
選派 Appoint to a post; depute.
選票 A vote.
選集 A selection; a choice selection; an anthology.
選舉 Election.
選擇 Choose; select; pick out; elect. Selection.
選舉人 An elector; a voter.
選舉場 A polling-place (station); a poll.
選舉權 Suffrage; franchise; the right to vote.
選美運動 A beauty contest.

**遺** yí (n.)- A residue; a surplus; a remainder; the leavings.
(v.)- Leave behind; lose; miss; forget; abandon; discard; forsake; desert. Make water.

遺失；遺落 Lost; gone.
遺志 The intention (object) of a deceased person.
遺忘 Neglected; forgotten; long out of mind.
遺尿 Incontinence of urine; bed-wetting.
遺物 A bequest; a legacy.
遺孤 A surviving child.
遺留 Leave; hand down.
遺產 Property left behind; an inheritance; a legacy.
遺棄 Discard; abandon; leave; give up.
遺像 Portrait of the dead.
遺漏 Omission; oversight; miss; omit.
遺精 Nocturnal pollution; wet dreams; spermatorrhea.
遺憾 Regret; a pity.
遺體 The body handed down by parents.
遺囑 A will; a testament.
遺產稅 Legacy duty.
遺傳性 Hereditary nature; transmissibility; heredity.
遺臭萬年 Leave a bad name myriads of years behind.
遺產繼承 Succession to a property.
遺憾萬分 It is a thousand pities. What a pity that it should be so!
遺產管理人 An administrator.
遺產繼承人 An heir to a property.

**遼** liáo (adj.)- Far; distant.
遼遠 Far; distant; a long way off.
遼寧（地）Liaoning.

遼闊 Vast; wide.
遼東半島（地） The Liaotung Peninsula.

**遽** (adj.)-Hurried; agitated; speedy; rash; hasty.
jù (v.)- Agitate; tremble.
(adv.)- Suddenly; hastily; quickly; hurriedly.
遽然 Suddenly; all at once; unexpectedly.

**避** (v.)- Avoid; shun; flee; escape; leave; quit; free from; keep away.
bì 避妊 Prevention of conception (fecundation); contraception.
避免 Avoid; get off; get clear; escape from.
避開 Avoid; evade; get out of the way; keep away from; keep clear of.
避債 Avoid creditors.
避暑 Summering. Go to a summer resort.
避禍 Avoid calamity.
避難 Take refuge; seek safety; evacuate.
避妊藥 A contraceptive.
避風所 A typhoon shelter.
避暑地 A summer resort (retreat).
避雷針 A lightning-rod (-conductor).
避免責任 Shirk one's responsibility.
避重就輕 Shirk the difficult and take the easy.

**邀** (v.)- Invite; meet; receive; request. Intercept. Send for; summon.
yāo 邀約 Request; invite; ask.
邀宴 Invite someone to a feast.
邀請 Invite.

**邁** (adj.)- Old; aged.
(v.)- Surpass; exceed; pass by; go on a journey; depart; far.
mài 邁進 Dash forward; push on; strive for.
邁開大步 Walk with great strides.

**邂** 邂逅 A chance meeting; meet unexpectedly; meet by chance.
xiè

**還** (v.)- Go or come back; return. Surround. Revolve; rotate. Repay; give back; recompense.
huán [hái] (adv.)- Still; furthermore; at once; forthwith; even; yet.
還有 There is still; further.
還早 Still early; plenty of time.
還拜 Return a visit.
還原 Get back to the original state. Be restored to health. (化) Reduction; deoxidation.
還家 Come (get) back; return home.
還清 All paid—as an account.
還債 Repay; pay a debt; pay back the money.
還鄉 One returns to his native town.
還價 Abate a price; beat down.
還原劑 A reducing agent.
還原作用 A reducing process.

**邊** Same as 边.
(n.)- A side; an edge, a margin.
biān A border; a boundary. A line.
邊地；邊境；邊疆 The frontier; the borderland.
邊防 Frontier-garrison.
邊門 Side door.
邊界 Border; limit.
邊旁 On the side.
邊緣；邊際 A rim; a raised edge.
邊關；邊塞 A frontier-pass.
邊防軍 Frontier forces.
邊界問題 Boundary question.

**邏** (v.)- Patrol; inspect; watch.
luó 邏輯 Logic.

# 邑 部

**邑** yì (n.)- A city; a town; a district.
邑人 Those of the same district.
邑廟 The district temple.

**那** nà (pron.)- Which? What? Who?
(adj.)- Plentiful; comfortable. That; those.
(adv.)- How.
那時 Then; that time.
那裏 There; in that place. Where? in which place?
那一個 Which? who? who is it?
那自然 That is a matter of course.
那能夠 How can it be? How is it possible?
那裏去 Where are you going?
那年那月 Which year and which month?

**邦** bāng (n.)- A state; a country; a nation; a kingdom; a realm.
邦交 Diplomatic relations.
邦國 States; nations; kingdom.

**邪** xié (adj.)- Wicked; dishonest; vicious; evil; wrong.
(adv.)- An interrogative particle, for which 耶 is now used.
邪心；邪念 An evil thought (desire, intention); a vicious mind.
邪法；邪術 Sorcery; magic; enchantment; black arts.
邪病；癲癇 Epilepsy.
邪氣 Noxious influence; vicious air.
邪教 A heretical religion; heterodoxy.
邪淫 Lewdness; lustful.
邪惡 Vice; wickedness; viciousness.
邪路 A wrong path or course.

**邯** hán 邯鄲(地) A district in Hopei.
邯鄲夢；黃粱夢 Evanescence of life.

**邱** qiū (n.)- A mound; a tumulus; a hillock.
邱陵 A mound.

**郁** yù (adj.)- Elegant; fragrant; beautiful; splendid; fine.
郁郁 Fragrant; odoriferous; odorous.
郁馨 Sweet scented.
郁郁紛紛 Brilliant and beautiful—as clouds.

**郊** jiāo (n.)- Country; suburb; outskirts.
郊外 In the wilds; in the country; outskirts of a town.
郊墟 The open country; wastes; wild fields.
郊遊野餐 Picnic.

**郎** láng (n.)- A gentleman; a young man; a son. A husband.
郎君；才郎 A husband.

**郡** jùn (n.)- A province; a district; a prefecture; a county; a shire.
郡王 A prince of the second rank; the grandson of an emperor.
郡主 A princess; daughter of a prince of the first rank.
郡城 A prefectural city; a county

town.
郡縣 A district.

部 (n.)- A class; a section; a family. A sort; a tribe; a genus. A
bù ministry; a board; a department. A volume.
部下 Those under the command; subordinates.
部分 A portion; a part; a section; a division.
部位 Locality.
部長 A minister; the head of a department.
部門 A class; a group; a department; a section.
部首 Radicals of Chinese characters.
部隊 A corps; a detachment.
部落 A tribe; a clan.
部署 Arrange the parts; assign places to.
部分的 Partial; sectional.

郵 (n.)- A post office. A hut.
(adj.)- Postal; mail.
yóu (v.)- Mail.
郵片 A postal card; a post card.
郵件 Mail matters; postal matters.
郵印；郵戳 A postmark.
郵局 A post-office.
郵車 Postal vans; mail cart.
郵政 Post service.
郵差 A postman; a post-boy; a letter-carrier.
郵區 Postal district.
郵票 A postage stamp.
郵寄 Send by post (mail); mail; post.
郵筒 A pillar-box.
郵費 Postage.
郵滙 Postal money order; remit by post.
郵局電滙 A postal telegraphic transfer.
郵局滙票 Postal order.
郵政指南 Postal guide.

都 (n.)- The metropolis or capital; a large city; a center city.
dū (adj.)- Beautiful; elegant; fine; graceful.
(adv.)- All; altogether; wholly.
都市；都會 A city; a town; a municipality.
都城 The capital; the metropolis.
都督 A military governor.
都市人口 Urban population.
都是一樣 All are alike.

鄂 (n.)- A name for the province of Hupeh (湖北).
è

鄉 (n.)- A village; the country; the native place; rural district.
xiāng 鄉下 One's native place; in the country.
鄉民 Villagers; rustics; country-folk (people).
鄉俗 Rural customs.
鄉紳 Country-gentry.
鄉親 Fellow country men; country cousin.
鄉政府 Township government.
鄉村生活 Village life.
鄉村自治 Municipal government; town government.

鄙 (n.)- A small district; a frontier town.
bǐ (adj.)- Mean; base; low; rustic; rude; vulgar; country like; miserly; stingy; niggard.
(v.)- Despise; slight.
鄙夫 A mean fellow; a rustic; a base man.
鄙劣 Unpolished; mean; vile; worthless.
鄙夷；鄙薄 Despise; speak ill of.

鄙俗 Rural custom.
鄙視 Despise; have contempt for.
鄙意；鄙見 My humble opinion.

**鄭** (n.)- A plain. A surname. The name of a place in Honan.
zhèng (v.)- Emphasize.
鄭重 Pay attention to. Earnest; sincere. Important; value; consider seriously.
鄭重其事 Handle a thing carefully (with care).

**鄰** (n.)- Neighbour; neighbourhood.
lín (adj.)- Near; neighbouring; next; close by; contiguous.
鄰人；鄰右 A neighbour.
鄰居 A neighbouring house; the next door.
鄰近 Near; close by.
鄰室 The next (adjoining) room.
鄰國 A neighbouring (an adjacent) country.
鄰境 Vicinity; the neighbourhood.

# 酉 部

**酊** (adj.)- Drunk; intoxicated.
dǐng

**酋** (n.)- Liquor after fermentation. A headman; the chief of a tribe.
qiú 酋長 A leader; a chieftain.

**酌** (v.)- Drink; pour out wine. Make a preferance; deliberate;
zhuó consult; discuss; consider.
酌定；酌奪 Deliberate and come to a decision; consult.
酌酒 Pour wine.
酌減 Propose to reduce.
酌量 Weigh; consider; take into consideration.
酌辦 Consider what course is to be taken.
酌議；斟酌 Deliberate; consult; discuss over.

**配** (n.)- A mate; one of a married couple; a wife. An equal.
pèi (v.)- Match; fit; assort. Marry a daughter to another. Accompany; repair; restore; fill up.
配合 Mate; pair; assimilate; fit; suit; conjugate.
配身 Fit or suit, as a dress.
配角 The cast of a play; a utility man; a supernumerary.
配偶 A married pair; a couple; a match.
配給 Distribution; ration.
配備 Equip.
配對 Couple; mate.
配製 Mix drugs; make up a prescription.
配給米 Rationed rice.
配藥所 Dispensary.
配尼西林 Penicillin.
配合得好 Well-matched; in harmony with.

**酒** (n.)- Liquor; wine; spirit.
jiǔ 酒店 An alehouse; a wine shop; a drinking-house; a public house; a tavern; a bar.
酒肴 Wine and food (dainties).
酒杯 A cup; a wine-cup (glass).

酒保 A waiter; a bar-tender.
酒宴；酒席 A banquet; a feast. Hold a banquet; give a feast.
酒瓶 A wine bottle.
酒量 Wine measure; drinking capacity.
酒窩 Dimples on the cheeks.
酒精；火酒 Spirit of wine; alcohol.
酒樓 A banqueting house.
酒醉 Get drunk; be (become) intoxicated.
酒館 A restaurant; a tavern.
酒精燈 A spirit (an alcohol) lamp.

**酗** xù (adj.)- Mad with drink; raving drunk; intoxicated.
酗酒 Mad with drink.

**酣** hān (adj.)- Merry from drinking.
酣飲 Drink to intoxication.
酣歌 Sing in a tipsy way.
酣睡 Sleep soundly; sleep heavily.
酣暢 Jovial; merry; cheerful.

**酥** sū (n.)- Curd; cheese.
(adj.)- Crisp; flaky; short; soft.
酥油 Butter.
酥酪 Cheese.
酥餅 Short cakes.

**酩** mǐng 酩酊 Drunkenness; intoxication.
酩酊大醉 Deadly drunk.

**酪** lào (n.)- Cream; cheese.
(adj.)- Fat.
酪酥 Cheese.
酪酸 (化) Butyric acid.

**酬** chóu Same as 醻.
(v.)- Entertain; treat a guest. Repay; return; requite.
酬金 A gratuity; earning; salary; remuneration.
酬答 Requite; repay.
酬勞 Reward services; compensate for one's trouble (service).
酬報 Requite; repay; reward.
酬愿 Make a thank offering.
酬謝 Remunerate; make a return present; return thanks.
酬勞金 A reward; a recompense.

**酵** jiào (n.)- Yeast; barm.
酵母 Yeast; ferment.
酵粉 Yeast-powder.
酵素 Enzyme.
酵餅 Yeast cakes.

**酷** kù (adj.)- Cruel; oppressive; violent; severe; tyrannical; harsh; hard-hearted.
(adv.)- Extremely; very; exceedingly.
酷刑 Cruel punishment; torture.
酷虐 Tyrannical; harsh; cruel; oppressive.
酷烈 Severe; harsh; intense.
酷暑 Severe summer (heat).
酷愛；酷好 Very fond of; devoted to.
酷熱 Exceedingly hot; scorching; sultry.

**酸** suān (n.)- An acid; a sour taste.
(adj.)- Painful; grieved. Sour; acid.
酸辛 Misfortunes; bitter; miserable.
酸味 Acidity; sourness.
酸性 Acidity.
酸素；養氣 Oxygen.
酸梅 Sour plumes.
酸楚 Sad; grieved; sorrowful.
酸醋 Vinegar.
酸澀 Sour and bitter.
酸化物 An oxidized substance; an oxide.

酸化劑 An oxidizing agent.
酸性反應 Acid reaction.
酸甜苦辣 Sour, sweet, bitter, astringent.

醃 yān (adj.)- Salted; pickled; cured.
(v.)- Salt; pickle.
醃肉 Salt meat; bacon.
醃魚 Salt fish; cure fish.
醃菜 Greens for salting; salted rape; salted greens.

醇 chún (n.)- Good wine. (化) Ethyl alcohol.
(adj.)- Good; pure; strong; thick as a sirup; generous; rich; liberal.
醇化(哲) Idealize.
醇酒 Good wine.

醉 zuì (adj.)- Drunk; intoxicated.
(v.)- Be under the table; crook the elbow; be in one's cup; get drunk.
醉酒 Drunk with wine; feel the effects of drink; get drunk (tipsy).
醉鬼；醉漢 A sot; a drunkard; a drink-sodden fellow.
醉醺醺 Drunkenness.
醉生夢死 Dream away one's life; live a life of dreams; live to no purpose.

醋 cù (n.)- Vinegar.
醋意 Jealousy.
醋酸 (化) Acetic acid.
醋酸鹽 Acetate.

醒 xǐng (v.)- Awake; wake up. Become sober; come to one's self; rose up; incite; excite to action.
醒悟 Come to oneself; realize; become aware or conscious of; awake from spiritual sleep.
醒覺 Be brought to one's senses; awakened.
醒目 To catch the eye; to attract attention.

醜 chǒu (adj.)- Ugly; shameful; hateful; awkward; disgraceful.
(v.)- Dislike. Compare.
醜名 Infamy; an ill name; bad repute.
醜事 A disgraceful affair.
醜陋 Ugly; ill-looking.
醜惡 Ugly; mishappen; ill-shaped; deformed.
醜話 Vile language.

醞 yùn (v.)- Brew. Foment; arouse.
醞釀 Brew wine. Agitate secretly; work underhand.

醣 táng 醣類；碳水化物 Carbohydrate.

醫 yī (n.)- A physician; a doctor; a surgeon.
(adj.)- Medical.
(v.)- Cure; heal; treat.
醫生；醫師 A doctor; a physician; a surgeon (外科).
醫治；治療 Medical treatment; medical care. Heal; cure; remedy.
醫科 Medical department.
醫院 A hospital.
醫學 Medical science; medicine.
醫藥 Medicine; a medicament.
醫學院 Medical college.
醫治無效 The medical treatment is not efficacious.
醫學博士 A doctor of medicine (D.M. or M.D.).
醫療用具 Medical instruments; surgical instruments.

醫療設施 Medical service.
醫療費用 Medical fees.
醫藥文獻 Medical literature.

醬 (n.)- Sauce; soy; condiment; pickles; jelly; jams.
jiàng 醬瓜 Pickled cucumbers.
醬油 Soy; bean sauce.
醬菜 Pickled vegetables; vegetables seasoned in soy.

醮 (n.)- A sacrifice; a thanksgiving service.
jiào (adj.)- Finished; emptied; exhausted.
(v.)- Offer drink. Sacrifice to the dead; celebrate the All-souls festival.

醱 (v.)- Brew; ferment.
醱酵 Fermentation.
pō

醵 (v.)- Contribute to a feast.
jù

釀 (v.)- Cause to ferment; brew; breed; generate; create; excite;
niàng cause.
釀母 Yeast.
釀酒 Ferment spirits; distil wines.
釀造 Brew; distil.
釀禍 Create trouble; hatch mischief.
釀蜜 Make honey—by bees.
釀酒所 A brewery; a distillery.
釀成大患 To bring about disaster.

釁 Same as 衅.
(n.)- A quarrel; a pretext; an
xìn offence; a dispute.
(v.)- Offer blood in sacrifices.
釁隙 A pretext for strife.
釁端 Cause of quarrel; beginning of strife.

# 采 部

采 (n.)- Bright colours.
(adj.)- Variegated; brilliant; ele-
cǎi gant.
(v.)- Pluck; gather; pick; snatch; pull off; choose; select; separate. Distinguish.
采輯 An anthology. Gather together.
采邑 Allotments to feudal nobles; a fief.

釋 (n.)- Buddhist.
(v.)- Unloose; release; free;
shì liberate. Explain.
釋放 Release; let go; set free; liberate.
釋罪 Pardon; let off.
釋縛 Set force; uncord; loose the bonds.
釋迦牟尼；釋尊 Sakya-Muni; Gautama.

# 里 部

**里** ㄌㄧ (n.)- Li, a linear measure of 1800 Chih (尺). A neighbourhood. A village. A lane; an alley. The native town.

里巷；里弄；胡同 A lane.
里門 The old home. Gate of a village.
里昂(地) Lyons.
里數；里程 Mileage; distance.
里程碑 A mile-post (-stone).
里斯本(地) Lisbon.
里比利亞(地) Liberia.
里約熱內盧(地) Rio de Janeiro.

**重** zhòng [chóng] (n.)- Weight.
(adj.)- Heavy; weight. Important; grave. Strong. Violent; severe. Deep; dull; lumpish; inactive.
(v.)- Weigh; respect; venerate; look up; think much of; give importance to. Double; repeat; multiply.

重九；重陽 Chung-Yeung Festival.
重大 Grave; important; serious; weighty.
重心 The centre of gravity.
重用 Appoint one to a position of trust; give one an important position.
重任 Reappointment. A heavy responsibility; an important duty. Reassume an office. Take up a responsible position.
重地 Reserved, secluded, or important places not open to the public.
重抄 Re-copy. Transcription.
重版 A second edition.
重油 Heavy (thick) oil.
重建 Re-construction; re-building.
重要 Important; essential; indispensable; momentous; significance.
重負；重累 Heavy burdens.
重音 Accent.
重病 A serious (severe) illness.
重做 Do over.
重修 Repair; revise.
重婚 Bigamy.
重視 Respect; esteem; make account of; value; attach importance to.
重稅 A heavy tax.
重量 Weight.
重傷 A severe (serious, mortal) wound (injury).
重圍 A close siege. Be closely hemmed in by the enemy.
重新 Afresh; anew.
重慶(地) Chungking.
重複 Be repeated; double; again and again; frequently; one after another; doubly; repetition.
重學；力學 Mechanics.
重壓 Overwhelm; overlay; oppress; weigh down.
重擔 A heavy load (burden).
重點(物) Point of weight.
重讀 Repeat; stress.
重工業 Heavy industries.
重金屬 Heavy metals.
重大事件 A grave (serious) affair.
重大問題 A question of great (vital) consequence.
重大損失 Heavy losses.
重重疊疊 In a pile; in layers; one upon another.
重要工業 The key industry.
重要地位 An important (a responsible) position.
重要關鍵 A vital point.
重量超過 Overweight.
重新做人 To turn over a new leaf.
重新開始 Resume; to make a fresh start.

**野** yě (n.)- A waste land; a moor; a wilderness; the country; the open country; uncultivated

region.
(adj.)- Wild; rustic; rude, savage; uncultivated; ambitious; uncivilized.
野火；野燒 A prairie fire.
野牛 A wild ox; a bison.
野心 Ambition.
野生 Growing wild.
野外 Out in the wilderness.
野味 Game; savoury dishes.
野兔 A hare.
野豬 A wild boar (hog).
野餐 A picnic; picnicking.
野獸 Wild animals (beasts).
野蠻 Savage; barbarous; brutal; fierce.
野心家 A man of ambition.
野戰軍 Field army.
野心勃勃 Ambitious; aspiring; burning with ambition.
野生植物 A wild plant.

**量** líǒng [liàng] (n.)- A measure; the capacity; a quantity.
(v.)- Measure; gauge; calculate; consider; deliberate; estimate.
量力 Measure one's strength.
量身 Measure one's height.
量杯 A measuring glass.
量器 A measure of capacity.
量角規；分度器 Protractor.
量力而行 Attempt nothing beyond your strength; do according to one's ability.

**釐** lí Same as厘.
(n.)- The thousandth part of a Chinese foot or a tael. A cash.
(adj.)- Small; minute.
(v.)- Arrange; adjust; regulate.
釐分 Minute; scanty; few.

# 金 部

**金** jīn (n.)- Metal. Gold. Money.
(adj.)- Yellow. Metallic. Golden. Precious.
金色 Golden colour.
金沙；金屑 Gold dust.
金言 Precious words; valuable advice; golden sayings.
金星(天) Venus.
金婚 A golden wedding, the 50th anniversary.
金魚 A goldfish.
金箔；金葉；金鉑 Gold foil; gold leaf.
金牌 A gold medal.
金銀 Gold and silver. Money.
金融 Currency; circulation of money; finance.
金錢 Money.
金錶 A gold watch.
金鎊 Pound sterling.
金額 A sum (an amount) of money; the sum; the amount.
金邊 Gilt-edged. (地) Pnompenh, Cambodia.
金屬 Metals.
金本位 Gold standard.
金字塔 A pyramid.
金融界 Financial circles.
金鋼石 The diamond.
金鋼鑽 Diamond for a small drill; a drill for boring porcelain.
金黴素 Aureomycine.
金碧輝煌 Glittering and bright.
金銀財寶 Money and valuables.
金髮女子 A blonde.

金融中心 A money (financial) centre.
金屬元素 Metallic elements.
金融市場 Money market.
金屬鑛物 Metallic minerals.
金鷄納霜 Quinine.

釘 dīng 〔dìng〕 (n.)- A nail; a spike; a peg.
(v.)- Nail.
釘子 A nail.
釘住；釘牢 Nailed fast.
釘匠 Nailer.
釘書；裝釘 Bind books.
釘馬脚 Shoe a horse.

釜 fǔ (n.)- A pan; a boiler; a kettle; a caldron.
釜山(地) Fusan, Korea.

針 zhēn Same as 鍼.
(n.)- A pin; a needle; a sting; a thorn; a spine.
(v.)- Probe; prick; pierce.
針灸 Acupuncture and cauterization (moxibustion).
針科(醫) Acupuncture.
針線 Needles and thread; needlework.
針刺麻醉 Acupunctural anaesthesia.

釣 diào (v.)- Fish; bait; angle; seek.
釣竿 An angling rod; a fishing rod.
釣魚 Angling.
釣鈎 A fish-hook; an angle.
釣餌 Fishing-worm; bait.
釣魚用具 Fishing-tackle (-gear).

釵 chāi (n.)- A hairpin.
釵釧 Hairpins and bracelets—women's ornaments in general.

釷 tǔ (n.)- (化) Thorium (Th).

鈀 pá (n.)- A drag; a harrow. (化) Palladium (Pd).
鈀地 Harrow.

鈉 nà (n.)- (化) Natrium (Na); sodium.

鈍 dùn (adj.)- Dull; stupid; thick-brained. Blunt; obtuse.
(v.)- Be blunt; become dull.
鈍刀 A blunt knife.
鈍角(幾) An obtuse angle.
鈍劍 A foil.

鈔 chāo (n.)- Paper money; bank notes; money.
鈔票 Paper money; bank notes.
鈔寫；抄寫 Copy; transcribe.

鈕 niǔ (n.)- A button; a knob; a handle.
鈕子 Buttons.
鈕門；鈕耳 Button-hole.

鈞 jūn (n.)- A weight of thirty catties. A porter's wheel.
(adj.)- Just; equal. Respectful; important.
(v.)- Equalize; classify.
鈞函 Your esteemed letter.

鈣 gài (n.)- (化) Calcium (Ca).

鈦 tài (n.)- (化) Titanium (Ti).

鈴 líng (n.)- A bell; a hand-bell; a door-bell.
鈴鳴；鈴響 A bell rings (tin-

kles); ring (push, press) the bell.
鈴聲 Ringing; the tinkle of a bell.

**鈷** gǔ
(n.)- (化) Cobalt (Co).

**鈸** bó
(n.)- Cymbals.

**鈺** yù
(n.)- Strong mental.

**鈾** yóu
(n.)- (化) Uranium (U).

**鈿** tián
(n.)- Silver or gold filigree; a hair ornament.
鈿盒 A hair-ornament case.

**鉀** jiǎ
(n.)- (化) Potassium; kalium (K).

**鉅** jù
(n.)- Steel. A hook.
(adj.)- Great; huge; gigantic; immense; large.
鉅款 A large sum of money.
鉅費 Great expenses.

**鉋** bào
(n.)- A plane.
(v.)- Plane; level off.
鉋子 A plane.
鉋木 Plane wood.
鉋花；鉋柴 Woodshavings.

**鉍** bì
(n.)- (化) Bismuth (Bi).

**鉑** bó
(n.)- A thin sheet of metal; mental foils (化) Platinum (Pt).
鉑絲 Platinum wire.
鉑金屬 Platinum metals.

**鉗** qián
(n.)- Tweezers; pincers; forceps; tongs; pliers.
(v.)- Pinch; clasp; grasp.
鉗子 Pincers; tweezers; tongs.
鉗夾 Nip it up.
鉗制 Force submission.

**鉛** qiān
(n.)- Lead; plumbum (Pb).
鉛片 Sheet lead.
鉛印 Printed from lead types.
鉛字 Lead type.
鉛粉；鉛華 White lead; ceruse.
鉛筆 A lead pencil; a pencil.
鉛絲 Lead wire.
鉛鑛 Lead ore.
鉛垂線 Plumb line; a vertical line.
鉛筆心 The lead of a pencil.
鉛筆畫 A pencil sketch (drawing).
鉛筆鉋 A pencil-sharpener.

**鉢** bō
Same as 缽.
(n.)- An earthenware basin. A Buddhist priest's alms-bowl.

**鉤** gōu
Same as 鈎.
(n.)- A hook; a scythe; a clasp; a sickle.
(v.)- Hook; tempt; seduce. Bend; curve; be crooked.
鉤形 Hooked; hook-shaped; unciform.
鉤起 Hook up.
鉤針 A hook; a crochet needle (編織用).
鉤緊 Hook fast.

**鉻** gè
(n.)- A hook. (化) Chromium (Cr).
鉻酸 (化) Chromic acid.
鉻鋼 Chrome steel; chromium

steel.
鉻黃色 Chrome yellow.
鉻鐵鑛 Chromite.

**銀** yín (n.)- Silver; silver coin; treasure.
銀匠 A silversmith.
銀行 A bank.
銀色 The touch or quality of silver. Silvery.
銀杯 A silver cup.
銀河(天) The Milky Way.
銀婚 A silver wedding, the 25th anniversary.
銀票 Bank notes; bank bills; cheques; cash note; silver note.
銀牌 A silver medal.
銀圓 Dollars; silver coins.
銀幕 Silver screen.
銀錢;銀幣 A silver coin; money.
銀灰色 A silver-grey colour.
銀行家 A banker.
銀行業 Banking business.
銀行支票 Bank cheque.
銀行存摺 A bank-book; a pass-book.
銀行股票 Bank stocks.
銀行條例 Bank act.
銀行滙票 Bank bill of transfer; bank draft; demand draft.

**銅** tóng (n.)- Copper; brass.
(adj.)- Brazen; coppery.
銅片 Copper sheets; copper plates.
銅匠 Coppersmith.
銅色 Copper-coloured; sun-burnt.
銅壺 A copper boiler.
銅牌 A copper medal.
銅絲 Copper wire.
銅鼓 Copper drum.
銅像 A bronze statue.
銅綠 Verdigris.
銅箔 Brass foil; tinsel.
銅幣 A copper coin.
銅器 Copper vessels or utensils; copperwares.
銅錢 Money; cash.
銅鑛 Copper mine; copper ore.
銅鑼 Copper gong.
銅器時代 The bronze age.
銅牆鐵壁 Impregnable (invulnerable) as walls of brass and iron.

**銑** xiǎn (adj.)- Bright; burnished.
銑鐵 Pig-iron.

**銘** míng (n.)- An epitaph; an inscription.
(v.)- Carve; inscribe; record; engrave words, as on metal or stone.
銘心 Impress (stamp) on one's mind; remember well.
銘刻 Engrave.
銘感肺腑 Make a strong and lasting impression; sink into or penetrate the mind.

**銜** xián (n.)- Rank; official position; a title.
(v.)- Contain; hold in the mouth.
銜名 Official title of an officer.
銜命 Act according to orders received.
銜恩 Feel grateful.
銜頭 A title.

**銨** ǎn Same as 鉦.
(n.)- Ammonium.

**銳** ruì (n.)- A sharp-pointed weapon.
(adj.)- Acute; keen; sharp; pointed. Zealous; valiant. Trifling; insignificant.
銳利 Sharp; keen; trenchant; sharp (keen)-edged.

銳角(幾) An acute angle.
銳角三角形 An acute-angled triangle.

銷 (v.)- Melt; fuse; waste; consume; spend; cancel; hand over; exhaust; clear off; sell.
xiāo 銷行 Put into circulation.
銷案 Settle a case in court; close a case; quash an indictment.
銷耗 Wear and tear; waste.
銷售 Sell; put into circulation.
銷路 Range of sale; area of consumption; salability.
銷貨清單 Account sales.

銻 (n.)-(化) Antimony; stibium (Sb).
tī

銼 (n.)- A file; an iron pan.
(v.)- File.
cuò 銼光 File; polish.

鋁 (n.)-(化) Aluminium (Al).
lǚ

鋅 (n.)- Zinc (Zn).
鋅版 Zincograph; zincotype.
xīn

鋇 (n.)-(化) Barium (Ba).
bèi

鋏 (n.)- A pair of pincers for use at a fire. A sword.
jiá

鋒 (n.)- A sharp point; a spear; a blade. The van of a troop; the front.
fēng
鋒利 Incisive; acute; sharp-pointed sharp.
鋒芒 Sword-point.
鋒鏑 Weapons.

鋤 Same as 鉏.
(n.)- A hoe; a mattock.
chú (v.)- Hoe; cultivate the fields; weed; dig.
鋤地 Hoe the ground.
鋤草 Root out; weed.
鋤頭 A hoe.

鋩 (n.)- A sharp point.
máng

鋪 (n.)- A shop; a store. A post-house.
pū (v.)- Spread out; arrange; lay in order.
鋪上 Lay on.
鋪瓦 Lay tiles.
鋪床 Make a bed.
鋪張 Paint in bright colours; display; show.
鋪路 Pavement.
鋪子 A shop.
鋪蓋 Bedclothes; bedding.

鋸 (n.)- A saw.
(adj.)- Serrated.
jù (v.)- Saw; split.
鋸木 Saw wood.
鋸匠 A saw-setter.
鋸開 Cut in two; saw asunder.
鋸齒 The teeth of a saw; saw-teeth.
鋸木廠 Saw mill.

鋼 (n.)- Steel.
(adj.)- Hard; strong.
gāng 鋼甲 Steel armour.
鋼板 Steel plate.
鋼勁 Vigorous; lusty.

鋼軌 Rail steel.
鋼盔 Helmet.
鋼琴 A piano.
鋼筆 A pen.
鋼琴家 Pianist.
鋼筆尖 A pen-point; a nib.
鋼筆畫 Pen-and-ink drawing.
鋼鐵工人 Steel working.
鋼骨建築 A steel-skeleton building.
鋼鐵工業 Iron and steel industry.
鋼筋混凝土 Reinforced concrete.

錄 (n.)- A record; a document; annals.
lù (v.)- Admit; accept. Record; note; write down; copy; transcribe. Select; choose.
錄下 Write down; take down.
錄用 Select for appointment; employ.
錄取 Select.
錄音 Sound-recording. Record on the disk.
錄錄；碌碌 Ordinary; common-place.
錄音室 A recording room.
錄音機 A recorder.
錄音帶 A tape.
錄音廣播 Electro-transcription broadcasting; broadcasting of a recorded speech.

錐 (n.)- An awl; a gimlet; the tip or point; a sharp pointed tool; a broach.
zhuī (v.)- Bore.
錐子 An awl; a gimlet; a drill.
錐孔；錐眼 Bore a hole with an awl; drive a gimlet into.
錐穿 Bore through.
錐刀之末 The tip of an awl–a trifle.

錘 (n.)- A hammer.
(v.)- Hammer.
chuí 錘煉 Hammer–as wrought iron.

錢 (n.)- Coin; cash; money; coppers; wealth.
qián 錢財 Money; wealth; property.
錢袋 A purse; a pouch.
錢票；錢鈔 Bank notes; paper money.
錢幣 Coin; money.
錢塘江(地) The Tsien Tang River in Chekiang.
錢幣學；古錢學 Numismatics.

錦 (n.)- Brocade; tapestry; embroidered silk.
jǐn (adj.)- Ornamented; flowery.
錦文 Fine writing.
錦旗 A brocade flag.
錦綢 Figured pongee.
錦標 Champion; champion flag.
錦標賽 A championship.
錦上添花 Add flowers to embroidery–superfluous.

錫 (n.)- Tin; stannum (Sn). A gift.
xī (v.)- Give; grant; confer; bestow.
錫石(鑛) Cassiterite; tinstone.
錫匠 A tinman; a tinsmith.
錫杖 A Buddhist abbot's staff.
錫蘭(地) Ceylon.
錫鑛 Tin ore.
錫蘭人 A Ceylonese; a Singhalese.
錫蘭語 Singhalese.

錯 (n.)- A grindstone. A mistake; an error.
cuò (adj.)- Confused. Ornamented.
(v.)- Mistake; be wrong; err. Be confused.
(adv.)- In confusion; in disorder.
錯刀 The name of an ancient coin shaped like a knife and inlaid with gold.
錯失；錯誤 Make a mistake; drift

(fall) into error. A mistake; an error.
錯字 Erratum; an erroneous character.
錯言 Erroneous expression.
錯怪 Blame the wrong person.
錯處 Fault; wrong; offence.
錯亂 Be thrown out of order; get confused.
錯臂 Tattoo the arms.
錯雜；複雜 Complicated; complex; intricate; tangled.
錯覺 Have (hold) an illusion.
錯過機會 Miss an opportunity.

錳 (n.)- (化) Manganese (Mn).
měng

錶 (n.)- A watch.
biǎo
錶匠 A watchmaker.
錶袋 Watch-pocket.
錶殼 Watch-case.
錶鍊 Watch chain.
錶帶 Watch guard.
錶面玻璃 Watch glass; crystal.

錨 (n.)- An anchor; a grapnel.
máo
錨起 Weigh (get up) anchor.
錨落 Cast (drop) anchor.
錨標 A mooring buoy.
錨繩；錨纜 A cable; a hawser.

鍊 (n.)- A chain.
liàn
(adj.)- Experienced; expert.
(v.)- Refine; train; drill; temper.
鍊仙 Become an immortal.
鍊金 Refine gold.
鍊熟 Well smelted; matured in; accustomed to.
鍊鋼廠 Steel mill or works; steel refinery.
鍊而愈精 The more it is refined, the purer it becomes.

鍋 (n.)- A pot; a caldron; a kettle; a pan; a boiler.
guō
鍋巴 The burnt rice that adheres to the sides of the pot.
鍋貼 Fried pastry with meat.
鍋蓋 A pot-lid; the cover of a pot.
鍋爐 A boiler.

鍍 (v.)- Overlay with metal; plate; gild.
dù
鍍金 Plate with gold; gild.
鍍銀 Plate with silver. Silver plating.
鍍金匠 A gold-plater.

鍘 (n.)- A lever-knife.
zhá
鍘刀 Lever-knife for cutting chaff, etc.

鍛 (v.)- Temper; forge. Train; drill.
duàn
鍛鍊 Temper; forge; train; perfect oneself.
鍛鍊本領 Improve one's art; train oneself.
鍛鍊精神 Train one's spirit; foster presence of mind.

鍵 (n.)- The bolt of a lock. The linchpin on the nave. The keys of an organ, piano-forte, etc.
jiàn
鍵孔 A keyhole.
鍵盤 Keyboard.

鍶 Same as 鎴.
sī
(n.)- (化) Strontium (Sr).

鍾 (n.)- An ancient measure, equal to four pecks. A cup; a goblet; a jar.
zhōng
(v.)- Bring together; concentrate. Love.

鍾情 Fall in love with.
鍾愛 Love dearly; dote on; treat with great tenderness.

鎂 (n.)- (化) Magnesium (Mg).
měi 鎂光燈 Magnesium light.

鎊 (n.)- A sterling pound; a gold coin.
bàng (v.)- Scrape off; level.

鎔 (v.)- Fuse; melt; dissolve.
róng 鎔化；鎔銷 Melt; fuse; thaw.
鎔度 Fusing point.
鎔解 Fusion; melting; smelting.
鎔爐 A smelting-furnace (-blasting); a cupola furnace.
鎔鑄 Cast; pour metal into a mould.
鎔化金銀 Melt gold and silver.

鎖 (n.)- A lock. Fetters; chains.
suǒ (v.)- Lock; bolt; blockade.
鎖門 Lock (fasten) the door.
鎖骨(解) The collar bone; the clavicle.
鎖匙；鎖鑰 A key.
鎖禁；鎖押 Confine in chains.
鎖鍊 Fetters; chains.

鎗 (n.)- A gun; a pistol; a rifle. A spear; a lance.
qiāng 鎗口 Muzzle.
鎗手 A gunman.
鎗托 The stock of a gun.
鎗身 Barrel of a gun.
鎗架 Rack for guns.
鎗彈 A shot; a bullet.
鎗機 The lock or trigger of a gun.

鎘 (n.)- (化) Cadmium (Cd).
gé

鎚 (n.)- A mallet; a hammer; a club.
chuí (v.)- Hammer; pound.
鎚打 Hammer.

鎢 (n.)- Tungsten; wolfram (W).
wū 鎢絲燈泡 A tungsten lamp.

鎧 (n.)-Armour; coat of mail.
kǎi 鎧甲 Armour; coat of fence.

鎬 (n.)- A stove.
gǎo (adj.)- Bright.

鎮 (n.)- A town; a market.
zhèn (v.)- Press down; reduce. Guard; keep quiet; quell; subdue.
鎮江(地) Chinkiang. Kiangsu.
鎮定 Keep presence of mind. Calm.
鎮服 Reduce to submission.
鎮靜 Quiet; compose; soothe. Tranquillity; calmness.
鎮壓 Repress; suppress; subdue; subjugate.
鎮痛劑 An anodyne; an antalgic; a balm.
鎮靜劑 A soothing medicine; a sedative.
鎮壓暴動 Put down a riot.

鎳 (n.)- (化) Nickel (Ni).
niè 鎳幣 Nickel coin.

鏈 (n.)- A chain.
liàn 鏈子 Chains; fetters.
鏈索 Chain cable.

鏑 (n.)- The sharp point of an arrow. (化) Dysprosium (Dy).
dī

**鏖** (n.)- Desperate fighting.
áo
鏖兵 Fight; slaughter.
鏖戰 A bloody battle.

**鏗** (n.)- The jingling of metals.
kēng
鏗鏘 The jingle of bells, etc.

**鏜** (n.)- The sound (toll) of a bell; other loud booming noises.
tāng

**鏞** (n.)- A large bell.
yōng

**鏟** (n.)- A spade; a shovel.
chǎn
(v.)- Shovel; smooth off; cut; pare.
鏟子 A spade-shaped instrument used as a slice in Chinese kitchens.
鏟除 Clear off.

**鏡** (n.)- A looking-glass; a mirror. A lens.
jìng
(v.)- Look in a mirror.
鏡台 A mirror-stand; a toilet-stand.
鏡頭 A camera lens.

**鏢** Same as 鑣.
biāo
(n.)- The point of a sword; a weapon.
鏢槍 Iron pointed spear.

**鏤** (n.)- Steel.
lòu
(v.)- Engrave; carve.
鏤板 Cut a block for printing.
鏤刻 Engrave; carve.

**鐐** (n.)- Shackles; fetters. Silver of the purest kind.
liào
鐐銬 Fetters for hands and feet.

**鐘** (n.)- A bell; a clock; a time-piece.
zhōng
鐘鳴 Toll; knell.
鐘樓 A belfry; a bell-tower; a bell turret. A clock tower.
鐘錶 Clocks and watches; a time-piece; a time-keeper.
鐘點 An hour; time.
鐘乳石 (鐘) Stalactite.
鐘錶店 A watchmaker's shop.
鐘鼎文 Ancient inscriptions on bronzes.

**鐫** (v.)- Engrave; carve. Degrade; cut.
juān
鐫石 Cut in stone.
鐫刻 Carve; engrave, as a printing lock.

**鐮** (n.)- A sickle; a scythe; a reaping hook.
lián
鐮刀 A sickle.

**鐲** (n.)- A small bell. Bracelets; wristlets; armlets.
zhuó
鐲子；手鐲 A bracelet.

**鐳** (n.)- A pot or jar. (化) Radium (Ra).
léi
鐳錠 Radium.
鐳錠療法 Radium treatment; radio-therapy.

**鐵** Same as 鉄，銕.
tiě
(n.)- Iron; ferrum (Fe).
(adj.)- Black; firm; brave.
鐵牛 A tractor.
鐵匠；鐵工 A blacksmith; an iron-worker.
鐵床 An iron bedstead.
鐵板 Iron plate; sheet iron.
鐵門 An iron gate.
鐵軌 Iron rails.

鐵泉(鑛) A chalybeate spring.
鐵柵 An iron railing (fence).
鐵屑 Iron filings (dust); scrap-iron.
鐵案；鐵證 Incontrovertible evidence.
鐵索；鐵鍊 Iron chains.
鐵釘 Iron nails.
鐵條 Rod iron.
鐵窗 A prison.
鐵筆 A graver; a burin. A stylus. A vigorous pen.
鐵絲；鐵線 Iron wire.
鐵路；鐵道 A railway; a railroad.
鐵管 An iron pipe (tube).
鐵廠 An iron-works.
鐵箱 An iron safe.
鐵蹄 A horseshoe.
鐵銹 Iron rust.
鐵器 Iron utensils; ironware; hardware.
鐵橋 An iron bridge.
鐵鍬 An iron shovel.
鐵鑛 An iron mine; iron ore.
鐵鑽 An iron auger.
鐵石英(鑛) Ferruginous quartz.
鐵索橋 Wire bridge.
鐵啞鈴 Iron dumb-bells.
鐵絲網 Barbed wire entanglements.
鐵路網 A network of railways; the railway system.
鐵路線 Railway line.
鐵道部 Ministry of Railways.
鐵石心腸 An iron will; a steadfast (dogged) resolution.
鐵路枕木 Sleepers of railway.
鐵路乘客 A railway passenger.
鐵路旅行 Travel by rail (by train).
鐵路運輸 Railway transport.
鐵道部長 The Minister of Railways.
鐵器時代 The iron age.
鐵甲巡洋艦 Armoured cruiser.

鐸 duó (n.)- A bell with a clapper.

鐺 dāng (n.)- Heater. Small gong struck by pedlars; the sound of a gong.
鐺鐺 The sound made by striking a gong.

鏽 xiù Same as 銹.
(n.)- Rust.
(v.)- Rust; corrode with rust.
鏽壞 Spoilt by rust; corrode.
鏽鐵 Corroded iron.

鑄 zhù (v.)- Cast metal; found.
鑄像 Cast an image.
鑄模 Cast a model.
鑄錢 Coin money.
鑄鐵 Cast iron.
鑄鐵廠 Foundry.

鑑 jiàn (v.)- Look into; be seen; reflect; examine; survey; revise.
鑑別 Distinguish; judge; discriminate.
鑑定 Expert evidence; judge; appraise; examine critically.
鑑於 In view of.
鑑察 Inspect; scrutinize; take into consideration.
鑑賞 Appreciate.
鑑定書 An expert opinion in writing. (法) Written expert testimony.
鑑賞家 A connoisseur; a virtuoso; an appreciator of art.

鑛 kuàng Same as 礦.
(n.)- A mine; the ore; a mineral.

鑪 lú Same as 爐，罏.
(n.)- A stove; a furnace; a kiln.
鑪鼎 A tripod, used in temples for burning incense.

鑰 yào (n.)- A lock. A key.
鑰孔 Keyhole.
鑰匙 A key.

鑲 xiāng (v.)- Inlay; set; insert. Put (fix) in. Clamp on; border.
鑲工 Inlaid work.
鑲牙 Artificial teeth. Insert teeth.
鑲板；格子 Panel.
鑲嵌 Inlay; put in; insert in; inset in.
鑲邊 Border. A border.

鑷 niè (n.)- Forceps; nippers; tweezers; pincers.
(v.)- Pull out; nip.
鑷子 A pair of tweezers.
鑷毛 Pull out hairs.

鑼 luó (n.)- A gong.
鑼鼓 Gong and drum.

鑽 zuān [zuàn] (n.)- A gimlet; an auger; a screw; a borer.
(v.)- Bore a hole; pierce; drill; penetrate.
鑽子 A drill.
鑽孔 Make a hole; perforate; puncture.
鑽井 To bore a well.
鑽石 A diamond.
鑽孔機 Drilling machine.

鑿 záo (n.)- A chisel; a punch.
(v.)- Chisel out; dig.
鑿山 Bore through a hill.
鑿子 A chisel.
鑿井 Well-drilling (sinking). Sink a well.
鑿石 Quarry.
鑿通 Bore a hole; open a way through; tunnel.
鑿開 Open out; cut a way into.
鑿鑿可據 Indisputable proof; thing is very certain.

# 長 部

長 zhǎng (n.)- Length. Head; chief; senior. A strong point.
(adj.)- Long, in time or distance. Distant; far. Elder.
(v.)- Increase; grow up; superior; prosper; rise; raise; excel.
(adv.)- Always; constantly; continually.
長子 The eldest son.
長大 Grow up; become a man.
長工 Regular employment; long-term labourers.
長女 The eldest daughter.
長久 A long time; permanent; everlasting; last long.
長兄 The elder brother.
長江(地) The Yangtze River.
長命 A long life; longevity. Enjoy a long life; live long; live to great age.
長夜 A long night.
長城 The Great Wall.
長春(地) Changchun.
長崎(地) Nagasaki, Japan.
長處 Advantages; good points; good qualities; strong points.
長途 A long distance (journey).
長期 A long term.
長凳 A bench.
長壽 Long-lived; a good old age.

長篇 A long piece; a voluminous work.
長輩 Seniors; those of a generation above the speaker.
長襪 Stockings; hose.
長方形 A rectangle; an oblong.
長生果(植) The groundnut or peanut.
長統靴 Jack (top) boots; high boots.
長頸鹿 Giraffe.
長臂猿 Gibbon.
長命百歲 Long-life to you.
長途賽跑 A long-distance race.
長途旅行 A long trip (journey).
長途電話 The long-distance telephone; trunk conversation.
長篇小說 A novel.
長篇大論 A long and minute statement.

# 門 部

門 (n.)- A door; a gate; an opening; a gateway. A valve. A family. A school. A department; a sect.
mén
門口 An entrance; a doorway.
門戶 The door. A family.
門牙 Front teeth; incisor.
門市 Sell retail over the counter.
門前 In front of a gate.
門牌 A doorplate; a door tablet.
門診 See patients at home or at hospital; as contrasted with visiting them in their homes.
門路 An opening; an introduction.
門鈴 A door bell.
門聯；門對 Door scrolls.
門檻 A door sill; a threshold.
門簾 Door screens.
門外漢 An outsider; a layman.

閂 (n.)- A gate-bar; a bolt.
(v.)- Bar; bolt; shut.
shuān
閂門 Bar the door.

閃 (n.)- A flash of light.
(v.)- Flash; shine; break forth, as a sudden light. Dodge; evade; avoid; shun.
shǎn
閃光 A flash (streak) of light; a gleam; a glitter.
閃閃 Flashing; gleaming; bright.
閃射 Flash; gleam.
閃耀 To twinkle.
閃電 Lightning; flash.
閃避 Elude by shifts and turns; dodge; move out of the way; avoid.
閃爍 Glitter; flashing, as metal.
閃光燈 A flash-lamp.
閃電戰 Blitzkrieg; a lightning war.
閃綠岩(礦) Diorite.
閃光攝影 Flash-light photography.

閉 (v.)- Close; shut; block up; obstruct; stop up.
bì
閉口 Shut the mouth.
閉戶；閉門 Shut (close) the door.
閉目；閉眼 Close the eyes. Die.
閉歇；倒閉 Become bankrupt; stop business.
閉會 Close a meeting. Adjournment.
閉塞 Obstruct; impede; choke; block up.
閉幕 Drop the curtain; close.
閉幕禮 The closing ceremony.
閉路電視 Closed-circuit.
閉關政策 A policy of seclusion.

開 (v.)- Open; reveal. Begin; commence; start; initiate; spread out; extend; make out; set forth; burst forth.
kāi

開刀 Kill; use knives. ( 醫 ) Operate.
開工 Begin work; set to work; commence work.
開口 Open the mouth; begin to speak.
開火 To open fire.
開支；開銷 Expense; outgo; outlay.
開水；滾水 Boiling water.
開心 Open the heart; be merry; feel happy.
開化 Civilized; enlightened; modernized.
開方(算) Evolution.
開行 Open a business. Start; set sail.
開年 Next year.
開言 Begin speaking.
開店 Set up a shop; start in business.
開花 Bloom; flower.
開門 Open a door.
開始 Begin; commence; start.
開封 Break a seal; open a letter. ( 地 ) Kaifeng.
開庭 Open (hold) a court.
開除 Deduct; dismiss; abrogate; expel from; sack; fire.
開船 Weigh anchor; set sail; cast off the moorings.
開動 Operate; start.
開國 The founding of a state.
開張 Commence business; open a shop.
開彩 Draw a lottery.
開設 Establish; open; start; found; set up.
開創 Found; originate; commence.
開發 Develop; exploit; open up. Disburse; pay–as wages.
開路 Make way; open a way; clear the track; give exit; open a door to.
開業 Open (commence) business; open a shop.
開會 Hold a meeting; open a conference.
開飯 Serve up a meal.
開演 Start a performance.
開價 Quote a price.
開學 Open (inaugurate) a school.
開燈 Light a lamp.
開導 Lead the way; be a guide; instruct.
開辦 Put in operation; begin; start.
開闊 Open; broad.
開鎖 Unlock.
開鎗 Open fire on; fire off a gun.
開顏 Smile.
開關 A switch.
開闢 Open out; extend; develop.
開平方(數) Extraction of the square root.
開立方(數) Extraction of the cube root.
開場白 Prologue.
開會詞 The opening address.
開幕禮 The opening ceremony; inauguration.
開藥方 Write a prescription.
開卷有益 Reading gives advantages.
開國紀念 National anniversary.
開路先鋒 A pioneer; the vanguard.
開闢道路 To open up a way; to pave the way.
開闊眼界 To widen one's breadth of vision.
開會歡迎 Give a reception.
開業執照 A licence.
開誠相見 Heart-to-heart meeting.
開學典禮 The school new term beginning ceremony.
開鑿隧道 Cutting of a tunnel.
開墾荒地 To open up waste land.

閏 (adj.)- Intercalary; extra; leap.
rùn
閏月 An intercalary month.
閏年 A leap year; an inter-

calary year.

閑 xián (n.)- A barrier; a bar; a fence.
(adj.)- Practised; accustomed; trained.
(v.)- Guard; close; restrain; defend; regulate by law.

閒 xián (n.)- Leisure; spare time.
(adj.)- Easy; vacant; unoccupied.
閒言；閒語 An idle talk; a chat; gossip.
閒空；閒暇 At leisure; in repose; not busy; at odd hours. Have no work to do; have time to spare.
閒事 Private affairs; unimportant matters.
閒遊 Take a stroll; stroll around; ramble idly; idle about.
閒談；閒話 A chat; an idle talk. Talk quietly; chat; have a cozy chat.
閒人莫入 No admittance except on business.

間 jiàn (n.)- A partition; an opening; a room; an apartment; a space; an interval.
(adj.)- Quiet; gentle; idle.
(prep.)- During; among; while; in the meanwhile; between; in the midst of.
(v.)- Set apart; separate; interrupt.
間日；隔日 Every other day.
間接 Indirect.
間隔 Have a space between; set apart; separate. An interval.
間隙 A crack; a crevice; an interspace. An offence; a grudge; an estrangement.
間諜 A spy; a secret agent.
間斷 Break off; intermit; interrupt; discontinue.

閔 mǐn (v.)- Pity; commiserate; mourn.

閘 zhá Same as 牐.
(n.)- A water gate; a lock in a canal; a sluice; a flood gate; a barrier; a dam.
閘口 Entrance to a lock.
閘門；閘板 A lock gate.

閣 gé (n.)- A hall; a cabinet; a pavilion; a shelf; council chamber.
閣下 You, Sir; your excellency.
閣員 A cabinet minister.
閣樓 Garret; mezzanine.
閣議 A cabinet (ministerial) meeting.

閥 fá (n.)- Merits of an official posted on the left-side door; lineage; clique.

閨 guī (n.)- A woman's apartment; a woman's room; a small door.
閨女 A damsel; a maiden; a girl; a virgin; a young unmarried lady.
閨秀 A lady writer; an authoress; a literary woman; graceful girls.
閨房；閨閣 A lady's apartment; a boudoir.

閩 mǐn (n.)- A name for Fukien (福建).
閩浙 Fukien and Chekiang.
閩粵 Fukien and Kwangtung.

閭 lǘ (n.)- A village of twenty-five families. The gate of a village; habitation.
閭里 A village; the country.

閭巷 A lane or alley.

閱 (v.)- Look at; inspect; read carefully; examine; review; go
yuè over; see; glance over.
閱兵 An inspection of troops; a review.
閱卷 Examine an essay. Mark examination.
閱報 Read newspapers.
閱覽 Read; review.
閱讀 Read; peruse.
閱覽室 A reading-room.

閹 (n.)- A eunuch.
(v.)- Castrate.
yān 閹雞 A capon; a castrated cock.

閻 (n.)- The gate to a village.
閻王；閻羅 *Yama*; the Chinese
yán Pluto; the King of Hades.

闊 Same as 濶.
(adj.)- Broad; wide. Rich; well-
kuò off. Liberal. Distant.
闊步 Take big strides; walk long steps.
闊胸 Broad breast.
闊狹 Wide and narrow.
闊別已久 Have long been separated.

闋 (n.)- A tune.
què

闌 (n.)- A door screen. A wristlet. A rail. Evening.
lán (v.)- Shut in or off; separate.
闌尾炎(醫) Appendicitis.

闔 (n.)- A leaf of a door.
(adj.)- All; whole; entire.
hé (v.)- Shut; close.

闔閭 Dwelling.
闔第光臨 Presence of your whole family is expected.

闖 (v.)- Intrude into; rush in suddenly; enter abruptly.
chuǎng (adv.)- Suddenly. Forcibly; rudely.
闖入；闖進 Burst in; trespass on; intrude into.
闖禍 Rush into calamity; make trouble.

關 Same as 関.
(n.)- A frontier gate; a custom-
guān house; a bar; a pass; a gate; a crisis; a turning point.
(v.)- Shut; fasten; cover; close; stop passage; involve; concern; connect; bear upon.
關口 A custom-house. A boundary pass; the guard-station at a barrier.
關心 Be interested in; give attention to; be concerned; be affected.
關於 Regarding; respecting; concerning; with regard to; in respect to; with reference to; with relation to.
關門 Shut the door. A barrier-gate.
關係 Connection; relation. Have relation to; be connected with.
關島(地) Guam.
關員 Custom-house officers.
關閉 Close; shut.
關連 In connection with... ; in relation to... .
關窗 Shut (close) the window.
關稅 Customs duty.
關鍵 A key. An important thing.
關懷 Be affected by; concerned with.
關節炎 Arthritis.
關心照料 Look after carefully.
關係密切 Intimate relationships.
關節風濕病 Articular rheumatism.

闡 (v.)- Open; express; disclose; enlighten.
chǎn 闡明 Clear up; explain.

闢 (v.)- Split open; burst forth; develop.
pì 闢謠 Dispute a rumour.

# 阜 部

阜 (n.)- A mound; a small hill.
(v.)- Make rich.
fù 阜財 Very wealthy.

阡 (n.)- A road leading north and south; a grave path; a
qiān foot path through the field.
阡陌 A footpath between fields.
阡陌縱橫 Numerous foot-paths in the field.

阬 (n.)- A pit. A mound.
(v.)- Entrap; put into a pit.
kēng 阬害 Injure; harass.
阬儒 Bury the scholars alive in a pit.

阱 Same as 穽.
(n.)- A pitfall; a catching pit; a
jǐng hole.

防 (n.)- Dyke; defence; protection; prevention.
fáng (v.)- Defend; guard against; protect from; ward off; keep away.
防火 Fire-proof; fire-resisting.
防水 Waterproof; watertight.
防止 Prevent; guard (take precautions) against; prohibit; check; hold (keep) in check.
防守 Guard; protect; defend.
防空 Air (aerial) defence.
防風 Protection against wind. (植) *Siler divaricatum.*
防患 Guard against calamities.
防備 Prepare for; be ready for.
防盜 Guard against robbers.
防線 A line of defence.
防範 Take precautions; guard against.
防禦 Defend; safe guard; fight in defence; take up arms for.
防濕 Damp-proof.
防癆 Anti-tuberculosis.
防水布 Water-proof cloth.
防水紙 Water-proof paper.
防火布 Fire-proof cloth.
防空洞 An air-raid shelter; a bomb-shelter.
防風林 A shelter-belt (- wood); a windbreak.
防疫所 Quarantine office.
防傳染 Prevent infection.
防腐劑 An antiseptic; a preservative.
防火設備 Fire-service arrangements; a safe-guard against fire.
防空演習 Anti-air-raid manoeuvres; an air-defence drill (training).
防禦工事 Defensive works; fortifications.

阻 (n.)- A dangerous pass.
(v.)- Hinder; prevent; put down;
zǔ impede; check; retard; stop; oppose; delay; suspect; obstruct.
阻力 Resistance.
阻路 Bar the way.

阻止；阻擋 Hinder; obstruct; check; hold back; stop; impede; hamper; retard.
阻塞 Stop up; obstruct; block up.
阻礙；阻害 Check; obstruct; impede; hamper; retard.
阻止進步 Arrest progress.

阿 ā (adj.)- Prejudiced; leaning against.
(v.)- Flatter; assent; incline to; lean against; show partiality.
阿婆 A term of respect for an old woman. Husband's mother.
阿諛 Flatter; truckle to; fawn upon.
阿芙蓉 Opium.
阿刺伯(地) Arabia.
阿根廷(地) Argentina.
阿富汗(地) Afghanistan.
阿司匹靈(退熱藥) Aspirin.
阿拉斯加(地) Alaska.
阿非利加(地) Africa.
阿刺伯人 An Arabian; an Arab.
阿刺伯文 Arabic; Arabian.
阿爾及爾(地) Algiers.
阿爾泰山 The Altai Mountains.
阿摩尼亞(化) Ammonia.
阿彌陀佛 Amitabha Buddha.
阿比西尼亞(地) Abyssinia.
阿爾巴尼亞(地) Albania.
阿爾卑斯山 The Alps.

陀 tuó (n.)- A steep bank.
陀螺 A top.

陂 pō (n.)- A pool. A march. Hillside; slope; declivity.
陂池；陂塘 A small pond.

附 fù (n.)- A supplement; an appendix; an inclosure.
(v.)- Subjoin; be near to; side with; append; annex; attach; follow; inclose; increase; add; join.
附加 Add; supplement; append.
附件 An enclosure.
附言 Additional remarks. Add a remark.
附近 Near to; neighbouring; close by; adjacent.
附記；附註 Remarks. Append; write on addition.
附錄 An appendix; a supplement.
附屬 Dependent; tributary; accessory. Belong to; be attached to.
附加稅 An additional tax; a supplementary tax; a surtax.
附屬品 Accessories; fittings; furnishings.
附屬小學 An attached elementary school.
附屬中學 An attached middle school.

陋 lòu (n.)- A rustic residence; a vile place.
(adj.)- Low; vulgar; rustic; rude; mean; sordid.
陋劣 Vile; base; mean; despicable.
陋巷 A narrow dirty alley; humble quarters; slums.
陋規 Bribes; illegalities in taking fees.
陋習 A corrupt custom; crusted habits.
陋賤 Low and poor.

陌 mò (n.)- A foot path between fields; a market street.
陌生 Strange.
陌路人 A stranger.

降 jiàng (v.)- Fall; come down; drop. Descend; go down; reduce in rank; degrade. Surrender; yield; submit.
降下 Fall; come down; descend; drop.

降低 Fall; abase; descend.
降雨 Rainfall. It rains.
降級 Degradation.
降雪 Snowfall.
降落 Descend; fall from; alight.
降旗 A flag of surrender; a white flag.
降禍；降災 Send down calamity.
降臨 Advent; condescend; visit; coming down.
降雨量 The amount of rainfall.
降落傘 A parachute.

**限** xiàn (n.)- A limit; a restriction; a boundary. A threshold.
(v.)- Limit; restrict; restrain; confine; set bounds to; fix the limits of.
限定 Fix a limit to; restrict; set out; determine.
限制 Set bounds; restrict; confine; qualify.
限界 A limit; a bound.
限度 A limit; limitation; restriction.
限期 A limit of time; a fixed time; a set period.
限量 A measure; an estimate.
限價 Price-limit.
限額 Limited amount.

**陛** bì (n.)- The throne; the emperor.
陛下 Your Majesty; the emperor.

**陝** shǎn (n.)- A mountain pass. The province of Shensi ( 陝西 ).

**陞** shēng Same as 升.
(v.)- Ascend; go up; mount.
陞官 Be promoted (advanced) to.
陞降 Promotion and degradation.
陞遷 Advance in seat.

**陡** dǒu (adj.)- Steep; high; slope of a hill.
(adv.)- Suddenly; unexpectedly.
陡峭 Precipitous.
陡然 All at once; suddenly.

**院** yuàn (n.)- A courtyard; a walled inclosure. A hall; a college; a public building; a hospital; a museum. An office.
院長 The dean of a college. The director of a hospital.

**陣** zhèn (n.)- An army. A battle. A moment; a little while.
陣亡 Die in battle; fall fighting.
陣地 Battle field; a position.
陣雨 Shower; rainfall.
陣線 Line of battle.
陣營 A camp; an encampment.

**除** chú (v.)- Deduct; divide. Appoint. Remove; get rid of; take away; cast off; do away with; wipe out; debar; shut out.
(prep.)- Besides; except.
除夕 The New Year's eve.
除去 Clear off; blot out; obliterate. Deduct; take away.
除外 Exception; exclusion. Except from; exclude from.
除邪 Remove noxious influences; exorcise.
除非 With the exception of; unless; only if.
除法(算) Division.
除根 Eradicate; root out; do away with entirely.
除害 Get rid of danger. Do away with an evil; remove evil.
除草 Mow (cut) grass; weed.

除號(算) The sign of division (÷).
除數(算) A divisor.
除四害 To wipe out the four pests.
除此以外 Besides this; with the exception of.
除舊布新 Change old things for the new.

陪 (adj.)- Secondary; subordinate.
(v.)- Attend; follow; accompany; assit; help; subordinate; match; add; repay; compensate.
péi
陪伴 A companion; a company; associate with.
陪送 Escort; see a guest out.
陪審員 A juryman; a juror. A jury (總稱).

陰 (n.)- Shadow. Shade. The privates; the genitals.
yīn (adj.)- Shady; cloudy; gloomy; dark; somber; obscure; dim. Cold. Mysterious; secret.
陰天 A dark or cloudy day; gloomy weather.
陰性 Female. Gloomy disposition. (電) Negative.
陰涼 Cool; shady.
陰乾 Dry in the shade.
陰溝 A covered drain.
陰暗 Gloomy; obscure.
陰電 Negative (minus) electricity.
陰影 A shadow; a shade.
陰謀 Conspire; intrigue; plan secretly. A secret plot; a close design; a conspiracy.
陰險 Crafty; subtle; cunning; wily; treacherous.
陰曆 The lunar calender.
陰極線 The cathode-ray.
陰謀家 A plotter; an intriguer; a conspirator.
陰謀詭計 Crafty schemes.

陳 (n.)- A surname.
(adj.)- Old.
chén (v.)- Arrange; exhibit; spread out.
陳久 Old; for a long time.
陳皮 Dried orange peel.
陳列 Arrange; show; exhibit; display; place in a row; demonstrate; lay before; be on view.
陳述 Give details; explain; state; give an account of.
陳貨；殘貨 Old stock.
陳舊 Antiquated; old-fashioned; stale.
陳列所 A showroom; an exhibition; a museum.
陳列品 An exhibited article; an article on view; an exhibit; the things on display.
陳列窗 A show-window.
陳腔濫調 Platitude.

陵 (n.)- A high mound; a hill. A tomb; a grave.
líng (v.)- Desecrate; insult; usurp; outrage; abuse. Ascend; climb; aim high.
陵弱 Insult the weak.
陵墓 Tomb; grave.

陶 (n.)- Earthenware; pottery.
(adj.)- Happy; cheerful; joyful.
táo 陶然 Happy; joyful; cheerful.
陶醉 Be intoxicated; be carried away; be in delirium.
陶器 Earthenware; pottery; chinaware; crockery.
陶鑄；陶鎔 Fuse; melt. Educate; cultivate.

陷 (adj.)- Overwhelmed; ruined.
(v.)- Fall; sink; subside; drop
xiàn into; entrap; beguile; capture; collapse.

陷入 Sink into.
陷阱；陷坑 A pitfall; a trap; a snare.
陷害 Get another into trouble.
陷落 Fall in; sink. Surrender; fall; capitulate.
陷於困難 Get into trouble (difficulties).

陸 lù (n.)- A surname. Land; continent. The shore.
(adj.)- Six.
陸地 Land.
陸軍 Land forces (troops); the army.
陸運 Transportation by land.
陸續 One after another; in succession; successively.
陸軍部 The Ministry of War.
陸戰隊 A landing party; a naval brigade; marines.
陸上貿易 Overland trade.
陸地動物 A land animal.
陸海空軍 A land, air and sea force.

陽 yáng (n.)- The positive side. The sun. The south of a hill.
(adj.)- Male; masculine. Sunny; light; bright; brilliant.
陽台 Balcony; veranda. Lovers' rendezvous.
陽光 Sunlight.
陽性 Masculine gender.
陽電 Positive electricity.
陽溝 An open drain.
陽曆 The solar calendar.

隄 dī Same as 堤 .
(n.)- A dike; a bank; an embankment.

隅 yú (n.)- A corner; a nook; an angle; a recess.
隅石；基石 A corner-stone.
隅坐 Sit at a corner.

隋 suí (n.)- The Sui dynasty (589–618 A.D.).

隆 lóng (adj.)- High; lofty; ample; generous; eminent; glorious; abundant; fertile; prosperous.
隆厚 Substantial; wealthy; generous.
隆恩 Great kindness; unusual mercy.
隆重 Honour; very beneficient.
隆起 Upheave; rise; bulge; protrude.
隆盛 Properous; flourishing; booming.
隆情；盛情 Great kindness; great favours.
隆重接待 Grand reception.
隆重開幕 To open ceremoniously.

隊 duì (n.)- A party; a company; a corps; a team; a squad; a band.
隊伍 The ranks.
隊形 A formation; the disposition of troops.
隊長 A commander; a captain.
隊商 A caravan.
隊球；排球 Volley ball.
隊伍整齊 In regular ranks; in perfect order.

階 jiē (n.)- A step; stairs. A rank; a grade; a degree.
階石 The stone steps; stepping stones.
階次；等級 Grade; rank; order; class.
階段 A grade; a stage. Steps; a staircase; a flight of steps.
階梯 Stairs; steps. A ladder.
階級性 Class nature.
階級利益 Class interest.
階級感情 Class feeling.
階級鬥爭 Class struggle.
階級社會 Class society.

隔 (n.)- A partition; separation; a division.
gé (adj.)- Separated; apart.
(v.)- Divide; obstruct; part; separate.
隔岸 On opposite bank; separated by a river.
隔夜 Overnight; last night.
隔開 Separate; set apart.
隔絕 Be far (away) from each other; be wide apart; be separated.
隔膜(解) A diaphragm.
隔壁 A partition. Next-door neighbours.
隔離 Separate; isolate; quarantine.
隔音裝置 A silencer; an anti-noise device.
隔牆有耳 Walls have ears.
隔離病人 An isolated patient.
隔離病房 An isolated ward.

隕 (n.)- Area.
(v.)- Roll down; fall from or
yǔn into; drop.
隕石 A meteorite.
隕星 A meteor.
隕落；隕墜 Fall to the ground; drop down.
隕於深淵 Fall into the abyss.

隘 (n.)- A pass; a narrow path; a defile.
ài (adj.)- Narrow; close; contracted; straitend; distressed; hampered; confined; obstructed. Narrow-minded.
隘口 The entrance to a pass.
隘害 A strategic point.

隙 (n.)- A fissure; a chink; a crack. An interval. A pretext.
xì 隙穴 A crevice; a chink; an opening.

際 (n.)- A border; a limit; the side. Intercourse. Line of junc-
jì tion.
(adv.)- Now; then.
(prep.)- In the midst; between; in course of; during; at.
際會 Meet by chance.
際遇 Meet with.

障 (n.)- A barricade; an embankment; a dike. A veil. A defence;
zhàng an intrenchment; an obstacle.
(v.)- Separate; shut up inside; protect; screen.
障害 Hinder; impede; be in the way; constitute an obstacle.
障礙 Hinder; prevent; obstacle; barrier.
障礙物 Hindrance; an impediment; an obstacle.

隧 (n.)- A tunnel; a subway.
隧道 A tunnel; a subway.
suì 隧道門 Portal of a tunnel.

隨 (v.)- Follow; comply with; accompany; wait on; come
suí after; accord with; obey. Let; allow.
隨手 Immediately; freely; without hesitation; ready at hand.
隨行 Accompany; follow.
隨同 Accompany; attend on.
隨地；隨處 Everywhere; in every place; here and there.
隨即 Immediately; forthwith; at once.
隨你 As you please.
隨便 At your convenience; at pleasure; at will; anyhow and everyhow.
隨後 Afterwards; in due course.
隨時 Anytime; at once; at one's convenience; at times.
隨從；隨員 Attendants; a suite.
隨筆 Stray notes; miscellaneous

writings; a miscellany.
隨意肌 A voluntary muscle.
隨軍記者 A war correspondent.
隨機應變 Adapt oneself to circumstances.

險 xiǎn (n.)- A defile; a narrow pass; an obstruction. Risk; danger; obstacle.
(adj.)- Dangerous; difficult of access; perilous; hazardous; steep; precipitous; malicious; evil.
險口；險隘 A dangerous pass.
險要 Perilous; dangerous; a strategic post.
險處 A dangerous place.
險詐；險猾 Treacherous.
險惡 Dangerous; perilous; threatening; inclement; serious; grave.

隱 yǐn (adj.)- Retired; tranquil in private life. Dark; obscure; hidden; secret; mysterious.
(v.)- Retire; conceal; keep secret; hide; withdraw; keep back.
隱士 A retired scholar; a hermit; a recluse.
隱名 Conceal one's identity.
隱伏 Lie concealed.
隱約 Indistinct; obscure; ambiguous.
隱蔽 Conceal; hide; keep dark.
隱藏 To hide.
隱瞞 Deceive; conceal from.
隱形眼鏡 Contact lens.
隱顯墨水 Sympathetic ink.

隴 lǒng (n.)- Grave; bank; dike; mound.
隴畝 Dikes and fields.

# 隶 部

隸 lì Same as 隷.
(n.)- Servants; retainers; slave; subordinates; underlings.
(prep.)- Under.
隸人 Criminals; convicts.
隸卒；皁隸 Lictors; official servants.
隸書 The square plain style of Chinese characters.
隸屬 Be under the jurisdiction (control) of; be subordinated to.

# 隹 部

隻 zhī (adj.)- One; single.
隻手 One hand; a single hand.
隻字 Single character.
隻身 Alone.
隻眼 An eye.
隻手不能遮天 A single hand cannot cover the sky.

雀 què (n.)- Birds; the sparrow.
雀麥(植) Oats.
雀鳥 Small birds.
雀巢 A bird's nest.
雀斑 Freckles.
雀噪 A sparrow chirps.
雀躍 Dance (leap) for joy.

**雁** (n.)- A wild goose.
yàn
雁行 Keep pace (abreast) with; go side by side.
雁帛 A letter.
雁影分飛 Separation of brothers.

**雄** (n.)- A male. A hero; a chief.
xióng
(adj.)- Masculine; male. Martial; heroic; brave; valiant.
雄牛 An ox; a bull.
雄壯 Burly; strong; brave; courageous.
雄性 Masculine gender.
雄姿 A brave (gallant) figure.
雄健 Virile; vigorous; stalwart.
雄偉；雄大 Grand; imposing; magnificent.
雄雞 A cock.
雄辯 Eloquence; declamation.
雄姿颯爽 In gallant trim.
雄霸一方 Seize a region by force.

**雅** (n.)- The crow.
yǎ
(adj.)- Elegant; polished; refined; graceful; nice; neat.
雅人 A man of refined taste.
雅片 Opium.
雅言 An elegant word; refined diction; classical language.
雅典(地) Athens.
雅致 Elegant; tasteful; graceful.
雅儀 Courteous manners; graceful manner.
雅利安人 Aryans.

**集** (n.)- A fair; a market. A gathering; a meeting. Literary works; miscellany; collection of essays and poems.
jí
(v.)- Assemble; collect; mix; blend; bring together; flock together; gather. Complete; accumulate.
集中 Concentrate; centralize; centre.
集合 Assemble; meet; crowd; gather; throng; collect together.
集捐 Obtain from contribution.
集款 Prepare funds; collect money.
集郵 Philately; stamp-collecting.
集會 Gather; hold a meeting; assemble. A meeting; a gathering.
集體 A body; a mass.
集中營 Concentration camp.
集郵家 A stamp-collector; a philatelist.
集中反映 To embody a concentrated reflection of.
集合名詞 A collective noun.
集會自由 Free assembly.
集體主義 Collectivism.
集體經濟 Collective economy.
集體勞動 Group work.
集體農場 A collective farm; a Kolkhoz.
集體領導 Collective leadership.

**雇** Same as 僱
gù
(v.)- Hire; employ; engage.
雇主 An employer; a hirer; a master.
雇員 An employee.
雇農 Employed peasantry.
雇傭兵 A hired soldier; a mercenary.
雇用期間 The term of employment.

**雌** (n.)- A female.
cí
(adj.)- Female. Weak; womanlike.
雌雄 Male and female; victory or defeat.
雌蕊 A pistil.
雌老虎 A tigress–a virago.
雌雄同體(動) Hermaphrodite.

**雍** (n.)- Harmony; union; concord.
yōng
(adj.)- Harmonious; concordant; congruous.
(v.)- Be harmonious.
雍和 Peace and harmony; at peace.
雍容 Peaceful and mild.

**雕** (n.)- A kite; an eagle.
(v.)- Carve; engrave; cut.
diāo 雕花 Carve figures or pictures.
雕刻 Engrave; cut out; carve; sculpture.
雕琢 Cut and polish gems.
雕像 A carved statue; a sculpture. Carve an idol.
雕刻圖章 Carve a seal.

**雖** (adv.)- Although; even if.
(conj.)- Although; if; supposing.
suī 雖然 Nevertheless; notwithstanding; although; for all that; after all; though.
雖然如此 Be that as it may.

**雙** Same as 双.
(n.)- A pair; a couple; a brace.
shuāng (adj.)- Two; both; double; even.
雙手 Both hands.
雙方 Both parties; both sides.
雙倍 Double; twofold; twotimes; twice.
雙層 Twofolds. Double-decker.
雙親 Both parents.
雙雙 In pairs; both.
雙生子 Twins.
雙掛號 Registered letter with return receipt.
雙關語 Ambiguous words. A pun; a phrase with a double meaning.
雙方同意 Mutual consent.
雙方滿意 Mutual satisfaction.
雙目失明 Blind in both eyes.
雙邊協定 A bilateral contract.
雙翼飛機 A biplane.
雙眼望遠鏡 A binocular telescope.
雙層公共汽車 A double-decked bus.

**雛** (n.)- A chicken; a young bird; a child.
chú 雛鳥 Young birds.
雛鴨；黃鴨 Duckling.
雛雞 A little chick.

**雜** (n.)- A mixture.
(adj.)- Various; mixed; mingled;
zá miscellaneous; sundry; promiscuous; confused; blended; variegated. Coarse; roughly made.
雜文 A miscellany.
雜色 Variegated; parti-coloured; motley.
雜技；雜耍 Various kinds of amusements; acrobatics.
雜役 An odd-job man.
雜念 Worldly thoughts.
雜物 Motley things; miscellaneous articles.
雜音 Noises.
雜草 Weeds.
雜碎 Chop-suey.
雜貨 Miscellaneous (sundry) goods.
雜費 Sundry expenses; miscellaneous (petty) expenses.
雜亂 Confused; disordered; out of order.
雜種 A mixed breed; a hybrid; an illegitimate child.
雜誌 A journal; a magazine.
雜談 Chat; gossip; have an idle talk.
雜題 Miscellaneous problems.
雜糧 Various cereals.
雜記簿 A note-book; a memorandum-book.
雜貨舖 A general store (shop); a grocer's shop; a grocery.
雜文作家 A miscellaneous writer; a miscellanist.
雜亂無章 All in confusion.
雜誌廣告 Magazine or periodical advertising.

**雞** (n.)- Domestic fowl; a cock; a hen; a chicken.
jī 雞子；雞蛋；雞卵 An egg; a

hen's egg.
雞肉 Chicken; meat of fowl.
雞眼 Corns.
雞痘；水痘(醫) Chicken-pox.
雞鳴；雞啼 Cock-crow. A cock crows.
雞毛箒 A feather-brush (-duster).
雞冠花 Cockscomb flowers.
雞蛋糕 Sponge cakes.
雞鳴報曉 The crowing cocks harbinger the dawn.

離 (v.)- Separate; part; leave; depart; retire. Fall into.
lí 離任 Leave one's post.
離別 Separation; parting. Bid farewell or adieu; part from; take leave of; say good-bye to.
離奇 Wonderful; quaint; thrilling, as a story.
離座 Leave one's seat.
離席 Leave the table.
離家 Leave home.
離婚 Divorce.
離開 Separate; leave; put apart; remain at a distance; refrain from.
離職-Give up one's post; off duty.
離籍 Excluded from the family register.
離合器 The clutch.
離心力(物) Centrifugal force.
離魂病 Somnambulism.
離別多年 Have separated for many years.
離鄉背井 To leave one's native place.
離經叛道 Wayward and rebellious.

難 Same as 难.
nán (n.)- Difficulty; trouble; distress; calamity; hardship; affliction.
(adj.)- Difficult; hard; not easy.
難民 People in distress; sufferers; refugees.
難免 Difficult to avoid; cannot be helped; unavoidable; cannot but.
難治；難醫 Hard to cure; almost incurable; beyond medical skill; fatal.
難事 A difficult matter; an awkward business.
難受 Not easy to bear or endure.
難怪 No wonder.
難看 Awkward; odd-looking; ugly.
難信 Hard to believe.
難症 A difficult case; a serious disease.
難產(醫) Difficult (hard) labour; a difficult delivery (birth).
難過 Sad; in trouble.
難題 A difficult (hard) problem; a hard nut to crack; the Gordian knot.
難聽 Unpleasant to hear; discordant.
難以形容 Indescribable.
難以說明 It is difficult to explain.
難題解決 Solve a hard problem.

# 雨 部

雨 (n.)- Rain; a shower.
yǔ (adj.)- Rainy.
(v.)- Rain; fall.
雨天 A rainy day.
雨水 Rain-water.
雨衣 A rain coat; a waterproof.
雨季 The rainy (wet) season.
雨蛙 A tree-frog.
雨傘 An umbrella.
雨量 The rainfall.
雨點 A rain drop.
雨天操場 A covered drill-ground; an

exercise room; a gymnasium.
雨後春筍 Spring up like mushrooms.

雪 (n.)- Snow.
(adj.)- Snowy.
xuě (v.)- Snow. Avenge; clean; wipe away; wash; make clean.
雪白 Snow-white; snowy.
雪花 Snow crystals; snow flakes.
雪茄 Cigars.
雪崩 An avalanche; a snowslide; a snowslip.
雪球 Snowball.
雪帽 Snowcap.
雪梨(植) Tientsin pears.
雪景 Snow scenery; a snow-covered land-scape.
雪花膏 Cold cream.
雪蘭莪(地) Selangor, Malaya.
雪中送炭 Send fuel in cold weather-timely assistance.

雲 (n.)- Cloud.
(adj.)- Cloudy.
yún 雲石 Marble from Yunnan.
雲母(礦) Mica.
雲南(地) Yunnan.
雲彩 Clouds of beautiful colours; red-tinged clouds.
雲集 Crowd; swarm; throng; gather in crowds.
雲腿 Hams from Yunnan.
雲漢；銀河 The Milky Way.

零 (n.)- Small rain; drizzle. Naught; zero. A fraction; a remainder.
líng (adj.)- Fractional; broken-up.
零丁 Lonely; solitary.
零件 Parts; accessory.
零度 Zero; the zero point.
零時 Twelve O'clock.
零落 Be stripped of leaves; scattered; fall low.
零賣；零售 Sell in small quantities; retail.
零錢 A petty sum of money.
零用錢 Pocket money.
零售者 Retailer; retail dealer.
零度以下 Below zero. Fall down below zero.
零售市場 Retail market.
零售價目 Retail price.

雷 (n.)- Thunder.
(adj.)- Thundering.
léi 雷公；雷神 The god of thunder; the Thunderer.
雷雨 A thunder-shower (-storm).
雷達 Radar.
雷電 Thunder and lightning; a thunderbolt.
雷管 A percussion-cap; a detonator.
雷鳴 The thunder rolls (rumbles, growls).
雷錠 Radium.
雷達網 Radar screen.

雹 (n.)- Hail; hailstones.
báo

電 (n.)- Lightning; electricity.
(adj.)- Electric
diàn 電力 Electric power.
電子 An electron.
電化 Electrification; electrization.
電文 Text of a telegram (cable).
電示；電令 Telegraphic instructions.
電光 A flash of lightning; electric light.
電池；電槽 An electric battery (cell).
電灶 An electric stove (heater).
電車 An electric car; a tramcar; a street car.
電表 Electrometer.
電波 An electric wave.

電流 An electric current.
電扇 An electric fan.
電梯 Lift; elevator.
電荷 An electric charge.
電場 An electric field.
電視 Television.
電椅 An electric chair.
電筒 An electric torch.
電路 Electric circuit.
電賀 Congratulations sent by telegram.
電滙 A telegraphic; transfer (T.T.); a cable order (transfer).
電源 A source of electricity.
電解 Electrolysis.
電報 A telegram; a telegraphic dispatch (message); a wire; a wireless.
電腦；電子計算機 Electronic brain; electronic calculator.
電話 A telephone; a phone.
電鈴 An electric bell.
電影 A moving picture; a film; a motion-picture.
電線 A telegraphic wire; an electric line.
電壓 Electric pressure; voltage.
電燈 An electric light (lamp).
電療 Electropathy; electric treatment.
電鍍 Electroplating.
電爐 An electric furnace.
電纜 A telegraph cable.
電子能 Electronic energy.
電單車 A motorcycle; a motorbike.
電車站 A car-stop; a tram-stop.
電車路 A tramway; an electric-car track.
電動機 An electric motor; a motor.
電風扇 An electric fan.
電唱機 An electric phonograph; an electrophone.
電報局 A telegraph office.
電話局 A telephone office.
電話室 A telephone room; a telephone booth.
電話費 Telephone charges.
電話機 A telephone.
電話簿 A telephone directory.
電解物 An electrolyte.
電磁石 An electromagnet.
電磁學 Electromagnetism.
電影院 A cinema (movie) hall (theatre); a cinema palace.
電燈泡 An electric bulb.
電飯煲 An automatic rice cooker.
電版印刷 An electrotype.
電氣工業 Electrical industry; electro-industry.
電氣冰箱 An electric refrigerator.
電氣熨斗 An electric iron.
電氣鐵路 An electric railway.
電話號碼 A telephone (call) number.
電影公司 A film-producing company.
電影明星 A film (movie) star; a screen-star.
電話接線生 A telephone operator; a "Hello" girl; a phone-girl.
電影製片場 A cinema studio.

需 xū (n.)- Necessity; need; requirement.
(v.)- Need; want; have occasion; expect; wish for; desire; require. Hesitate.
需求 In demand.
需要 Need; necessity; demand; want.
需用經費 Necessary expenses.

霆 tíng (n.)- Thunder; the noise of thunder.

震 zhèn (n.)- Terror; fear; trembling; shaking.
(v.)- Shake; quake; tremble; quiver; vibrate; shock; agitate; terrify. Astound; move.
震耳 Ring in the ear; thunder in the ear.

震動 Vibrate; shake; quake.
震撼 Strike with awe; shake.
震駭 Stun with amazement; astound; terrify.
震盪 Shake; give a shock.
震驚 Startle; alarm; strike with alarm; terrify.
震天動地 Amaze (electrify) the whole world.
震耳欲聾的 Deafening.

霉 méi
Same as 黴.
(n.)- Mildew; mould; rotten.
(adj.)- Mouldy; damp.
(v.)- Become (grow) mouldy; be mildewed.
霉天 The damp weather; the rainy season.
霉氣 Musty; fusty; stale.
霉爛 Mouldy and rotten.

霍 huò
(n.)- Speed; celerity.
(adv.)- Suddenly; quickly.
霍然 Suddenly; quickly.
霍亂 Cholera.
霍爾蒙 Hormone, as male or female sex hormone.

霎 shà
(n.)- Slight shower; passing rain. An instant.
霎時 Suddenly; in a moment; a little while; at a bow.
霎眼 Wink.
霎然間 In a moment; suddenly.

霓 ní
Same as 蜺.
(n.)- Coloured clouds; a rainbow.
霓虹燈 A neon sign (lamp).

霑 zhān
(v.)- Become wet; soak; drench.
霑濕 Wet through; soaked.

霖 lín
(n.)- A continuous rain of three days or more.
霖雨 A long spell of rain; a long-continued rain.

霜 shuāng
(n.)- Frost; hoar-frost.
霜季 Frosty weather.
霜晨 A frosty morning.

霞 xiá
(n.)- Rosy clouds.
霞光 Rosy rays of light.

霧 wù
(n.)- Fog; mist.
(adj.)- Foggy.
霧季 Season of fog.
霧氣；雲霧 Mist; fog.

露 lù
(n.)- Dew.
(v.)- Disclose; expose; exhibit; manifest; show through.
露水 Dew.
露天 Open to the sky; expose to the air; in the open air.
露出 Disclose; let out; expose; bare; come out; open up.
露台 A balcony.
露形 Expose one's form; show the real form.
露營 Camping; bivouac; camp out; encamp for the night.
露點 Dew point.
露天礦 An open mine; surface digging.
露馬脚 Show the cloven hoof (foot); reveal one's evil character.

霸 bà
Same as 覇.
(n.)- A leader; a conqueror; an oppressor; a fedual chief; a tyrant.
(v.)- Rule by force; dominate over.
霸王 One who rules by force; a conqueror.

霸業 Achievement of a conqueror.
霸佔 Encroach upon; usurp; annex; occupy by force and arms.
霸道 The rule of might.
霸權 Supremacy; hegemony.

**霹** (n.)- The crash of thunder; a thunderclap.
pī 霹靂 A sudden peal of thunder.
(地) Perak, Malaya.
霹靂一聲 A clap of thunder.

**靂** (n.)- A thunder-clap.
lì

**靄** (n.)- Cloudy sky.
ǎi

**靈** Same as 灵.
(n.)- The spirit; the soul.
líng 靈丹 Efficacious pills.
靈巧 Ingenious; skilful. Handy.
靈活 Bright and lively; active and intelligent.
靈敏 Intelligent; keen; acute; quick; smart; bright.
靈感 Inspiration.
靈魂 The soul; the spirit.
靈藥 A miraculous medicine; a panacea.

# 青 部

**青** (adj.)- Dark green; blue.
青玉(礦) Sapphire.
qīng 青年 A youth; a young man; the spring time of life.
青竹 A green bamboo.
青豆 Green peas.
青盲 Green-blindness.
青果；橄欖 The Chinese olive.
青春 Youth; the prime (springtime) of life; the bloom of youth; juvenility.
青苔 Green moss (lichen).
青島(地) Tsingtao.
青草 Green grass.
青海 A blue sea. (地) Chinghai.
青蛙 A green-frog; a tree-frog.
青菜 Vegetables; greens; green stuff.
青銅 Bronze.
青年會 Young Men's Christian Association (Y.M.C.A.).
青黴素 Penicillin.
青年時代 Young days (years); youth.
青銅器時代 The bronze age.

**靖** (n.)- Peace; tranquillity.
(adj.)- Quiet; tranquil; peaceful;
jìng calm.

**靚** (adj.)- Beautiful; particularly said of the painted face of a
liàng woman.
(v.)-Ornament; powder the face.
靚衣 Fine clothes; gay dress.
靚妝 Powder the face.

**靛** (n.)- Indigo.
靛青；藍靛 Indigo.
diàn

**靜** (n.)- Peacefulness; silence; stillness; quietness.
jìng (adj.)- Quiet; motionless; noiseless; calm; still; tranquil; silent; peaceful; solitude. Pure.

(v.)- Think carefully on. Judge or examine.
(adv.)- Quietly; silently.
靜止 Rest; repose; stillness.
靜坐 Sit quietly.
靜夜 Stilly night.
靜思 Meditation; think quietly.
靜脈 Veins.
靜電 Static electricity.
靜養 Rest; recuperation; a rest cure. Keep quiet and take care of oneself; take a good rest; quiet nourishment.
靜默 Silence; hold one's peace; stillness.
靜物畫 A picture of still life.
靜悄悄 Quietly; stealthily.
靜電學 Electrostatics.
靜靜的 Quietly; calmly.
靜坐罷工 Sit down strike; sit-in.
靜默三分鐘 Silence of three minutes.

# 非 部

非 fēi (adj.)- Bad; wrong; unreal; fake; not right.
(v.)- Blame; deny; reproach; scorn at.
(adv.)- Not.
非凡 Uncommon; unusual; out of the common; extraordinary.
非法 Illegal; unlawful.
非洲(地) Africa.
非常 Unusual; uncommon.
非禮 Indecent; improper; disreputable; impolite.
非正式 Informal; irregular; unofficial; private.
非金屬 A non-metal; a metalloid.
非賣品 "Not for sale"; an article not for sale.
非凡之才 An unusual gift; an unusual talent.
非法行爲 An illegal act.
非常時期 In an emergency; in a period of emergency.
非常會議 Extraordinary session.
非武裝地帶 A demilitarized zone.
非營業日期 Non-business days.

靠 kào (v.)- Lean; depend on; rely on.
靠山 Lean against a hill. A protector.
靠近 Near to.
靠攏 Alongside; near to the side of.
靠不住 Untrustworthy; unreliable; not to be trusted.
靠背椅 A chair with a high back.
靠得住 Trustworthy; reliable.

靡 mí (adj.)- Dispersed. Extravagant; profuse; prodigal. Small. Defeated.
(v.)- Waste; destroy. Scatter; disperse. Involve in crime.
(adv.)- Not; without.
靡費；侈靡 Extravagant; wasteful.
靡靡 Slowly.

# 面 部

**面** (n.)- The face. The front; the surface. A plane. A side.
miàn (v.)- Front; face; show the back.
面巾 A towel.

面子 One's face; honour; credit.
面孔 The face; features; looks; a countenance.
面色 Complexion; countenance.
面具 A mask.
面前 In the presence of; in the sight or company of; before one's face; in front of.
面盆 A basin.
面容；面貌 Appearance; countenance; face and form.
面臨 To be faced with.
面部 The face.
面試 Oral examination.
面熟 Know by sight; familiar with.
面談 Discuss verbally; talk personally; have an interview.
面積 Area; dimensions.
面皮厚 Brazen-faced; brass-visaged; shameless.
面色好 Look well (fresh).
面對面 Face to face.
面貌全新 Put on (wear) a new aspect; change the appearance.
面面相覷 Looking at each other; at a loss about what to do.
面黃肌瘦 Flesh emaciated and face yellow.
面貌和善 Have a good-natured countenance.

# 革 部

**革** (n.)- Hides; leather. Defensive armour. A wing.
gé (v.)- Change; renew; reform. Dismiss; remove.

革命 A revolution.
革除 Get rid of; abolish; expel.
革新 Reform; renovate.
革職 To dismiss; remove.
革命家 A revolutionist; a revolutionary.
革命戰爭 A revolutionary war.
革新運動 A renovation movement.

**靴** (n.)- Boots.
xuē

**靶** (n.)- The splashboard of a chariot. A target; a mark.
bǎ 靶子 A target.
靶子場 The rifle range.

**鞋** Same as 鞵.
(n.)- Shoes; slippers.
xié 鞋匠 A shoemaker.
鞋店 A shoe-store; a boot-shop.

鞋刷 A shoe brush.
鞋底 The sole of a shoe.
鞋油 Shoe polish; shoe-shine.
鞋套 A pair of over-shoes.
鞋帶 Shoe laces (strings).

**鞏** (adj.)- Firm; strong.
(v.)- Strengthen; guard.
gǒng 鞏固 Well-guarded; secure; firm; strong; solid. Make solid; consolidate; solidify.

鞏固地位 Strengthen one's position.

**鞠** (v.)- Nourish; rear; bring up. Investigate. Exhaust. Address;
jú inform. Bend as the body.

鞠躬 Bow; bend the body.
鞠躬盡瘁 Give oneself entirely to the public service.

**鞦** (n.)- A crupper. The traces of a carriage.
qiū
鞦韆 A swing.

**鞭** (n.)- A whip; a lash.
biān
(v.)- Flog; slash; whip.
鞭子 A whip.
鞭打；鞭笞 Whip; lash; flog.
鞭炮 Firecrackers.
鞭策 A whip; a lash. Urge; encourage; spur on.

**韁** (n.)- A bridle, particularly the reins of a bridle.
jiāng
韁繩 A bridle; the reins.

**韃** (n.)- Tartar, a nomadic tribe which formerly dwelt in the North-west.
dá
韃靼人 A Tartar.

# 韋 部

**韌** (adj.)- Soft but tough; elastic.
rèn
韌性 An obstinate disposition.

**韓** (n.) A surname. A small feudal state. An old name of Korea.
hán

**韜** Same as 弢.
tāo
(n.)- Strategy. A bow-case; a scabbard.
(v.)- Hide; conceal; sheathe.
韜晦 Keep quiet, so as to escape observation.
韜藏 Hide; conceal.

# 韭 部

**韭** Same as 韮.
jiǔ
韭菜 Leeks; scallions; Chinese chive.

# 音 部

**音** (n.)- A sound. A musical note; a tone. Pronunciation.
yīn
音色 Timbre; tone; the quality of a sound.
音波 A sound-wave.
音信 News; tidings.

音符 Phonogram; a musical note.
音階 The musical scale; the gamut.
音程 A musical interval.
音量 The volume of one's voice.
音節 A syllable.
音樂 Music.
音標 Phonectic symbols.
音調 A tone; a tune.
音樂界 Musical circles.
音樂家 A musician.
音樂會 A musical entertainment; a concert.
音樂隊 A musical (brass) band.
音樂喜劇 Musical comedy.
音標文字 A phonetic character (sign).

**韶** (adj.)- Harmonious; excellent; beautiful.
sháo 韶光；韶華 The beauties of spring; spring time.

**韻** (n.)- A rime (rhyme); harmony of sound.
yùn (adj.)- Refined; polished; elegant.
韻士；詩人 A poet.
韻文 Verse; poetry.
韻律 A metre; a rhythm.
韻律學 Metrics.

**響** Same as 响.
(n.)- A noise; a sound; an echo;
xiǎng reverberation.
(adj.)- Noisy; clamorous.
響亮 A loud, distinct sound.
響應 Answer quickly; respond promptly.
響尾蛇 A rattlesnake.

# 頁 部

**頁** (n.)- A page; a leaf; a sheet; a folio.
yè 頁數 The number of pages in a book.

**頂** (n.)- The top; the crown of the head; the head.
dǐng (adj.)- Topmost; extreme; very.
(v.)- Wear on the head. Opposed the head to. Substitute.
頂上 The top; the summit; the highest peak. The very best.
頂大 The largest.
頂好 The very best; first rate.
頂替 Substitute.
頂點 The apex; the top; the vertex; the height; the climax.
頂壞 Worst; basest.
頂頭風 A head wind.
頂峯會議 A summit conference.

**頃** (n.)- The head inclined. A while; an instant; a moment. An
qǐng area of one hundred mow (畝); hectare.
(adv.)- Presently; just now.
頃刻 In a moment.
頃間 Just; recently; of late.

**項** (n.)- The nape of the neck. A sort; an item; a kind.
xiàng 項目 An item; an article.
項圈；項巾 A neckerchief; a scarf; a tippet.
項頸 The neck.
項鍊 A necklace.

**順** (adj.)- Obedient. Agreeable; favourable. Happy. Convenient.
shùn (v.)- Accord with; obey; yield to; follow.

順次 In regular order; by turns.
順序 Regular order; by turns.
順利 Prosperous; flourishing; no trouble with; easy; manageable; successful.
順便 At one's convenience; favourable; suitable; when convenient.
順風 With the wind.
順流；順水 With the stream; with the tide. A fair tide.
順從 Obedient. Obey; comply with.
順序不同 In different order.
順序錯亂 Be out of order; not in order.
順序顛倒 Invert the order.

**須** (n.)- The beard.
(adj.)- Necessary. Serviceable.
xū (v.)- Wait for. Ought; should be.
(adv.)- Certainly; by all means.

須用 Necessary.
須知 Take note; necessary to be known.
須臾 Momentarily; for a little while; for a short time.
須要；必須 Must; absolutely necessary.

**頌** (n.)- A song of homage; ballads; odes.
sòng (v.)- Praise; admire; commend.
頌揚 Laud; praise.

頌詞 A panegyric; commendatory odes; a eulogy.
頌歌 Hymns.
頌讚 Panegyrize; eulogize; commend.

**預** (adj.)- Prepared. Easy.
(adv.)- Beforehand; previously.
yù 預支 Take an advance of wages.
預先 Beforehand.

預定 Scheduled.
預防 To prevent.
預估 Estimate.
預訂 Pre-engage.
預計 Anticipate; premeditate.
預科 A preparatory course.
預備 To be prepared; make ready; make preparations.
預斷 Prejudge; decide beforehand; forecast.
預付金 Prepayment money.
預備金 Reserve funds.
預防天花 Protection against smallpox.
預防傳染 Prevent infection.
預定時間 On scheduled time; at the appointed time.
預定座位 Book a seat in advance; reserve a seat.
預約出版 Publication by subscription.
預備會議 A preliminary conference.

**頑** (adj.)- Stupid. Obstinate; stubborn.
wán (v.)- Play.
頑皮 Mischievous, as a child; perverse and obstinate.

頑抗 Stand (fight) against; offer resistance.
頑固 Obstinate; stubborn; stiff-necked.
頑童 A naughty youth or boy.
頑強 Tenacious; stiff; dogged; resolute.
頑固黨 The reactionary party.
頑強抵抗 Make a stubborn resistance; fight stubbornly.

**頒** (v.)- Bestow; grant; confer; donate. Distribute; publish
bān abroad; proclaim; promulgate; issue; send out.

頒布 Issue; publish; make known.
頒行 Publish; promulgate.
頒授(學位)；頒賜 Confer upon-by authority.
頒賞 Give rewards or bounties.

**頓** (n.)- A time; a moment; a turn. A meal. An inn. A rest in music.
dùn
(adv.)- Suddenly; immediately.
頓足；頓脚 Stamp the foot.
頓時 At once; forthwith.
頓口無言 Not a word to say in reply.

**頗** (adv.)- Very; rather.
pō
頗久 For a considerable time; very long.
頗有 Rather too much.
頗好 Pretty good; pretty well.
頗多 Too much; a great deal.
頗願 Very anxious.
頗爲滿意 Feel fairly satisfied.

**領** (n.)- The neck; the collar. A commander; a leader.
lǐng
(v.)- Receive. Guide; direct; lead.
領土；領地 Territory; dominion.
領去 Lead away.
領收；領受 Receive; accept.
領回 Receive back.
領取 Accept; receive.
領空 Air space.
領事 A consul.
領海 Territorial waters.
領帶 A necktie.
領情 Receive a favour; be obliged.
領袖 A chief; a headman; a leader.
領章 Collar badge.
領港 A pilot.
領會 Understand; perceive; comprehend.
領導 Lead; guide.
領導權 Hegemony.
領土權 Territorial rights.
領事館 A consulate.
領土主權 Territorial sovereignity.
領導集團 Leading group.
領事館員 A consular officer. The staff of a consulate (全體).

**頤** (n.)- The chin; the cheek.
yí
頤和園 (地) The Summer Palace in Peking.

**頭** (n.)- The head; the top; the end; the chief; the first; the beginning.
tóu
頭上 Above; on the head; overhead.
頭巾 A cap; a kerchief; a turban; a hood.
頭彩 First prize in a lottery.
頭家 One who takes a percentage from a gambling party.
頭部 The head.
頭痛 Headache.
頭號 Number one; the best; first class.
頭腦；頭目 A chief; a headman; a boss.
頭暈 Giddy; dizzy.
頭銜 Official titles.
頭髮 The hair.
頭一回 The first occasion; the first round.
頭等艙 First cabin or saloon.
頭蓋骨 The skull; the cranium.
頭等貨物 First class goods.
頭腦胡塗 Have no brains; be weak in the head; be dull-witted.
頭腦清楚 Have a clear head (brain); be clear-headed.
頭頭是道 Everything clear and straightforward.

**頰** (n.)- The cheeks.
jiá
頰骨 The cheek-bone.

**頷** (n.)- The chin; the jaws.
hàn
頷首 Nod; nod assent.

頸 (n.)- The neck.
jǐng 頸部 The neck; the cervical region.
頸項 The neck.
頸鍊 A necklace; a neck-chain. A collar (犬).

頹 (n.)- A scorching whirlwind.
(adj.)- Submissive; fallen.
tuí (v.)- Fall; crumble; go to pieces; collapse.
頹唐 Decrepit; failing.
頹廢 Ruined; destroyed; be corrupted; fall into decay; be degenerated.
頹廢派 The decadent school.

頻 (adj.)- Urgent; hurried; precipitate; incessant.
pín (adv.)- Frequently; repeatedly; often.
頻年 Year after year.
頻速 Hurriedly; quickly.
頻數；頻頻 Frequently; often; repeatedly.
頻繁 Frequently; very often; in rapid succession; continually.

顆 (n.)- A lump.
kē 顆粒 A grain; a lump; a pill.

顋 Same as 腮.
(n.)- The lower part of the face;
sāi the jaw. The gills of a fish.

題 (n.)- The forehead. A heading; a theme; a subject; a proposition.
tí (v.)- Compose. Look at. Discuss; criticize. Name.
題目 A theme; a subject; a heading.
題名 A title; a heading; a caption. Entitle.
題材 A subject-matter; a theme.
題評 Criticize.
題詩 Compose verses.
題綱 An outline.
題辭 A preface; an epigraph.

額 Same as 頟.
(n.)- The forehead. A fixed
é number or quantity.
額外 Beyond the stated quantity; supernumerary; excess.
額角 The temples.
額數 A fixed number.
額外稅；附加稅 Super tax.
額外折扣 Extra discount.
額面價值 Face-value; par value.

顎 (n.)- High cheek bone.
è

顏 (n.)- The face; the countenance; feature; look. Colour.
yán 顏色 Colour; complexion.
顏料 Dyeing materials; paints; pigments.
顏容 Feature; look; face and form.

願 (n.)- A wish; a desire; a vow; a preference.
yuàn (v.)- Wish; desire. Be willing.
願望 Hope; expectation; intention.
願意 Willing; voluntary.

顛 (n.)- The top. The beginning.
(adj.)- Mad; lunatic.
diān (v.)- Fall; overthrow; turn over; upset.
顛倒 Overturn; upset; reverse; turn upside down.
顛覆 Subvert; overthrow; upset.
顛簸 Joggle; jolt.

顛三倒四 Topsy-turvy.
顛倒次序 Invert the order; follow an inverse (a wrong) order.
顛倒黑白；顛倒是非 Confound black and white (right and wrong).
顛覆活動 Subversive activities.
顛撲不破的 Unbreakable.

類 lèi (n.)- A class; a sort; a species; a kind; a race; a type; a group.
(adj.)-Similar; resembling; alike.
(v.)- Classify; sort; become equal with.
類次 Classify.
類似 Resemble; bear resemblance to; be similar to; be alike.
類別 Classification. Classify.
類型 A type.
類人猿 An anthropoid.
類似事件 A similar (like) case.

顧 gù (v.)- Mind; attend to; observe; care for; regard; look after.
顧及 Mind; pay attention to; take into account.
顧主；顧客 A customer; a patron.
顧問 An adviser; a counsellor.
顧慮 Take thought for; be anxious about; have regard to; consider; regard.
顧全大局 In order to come to a satisfactory arrangement of the whole matter.

顫 zhàn (adj.)- Shivering; trembling.
(v.)- Shiver; tremble.
顫抖 Tremble; shiver.
顫動 Shiver; shake; tremble; vibrate.

顯 xiǎn (adj.)- Manifest; evident; clear. Illustrious. Bright; glorious.
(v.)- Make plain; display; cut a figure; become famous. Appear; show; exhibit.
顯示 Reveal; display to view.
顯明 Clear; evident; make plain.
顯要 Important; prominent.
顯然 Clearly; distinctly; evidently; conspicuously.
顯著 Manifest; conspicuous; plainly visible; notable.
顯露 Disclose; come to light; be laid bare; be found out.
顯微鏡 A microscope.
顯像液；顯影藥 Developer.
顯要人物 Prominent persons.
顯著利益 Notable advantage.
顯而易見的 Obvious; clear as day.

顱 lú (n.)- The skull; the head.
顱頂骨 Parietal bones.

顴 quán (n.)- The cheek bones.
顴骨高聳 High cheek bones.

# 風 部

風 fēng (n.)- A wind; a gust; a gale; a breeze. Manner; style; custom; habit; example; usage.
風力 The force of the wind.
風水 Wind and water—geomancy.
風化 Reform by example. Public morals.
風向 The direction of the wind.

風光 Scenes; manners and appearance.
風車 A windmill.
風災 Damages from a storm.
風味 Flavour; taste.
風波 Waves; a storm. Disputes and quarrels.
風俗 Customs; usages.
風流 Elegant; tasteful; romantic.
風度 Bearing; graceful manner; behaviour; address.
風氣 The prevailing spirit of a place; custom; modernism.
風格 Character; personality.
風浪 Wind and waves.
風扇 An electric fan.
風疹 Rubeola; rubella; German measles.
風琴 An organ.
風景 A scene; a landscape; a view; scenery.
風傳；風聞 Wild reports; rumours.
風箏 A kite.
風箱 Bellows.
風趣 Charm; flavour.
風濕 Rheumatic; malarious.
風聲 Rumour.
風騷 Poems. Bewitching; fascinating; seductive manner.
風土誌 Topography.
風景畫 A landscape.
風土人情 Local manners and customs.
風平浪靜 Calm and unruffled sea.
風光明媚 Great scenic beauty; superb scenery.
風景畫家 A landscape-painter.

颯 sà (n.)- The sound of wind.
颯爽 Lively.

颱 tái (n.)- A typhoon.
颱風 A typhoon.
颱風中心 The typhonic centre; the eye of a storm.

颶 jù (n.)- A high wind; a storm; a cyclone; a typhoon.
颶風 A typhoon; a high wind; a cyclone; a tornado; a hurricane.

颺 yáng (v.)- Tossed by the wind or the waves; soar; fly.
颺言 Speak loudly and quickly.

飄 piāo (adj.)- Floating. Graceful.
(v.)- Whirl; blow. Drift; float.
飄泊 Wandering.
飄流 Floating about; adrift.
飄洋；飄海 Blown over the seas.
飄動 Waving; fluttering, as a flag.
飄揚 Waft; blown into the air.
飄蕩 Be blown about by the wind. Rolling; afloat; adrift.
飄飄 Buoyantly; flying; floating.
飄渺 Obscure; misty; unfeasible.
飄飄然 Airy and graceful.

# 飛 部

飛 fēi (adj.)- Flying. Quick; speedy. Airy; high up.
(v.)- Fly; flit; move with high speed; soar; take wing.
飛去 Fly away (off).
飛行 Aviation; flying. Fly; make a flight.
飛往 To fly to; to leave by air.

飛速 Quickly; swiftly; promptly; at once.
飛魚 A flying-fish.
飛鳥 A flying bird; a bird on the wing.
飛翔 Fly; soar.
飛揚 Be raised, as dust; spread, as fire.
飛雁 The wild goose.
飛艇 An air ship; a flying-boat.
飛彈 A missile.
飛機 A flying machine; an aeroplane; an airplane; a plane.
飛濺 Sputter.
飛騰 Fly upwards; get rapidly promoted. (物價) Soar.
飛躍 A leap; a jump; activity.
飛行員 A pilot.
飛機庫 Hangar.
飛機場 An air-field; an aerodrome; an air port.
飛行堡壘 Flying fortress.
飛禽走獸 Birds and beasts.
飛躍發展 Make rapid progress; take (make) great (rapid) strides.
飛機鳥瞰圖 An aeroview.
飛機發動機 An aero-engine; an aero-motor.
飛機製造廠 An aeroplane (aircraft) factory.

# 食 部

**食** shí (n.)- A meal; food; fare. An eclipse.
(v.)- Eat; devour; take; live on; feed on.
食米 Rice.
食物；食品 Food; eatables; victuals.
食品 Food stuffs.
食指 The forefinger; the index-finger.
食堂 A dining-room (-hall); a refreshment-room.
食道 The gullet; the oesophagus.
食慾 Appetite; relish.
食餌 A bait.
食糧 Food; provisions.
食譜 A food recipe.
食鹽 Table salt.
食道炎 Oesophagitis.
食道癌 Cancer of the oesophagus.
食蟻獸 An ant-eater.
食鹽水 A solution of salt; a saline solution.
食物小心 Be careful about your food (diet).
食物中毒 Food poisoning; disagreement of food.
食慾不振 Have no appetite.

**飢** jī Same as 饑.
(n.)- Hunger.
(adj.)- Hungry; insufficient.
(v.)- Be hungry; starve.
飢民 Hunger-stricken people; starvelings.
飢荒 Famine.
飢寒 Hunger and cold.
飢渴 Hunger and thirst.
飢餓 Hunger; famishing; starvation.
飢寒交迫 Suffer from hunger and cold.

**飪** rèn (n.)- Cook food thoroughly.

**飲** yǐn (v.)- Swallow; drink. Receive. Suffer.
飲水 Drink water. Water to

drink; drinking water.
飲食 Eat and drink. Eating and drinking; food and drink.
飲酒 Drink wine; drinking.
飲茶 Drink tea.
飲料 A drink; a beverage; drinkables.
飲醉 Get drunk.
飲盡；飲乾 Drink off (up); drain one's glass; toss off.
飲食物 Food and drink.
飲食店 An eating-house; a restaurant.
飲水思源 When drinking the water, give a thought to the fountain.

飯 (n.)- A meal; cooked rice; food.
fàn 飯店 A restaurant; an eating house.
飯後 After the meal.
飯桌 A dining table.
飯時 Meal (dinner) time.
飯碗 A rice bowl.
飯館 A restaurant.
飯廳 A dining room.

飴 (n.)- Sweetish syrup or jelly made from various kinds of grains.
yí 飴糖 Sweet meats; sugar-plums.

飼 (v.)- Feed; nourish.
sì 飼料 Forage; fodder; feeds.
飼養 Breed; raise; rear. Breeding of live stock.
飼養法 The method of breeding (rearing); culture.
飼養家畜 Rear domestic animals.

飽 (adj.)- Full of food. Satisfied.
bǎo (v.)- Eat enough; be satiated; be satisfied.
飽和 Saturation. Saturate; be saturated.
飽暖 Well fed and clothed. Be in good keep.
飽滿 Full—as a face; inclusive; complete.
飽和點 The point of saturation.
飽學之士 A very learned man.
飽和化合物 A saturated compound.

飾 (v.)- Ornament; adorn; decorate; embellish. Deceive; gloss over.
shì 飾物 An ornament; a decoration.
飾詞 Use fair words; trump up a story; an excuse.
飾非文過 Gloss over faults.

餃 (n.)- A dumpling.
jiǎo 餃子 A boiled dumpling made of dough and containing meat, etc.

餉 (n.)- Rations or pay for troops.
xiǎng (v.)- Give or send food; give a present.
餉源 Sources of revenue.
餉銀 Soldiers' pay.

養 (v.)- Nourish; rear; bring up. Support; maintain; sustain; keep. Care for; refresh.
yǎng 養女 An adopted (a foster) daughter.
養子 An adopted son.
養父 A foster-father.
養母 A foster-mother.
養成 Educate; foster; train.
養育 Rear; nourish; bring up; foster.
養病 Nurse one's health; seek a cure for disease; recuperate one's health.
養料 Nutrition.
養氣；氧 Oxygen.

養蜂 Bee-keeping; apiculture.
養化物 An oxide.
養老金 An old-age pension.
養老院 An asylum for the aged; an old people's home.
養育院；普濟堂 A poorhouse; an asylum; an almshouse.
養魚場 A fish-farm; a breeding-ground.
養蜂場 A bee-farm (-yard); an apiary.
養猪場 A swinery (piggery).
養雞場 A poultry-yard; a poultry-farm.
養蠶所 A cocomery.
養蠶業 The silk-raising industry.
養成良好習慣 Cultivate (form) a good habit.
養成獨立精神 Cultivate the spirit of self-reliance.

餐 cān (n.)- A meal.
(v.)- Eat.
餐車 A dining-car; a restaurant-car; a buffet-car.
餐具 A dinner-set.
餐室 A dining-room; a restaurant.

餑 bō (n.)- Biscuits; cakes.
餑餑 Cakes.

餒 něi (adj.)- Hungry; famished. Putrid.
餒怯 Weak and timid.

餓 è (n.)- Starvation; hunger.
(adj.)- Starved; hungry.
(v.)- Suffer from hunger; starve.
餓死 Be starved to death; die of hunger; death from starvation.

餘 yú (n.)- The remainder; the surplus; the rest; the balance.
(adj.)- Superabundant; more than.
餘弦(算) A cosine (cos.).
餘事 Other things; the rest.
餘物 Remains; remnants; what is left.
餘剩 Remainder; what is left over; balance.
餘款；餘錢 The remaining money; surplus money; money to spare. Balance in hand.
餘暇 Leisure; spare time.
餘蓄 Savings.
餘數 The balance; the remainder in division.
餘震 An after-quake; a secondary shock.

餚 yáo Same as 肴.
(n.)- Food; delicacies; meats; a feast; dishes.

餛 hún (n.)- A kind of dumpling.
餛飩 A kind of dumpling.

餞 jiàn (n.)- Provisions preserved with sugar. A parting present of money or food.
(v.)- Entertain a departing friend; give a farewell dinner.
餞行；餞別 Give a farewell feast to a friend.
餞禮 Presents to a parting friend.

餅 bǐng (n.)- A cake; a biscuit; pastry.
餅店 A cake shop.
餅乾 Biscuits or crackers.
餅食 Pastry; cakes.

館 guǎn Same as 舘.
(n.)- An inn; a lodging. A hall. An office. A saloon. A restaurant. A school-room.
館子 An inn; an eating-house.
館所 A public hall.

餬 hú (n.)- Congee; porridge; gruel; paste.
餬口 Make a living; earn one's livelihood.

餵 wèi Same as 喂.
(v.)- Feed animals or children.
餵養 Keep; rear.

餽 kuì Same as 饋.
(n.)- A present. A sacrifice.
(v.)- Give a present; offer in sacrifice.
餽禮 Make presents.
餽贈；餽送 Make one a present; make a present of.

饅 mán (n.)- Steamed dumplings; bread.
饅頭 Steamed bread; bun.

饉 jǐn (n.)- A dearth; a scarcity of vegetables.
饉贈 To offer (as a present).

饌 zhuàn (n.)- Delicacies; dainties.
(v.)- Provide food; feed.

饑 jī (n.)- Famine.
饑民 Famine sufferers.

饒 ráo (n.)- Plenty; abundance.
(v.)- Be liberal; spare; excuse; forgive.
饒舌 Talkative; wrangle; chattering. Speak glibly.
饒命 Spare one's life.
饒恕 Forgive; pardon.

饗 xiǎng (n.)- A feast; a banquet; a treat; a sacrifice.
饗供；饗祭 Sacrifice.
饗宴 A feast; give (hold) a banquet (dinner).

饜 yàn (v.)- Be sated with; have enough of.
饜足 Be sufficient; be enough.
饜飽 Have enough of; be satiated.

饞 chán (adj.)- Greedy; gluttonous; rapacious; voracious.
(v.)- Love eating.
饞涎 The mouth waters. Saliva.
饞嘴 Devour (eat) greedily.

# 首 部

首 shǒu (n.)- The head. A chief; a leader. The beginning.
(adj.)- First.
首句 The opening sentence.
首先 First; in the first place.
首次 First time.
首名 The first name.
首府 The head prefecture; the capital of a province.
首尾 Head and tail; beginning and end.
首相；首揆 The prime minister; the premier.
首要 The principal; head; chief.
首映（電影） A gala premiere.
首座；首席 The head of a table; the seat of honour; the chief seat.
首創 The founder; the original manufacturer. Originate.

首都 The capital.
首飾 Ornaments for the head; head-dress.
首領 The leader; the chief.

# 香 部

香 (adj.)- Fragrant; sweet-smelling; odoriferous; scented; aromatic.
xiāng 香水 A perfume; perfumed (scented) water; a scent.
香瓜 The musk-melon.
香味 Aromatic flavour; spicy taste; savour.
香氣 Fragrance; perfume; sweet smell (scent).
香烟 Cigarettes.
香料 Spices; spicery; perfumery.
香粉 Cosmetics and face powder.
香草 Fragrant plants.
香荽；香菜 Coriander.
香港(地) Hongkong.
香蕉 Bananas.
香燭 Incense and candles.
香艷 Bewitching; fascinating.
香爐 A censer; an incense-burner.
香檳酒 Champagne.

馥 (n.)- A fragrant smell; odour. (adj.)- Fragrant; odoriferous.
fù 馥郁 Fragrant; odoriferous; sweet-smelling.

馨 (n.)- Sweet incense; fragrant odours.
xīn 馨芳 Perfumes of flowers.
馨香 Fumes of offerings.

# 馬 部

馬 (n.)- A horse; a mare; a colt.
馬力 Horse power (h. p.).
mǎ 馬上 On horseback. Quickly; at once.
馬夫 A groom; a stableman; an ostler.
馬匹 Horses.
馬肉 Horse-flesh.
馬克 Mark—a German coin.
馬車 A carriage; a coach; a cart.
馬房 A stable.
馬面 A long face.
馬將；麻將 Mahjong game.
馬票 A pool-ticket; a pari-mutuel ticket.
馬術 Horsemanship; horse-riding.
馬路 A highroad; a drive-way; a carriage-road; an avenue.
馬會 A horse-race club; a jockey club.
馬蹄 A horse's hoof.
馬嘶 Neigh.
馬鞍 A saddle.
馬賽(地) Marseilles.
馬戲 Circus; equestrian feats.
馬蟥 Horse-leeches.
馬鞭 A riding whip.
馬關(地) Shimonoseki, Japan.
馬繮 A bridle; a rein.
馬口鐵；白鐵 Tinplates.

馬尼剌(地) Manila.
馬將牌；麻將牌 A mahjong piece.
馬鈴薯 A potato.
馬德里(地) Madrid, Spain.
馬蹄形 Hoof-(U-) shaped; horseshoe.
馬蹄鐵 Horseshoe.
馬糞紙 Strawboard; cardboard.
馬賽曲 Marseillaise.
馬上就來 Will be here in a minute.
馬來半島(地) Malay Peninsula.
馬來西亞(地) Malaysia.
馬克思主義 Marxism.
馬拉松賽跑 A marathon race; a long-distance race.
馬爾塞斯主義；馬爾塞斯人口論 Malthusianism.

馭 yù Same as 御.
(v.)- Drive; ride; control; rule.
馭車 Drive a carriage.
馭者 A driver; a coach man.
馭馬 Ride a horse.

馮 féng (n.)- A surname. A horse running swiftly.
(adj.)- Very angry. Dissatisfied.
馮怒 Very angry; in a great passion.

馱 tuó (n.)- A load; a burden.
(v.)- Bear; carry on the back.
馱負 Carry a load.

馳 chí (v.)- Gallop; ride fast; run. Spread abroad.
馳名 Famous; well-known; reputed known far and wide.
馳赴 Go directly to; hasten; speed.
馳躍 Running; jumping.

馴 xùn (adj.)- Well-bred; polished; mild; trained; docile; tractable.
(v.)- Tame. Attain to gradually.
馴良 Tame; tractable; docile; mild.
馴服 Tame; subdued.
馴畜 Tame; trained animals.
馴養 Domesticate.
馴獅人 A lion-tamer.
馴獸者 A tamer.

駁 bó (v.)- Dispute; argue; contradict; criticise; refute; oppose. Tranship.
(adj.)- Mixed; diverse; particoloured; variegated.
駁斥 Expose an error; find fault with.
駁倒 Run down in argument.
駁船 Transfer goods to another boat. A lighter.
駁貨 Tranship goods.
駁運 Tranship; transport.

駐 zhù (v.)- Halt; stop; stay; sojourn.
駐屯；駐紮 Station; be stationed; be quartered.
駐守；駐防 Occupy, as troops.
駐軍 A garrison.
駐留 Remain; stay.
駐營 Encampment.
駐外公使 Ministers to foreign countries.
駐在領事 The resident consul.

駒 jū (n.)- A colt; a young horse; a pony.
駒影 The sun's shadow.
駒光易逝 Time flies.

駕 jià (v.)- Prepare the carriage. Yoke; drive; ride.
駕車 Harness a horse to a cart; drive a car.
駕船 Be or sail in a ship.
駕駛 Steer; navigate; sail; drive a car.
駕臨 Your presence.
駕駛盤 The driving wheel.

駕駛執照 A driving license.

駛 (v.)- Move fast; sail; drive; run swiftly as a horse.
shǐ 駛入 Sail into.
駛行 Sail; drive; proceed.
駛回 Sail back.

駝 (n.)- A camel.
tuó 駝子 A humpback; a hunchback.
駝毛 Camel's hair.
駝背 Humpbacked.
駝峯 The hump of a camel.
駝鳥 An ostrich.

駭 (n.)- Take fright; disperse; be frightened.
hài (adj.)- Startled; frightened; terrified.
駭怕 Be frightened; be scared; surprise; amazed.
駭浪 Fearful waves.
駭然 In astonishment.
駭人聽聞 Frightful to the ear.

駱 (n.)- A white horse with a black mane.
luò 駱駝 A camel; a dromedary (單峯駝).
駱駝絨 Camel's hair cloth.

駿 (n.)- A swift horse; a noble steed.
jùn (adj.)- Swift; fleet; rapid. Great; lofty.
駿才 A man of talent.
駿馬 An excellent horse; a fleet steed.
駿速 Very fleet; swift; rapid.

騁 (v.)- Hasten on; run away; run fast; gallop a horse.
chěng 騁能 Show off one's talents.

駢 (n.)- A pair of horses.
(adj.)- Joined together.
pián 駢字 Two-word phrases or terms.
駢肩 Shoulders together—a crowd.

騎 (n.)- A horseman; a cavalier; a saddled horse.
qí (v.)- Ride; ride on; mount.
騎士 A horseman. A knight.
騎兵 A cavalryman; a horseman. Cavalry; horse (隊).
騎師 A rider; a jockey.
騎馬 Horse-riding. Ride a horse.
騎術 Equitation.
騎牆派 People who takes no side; fence sitters.
騎虎難下 The man riding a tiger cannot get off its back—in an awkward position.

騖 (adj.)- Swift; rapid.
wù

騙 (v.)- Deceive; cheat; swindle; palm off; impose on; defraud.
piàn 騙子 A swindler; a deceiver; a crook; a cheat.
騙取 Obtain by fraud.
騙術 Tricks; wiles; swindles.
騙錢 Obtain money by fraud; swindle money from (out of) one.

騰 (v.)- Leap on. Ascend; mount; gallop; run. Move; turn out.
téng 騰出 Turn out.
騰空 Soar; mount to heaven.
騰起 Rise; go up.
騰達 Get on in life; become prosperous.
騰出地方 To make room for ... . To clear a space for ... .
騰出時間 To set aside time.

**騷** (n.)- Grief; sorrow; sadness.
(adj.)- Sad; unhappy; sorrowful.
sāo Disturbed; agitated; disquieted. Poetic. Charming.
(v.)- Disturb; disquiet; trouble.
騷動 Excite; stir up; agitate.
騷亂 Disturb; trouble; raise an uproar (a commotion).

**騾** (n.)- A mule; the offspring of an ass and a mare.
luó 騾夫 A muleteer.
騾馬 Mules and horses.

**驀** (v.)- Leap on a horse; leap over.
mò 驀然；驀地 Suddenly.

**驃** (n.)- A war horse; cream coloured horse.
piào (adj.)- Brave; valiant; daring; courageous.
驃勇 Valiant horseman; brave.

**驅** (v.)- Drive; urge onward; spur on; force; expel; compel. Gallop; run rapidly.
qū 驅入 Drive into.
驅使 Drive to work; urge on by force.
驅車 Drive a carriage.
驅逐 Expel; drive out; get rid of; turn out; chase; keep off; do away with.
驅散 Scatter; disperse.
驅風藥；通氣藥 Carminative.
驅逐機 Chaser; pursuit plane.
驅逐艦 A destroyer.
驅逐出境 Banish; deport.
驅逐艦隊 A destroyer flotilla.

**驕** (adj.)- Proud; arrogant. Ungovernable; haughty; disdainful.
jiāo (v.)- Boast; be proud of; be arrogant; glory in.
驕兒；驕子 A beloved son.
驕傲 Arrogant; proud; haughty; boastful; high-flown; be proud and insolent.
驕態 A proud bearing; a haughty manner.
驕者必敗 Pride goes before a fall.

**驗** Same as 騐.
(n.)- Effect; proof; testimony;
yàn evidence. Examination.
(v.)- Examine. Prove; test; verify; ascertain. Come true.
驗血 Examine blood.
驗尿 Examine one's urine.
驗查 Examine; inspect.
驗屍 An autopsy. Make a post-mortem examination.
驗病 Examine disease. Medical examination.
驗貨 Examine goods at the Customs.
驗算 Go over the accounts.
驗屍官 A coroner.
驗眼鏡 An ophthalmoscope.
驗看護照 Examine passports.

**驚** (adj.)- Frightened; afraid; alarmed; astonished; terrified; sur-
jīng prised; apprehensive.
(v.)- Terrify; fear; make confusion; astonish; surprise; amaze.
驚人 Terrifying; shocking; dreadful.
驚險 Dangerous.
驚悉 Shocked to learn.
驚奇 Surprised.
驚異 Wonder at; marvel at.
驚動 Disturb; annoy; molest; excite.
驚訝 Wonder; amaze; surprise.
驚慌 Frightened; alarmed; startled; terrified; out of wits.
驚嘆 Be lost in wonder (admiration); wonder at.

驚醒 Be startled from sleep.
驚弓之鳥 A scalded cat dreads cold water.
驚天動地 Astounding; tremendous.
驚心動魄 Be seized with a panic.
驚惶失措 Be frightened out of one's wits.

驟 (adj.)- Suddenly; frequently; quickly; urgently.
zhòu (v.)- Trot; gallop; race.
驟行 Instantly; immediately.
驟雨 A squall of rain; a shower.
驟然而來 Come in abruptly.

驢 Same as 馿.
lǘ (n.)- A donkey; an ass.
驢子 A donkey; an ass.
驢車 Donkey's cart.

驥 (n.)- A fast horse; a noble steed.
jì 驥尾 Follow one's lead; play second fiddle to one.

驪 (n.)- A black horse.
lí 驪歌 A farewell song.
驪駕 A pair of horses.
驪駒 A gallant steed.

# 骨 部

骨 (n.)- A bone. A rib (傘扇等).
gǔ (adj.)- Bony.
骨干 A backbone.
骨灰 Bone ash; ashes; remains.
骨肉 Flesh and bones. Kinsmen; blood relations.
骨炎 Osteitis.
骨格 Frame; build.
骨粉 Ground bones; bone-dust.
骨痛 Osteocope; bone-ache.
骨節 A bone-joint.
骨頭 A bone.
骨骼 A skeleton.
骨癌 Cancer of a bone.
骨髓 The marrow.
骨肉相殘 Dog eats dog.
骨瘦如柴 Thin and emaciated like a stick—be reduced to a skeleton.
骨骼系統 Osseous system.

骯 (adj.)- Fat; dirty; fleshy.
āng 骯髒 Dirty; filthy.

骷 (n.)- A skelton; bones of the body.
kū 骷髏 Skull of the dead.

骸 (n.)- The bones of the body. Dry bones.
hái 骸骨 A skeleton; the bones of the body; dried bones.

髒 (adj.)- Dirty; filthy; greasy; dusty; dingy.
zāng

髓 (n.)- The pith; the marrow of bones. The essence of a thing.
suǐ

體 Same as 体.
tǐ (n.)- The body; the trunk. A solid. Style; form; fashion. The substance.
(v.)- Embody. Represent in. Have sympathy with; show of com-

passion to. Partition.
體力 Physical strength.
體系 A system.
體制 Organization; system.
體育 Physical education (culture; training).
體重 The weight of the body.
體面 Dignity; appearance; decency; honour; reputation.
體現 Embody; give a concrete form to.
體健 Strong; healthy.
體溫 One's temperature; the animal heat.
體貼 Having sympathy with; being concerned with.
體裁 Style.
體會 Comprehend; take in an idea.
體質 Physical constitution.
體操 Physical (gymnastic) exercise; gymnastics; athletic exercise; drill (軍隊).
體態 Deportment; form; attitude.
體積 Volume.
體育家 A physical educator.
體育會 An athletic association; an athletic club.
體育館 A gymnasium.
體育精神 Sportsmanship.
體重增加 Gain in weight.
體格强壯 Stout body.
體格檢查 Physical examination.
體質健康 Healthy body.
體操教師 A gymnastics teacher; a gymnast; a drill-master.
體力勞動者 A manual worker (labourer).

# 高 部

高 gāo (adj.)- High; elevated; lofty; tall. Dear; expensive. Old; aged. Loud.
高大 High; tall; lofty.
高山 A high (lofty) mountain.
高見 Elevated views; far sight. Your esteemed opinion (review).
高低 High and low; rise and fall.
高尙 High-minded; high-principled; magnanimous; noble; lofty.
高明 Bright; intelligent.
高門 A noble family (house).
高度 Altitude; height.
高音 A high pitch tone; a loud voice. A high (loud) key; soprano.
高級 High class; senior.
高峻 Lofty and steep.
高原 A plateau.
高峯 A high (lofty) peak.
高棉；柬埔寨(地) Cambodia.
高貴 Noble; exalted; high and noble.
高雅 Graceful; elegant; refined.
高等 Advanced; first-class; high-grade.
高傲 Haughtiness; arrogance.
高漲 The tide rises. Go up (rise) in price.
高樓 A lofty (tall) building.
高潮 The high tide. The climax; the culmination.
高壓 High pressure (氣壓); high tension (電流).
高舉 Raised to high honours; extol; lift up high.
高燥 High and dry; arid; elevated.
高齡；高年 Aged; old; advanced in years; of advanced age.
高血壓 High blood pressure.
高利貸 Lend at usury (high interest).

高射砲 An anti-aircraft gun; an aero-gun.
高速度 High speed.
高跟鞋 High-heeled shoes.
高粱酒 Kaoliang wine.
高薪水 A high salary. High-salaried; highly-paid.
高麗參 Korean ginseng.
高利貸者 A usurer; a loan shark.
高低不平；高高低低 Uneven; rugged; unlevel.
高尚優美 High-toned and refined (elegant); graceful.
高枕無憂 Sleep free from care (in peace); sleep without anxiety; rest assured.
高架鐵道 An elevated railroad; an overhead (a high-level) railway.
高級中學 Senior middle school.
高等法院 The High Court of Justice.
高等教育 High (advanced) education.
高等數學 Higher mathematics.
高爾夫球 Golf.
高壓政策 A high-handed policy.
高壓電線 A high-tension wire.
高聲朗誦 Read aloud.
高等小學校 A higher primary school.
高等師範學校 Higher normal school.

# 髟 部

**髣** fǎng (adj.)- Resembling; like.
髣髴；彷彿 Resemble closely; similar to. Appear dimly.

**髯** rán Same as 髥.
(n.)- The beard; the whiskers.
髯翁 An old man.

**髦** máo (n.)- Hair.
(adj.)- Eminent; distinguished.

**髮** fà (n.)- Hair.
髮刷 A hairbrush.
髮油 Pomade; hair-oil.
髮妻 A wife.
髮針 Hair-pin.
髮釵 Hair-fork.
髮辮 A queue; a pigtail.

**鬃** zōng (n.)- The back-hair of a lady's head-dress. Horse mane.
鬃毛 Horse mane.

**鬆** sōng (adj.)- Loose; relaxed; shaggy; soft and crisp; spongy. Confused; disordered.
(v.)- Relax; let go.
鬆手 Let go.
鬆脆 Crisp and soft.
鬆髮蓬頭 Her tresses all in confusion.

**鬍** hú (n.)- The beard or moustache.
鬍鬚 The beard.

**鬚** xū (n.)- The beard and whisker.
(adj.)- Bearded; hairy.
鬚根(植) Fibrous root.
鬚梳 A whisker comb.
鬚髮 Beard and hair.
鬚髮均白 One's hair and beard all turned grey.

**鬢** bīn (n.)- The hair on the temples; curls.
鬢髮 The hair on the temples.

# 鬥 部

**鬧** nào (n.)- Noise; bustle; roaring; confusion; disturbance.
(adj.)- Noisy; bustling.
(v.)- Make a disturbance; embroil; disturb.

鬧市 A noisy and busy street.
鬧吵 Uproar; riot.
鬧事 Make a disturbance.
鬧鐘 An alarm clock.
鬧脾氣 Be bad-tempered.
鬧意見 Be on bad terms; to make a row.
鬧亂子 Cause trouble; start a riot.

**鬨** hòng (n.)- The din of battle; noise of fighting; war-cry.
(v.)- Fight; wrangle.

鬨堂 Laugh loudly.
鬨嚷 Clamour; uproar.

**鬭** dòu Same as 鬥，鬪.
(v.)- Fight; struggle for; strive with; contend.
鬭力 Wrestling.

鬭牛 A bull-fight.
鬭志 Fighting spirit; pugnacity.
鬭爭 Struggle; fight; contest.
鬭牛者 A bull-fighter; a toreador; a matador.
鬭牛場 A bull-ring.
鬭雞眼 Cross-eyed.
鬭雞場 A cockpit.
鬭志昂揚 High in spirits, firm in determination.

# 鬯 部

**鬱** yù (n.)- A fragrant herb.
(adj.)- Anxious; harassed; irriated; melancholy. Bushy.
鬱郁 Fragrant.

鬱結；鬱悶 Depressed; melancholy; grieved.
鬱葱 Dense; luxuriant; thick.
鬱金香 A tulip.
鬱鬱不樂 Cheerlessly; melancholy. Be despondent; be in the blues.

# 鬼 部

**鬼** guǐ (n.)- A spirit; a ghost; a devil; a demon.
鬼火 The will-o'-the-wisp; the jack-o'-lantern; fatuous fire.

鬼怪 Strange beings; ghost; devil.
鬼話 Empty words; falsehood; lying.

鬼混 Live an idle; slovenly life.
鬼魂 Ghosts; disembodied spirits.
鬼魅 Evil spirits.
鬼主意 Villainy scheme.
鬼門關 The gate to devils' home; the ominous (calamitous) direction.
鬼鬼祟祟 Devilish; impish; tricky.

**魁** kuī (n.)- The head; the chief; the best.
(adj.)- Great; eminent.
魁士 An eminent scholar.
魁首 The first; the chief; the best.
魁梧 Stalwart, gigantic stature; great and strong.
魁偉 Of great stature; stalwart; well-built.

**魂** hún (n.)- The soul; the spirit.
魂飛；失魂 Lose one's wits.
魂魄 The soul.

**魄** pò (n.)- The soul; the spirit. The body; figure; shape.
魄力 Courage; power.

**魅** mèi (n.)- A devil spirit; a demon; evil spirit.
魅力 Fascinating; attractiveness.

**魍** wǎng (n.)- An elf; a sprite.
魍魎 The spirits of the waters.

**魑** chī (n.)- A mountain elf.
魑魅魍魎 Evil spirits of mountains and rivers; mischievous imps.

**魔** mó (n.)- A devil; a demon.
魔力 Fascination; magical power; the power to charm.
魔鬼 A devil; an evil spirit.
魔術 Magic; magical art; witchcraft.

# 魚 部

**魚** yú (n.)- Fish.
魚子；魚卵 Fish-eggs; roe; milt; spawn.
魚池；魚塘 A fishpond; a fish-pool.
魚肚；魚胞 Fish maw.
魚油 Fish-oil; fish-fat.
魚竿 A fishing rod.
魚苗；魚秧 Small fry; minnows.
魚翅 Fish's fins; shark's fins.
魚鉤 A fish-hook.
魚雷 A torpedo.
魚業 Fishery.
魚膠 Fish glue; isinglass.
魚網 A fishing-net.
魚餌 Fish-bait.
魚鰭 Fin.
魚鱗 Fish scales.
魚肝油 Cod-liver oil.
魚雷艇 Torpedo-boat.

**魯** lǔ (adj.)- Stupid; vulgar; simple; dull; silly; blunt.
魯莽 Rash; careless; rude; rough.
魯鈍 Dull of understanding; stupid.

**鮑** bào (n.)- Dried fish; pickled or salted fish.
鮑魚 Awabi; a sea-ear; abalone.

**鮓** zhǎ (n.)- Preserved fish; salted fish; condiment of fish.

**鮭** guī (n.)- A white porpoise. A salmon.

**鮮** xiān (n.)- Fresh fish; fresh game.
(adj.)- Fresh; new; pure; bright; clean. Few; rare; uncommon.
鮮血 Fresh blood.
鮮肉 Fresh meat.
鮮果 Fresh fruit.
鮮美 Delicious.
鮮明 Clearness; distinctness; vividness. New; fresh and bright.
鮮花 Fresh-cut flowers.
鮮紅 Bright red; fresh and ruddy.
鮮艷 Beautiful as flowers; respledent (fresh) beauty.
鮮艷奪目 Attractive to the eyes.

**鯉** lǐ (n.)- The carp.
鯉魚 The carp.

**鯊** shā (n.)- The shark.
鯊魚 The shark.
鯊魚皮 Shagreen.

**鯖** qīng (n.)- Mackerel; mullet.
鯖魚；青花魚 Spotted mackerel.

**鯨** jīng (n.)- A whale.
(adj.)- Vast. Overwhelming.
鯨油 Blubber; whale-oil.
鯨魚肉 Whale-meat.

**鯽** jì (n.)- A kind of carp.
鯽魚 Golden carp.

**鰌** qiū Same as 鰍.
(n.)- Giant loach.

**鰓** sāi (n.)- The gills of a fish.

**鰥** guān (n.)- An unmarried man; a widower; a bachelor. Name of a huge fish.
(adj.)- Solitary.
(adv.)- Alone.
鰥夫 A widower; a bachelor.
鰥寡 Widowers and widows.

**鰱** lián (n.)- Silver carp.

**鰵** mǐn (n.)- Cod-fish.
鰵魚肝油 Cod-liver oil.

**鰻** mán (n.)- An eel.

**鰾** biào (n.)- Air bladders of fishes.

**鱖** guì (n.)- A kind of perch.
鱖魚 The mandarin fish.

**鱑** huáng (n.)- The sturgeon.

**鱔** shàn Same as 鱓.
(n.)- Yellow eel.
鱔羹 Eel stew.

**鱗** (n.)- The scale of a fish.
lín
鱗甲 Scales; armour-plates.
鱗狀 Scaly; squamose.

**鱠** Same as 膾.
kuài
(n.)- Minced meat; hashed flesh; hashed fish.

鱠鯉 Minced carp.
鱠殘魚；銀魚 The Chinese white-bait.

**鱷** Same as 鰐.
è
(n.)- The crocodile; the alligator.
鱷魚 A crocodile; an alligator.

# 鳥 部

**鳥** (n.)- A bird; the feathered tribe.
niǎo
鳥羽 A feather; a plume.
鳥巢 A bird's nest; an aviary.
鳥啼 The singing of a bird.
鳥喙 Beak; bill.
鳥鎗 A fowling piece; a gun.
鳥獸 Birds and beasts; fur and feather.
鳥類 Aves; birds; the feathered tribe.
鳥籠 A cage; a bird-cage.
鳥瞰圖 A bird's-eye view; an aeroview.
鳥類學 Ornithology.

**鳧** (n.)- Wild duck.
fú
鳧水 Swim.
鳧趨 Waddle; walk slowly.

**鳩** (n.)- The turtle-dove; the pigeon; the cuckoo.
jiū
鳩居 My humble abode.
鳩集；鳩合 Bring together; call people together; assemble.

**鳳** (n.)- The male phoenix; a fabulous bird.
fèng
鳳梨 A pineapple; an ananas.
鳳凰 The male and female phoenix; a fabulous bird.
鳳凰于飛 Conjugal affection.

**鳴** (n.)- The cry of a bird or animal. A sound.
míng
(v.)- Sound; sing; cry; chirp; hum; ring.
鳴冤 Cry out for redress.
鳴鼓 Beat a drum.
鳴謝 Express thanks.
鳴鑼；鳴金 Beat a gong.
鳴禽類 Passeriformes.
鳴炮致敬 To fire a salute.

**鴉** (n.)- A crow; a raven.
yā
鴉片 Opium.
鴉片精；嗎啡 Morphia or morphine.
鴉片戰爭 The Opium War.
鴉雀無聲 Not even the sound of a crow or a magpie's cawing—a dead silence.

**鴕** (n.)- An ostrich.
tuó
鴕鳥 An ostrich.
鴕鳥政策 An ostrich policy.

**鴛** (n.)- The male (or drake) of the mandarin duck.
yuān
鴛鴦 A pair of mandarin ducks.
鴛鴦枕 A double pillow for married couple.
鴛鴦劍 A pair of twin swords.

**鴞** xiāo
Same as 梟
(n.)- An owl.

**鴟** chī
(n.)- An owl; a kite; the white-horned owl.
鴟鴞 An owl; the eared owl.

**鴦** yāng
(n.)- The female of mandarin duck.

**鴣** gū
(n.)- A partridge.

**鴨** yā
(n.)- A duck; a drake ( 雄 ); a teal ( 水鴨 ); a duckling ( 小鴨 ).
鴨叫 Quack.
鴨蛋 Duck's eggs.
鴨綠江(地) Yalu River.
鴨嘴獸 The ornithorhynchus; a duck-bill.

**鴻** hóng
(n.)- A large wild goose; a wild swan.
(adj.)- Huge; great; vast; profound.
鴻才 Great talents.
鴻毛 The swan's-down–very light; matter of no importance or value.
鴻名 A famous name; great fame.
鴻恩 Great favour (kindness); boundless grace.
鴻雁 The wild goose.
鴻業 A glorious achievement; the great undertaking.
鴻圖 A big plan.
鴻鵠之志 Soaring ambitions.

**鴿** gē
(n.)- A dove; a pigeon.
鴿傳信 A pigeon message.

**鵑** juān
(n.)- A cuckoo.

**鵝** é
(n.)- The domestic goose.
鵝毛 Down of a goose–petty trifles.
鵝絨 Velvet.
鵝黃 A fine yellow, like that of a gosling.
鵝口瘡 Thrush.
鵝毛扇 A goose-feather fan.
鵝蛋臉 Oval face.
鵝喉症；咽喉炎 Sore throat.

**鵠** gǔ
(n.)- The snow goose. A target.
鵠候回音 Awaiting your reply.

**鵡** wǔ
(n.)- A parrot.

**鵬** péng
(n.)- A fabulous bird of enormous size; the roc.
鵬鳥 The roc.
鵬程 A great prospect.
鵬程萬里 A roc can reach a destination of a myriad miles away at one jump–said of those who have a bright future.

**鵰** diāo
(n.)- The eagle; the vulture; the hawk.
鵰扇 A fan of eagle's feather.

**鵲** què
(n.)- A magpie; a pica.

**鶩** wù
(n.)- The wild duck.

鶯 (n.)- The Chinese oriole; the mango bird; the warbler; the eastern nightingale.
yīng
鶯粟；罌粟 Poppy.
鶯燕 A courtesan; a whore.
鶯簧；鶯聲 The song of a warbler.
鶯花爛漫 The beauty of spring.
鶯歌妙舞 Singing and dancing; merry-making.

鶴 (n.)- A crane; a stork.
hè
鶴立 Anxiously waiting.
鶴壽；鶴算 Long life.
鶴頸 Long-necked.
鶴嘴鋤 A mattock; a pickaxe.
鶴立雞羣 One who towers above the common herd. A Triton among the minnows.

鷂 (n.)- A kite; a sparrow hawk.
yào
鷂子；紙鳶 A kite.

鷓 (n.)- The common partridge.
zhè
鷓鴣 The common partridge; a Chinese francolin.

鷗 (n.)- A sea-gull.
ōu

鷲 (n.)- A vulture; an eagle; a hawk.
jiù

鷸 (n.)- The turquoise kingfisher; the snipe.
yù
鷸蚌相爭 Contention between a snipe and a clam—a beneficial chance to fisherman to catch both.

鷺 (n.)- An egret; a paddy bird; a snowy heron.
lù
鷺鷥 A Chinese egret.

鷹 (n.)- A falcon; an eagle; a hawk; king of birds.
yīng
鷹子 An eaglet.
鷹眼 Eagle eyes; sharp-sighted as an eagle.

鸚 (n.)- A parrot.
yīng
鸚鵡；鸚哥 A parrot.
鸚鵡學舌 Echo another's words.

鸛 (n.)- A crane; the common stork.
guàn

鸝 (n.)- The oriole.
lí

鸞 (n.)- A fabulous bird. A bell.
luán
鸞車 An imperial carriage.
鸞鳳和鳴 Female and male in harmony—of marriage.

# 鹵 部

鹵 (n.)- Rock salt; salt marsh.
lǔ
(adj.)- Dull; obtuse; insolent; prude.
(v.)- Plunder; rob.
鹵田 Salt field.
鹵莽 Rash; careless; abrupt; rude.

鹵獲文件 Captured documents.

**鹹** (adj.)- Salt; salty.
xián
鹹土 Sour saltish land.
鹹肉 Salted meat; becon.
鹹味 A salty taste; saltiness.
鹹蛋 Salted eggs.
鹹魚 Salted fish.
鹹菜 Pickled cabbage; salted vegetable.
鹹湖 A lagoon; a salt lake.
鹹牛肉 Salted beef.
鹹水魚 A salt-water fish.
鹹水湖 A salt-water lake.
鹹肉糉 Salt-meat dumplings.
鹹橄欖 Salted olives.
鹹猪肉 Salted pork.

**鹼** (n.)- Lye; soap.
jiǎn
鹼水 Lye.
鹼土 Alkaline soil.
鹼性 Alkalinity.
鹼性反應 Alkaline reaction.

**鹽** Same as 塩 .
yán
(n.)- Salt.
鹽田 A salt field; brinepan.
鹽池 Salt lake.
鹽味 Saltiness; a flavour (taste) of salt.
鹽場 A salt-farm.
鹽酸(化) Hydrochloric acid.
鹽化物 A chloride.
鹽水灌腸 Salt enema.

# 鹿 部

**鹿** (n.)- A deer; a stag ( 雄 ); a hind ( 雌 ); a fawn ( 小鹿 ).
lù
鹿角 Deer's horns. An abatis.
鹿茸 Deer's antlers.
鹿豕 Rustic; vulgar; unlettered.
鹿苑 A deer park.

**麒** (n.)- The male of the Chinese unicorn.
qí
麒麟 A fabulous animal of good omen.
麒麟兒 A wise child.

**麓** (n.)- The foot of a hill.
lù

**麗** (n.)- A pair.
lì
(adj.)- Beautiful; handsome; fine; pretty; splendid. Glorious; ornamented; magnificent.
(v.)- Tie; fasten.
麗人 A beauty; a belle.
麗都 Beautiful; magnificent.
麗日光天 Beautiful (lovely) weather.

**麝** (n.)- The musk deer; the civet.
shè
麝香 Musk.

**麟** (n.)- The female of the Chinese unicorn.
lín
麟角 Rare; few; scarce.

# 麥 部

麥 (n.)- Wheat; barley; oats; rye.
mài
麥田 A wheat (barley) field.
麥片 White oats.
麥粉 Wheat flour.
麥酒 Beer.
麥穗 Wheat ears.
麥克風 A microphone.
麥芽糖 Maltose; malt-sugar.

麩 (n.)- Bran.
fū
麩皮 Bran.

麪 Same as 麵 .
miàn
(n.)- Wheat flour. Vermicelli.
麪包 Bread.
麪粉 Flour.
麪食 Wheaten food.
麪條 Vermicelli; noodle.
麪筋 Wheat gluten.
麪包店 A bakery.
麪包師 A baker.
麪包屑 Bread-crumbs.
麪粉廠 A flour mill.
麪包一片 A piece (slice) of bread.

## 麻 部

麻 (n.)- Hemp.
mó
(adj.)- Pock-marked.
麻子 Pockmark.
麻木 Numbed; without sensation of feeling.
麻布 Hemp cloth; linen.
麻疹 The measles.
麻袋 A hemp sack.
麻雀 A sparrow.
麻煩 Troublesome.
麻痺 Be paralyzed; benumbed; go numb.
麻醉 Anaesthetize; narcotize; render insensible.
麻點 Pit.
麻繩 A hempen rope (cord).
麻藥；麻醉劑 An anaesthetic; a narcotic; an opiate.
麻醉藥 Chloroform.

麼 (n.)- A sort.
mó
(adj.)- Small; delicate; minute.
An interrogative sign.

麾 (n.)- A signal flag; a standard.
huī
(v.)- Beckon; call; make motion with the hand.
麾手 Wave the hand.

## 黃 部

黃 (adj.)- Yellow.
huáng
黃土；黃壤 Loess; yellow soil.
黃瓜 The cucumber.
黃色 Yellow colour.
黃豆 Soy-bean.
黃昏 Twilight; the eventide; dusk.
黃河(地) The Yellow River.
黃金 Gold.
黃冠 A Taoist priest.
黃海(地) The Yellow Sea.

黃麻 Jute.
黃蜂 A wasp.
黃銅 Brass.
黃種 The Yellow Race.
黃糖；赤糖 Brown sugar.
黃芽菜 Celery cabbage.
黃金色 Golden; of golden colour.
黃疸病 Yellow jaundice.
黃梅天；雨季 Rainy season.
黃鼠狼 The weasel.
黃銅礦 Copper pyrites; chalcopyrite.
黃褐色 Yellowish brown; tawny.
黃熱病 The yellow fever.
黃鐵礦 Iron pyrites.
黃金海岸(地) The Gold Coast.
黃金時代 The golden age.

# 黍 部

黍 shŭ (n.)- The glutinous, panicled millet. A unit of weight, dry measure, or length.
黍子 Millet.
黍稷 Varieties of millet.

黎 lí (n.)- Black; black-haired. Many.
黎人 The aborigines of Hainan.
黎明 Early dawn; daybreak.
黎明期 The dawn of a new age (era).

黏 nián Same as 粘.
(adj.)- Sticky; glutinous; adhesive.
黏土 Clay; slime.
黏米 Glutinous rice.
黏性 Viscosity; cohesion.
黏液 Mucus; viscous liquid.
黏膜 A mucous membrane.
黏土質 Clayey; argillaceous.
黏液質 Phlegmatic temperament.
黏質石灰土 Clay lime soil.

# 黑 部

黑 hēi (adj.)- Black; dark; dull; obscure.
黑人 A negro.
黑心 Villainous; evil-hearted.
黑市 Black market.
黑奴 Negro slaves.
黑白 Black and white; right and wrong.
黑色 Black colour.
黑豆 Black soy-bean.
黑夜 Night; the dark night.
黑板 A blackboard.
黑炭；烟煤 Blackcoal; soft coal.
黑海(地) The Black Sea.
黑痣 A mole.
黑棗 Black dates.
黑暗 Dark; dim; dusky; murky.
黑影 A dark shadow.
黑點 A dark (black) spot.
黑名單 A black list.
黑死病 Pest; the black plague; black death.
黑板刷 A blackboard-rubber; an eraser; a wiper.
黑啤酒 Dark-brown beer; stout; porter.

黑雲母 Biotite.
黑熱病 Kalaazar.
黑龍江(地) The Amur River.
黑白顚倒 Talk black into white.
黑花崗石 Syenite.
黑漆漆的 Intense dark; in deep black; boldly in black.

黔 qián
(n.)- The Province of Kweichow.
(adj.)- Black.
黔黑 Black.

默 mò
(adj.)- Still; silent; secret.
默然 Silently; in silence.
默想；默念 Muse; meditate on; be sunk in thoughts.
默認 Give a silent (tacit) consent; acquiesce.
默誦；默讀 Repeat in the mind; read silently.
默寫；默書 Write from memory; dictation.
默禱 A silent prayer; pray in silence.
默不作聲 Be silent; hold one's tongue; shut one's mouth.
默默無言 Silently; without a word.
默默靜聽 Silently listening.

黛 dài
(n.)- Black for the eyebrows; eyebrow-paint.
(adj.)- Umber-black.
黛眉 Black eyebrows.

黝 yǒu
(adj.)- Black; dark green.
黝黝 Gloomy and dark.

點 diǎn
Same as 点.
(n.)- A black spot; a dot; a speck. A period; a full stop.
(v.)- Punctuate. Light. Point out.
點子 A spot; a dot.
點心 Sweets; refreshment; pastry.
點火 Light; kindle; ignite.
點名；點卯 A roll-call. Call the roll.
點明 Mark off; reckon over.
點菜 Order a dinner; select the dishes.
點號 A full stop; a period.
點滴 Drops; drippings; a drop of water.
點綴 Dot; stud; intersperse; embellish.
點數 Points; the number of marks; a score.
點頭；點首 Nod; nod assent.
點燈 Light; light the lamp; switch on a light.
點名册 A roll.
點眼藥水 Apply eye-lotion.
點點滴滴 Drop by drop.

黨 dǎng
(n.)- An association; a party; a league. Kindered. Companions.
黨人；黨員 A member of a party; a partyman; a partisan; a factionist.
黨性 Partyism; partisan spirit.
黨紀 Party discipline.
黨派 A party; a faction.
黨章 Party regulations.
黨魁 The leader of a party.
黨綱 The platform of a party.
黨籍 The party register.

黯 àn
(adj.)- Black; dark.
黯然 Gloomily; sadly; in a melancholy way.

黴 méi
(n.)- Mould; mildew.
(v.)- Mould; become mouldy (musty).
黴菌 A germ; a bacillus; a bacterium.
黴毒性 Syphilitic.
黴菌學 Bacteriology.

## 黽 部

鼈 (n.)- A river turtle; the fresh-water turtle.
biē 鼈甲 Tortoise-shell.

鼈蛋 A turtle's egg.

## 鼎 部

鼎 (n.)- A tripod with two ears; a cauldron; a sacrificial utensil.
dǐng (adj.)- Firm; settled; steady.
鼎力：大力 Great strength; your influence.
鼎立 Take a triangular position.
鼎臣 A high minister of state.
鼎盛 Prosperous; flourishing.

## 鼓 部

鼓 (n.)- A drum.
gǔ 鼓手；鼓吏 A drummer.
鼓吹 Praise; extol; advocate.
鼓動 Rouse; excite; instigate.
鼓脹(醫) Tympanites.
鼓掌 Clap the hands in applause.
鼓舞 Encourage; raise; inspire; rouse.
鼓勵 Stimulate; encourage; hearten.
鼓舞士氣 Stiffen (stimulate) the morale of troops.

鼕 (n.)- The sound of drums.
dōng 鼕鼕響 The great clamour of drums.

## 鼠 部

鼠 (n.)- A rat; a mouse.
shǔ 鼠目 Rat's eyes—sharp, cunning.
鼠疫 Pest; the bubonic plague; the black plague (death).
鼠技 Little ability unfit for use.
鼠竄 Flee like rats; dash away.

鼯
wú 鼯鼠 Flying squirrel.

鼷 xī (n.)- A mouse.
鼷鼠 Common mouse.

鼹 yǎn (n.)- A mole.
鼹鼠 Mole.

# 鼻 部

鼻 bí (n.)- A nose; a trunk (象); a muzzle ( 犬馬等 ); a snout (豕).
鼻孔 The nostrils; nares.
鼻炎 Nasal catarrh.
鼻音 A nasal sound (voice).
鼻屎 Nose-dirt; nose-wax.
鼻祖 The founder of the family; the first ancestor.
鼻涕 Nasal mucus; snivel.
鼻樑 Nose bridge; the bridge (column) of the nose.
鼻腔 The nasal cavity.
鼻管 Nasal duct.
鼻鼾 Snore.
鼻出血 Bleed through the nose.

鼾 hān (n.)- A snore.
(v.)- Snore.
鼾睡 Heavy sleep with snoring.
鼾聲 Snoring; a snore.
鼾聲如雷 One snores loudly.

# 齊 部

齊 qí Same as 齐.
(n.)- Name of a state.
(adj.)- Even; uniform; regular. All like.
(adv.)- Alike; together.
齊心 Of one mind; unanimous.
齊全 Complete; perfect.
齊集 All assembled.
齊備 All ready; all arranged.
齊整 Orderly; neat; well-arranged; even.
齊心努力 Put forth a united effort.
齊齊哈爾(地) Tsitsihar.

齋 zhāi Same as 斋.
(n.)- Fasting. Vegetable diet. A study.
(adj.)- Pure. Dignified.
(v.)- Abstain from a meat diet. Purify. Respect.
齋戒 Fasting and purification.
齋期 A fast day.
齋飯 Monastery meal.

# 齒 部

齒 chǐ (n.)- The teeth. Age. A notch.
齒垢 Tartar (impurities) on the teeth.
齒音 A dental sound; a sibilant.
齒根 The fang (root) of a tooth.
齒腔 The pulp cavity of teeth; a dental cavity.
齒痛 Toothache. Have a toothache.
齒落 Toothless.
齒輪 A toothed wheel; a cog-wheel; a gear wheel.
齒齦 The gums.
齒髓 The dental pulp.

齟 jǔ (n.)- Teeth which do not fit one against another.
(adj.)- Irregular; incongruous; discordant.
齟齬 Irregular; discordant; not in harmony. Quarrel; disagree; contradict; conflict with.

齠 tiáo (adj.)- Young; youthful.
(v.)- Shed the milk teeth.
齠年；齠齡 Young; youthful; of tender years. A child.

齡 líng (n.)- Age; one's age.

齲 qǔ 齲齒 A decayed tooth.

齷 wò (adj.)- Dirty. Mean.
齷齪 Dirty. Mean.

# 龍 部

龍 lóng (n.)- The dragon. The sovereign.
(adj.)- Imperial; royal.
龍舟 Dragon boats.
龍眼 The longan.
龍蝦 Lobster.
龍芽茶 Agrimony.
龍肝鳳肺 Rare food.
龍爭虎鬥 A well-matched fight.
龍馬精神 Vigorous old age, like that of a dragon or a horse.
龍章鳳姿 Noble-looking.

龐 páng (n.)- A lofty house.
(adj.)- Confused. Great.
龐大 Great; huge; gigantic.
龐然 Bountiful; liberally; proud.

# 龜 部

龜 guī (n.)- A tortoise.
龜甲；龜板；龜殼 A tortoise-shell; a carapace.
龜裂 A crack; a crevice; a cleft. Be cracked.
龜齡 Long life.
龜甲形 A honeycomb pattern.
龜鼈類 Chelonia.

# 筆畫檢字表

## 五畫



## 六畫

## 七畫

## 八畫

## 九畫

## 十畫

## 十一畫

## 十二畫

## 十三畫

## 十四畫

## 十五畫

## 十七畫

## 十九畫

## 二十畫

## 二十一畫



## 二十二畫



## 二十三畫

# 漢語拼音檢字表


a

阿 509

ai

哀 66
哎 67
唉 67
埃 79
愛 146
挨 167
曖 203
癌 303
矮 319
礙 324
艾 391
藹 406
隘 513
靄 521

an

安 100
岸 115
按 166
暗 201
案 216
菴 399
諳 440
鞍 496
黯 551

ang

昂 196
盎 309
骯 539

ao

傲 25
凹 37
奧 91
懊 151
澳 265
熬 275
翺 367
襖 423
遨 483
鏖 501

ba

八 32
壩 84
巴 119
扒 157
把 160
拔 164
疤 299
笆 339
罷 363
耙 369
芭 391
跋 462
霸 520
靶 523

bai

伯 15
拜 165
擺 181
敗 187
柏 213
白 306
百 307

ban

伴 15
半 51
坂 78
扮 158
拌 163
搬 176
斑 190
板 211
版 280
班 288
瓣 291
絆 353
般 389
辦 471
頒 526

bang

傍 24
幫 122
棒 218
榜 221
浜 250
磅 323
綁 355
蚌 409
謗 441
邦 486
鎊 500

bao

保 20
刨 40
剝 42
包 48
堡 81
報 81
寶 107
抱 161
暴 202
爆 278
胞 376
苞 393
葆 400
褒 423
豹 449

鉋 495
雹 518
飽 532
鮑 543

bei

倍 22
備 24
北 49
卑 51
悖 142
悲 143
憊 149
杯 210
盃 309
碑 322
背 375
蓓 402
被 419
貝 449
輩 469
鋇 497

ben

奔 90
本 209
畚 297
笨 340
苯 395

beng

崩 116
繃 360

bi

俾 21
匕 48
壁 83
婢 96
幣 122
庇 125
弊 128
彼 133
必 137
敝 187
斃 189
比 235
璧 291
畢 297
碧 322
秕 330
筆 340
篦 343
臂 382
荸 397
蓽 399
蓖 402
蔽 403
裨 421
逼 479
避 485
鄙 487
鉍 495
閉 504
陛 510
鼻 553

bian

便 19
徧 135
扁 156
編 358
辮 361
蝙 412
褊 422
變 445
貶 452
辨 471
辯 471
遍 480
邊 485
鞭 524

biao

婊 96
標 223
表 418
錶 499
鏢 501
鰾 544

bie

別 40
癟 303
蹩 465
鼈 552

bin

儐 27
彬 132
殯 233
濱 266
瀕 267
繽 361
賓 454
鬢 541

bing

丙 5
並 5
併 21
兵 33
冰 35
幷 123
檳 226
炳 269
病 300
秉 329
稟 331
餅 533

bo

伯 15
剝 42
勃 45
博 52
帛 120
搏 175
撥 178
播 178
柏 213
泊 245
波 246
渤 257
玻 288
箔 342
簸 344
膊 380
舶 389
菠 398
薄 404
跛 462
鈸 495
鉑 495
鉢 495

櫬 423
趁 460
辰 472
陳 511

cheng

丞 5
乘 7
呈 63
城 79
懲 152
成 153
承 159
撐 178
橙 224
澄 265
秤 330
程 331
稱 332
蟶 414
誠 436
逞 477
騁 537

chi

侈 18
匙 49
叱 59
吃 60
呎 66
喫 70
嗤 72
弛 130
恥 141
持 166
斥 191
池 241
熾 276
癡 303
笞 339
翅 366
褫 423
豉 447
赤 459
遲 483
馳 536
魑 543
鴟 546
齒 554

chong

充 28
寵 107
崇 115
沖 243
蟲 414
衝 417
重 492

chou

丑 4
仇 12
惆 144
愁 145
抽 162
稠 331
籌 345
綢 356
臭 384
讎 445
躊 465
酬 489
醜 490

chu

儲 28
出 37
初 39
廚 127
楚 220
楮 220
畜 297
矗 317
礎 324
耡 369
芻 392
處 408
觸 428
躇 465
鋤 497
除 510
雛 516

chuan

串 6
傳 25
喘 70
川 117
穿 334
船 389
遄 479

chuang

創 43
牀 279
瘡 302
窗 335
闖 507

chui

吹 64
垂 79
捶 169
搥 176
椎 219
槌 222
炊 268
錘 498
鎚 500

chun

春 198
純 350
脣 377
舂 386
蠢 414
醇 490

chuo

綽 356
輟 469

ci

伺 16
刺 41
慈 147
次 227
此 230
瓷 292
疵 300
磁 323
祠 326
茨 395
詞 432
賜 455

辭 471
雌 515

cong

匆 48
叢 57
從 134
聰 372
葱 401

cou

湊 258
輳 469

cu

促 19
簇 344
粗 346
蔟 403
蹙 465
醋 490

cuan

竄 336
篡 343

cui

催 25
摧 177
瘁 302
粹 346
翠 367
脆 377
萃 399

cun

吋 62
存 98
寸 107
村 210

cuo

挫 167
措 173
搓 175
撮 179
磋 323
蹉 464
銼 497
錯 498

da

大 87
打 157
搭 176
答 341
達 481
韃 524

dai

代 13
呆 64
帶 121
待 133
怠 139
戴 155
歹 231
殆 232
獃 285
玳 287
袋 419
貸 452
迨 473
逮 478
黛 551

dan

丹 6
但 16
啖 69
單 71
擔 180
旦 195
氮 238
淡 254
眈 313
耽 370
膽 381
蛋 410
誕 435
躭 466

dang

擋 180
檔 226
當 298
盪 311
蕩 404
鐺 502
黨 551

dao

倒 22
刀 38
到 40
叨 59
導 109
島 115
悼 143
搗 176
盜 310
禱 328
稻 332
蹈 464
道 481

de

得 134
德 136

deng

凳 37
櫈 226
燈 276
登 304
瞪 317
等 340

di

低 16
地 78
堤 81
娣 95
嫡 97
帝 120
底 125
弟 130
抵 161
敵 188
柢 213
滌 260
滴 261
狄 284
的 307

砥 320
笛 339
第 340
締 357
蔕 401
詆 432
諦 439
遞 482
鏑 500
隄 512

dian

佃 16
典 33
墊 82
奠 90
巔 116
店 125
殿 234
澱 265
玷 287
癲 304
碘 322
電 518
靛 521
顛 528
點 551

diao

凋 36
刁 38
弔 129
彫 132
掉 170
碉 322
調 437
貂 449
釣 494
雕 516
鵰 546

die

喋 70
爹 279
牒 280
疊 298
碟 322
蝶 412
諜 439
跌 462
蹀 464
迭 474

ding

丁 2
叮 59
定 102
疔 299
碇 322
訂 428
酊 488
釘 494
頂 525
鼎 552

diu

丟 5

dong

冬 35
凍 36
動 46
恫 141
懂 151
東 211
棟 218
洞 248
董 401
鼕 552

dou

兜 30
抖 161
斗 190
痘 301
竇 336
荳 396
蚪 410
豆 446
逗 476
陡 510
鬬 542

du

堵 81
妒 93
度 125
杜 210
毒 235
渡 257
瀆 266
牘 280
獨 285
督 316
睹 316
篤 343
肚 374
蠹 415
覩 426
讀 444
賭 456
都 487
鍍 499

duan

斷 192
段 233
短 318
端 338
緞 357
鍛 499

dui

兌 29
堆 81
對 109
隊 512

dun

噸 73
囤 75
墩 83
敦 187
沌 243
燉 276
盾 313
蹲 465
躉 465
遁 479
鈍 494
頓 527

duo

剁 41

咄 65
墮 83
多 86
奪 91
惰 145
朵 209
舵 389
跺 462
踱 464
躲 466
鐸 502

e

俄 19
厄 54
噩 73
堊 81
娥 95
婀 95
惡 144
愕 146
扼 159
腭 379
蛾 411
訛 430
遏 481
鄂 487
額 528
顎 528
餓 533
鱷 545
鵝 546

en

恩 141

er

二 9
兒 30
爾 279
而 369
耳 370
貳 452

fa

乏 7
伐 15
法 245
琺 290
發 304
筏 341
罰 363
閥 506
髮 541

fan

凡 36
反 56
帆 120
梵 217
氾 240
汎 240
泛 246
煩 274
犯 283
番 297
礬 324
範 343
繁 360
繙 360
翻 367
范 394
蕃 403
藩 406
販 451
返 473
飯 532

fang

仿 14
倣 22
坊 78
妨 93
彷 132
房 156
放 185
方 192
紡 351
芳 392
訪 431
防 508
髣 541

fei

匪 49
吠 63
啡 69
廢 127
扉 156
沸 244
痱 302
緋 357
翡 367
肥 375
肺 375
菲 399
誹 437
費 452
非 522
飛 530

fen

份 14
分 38
吩 63
墳 83
奮 91
忿 138
憤 150
汾 242
焚 270
粉 345
糞 348
紛 350
芬 391

feng

丰 6
俸 21
奉 90
封 108
峯 115
楓 220
烽 270
瘋 302
縫 359
蜂 411
諷 440
豐 447
逢 478
鋒 497
風 529
馮 536
鳳 545

**fou**

否 63

**fu**

付 13
伏 15
佛 17
俘 20
俯 21
傅 24
副 43
咐 66
夫 89
婦 96
富 105
幅 122
府 125
彿 133
復 135
扶 158
拂 162
撫 178
斧 191
服 207
氟 237
浮 250
父 279
甫 295
福 327
符 339
縛 358
脯 378
腐 379
腑 379
腹 380
膚 380
芙 391
莩 397
蜉 411
蝠 412
複 422
覆 425
訃 429
負 449
賦 456
賻 457
赴 460
跗 462
輔 468
輻 469
釜 494
阜 508
附 509
馥 535
鳧 545
麩 549

**gai**

丐 4
改 184
概 222
漑 262
蓋 402
該 434
鈣 494

**gan**

乾 8
坩 79
干 122
幹 124
感 147
敢 187
杆 210
柑 213
桿 216
橄 224
甘 292
疳 300
稈 331
竿 339
肝 374
贛 458
赶 460

**gang**

剛 42
岡 115
崗 116
槓 222
港 258
綱 356
缸 362
肛 374
鋼 497

**gao**

告 64
槁 221
睪 316
稿 332
篙 343
糕 347
羔 365
膏 380
誥 436
鎬 500
高 540

**ge**

個 21
割 43
各 60
哥 67
戈 153
擱 181
格 215
歌 228
疙 299
胳 376
膈 380
蛤 410
鉻 495
鎘 500
閣 506
隔 513
革 523
鴿 546

**gei**

給 354

**gen**

根 215
跟 462

**geng**

哽 67
庚 125
更 204
梗 217
羹 366

耕 369
耿 370

**gong**

供 18
公 32
共 33
功 44
宮 103
工 117
弓 129
恭 141
拱 165
攻 184
汞 241
肱 375
貢 450
鞏 523

**gou**

佝 17
勾 48
垢 79
媾 96
枸 213
構 221
溝 259
狗 284
苟 393
覯 426
購 457
鉤 495

**gu**

估 15
僱 26
古 58
呱 65
固 75
姑 94
孤 99
故 185
沽 245
痼 302
穀 332
箍 341
股 374
臌 382
菇 398
蠱 415
詁 432
谷 446
賈 454
辜 471
鈷 495
雇 515
顧 529
骨 539
鴣 546
鵠 546
鼓 552

**gua**

刮 40
剮 43
卦 53
寡 106
挂 166
掛 171
瓜 291
褂 422

**guai**

乖 7
怪 140
拐 163
枴 212

**guan**

倌 21
冠 34
官 101
慣 148
棺 219
灌 267
盥 311
管 342
綸 356
罐 362
觀 427
貫 451
關 507
館 533
鰥 544
鸛 547

**guang**

光 29
廣 127

**gui**

劊 44
桂 216
櫃 226
歸 231
瑰 291
規 425
詭 433
貴 452
跪 463
軌 467
閨 506
鬼 542
鮭 544
鱖 544
龜 554

**gun**

棍 218
滾 261

**guo**

國 75
果 212
菓 398
裹 422
過 480
鍋 499

**ha**

哈 67

**hai**

孩 99
害 103
氦 238
海 251
還 485
駭 537
骸 539

**han**

函 38
含 63
喊 69

寒 105
悍 142
憨 150
憾 150
捍 168
撼 179
旱 196
汗 240
涵 253
漢 263
罕 363
翰 367
邯 486
酣 489
韓 524
頷 527
鼾 553

hang

杭 210
航 388
行 416

hao

壕 84
好 92
毫 236
浩 250
濠 266
皓 308
耗 369
號 409
蠔 414
豪 448

he

何 17
合 60
呵 65
和 65
喝 70
壑 83
核 215
河 244
涸 253
盒 309
禾 328
荷 396
褐 422
訶 431
貉 449
賀 453
赫 459
闔 507
鶴 547

hei

黑 550

hen

很 133
恨 141
狠 284
痕 301

heng

亙 10
亨 11
恆 140
橫 225
衡 417

hong

哄 66
宏 101
洪 248
烘 270
紅 349
虹 409
訌 429
轟 470
鬨 542
鴻 546

hou

侯 19
候 22
厚 54
后 62
吼 64
喉 69
後 133
猴 285

hu

互 9
呼 65
囫 75
壺 85
弧 130
忽 138
戶 155
湖 258
滬 261
滸 261
狐 284
琥 290
瑚 290
糊 347
胡 376
葫 401
虎 407
蝴 412
護 444
餬 534
鬍 541

hua

划 39
劃 43
化 48
樺 224
滑 261
猾 285
畫 297
花 391
華 398
話 434
譁 442

huai

壞 84
懷 152
槐 222
淮 255
踝 464

huan

喚 70
圜 77
宦 103
幻 124
患 143
換 175
歡 229

| 浣 | 250 | 卉 | 51 | **hun** | | 及 | 56 | 稷 | 332 |
| 換 | 257 | 回 | 74 | | | 吉 | 61 | 稽 | 332 |
| 煥 | 274 | 彗 | 131 | 婚 | 96 | 基 | 80 | 積 | 333 |
| 獲 | 286 | 彙 | 131 | 昏 | 197 | 姬 | 93 | 箕 | 342 |
| 環 | 291 | 徽 | 136 | 混 | 256 | 嫉 | 97 | 籍 | 345 |
| 緩 | 358 | 恢 | 141 | 渾 | 258 | 季 | 99 | 紀 | 348 |
| 繯 | 446 | 悔 | 142 | 葷 | 401 | 寂 | 104 | 級 | 350 |
| 豢 | 448 | 惠 | 144 | 餛 | 533 | 寄 | 104 | 緝 | 357 |
| 雛 | 449 | 慧 | 148 | 魂 | 543 | 己 | 119 | 績 | 360 |
| 還 | 485 | 揮 | 175 | | | 幾 | 124 | 繼 | 361 |
| **huang** | | 晦 | 199 | **huo** | | 忌 | 137 | 羈 | 364 |
| | | 暉 | 201 | 伙 | 15 | 急 | 139 | 肌 | 374 |
| 凰 | 36 | 會 | 205 | 夥 | 87 | 悸 | 143 | 脊 | 377 |
| 恍 | 140 | 毀 | 234 | 惑 | 144 | 技 | 159 | 覬 | 426 |
| 惶 | 145 | 灰 | 268 | 或 | 154 | 擊 | 179 | 計 | 429 |
| 慌 | 148 | 煇 | 273 | 活 | 248 | 擠 | 180 | 記 | 430 |
| 煌 | 273 | 燬 | 277 | 火 | 267 | 既 | 194 | 譏 | 443 |
| 皇 | 307 | 穢 | 333 | 獲 | 286 | 墍 | 202 | 跡 | 462 |
| 簧 | 344 | 繪 | 361 | 禍 | 327 | 棘 | 218 | 蹟 | 464 |
| 荒 | 396 | 茴 | 395 | 穫 | 333 | 楫 | 220 | 輯 | 469 |
| 蝗 | 412 | 蕙 | 404 | 藿 | 407 | 極 | 220 | 際 | 513 |
| 蟥 | 413 | 蛔 | 410 | 豁 | 446 | 機 | 224 | 集 | 515 |
| 謊 | 441 | 誨 | 434 | 貨 | 450 | 汲 | 241 | 雞 | 516 |
| 遑 | 481 | 諱 | 436 | 霍 | 520 | 激 | 265 | 飢 | 531 |
| 鰉 | 544 | 譓 | 440 | | | 濟 | 266 | 饑 | 534 |
| 黃 | 549 | 賄 | 454 | **ji** | | 畸 | 298 | 驥 | 539 |
| **hui** | | 輝 | 469 | 几 | 36 | 疾 | 300 | 鯽 | 544 |
| | | 迴 | 474 | 劑 | 44 | 瘠 | 302 | **jia** | |
| 匯 | 50 | 麾 | 549 | 即 | 54 | 祭 | 327 | | |

| 佳 | 17 | 劍 | 44 | 見 | 425 | 僥 | 26 | 轎 | 470 |
| 假 | 23 | 堅 | 80 | 諫 | 439 | 傲 | 27 | 郊 | 486 |
| 傢 | 24 | 奸 | 92 | 賤 | 456 | 剿 | 43 | 酵 | 489 |
| 價 | 27 | 姦 | 94 | 踐 | 463 | 勦 | 47 | 醮 | 491 |
| 加 | 45 | 尖 | 111 | 鍵 | 499 | 叫 | 59 | 餃 | 532 |
| 嘉 | 72 | 建 | 128 | 鑑 | 502 | 嚼 | 73 | 驕 | 538 |
| 夾 | 89 | 戔 | 154 | 間 | 506 | 姣 | 94 | | |
| 嫁 | 96 | 揀 | 173 | 餞 | 533 | 嬌 | 97 | **jie** | |
| 家 | 104 | 柬 | 214 | 鹼 | 548 | 徼 | 136 | 介 | 12 |
| 挾 | 168 | 檢 | 226 | | | 攪 | 182 | 借 | 22 |
| 架 | 212 | 檻 | 226 | **jiang** | | 教 | 186 | 傑 | 24 |
| 枷 | 213 | 礦 | 233 | 僵 | 26 | 校 | 214 | 劫 | 45 |
| 甲 | 295 | 減 | 257 | 匠 | 49 | 椒 | 219 | 嗟 | 71 |
| 稼 | 332 | 漸 | 263 | 獎 | 91 | 澆 | 265 | 姊 | 93 |
| 笳 | 340 | 澗 | 264 | 將 | 108 | 焦 | 272 | 孑 | 98 |
| 莢 | 397 | 濺 | 266 | 漿 | 222 | 狡 | 284 | 屆 | 113 |
| 峽 | 411 | 煎 | 273 | 殭 | 233 | 皎 | 308 | 戒 | 153 |
| 鉀 | 495 | 監 | 310 | 江 | 241 | 矯 | 319 | 截 | 154 |
| 鋏 | 497 | 箋 | 341 | 槳 | 263 | 礁 | 323 | 拮 | 165 |
| 頰 | 527 | 箭 | 342 | 疆 | 298 | 窖 | 335 | 捷 | 169 |
| 駕 | 536 | 簡 | 344 | 繮 | 361 | 絞 | 354 | 接 | 172 |
| | | 縅 | 357 | 薑 | 404 | 繳 | 361 | 揭 | 175 |
| **jian** | | 繭 | 361 | 講 | 441 | 腳 | 380 | 潔 | 264 |
| 件 | 14 | 翦 | 367 | 醤 | 491 | 膠 | 381 | 界 | 296 |
| 健 | 23 | 肩 | 375 | 降 | 509 | 茭 | 395 | 疥 | 299 |
| 僭 | 26 | 艦 | 389 | 韁 | 524 | 蕉 | 403 | 癤 | 303 |
| 儉 | 27 | 艱 | 390 | | | 蛟 | 410 | 皆 | 307 |
| 兼 | 33 | 菅 | 398 | **jiao** | | 角 | 427 | 睫 | 316 |
| 剪 | 43 | 薦 | 404 | 交 | 10 | 較 | 468 | 竭 | 338 |

攫 183
決 241
爵 279
絕 353
蕨 404
覺 426
訣 431
蹶 465
蹻 465

jun

俊 19
君 62
均 79
峻 115
竣 338
菌 398
軍 467
郡 486
鈞 494
駿 537

ka

卡 53
咖 66
咯 66
喀 69

kai

凱 37
嘅 72
慨 149
揩 174
楷 221
鎧 500
開 505

kan

刊 39
勘 46
坎 79
堪 81
看 313
瞰 317
砍 320

kang

伉 14
康 126
慷 149
扛 158
抗 161
炕 269
穅 332
糠 348

kao

拷 165
烤 270
考 368
靠 522

ke

克 29
刻 41
可 59
咳 66
壳 84
客 102
柯 214
棵 219
殼 233
渴 258
疴 300
瞌 316
磕 323
科 329
窠 336
苛 393
蝌 412
課 437
顆 528

ken

啃 69
墾 83
懇 151
肯 375

keng

坑 79
鏗 501
阬 508

kong

孔 98
恐 140
控 172
空 334

kou

口 58
叩 59
寇 105
扣 158
蔻 403

ku

哭 67
庫 126
枯 212
窟 336
苦 393
褲 419
酷 489
骷 539

kua

胯 376
誇 434
跨 462

kuai

儈 27
塊 81
快 138
會 205
筷 341
膾 381
鱠 545

kuan

寬 107
款 228

kuang

匡 49
曠 203
框 216
況 245
狂 283
眶 314
礦 324
筐 341
誆 435

鑛 502

kui

傀 24
奎 90
愧 147
潰 264
盔 309
窺 336
葵 401
虧 409
餽 534
魁 543

kun

困 75
崑 115
捆 168
昆 196
睏 315
綑 355

kuo

廓 126
括 165
擴 181
闊 507

la

喇 69
垃 79
拉 163
瘌 302
臘 382
蠟 414
辣 471

lai

來 18
癩 304
賴 457

lan

嵐 116
懶 152
攔 182
攬 183
欄 227
欖 227
濫 266
瀾 267
爛 278
籃 345
纜 362
藍 405
蘭 407
襤 423
覽 427
闌 507

lang

廊 126
朗 207
浪 250
狼 284
琅 289
螂 412
郎 486

lao

勞 47
嘮 72
姥 94
撈 177
烙 270
牢 281
癆 303
老 368
酪 489

le

勒 46
肋 374
樂 222

lei

壘 84
擂 179
淚 254
累 351
纍 361
羸 366
蕾 404
鐳 501
雷 518
類 529

leng

冷 35
楞 220
稜 331

li

例 18
俐 19
俚 20
儷 28
利 40
力 44
勵 47
厘 54
厲 55
吏 62
哩 67
慄 147
曆 202
李 210
栗 214
梨 217
歷 231
浬 250
涖 253
瀝 267
犁 283
狸 284
理 289
璃 291
痢 301
癧 304
礫 324
禮 328
立 337
笠 339
籬 345
粒 346
罹 364
荔 395
莉 397
莅 402
蠡 414
蠣 414
裏 420
詈 432
貍 449
里 492

蠡 493
隸 514
離 517
靂 521
驪 539
鯉 544
鸝 547
麗 548
黎 550

lian

奩 120
廉 126
憐 150
戀 152
斂 189
殮 233
漣 263
煉 273
簾 344
練 358
聯 371
臉 382
蓮 403
連 478
鍊 499
鏈 500
鐮 501
鰱 544

liang

亮 11
倆 21
兩 31
晾 201
梁 216
樑 223
涼 253
粱 346
糧 348
良 390
諒 439
踉 463
輛 468
量 493
靚 521

liao

了 8
僚 26
嘹 72
寥 106
寮 107
料 190
潦 264
燎 276
療 303
瞭 317
聊 370
遼 484
鐐 501

lie

冽 36
列 39
劣 45
烈 269
獵 286
裂 420

lin

凜 36
吝 62
懍 151
林 212
淋 253
燐 276
琳 290
磷 324
臨 382
賃 453
躪 466
鄰 488
霖 520
鱗 545
麟 548

ling

令 13
伶 15
另 58
嶺 116
淩 254
玲 287
綾 356
羚 365
翎 366
聆 370
菱 399
鈴 494
陵 511
零 518
靈 521
領 527
齡 554

liu

六 33
柳 214
榴 221
流 249
溜 259
琉 290
留 296
瘤 302
硫 321

long

壟 84
弄 128
攏 182
礱 324
籠 345
聾 373
隆 512
隴 514
龍 554

lou

僂 26
摟 177
樓 223
漏 262
簍 344
螻 413
鏤 501
陋 509

lu

廬 128
擄 179
櫓 226
爐 278
盧 311

碌 322
綠 355
艫 389
菉 398
蘆 407
虜 408
賂 453
路 463
轆 470
錄 498
鑪 502
陸 512
露 520
顱 529
魯 543
鷺 547
鹵 547
鹿 548
麓 548

luan

亂 8
卵 53
孿 100
巒 116
鸞 547

lun

倫 22
圇 75
淪 255
論 439
輪 469

luo

倮 23
囉 74
洛 248
籮 345
絡 354
羅 364
落 400
蘿 407
螺 413
裸 422
邏 485
鑼 503
駱 537
騾 538

lü

侶 19
呂 64
屢 114
履 114
律 133
慮 149
旅 193
櫚 226
氯 238
濾 266
縷 359
鋁 497
閭 506
驢 539

lüe

掠 171
略 297

ma

嗎 71
媽 96
瑪 291
痳 302
碼 323
罵 364
螞 412
蟆 413
馬 535
麻 549

mai

埋 79
脈 377
買 452
賣 455
邁 485
麥 549

man

慢 148
曼 204
滿 261
漫 263
瞞 317
蔓 403
蠻 415
謾 442
饅 534
鰻 544

mang

忙 137
盲 311
芒 391
茫 395
莽 397
蟒 413
鋩 497

mao

冒 34
帽 122
毛 236
矛 317
茂 394
茅 394
蝥 413
貌 449
貓 449
貿 453
錨 499
髦 541

mei

妹 93
媒 96
媚 96
寐 105
昧 198
枚 212
梅 217
楣 220
每 234
沒 243
湄 258
煤 273
玫 287
眉 313
美 364
袂 419
鎂 500
霉 520
魅 543

黴 551

men

們 22
悶 143
門 504

meng

夢 86
曚 203
朦 208
氓 237
濛 266
猛 284
盟 310
矇 317
艋 389
萌 399
蒙 401
虻 409
蜢 411
錳 499

mi

密 105
彌 131
泌 245
瀰 267
祕 325
米 345
糜 347
蜜 411
覓 425
謎 441
迷 474
靡 522

mian

免 29
冕 34
勉 46
娩 95
棉 218
眠 314
綿 357
緬 358
面 523
麪 549

miao

妙 93
廟 127
描 174
杪 210
渺 259
眇 313
瞄 316
秒 330
緲 358
苗 393
藐 405

mie

滅 260
篾 344
蔑 403

min

敏 187
民 236
泯 247
閔 506
閩 506
鰵 544

ming

冥 35
名 61
命 65
憫 150
明 196
暝 201
瞑 316
茗 395
螟 413
酩 489
銘 496
鳴 545

miu

謬 442

mo

墨 83
寞 105
抹 162
摩 177
摸 177
摹 177
末 209
模 223
歿 232
沒 243
沫 243
漠 263
磨 323
膜 381
茉 394
莫 397
謨 442
陌 509
驀 538
魔 543
麼 549
默 551

mou

某 213
牟 281
眸 314
謀 440

mu

募 47
墓 82
幕 122
慕 148
拇 162
暮 202
木 208
母 234
沐 243
牡 281
牧 281
畝 297
目 311
睦 316
穆 333

na

吶 63
拿 166
納 349
那 486

鈉 494

nai

乃 7
奈 90
奶 92
柰 214
氖 237
耐 369

nan

南 52
楠 220
男 296
赧 459
難 517

nang

囊 74

nao

惱 145
撓 178
瑙 290
腦 379
鬧 542

ne

訥 431

nen

嫩 97

neng

能 377

nei

內 30
餒 533

ni

你 15
匿 50
呢 64
尼 112
擬 181
泥 246
溺 260
膩 381
逆 475
霓 520

nian

年 123
念 138
拈 162
捻 169
碾 323
蹍 464
輦 469
黏 550

niang

娘 95
釀 491

niao

尿 112
裊 420
鳥 545

nie

揑 168
躡 466
鎳 500
鑷 503

ning

凝 36
寧 106
擰 181
檸 226
獰 286

niu

忸 138
扭 158
牛 281
紐 350
鈕 494

nong

儂 27
濃 265
膿 381
農 472

nu

努 45
奴 91
弩 130
怒 138

nuan

暖 201

nuo

懦 151
挪 167
糯 348
諾 440

nü

女 91

nüe

瘧 303
虐 408

ou

偶 24
嘔 72
歐 228
毆 234
甌 292
耦 369
藕 406
謳 442
鷗 547

pa

帕 120
怕 139
杷 211
爬 278
琶 290
鈀 494

pai

俳 21
徘 134
拍 163
排 170
派 249
湃 258

牌 280

pan

判 40
叛 57
攀 182
泮 247
畔 296
盤 310
盼 313
磐 323
蟠 413
蹣 465

pang

旁 193
滂 260
胖 376
膀 380
螃 412
龐 554

pao

刨 40
咆 65
拋 163
泡 246
炮 269
礮 324
袍 419
跑 462

pei

佩 17
培 80
沛 243
胚 376
賠 455
配 488
陪 511

pen

噴 73
盆 309

peng

彭 132
抨 164
捧 169
朋 207
棚 218
澎 265
烹 270
硼 321
篷 343
膨 381
蓬 403
鵬 546

pi

僻 27
劈 44
匹 50
啤 69
屁 112
批 159
披 161
枇 211
琵 290
疋 299
疲 299
痞 301
癖 303
皮 308
砒 320
脾 378
譬 444
貔 449
辟 471
闢 508
霹 521

pian

偏 23
片 280
篇 343
翩 367
蹁 464
駢 537
騙 537

piao

嫖 97
殍 232
漂 262
瓢 291
票 326
飄 530
驃 538

pie

撇 177
瞥 317

pin

品 66
姘 95
拚 164
聘 371
貧 450
頻 528

ping

乒 7
凭 36
坪 79
娉 95
屏 113
平 122
憑 150
瓶 292
萍 399
蘋 407
評 432

po

坡 79
婆 96
潑 264
珀 288
破 320
粕 346
迫 473
醱 491
陂 509
頗 527
魄 543

pou

剖 42

pu

仆 12
僕 26
匍 48

| 卜 | 52 | 憩 | 150 | **qia** | | 錢 | 498 | 磽 | 323 |
| 圃 | 75 | 戚 | 154 | | | 阡 | 508 | 竅 | 336 |
| 埔 | 80 | 旗 | 194 | 恰 | 142 | 黔 | 551 | 翹 | 367 |
| 撲 | 179 | 期 | 208 | 洽 | 249 | | | 蕎 | 404 |
| 普 | 199 | 棄 | 218 | 袷 | 420 | **qiang** | | 譙 | 443 |
| 曝 | 203 | 棋 | 218 | | | | | 曉 | 465 |
| 樸 | 224 | 棲 | 219 | **qian** | | 嗆 | 71 | | |
| 浦 | 250 | 欺 | 228 | | | 強 | 130 | **qie** | |
| 瀑 | 266 | 歧 | 230 | 前 | 42 | 搶 | 176 | | |
| 舖 | 387 | 气 | 237 | 千 | 50 | 槍 | 222 | 且 | 4 |
| 菩 | 398 | 氣 | 237 | 堅 | 82 | 牆 | 280 | 切 | 39 |
| 葡 | 401 | 汽 | 242 | 嵌 | 116 | 腔 | 379 | 妾 | 93 |
| 蒲 | 402 | 泣 | 246 | 欠 | 227 | 薔 | 404 | 怯 | 140 |
| 譜 | 443 | 凄 | 254 | 歉 | 228 | 蜣 | 411 | 愜 | 147 |
| 蹼 | 465 | 溪 | 259 | 淺 | 256 | 蹌 | 464 | 竊 | 336 |
| 鋪 | 497 | 漆 | 262 | 潛 | 264 | 鎗 | 500 | 篋 | 343 |
| | | 砌 | 320 | 牽 | 282 | | | 茄 | 394 |
| **qi** | | 磧 | 323 | 箝 | 342 | **qiao** | | | |
| | | 祈 | 325 | 簽 | 344 | | | **qin** | |
| 七 | 2 | 綺 | 356 | 籤 | 345 | 俏 | 19 | | |
| 乞 | 8 | 臍 | 382 | 茜 | 395 | 僑 | 26 | 侵 | 19 |
| 企 | 14 | 萁 | 401 | 蕁 | 403 | 喬 | 71 | 勤 | 47 |
| 其 | 33 | 訖 | 430 | 虔 | 408 | 峭 | 115 | 寢 | 106 |
| 敧 | 69 | 豈 | 446 | 謙 | 441 | 巧 | 118 | 懃 | 151 |
| 器 | 73 | 起 | 460 | 譴 | 444 | 悄 | 142 | 擒 | 180 |
| 奇 | 90 | 迄 | 472 | 遣 | 483 | 憔 | 150 | 欽 | 228 |
| 契 | 90 | 騎 | 537 | 遷 | 484 | 敲 | 188 | 沁 | 242 |
| 妻 | 93 | 麒 | 548 | 鉗 | 495 | 樵 | 224 | 琴 | 290 |
| 崎 | 115 | 齊 | 553 | 鉛 | 495 | 橇 | 224 | 禽 | 328 |
| 棲 | 143 | | | | | 橋 | 224 | 秦 | 330 |
| | | | | | | 瞧 | 317 | 芹 | 392 |

衾 419

qing

傾 25
卿 54
情 143
慶 149
擎 178
晴 200
氫 238
清 256
磬 323
罄 362
菁 397
蜻 411
請 438
謦 442
輕 468
青 521
頃 525
鯖 544

qiong

瓊 291
穹 334
窮 336

qiu

丘 5
囚 74
毬 236
求 240
泅 245
球 289
秋 329
虬 409
蚯 410
裘 420
邱 486
酋 488
鞦 524
鰌 544

qu

區 50
去 55
取 57
娶 95
屈 113
嶇 116
曲 203
渠 257
蛆 410
趣 461
趨 461
軀 466
驅 538
齲 554

quan

全 31
券 41
勸 47
圈 75
拳 165
權 227
泉 245
犬 283
痊 301
顴 529

que

確 322
缺 362
闋 507
雀 514
鵲 546

qun

羣 365
裙 420

ran

冉 34
染 213
然 272
燃 276
苒 392
髯 541

rang

嚷 73
壤 84
攘 182
讓 445

rao

擾 182
繞 360
饒 534

re

惹 145
熱 275

ren

人 11
仁 12
仞 13
任 14
妊 93
忍 137
荏 396
認 435
軔 467
韌 524
飪 531

reng

仍 13

ri

日 194

rong

容 104
嶸 116
戎 153
榕 221
榮 221
毧 236
溶 260
熔 275
絨 354
羢 365
茸 395
融 412
鎔 500

rou

揉 173
柔 213
肉 374
蹂 464

ru

乳 8
入 30
如 92
孺 100
汝 241
茹 395
蠕 414
褥 423
辱 472

ruan

軟 467

rui

瑞 290
蕊 403
銳 496

run

潤 264
閏 505

ruo

弱 130
若 393

sa

撒 178
灑 267
颯 530

sai

塞 82
腮 379
賽 457
顋 528
鰓 544

san

三 2
傘 24
散 188

sang

喪 70
嗓 71
桑 216

sao

嫂 97
掃 169
搔 176
繅 360
騷 538

se

澁 265
瑟 290
色 390

sen

森 219

seng

僧 26

sha

傻 27
剎 41
殺 233
沙 243
煞 274
痧 301
砂 320
紗 350
霎 520
鯊 544

shai

曬 203
篩 343

shan

刪 40
善 69
姍 94
山 114
扇 156
擅 179
杉 210
汕 240
煽 274
珊 288
疝 299
繕 360
膳 381
舢 388
芟 391
蟮 414
衫 418
訕 430
贍 458
跚 462
閃 504
陝 510
鱔 544

shang

上 2
傷 25
商 68
尙 111
晌 199
裳 421
賞 455

shao

勺 48
哨 67
少 111
梢 217
燒 276
稍 331
筲 341
紹 352
韶 525

she

奢 90
射 108
捨 169
攝 182
涉 253
社 325
舌 387
舍 387
蛇 410
設 431
賒 454
赦 459
麝 548

shen

什 12
伸 15
參 55
呻 65
娠 95
嬸 97
審 106
慎 147
深 255
滲 261
瀋 266
甚 293
申 296
神 326
紳 352
腎 379
莘 397
蜃 411
身 466

sheng

剩 43
勝 46
升 51
昇 196
牲 282
生 293
甥 294
盛 309
省 313
笙 339
繩 360
聖 370
聲 372
陞 510

shi

世 4
事 9
什 12
仕 13
似 16
使 18
侍 18
勢 47
匙 49
十 50
史 60
嗜 71
士 84
失 89
始 93
室 103
實 106
尸 112
屍 113
屎 113
峙 115
市 119
師 121
式 129
弑 129
拭 165
拾 165
施 193
是 198
時 198
柿 212
氏 236
溼 260
獅 285
矢 318
石 319
示 324
舐 387
虱 409
蝕 412
視 426
試 433
詩 433
誓 435
識 443
豕 447
逝 477
適 483
釋 491
食 531
飾 532
駛 537

shou

受 57
售 67
壽 85
守 100
手 156
授 170
收 183
狩 284
獸 286
瘦 302
首 534

shu

叔 57
塾 82
墅 82
孰 99
屬 114
庶 126
恕 140
數 188
暑 201
曙 203
書 204
束 210
梳 217
樞 223
樹 224
殊 232
淑 254
漱 263
熟 275
疏 299
署 363
舒 387
菽 399
蔬 403
薯 405
蜀 411
術 417
豎 447
贖 458
輸 469
述 474
黍 550
鼠 552

shua

刷 41
耍 369

shuai

帥 121
摔 177
率 287
蟀 413
衰 418

shuan

拴 167
栓 214
閂 504

shuang

爽 279
雙 516
霜 520

shui

水 238
睡 316
稅 331
誰 437

shun

吮 63
瞬 317
順 526

shuo

朔 207
碩 322
說 436

si

司 60
嗣 71
嘶 72
四 74
廝 127
思 139
撕 178
斯 191
死 231
寺 108
祀 325
私 329
絲 354
肆 373
鍶 499
飼 532

song

宋 101
悚 142
松 211
淞 254
聳 372
菘 398
訟 430
誦 436
送 475
頌 526
鬆 541

sou

叟 57
嗽 72
搜 176
艘 389

su

俗 20
塑 81
宿 104
溯 260
粟 346
素 350
肅 373
蘇 407
訴 431
速 477
遡 482
酥 489

suan

算 342
蒜 402
酸 489

sui

歲 231
燧 277
碎 322
祟 326
穗 333
綏 355
遂 479
隋 512
隧 513
隨 513
雖 516
髓 539

sun

孫 99
損 175
筍 341

suo

唆 67
所 156
梭 217
瑣 290
索 351
縮 359
鎖 500

ta

他 13
塔 81
它 100
榻 221
獺 286
踏 463

tai

台 59
太 89
態 148
擡 180
檯 226
汰 241
泰 247
胎 376
臺 385
苔 392
鈦 494
颱 530

tan

嘆 72
坍 78
坦 79
壇 83
彈 131
探 172

攤 182
曇 202
檀 225
歎 228
毯 236
潭 264
灘 267
炭 269
痰 301
癱 304
碳 322
談 438
譚 443
貪 451

tang

倘 22
唐 67
堂 80
塘 82
搪 176
棠 219
湯 259
燙 277
糖 347
膛 381
螳 413
躺 466
醣 490
鏜 501

tao

叨 59
啕 69
套 90
掏 173
搯 176
桃 216
淘 254
滔 261
濤 266
絛 354
討 429
逃 475
陶 511
韜 524

te

特 282

teng

疼 300
籐 345
藤 406
謄 441
騰 537

ti

剃 41
剔 42
啼 69
嚏 73
屜 113
惕 144
提 174
替 204
梯 217
涕 253
踢 464
蹄 464
銻 497
題 528
體 539

tian

填 82
天 88
恬 141
添 257
甜 293
田 295
鈿 495

tiao

佻 18
挑 167
條 217
眺 315
窕 335
苕 393
調 437
跳 463
迢 473
齠 554

tie

帖 120
貼 453
鐵 501

ting

亭 11
停 23
婷 96
庭 126
廳 128
廷 128
挺 168
汀 240
聽 372
艇 389
霆 519

tong

僮 26
同 61
桐 216
桶 216
痛 301
瞳 317
童 338
筒 341
統 354
通 476
銅 496

tou

偸 24
投 160
透 476
頭 527

tu

兎 30
凸 37
吐 62
圖 77
土 77
塗 82
屠 113
徒 134
禿 329
突 335
荼 397
途 476
釷 494

tuan

團 77
湍 258
糰 348

tui

推 173
腿 380
蛻 411
褪 423
退 474
頹 528

tun

吞 62
屯 114
臀 381
豚 447

tuo

唾 68
妥 93
托 158
拓 163
拖 164
橢 225
脫 378
託 430
陀 509
馱 536
駝 537
鴕 545

wa

哇 67
娃 95
挖 167
瓦 292
窪 336
蛙 410
襪 423

wai

外 85
歪 231

wan

丸 6
剜 42
婉 96
完 101
宛 102
彎 131
挽 168
晚 199
灣 267
玩 287
皖 308
碗 322
紈 349
腕 379
萬 399
蜿 412
豌 447
輓 468
頑 526

wang

亡 10
往 133
忘 137
惘 144
旺 196
望 207
枉 211
汪 241
王 287
網 356
罔 363
魍 543

wei

位 16
偉 23
偎 23
僞 26
危 53
味 65
唯 68
圍 76
委 94
威 95
尉 108
尾 112
巍 116
帷 121
微 135
惟 144
慰 149
未 208
桅 216
煨 274
爲 278
猥 285
畏 296
維 356
緯 358
胃 375
萎 399
葦 401
蔚 403
薇 404
蝟 412
衞 417
諉 438
謂 441
違 481
餵 534

wen

刎 39
吻 64
問 68
文 189
溫 259
瘟 302
穩 333
紊 349
紋 349
聞 371
蚊 409

weng

嗡 71
甕 292
翁 366

wo

我 154
握 175
斡 190
沃 242
渥 257
渦 257

窩 336
臥 382
蝸 412
齷 554

wu

五 9
伍 15
侮 19
務 46
勿 48
午 51
吳 63
吾 64
喔 70
嗚 71
塢 82
屋 113
巫 118
悟 142
戊 153
无 194
晤 199
梧 217
武 230
毋 234
汚 241
烏 270
無 270
物 281
舞 388
蕪 404
蜈 411
誣 436
誤 436
鎢 500
霧 520
騖 537
鵡 546
鶩 546
鼯 552

xi

係 19
兮 33
吸 63
喜 70
嘻 72
夕 85
媳 96
嬉 97
希 120
席 121
徙 134
息 142
悉 142
惜 144
戲 155
昔 197
晰 200
析 211
檄 225
汐 240
洗 247
溪 259
熙 273
熄 274
犀 283
犧 283
晳 308
矽 320
禧 327
稀 330
系 348
細 351
繫 361
習 366
膝 381
蓆 402
蜥 411
蟋 413
襲 423
西 424
谿 446
蹊 464
錫 498
隙 513
鼷 553

xia

下 3
俠 20
匣 49
厦 55
嚇 73
夏 85
峽 115
暇 201
狹 284
瑕 290
瞎 316
蝦 412
轄 470
遐 481
霞 520

xian

仙 13
先 28
咸 66
啣 71
嫌 97
嫻 97
弦 130
憲 150
掀 169
暹 202
涎 253
獻 286
現 288
癇 303
絃 352
線 357
縣 359
纖 362
羨 365
腺 380
舷 389
莧 397
蘚 407
蜆 411
賢 455
跣 462
躚 465
銑 496
銜 496
閑 506
閒 506
限 510
陷 511
險 514
顯 529
鮮 544
鹹 548

**xiang**

享 11
像 26
向 62
嚮 73
巷 119
廂 126
想 145
橡 225
湘 259
相 312
祥 326
箱 342
翔 366
襄 423
詳 434
象 447
鄉 487
鑲 503
響 525
項 525
餉 532
饗 534
香 535

**xiao**

削 42
効 45
哮 67
嘯 72
囂 73
孝 99
宵 103
小 110
效 186
曉 203
校 214
梟 217
消 252
瀟 267
硝 321
笑 339
簫 344
肖 374
蕭 405
逍 476
銷 497
鴞 546

**xie**

些 10
偕 23
協 52
卸 54
寫 107
屑 113
懈 151
攜 182
斜 190
械 217
楔 220
歇 228
泄 245
瀉 266
脅 377
蝎 412
蟹 414
蠍 414
褻 423
諧 439
謝 441
邂 485
邪 486
鞋 523

**xin**

信 20
心 136
新 191
欣 227
薪 405
辛 470
釁 491
鋅 497
馨 535

**xing**

倖 22
刑 39
型 79
姓 94
幸 123
形 132
性 139
惺 145
星 197
杏 210
猩 285
腥 379
興 386
行 416
醒 490

**xiong**

兄 28
兇 28
凶 37
匈 48
洶 248
熊 275
胸 377
雄 515

**xiu**

休 15
修 21
嗅 71
朽 209
秀 329
繡 361
羞 365
脩 378
袖 419
鏽 502

**xu**

敘 57
噓 72
墟 83
壻 85
序 125
徐 134
恤 141
戌 153
敍 186
旭 196
栩 216
煦 274
絮 354
緒 357
續 361
胥 376

蓄 402
虛 408
許 431
酗 489
需 519
須 526
鬚 541

xuan

喧 70
宣 102
懸 152
旋 194
暄 201
炫 269
玄 287
癬 304
眩 314
萱 400
衒 417
諠 439
軒 467
選 484

xue

削 42
學 99
穴 334
血 415
雪 518
靴 523

xun

勳 47
尋 109
巡 117
徇 133
循 135
旬 196
殉 232
汛 241
洵 248
熏 275
薰 405
訊 429
訓 429
詢 433
迅 472
遜 482
馴 536

ya

丫 5
亞 10
啞 69
壓 84
崖 116
押 162
氬 238
涯 253
牙 280
芽 392
蚜 410
衙 417
訝 430
雅 515
鴉 545
鴨 546

yan

厭 55
咽 66
唁 67
嚴 73
堰 81
奄 90
妍 94
嫣 97
宴 103
岩 115
巖 116
延 128
彥 132
懨 151
掩 173
晏 199
檐 226
沿 245
淹 256
湮 259
演 262
炎 268
焉 270
焰 272
煙 273
燄 276
燕 277
眼 315
研 321
硯 321
筵 341
簷 344
胭 376
艷 391
菸 399
衍 417
言 428
諺 440
豔 447
贗 458
醃 490
閹 507
閻 507
雁 515
顏 528
饜 534
驗 538
鹽 548
鼴 553

yang

仰 14
佯 17
央 89
揚 174
楊 220
樣 223
殃 232
氧 238
泱 247
洋 247
癢 303
秧 330
羊 364
陽 512
颺 530
養 532
鴦 546

yao

咬 66
夭 89
妖 93
姚 94

| 字 | 頁 |
|---|---|
| 傜 | 135 |
| 搖 | 176 |
| 杳 | 211 |
| 瑤 | 290 |
| 窈 | 335 |
| 窯 | 336 |
| 耀 | 367 |
| 腰 | 379 |
| 舀 | 386 |
| 藥 | 406 |
| 要 | 424 |
| 謠 | 441 |
| 遙 | 482 |
| 邀 | 485 |
| 鑰 | 503 |
| 餚 | 533 |
| 鷂 | 547 |
| **ye** | |
| 也 | 8 |
| 冶 | 35 |
| 叶 | 60 |
| 夜 | 86 |
| 曳 | 204 |
| 椰 | 219 |
| 業 | 220 |
| 液 | 253 |
| 爺 | 279 |
| 耶 | 370 |
| 腋 | 378 |
| 葉 | 400 |
| 謁 | 440 |
| 野 | 492 |
| 頁 | 525 |
| **yi** | |
| 一 | 1 |
| 乙 | 7 |
| 亦 | 11 |
| 以 | 14 |
| 伊 | 14 |
| 佚 | 17 |
| 依 | 18 |
| 倚 | 22 |
| 儀 | 27 |
| 億 | 27 |
| 囈 | 73 |
| 壹 | 85 |
| 姨 | 94 |
| 宜 | 102 |
| 已 | 119 |
| 役 | 132 |
| 怡 | 139 |
| 意 | 146 |
| 憶 | 150 |
| 抑 | 160 |
| 揖 | 174 |
| 易 | 197 |
| 椅 | 219 |
| 毅 | 234 |
| 溢 | 259 |
| 異 | 298 |
| 疑 | 299 |
| 疫 | 299 |
| 益 | 309 |
| 矣 | 318 |
| 移 | 330 |
| 繹 | 358 |
| 義 | 365 |
| 翌 | 366 |
| 翼 | 367 |
| 肄 | 373 |
| 胰 | 376 |
| 臆 | 382 |
| 藝 | 406 |
| 蟻 | 414 |
| 衣 | 418 |
| 裔 | 420 |
| 詣 | 433 |
| 誼 | 437 |
| 譯 | 444 |
| 議 | 444 |
| 貽 | 453 |
| 迤 | 473 |
| 逸 | 479 |
| 遺 | 484 |
| 邑 | 486 |
| 醫 | 490 |
| 頤 | 527 |
| 飴 | 532 |
| **yin** | |
| 印 | 53 |
| 吟 | 63 |
| 因 | 75 |
| 姻 | 94 |
| 寅 | 105 |
| 廕 | 126 |
| 引 | 129 |
| 殷 | 233 |
| 淫 | 255 |
| 茵 | 395 |
| 蔭 | 403 |
| 蚓 | 409 |
| 銀 | 496 |
| 陰 | 511 |
| 隱 | 514 |
| 音 | 524 |
| 飲 | 531 |
| **ying** | |
| 嬰 | 97 |
| 影 | 132 |
| 應 | 151 |
| 映 | 198 |
| 櫻 | 226 |
| 荧 | 275 |
| 營 | 277 |
| 瑩 | 291 |
| 盈 | 309 |
| 硬 | 321 |
| 穎 | 333 |
| 縈 | 358 |
| 罌 | 362 |
| 膺 | 381 |
| 英 | 394 |
| 螢 | 413 |
| 蠅 | 414 |
| 贏 | 458 |
| 迎 | 473 |
| 鶯 | 547 |
| 鷹 | 547 |
| 鸚 | 547 |
| **yong** | |
| 俑 | 19 |
| 傭 | 25 |
| 勇 | 45 |
| 咏 | 66 |
| 壅 | 83 |
| 庸 | 126 |
| 恿 | 142 |
| 擁 | 179 |
| 永 | 239 |
| 泳 | 247 |

折 161
摺 177
柘 213
浙 250
者 368
蔗 403
蜇 411
蟄 413
褶 423
謫 442
轍 470
這 476
遮 483
鷓 547

zhen

偵 24
振 167
斟 190
枕 211
珍 288
甄 292
疹 300
眞 314
砧 320
禎 327
箴 342
診 431
貞 449
賑 454
針 494
鎭 500
陣 510
震 519

zheng

崢 116
幀 122
征 133
徵 135
拯 165
掙 171
政 185
整 189
正 229
烝 270
爭 278
猙 284
症 300
睜 315
箏 342
蒸 402
諍 439
證 442
鄭 488

zhi

之 7
値 22
制 41
只 59
址 78
執 80
姪 94
幟 122
志 137
指 166
擲 181
支 183
旨 195
智 200
枝 212
植 219
止 229
殖 232
汁 240
治 244
滯 261
炙 269
痔 301
痣 301
直 311
知 318
祇 325
秩 330
稚 331
窒 335
紙 350
緻 359
織 360
置 363
職 372
肢 374
脂 377
至 385
致 385
芝 391
芷 392
蛭 410
蜘 411
製 422
誌 434
質 456
贄 457
趾 461
跖 462
蹠 465
隻 514

zhong

中 5
仲 14
忠 137
盅 309
眾 315
種 331
終 352
腫 379
衆 416
衷 419
踵 464
重 492
鍾 499
鐘 501

zhou

胄 34
周 64
咒 65
宙 102
州 117
帚 120
晝 199
洲 248
皺 308
籀 342
粥 346
縐 358
肘 374
舟 388
軸 468
週 478
驟 539

zhu

主 6
住 16
侏 18
助 45
囑 74
朱 209
柱 214
株 215
注 247
煮 273
燭 277
猪 285
珠 288
矚 317
硃 321
祝 326
竹 339
竺 339
築 343
苧 394
著 400
蛀 410
蛛 410
註 432
誅 434
諸 440
豬 448
貯 451
躅 465
逐 476
鑄 502
駐 536

zhua

抓 160
撾 179

zhuan

專 108
撰 179
甎 292
篆 343
賺 457
轉 470
饌 534

zhuang

壯 84
妝 93
撞 178
樁 222
狀 283
粧 346
莊 397
裝 421

zhui

墜 82
椎 219
綴 356
贅 457
追 474
錐 498

zhun

准 36
準 259
諄 438

zhuo

卓 52
啄 68
拙 164
捉 168
桌 216
濁 265
灼 268
琢 290
着 315
茁 394
酌 488
鐲 501

zi

咨 66
姿 95
子 98
字 98
梓 217
滋 260
滓 261
漬 263
玆 287
籽 345
紫 351
自 383
茲 395
諮 440
資 454

zong

宗 101
棕 220
糉 347
綜 355
縱 359
總 359
蹤 465
鬃 541

zou

奏 90
走 459

zu

卒 51
族 194
祖 325
租 330
組 352
詛 432
足 461
阻 508

zuan

纂 361
鑽 503

zui

嘴 72
最 205
罪 363
醉 490

zun

尊 108
樽 224
遵 484

zuo

佐 16
作 17